Child and Adolescent Development for Educators

Child and Adolescent Development for Educators

Second Edition

Judith L. Meece

*University of North Carolina
at Chapel Hill*

Boston   Burr Ridge, IL   Dubuque, IA   Madison, WI   New York
San Francisco   St. Louis   Bangkok   Bogotá   Caracas   Kuala Lumpur
Lisbon   London   Madrid   Mexico City   Milan   Montreal   New Delhi
Santiago   Seoul   Singapore   Sydney   Taipei   Toronto

McGraw-Hill Higher Education

*A Division of The **McGraw-Hill** Companies*

CHILD AND ADOLESCENT DEVELOPMENT FOR EDUCATORS

3 4 5 6 7 8 9 0 D O W / D O W 0 9 8 7 6 5 4 3 2

ISBN 0-07-232235-7

Editorial director: *Jane Karpacz*
Sponsoring editor: *Beth Kaufman*
Developmental editor: *Cara Harvey*
Senior marketing manager: *Daniel M. Loch*
Project manager: *Laura Griffin*
Production supervisor: *Susanne Riedell*
Media technology producer: *Lance Gerhart*
Photo research coordinator: *Judy Kausal*
Supplement producer: *Matthew Perry*
Senior designer: *Pam Verros*
Interior design: *JoAnne Schopler*
Cover design: *JoAnne Schopler*
Cover photographs: *Rob Gage/ © FPG, Mel Yates/ © FPG, © PhotoDisc, © Eyewire*
Printer: *R. R. Donnelley & Sons Company*
Typeface: *10/12 Times Roman*
Compositor: *GAC Indianapolis*

Library of Congress Cataloging-in-Publication Data

Meece, Judith L.
    Child and adolescent development for educators / Judith L. Meece.—2nd ed.
        p. cm.
    Includes bibliographical references (p.) and index.
    ISBN 0-07-232235-7 (alk. paper)
    1. Child development. 2. Adolescence. 3. Constructivism (Education) 4. Cognition in children. 5. Children–Language. I. Title

LB1115 .M266 2002
370.15'1—dc21

www.mhhe.com   00-066439

About the Author

Judith L. Meece is professor of education at the University of North Carolina-Chapel Hill, where she teaches in the School of Education. *Child and Adolescent Development for Educators* draws on over 20 years' experience in teaching child and adolescent development courses to preservice teachers and graduate students. Before coming to Chapel Hill, Meece taught at Purdue University and completed a post doctoral fellowship at the Learning Research and Development Center of the University of Pittsburgh. She received her PhD in educational psychology from the University of Michigan in 1981. Meece's research focuses on academic motivation, gender differences in mathematics and science achievement, and teachers' beliefs about children's development. She has authored or coauthored numerous articles and chapters on these topics. Currently, she serves on the editorial board of the *Educational Psychologist* and *Journal of Early Adolescence.* She also is helping to design a gender-specific educational and treatment program for female juvenile offenders in North Carolina and working on two new books—one on children's development in multiple contexts and the other on schooling and development.

For Cheryl, Dean, and Julie

Contents in Brief

Contents

Chapter 1

Studying Children's Development   3

Chapter 2

Physical Development   59

Chapter 3

Cognitive Development: Piaget's and Vygotsky's Theories   119

Chapter 4

Cognitive Development: Information Processing and Intelligence Theories 175

Chapter 5

Language and Literacy Development   239

Chapter 6

Children with Exceptional Learning Needs   315

Chapter 7

Self-Concept, Identity, and Motivation 377

Chapter 8

Peers Relations and Moral Development   435

Chapter 9

The Family: Partners in Education   477

List of Features

Focus on Research

Focus on Teaching

Focus on Development

Preface

My decision to write *Child and Adolescent Development for Educators* was motivated by a desire to create positive school environments for children and adolescents. Young people spend more than 15,000 hours in some form of school setting. Research now shows that the experiences and interactions they have in those settings have a lasting influence on almost every aspect of their development. Moreover, for many young people today, schools play an influential role in protecting them from the adverse effects of poverty, dangerous neighborhoods, or difficult home environments.

This development text also grows out of my work as an educator and researcher. I have more than 20 years of experience teaching child and adolescent development courses to education students. Until my first edition was published, I relied on child and adolescent texts written for psychology students. Although there are many fine texts available, few focus on children's development in school settings. As an educational researcher, I was aware of a growing research literature on the effects of schools on child and adolescent development, and the many ways this research can be applied in educational settings. Thus, I wrote the first edition of *Child and Adolescent Development for Educators* with the idea of designing a text appropriate for educators but including a strong research base on schooling and development. Most important, I wanted to write a development text that would reflect the important role of teachers and schools in children's lives. It was the first book of this type in education.

OVERALL APPROACH: A DEVELOPMENT TEXT FOR FUTURE TEACHERS

Child and Adolescent Development for Educators is a text written for teachers. It presents the content future teachers need to know in order to understand the development of their students. From its inception, this book was designed to meet the special needs of teacher education students. For example, in addition to focusing exclusively on school-age development, each chapter opens with a school or classroom vignette that sets the stage for the material that follows and then punctuates each discussion with an abundance of school and classroom examples. The Focus on Research and Focus on Teaching features show students how to connect and apply developmental research to the classroom and provide them with extended classroom examples. In addition, each chapter concludes with an assortment of observation, interview, and reflection activities designed to apply key topics. Topic coverage reflects the realities of teaching as well, with a third of the text devoted to cognitive and language development. The importance of social and cultural context on development is also emphasized throughout the book.

COVERAGE AND ORGANIZATION

The text takes a topical approach. The content is focused on those topics of most interest to educators—cognitive development, literacy, social and emotional development, children with special learning needs, and family involvement in education. Because of its teaching focus and modest price, it can be used as a core text with supplemental readings and materials.

The text is organized into nine chapters. Chapter 1 stresses the importance of studying children's development in education and provides an overview of the theories and the methods used in child development research. This chapter emphasizes the important role that schools and teachers play in children's development. Chapter 2 examines children's physical development, with a focus on brain development, puberty, genetic and environmental risk factors, and special health concerns in childhood and adolescence. A special section discusses the implications of brain research for education. There are two chapters on cognitive development, and each provides suggestions for using cognitive theories in the classroom. Chapter 3 focuses on Piaget's cognitive development theory and Vygotsky's sociocultural theory. Both theories serve as theoretical foundations for constructivist approaches in education. Chapter 4 presents information processing and psychometric approaches to understanding children's intellectual development and discusses how individual variations in cognitive development are measured and explained. A special section focuses on the influence of television and computers on children's learning.

The focus of Chapter 5 is children's language and literacy development, and new approaches to teaching reading and writing are highlighted. This chapter also contains information on literacy development in non-English-speaking children. Chapter 6 presents a comprehensive introduction to the development of children with special learning needs. The chapter is organized by the prevalence of different exceptionalities in the school population, beginning with high-prevalence conditions such as learning disabilities, communication disorders, attention deficit hyperactive disorder, and so on.

The last three chapters focus on children's emotional and social development and the role of the peers and families in development.

Chapter 7 addresses the development of emotional competence, conceptions of the self, and motivation. It begins with an overview of Erikson's theory of psychosocial development, and each section concludes with a set of suggestions for how teachers can help to foster emotional competence, positive self-conceptions, and academic motivation. Chapter 8 turns to children's social understanding and relations, focusing on the development of social cognition, peer relations, peer groups, and moral development. The chapter addresses how educators can create a caring and supportive environment that promotes social understanding and acceptance. The final chapter, Chapter 9, is devoted to the important role of the family in children's development, including a discussion of family diversity and transitions. For educators, it includes important information on child care, helping children cope with divorce, and child maltreatment. Most important, the chapter concludes by suggesting some ways educators can form partnerships with parents and other family members.

NEW TO THE SECOND EDITION

The first edition of *Child and Adolescent Development for Educators* was embraced by instructors of future teachers because of its emphasis on classroom application and the content that teachers need to know. The second edition was based on substantial feedback from instructors using the text as well as other instructors of education majors. All of the feedback was closely considered and used to revise the text to best meet the needs of instructors of future teachers.

Key revisions included in the second edition include:

Two New Chapters: Two chapters are added to the second edition. The coverage of personal, social, and moral development is expanded and divided into two chapters—Chapter 7: Self-Concept, Identity, and Motivation and Chapter 8: Peer Relations and Moral Development. A new chapter, Chapter 9: The Family: Partners in Education, is also included.

Expanded Content and Depth: Each chapter is heavily revised to ensure complete coverage of topics future teachers need to understand. At least two or three new sections are added to each chapter. Specific added content includes new research on brain development, early puberty in girls, play, social cognition, computers and learning, language-minority students, development precursors of learning disabilities, emotional competence, ethnic identity development, peer groups, quality preschool programs, teacher-student relations, family influences on development, and parental involvement in education. The text is also expanded to include more information on early childhood and adolescent development.

New Pedagogical Features: Two pedagogical features new to the text are Focus on Teaching and Focus on Development. Focus on Teaching features classroom applications, and Focus on Development serves as a chronological summary to aid students' understanding of key developmental concepts.

Full-Color Design and Visual Program: A new interior design uses full color, 50 photos, and numerous figures to engage students. The resulting *Child and Adolescent Development for Educators* is now one of the most attractive development texts available!

Updated and Expanded Scholarship: The scholarship of the first edition is updated and expanded to reflect new studies. Approximately 30 to 40 references added to each chapter ensure a comprehensive and current research base. The relevant Focus on Research feature and the solid foundation of scholarship that supports the text make *Child and Adolescent Development for Educators* the most research-based development text for educators.

A Wealth of Supplements: A new supplements program to the text meets additional needs of the instructor and the student. Key supplements include an instructor's manual and test bank, an Online Learning Center at www.mhhe.com/meece that includes numerous instructor resources and a student study guide, and a *Making the Grade* CD-ROM with practice tests that is packaged with each new copy of the text. Also available through McGraw-Hill is *Understanding Children: An Interview and Observation Guide for Educators*, a text by Denise Daniels, Florence Beaumont, and Carol Doolin.

Improved by the above revisions, *Child and Adolescent Development for Educators* remains brief and affordable.

SUPPORTING STUDENT LEARNING

The second edition maintains the same *student-friendly writing style* as the first edition. The pedagogical structure was developed to support and guide the student's learning. Each chapter begins with an *outline* listing the key topics covered in the chapter. An *opening vignette* set in a school or classroom invites the student into the chapter by providing an immediate engagement. *Focus on Development* boxes provide chronological summaries to help clarify types of development. *Key ideas* are listed in the margins and bolded *key terms* help students focus on the most important aspects of the chapter. At the end of the chapter, a comprehensive *summary* and *listing of key terms* with page references aid the student's review.

APPLIED FEATURES

Several features were developed to encourage students to apply the developmental theory they read about. Each chapter contains a section or two that discusses the educational implications and applications. Several charts and tables are included that also describe educational implications for the various theories discussed. A set of activities at the end of each chapter provides opportunities for the student to use and apply the learning material as well.

Focus on Research features summarize developmental research and show how the research can be applied— and the importance of the application—to the classroom.

Focus on Teaching boxes provide students with a look inside classrooms, give examples of how teachers approach different situations, and take a look at the role development plays in the classroom setting.

SUPPLEMENTS

The second edition of the text is accompanied by an extensive supplements program developed to support both the instructor and student.[*]

FOR THE INSTRUCTOR

Instructor's Manual and Test Bank

The new instructor's manual and test bank provides the instructor with additional resources, as well as traditional support. The test bank is also available on a dual-platform CD-ROM.

[*]The following supplements are available. Please contact your sales representative for more information.

The Online Learning Center provides numerous instructor resources including *text-specific PowerPoint slides;* suggested research topics; and supplemental lecture topics, activities, critical thinking exercises, and audio-visual suggestions *in addition* to those found in the instructor's manual.

PageOut

Create your own course website! Simply plug your course information into a template and click on one of 16 designs, and you can create your own professional-looking website. Powerful features include an interactive course syllabus that lets you post content and links, an online gradebook, lecture notes, bookmarks, and even a discussion board where students can discuss course-related topics.

Also available for the instructor are the **McGraw-Hill Overhead Transparencies for Child Development** and the McGraw-Hill *Video Cases in Human Development: Childhood.*

FOR THE STUDENT

Making the Grade Student CD-ROM

This CD-ROM is packaged for free with each new copy of the text. It includes *practice quizzing* for each chapter; a *Learning Styles Assessment* to help students understand how they learn and, on the basis of that assessment, how they can use their study time most effectively; and two *guides to the Web.* The *Internet Primer* explains the essentials of online research, including how to get online and then find information once you are there. The *Guide to Electronic Research* guides students through Web-based information databases and explains how to evaluate the quality of information gathered online.

The Online Learning Center provides students with a *student study guide* that includes: a chapter outline, objectives, a chapter overview, multiple choice questions, matching questions, essay questions, key terms, a key terms practice exercise, a critical thinking exercise, annotated Web links, and additional resources.

One such additional resource, *Understanding Children: Interview and Observation Guide for Educators* by Denise Daniels, Florence Beaumont, and Carol Doolin, provides guidelines observing children in the school setting. Each chapter includes several observation activities and sample forms, and concludes with a "Tips for Teachers" section that discusses the implications of the observations for the future teacher.

Acknowledgments

With great appreciation, I would like to thank the many individuals who assisted with this project for their generous support and encouragement. First, I gratefully acknowledge Jane Danielewicz and Marge Terhaar-Yonkers for their excellent chapters in the first edition. Their high-quality chapters on language and literacy development (Danielewicz) and children with exceptional needs (Terhaar-Yonkers) made the task of revising an easy one. For the second edition, I am indebted to Ryan Kinlaw for his assistance with the family chapter, to Julie Schock for her assistance with revising the material on exceptional learners, and to Phillip Herman and Amanda Knight for their assistance with library research. Emily Cooper and Julie Johnston provided much needed assistance with preparing the reference list. My colleague, Jill Hamm, provided new ideas for the peer chapter; and my teaching colleague, Dwight Rogers, shares my passion for helping new teachers understand children's development. My developmental editor, Cara Harvey, offered many helpful suggestions for the second edition, and Laura Griffin, who managed the production process, kept everything running smoothly despite the many delays. I am grateful to each of them.

Many individuals have helped to strengthen the book by reviewing one or several chapters. For the first edition, the contributions of the following reviewers are gratefully acknowledged: Kay Alderman, University of Akron; Linda Anderson, Michigan State University; Hilda Borko, University of Colorado; Carol Anne Kardash, University of Missouri; Paul Pintrich, University of Michigan; Gary Stuck, University of North Carolina; Allan Wigfield, University of Maryland. A special thanks is also extended to reviewers of the second edition, whose comments led to important improvements and refinements:

Julie Alexandrin, Eastern Connecticut State University; Kay Alderman, University of Akron; David Andrews, Indiana State University; Rosenna Bakari, State University of New York at Oneonta; Audrey W. Beard, Albany State University; Katherine Benson, University of Minnesota, Morris; Navaz Bhavnagri, Wayne State University; J. T. Binfet, California State University, San Bernardino; James P. Byrnes, University of Maryland; Clara Carroll, Harding University; Heather Davis, University of Georgia; Sandra Deemer, Millersville University; Darlene DeMarie,

University of South Florida; C. Timothy Dickel, Creighton University; Maribeth Downing, Harding University; Saralee S. Goodman, Goucher College; Michele Gregoire, University of Florida; Mary Anne Hannibal, Indiana University of Pennsylvania; Susan Hegland, Iowa State University; Young Suk Hwang, California State University, San Bernardino; Wilsie G. Jenkins, Fort Valley State University; Evelyn Jordan, LaGrange College; Deborah L. Kalkman, Northern Illinois University; Carol R. Keyes, Pace University; Gary W. Ladd, University of Illinois; Sheila Marino, Lander University; Kathy Morrison, University of Texas, Arlington; Jack Piel, University of North Carolina, Charlotte; Evan R. Powell, University of Georgia; F. Thomas Scappaticci, King's College; Shereen F. Sheehan, University of Houston, Clear Lake; Stephen Sherblom, University of Missouri, St. Louis; Susan Sze, Niagara University; Dennis Thompson, Georgia State University; Theresa Thorkildsen, University of Illinois, Chicago; Jayne White, Drury College; Allan Wigfield, University of Maryland; Barbara Yunker, Jacksonville State University

Finally, I would like to acknowledge the generous support of my family and friends. Thanks especially to Susan Griffith, Jane Bulter Kahle, Kate Scantlebury, and Ann Schulte, for their continuing encouragement and assistance. I am also especially grateful for the long-distance support from my sister, Cheryl Meece. A heartfelt thanks to you all.

Judith L. Meece

Child and Adolescent Development for Educators

Chapter 1

Studying Children's Development

During a lunch break, a group of middle school teachers are discussing why adolescents are so difficult to teach. This issue sparks a lively debate.

Darren says, "Look, I've been teaching these kids a long time, and I think it's just a stage that all adolescents go through. There's not much we can do. I remember when I was their age. As soon as those hormones started to kick in, all I wanted to do was look at girls, play soccer, and hang out with my friends! They'll grow out of it. Meanwhile, we just have to live with them."

Lucia replies, "I may be new at teaching, but I don't think it's that simple. Sure these kids are going through some physical changes, but isn't there more that we could do for them? I think they're just bored with school, and that's why they're so difficult to teach. Maybe there are some ways we can make learning more meaningful to them. I'm going to start using more cooperative learning activities in my classroom. I'm also going to let them have a bigger say in deciding how we do things. They're old enough to take on more responsibility for their own learning."

Frank, a seventh-grade social studies teacher, just shakes his head. "Where have you been? Haven't you read the papers? Kids today need a firm hand. They need discipline. That's the problem. Teachers like you are way too permissive. We can change these kids if we

Chapter opener photo: © David Young-Wolff/PhotoEdit, Inc.

3

reward the good ones and punish the bad ones. Taxpayers are paying for their education, and they should be expected to learn so they can get jobs when they graduate. Learning isn't fun, it's hard work. You won't find any fooling around in my classes. My students know that they have to finish their work or stay after school. It's that simple."

As this scenario suggests, teachers often disagree about how children learn, what factors influence their development, and whether teachers can facilitate learning and development. Darren, for example, thinks that children are simply programmed to pass through different stages of development. Parents and teachers should just let nature take its course. In contrast, Frank believes that adults can change behavioral patterns through rewards and punishments. His statements imply that the environment determines how children develop. Lucia, on the other hand, is expressing a more complex view of development. Her statements suggest that changes in behavior come from sources within and outside the student. Problems arise when teachers do not respond appropriately to new behavioral patterns that emerge as students mature.

Studying children's development helps teachers match their instruction to children's developmental levels and understand student variability.

In this chapter, we begin to explore different theories of child development and their implications for teaching. This research can help teachers answer questions about how thinking processes unfold, how children determine right from wrong, when children begin to understand the feelings of others, why children lose interest in learning, how children learn self-discipline, why some adolescents are rejected by their peers, why some youths become aggressive and violent, and so forth. More important, child development research can help educators to identify those behaviors that place children at risk for not succeeding in school. Lastly, child development research can help educators to create an educational environment that promotes the healthy development of all children. The Focus on Research box describes how child development research can help guide school reform efforts.

The first two sections of this chapter focus on the question: Why study children's development? Subsequent sections discuss the history of childhood and the status of children today. We then turn to the theories of development that serve as the focus for this book.

Why Study Children's Development?

Teachers' Understanding of Children's Development

We have seen that teachers hold varying points of view about children's development. Look at the photograph on the next page of the middle school students who are being supervised during in-school suspension? What beliefs about children are guiding the practices shown here? How do teachers form these ideas? Some teachers may have taken a formal course on child psychology, whereas others may construct a naive or commonsense theory of development from their own personal experiences and observations. Children, according to most people, act the way they do because they have not been educated or socialized. At the same time, most people recognize that many fundamental human characteristics (e.g., intelligence, temperament, etc.) appear without training because they are innate (Baldwin, 1967).

Society also offers some "ready-made" ideas about children (Goodnow, 1985). Every culture has a set of concrete beliefs about what the child can be expected to do and to learn at each age. These beliefs vary from society to society. For example, American teenagers

SOURCE: News &
Observer.

These middle school students have been assigned to in-school suspension, with an adult supervisor. What child development practices are guiding the practices shown here?

are expected to delay sexual reproduction for many years after they reach sexual maturity; but in some societies young people are permitted to, and even expected to, have sexual relations as soon as they reach puberty. As we will see, American society viewed children as miniature adults until the beginning of the twentieth century. Several child observers have identified a trend toward "adultification" in American images of childhood that may carry negative implications for children's well-being and development (Elkind, 1983).

Regardless of how beliefs are formed, teachers' intuitive understanding of children's development can influence how they teach. Teachers who believe that behavioral differences are innate may not try to remediate students' learning problems. Teachers who view development as being strongly influenced by environmental factors may be too controlling. Other teachers may adopt a teaching approach that acknowledges both the role of the child and the environment in the learning process. In the example presented at the beginning of the chapter, Lucia implies that she wants to adapt her teaching to students' interests and abilities in order to reduce learning problems.

A study of school readiness by Mary Lee Smith and Lorrie Sheppard (1988) demonstrated the important influence of teachers' beliefs about child development on teaching practices. Using a set of open-ended questions, the researchers asked 40 kindergarten teachers in one school district to think about particular children who were not ready for school and to speculate about the reasons for their lack of readiness. The researchers then examined teachers' statements to identify beliefs about (a) the nature of development and early learning; (b) rates of development; (c) causes of unreadiness; and (d) methods of remediation. In this study, the concept of teachers' beliefs referred to those propositions a teacher "holds to be true" (p. 309).

Studies indicate that teachers have different views about children's development that have implications for the way they teach.

Dr. James P. Comer: Putting Children First

Dr. James P. Comer is considered one of America's leading architects of school reform and perhaps the only prominent reformer who views children's development as the center of all educational programs. In a 1997 interview for *Phi Delta Kappan*, Dr. Comer stated, "I have maintained a steady focus on child development and this is what I have tried to bring to education. Even people in education who are sensitive to child development focus on curriculum/instruction/assessment first, and I argue that it should be development first and that development should guide everything else" (Goldberg, 1997, p. 599).

For more than 25 years, Comer has been working with schools using a collaborative process of reform that brings together teachers, principals, parents, health professionals, and community members to create educational programs that foster the development of children. The basic premise of Comer's School Development Program (SDP) is that "all children have the potential to succeed in school and in life, and that the realization of this potential depends on how well educators, families, and communities work together to create environments that support child development; children who are developing well can learn adequately" (Comer & Haynes, 1999, p. 601). The SDP has three important components: (a) a governance and management team that develops a comprehensive school plan, assessment strategy, and staff development program; (b) a mental health or school support team; and (c) a parents' program (Comer, Haynes, Joyner, & Ben Avie, 1996). These three teams work together to promote students' learning and development using Comer's guiding principles of collaboration, consensus, and no-fault problem solving to create a climate of competence, mutual respect, and trust in the school. Additionally, the SDP team uses six developmental pathways as a framework for making decisions that benefit students. These are physical, cognitive, language arts, social, psychological, and ethical. To educate the whole child, Comer believes that schools must develop a balanced curriculum that is not only focused on cognitive development but also addresses a broad spectrum of children's developmental needs.

One of the first schools to implement the Comer program was Martin Luther King Jr. Elementary School in New Haven, Connecticut—a predominantly African-American, low-income, inner-city school. At the beginning of the project in 1968, its students were an average of 19 months below grade level in language arts and 18 months below grade level in reading. Students' scores in both areas were at grade level in 1979 and were 12 months above grade level in 1984. Additionally, parent involvement had increased, school absences and behavior problems had decreased, and staff turnover was nearly zero. These changes occurred without any dramatic change in the socioeconomic backgrounds of the children attending the school.

Today, Comer's School Development Program is operating in more than 700 elementary, middle, and high schools across the United States, and in Trinidad and Tobago. *For Dr. James Comer, education and development are one in the same.*

The study showed several noteworthy findings. First, the teachers differed in the extent to which they viewed the development of school readiness as influenced by internal or environmental processes. Nearly half the teachers were labeled "nativists" because they construed development as a maturational process that was "largely or completely outside the influence of parents or teachers" (p. 314). The remaining teachers all believed that school readiness could be influenced by teachers, parents, and other environmental forces, but they differed with respect to the sort of intervention they would recommend for a child who was not ready for school. A large majority of this group believed that additional instruction would increase readiness (remediationist teachers) or would correct specific deficits in readiness (diagnostic-prescriptive teachers). Only 3 of the 40 teachers viewed the development of school readiness as a complex interaction between the child's characteristics and the environment provided by the caregivers.

Second, the results of this study indicated that teachers' beliefs about the development of school readiness influenced their decisions to recommend an extra year of kindergarten. Figure 1.1 shows how different types of teachers (e.g., nativist, remediationist) responded to the question "Is there anything the teacher can do about a child who is not prepared for first grade?" Teachers who held nativist beliefs were the most likely to recommend retention, whereas teachers with nonnativist views reported lower rates of retention.

Other studies have suggested that teachers and principals have unrealistic expectations for children's development. In one such study, Donna Bryant, Richard Clifford, and Ellen Peisner (1991) examined the extent to which developmentally appropriate teaching practices and learning materials were employed in 103 randomly selected kindergarten classes in North Carolina. Examples of developmentally appropriate practices included opportunities for free play, exploration, and creative activity; use of hands-on and child-selected activities; and use of materials to promote self-esteem, physical, mental, and language development. The results indicated that 60 percent of the classes observed did not provide teaching activities and practices that were developmentally suited to the learning styles of 5-year-olds. This finding is significant because grade retention rates are often higher for kindergarten than for any other grade level.

Many studies indicate that teachers need a better understanding of how children develop and learn.

This study further suggested that the quality of the kindergarten program was not related to the region of the state, the size of the school, per pupil expenditures, or other expected predictors. What predicted a better classroom quality was a high level of knowledge and belief in developmentally appropriate practices. The authors concluded: "Providing even more knowledge about developmental teaching and increasing the strength of that conviction (or both) would be likely to improve kindergarten teaching" (p. 799).

Another research report, *Years of Promise* (Carnegie Task Force on Learning in the Primary Grades, 1996), indicates that children begin school with high hopes and a strong desire to learn. However, many lose their confidence by the time they reach the fourth grade. The authors of this report write, "Something happens to many American children as they progress to and through the elementary grades—something elusive and disturbing: over the years, they lose their natural curiosity and their enthusiasm for learning" (p. 4). Recent research indicates that patterns of school disengagement and withdrawal appear early in elementary school and predict a student's inclination to drop out of high school (Alexander, Entwisle, & Horsey, 1997).

Another well-publicized report, *Turning Points: Preparing American Youth for the 21st Century* (Carnegie Council on Adolescent Development, 1989), raised concerns about developmental mismatches in educational programs for young adolescents. Among the problems highlighted were the placement of young adolescents in large impersonal environments, when they need stable trusting relations with adults and peers; a middle grades curriculum that emphasized rote learning, practice, and basic skills, when most

In an interview study, Mary Lee Smith and Lorrie Shepard asked 40 kindergarten teachers, "Is there anything the teacher can do about (a particular) kindergartner who is not prepared for first grade?" The responses here represent examples of the different views expressed by teachers.

Nativist View

He's young. He's a boy and very low in a lot of those areas like following directions, attending, and things like that. I just feel he needs another year to get him ready for first grade. Just to give him a big start. If he doesn't, school's going to be a struggle for him. If he's struggling now in kindergarten what will it ever be like in first and second grades? When I present that to parents, I just say they need another year just to grow and to catch up.

Remediationist View

I think we as educators have to give them the most benefit of the doubt or do something different and help that child. And maybe the way we taught it is not correct. Maybe we ought to change teaching our style or do something different and help that child. And I think if you marked them and said, "If he doesn't get it now, he'll never get it. We'll try for another year of maturity, maybe he'll get it next year," I think you give up.

Diagnostic-Prescriptive View

You always have children who can handle everything else but have problems with visual-motor coordination, and those children probably are going to have those problems so that shouldn't be any reason for retention. We have our academic assistance program, and children who are showing these problems work there. If a child absolutely couldn't listen, I'd certainly try very hard to find out what the problem is before wanting to keep him in kindergarten another year. The reason he can't attend may be because he has an auditory problem. If he has this block or a problem, then he's got to learn to work around that to compensate for it, and that's what we'll try to give him, ways to compensate.

Interactionist View

With the variety of materials we have in experiential education, a child will plug in right where he is comfortable. And you can see right away by the way the child works with materials the kinds of experiences he is going to need that year. When there is a wide range of kids, you've got to offer a wide range of experiences.

FIGURE 1.1

Teachers' Beliefs and Practices

SOURCE: After Smith & Shepard (1988).

adolescents are able to engage in critical and higher-order thinking; and lack of attention to their emotional, physical, and social development. The authors of this report recommended that schools hire teachers and principals with special training in adolescent development.

Following the release of *Turning Points,* the Carnegie Corporation of New York began a decade-long program to promote the implementation of the report's recommendation. To date, 225 middle schools nationwide have participated in this school reform program. However, a recent report suggests that the reforms did not go deep enough (Jackson & Davis, 2000). Many middle schools today are "warmer, happier, and more peaceful places for students and adults...[yet most schools] have not moved off this plateau and taken the critical

Teenagers

- Believe education is essential.

- Want to do well in school and go on to college.

- Want teachers who give individual help, are enthusiastic and excited, care personally, are compassionate and respectful of them, emphasize class discussions.

- Want standards that challenge them personally.

- Need close and unwavering attention of teachers to help them want to learn and help them value learning.

- See most of what they learn as tedious and irrelevant.

- Complain about lack of respect from teachers and other students.

- Want more structure, firmness, and consistency.

- Complain that schools have too many disruptive students, poor discipline, and crowded classes.

- See drugs and violence as serious concerns in their lives.

FIGURE 1.2
Getting By: What Teenagers Really Think about Their Schools
SOURCE: Public Agenda, 1997.

next step to develop students who perform well academically, with the intellectual where-withal to improve their life conditions" (Lipsitz, Mizell, Jackson, & Austin, 1997, p. 535).

Finally, the students themselves tell us that schools and teachers are not promoting their development or meeting their needs. In a 1996 study of 20,000 teenagers in California and Wisconsin, Lawrence Steinberg and his colleagues reported that approximately 40 percent of high school students, regardless of their socioeconomic background, stated that they were just "going through the motions" (Steinberg, 1996, p. 67). One-third of the students surveyed showed signs of being emotionally disengaged from school. They reported that they had lost interest in school, they were not learning much, and they got through the day by "goofing around with their classmates" (Steinberg, 1996, p. 71). A 1997 study, *Getting By: What American Teenagers Really Think about Their Schools* (Public Agenda, 1997) reported similar findings. A majority of the 1,000 randomly surveyed teens stated that "they could do better in school if they tried" and wanted standards that challenged them personally. Other important themes are shown in Figure 1.2. In summary, the most fundamental reason why teachers should study children's development is to improve their teaching skills and to better meet the needs of their students.

Along with the family and peer group, schools have a powerful influence on children's development.

Schools as a Context for Development

Along with the family and the peer group, schools are one of the most influential contexts for children's development in our society. Some experts have argued that when children and youths are not connected with adults or communities who are concerned about their well-being, then schools must serve as the primary socializing influence in children's lives (Comer et al., 1996).

Amount of Time Spent in School

By the time students graduate from high school they will have spent more than 10,000 hours in school. Figure 1.3 indicates that approximately one-third of an adolescent's waking life is spent in some type of school environment (Csikszentmihalyi & Larson, 1984). Furthermore, students start school earlier and stay in school longer than young people in past generations. In 1920, the average school year was 120 days. The length of the school term is now 180 days for American students, and according to 1999 data, more than 2 million students in 597 districts in the United States and Canada are being educated in some model of year-round schooling (Shields & Oberg, 1999).

Since the early 1900s, there have been significant increases in the percentage of children who attend school. Figure 1.4 shows that the percentage of 3-, 4-, and 5-year-olds enrolled in school has more than doubled in the last 50 years. About two-thirds of 3- to 5-year-olds attended preprimary programs in 1999. High school graduation rates for 17-year-olds have also increased from 59 percent to 71 percent in the last 50 years (National Center for Education Statistics, 1999).

The fact that children and adolescents spend so much time at school makes this context a potentially powerful influence on their development. Teachers, classmates, and curricula all play an important role in a child's development. But the effects of schools are not easy to assess.

Assessing the Effects of Schools on Children's Development

Since schools were first established, there has been no clear consensus concerning what should be the purpose and function of schools in children's lives. Should schools focus exclusively on students' intellectual development? Should schools be concerned about students' social and emotional lives? Should schools teach health, sex education, family life, personal finance, driver's education, and other courses to prepare students for adulthood? Should schools help solve social problems such as poverty, drug abuse, and racism? Ask your classmates and friends these questions, and you will find a wide range of opinions.

For the most part, the debate has focused on whether schools should train basic intellectual skills or provide a more comprehensive training for life that includes both intellectual and emotional development. The school environment changes as one set of goals is emphasized over the other. In the 1960s, for example, educational reformers claimed that schools were not providing learning experiences that were relevant to students' lives. Programs were implemented so that students could receive more "hands-on" and "real world"

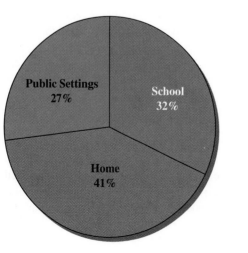

FIGURE 1.3

Percentage of Time Adolescents Spend in Different Settings

SOURCE: Csikszentmihalyi & Larson (1984).

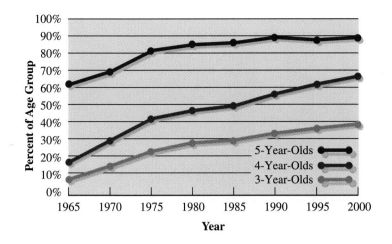

FIGURE 1.4

Percent of 3-, 4-, and 5-Year-Olds in Preschool Programs

SOURCE: National Center of Education Statistics (2000a).

learning experiences. Since the 1980s, the "back-to-basics" movement has gained momentum because policy makers believe we are losing our competitive edge in the world economic market. Some proposals call for more demanding academic curricula, tougher academic standards, more homework, more tests, longer school days, and the end of social promotion. At times, the school has been viewed as an agent of social reform, as seen in the desegregation and mainstreaming movements of the 1970s, which continue to have an influence on schools today.

It also is difficult to assess the effects of schools on children's development because schools differ greatly with respect to philosophy, resources, learning opportunities, and social climate. Some students have well-equipped classrooms, large libraries, the latest computer technology, small classes, modern school facilities, and access to two or more gymnasiums. Other students are expected to learn in schools with outdated textbooks, overcrowded classrooms, poorly paid teachers, and metal detectors at the front door. Many of these students come from poor families who cannot provide additional resources to support their children's learning at home. Because of tremendous disparities in the way public schools are funded in this country, the poor get a poorer quality of education. In his book *Savage Inequalities,* Jonathan Kozol (1991) speculated that some children have a better chance of learning math and reading on the street than they do in school. For some students, the conditions of schooling have not improved much in the last 10 years.

An ongoing debate for schools is a singular focus on intellectual development versus a broader focus on both intellectual and social/emotional development.

Effects of Schooling on Development

Despite difficulties in assessing the effects of schools on development, a growing body of evidence indicates that schools do have on impact on the achievement, socialization, and psychological well-being of children and adolescents. Consider, for example, the consequences of dropping out of school. High school dropouts generally perform more poorly on standardized tests of achievement than same-age peers with more years of schooling do (Alexander, Natriello, & Pallas, 1985). There is also a strong relation between intelligence test (IQ) scores and highest grade completed in school, although it is quite possible that some other factor such as poverty can explain this relationship (Ceci, 1991). However, even after controlling for differences in social background, the relationship between IQ and years of school is still fairly strong. According to Stephen Ceci (1990), this relationship is partly explained by the fact that schools teach the basic skills and cultural knowledge that are included in standardized tests of achievement and intelligence (e.g., "What is the boiling point of water?" "What is the capital of the United States?").

FIGURE 1.5

Average Percentages of Concepts in 8th Grade Mathematics Lessons That Were Stated vs. Developed

SOURCE: National Center of Educational Statistics (1995).

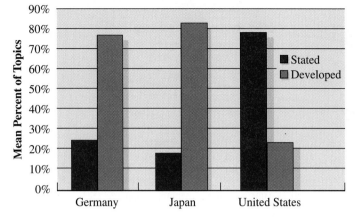

Studies indicate that cross-cultural differences in students' academic achievement is mostly related to cultural differences in schooling and teaching practices.

In general, children in the United States do consistently worse than children in many Western industrialized countries on measures of academic achievement. Cross-national differences are particularly large for secondary students. In the Third International Mathematics and Science Study (TIMSS), the largest cross-national study of educational achievement ever conducted, eighth graders in the United States scored slightly below the international average in mathematics and had scores lower than 14 other countries. U.S. students were slightly above the international average for eighth graders in science but scored below students in Canada, Czech Republic, Hungry, Japan, Singapore, Slovak Republic, and Sweden (International Association for the Evaluation of Educational Achievement, 1997). By the twelfth grade, the mathematics and science scores of U.S. students were well below international averages.

These discrepancies are not simply due to innate differences in cognitive abilities (i.e., Asians do not have better math genes). Researchers have found that American, Japanese, and Chinese students perform equally well on general tests of cognitive functioning (Stevenson & Stigler, 1992). The differences result in part from the instructional practices of teachers in different countries. Both Japanese and Chinese teachers spend more time than American teachers on mathematics instruction (Stevenson & Stigler, 1992). Additionally, U.S. mathematics teachers tend to teach students how to solve a particular problem, then ask the students to solve it on their own. In contrast, Japanese teachers often give students problems that they have not seen before to develop their thinking skills and to prepare them for later instruction (Stigler & Hiebert, 1999). As you can see in Figure 1.5, teachers in other countries also spend more time explaining and developing new concepts in mathematics lessons (Stigler, Gallimore, & Hiebert, 2000). Some important lessons that can be learned from international studies of teaching are described in the Focus on Teaching box.

Schools not only affect students' academic achievement but also influence the way they organize their thoughts and cognition. Cross-cultural research has helped psychologists to disentangle the extent to which advances in cognitive functioning are related to formal schooling or to age differences (Ceci, 1990; Rogoff, 1981; Rogoff & Morelli, 1989; Sharp, Cole, & Lave, 1979). Individuals with more formal schooling are better at remembering disconnected bits of information, and they spontaneously engage in cognitive processes that lead to better recall of information, such as rehearsal and organizational strategies. Additionally, schooled individuals are more likely to sort objects into abstract categories (tools and food items) than into functional groups (e.g., knife with apple, shovel with potato).

Focus on Teaching

Learning from the World's Teachers

James Stigler and his colleagues conducted a videotape study of mathematics classrooms as part of the Third International Mathematics and Science Study (TIMSS) (Stigler, Gonzales, Kaawanaka, Knoll, & Serrano, 1999). Previous large-scale international studies relied on questionnaires to collect information about teaching practices and student learning. The TIMSS Videotape Study was the first of its kind to videotape national samples of teachers teaching in their classrooms. The study focused on eighth-grade mathematics classrooms in three countries: Germany (50 classrooms), Japan (50 classrooms), and the United States (100 classrooms). The summary that follows focuses on comparisons between American and Japanese classes and presents some important lessons for educators. For a more detailed account of this study, see *The Teaching Gap* (1999) by J. W. Stigler and J. Hiebert. As you read these lessons, it is important to keep in mind that Japan and the United States have very different economic, political, and educational systems that need to be considered when making cross-cultural comparisons. For a critique of cross-national comparisons, see *Manufactured Crisis* (1995) by D. C. Berliner and D. J. Biddle.

Lesson One: A Focus on Teaching Methods Is Essential for Improving Education

Many policymakers and educational reformers in the United States view improvements in the quality and competence of teachers as critical for improving student achievement and learning. Although variability in teacher competence within counties was evident in the TIMSS Videotape Study, cultural differences in *teaching methods* were considerably greater and more influential. Students' daily experiences in the classroom are mainly determined by the quality of the teaching methods used. Many highly trained and competent American teachers of mathematics employ limited methods that, for the most part, focus on a narrow range of *procedural skills*. As a result, American students spend most of their time in mathematics classes acquiring isolated skills through repeated practice. In contrast, teachers in Japan teach mathematics in a deeper way: They teach for *conceptual understanding*. Their students spend as much time solving challenging problems as they do practicing skills.

Lesson Two: Teaching Is a Cultural Activity

Teaching is influenced by a small and tacit set of cultural beliefs about how students learn, about what role teachers play in the classroom, and about the nature of their subject matter. Although teaching methods may vary within a culture, there is a shared set of cultural beliefs and expectations that underlie teaching. In part, this is explained by the fact that teachers enter their profession with an image of teaching that they have constructed from their many years as a student.

The Videotape Study revealed that mathematics in American classrooms is taught as a set of isolated facts, procedures, or skills to be learned incrementally, piece by piece. The teacher's role is to break down complex tasks into manageable pieces and to provide plenty of opportunities for practice. When students get confused or frustrated, teachers must quickly assist students by providing information to get them back on track. Many teachers learned mathematics this way, and many parents expect their children to learn mathematics the same way they did.

By contrast, mathematics teaching in Japan reflects a different set of cultural beliefs. Japanese teachers want their students to see relationships between mathematical ideas and concepts. They believe that students learn best by first struggling to solve mathematics problems, then participating in discussions about different problem solutions. The teacher's role in the classroom is to find challenging problems to begin a lesson and to observe how their students solve problems on their own for follow-up discussions. Frustration and confusion are viewed as a natural part of the learning process, and Japanese teachers encourage students to keep struggling in the face of difficulty. They may offer hints to support students' progress, but they refrain from telling or showing students how to solve the problem.

Lesson Three: There Are No "Quick Fixes" for Improving Education

Perhaps the most important lesson of the TIMMS Videotape Study is that there are no "quick fixes" or "magic bullets" to improve education. Despite decades of educational reform in the United States, research suggests that classroom teaching has changed little during this time. By contrast, teaching practices in Japan have changed markedly over the last 50 years. What accounts for this difference?

Whereas American educators have sought major changes with a short period of time, Japanese educators have instituted a system of educational reform that leads to gradual, incremental improvement over time. In Japan, teachers are not

---

Schools affect a wide range of developmental outcomes, including cognition, language, social relationships, and emotional well-being.

Schooling also influences the ability of individuals to perceive abstract visual-spatial relations (e.g., mental rotation of objects) and to make figure-ground discriminations (e.g., find hidden objects in puzzles). Taken together, cross-cultural research suggests that formal Western-style schooling fosters a certain way of thinking, reasoning, and problem solving (Rogoff, 1981).

In addition to cognitive development, schools have a strong influence on students' social and emotional development. The quality of children's school experiences influences a wide range of outcomes including vocational aspirations, feelings of competency and self-worth, academic motivation, identity formation, peer relations, racial attitudes, gender-role beliefs, and even standards of right and wrong. We will discuss many of these influences in later chapters. A few examples include:

- Head Start programs for economically disadvantaged preschool children can help offset some of the effects of poverty, such as truancy, high school dropout, teenage pregnancy, and unemployment.
- Children who are rejected by their peers in school are at greater risk for later psychological disturbance and criminal behavior.
- Children become less intrinsically motivated to learn and less confident of their abilities as they progress in school.

considered competent because they have graduated from college or have completed a standardized test of teacher competency. Japanese teachers are expected to participate in school-based professional development once they enter the teaching profession. *Kounaikenshuu* is the word used to describe the continuous process of school-based professional development in Japan.

One of the most important components of *Kounaikenshuu* is what is known as "lesson study" (*jugyou kenkyuu),* in which groups of teachers work on improving one or several "research lessons." Lesson study involves identifying a problem that poses a challenge to students, and planning, with teacher colleagues, a lesson to achieve a particular learning goal. The lesson is taught by one of the teachers in the lesson-study group, after the other teachers have helped to prepare the design and materials for the lesson. The lesson is then observed by other members of the group. On the basis of the group's observations and discussion of the lesson, the lesson may be revised and taught again. Rather than focusing on a particular weakness of a teacher, group discussions focus on lesson design and teaching methods. Once the lesson-study group has successfully designed and implemented a lesson, it is then shared with other educators. Some Japanese schools may host a "lesson fair" at the end of the school year and invite teachers from other schools to observe the research lessons they have produced in different subjects. Compared with teachers in the United States, Japanese teachers who participate in lesson studies view themselves as contributing to the development of knowledge about teaching as well as contributing to their own professional development.

SOURCE: Adapted from Stigler & Hiebert, 1999.

- Cooperative learning programs, if properly implemented, can promote positive race relations and increase acceptance of handicapped students.
- Schools that foster high self-esteem and academic success can reduce the likelihood of emotional problems, behavioral disturbance, and delinquency.

At this point in the history of child development research, the question is no longer *whether* schools influence children's development, but rather *what* types of schools or schooling experiences exert a positive influence (Linney & Seidman, 1989). As we shall see, there is a large body of research that teachers can draw on to create learning environments suited to the developmental needs of young people.

History of Childhood

The Invention of Childhood and Adolescence

Most people tend to view childhood as a time of innocence, when children need special care and protection. However, historical records reveal that this romantic conception of childhood did not appear in the United States until after the Civil War. In fact, according to some historians, the concept of childhood itself is a fairly recent cultural invention (Aries, 1962; Kessen, 1979). It was not until the last few hundred years that adults began to view children as needing to be nurtured, coddled, and protected. Before examining different theories of child development, it is important to recognize how our ideas about childhood and about children themselves are shaped by social, economic, and historical circumstances.

Until fairly recently, most children in Western society were viewed as miniature adults expected to assume adult roles and responsibilities.

In colonial America, children were viewed as "miniature adults" who could assume adult roles and responsibilities. Most children started to work as either a servant or an apprentice in other people's homes around the age of 7. By puberty, children knew how to farm, to cook, to care for children, and so on. Many immigrant children entered America as indentured servants or as slaves. Children of wealthier parents were sent out of the home to attend boarding school at the age of 7, and most received the equivalent of a college education before the age of 18. For poor and rich children alike, the transition from childhood to adulthood was brief.

The transition to adulthood was equally brief, and perhaps more difficult, for children of the early nineteenth century. During the early periods of industrialization, children were viewed as a cheap source of unskilled labor. Many children worked in textile mills, sweatshops, and mines. According to an 1870 census report, one out of eight children between the ages of 10 and 15 in the United States worked as child laborers (Lomax, Kagan, & Rosenkranz, 1978). Like adults, these children were expected to work between 12 and 14 hours a day performing menial tasks under dirty and hazardous working conditions. Corporal punishment was frequently used if children were lax at their work, as they frequently were, due to immaturity, poor health, or fatigue. As before, childhood experiences were conditioned by social class and ethnicity. Children of wealthier parents attended school longer because their parents could afford to forgo their meager wages.

The "discovery" of adolescence as a distinct stage of development came about as the result of economic and social changes in the late nineteenth century (Kett, 1977). The nature of the economy changed in favor of workers with a formal education, which led to the expansion of the public high school system. Between 1870 and 1900, there was a fivefold increase in the number of adolescents attending high school (Rury, 1991). At the same time, social reformers began to emphasize the state's responsibility to protect the welfare of the child and to eliminate inequalities in education. Between 1870 and 1920, many states restricted the use of child labor and established compulsory education laws for youths under the age of 14 or 16. Most important of all, G. Stanley Hall (1904), one of the first American

Compare these two images of classrooms from the 1950s (left) and 1990s (right). What changes do you see in teaching practices?
SOURCE: Jack Moebes/CORBIS and Will Hart/Photo Edit.

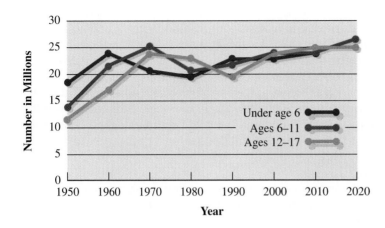

FIGURE 1.6

*Number of Children
in the United States:
1950 to 2020
(Projected)*

SOURCE: Forum on
Child and Family
Statistics (1999).

child psychologists, proclaimed that puberty should be viewed as new birth, "for the higher
and more completely human traits are born" (p. xiii). Hall believed that a prolonged period
of development was necessary in order for the highest human capabilities to emerge.

This brief historical analysis shows that society's beliefs about what children are like
and how they should be treated have changed dramatically over time. There is also considerable variability in the definition of childhood from society to society. Historians argue
that adolescence as a distinct stage of development exists mainly in those societies where
prolonged education and socialization is believed to be necessary for people to become
competent members of a community (Aries, 1962; Modell & Goodman, 1990).

Even within Western society today, there is considerable variability in the worlds of
childhood among different social groups. For large numbers of immigrant, poor, and minority children, the circumstances of childhood are far from the romantic ideals of goodness and innocence proposed by social reformers at the turn of the century. In the next
section, we will see that childhood at the beginning of the twenty-first century continues to
be affected by social and economic change as well as by ethnicity and social class.

Current Status of Children and Adolescents

Increases in the Population of Schoolchildren

During what was know as the "baby boom" period following World War II (1946 to 1964),
there was a dramatic increase in the number of children in the United States. Fluctuations
in child population over the last 50 years can be seen in Figure 1.6. Enrollment in public
schools peaked in the early 1970s. From 1971 to 1984, the school-age population declined
by 10 percent, but enrollment in public schools started to increase again and hit record enrollment levels in the mid 1990s (NCES, 1999). In 1999, the number of children under the
age of 18 was estimated to be about 70 million (Forum on Child & Family Statistics, 1999).
Over the next several decades the number of children under the age of 18 in the United
States is expected to rise to approximately 77 million by the year 2020.

Increases in the Ethnic Diversity of Schoolchildren

One of the most important demographic trends in the last 20 years is the increased racial
and ethnic diversity of America's children. As recently as 1980, nearly 75 percent of all
children in this country were non-Hispanic whites. By the year 2010, this group is expected
to constitute just over half (60 percent) of the U.S. child population. Prior to 1997, African

FIGURE 1.7

Portrait of America's Kindergartners: Class of 1998/1999

SOURCE: National Center for Educational Statistics (2000b).

In the fall of 1998, approximately 4 million children were attending kindergarten in the United States, many for the first time. According to a national study by the U.S. Department of Education, the ethnic backgrounds of the kindergarten class of 1998/1999 were 58 percent white, 19 percent Latino, 15 percent African American, 3 percent Asian, 2 percent American Indian or Alaskan Native, and 1 percent Hawaiian Native or Pacific Islander. A majority of America's kindergartners (75 percent) live with two parents, and nearly half have mothers with some college education or a college degree. Other key findings of this study were:

- Prior to kindergarten, four out of five children received care on a regular basis from someone other than a parent.

- As children enter kindergarten for the first time, parents report that 92 percent are eager to learn and 75 percent persist at tasks very often.

- Nearly half of parents report that a family member reads or sings to their kindergarten-age child on a regular basis.

- Approximately 66 percent of first-time kindergarten students can recognize their letters, and 94 percent can recognize numbers and count to 10.

- Teachers report that 75 percent of kindergartners are able to make friends, to join others in play, and to form friendships. Fewer than 10 percent have difficulty getting along with others.

- About 12 percent of boys and 11 percent of girls have a body mass index that places them at risk for becoming overweight.

It is important to note that the above characteristics varied by family type, income level, ethnicity, language spoken at home, and maternal education.

Americans were the largest minority group in the United States. Currently, African Americans and Latinos each represent approximately 15 percent of the child population in the United States. These numbers are followed by Asian Americans at 4 percent and Native Americans at 1 percent. The number of Latino children has increased faster than that of any other racial or ethnic group. Figure 1.7 presents a portrait of the kindergarten class of 1998/1999. As you can see, there is considerable diversity in the children coming to school. By the year 2020, more than one in five children in the United States will be of Hispanic origin. The Asian-American child population is also expected to increase from 4 percent to 6 percent by 2010 (Forum on Child & Family Statistics, 1999). Figure 1.8 shows the growing diversity of the school-age population.

A major contributor to the increased diversity of America's school children is immigration. The United States is a nation of immigrants, but rates of immigration have varied considerably over different periods of our history. Currently, the United States is experiencing a period of high immigration, which began in the 1960s. By 1995, the number of foreign-born persons residing in the United States reached 25 million, and this figure was projected to grow to 28 million by the year 2000 (National Research Council, 1997). Before 1965, the majority of legal immigrants came from Canada and Europe. However, Asia and Latin America are now the major sources of immigration into the United States.

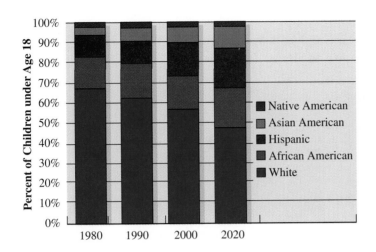

FIGURE 1.8

Changing Demographics of U.S. School Population

SOURCE: Forum on Child and Family Statistics (1999).

Immigrants tend to settle in areas where there are people of similar backgrounds and nationalities. In the 1990s, the majority of the immigrants who arrived in the United States settled in only six states: California, New York, Texas, Florida, New Jersey, and Illinois. In addition, according to 1990 census data, more than 90 percent of the foreign-born population resides in metropolitan areas, including Los Angeles, New York, Miami, Anaheim, Chicago, Washington, D.C., Houston, and San Francisco (National Research Council, 1997). However, geographic concentrations of immigrants are not static, and other states have experienced an influx of these residents in recent years. For example, the number of Hispanic children enrolled in North Carolina's schools increased 250 percent from 1997 to 1998 (N.C. Department of Public Instruction, 1998).

Due to recent increases in the number of immigrants living in the United States, schools are becoming more culturally and linguistically diverse. The number of children who spoke a language at home other than English or who had difficulty speaking English was 2.4 million in 1995, an increase from 1.3 million in 1979 (Forum on Child & Family Statistics, 1999). This number represents approximately 5 percent of school-aged children in the United States.

By the year 2020, more than two-thirds of America's schoolchildren will be African American, Latino, Asian, or Native American.

The United States has the highest poverty rate of any industrialized country.

Changes in Rates of Childhood Poverty

Another significant factor affecting the status of America's children today is child poverty, which has both immediate and long lasting negative effects on children's development. As you can see in Figure 1.9, rates of poverty among children under the age of 18 have fluctuated since the early 1980s, and these poverty levels depend on the racial or ethnic background of the child. Childhood poverty reached a peak in 1993, when more than 22 percent of children under the age of 18 lived in poverty. In 1998, 13.5 million or 19 percent of children were poor. This year was the first time childhood poverty rates have been below 20 percent since 1980. However, children continue to represent a large proportion (37 percent) of the poor population in the United States. Poverty rates are the highest for children under the age of 18 than for any other age group. Additionally, 8 percent of children in 1998 lived in families with total incomes of less than half of the poverty line, or $8,200 a year for a family of four (Forum on Child & Family Statistics, 1999). Overall, the United States has the highest child poverty rate of any industrialized country. U.S. child poverty rates are two to three times higher than those reported by the United Kingdom, Canada, Germany, Sweden, or France.

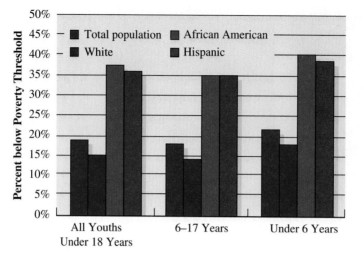

FIGURE 1.9

Percent of Poverty by Age Group

SOURCE: Forum on Child and Family Statistics (1999).

Poverty rates tend to be higher among African American and Hispanic populations.

Contrary to cultural stereotypes, a majority of poor children are non-Hispanic whites. In actual numbers, approximately 9 million white children live in poverty. Poverty rates, however, tend to be higher among African American and Hispanic populations. Because African American and Hispanic children make up a smaller proportion of the total child population, the percentage of poor children in these groups is considerably higher than that of non-Hispanic whites, as shown in Figure 1.10. Whereas 10 percent of the total population of white children in 1998 were poor, the comparable figures were 36 percent for African American children and 34 percent for Latino children (Forum on Child & Family Statistics, 1999).

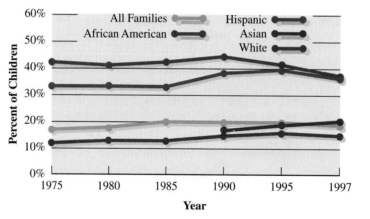

FIGURE 1.10

Percent of U.S. Children under 18 Living in Poverty by Ethnic Group

SOURCE: Forum on Child and Family Statistics (1999).

Changes in Family Structures

Another significant change affecting the status of children today is the rise of single-headed households. The number of parents living with a child is generally linked to quality of care and amount of economic resources available to that child. Research indicates that children who live with just one parent are more likely to have family incomes below the poverty line. The percentage of American children living with two parents has declined from 85 percent in 1970 to 68 percent in 1999 (Forum on Child & Family Statistics, 1999). We will examine some of these changes more closely in Chapter 9.

One in two preschoolers has a mother in the labor force.

One in two will live in a single-parent family at some point in his or her childhood.

One in two will never complete college.

One in three is born to unmarried parents.

One in three will be poor at some point in his or her childhood.

One in three is behind a year or more in school.

One in four lives with only one parent.

One in four was born poor.

One in five is poor now.

One in five was born to a mother who did not graduate from high school.

One in five has a foreign-born mother.

One in six is born to a mother who did not receive prenatal care in the first three months of her pregnancy.

One in six has no health insurance.

One in eight will never graduate from high school.

One in eight was born to a teenage mother.

One in 12 lives at less than half the poverty level.

One in 12 has a disability.

One in 13 was born with low birthweight.

One in 24 lives with neither parent.

FIGURE 1.11

A Portrait of America's Children

SOURCE: Children's Defense Fund (2000).

Implications for Schools

A summary portrait of America's children today is presented in Figure 1.11. How will the current status of children and youth affect schools? First, as mentioned, there are record numbers of elementary and secondary students enrolling in private and public schools today. Since 1990 school enrollment figures have increased by 14 percent, or 4.4 million elementary and secondary students, and this trend is expected to continue throughout the rest of the twenty-first century (U.S. Department of Education, 2000). Increases in the school population are placing an added burden on schools that are already dealing with overcrowded classrooms, rundown facilities, and teacher shortages. In addition, statistics indicate that the majority of teachers today are in their mid forties, and this group of teachers is expected to retire within the next 5 to 10 years. An estimated 2.2 million new teachers will be needed over the next 10 years to replace those teachers and to meet enrollment increases.

As described, an increasingly diverse group of schoolchildren is coming to school. One of the challenges for educators will be to provide equal educational opportunities to students from various cultural backgrounds. Despite 30 years of desegregation and bilingual education legislation, national test scores of Hispanic and African American students lag behind those of white and Asian students. For example, the most recent NAEP assessment showed that the average scores of 17-year-old African American students were about the same as those of 13-year-old white students in mathematics and reading (National Center for Educational Statistics, 2000c). Compared with white and Asian students, African American and Hispanic students are less likely to take advanced courses in mathematics and science (National Center for Educational Statistics, 2000c), and they have lower graduation rates.

The educational progress of some students is complicated by language barriers. As has been mentioned, approximately 5 percent of schoolchildren speak a language other than

Schools today are ill prepared to educate the growing numbers of ethnically diverse students.

English at home. The majority of these children speak Spanish at home, and most language-minority children are found in kindergarten through fourth grade (August & Hakuta, 1997). As the Latino population expands, more and more teachers will be working with students with limited English proficiency, or English-language learners. However, a National Research Council study indicated that approximately 55 percent of teachers of students with English-language learners had taken a relevant college course or received in-service professional development related to working with these students (August & Hakuta, 1997). Only one-third of the teachers had taken college courses focusing on cultural diversity. At present, teachers and administrators are not sufficiently prepared to teach these language-minority children.

More important, as has been discussed, a disproportionate number of both Hispanic and African American families are poor. Poverty rates also tend to be more persistent among ethnic minority families. One study showed that 24 percent of African American children who were under 4 in 1968 lived in poverty for 10 of 15 years. The comparable figure for white children was less than 1 percent (McLoyd, 1990).

The negative consequences of poverty on children's development are well documented (Sherman, 1997; Duncan & Brooks-Gunn, 1997). Poor children are more likely to be born prematurely or at a low birthweight, and they are at greater risk for malnutrition and health problems during early development. Poor children are twice as likely as other children to have impaired vision, hearing problems, and anemia. Many poor children live in substandard houses where they are exposed daily to structural, electrical, and sanitation hazards. It is estimated that 12 million children younger than 7 years old live in homes that contain lead paint, which if inhaled or ingested can cause comas, convulsions, mental retardation, and even death in extreme cases (Sherman, 1997).

Poor families also make up a large percentage of homeless people in the United States. In 1997, the U.S. Department of Education estimated that there were 625,000 homeless school-age children, but fewer than half of these children were attending school (National Center for Educational Statistics, 1997). The Focus on Teaching on pp. 24–25 presents a summary of different school programs for homeless children.

In terms of school performance, poor children are likely to experience many educational setbacks. By the time they enter school, poor children are already behind their middle-class classmates on scores in standardized tests of achievement and intelligence (Sherman, 1997; National Center for Educational Statistics, 2000b). Illness and malnutrition can cause children to be less attentive, less motivated, and more irritable, which can lead to behavioral and learning problems in the classroom. As a result, a disproportionate number of low-income children are placed in special education or are retained in a grade.

The educational problems of poor children are further complicated by schools they attend. A relatively high percent attend

The school population in the United States is more diverse than ever before.

poor schools with fewer financial and material resources to help these students. For example, teachers in poor schools are two to four times more likely to report inadequate supplies of books, learning materials, and audiovisual equipment, including computers (Sherman, 1997). By the time they reach adolescence, children from low-income families are more likely to drop out of school early. Rates of school truancy, juvenile delinquency, and teenage pregnancy are also higher among children from poor families.

It is clear that poverty can have negative pervasive effects on children. However, many children are resilient and able to overcome tremendous obstacles. That is, not all poor children grow up to be high school dropouts, juvenile delinquents, or teenage parents. As we shall see later, some children are less vulnerable than others to the effects of poverty. Parents, schools, and resources in the community can protect children from the devastating effects of poverty.

Children who grow up in poverty experience many educational setbacks.

Perspectives on Children's Development

So far we have discussed various reasons why teachers need a working knowledge of children's development and of the status of children today. In this section, we will begin to examine the theories child development experts use to explain children's development. First, we will discuss how theorists define development and what they view as the important issues of debate. Next, we will look at five different perspectives on children's development: biological, psychoanalytic, behavioral, cognitive, and contextual. This section serves as an introduction to the theories that will be discussed in later chapters.

Why so many theories of development? Suppose you have a girl in your classroom who frequently starts fights with classmates. How would you explain her behavior? There are a number of possible explanations. Perhaps she is not getting enough care and affection at home and is, therefore, acting out to get attention. Perhaps she has not learned how to control her emotions. Perhaps she has not learned more socially acceptable ways of relating to others. Or, it may be that this student is watching too many violent television shows and is simply imitating the behavior of television characters. Each of these explanations suggests a different form of intervention. Developmental theories provide several frameworks for understanding and interpreting children's behavior. Generally, there are multiple explanations for a particular pattern of behavior, and most theorists agree that one theory of development is not sufficient to explain all we know and observe about children. Therefore, it is best to have a repertoire of different child development theories from which to draw.

Definitions and Issues

Development as used in this text refers to changes in the child that occur *over time*. Although there are differences among theorists, most agree that development represents systematic and successive changes that enhance a child's overall adaptation to the environment. Development is not just any change that occurs as the child matures. To be labeled *developmental,* the changes must follow a logical or orderly pattern that moves toward greater complexity and enhances survival. Developmental changes in language, for example, involve more complex forms of speech and language that enable children to better communicate with people in their environment.

For the purposes of this discussion, we define a **theory** as a set of general statements (rules, assumptions, propositions, or principles) used to explain facts. When applied to child development, a theory provides a framework for observing, interpreting, and

A developmental change follows a logical or orderly pattern that moves toward greater complexity and enhances survival.

School Programs for Homeless Children

The homeless population, once stereotyped as the fate of unemployed alcoholics or schizophrenic bag ladies, has experienced a demographic shift leaving an estimated over half a million children sleeping homeless each night (U.S. Department of Education, 1997). Homeless families face a number of barriers upon enrolling their school-age children in school, and if enrollment is in fact allowed, the children may experience difficulties of acceptance, misplacement, and misunderstanding among peers and teachers.

The U.S. Congress passed the Stewart B. McKinney Homeless Assistance Act of 1987 to facilitate the enrollment of homeless children into public schools. The act makes provisions for each state to have an Office for Coordination of Education of Homeless Children and Youth, and to review and revise practices that impede homeless children's access to public school. Each state is also required to have an approved plan for addressing problems associated with the children's enrollment, attendance, and success in school (U.S. Department of Education, 1999). With the increasing prevalence of homeless children in schools today, it is essential that comprehensive, support programs are available to help schools address the emotional, social, developmental, educational, or health problems that often afflict homeless children. Some examples of such school programs that can serve as models for further development include:

- **City Park School in Dallas, Texas.** Staff members have been successful in assisting new students in feeling accepted, and they provide support for academic and psychosocial needs. There is a strong emphasis on basic skills. School supplies are given to the students, and parents are referred to medical and social services.

explaining changes in the child over time. More specifically stated, the three purposes of a developmental theory are to describe how children differ from one age to the next; describe how different aspects of development are interrelated (e.g., influence of cognitive development on peer relations); and explain why development proceeds in a certain direction.

It would be easy to understand children's development if there were just one overarching theory. But, as suggested earlier, there are several different theories of development. Each theory gives the "facts" of development a different meaning by organizing them differently, focusing on different aspects of development, and emphasizing different causal factors. For example, some theories focus on intellectual development, whereas other theories focus on physical or social development. Theories of development also differ with respect to the position they take on certain basic core issues. Among the issues most relevant to educators are the following:

Nature versus nurture. To what extent is development a function of innate biological processes, environmental conditions, or some interaction of the two?

- **Our House, in Decatur, Georgia.** This agency provides free quality day care to homeless children between the ages of 2 months and 6 years who live in shelters in the county. Children are cared for on an emergency basis until they can begin school. The program provides a safe space, a healthy diet, health care, cognitive stimulation, and emotional support to young children.

- **Grace Hill Family Center in St. Louis, Missouri.** This program provides shelter-based educational services for homeless parents and children. The program's first priority is to enroll shelter children in school. A peer counselor works with school officials and families to place children in preferred schools, ensuring that records are transferred, transportation is arranged, and teachers are informed of any special needs. Volunteers provide child care for children or parents looking for employment and tutoring for school-aged children.

- **First Place in Seattle, Washington.** This elementary school project is designed to meet the educational and emotional needs of homeless children. Space as well as transportation from shelters is provided by the Seattle public schools. The program operates in two classrooms for children from kindergarten through sixth grade. The program offers nutritious meals, academic work, and a quiet time for reading. Teachers give individual attention, counseling, and extra help with schoolwork when needed.

SOURCE: Stronge & Reed-Victor (2000)

Stability versus plasticity. Are there critical periods in which a child must have certain social or cognitive experiences in order to develop normally? Are developmental processes highly malleable and open to change at any point in the course of development?

Continuity versus discontinuity. Is development a continuous process that occurs gradually in small increments? Is development a series of discrete stages that represent major and abrupt transformations in functioning?

Passive versus active child. What is a child's role in the developmental process? Is the child a passive organism that is simply shaped by genetic or environmental influences? Are children active agents who shape, control, and direct their own development?

Endpoint versus no endpoint. What is it that develops? Is there an endpoint to development? Do all children follow a universal sequence of development?

As a general introduction to the theories that will be discussed in later chapters, we will compare different theoretical perspectives on development with regard to their positions on

Developmental theories are important because they influence the beliefs and practices of both teachers and educational policy makers.

The Educational Legacy of Locke and Rousseau

Two early philosophers, John Locke and Jean-Jacques Rousseau, are considered the philosophical forefathers of developmental psychology. From the eighteenth century until today, these philosophers have greatly influenced our beliefs about the nature of children and how they should be educated. Current debates concerning the role of education in children's lives can be traced back to these early philosophers.

John Locke (1632–1704)

The English philosopher John Locke proposed that the child's mind is a blank slate, or *tabula rasa*, on which experience makes its imprint. Children are neither good nor bad; they become that way by virtue of how they are treated. In his book *Some Thoughts Concerning Education* Locke (1902) compared the formation of the child's mind and attitudes to the "fountains of some rivers, when a gentle application of the hand turns the flexible waters into channels, that make them take quite contrary courses" (pp. 1–2). Locke recognized that children were born with different temperments and propensities, but he believed that a child could be infinitely improved and perfected through experience, humane treatment, and education. Locke further believed that adults could mold children's moral character and intellect by conditioning them to have the right habits. In Locke's conception of children we find the roots of behavioral approaches to education, which emphasize the importance of reward and punishment in shaping children's behavior. Key to this perspective is the assumption that children are mostly a product of their environment.

Jean-Jacques Rousseau (1712–1778)

Jean-Jacques Rousseau, a Swiss-born philosopher, introduced a romantic conception of childhood. For Rousseau, a child is born in a state of natural goodness. Adults should not shape children forcibly but protect them from the pressures of society and allow them to develop naturally. Rousseau (1762/1911) presented his views on education in *Emile*, a story about a boy and his tutor. Emile passes through several stages of development, and the tutor provides experiences that are appropriate to his needs at the time. Rousseau believed that each dimension of development (physical, mental, social, and moral) followed a particular schedule that should be respected and protected. According to Rousseau, children are incapable of true reasoning until the age of 12. During the early period of development,

the basic issues described above. An understanding of these issues is important for two reasons. First, debates about children's development often play a major role in educational reform movements. As described in the Focus on Research box, educational reformers often share different beliefs about the nature of children and how they should be educated. Second, we have seen that teachers use different theories to explain children's behavior and to make instructional decisions. These theories, in turn, involve different assumptions about the nature of the child, the sources of development, the nature of development, and so forth. In adopting one or the other view, teachers need to be cognizant of the assumptions they are making about children's development.

children should be permitted to learn through discovery and experience. In Rousseau's conception of the child, we find the roots of child-centered approaches to education. Key to this perspective is the assumption that the curriculum must evolve from the natural capacities and interests of the child, and it must foster the child's progression toward higher stages of development.

Locke, Rousseau, and Education Today

Locke and Rousseau expressed very different views about the role of education in children's lives. The concept of the child as a blank slate allowed early educational reformers to "dream of schools as institutions for creating a perfect society" (Spring, 1994, p. 29). Because Locke's conception of the child stressed the role of the environment in children's development, it continues to have a powerful influence on education. Today, traces of Locke's "malleable child" can be found in educational reforms that call for higher test scores, tougher promotion standards, stricter discipline, more homework, and better trained workers.

Rousseau's romantic view of children had the most influence on educational reformers of the twentieth century who rejected the emphasis on passivity, conformity, and authority in schools (Spring, 1994). Elements of Rousseau can be found in the writing of John Dewey (1859–1952), one of the most influential educational reformers of this century. In *The Child and Curriculum,* Dewey expressed the basic principles of child-centered education:

> The child is the starting point, the center, and the end. His development, his growth, is the ideal. It alone furnishes the standard (Archambault, 1964, pp. 342–343).

Dewey's approach to education emphasized student interest, student activity, group work, real-life learning experiences, and cooperation. Dewey's philosophy influenced educational reforms in the progressive period of the early 1900s and in the mid 1960s to early 1970s, when open classrooms, discovery learning, and other activity-based curricula were introduced. In recent years, the view that education should be appropriate to a child's stage of development has influenced efforts to reform public school programs for young children (Bredekamp, 1987) and young adolescents (Carnegie Council on Adolescent Development, 1989).

Biological Theories

Early pioneers in developmental psychology explained children's development in terms of innate biological processes. Human characteristics "bloom" like a flower according to a predetermined biological timetable. A child goes through invariant, predictable stages of growth and development. According to this perspective, the environment provides the basic nutrients for growth, but it plays little or no role in determining the sequence of development. Moreover, children passively respond and adjust to the changes that occur with age.

Biological theories have been used to explain changes in height, weight, language, mental abilities, motor skills, and many other characteristics. One of the most influential maturational theorists in education was Arnold Gesell (1880–1961) who, along with his colleagues at the Yale Child Development Clinic, established age norms for growth and behavioral change in 10 major areas of development (Gesell & Ilg, 1946; Gesell, Ilg, & Ames, 1956). Gesell and his colleagues also introduced the concept of *readiness.* Learning could occur only if a child was biologically "ready." If a child is unable to perform the activities predicted to be achievable at a specific age, he or she simply needs more time to mature. This view comes closest to the *nativist* theory of development described previously in the section on teachers' beliefs.

A more contemporary version of this biological perspective on development can be found in the work of **behavioral geneticists.** Geneticists tell us that many of our physical characteristics (e.g., body type, eye and hair color, skin color) are inherited. Moreover, many of the traits that make us uniquely human (e.g., ability to stand on two legs, speak, think abstractly) are also inherited. We also know that some forms of mental retardation, such as Down's syndrome, are caused by chromosomal abnormalities. Behavioral geneticists study the degree to which psychological traits (sociability, aggression, criminality, affective disorders) and mental abilities (intelligence or creative talents) are inherited. Just as many of our physical characteristics are determined by heredity, behavioral geneticists argue that many of our psychological attributes also have a genetic component. For example, as we will discuss in Chapter 4, some researchers have argued that as much as 60 percent of the variation in intelligence within a given population is due to genetic differences (Hernnstein & Murray, 1994). The comparable statistic for personality traits can range from 5 percent to 40 percent. In reviewing research on behavioral genetics, one researcher concluded: "Genetic influence is so ubiquitous and pervasive that a shift in emphasis is warranted: Ask not what is heritable, ask what is not heritable" (Plomin, 1989, p. 108).

Although research on behavioral genetics suggests that many of a child's traits and abilities may be influenced by biological factors, most theorists today recognize the important roles of the environment and experience in this developmental process. A child born with a genetic predisposition, such as shyness, may not necessarily grow up to be a shy adult. The actual emergence or appearance of this genetic trait will depend on the child's environment. However, a child's genetic traits can shape that environment in several interesting ways. Shy children, for example, may elicit different reactions from others or choose to engage in more solitary activities than highly sociable children. Therefore, the child's genotype and environment are often strongly related (Plomin, DeFries, & Loehlin, 1977; Scarr & McCartney, 1983). In Chapter 2, we will discuss in more detail how genetic and environmental factors can work together to influence children's development. Current research on behavioral genetics suggests that development is a complex interplay between genes and the environment (Plomin, 1990).

Psychoanalytic Theories

Psychoanalytic theories focus on developmental changes in the self and personality. Psychoanalytic theorists like Sigmund Freud (1856–1939) and Erik Erikson (1902–1994) saw development as a *discontinuous process* that follows a series of discrete stages. At each stage of maturation, certain drives, needs, or conflicts emerge that influence the way a child relates to the environment. These stages are summarized in Table 1.1. Each stage builds on the previous one and represents *qualitative changes* in the child's personality structures or sense of self.

Table 1.1	Stage Views of Development		
Age	**Freud**	**Erikson**	**Piaget**
Infancy (Birth to 2½ years)	Oral Anal	Trust vs. mistrust Autonomy vs. shame	Sensorimotor
Early childhood (2½ years to 6 years)	Phallic	Initiative vs. guilt	Preoperations
Middle childhood (6 to 12 years)	Latency	Industry vs. inferiority	Concrete operations
Adolescence (12 to 19 years)	Genital	Identity vs. role confusion Intimacy vs. isolation	Formal operations

According to psychoanalytic theories, the ways in which children deal with their needs at different ages set the patterns for personality development. For example, toddlers who are harshly punished for accidents during toilet training could develop feelings of shame and self-doubt that affect later development. Erikson, more than Freud, recognized that societies have agreed upon ways of meeting a child's needs, but maturation still determines when certain personality dimensions emerge. In addition, Erikson believed that development is a lifelong process, whereas Freud maintained that the basic structures of the child's personality are laid down within the first five years of life. In other words, there is a **critical period** for personality development.

Erikson believed that development was a lifelong process.

Behavioral Theories

At the opposite end of the nature–nurture continuum are behaviorist perspectives on development. Behaviorists maintain that developmental changes in behavior are influenced by the environment, and the major mechanisms of development are principles of learning. A child's level of maturation was of little importance to early theorists, but most behaviorists today take a more moderate position, which recognizes certain biological constraints on development (Miller, 1993).

Behavioral theories have been used to explain children's development in several areas. John Watson (1878–1958), known as the father of behaviorism, examined the role of **classical conditioning** in the development of children's emotions. Watson conditioned a young boy, Albert, to be afraid of a white rat by making a loud noise whenever the rat appeared. The child's innate fear of loud noises (unconditioned response) became associated with the rat (conditioned response). After several learning trials, Albert showed the same fearful reaction when the rat alone appeared.

B. F. Skinner (1904–1990) argued that parents influence their child's language development through the principles of **instrumental** or **operant conditioning.** When babies begin to babble, parents react positively, repeat sounds, and reinforce the child for attempting to communicate. Parents respond more positively to sounds that resemble words than to sounds they cannot recognize as words. According to Skinner, this differential reinforcement increases the likelihood that certain sounds will be made again by the child. Behaviorists argue that the meaning of words and rules of grammar are acquired through the same principles of reinforcement.

Behavioral theories of development assume that learning, conceived as a series of passive responses to incoming stimuli, controls children's development.

Behaviorists also believe that children acquire new behaviors through the processes of *observation* and *imitation*. That is, children do not have to be explicitly reinforced for a behavior; they can simply observe a model, remember the behavior, and repeat it later. Observational or social learning theories have been used to explain developmental changes in aggression, social skills, sex-role behavior, attitudes, moral judgments, and standards of conduct (Bandura, 1989).

Behaviorists believe development is a gradual, *continuous* process. It represents small, *quantitative changes,* as the child acquires new skills and behaviors. Similar to maturational theories, children have a *passive role* in this developmental process. They simply respond to environmental inputs and store them away for later use. In addition, there is *no critical stage* for developing various cognitive, language, or social skills. If children are deprived of certain experiences early in development, they can acquire these skills later on. According to this view, there is a good deal of plasticity in development. Furthermore, there are no universal patterns of development because inputs are provided by the environment, which can vary from child to child.

Cognitive Theories

Cognitive theorists focus on the ways children construct their own understandings of their environment. Development occurs through the interplay between a child's emerging mental capabilities and his or her environmental experiences. These theories support the belief that both nature and nurture explain children's development. For this reason, the cognitive theories that we will examine represent an *interactional perspective*. That is, development takes place through the interaction of innate and environmental theories. In subsequent chapters, we will study three different cognitive theories of development: cognitive developmental theory; information processing theory; and social learning theory. Each of these theoretical perspectives is introduced here.

Cognitive theories of development assume that development is the product of children's purposefully interacting with their environment.

Cognitive Developmental Theory

Jean Piaget (1896–1980) is probably the best-known developmental psychologist in education. Piaget proposed that children pass through an invariant sequence of stages, each characterized by qualitatively different ways of organizing information and learning about the world. He divided cognitive development into four distinct stages, which were presented in Table 1.1. Key to this sequence is the development of symbolic thought, which begins in infancy and continues until thought processes are governed by principles of formal logic.

Piaget believed development represented *qualitative changes* in children's cognitive processes and structures. He also believed that all children pass through these cognitive stages in the same order, but not necessarily at the same age. That is, there is a *universal pattern* to children's cognitive development. In keeping with an interactional perspective, Piaget proposed that development takes place through the interaction of innate and environmental factors. As a child matures, new possibilities become available that stimulate further development. These experiences, in turn, are interpreted in terms of what the child already knows. In this way, children play an *active role* in their own development.

Information Processing Theory

Information processing theories provide another interactional view of development. Rather than focusing on how knowledge is organized at various stages of development, these theories focus on the precise steps involved in performing mental tasks. Information processing

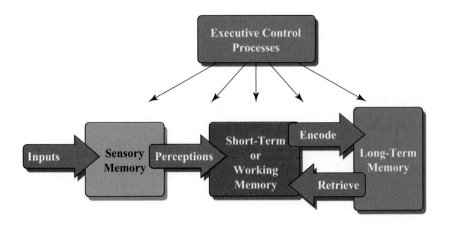

FIGURE 1.12

Model of Human Information Processing System

theorists use the computer as a model of human thinking. As with the computer, data must be entered, processed, and stored in a child's memory. The components of this information processing system are shown in Figure 1.12. The sense organs receive and pass along information, which is then transformed and recorded into memory by the child for later retrieval. According to this perspective, cognitive advances in thinking result from gradual improvements in children's attention, memory, and strategies for acquiring and using information. Therefore, development involves both *quantitative* (increases in amount of information stored) and *qualitative* (new strategies for information storage and retrieval) changes.

In a view similar to Piaget's, information processing theorists maintain that development results from an interplay between information from the environment and the state of a child's information processing system. The child's existing knowledge and cognitive skills influence their ability to acquire new understandings. Although information processing theorists recognize the importance of neurological development, they assume that the development of some cognitive skills can be accelerated with training. Numerous investigations have examined how children can be taught to use more sophisticated memory and learning strategies, but the positive effects of this training for young children are often short-lived.

Both Piagetian theorists and information processing theorists believe that children's existing knowledge and their cognitive skills influence their ability to acquire new information.

Social Learning Theories

Social learning theories help explain how children learn social behaviors, such as acts of helping and caring for others, aggressive tendencies, and behaviors appropriate for their gender. Early social learning theories proposed that children learn new behaviors through observation and imitation. In a reformulation of this theory, referred to as *social-cognitive theory,* Albert Bandura (b. 1925) specified a number of cognitive factors that influence the process of social learning. In order to imitate models, children must be able to process and store information about social behaviors, to anticipate consequences for certain actions, and to regulate their own behavior. As these cognitive processes change with age, children become better able to learn from their social environments.

Similar to Piagetian and information processing approaches, social cognitive theory maintains that children form mental representations of their social world. For this reason, a child has as much influence on the environment as the environment has on the child. This interplay between the child and the environment is captured in Bandura's concept of **reciprocal determinism** (Bandura, 1986). Children's mental representations of a situation or event influence the way they act and feel, which determines how others perceive and respond to them. These reactions, in turn, influence children's thinking and behavior in

Along with Piagetian and information processing theories, contemporary theories of social learning also suggest that children form mental representations of their social world.

subsequent situations. Because social cognitive theory stresses reciprocal relations between a child's internal states (mental representations, perceptions, and emotions) and the environment, it represents an interactional perspective.

Contextual Theories

This last group of theories focuses on the influence of the social and cultural context on children's development. We know from cross-cultural research that there is considerable variability from culture to culture in what children are expected to learn, how they are expected to acquire information and skills, what types of activities children participate in, when children are allowed to participate in those activities, and so on. Contextual theories help to explain these social influences on children's development.

Contextual theorists assume a child has an *active role* in shaping his or her own development. As children mature, they actively seek different social and physical contexts. Activities within these contexts, in turn, change the children, which subsequently changes how they select and respond to activities in the future. However, in contrast to the interactional theories discussed earlier, contextualists emphasize that both the child and the environment are constantly changing, and changes in one often lead to changes in the other. Therefore, there can be *no universal patterns or endpoints* for development. Contextual theories offer a more complex view of development than other developmental theories. According to this perspective, development cannot be separated from the context in which it takes place. A brief description of two theories that fit the contextual framework—social-cultural theory and ecological theory—are presented here.

Social-Cultural Theory

Lev Vygotsky (1896–1934) was one of the first developmentalists to consider the influence of a child's social and cultural context. In his social-cultural theory of language and cognitive development, knowledge is not individually constructed; rather it is coconstructed between people. Vygotsky believed that children are endowed with certain "elementary functions" (perception, memory, attention, and language) that are transformed into higher mental functions through interactions with others. Vygotsky proposed that talking, thinking, remembering, and problem solving occur first on a social plane between two people. As a child gains new skills and knowledge, the other person involved in an interaction adjusts his or her level of guidance and assistance, which allows the child to assume more and more responsibility for the activity. These social exchanges are subsequently transformed and organized by the child into internal actions and thoughts the child uses to regulate his own behavior. Vygotsky believed that development involved *qualitative changes* as the child moves from elementary to higher forms of mental functioning, but he did not specify a set of developmental stages. There are no universal patterns of development in Vygotsky's theory, because cultures differ with respect to goals for children's development.

Vygotsky believed that people structure a child's environment and provide the tools (e.g., language, mathematical symbols, art, writing) for making sense of it. Observe some mothers talking with their 3-year-olds, and you can see Vygotsky's ideas in action. The mothers' speech is slow, simple, and repetitive so that the children can understand what they are saying. Such children are fortunate, because not all mothers talk "baby talk" to their children. When one does, the mother and child are trying to negotiate a shared understanding of language. The child can understand simple sentences under these conditions, but this understanding may not generalize to other language contexts. A key assumption of Vygotsky's theory is that children may be able to demonstrate a higher level of cognitive competence under the guidance of more capable peers and adults.

Contextual theories of development assume that children actively seek out and interact with new social and physical contexts that help shape their development.

A key assumption of Vygotsky's theory of social-cultural development is that individuals are able to demonstrate higher levels of competence under the guidance of a more capable peer or adult.

Ecological Theories

Urie Bronfenbrenner (b. 1917) offers another contextual model of development. He envisions development as embedded in multiple contexts. In his view, "a child's world is organized as a set of nested structures, each inside the next, like a set of Russian dolls" (Bronfenbrenner, 1979, p. 22). As shown in Figure 1.13, the child is at the center of this model; the child is born with certain temperamental, mental, and physical characteristics that create the biological context for his or her development. The child, however, does not develop in a vacuum. The next circle represents the child's immediate physical and social environment. It includes physical objects (toys, books, television, computer, etc.), as well as the family, school, peer group, and neighborhood. These settings are all embedded in a broader social and economic context. The outermost circle is the cultural context. It represents the shared beliefs, values, and customs of a culture, as well as subgroups within the culture. This larger context also includes major historical events, such as wars and natural disasters, that affect other ecological contexts.

A major assumption of Bronfenbrenner's model is that various subsystems (family, school, economic conditions) of this ecological scheme change over the course of development. Change can originate from within the child, as when the child enters puberty or suffers from a severe accident, or it can originate outside the child, as when there is a change in family status or a major historical event such as the Great Depression. Bronfenbrenner (1989) stated, "Whatever the origin, the critical feature of such events is that they alter the existing relation between the person and environment, thus creating a dynamic that may instigate developmental change (p. 201).

Another major assumption of Bronfenbrenner's ecological model is that changes at one level of the context can influence what occurs at other levels. For example, physical

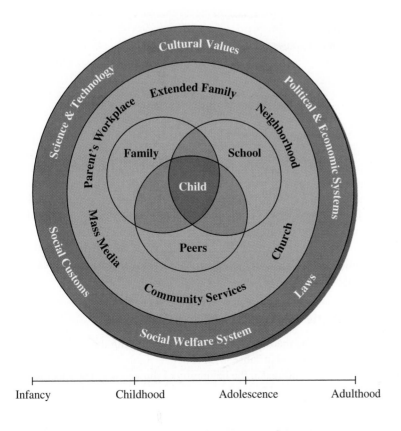

FIGURE 1.13

Bronfenbrenner's Ecological Model

SOURCE: After Bronfenbrenner (1979).

Issues	Biological	Behavioral	Interactional	Contextual
Table 1.2 Summary of Major Theoretical Perspectives and Assumptions				
Nature vs. nurture	Primary focus is on biological influences	Primary focus is on environmental influences	Focus on interactive influence of biology and environment	Focus on interactive influence of biology and environment
Stability vs. plasticity	Critical periods for development	Considerable plasticity in development	Some plasticity in development	Considerable plasticity in development
Continuity vs. discontinuity	Continuous in Gesell's theory; discontinuous in Freud's and Erikson's theories, stage view	Discontinuous, nonstage view	Discontinuous in Piaget's theory; continuous in information processing theory	Continuous, nonstage view
Passive vs. active child	Passive child	Passive child in traditional theories; moderately active child in social learning theory	Active child	Active child
Endpoint vs. no endpoint	Universal sequences in physical, mental, and personality development	No universal sequence in cognition, language, or social behavior	Universal sequence in cognitive stages and cognitive processes	No universal sequence in goals of development

Ecological theories of development are important for understanding the complex interplay between biological and environmental influences on development.

changes at puberty can lead to changes in the child's social relationships with peers, parents, and teachers, but these changes are also influenced by social conditions and by cultural expectations. We mentioned how in different cultures children are expected to assume adult responsibilities when they reach puberty. However, the specific nature of those expectations varies depending on the child's gender and economic situation within a particular culture as well. Bronfenbrenner's theory is useful for understanding complex interactions between biological and environmental effects, as well as relations between different environmental contexts (e.g., home and school). It also helps us understand that the environment in which children live is so complex and intertwined that development cannot be reduced to any one single source.

Importance of Multiple Theories

We have just described some of the theoretical assumptions underlying the various developmental theories that will be discussed in subsequent chapters. Table 1.2 summarizes each viewpoint's position on the issues outlined at the beginning of this section. The specifics of each theory will be described in more detail later. For now, it is enough to recognize the importance of examining children's development from different theoretical perspectives. Some theories may provide a more adequate explanation than others, but all have a place in a teacher's repertoire. In combination they provide a better explanation of children's behavior than any single theory alone can.

It is also important to recognize that the theories presented in this chapter are themselves human constructions that reflect a certain situation, time, and place. Because theories are human constructions, many of the "facts" of development discussed in subsequent chapters are open to question and further interpretation. It is helpful to think of these theories not as statements of "essential truths," but as ways of thinking and talking about children's and adolescents' development in the classroom.

Studying Children's Development

We have just discussed some different theoretical frameworks for understanding children's development. Now let's examine how researchers actually study various aspects of children's development. An understanding of research methods is important for prospective teachers for two reasons. First, as a professional teacher you will attend conferences and read articles that focus on different aspects of children's development. To be a critical consumer of this research, you must be able to judge the quality and validity of different studies. Some methods of study are thought to be more valid and reliable when compared to other methods. Second, as a teacher you will function as a researcher in your own classroom. For example, a teacher might be interested in the following sorts of questions: Are students more involved in learning when I give them a choice of activities? Does concept mapping help students to organize and to retain information? Does peer tutoring have a negative or positive effect on children's learning and confidence? Does it have the same effect on both low- and high-achieving students?

Observations, interviews, experiments, and surveys can help teachers understand how best to facilitate children's learning and development in their own classrooms. In this last section, we will examine the various research designs and methods researchers use to describe and to explain children's development. After reading this section, you will better understand the research findings discussed in later chapters. We will also discuss how to judge the quality of a study. And finally, we will consider ethical issues in child development research.

Research Designs

A **research design** is the plan or structure of an investigation. The type of design selected depends, in part, on the investigator's research question. The first step in any scientific study is to define the question to be studied. For example, a researcher may want to know, Does aggression increase or decrease with age? The researcher then reads existing research on this topic and formulates a hypothesis. A **hypothesis** is a statement derived from theory that has not yet been validated. In the example here, the researcher may hypothesize that children become more aggressive as they get older. Having formulated a research hypothesis based on previous studies, the next step is to choose an appropriate design for testing the hypothesis.

The type of research design selected depends on the investigator's research question.

The six most commonly used research designs in developmental research are single-subject cases, correlational studies, longitudinal designs, cross-sectional designs, cross-sequential designs, and experimental interventions. These research designs for describing

Table 1.3   Advantages and Disadvantages of Different Research Designs

Type of Design	Advantages	Disadvantages
Case study	Provides detailed information of one person's behavior. Can be used as starting place for future investigations.	May reflect observer bias. May not generalize to other situations.
Correlational studies	Can be used with large samples for testing associations between different variables (e.g., age and self-esteem).	Cannot be used to test cause-and-effect relations.
Longitudinal studies	Provides information on changes in individual behavior over time. Can be used to test the stability of behaviors and cause-and-effect relations.	Very costly and take years to complete. If study spans several years, subjects can become test-wise and historical events can affect results. Subjects can drop out of the study and bias the results.
Cross-sectional studies	Can be used with large samples to examine developmental changes. May be completed within a few months. Useful for establishing age norms.	Cannot establish cause-and-effect relations. Do not provide information on the stability of behavior.
Cross-sequential studies	Combine the advantages of longitudinal and cross-sectional designs.	Not frequently used or well understood.
Experimental interventions	Conditions of study are well controlled. Degree of control is highest in laboratory studies and least in natural experiments.	Involve small samples and if conducted in the laboratory may not generalize to other settings.

and explaining children's development differ with respect to complexity, efficiency, and the kinds of questions they can answer. As summarized in Table 1.3, each has its own advantages and disadvantages.

Case Studies

A **case study** is an in-depth investigation of one person or of a small group of individuals (e.g., a family, a peer group). Some of the earliest discoveries about children's development have been based on case studies. In the 1800s, for example, Charles Darwin kept a detailed diary of his son's emotional expressions. This diary became the basis for his theory of emotional development in infants and children. Freud kept detailed notes of individual patients that he and other psychoanalysts relied on heavily in their research. Piaget recorded the developmental progress of his children and incorporated his findings into his theory of children's cognitive development.

A case study that has helped researchers understand language development is the story of Genie (Curtiss, 1977). Genie (not her real name) was confined to a small room where no one spoke to her from the age of 20 months until a caseworker found her when she was $13\frac{1}{2}$ years old. When she was discovered, she weighed only 59 pounds and could not speak. During the next 9 years, Genie received intensive therapy to help her learn to speak. However, her language development never approached that of a normal adult. At last report, Genie, in her 30s, was living in a group home for retarded adults, and her language was still not normal.

Case studies provide useful, in-depth information about an aspect of development, such as language or cognition. From studies on subjects such as Genie, we have learned much about the effects of social isolation on language acquisition. This case study also suggests there may be a critical period for language development, because Genie was never able to acquire normal language taught to her as an adolescent and adult. The chief limitation of a case study is that it is difficult to make general statements about development from a single case: The results may be unique to the individual being studied. In Genie's case, for example, it may be that poor nutrition and physical abuse, both of which can cause brain damage, prevented her from acquiring a language. It is not possible to make conclusions about cause-and-effect relationships. Furthermore, case studies are vulnerable to "observer bias." That is, the researcher may emphasize one aspect of development and ignore other areas. Thus, case studies may provide valuable information about an individual child, but their results may not tell us much about children in general.

Case studies provide an in-depth look at one person or group, but the findings can't be generalized to larger populations.

Correlational Studies

Correlational studies are perhaps the most widely used design in developmental research. These studies tell us what factors influence or are associated in a positive or negative way. For example, it is commonly believed that school achievement is positively related to self-esteem; students who do well in school feel good about themselves. A researcher could test this hypothesis by administering a measure of self-esteem to a large sample of children and collecting information on their school achievement (grades, tests scores, teacher ratings, etc.). After collecting these data, the researcher would then examine relations between the measures of self-esteem and school achievement.

The strength of relations between measures is expressed by a statistic called a **correlation coefficient.** Correlations can vary from -1.0 to $+1.0$. If two measures are unrelated, then the correlation would be near zero. This finding would be interpreted to mean that higher or lower scores on one measure did not correspond with higher or lower scores on the other. If higher scores on the self-esteem measure corresponded with higher achievement test scores, then the correlation would be positive, somewhere between 0 and 1.0. If, however, higher scores on one measure were associated with lower scores on the second measure, then the correlation would be negative, somewhere between 0 and -1.0. This finding means that as one score goes up, the second score goes down. A correlation is **statistically significant** when the relation between the two measures is stronger than would be predicted by chance alone.

As an example, most studies report a significant positive correlation between self-esteem and school achievement. However, a positive correlation does not mean that there is a **causal relationship** between the two factors (i.e., changes in one factor *cause* changes in the other). The results merely tell us the two factors are related in some systematic manner. We cannot tell whether higher self-esteem contributes to better school achievement or whether better school achievement contributes to higher self-esteem. That is, the direction of causality is unclear. In fact, both statements of causality could be correct. Moreover, a third variable, the home environment, could have a causal effect on both self-esteem and school achievement (see Figure 1.14). *Therefore, correlational studies cannot be used to establish cause-and-effect relationships.* They are simply used to establish relations or associations among different measures.

Correlational studies establish a general relationship between two factors, but they can't determine a cause-and-effect relationship.

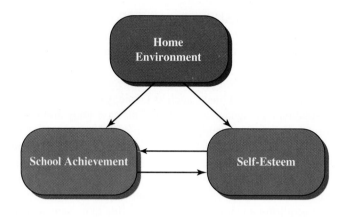

FIGURE 1.14

*Model of Positive
Correlation between
School Achievement
and Self-Esteem*

A positive correlation does not mean that positive achievement *causes* children to
have self-esteem. It is possible that positive self-esteem can lead to higher school
achievement. In addition, a positive or negative home environment can affect both
self-esteem and school achievement and explain their positive correlation.

Longitudinal, Cross-Sectional, and Cross-Sequential Studies

As you recall, development involves changes in behavior over time. We discussed how correlational studies can be used to examine relations between age and various behaviors, such
as aggression or self-esteem. Two other research designs are widely used to study changes
in behavior over time: longitudinal and cross-sectional designs.

In a **longitudinal study,** the development of one group of children is tracked over several years. Data of different aspects of development are collected on a regular basis. One
well-known longitudinal study is Lewis Terman's *Genetic Studies of Genius* (Terman,
1925; Terman & Oden, 1959), which began in 1922 and followed the lives of 1,500 individuals for 70 years. The initial selection criteria for this study was a superior score (top 1
percent of range) on an intelligence test at age 11. During the next 70 years, researchers
collected data on the child's early childhood experiences, education, personality characteristics, careers, families, physical and mental health, and adjustment to retirement.

Longitudinal studies can provide valuable information about individual development
over time, so it is possible to examine the impact of early events on later development. For
example, many working parents want to know how infant day care may affect their child's
development in the long run. Longitudinal studies also allow researchers to identify differences in behavior at different points of development (e.g., increases or decreases in aggression with age). In addition, it is possible to examine the stability of a behavior for
individual children. For example, do shy children become lonely adults? In Chapter 4, we
will discuss the stability of intelligence from childhood to adulthood. This information is
drawn from longitudinal studies.

*Longitudinal
studies, which
follow the same
subjects over
time, allow
researchers
to trace
developmental
changes over
time and to study
the impact of
early events
on later
development.*

Although longitudinal studies have several advantages, there are several disadvantages
that must be considered as well. First, longitudinal studies are costly and take years to complete. A researcher would need to wait 5 years or more, for example, to determine whether
aggression increases or decreases during childhood. It is often difficult to keep the sample
group intact, especially in our mobile society. There is also the danger that individuals become very "test-wise" if they are repeatedly assessed. And finally, the conclusions drawn
from longitudinal studies must be considered in relation to when the study was completed.
For example, the Great Depression and World War II probably had a strong influence on

the lives of both men and women in the Terman study. Also, gender roles have changed a great deal since the 1940s, when most of the participants probably raised their families. The experiences of children and adults today are likely to be very different from those of children in the 1920s.

Another well-known design for studying developmental changes in children is a **cross-sectional study.** In a cross-sectional study, researchers select children of different ages and measure the factor under study. To use our familiar example, a researcher could study whether the nature and frequency of aggressive acts differ with age by measuring aggression in children of different ages (e.g., 5, 7, 9, and 11 years). Each age group should have a similar profile with regard to ethnic and gender ratios, socioeconomic background, schooling experiences, and so forth. The researcher would then compare groups in terms of their scores on some measure of aggression, such as frequency of fights at school as reported by peers and teachers. If the results showed a greater incidence of fighting among 9- and 11-year-olds than younger children, then the researcher would have evidence to suggest that aggression increases with age. Before drawing this conclusion, the researcher might check to make sure the finding was consistent for boys and girls and for different ethnic groups.

Cross-sectional studies are certainly faster and less costly than longitudinal studies. They can involve a wide age range of subjects and be completed within a couple of months. Cross-sectional studies are, therefore, useful for establishing **age norms**—the age at which certain characteristics emerge. Because the participants are sampled only once, there is less chance that the assessments will affect their behavior.

As with correlational and longitudinal studies, cross-sectional studies have some disadvantages that must be considered. First, this design does not actually study changes in behavior over time; it provides only an estimate of those changes. In addition, cross-sectional studies cannot provide information on early determinants of behavior. For example, it would not be possible to establish the effects of early cognitive stimulation on later intellectual development. Furthermore, as suggested, the participants for each age group must be carefully selected in order to rule out differences, other than age, that could bias the results. Last, a cross-sectional study cannot provide information about the stability of behaviors over time, because the same children are not followed over time. If you recall, one of the issues of debate in developmental research is the continuity versus discontinuity of development. To answer this question, longitudinal assessments of the same children are needed.

Cross-sectional studies compare behaviors of similar subjects in different age groups and are used to establish the point at which certain characteristics emerge.

A compromise between longitudinal and cross-sectional studies is the **cross-sequential study.** In a cross-sequential study, children of different ages are selected and then followed for two to three years. Because there is a wide range of ages to begin with, this design is more efficient than a longitudinal study. By studying the same group of children over time, it is also possible to identify antecedents of behavior, as well as to assess the stability of behavioral patterns. Although sequential designs blend the best features of cross-sectional and longitudinal designs, they are not widely used. Most of the findings related to children's development over time come from either longitudinal or cross-sectional studies.

Experimental Studies

For testing cause-and-effect relations, most researchers rely on experimental designs. These studies are believed to yield the most conclusive cause-effect evidence. In an **experimental study,** the participants are carefully selected and matched on a number of variables that could potentially affect the results (gender, ethnicity, family background, school achievement, etc.). The children are then randomly assigned to either of two conditions: an experimental or a control group. In the experimental condition, the children receive a treatment

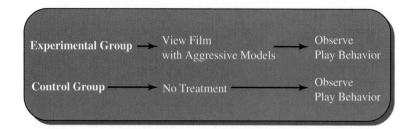

FIGURE 1.15

Model of the Bobo Doll Experiment

Experimental studies are used to establish cause-and-effect relationships in laboratory settings, but the findings don't always hold true for natural settings.

(independent variable) of some type. The treatment is presumed to cause a certain behavior or outcome. In the control condition, the children do not receive the treatment. After the experiment, children are measured on some outcome measure, known as the *dependent variable*. If there is a significant difference between the two groups on this outcome measure, then the results support the hypothesis that the treatment *caused* a change in behavior.

Returning to our question about what causes childhood aggression, let's look at an example of an experimental study. In a classic study, a group of researchers examined the effects of adult models on children's aggression (Bandura, Ross, & Ross, 1963). The research design is outlined in Figure 1.15. Children who were assigned to the experimental condition observed a film in which adults showed aggressive behaviors toward a plastic "Bobo doll" or clown. After watching the film, the children played in a room that contained the doll and some other toys. Children in the control condition did not observe the film but were allowed to play in the room with the Bobo doll. The researchers observed the behavior of each child for 20 minutes through a one-way mirror. They used a behavioral checklist to assess children's aggressive and nonaggressive behaviors. The researchers hypothesized that children who viewed the aggressive model would act more aggressively afterward. The results confirmed the researchers' hypothesis that children can become more aggressive when they are exposed to aggressive models.

One of the shortcomings of experimental research is that findings are confined to laboratory situations. It is not clear that the findings would be found in natural settings, such as in the school classroom or on the playground where there are rules for proper conduct. For this reason, experiments like the one with the Bobo doll are often replicated outside the laboratory setting. Interestingly, research suggests that similar principles apply for learning aggression through models at school as in the laboratory (Parke & Slaby, 1983).

Many other examples of experimental studies can be found in child development literature. Early studies of cooperative learning used experimental designs to assess the effects of these programs on children's learning, confidence, and motivation to learn. In Chapter 4 we will discuss the effects of early childhood programs on children's development. These studies used an experimental design to assess the effects of an early intervention, such as Head Start programs, on children's cognitive development.

As stated previously, experiments, with their carefully controlled conditions, provide more conclusive evidence about cause-and-effect relations. It is possible to test whether the variable being manipulated (the treatment) actually causes a change in behavior. The major disadvantage of an experiment is that the situation may be so controlled that it does not resemble the real world. In settings outside the laboratory, as Bronfenbrenner's model suggests, behavior is likely to be influenced by multiple causes that cannot be easily isolated or manipulated. For this reason, many investigators are conducting their research on children in natural settings, such as the home, school, playground, and so forth. An example of a natural experiment is described in the Focus on Research box. It is hoped that these studies will provide a more complex view of children's development.

Focus on Research

Frederick Morrison and his colleagues (1995) have conducted a "natural experiment" to assess the effects of age and education on children's cognitive development. The study uses what is known as the *school cut-off method.* Each school system specifies a certain cut-off date to determine when children can enter kindergarten or first grade. A child's birthday must precede this date. For some schools, this cut-off date is December 31, whereas for other schools the date can be as early as March 1.

In Morrison's research, "old kindergarten" children, who just missed the March school-entry date, were compared with "young first-grade" children, who just made the cut-off date. On average, this second group of children were 41 days older than the first group, but they had received an additional year of schooling. The two groups were carefully matched in terms of IQ, parental and occupational similarities, and day care experience at the time of school entry. Morrison's cut-off method provides a way to separate the effects of age (maturation) and experience (education) on cognitive development. If the two groups are equal on cognitive measures, then age is assumed to be the primary driving force. On the other hand, if the young first graders out perform the old kindergartners, then educational experiences can be assumed to play a primary role in cognitive development.

The results of Morrison's natural experiment suggested that school-related experiences rather than age alone have a major impact on cognitive development. The young first graders showed better recall on a memory task than did the old kindergartners. The young first graders also showed greater improvement in their memory skills and performance during the school year than did the old kindergartners. In addition, the young first graders demonstrated greater phonemic awareness (i.e., ability to divide words into syllables or to differentiate sounds within one syllable words) than did the old kindergartners. Both groups showed improvements in this area during the school year, but the young first graders made greater gains.

Because the two groups of children were about the same age, the development of memory and reading skills is not simply due to growing older. Rather, the results of this natural experiment clearly suggest that experience is an important factor in this developmental process. The young first graders performed better on memory and reading tasks than old kindergartners because they had more formal schooling. That is, their performance on these cognitive tasks was directly enhanced by schooling experiences that emphasized memorization and beginning reading skills. This research supports the conclusion that schools can have a powerful influence on children's cognitive development.

Action Research

Before we turn to data collection methods, it is important to discuss another form of inquiry found in schools today. **Action research** is carried out by teachers, administrators, and other change agents in the school to improve the educational environment for their students. The goal of action research is not to understand general principles of children's development and learning but to understand a specific problem or to improve teaching practices within a specific classroom or school setting. The Japanese "lesson study," discussed earlier, was a form of action research.

Action research has many benefits for teachers. It empowers them to think critically about their own teaching practices, to identify areas in need of change, to find effective solutions, and to improve learning conditions for children under their care. Rather than to function as the recipients of research and knowledge, action research encourages teachers to be problem solvers and continuous learners.

Although there are a number of different models of action research, the basic process involves four steps. These are (1) selecting an area of focus and inquiry; (2) collecting data and information; (3) analyzing and interpreting the data; and (4) developing and implementing a plan for action.

The first step of the process involves *selecting an area of focus or inquiry*. It is recommended that educators choose areas that involve a topic or problem related to teaching and learning they can change or improve, and then state a specific purpose or objective for their investigation. This statement should include the specific research questions that will be addressed, a definitions of variables, and the types of data to be collected (Mills, 2000). For example, a middle school teacher might want to study the social networks of her classroom to determine if students are interacting across ethnic or gender lines. She would need to define the type of interactions of interest and to identify some ways to collect information on interactions in her classroom.

The second step is to *collect data and information* that is appropriate and accessible. Several different data collection methods are described below and may be used in an action research plan. Generally, the nature of research problem or question determines the types of data collected, but sources may include archival records, interviews, focus groups, performance assessments, classroom observations, classroom maps or videos, surveys, journals, and other artifacts. It is best not to rely on one single source of data but to use multiple sources of information to identify common themes across data sources. The use of multiple data collect methods to compare findings across sources is known as **triangulation.**

Having collected relevant data and information, the next step is to *analyze and to interpret* those data. The goal of analysis and interpretation is to summarize the data in a reliable and accurate manner. It is important to use the research questions to guide this analysis process, but new questions may emerge during data analysis that require additional data collection. Figure 1.16 portrays the spiral nature of action research. In interpreting the data, it is important to relate the results to findings in the literature or to theories of teaching and learning. The Focus on Teaching box on page 44 describes an action research study in which learning theories were used to interpret the influence of technology on mathematics learning.

The final step of action research is to articulate a *plan for*

The goal of action research is to improve teaching practices within a specific classroom or school setting.

An action plan specifies what needs to be done to change or to improve the educational environment, who is responsible for making the changes, and how progress will be monitored.

SOURCE: David Young-Wolff/PhotoEdit

This teacher is sharing her classroom with an educational researcher. Classroom observations provide valuable and rich information about how children learn.

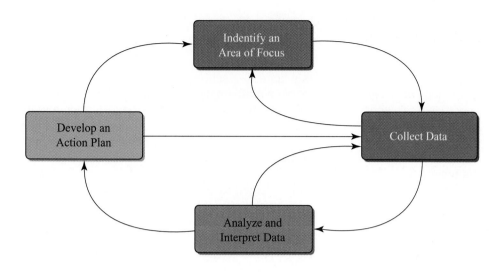

FIGURE 1.16

The Action Research Spiral

action. In developing an action plan, the teacher-researcher specifies what needs to be done related to the findings, who is responsible for carrying out the actions, who needs to be consulted or informed about these recommended actions, and how the effects of the actions will be monitored or evaluated. As we suggested in Figure 1.16, the implementation of an action plan can lead to additional research and data collection. Throughout the action research process it is important to keep in mind that the overall goal is to change or improve the educational environment for children.

Data Collection Methods

We have just discussed different designs for describing and explaining children's development. In this discussion, several methods for collecting data on children were mentioned (e.g., standardized performance measures, behavioral checklists, self-ratings). The choice of a specific collection method will depend on the hypotheses being tested by the investigator. As we have seen with different research designs, each method of data collection has advantages and disadvantages.

Observations

Information on the development of young children is often collected through *direct observation,* a technique that is very important for teachers to master. When a child is observed in a controlled environment, like a laboratory, this method is called a **structured observation.** Bandura's experiment with the Bobo doll involved a structured observation of children in a carefully controlled setting. When children are observed in their own environments, these data are called **naturalistic observations.** Regardless of which method of observation is used, observers must record their observations in some way. In some cases, the observer writes down everything the child is doing. In other cases, the observer may only be interested in, and therefore record, certain behaviors, such as acts of aggression. This technique is known as **event sampling.** Alternatively, the observer may use an observation coding sheet that contains a list of behaviors. The observer then checks off the behaviors that occurred within a predetermined time frame (e.g., every 5 minutes). This technique is known as **time-sampling.** One disadvantage of this observation method is that the behavior of interest (e.g., fighting) may be so infrequent that the observer may have to wait a long time

Structured observations allow observers to study children's behavior in a controlled (artificial) environment, but the results may not transfer to the real world.

Using Technology to Enhance Mathematics Learning

Billabong Elementary School is a large K–7 school that has embraced the use of technology as a key component of its mathematics curriculum reform efforts. The principal of this school is described by his teachers as a visionary leader, and the school has a large collection of computer hardware and software because of the principal's grant-writing efforts. The principal is committed to the use of technology at Billabong because he believes that it is necessary to prepare children for the twenty-first century.

A team of teachers at Billabong decided to conduct an action research project focusing on the impact of technology on student achievement. They decided to observe each others' classrooms, interview teachers and children, analyze test data, and compare the mathematics curriculum taught with the teaching and learning standards proposed by the National Council of Teachers of Mathematics (NCTM). When the team presented its project to the rest of the faculty, all the teachers and the principal indicated that they would cooperate with the research team's request for access to classrooms, curriculum materials, and so on.

The team's initial visits to classrooms revealed that students had good access to computers, scanners, and printers. Most classrooms had at least six computers, and all children in one classroom had laptop computers to use for the year. The students were observed using the computers for their class assignments, creating hypercard stacks for creative writing, playing math games, and so on. Math centers featured different math manipulatives: base 10 blocks, place value charts, colored chips, tangrams, geo-boards, and so on.

However, a closer look at the classrooms revealed a different story. In many of the classrooms, for example, children busily engaged with computers were playing math mazes. For the most part, the children were engaged in low-level activities, and the purpose of the learning activity was lost. Many children were also engaged in "drill-and-kill" activities that had little relevance to their math learning. In these classrooms, the computers seemed to function as an electronic worksheet to keep the students busy once they had completed their math assignments.

Time-sampling is a frequently used method of recording behavior in observational settings.

before seeing it. For this reason, some researchers may try to structure the situation so that the behavior is more likely to occur. For example, the researcher may place a very attractive toy in the toddler unit of a day care center as a way to increase the chances that children may fight over the toy. But as suggested earlier, this modification could make the observation situation more contrived.

In general, some type of time-sampling is generally used in most observational studies. The main advantage is that it provides a systematic way of collecting observational data, making it possible to compare different children's behavior. The main disadvantage is that the coding procedure may not pick up infrequent behaviors. In addition, most time-sampling coding procedures provide only counts of behaviors. In some cases, researchers may want to know what preceded or followed a particular behavior. Figure 1.17 presents a very simple set of procedures that teachers can use to observe their students' behavior in the classroom.

Interviews with children were equally revealing. When conducting the interviews, the research team asked the children to be honest and assured them that their responses would be strictly confidential. As it turns out, some children were brutally honest, telling in great detail the kinds of math activities their teachers used on the computers. Some activities were singled out by the children as a "waste of time," and others described some teachers as "not having a clue" about how the computers were really being used.

Interviews with teachers revealed other problems. Many of the teachers knew very little about the NCTM standards and continued to use their "tried and proven" curriculum in spite of a new textbook adoption by the principal. In fact, some of the teachers were very unhappy about the textbook adoption because no teachers had been consulted in the process.

Compared to those at other schools in the district, Billabong's students performed below average on statewide assessments. This information surprised teachers, who thought that their pupils were doing well in most math strands, with the exception of open-ended problem solving and algebraic relationships. These teachers thought the problem was with the appropriateness of the tests, not the use of technology to enhance teaching and learning.

Before the research team could share its results with the rest of the faculty, a number of issues needed to be considered. The team wanted to share its results without hurting individual teachers and without alienating the teachers from the principal. They decided to adopt a "hold harmless" approach. The team shared the general findings at a faculty meeting and then invited teachers, on a voluntary basis, to meet with team members to discuss the data for their classrooms. Similarly, they invited the principal to meet with them to discuss the implications of the findings for future professional development opportunities.

SOURCE: Adapted from Mills (2000)

Self-Reports

Another method of collecting information on children is **self-reports.** Children can report on their own behavior, their parents' and teachers' behavior, or their peers' behavior. Parents, teachers, and friends can also report on the child's behavior. Self-reports can take several different forms. The individuals being studied can complete a *questionnaire* that contains a number of carefully structured questions that they must answer. Another type of self-report measure is the *rating scale*. Here individuals are given a set of behaviors or attributes to rate. For example, teachers may be asked to rate a child's effort, persistence, or ability to work independently in the classroom. An example of a rating scale is shown in Figure 1.18. Clearly these two self-report measures—questionnaires and rating scales—can be used only with children and adults who can read. These measures are generally less reliable for children under the age of 8 or 9. For younger children, an *interview* may be more appropriate. Using this method, children or adults are asked a set of questions. Some interviews are highly

Time	Activity	Observation	Interpretations/Questions

1. When collecting observations of students, be sure to note the time and setting of the observation. Record facts about what is happening. Try to write down as much as you can about what the student(s) is/are saying and doing. Look for behaviors that precede or follow a particular event. Do not try to interpret what the student(s) is/are doing; pretend you are a video camera recording the event. Many teachers and researchers find the above format useful for collecting observational records. Note that there is space in the right margin for interpretations and questions.

2. After completing a set of observations, begin to interpret what might be going on in the situation and what the actions might mean to the people involved. Also, record any questions this observation might provoke for further investigation. Begin to look for patterns and consistencies in behavior and record them in the interpretation section. Begin to formulate hypotheses to explain the events you are observing.

3. In drawing conclusions from your observations, look for consistencies in behavior across situations. Identify events that preceded and followed the behavior of interest. Formulate a theory to explain the students' behavior. What type of evidence do you have to support your theory? Finally, consider alternative explanations and interpretations for what you are observing. What type of information might you need to either confirm or reject this explanation?

4. In collecting and analyzing observational records, be careful to avoid some common pitfalls. First, we have a tendency to see "what we want to see." If, for example, we assume teachers treat high and low achievers differently, then we are likely to bias our observations in this way. That is, our own beliefs, expectations, and past experiences can lead us to select and interpret our observations according to prior assumptions. It is important to remove these "perceptual blinders" as much as possible. Be objective. When observing, be sure to collect information that might counter preexisting assumptions and expectations. Second, avoid premature conclusions or interpretations. As suggested earlier, look for patterns of behavior across time and situations. In making a conclusion or interpretation, be sure to cite concrete examples that support your statements. Conclusions are more trustworthy if you can cite several instances of a behavior to support them. Last, be aware of how the situation can influence a student's behavior. In observing other people, we have a tendency to attribute behavior to stable dispositions (i.e., she is shy), rather than to the situation (i.e., she is quiet in class). For this reason, it is important to collect information about a student across situations. If a behavior pattern (i.e., shyness) appears in several settings with different people, then it is appropriate to make inferences about underlying dispositions.

FIGURE 1.17

Suggestions for Collecting Observations in the Classroom

SOURCES: After Brophy & Good (1974) and Florio-Ruane (1985).

Directions: Rate how often each student exhibits the following behaviors in class. Rate each behavior on a 1 to 4 scale. Circle 1 if the student *never* shows the behavior, 2 if the student *sometimes* shows the behavior, 3 if the student usually shows the behavior, 4 if the student *frequently* shows the behavior.

	Never	**Sometimes**	**Usually**	**Frequently**
Gets along with others	1	2	3	4
Enjoys challenging activities	1	2	3	4
Works independently	1	2	3	4
Helps others	1	2	3	4
Gives up easily	1	2	3	4

FIGURE 1.18

Examples of Rating Scale Items

structured and standardized, whereas others are more loosely organized. Interviews are useful for understanding why a person is acting or feeling a certain way.

Because questionnaires and rating scales are efficient ways of collecting information about children, they are widely used in research on children's development, especially if the researcher is collecting information on a large sample of children. However, these data collection methods have some serious disadvantages. First, it's not clear that all children and adults interpret rating scale and questionnaire items in the same way. For example, "works independently" may be interpreted as working alone by one teacher and as completing independent assignments by another teacher. Second, children and adults may not be motivated to complete questionnaires, particularly if they are time-consuming. They may leave answers blank or respond to questions randomly. In addition, children and adults may not be good reporters of their own behaviors. They sometimes answer questions according to how they think you want them to respond. This problem is most likely to occur if children are asked to report on undesirable behaviors, such as fighting, cheating, stealing, and so forth. Similarly, adults are not likely to provide accurate reports of behaviors that are inappropriate or undesirable, such as hitting a child. In general, individuals have a tendency to overestimate desirable behaviors and to underestimate undesirable behaviors. This problem is known as **social desirability.**

Interview questions are less likely to be misinterpreted than questionnaire questions. The interviewer can also probe an individual's responses. Interviews can provide more elaborate and richer data about different events. However, interviews are very time-consuming. Children are more difficult to interview than adults because they are less attentive, slower to respond, and have difficulty understanding questions. In addition, the interview must be transcribed and analyzed according to a coding scheme. Also, the problem of social desirability may be more likely to occur in face-to-face interviews, in which individuals are not likely to divulge feelings, attitudes, or behaviors that others may view as undesirable or inappropriate.

When self-report measures are used, it is best to gather additional information. For example, researchers often collect information about a child's behavior from multiple sources, such as teachers, parents, and peers. If there is a convergence in the information collected from these various sources (e.g., a child is rated as popular by two or more sources), then results are more likely to be accurate. In addition, self-report measures are often used in conjunction with other data collection strategies, such as observations and performance assessments.

Information gathered through self-reports (questionnaires, rating scales, interviews) needs to be confirmed by more than one source, as people tend to overestimate their desirable behaviors.

Performance Assessments

Sometimes the best way to collect information about children's development is through **performance assessments,** which seek to measure children's ability to perform specific tasks correctly. These methods are generally used to assess children's physical and cognitive development. For example, asking a group of preschool children to skip around the gym is one way to assess their large motor skills. Intelligence and achievement tests are also performance assessments in which individuals are given a set of cognitive tasks to perform. For example, a subtest of the *Wechsler Scale of Intelligence for Children* (Wechsler, 1991) asks children to make designs with blocks that match a model. Achievement tests also include a standard set of problems for students to solve. In recent years, however, educators have moved away from multiple-choice tests of achievement toward performance assessments in which students are given authentic tasks to perform. Asking fifth-grade students to use their mathematical knowledge to design and to furnish a "dream house" is an example of a performance assessment.

In Chapter 3, we will learn that Piaget used performance assessments in much of his research on children's cognitive development. One of his most famous tasks involved the conservation of water. As shown in Figure 1.19, children are first shown two glasses of water and asked if the two glasses contain the same amount of water. Next, the water from one glass is poured into a taller, thinner glass, and the children are again asked if the two glasses contain the same amount of water. A child who does not understand the concept of conservation would say, "No, the taller glass has more." In Piaget's research, children were then asked to explain their answers. This technique of probing children's reasoning processes was known as the **clinical interview method.** It is a good example of how performance assessments can be combined with interviews to assess children's cognitive functioning.

Performance assessments have several advantages. First, they provide a behavioral measure of a child's level of development in a certain area. These assessments are likely to be more accurate than self-reports. Second, performance assessments can show which tasks and problems children can solve at specific ages. Because the tasks, procedures, and conditions can be standardized across situations, the child's performance can be compared with previously established norms. For example, standardized achievement tests have national

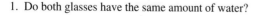
1. Do both glasses have the same amount of water?

2. Now do the glasses have the same amount of water?

Figure 1.19   *Conservation of Liquid Problem*

or state norms, which allow teachers to compare their students' performance with other students of the same age. The disadvantage of performance assessments, particularly standardized tests, is that they do not provide information on the cognitive processes children use to solve problem. This information must be inferred from the child's performance. However, Piaget's method of combining performance assessments and clinical interviews may be a way of overcoming this problem.

Judging the Quality of a Study

You have just read about different approaches for studying children's development and their various strengths and limitations. The next question is, How do you know whether research findings can be trusted? To answer this question, several important criteria should be considered.

Generalizability

In judging the quality of a study, it is important to examine how the sample was selected. If the sample is limited in some way (e.g., all white males), then the findings should not be generalized to other groups of children. The **generalizability** of research findings has to do with how well the findings apply to another sample or to the general population. Case studies, for example, have limited generalizability because they involve one individual or a small group of individuals. In addition, many developmental studies have been criticized because they are based on white, middle-class samples. Results from these investigations cannot be applied to poor or ethnic minority children. Because a child's social and cultural context can influence behavior, care must be taken to select a representative group of children who vary with respect to ethnicity, social class, and sex. When findings are consistent across different samples of children, then we can be more confident that the results apply to a broad range of children.

Reliability and Validity

In judging the quality of a study, it is also important to examine the reliability and validity of the measures used. **Reliability** refers to the consistency or precision of a measurement when repeated under similar circumstances. For example, there are numerous measures of self-esteem. In choosing a scale, the researcher wants one that provides a reliable estimate. One method for assessing the reliability of a measure is to administer it several times within a short interval of time (a few weeks is acceptable) and to examine the consistency of scores across time. Of course, the same group of individuals should complete the measure each time. Reliable measures yield more consistent scores within a short interval of time. This measure of consistency is called **test-retest reliability.** Studies that use a test, performance measure, or questionnaire should report this information.

A different reliability estimate is used in interview and observation studies. When analyzing observation or interview data, researchers typically identify different categories or patterns of behavior. This analysis process involves subjective interpretations and judgments. To establish the reliability of coding procedures, researchers generally ask two or more people to observe or code the same events. The researcher then computes the degree of agreement between the observers or the raters. Whereas one observer may interpret an intense look as a threat, another observer may not interpret it that way. This estimate of agreement is called **interobserver** or **interrater** reliability. When observers agree in their assessments, the resulting measures are more reliable.

The reliability of a research instrument is established if it generates consistent measures when repeated under similar circumstances.

Along with providing a reliable measure of a behavior, a research instrument must provide a valid measure. The **validity** of a measure refers to whether or not it provides an accurate measure of the phenomenon being studied. That is, does the instrument really measure what it purports to measure? It is possible to get a reliable estimate of a behavior, but the instrument used to obtain this assessment may not really assess what it is supposed to. This point is often confusing to many readers. Suppose a researcher thinks, as early researchers did, that the size of a person's head was a measure of intelligence. It is possible to obtain a reliable estimate of an individual's head size, but who today believes that head size is a valid measure of intelligence? This simple example should help clarify the difference between the reliability and validity of a measure.

There are many factors that can threaten the validity of a measure. In Chapter 4, we will discuss the validity of contemporary tests of intelligence. Although there are many different definitions of intelligence, IQ tests are currently based on a narrow definition of intelligence. If a child does not perform well on these tests, is it correct for the researcher to conclude that the child has low intelligence? Perhaps, as some critics argue, these tests are really a measure of a child's familiarity with white, middle-class American culture since this is the cultural background of most testmakers. Given that children's abilities to focus and concentrate for long periods of time can affect how well they perform on IQ tests, perhaps these tests are really measuring attention span. To establish the validity of a measure like an IQ test, a researcher must relate it to other valid and reliable measures of the same attribute or behavior. In the case of IQ tests, the scores could be related to other valid tests of intelligence, cognitive abilities, or academic achievement. If a measure is valid, it should show strong relations with these other measures.

The validity of a research instrument is established if it measures the characteristics it purports to measure.

Replication

Ultimately in the scientific community, the quality of a research study is judged in terms of its ability to be replicated. Replication involves testing a hypothesis with multiple samples and with different but parallel methods. If the findings replicate, then it is unlikely that the results are due to a particular group of individuals or to a certain research method. Research findings are more trustworthy when they are found across studies that use different samples and methods of collecting data, as well as conducted by different researchers.

Research Ethics

As a prospective teacher or parent, you and your children may at some point be asked to participate in a study. It is important, therefore, that you understand **research ethics,** the ethical standards that researchers must follow when conducting research on human subjects. The guidelines shown in Figure 1.20 have been developed to protect you and your children from dangerous procedures. Because children are often too young to understand the issues involved in a study, parents must provide informed consent for their child to participate. Even when children have parental consent to participate in a study, the child can still refuse to participate or can withdraw from the study at any point without penalty. More important, the participants and their parents have a right to information about the results of the study. If you participate in a study, do not hesitate to ask for its results. The information should be presented in a way that protects the identities of the individual participants.

Research ethics dictate that research subjects give informed consent, their identities remain confidential, and they have access to the findings.

Teachers and parents are often reluctant to participate in a study because of the amount of time involved. However, it is important to keep in mind that researchers continue to

1. In most cases, researchers must have their study reviewed by a school or institutional review board. Researchers must reveal all relevant information about the study.

2. Researchers must not use any methods or procedures that would cause physical or psychological harm to the child. The benefits of the study must outweigh its possible risks.

3. If participants are under the age of 18, researchers must inform the parents, guardians, or others responsible for the child's care about the research procedures and obtain their written consent before beginning the study.

4. If the participant is old enough to understand the research procedures, they must be informed and asked for their verbal consent before participating in the study. Participants must be informed that they can withdraw from the study at any time.

5. Researchers must keep all information about the participants confidential. In all reports of the investigation and in casual conversations about the study, the identities of the participants cannot be revealed.

6. Researchers must inform parents, guardians, or other responsible adults if they obtain information that threatens the child's well-being. For example, if during the study, the researcher discovers that a child is seriously depressed, the researcher must contact a person who can help the child obtain psychological treatment.

7. Each participant has a right to the results of the study. Researchers are obligated to share their research findings with interested parties (e.g., participants, parents, guardians, school officials, and staff). As stated previously, the identities of the participants must be protected in research summaries.

8. Each child participant has the right to the benefits of a treatment provided to other participants. For example, if the experimental treatment is shown to be beneficial, then participants in the control group who did not receive the treatment have a right to beneficial treatments at some later time.

SOURCE: SRCD Committee on Ethical Conduct in Child Development Research (1990).

FIGURE 1.20

Guidelines for Conducting Research with Children

make new discoveries about children's development. They are turning more and more to natural environments, such as the classroom or home, as the setting for their studies to ensure their research is a valid description of children's development. All research projects conducted by individuals from institutions who receive federal funds must be reviewed by an ethics review board. In order for a research project to be approved, the perceived benefits of the study for children must outweigh the costs to their time and effort. In any research study, the needs of children and their families should come first.

Chapter Summary

Why Study Children?

- Child development research can help teachers understand how children change over time and what explains the observed changes.

- Instructional decisions are influenced by teachers' beliefs about children's development. Teachers have varying points of view about development, but a large number believe that development is primarily a biological process.

- Several recent studies have raised questions about teachers' understanding of child and adolescent development. Many teachers appear to have a limited understanding of the age group they teach.

- Schools play an important role in children's intellectual, social, and emotional development. Schooling not only affects children's level of intellectual development, but also influences their ways of thinking, problem solving, and reasoning. Schooling experiences shape children's feelings of competency, sense of self, peer relations, and social attitudes as well as many other aspects of social development.

Perspectives on Children's Development

- Cultural beliefs about the nature of children and how they should be treated has changed dramatically over the last 100 years. Before the industrial revolution, children were considered miniature adults. The idea of childhood occurred as a result of social and economic changes during the early decades of the twentieth century. Children's lives continue to be conditioned by social, economic, and historical circumstances.

- Most theorists believe that development involves systematic and orderly changes that enhance a child's overall adaptation to their environment. Theories of development provide a coherent framework for interpreting, explaining, and understanding those changes. Developmental theories make different assumptions concerning the nature of child, the nature of development, and the sources of development.

- Biological theories assume that human characteristics unfold according to a biological timetable. The environment plays little role in shaping the course of development. Development is viewed as either continuous or discontinuous, depending on the theorist. Two early maturational theorists were Hall and Gesell.

- Psychoanalytic theories focus on changes in the self and personality. At different stages of physical development, new drives, needs, and conflicts emerge that influence the way children relate to the environment. The way in which children satisfy their needs at different ages can set the pattern for personality development. Key psychoanalytic theorists are Freud and Erikson.

- Behavioral theories emphasize the role of the environment in determining the course of development. Development is gradual and continuous, as a child acquires new skills and behavior through various principles of learning (conditioning, reinforcement, imitation). There are no universal patterns of development because inputs are provided by the environment, which can vary from child to child. Some well-known behavioral theorists who have studied children's development are Watson and Skinner.

- In Piagetian, information processing, and social cognitive theories, development results from an interplay between a child's developing mental abilities and environmental experiences. Children actively seek out information about their environment and attempt to make sense of it using existing knowledge and cognitive processes. Piaget's theory emphasizes qualitative changes in how children organize information, whereas information processing and social cognitive approaches emphasize developmental changes in the efficiency of children's cognitive processes.

- Contextual theories emphasize relations between a developing child and a changing environment. Development cannot be separated from the context of culture in which it takes place. In Vygotsky's theory, people structure the environment in ways that facilitate children's cognitive development. Qualitative shifts in children's thinking occur as children transform innate abilities into higher mental functions through interactions with others. Brofenbrenner proposed that children's development is embedded in multiple environments. Changes in one system (parents' divorce) can influence changes that occur in other systems (child loses interest in schoolwork). For contextualists, development does not follow a universal sequence because the child and environment are constantly changing.

- There are multiple perspectives on children's development. Because no single theory alone can explain all that we know and observe about children, it is important to have a repertoire of child development theories. A familiarity with several theories provides various ways of thinking and talking about children's development.

Studying Children's Development

- Studies of children can take several different forms. The most commonly used research designs in child development are case studies, correlational studies, longitudinal and cross-sectional studies, and experimental intervention. Correlational studies examine associations between two events or variables, whereas longitudinal and cross-sectional studies are used to study development over time. Correlational and cross-sectional studies can be conducted with large samples. Longitudinal studies are the most useful for identifying antecedents of developmental changes and for establishing the stability of individual behavior. Experiments are used to test cause-and-effect relations, but their findings may not generalize to other settings.

- There are numerous methods for collecting data on children's development. Children can be observed in a structured or unstructured environment, and various behaviors can be recorded and analyzed for frequency of occurrence. The advantage of this method is that it provides detailed information on actual behavior, but the observer may influence the person's behavior. Information on children can also be collected through rating scales, questionnaires, and interviews. These methods are efficient, but subjects may not be accurate or truthful in their reporting. Like observations, performance assessments provide behavioral data. These assessments are more accurate than self-reports but do not provide information on the processes involved in performing specific tasks.

- There are several criteria for judging the quality of a study. Characteristics of the study's sample or setting can influence how well the results generalize to other samples and situations. The reliability (precision) and validity (accuracy) of a measure or instrument are also important for judging the quality of a study. Studies should provide a reliable and valid estimate of the phenomenon being studied. Most theorists, however, judge a study in terms of its ability to be replicated. Research findings are more trustworthy when they are found across studies that use different samples and methods.

- Research studies involving children and adults must follow a set of ethical guidelines. The perceived benefits of a study must outweigh its potential risks and costs in terms of time and effort. Informed consent must be obtained before the study is conducted, and the identities of all participants must remain confidential. Research participants should be provided with a summary of the research findings when the study is completed, and each participant has the right to the benefits of a treatment provided to other research participants.

Key Terms

action research (p. 41)

age norms (p. 39)

behavioral genetics (p. 28)

case study (p. 36)

classical conditioning (p. 29)

clinical interview method (p. 48)

correlation coefficient (p. 37)

correlation study (p. 37)

critical period (p. 29)

cross-sectional study (p. 39)

cross-sequential study (p. 39)

development (p. 23)

event sampling (p. 43)

experimental study (p. 39)

generalizability (p. 49)

hypothesis (p. 35)

longitudinal study (p. 38)

natualistic observation (p. 43)

operant conditioning (p. 29)

performance assessment (p. 48)

reciprocal determinism (p. 31)

reliability (p. 49)

research design (p. 35)

research ethics (p. 50)

self-reports (p. 45)

social desirability (p. 47)

structured observation (p. 43)

theory (p. 23)

time sampling (p. 43)

triangulation (p. 42)

validity (p. 50)

Activities

1. Interview two to five teachers of different grade levels about their knowledge of child or adolescent development. Were they required to take a child or adolescent psychology course as part of their teacher preparation program? What type of issues or concerns do they have about children's development? How do they use information about children's development in planning learning activities, organizing the classroom, identifying students with special learning needs, and disciplining a child? Try to determine the extent to which the teachers' instructional decisions are based on child development research or their own experiences and intuitions. Summarize your findings in a paper you can share with your classmates.

2. Listed below are questions about children's development (adapted from Martin & Johnson, 1992). Read each item and mark the item you think provides the best answer.

   a. When do children follow rules?

   _____ They reach a stage when they can do things alone.

   _____ Parents praise them for doing things on their own.

   _____ They have a desire to experiment with new ideas and actions.

   b. How do children come to understand differences between plants and animals?

   _____ The distinction is obvious when children reach a certain stage.

_____ They formulate the concept by observing and analyzing differences between the two groups.

_____ They are taught the important characteristics of each group.

c. Why do children's misconceptions about the world eventually change?

_____ Adults present the correct information.

_____ As they get older they outgrow immature ideas.

_____ Their curiosity motivates them to find out more about their ideas.

d. Why do children make up imaginative stories?

_____ Make-believe is a natural part of childhood.

_____ Adults encourage the child's imagination.

_____ The child's imagination develops from playing with others and thinking about objects.

e. How do children know that a candy bar broken into pieces is still the same amount of candy?

_____ While playing with objects, children discover the relationship between parts and wholes.

_____ Adults tell them the amounts are the same.

_____ Children naturally know this when they reach a certain age.

f. How do children learn to resolve conflicts with their friends?

_____ Some children are naturally more agreeable or cooperative than others.

_____ Through interacting with others, they discover that cooperation reduces conflicts.

_____ They are encouraged by adults to get along.

g. How do young children come to understand that cartoon characters are not real?

_____ Adults tell them that the stories are make-believe.

_____ The difference is obvious to children when they reach a certain stage.

_____ Their everyday experiences help them to figure out that cartoon characters cannot be real.

h. How do children acquire a desire to learn?

_____ Children have a natural curiosity about things.

_____ They imitate parents who like to learn.

_____ As children learn ideas and skills, they seek out new learning experiences.

i. How do children come to realize the consequences of their actions?

_____ Children gradually become more aware of how things happen as they grow older.

_____ They discover through interactions with others that it is important to consider the possible outcomes of different actions.

_____ Adults praise their good behavior or ignore their bad behavior.

After answering the questions, decide with a classmate which of the statements for each item represent the following points of view discussed in this chapter (see pages 00–00):

> _Biological._ Characteristics of the child naturally unfold as the child matures; changes in development are independent of training or experience.

Behavioral. Changes in the child are determined by the environment. The mechanisms that lead to change are direct instruction, reward, punishment, imitation, and so forth.

Cognitive. Changes in the child are due to a dynamic interaction between the child's existing knowledge and the environment. The child plays an active role in his or her own development through the construction of knowledge.

Review your answers to examine which of these points of views you used most frequently to explain children's behavior. Discuss with your classmates how your beliefs might influence the way you teach.

3. For the last century, two major approaches have dominated children's educational programs. Some teachers favor a child-oriented approach in which knowledge is "discovered" or "constructed," and others favor a teacher-oriented approach in which knowledge is "transmitted" or "presented." These approaches can be traced back to the views of Locke and Rousseau on children's development and education. Observe at least two classrooms focusing on the types of materials used, instructional and discipline practices, and classroom organization. Make a list of characteristics that would be associated with a child-oriented or teacher-oriented approach. How would you characterize the classrooms you observed? Compare your findings with the rest of the class.

4. If you have access to a classroom, you can do your own action research project. Consult with the teacher to find a problem or issue of mutual interest. Review pages 000–000 to develop a plan for your project. Be sure to define the problem and to identify appropriate data collection methods. After collecting and analyzing the information, develop an action plan and share it with your teacher and classmates.

Chapter 2

Physical Development

I'm not sure how I feel about starting high school next year. I think the hardest thing will be that the school is bigger, and I won't be the oldest student anymore. The older kids might tease us and say, "Look at those little ninth graders walking down the hall. They look funny." My best friend is moving away this summer, and I really won't have any friends at the new school. Most of the girls my age act and look younger. I got my period before they did. I hope I can meet some kids who are more like me at the new school. I'd really like to go out on dates with older guys, but my parents worry that I might get into trouble. They think all teenagers drink, smoke, and do bad things. I don't think high school kids are that way. I wish they wouldn't say those things.

Chapter opener photo: Corbis #az001710.

This vignette describes the feelings of a 14-year-old girl who is about to enter her first year of high school. As you can see, she has many concerns as she makes this transition to a new school environment. Her feelings are typical of girls who reach puberty early for their age group. These girls are often the envy of less mature girls, but they, themselves, begin to feel out of place. Young people who mature early tend to seek out older peers who are more like them. Unfortunately, parents of these children do have cause for concern. Research suggests that early-maturing girls and boys may begin to engage in activities, such as early dating, they are not emotionally prepared to handle. Early maturity can also have a strong influence on a young person's relationships with parents, self-esteem, peer popularity, and even school achievement.

In this chapter, we examine the influence of biological changes on child and adolescent development. The chapter will focus on many different questions of interest to educators: How does heredity influence a child's development? Why are boys more likely than girls to develop inherited diseases or disorders? How does the brain develop? When can children hold a pencil or hit a ball like an adult? When do young people begin puberty? How can parents and teachers help support young people as they make the transition into adolescence?

Because some physical and cognitive problems have a biological basis, the chapter begins with a discussion of the role of heredity in development. We then look at the process of prenatal development and the factors that can place a child at risk for later development. The following sections describe the development of the brain, perceptual abilities, and motor skills. Next, we explore various aspects of physical development, including changes in height and weight in childhood and at the onset of puberty. Here we will examine the psychological impact of puberty and what can be done to support young people through this transition. In the last section, we discuss eating disorders, drug and alcohol abuse, adolescent sexuality, and other health concerns.

Prenatal Development

The time from conception to birth is called the prenatal development period, and although it is primarily controlled by genetic influences, some external forces, such as diet, disease, and drugs, contribute to variations in human development.

Developmental processes are set into motion at the moment of human conception, when a male sperm penetrates and fertilizes a female egg. Within this fertilized egg, there are complete instructions for creating a new human being. The time from conception to birth is known as the prenatal development period. Similar to other developmental processes, prenatal development follows a universal sequence that is mainly directed by genetic influences. However, the environment can still influence what takes place during prenatal development. A variety of adverse conditions and agents, such as dietary deficiencies, radiation, drugs, and maternal diseases, can contribute to variations in the development of an unborn child.

In this section, we examine the developmental processes that give birth to a child. The first section describes the role of genes and chromosomes. Next, we examine the stages of prenatal development. We also discuss the effects of genetic and environmental factors on the unborn child. In the final section, we consider the effects of birth complications (e.g., low birth weight and prematurity) that can affect a child's status at birth and during later development.

Genes and Chromosomes

Human development begins, as mentioned previously, when a male sperm penetrates a female ovum at the point of conception. The sperm and ovum each contain over 1 billion chemically coded genetic messages that, when combined, serve as the blueprint for human

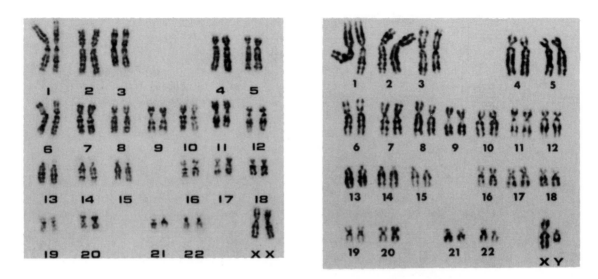

Figure 2.1 *Human Chromosomes*
SOURCE: After Hetherington & Parke (1993).

life. The **human zygote** is the cell that is formed by the union of the sperm and ovum. It contains one set of 23 **chromosomes** from the mother and another set of 23 chromosomes from the father. As shown in Figure 2.1, the 46 chromosomes are arranged into 23 pairs. At birth, an infant has approximately 10 trillion cells, with each cell containing the same 23 pairs of chromosomes as the one-cell zygote. Chromosomes are composed of long thread-like molecules of **deoxyribonucleic acid** (DNA), which twist around to form a spiral staircase or a double helix, as pictured in Figure 2.2. It is believed that this DNA contains approximately 100,000 **genes,** the basic units of heredity (Ezzell, 2000).

Whereas some traits, such as Huntington's disease, are caused by a single gene, most human traits are a combined effect of many different genes. Human characteristics, such as skin color or height, which result from the interplay of multiple genes are called **polygenetic traits.** Some genes are not always expressed, because their genetic directions are masked by the genes of the other parent. For example, a child who inherits a gene for blonde hair from one parent and a brown hair gene from the other parent will have brown hair. In this case, the trait not expressed—blonde hair—is the **recessive gene,** whereas brown hair is caused by a **dominant gene.** To produce blonde hair, a recessive gene must be inherited from each parent. Some traits that are caused by recessive genes include blue eyes, baldness, color blindness, hemophilia, and sickle-cell anemia. Abnormalities caused by recessive genes will be discussed in a later section. Other examples of traits caused by dominant genes are curly hair, color vision, and farsightedness.

A child's sex is determined by the twenty-third chromosomes, which are known as the **sex chromosomes.** Males have two types of sex chromosomes: an X and a Y chromosome, whereas females have two X chromosomes. At the point of conception, if an X-bearing sperm fertilizes an ovum that contains an X chromosome, the fertilized egg will develop as a female (XX). If the sperm contains a Y chromosome, the fertilized egg will develop into a male (XY).

It is believed that sperm that are genetically coded to create male offspring have a greater likelihood of penetrating the ovum than sperm coded to produce females. Approximately 160 males are conceived for every 100 females. However, only 105 boys for every

The human zygote, the cell formed by the union of sperm and ovum, contains the genetic blueprint for human life.

Traits, such as intelligence, skin color, and height, result from an interplay of multiple genes.

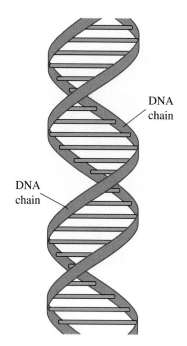

DNA
chain

DNA
chain

FIGURE 2.2

A DNA Molecule

Monozygotic twins develop from the splitting of an egg, with each half containing identical genetic instructions, whereas dizygotic twins develop from two different eggs and are not genetically identical.

100 girls are born. Some theorists speculate that females may be better equipped than males to survive the process of prenatal development.

Another interesting fact is that some recessive genes are carried on the sex chromosome. These traits are called **sex-linked characteristics,** because they are carried on the female sex chromosome. For example, baldness, color blindness, and hemophilia are all sex-linked characteristics. Females are the carriers of these disorders, but males have a higher likelihood of inheriting them. The greater genetic vulnerability of males occurs because a recessive gene on the X chromosomes has no matching dominant gene on the Y chromosome to mask its expression. The higher rate of miscarriage and infant mortality for male offspring is partly attributable to their greater vulnerability to sex-linked disorders.

Generally, most pregnancies result in a single birth, but multiple births are becoming more and more frequent, due to the use of hormones to treat infertility problems. There are two ways multiple births occur. First, during the early stages of cell division, a fertilized egg can divide into two clusters that develop into two different fetuses. These are called identical or **monozygotic twins,** because they come from the same fertilized egg and contain the same genetic instructions. Sometimes more than one egg or ova are released from a woman's ovaries at the same time, and both are fertilized. The babies that develop under these conditions are called fraternal or **dizygotic twins,** because they develop from two different eggs. Genetically, dizygotic twins are only as similar as biological siblings, but they share the same prenatal and postnatal environment. Dizygotic twins (8 per 1,000 births) are more common than monozygotic twins (4 per 1,000 births). The factors linked to fraternal twinning are maternal age, ethnicity, nutrition, number of births, and exposure to fertility drugs (Cohen, 1984).

Genetic and Chromosomal Abnormalities

Every person is the carrier of at least 20 genes that could produce genetic disorders or diseases in their offspring (Milunsky, 1989). Many of these disorders are attributable to recessive genes, so that a person will not inherit a particular condition unless both parents are carriers of the disease. Table 2.1 presents a list of common genetic diseases and conditions caused by recessive genes. The disorder Huntington's disease, mentioned earlier, is caused by a dominant gene, but its occurrence is rare (1 out of 18,000 to 25,000 births). Some, but not all, genetic disorders can be detected through genetic counseling or prenatal diagnosis. Couples who already have a child with a genetic disorder, who belong to an ethnic group known to be at risk for a genetic disorder, or who have experienced a series of miscarriages should seek genetic counseling. By taking the couple's genetic history and examining tissue samples, experts are able to determine the risk of genetic disorders that can be identified this way (e.g., sickle-cell anemia, hemophilia, and phenylketonuria—known as PKU). As will be discussed, prenatal tests performed in the third and fourth month of a pregnancy

Some genetic or chromosomal disorders can be detected early through genetic counseling or prenatal tests.

Table 2.1	Common Genetic Diseases and Disorders			
Name	**Mode of Inheritance**	**Incidence**	**Description**	**Test Available**
Cystic fibrosis	Recessive gene	1 in 200 Caucasians; 1 in 16,000 African Americans	Mucous obstructions in lungs and digestive organs that lead to breathing difficulties	Yes
Congenital diabetes	Recessive gene	1 in 2,500 males	Abnormal metabolism of sugar; body does not produce enough insulin	No
Hemophilia	Recessive gene	1 in 1,000 males	Absence of clotting factor in blood	Yes
Huntington's disease	Dominant gene	1 in 18,000 births	Degeneration of central nervous system; symptoms do not appear until age 35 or later	Yes
Muscular dystrophy	Recessive gene	1 in 3,000 males	Degenerative muscular disease	Yes
Phenylke-tonuria (PKU)	Recessive gene	1 in 8,000 births	Inability to neutralize amino acid phenylalanine, which is present in many proteins; causes severe damage to central nervous system	Yes
Sickle-cell anemia	Recessive gene	1 in 500 African Americans	Abnormal red blood cells cause oxygen deprivation, tissue damage, and susceptibility to infections	Yes
Tay-Sachs disease	Recessive gene	1 in 3,600 births to Jews of European descent	Inability to metabolize fatty substances in neural tissue, which leads to death by age 3 or 4	Yes

SOURCE: After McKusick (1992).

Table 2.2	Risk Rates of Down Syndrome
Maternal Age (Years)	**Rate of Risk**
20	1 in 1,900 births
25	1 in 1,200 births
30	1 in 900 births
33	1 in 600 births
36	1 in 300 births
39	1 in 140 births
42	1 in 70 births
45	1 in 30 births

can also reveal a small number of serious genetic disorders. Some parents then have to decide whether or not to continue the pregnancy, which is not an easy decision for any parent.

Some genetic disorders are caused by defects in a chromosome. Most developmental problems of this type occur when genetic instructions go awry during early pregnancy. A chromosome pair does not separate properly, or part of a chromosome breaks off or is damaged. Since the problem does not involve just a single gene, these chromosomal abnormalities usually cause disorders with many physical and mental symptoms.

The best-known genetic disorder of this type is trisomy-21, or **Down syndrome.** A child with Down syndrome has an extra twenty-first chromosome or a piece of one. This disorder occurs in 1 out of 800 live births. As shown in Table 2.2, incidence of Down syndrome has been linked to the age of the mother. The risk of conceiving a child with Down syndrome is higher among mothers over 35 years old, because there is a greater likelihood that a woman's ova has been exposed to diseases, environmental pollutants, and other damaging effects. Children with Down syndrome have a very characteristic appearance. Their heads tend to be smaller and rounder than other children, their eyes are almond shaped, and their limbs are short. Children with Down syndrome also have a range of physical and mental handicaps. They are susceptible to heart defects, infectious diseases, and other health problems. Although most Down syndrome children have below-average intelligence, they have more learning potential than was assumed 15 to 20 years ago, when the majority of Down syndrome children were institutionalized. It is important to remember that not all children with Down syndrome are alike. Depending on how much extra genetic material is present, some children with this disorder exhibit practically normal characteristics (Rosenberg & Pettigrew, 1983). About 20 percent of children with Down syndrome die by age 10, but many live until middle adulthood.

Another chromosomal disorder, **fragile-X syndrome,** is one of the leading causes of mental retardation and developmental disabilities (Bailey & Nelson, 1995). Caused by a single gene, fragile-X syndrome is more common in males than females: 1 in 1,000 males versus 1 in 5,000 females. Males with this disorder have more serious symptoms than females, perhaps because the female carries another normal X chromosome. In females, fragile-X syndrome may result in mild forms of retardation, but about 25 percent of females who have this disorder have normal intelligence (Barnes, 1989). Of the males who inherit a fragile-X chromosome, 20 percent will have normal intelligence, 33 percent will be mildly retarded, and the rest will be severely retarded. Delays are generally evident in all developmental domains, although cognitive and communication skills tend to be the

The risk of conceiving a child with Down syndrome increases after a woman reaches the age of 35 because there is greater likelihood that the ova has been exposed to diseases.

most affected. In both boys and girls, fragile-X syndrome is associated with cleft palate, abnormal EEGs, disorders of the eyes, and a characteristic facial appearance. It is also associated with attention deficits, hyperactivity, language deficits in males, and increased depression in females. The social relationships of children with fragile-X syndrome are often affected due to poor communication skills. Boys with fragile-X syndrome may display an unusual style of interacting with other people. They tend to avoid direct eye contact during conversation and hand-flapping or hand-biting is common (Hagerman & Silverman, 1991).

Fraternal twins with Fragile-X Syndrome.

Compared with Down syndrome, this chromosomal abnormality appears to have more variable effects, which may depend partly on the influence of the environment. It is important to keep in mind that the quality of the family and school environment can moderate the effects of chromosomal anomalies (Bender, Linden, & Robinson, 1987).

Fragile-X syndrome can be detected through genetic screening and DNA analysis. Down syndrome can also be detected, and older mothers are generally counseled to have prenatal tests to identify any unexpected chromosomal abnormalities. The tests used for a prenatal diagnosis are described in Table 2.3. Amniocentesis is the most widely used procedure, but it cannot be performed before the fourth month of pregnancy. It involves inserting a needle through the abdominal wall to withdraw a small amount of amniotic fluid. The fetal cells are then examined for abnormalities. There are several newer tests for detecting genetic defects, but they cannot identify all disorders, and they may be less reliable. Scientists are currently working on methods for correcting some genetic defects before the fetus is born.

Prenatal tests, such as amniocentesis, which is reliable but cannot be used before the fourth month of pregnancy, can detect many genetic disorders.

From Genotype to Phenotype

To understand the effects of genetic influences on development, it is important to distinguish between a person's genotype and phenotype. The genes a person inherits from both parents for any particular trait make up his or her **genotype.** The actual expression of these traits is his or her phenotype. We have already learned that some traits are only expressed when both parents donate a recessive gene, such as with blonde hair. When individuals receive a recessive gene from one parent and a dominant gene from another parent, their genotype will be different from their **phenotype.** That is, they may have a recessive gene for the disease PKU, but because it is paired with a normal gene it is not expressed. Genes can also interact in an additive fashion to influence a person's phenotype. The several genes

The genes a person inherits for any particular trait make up his or her genotype; the actual expression of these traits is his or her phenotype.

Table 2.3	Description of Prenatal Tests

Type of Test	Description
Ultrasound	High-frequency sound waves used to form electronic picture of fetus; may have long-term effects on mother and fetal tissue
Amniocentesis	Sample of fluid extracted from amniotic sac; procedure typically performed at 15 to 18 weeks: can detect presence of over 100 disorders and sex of fetus; may result in uterine cramping and miscarriage
Chorionic villi sampling	Hollow tube inserted into the chorion, which surrounds the embryo in early weeks of gestation; procedure performed between twelfth and eighteenth week; scope of analysis is limited; some risk of infection
Alpha fetoprotein (AFP) testing	Sample of mother's blood tested for AFP substance between week 15 and 18; procedure can detect defects in neural tube (e.g., spina bifida); recommended for all pregnancies, especially if there is a history of neural tube defect

that influence height, temperament, intellectual abilities, and many other human traits are believed to interact in an additive way. Thus, genes interact among themselves to influence the actual expression of inherited traits.

A person's observable characteristics are also influenced by ongoing interactions between the genes and the environment. Some genes are not expressed, because the environment does not facilitate their appearance. For instance, a person may have inherited a set of genes for high intellectual ability, but if that talent is not encouraged or stimulated, it may not develop to its fullest. In other cases, the environment can modify the expression of some genes so that the inherited genes do not affect a person's phenotype. The disease PKU, for example, is associated with mental retardation. If a child with PKU is placed on a special diet from birth, mental retardation will not occur. In this case, the environmental effect of a special diet modifies the effects of a particular genotype (PKU), caused by two recessive genes.

Two people with the same set of genetic instructions (genotype) can develop different characteristics (phenotypes) if reared in vastly different environments.

Researchers use the concept of **reaction range** to understand genetic and environmental influences. This concept refers to a person's unique, genetically determined response to environmental influences. Two people with the same set of genetic instructions (genotypes) can develop different characteristics (phenotypes) if reared in vastly different environments. Conversely, people with different genotypes will respond differently to the same environments. The concept of reaction range helps us to understand that children differ in their responses to the environment. Our genes determine the upper and lower boundaries for our development, but the environment can facilitate or impede that development. The reaction range defines the degree to which the environment can affect the development. Figure 2.3 shows a graphic representation of the reaction range concept. Child A and Child B, in the diagram, differ in their genetic inheritance for height. Child A can benefit more from an enriching environment than Child B.

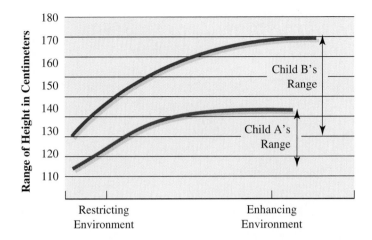

FIGURE 2.3

Range of Reaction

A child's genetic inheritance establishes the range of reaction when which environmental influences can affect development.

Stages of Prenatal Development

The average period of human gestation is 34 weeks. Within the first weeks of prenatal development, the head, limbs, vital organs, central nervous system, and skeleton are all formed. This period of development is the most rapid in the human life span. The Focus on Development box shows the stages of prenatal development. It is divided into three major stages: the *germinal period*, the *embryonic period*, and the *fetal period*. Developmental processes are most susceptible to disruption when the basic human structures are developing. The important changes that occur in each stage are briefly summarized here.

The first stage of prenatal development, the germinal period, encompasses the first 2 weeks of fetal development. In this stage, the fertilized ovum, or zygote, travels down the fallopian tube to the uterus, making new cells through the process of **mitosis.** During mitosis, chromosomes produce duplicate copies of themselves and divide into new cells. Within approximately 4 days, the zygote reaches the uterus, and the fertilized egg now contains 60 to 70 cells formed into a hollow ball. Before the zygote attaches itself to the uterine wall, cell differentiation takes place. The outer edge of the zygote will develop into the embryo, while other cells become the structures that protect and nourish the embryo, such as the placenta, the umbilical cord, and the amniotic sac. By day 6, the zygote develops threadlike structures or villi that enable it to draw nourishment from the uterine wall. Full implantation to the uterine wall does not occur until 12 days after conception, and it is not automatic. An estimated 58 percent of all zygotes fail to implant properly, thereby terminating pregnancy. Only 31 percent of all conceptions become living newborns.

Implantation of the zygote marks the beginning of the next stage of prenatal development, the **embryonic period.** From weeks 2 to 8, all the basic structures of the child are established. During the early days of the embryonic period, the **placenta, umbilical cord,** and **amniotic sac,** which were present at implantation, mature and begin to function. These structures are the life support system for the developing embryo. At the same time, the embryonic structure develops three distinctive layers of cells. The outermost layer, the **ectoderm,** will become the nervous system and skin. The middle layer, the **mesoderm,** will become the skeleton and muscles, and the innermost layer, the **endoderm,** will become the digestive tract and vital organs. This remarkable process of cell differentiation appears to

During the first 2 weeks of fetal development, called the germinal period, the zygote travels down the fallopian tube and implants itself on the uterine wall.

Focus on Development

Stages of Prenatal Development

Stage	Time	Changes
Germinal	0 to 4 days	Fertilization; cell division; zygote travels down fallopian tube to uterus
	4 to 8 days	Implantation begins
	12 to 13 days	Implantation completed
Embryonic	2 weeks	Placenta begins to form
	3 to 4 weeks	Heart begins to beat; eyes, blood vessels, and nervous system begin to develop
	5 to 6 weeks	Arms and legs begin to form; gonads begin to form
	8 weeks	Development of major organs completed; pregnancy detectable by physical exam
Fetal	8 to 12 weeks	Appearance of genitals; leg and arm movements occur; circulation system functions
	10 weeks	Responds to stimulation
	13 to 16 weeks	Skin and hair develop; skeleton hardens
	20 weeks	Heartbeat can be heard; vigorous movement
	25 to 28 weeks	Begins to gain weight; sucking movements visible
	26 weeks	Eyes open
	28 weeks	Respiratory system matures; survival outside womb possible
	30 weeks	Gains layer of fat under skin
	32 to 26 weeks	Survival outside womb probable
	38 weeks	Normal birth

From weeks 2 to 8, the embryonic period, all the basic structures of the developing child are established, with sex differentiation occurring between weeks 6 and 8.

be regulated by chemical reactions around the cells. Before differentiation, every cell of the embryo is virtually identical, but some cells will become brain cells while others will become the lining of the stomach, due to their location in the embryo and to the chemical messages they receive from their surrounding environment. In other words, genetic and environmental interactions are already taking place that will influence the process of human development.

During the third and fourth weeks of prenatal development, the heart and neural tube that will become the central nervous system begin to form, and ears and teeth buds under the gum appear in week 6. Between weeks 6 and 8, sex differentiation occurs. If a Y chromosome is present, gonadal tissue begins to differentiate into testes, the male sex organ. If no Y chromosome is present, the gonadal tissue begins to form into female ovaries. The sex chromosomes have now completed their mission; prenatal hormones secreted by the male and female sex organs (testes and ovaries) shape sexual differentiation from here on, including the formation of external genitalia.

By the end of week 8, all the embryo's basic organs and structures (heart, liver, digestive system) are in place, and some begin to function. All this development takes place when the embryo is barely 1 inch long! The rapid development of new organs and systems makes the embryonic period particularly vulnerable to environmental agents that can cause congenital anomalies (see Focus on Development). Most miscarriages, or spontaneous abortions, occur within this period. It is nature's way of eliminating the embryos with gross chromosomal or genetic abnormalities that are not likely to survive on their own.

The last and longest stage of prenatal development is called the **fetal period.** During this time (from 8 weeks until birth), the size of the fetus increases. In the fourth

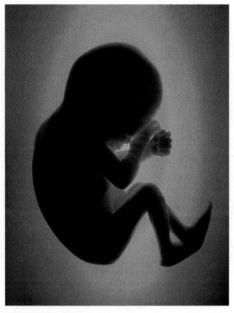

Fetus in Womb.

SOURCE: Alex Bartel/Science Photo Library/Photo Researchers, Inc.

and fifth months, the weight of the fetus increases tenfold! Eyelids, fingernails, taste buds, and hair form. By the fifth month, the fetus is generally active and gains another 3 to 4 pounds in the eighth and ninth months. At this time, the respiratory system matures to enable breathing after birth. If the baby is born in the seventh month, it can often survive but will need special support systems. By the ninth month, the fetus is cramped for space, and it is an uncomfortable time for mother and baby alike. Toward the end of this month, the baby moves to a head-down position. When this happens, birth is very near.

Environmental Effects on Prenatal Development

Prenatal development, for the most part, is directed by genetic factors. However, as mentioned previously, environmental conditions can interfere with normal fetal development. For this reason, radiologists generally ask women if they are pregnant before taking an X-ray. Doctors and pharmacists also inquire about a woman's status before prescribing a drug. In some work environments, women of child-bearing ages are protected from areas that would expose them to toxic agents.

Any environmental substance or disease that causes abnormal development of the fetus is called a **teratogen.** Forty years ago, many women continued to smoke cigarettes and to drink caffeine or alcohol while pregnant. Scientists have now shown that nicotine, caffeine, and alcohol all can have harmful effects on the development of a fetus. The frequent use of alcohol during pregnancy is one of the leading causes of mental retardation in industrialized countries (Cramer & Davidhizar, 1999). Other substances that can negatively affect the development of the fetus are prescription drugs, radiation, environmental pollutants (e.g., lead, mercury, PCBs), illegal drugs, and synthetic hormones. The effects of selected teratogens are summarized in Table 2.4.

Certain diseases contracted by the mother during pregnancy, such as rubella, mumps, chicken pox, and malaria, also can have harmful effects on a developing fetus. Similarly, sexually transmitted diseases, such as chlamydia, syphilis, genital herpes, and gonorrhea,

The last and longest stage of prenatal development (8 weeks until birth) is called the fetal period, and during this period the fetus increases its weight tenfold.

A teratogen is any environmental substance (e.g., alcohol or cigarettes) or disease that causes abnormal development of a fetus.

Table 2.4	Effects of Selected Drugs and Chemicals on Prenatal Development

Agent or Substance	Possible Effects
Analgesics (painkillers)	Respiratory problems
Anesthetics	Respiratory problems
Aspirin (large quantities)	Respiratory problems; low birth weight; poor motor development; fetal or infant death
Alcohol	Facial abnormalities; lower IQ; heart problems; developmental lag; poor attention and social skills
Antihistamines	Malformations; fetal death
Caffeine	Increased risk of retarded fetal growth and low birth weight
Cocaine	Structural damage; delayed growth; prematurity and low birth weight; hypersensitivity to stimuli; convulsions and seizures that can cause brain damage; poor attention and social skills
Diethylstilbestrol (DES)	In female offspring, increased risk of vaginal cancer, abnormal uterus, and high-risk pregnancies; in male offspring, increased risk of genital abnormalities and cancer of the testes
Heroin, morphine	Newborn withdrawal symptoms; prematurity and low birth weight; convulsions and tremors; developmental delays; infant death
Marijuana	Impairment of central nervous system; retarded fetal growth; prematurity and low birth weight; fetal or infant death; poor language and memory skills
Nicotine	Stunted fetal growth; prematurity and low birth weight; respiratory problems; convulsions; abnormal heart rate; cleft palate and lip; reduced head size; increased risk of infant death; learning problems
Oral contraceptives	Increased risk of heart and limb deformities
Streptomycin	Hearing loss
Tetracycline	Discolored teeth, slow bone growth
Valium	Cleft palate and lip

are dangerous as well. These diseases, caused by a viral or bacterial infection, are passed to the fetus through the placenta, infecting the fetus. Genital herpes is not passed to the fetus unless the infection is active at the time of delivery. Acquired immune deficiency syndrome (AIDS), which destroys the immune system, is another deadly disease that can be passed on to an unborn child. The Focus on Research box on p. 72 describes new methods for reducing the transmission of HIV to infants.

The effects of these teratogens on prenatal development are neither simple nor straightforward. As discussed earlier, a fetus is most vulnerable to environmental influences in the early stages of pregnancy, when the body parts and major organs are developing. In the 1950s, the drug thalidomide was prescribed to expectant women to prevent nausea and sleeplessness. It was used in 28 countries other than the United States, because it did not receive approval from the U.S. Food and Drug Administration (FDA). Women who took the drug between 38 to 46 days after conception gave birth to babies with deformed arms. If exposed to the drug between 46 to 48 days, the babies were born with deformed legs. In contrast, women who took the drug after 50 days gave birth to babies with normal limbs.

This tragic example shows clearly the varying influence of teratogens on unborn babies as well as sensitive periods for development.

Besides the timing of exposure, the level of dosage moderates the effects of teratogens on the fetus. In general, the more frequent the exposure and the higher the dose, the more severe the damage. Some teratogenic agents have a cumulative effect. For example, every cigarette smoked by a pregnant woman reduces an infant's birth weight by several milligrams. Other teratogens have a threshold effect; the substance is harmless unless its use reaches a certain frequency or dosage level. One or two aspirins during pregnancy may not harm a fetus, but frequent use of aspirin can lower a baby's birth weight, increase fetal or infant death, and impair motor development after birth (Barr, Streissguth, Darby, & Sampson, 1990). Finally, a woman's health status can reduce or increase the effects of teratogens. Poor nutrition, lack of prenatal care, poor health, or the presence of other teratogens can worsen the effects of a single harmful agent. On the other hand, doctors now know for certain that ensuring the level of some nutrients, such as folic acid, can prevent some common birth defects, such as cleft lip and palate and spina bifida.

Timing and dosage of teratogens change the effect they have on an unborn baby.

High-Risk Infants

Most babies are born between 38 and 42 weeks after conception and weigh between 5 and 10 pounds at birth. Babies both within this time period and weight range tend to be at minimal risk for complications. However, 7.6 percent of babies born in the United States weigh less than 5.5 pounds, or 2,500 grams, and 11.6 percent are born preterm (Center for Disease Control and Prevention, 2000). Babies who are small for gestation are called **low birth weight.** Not all low-birth-weight babies are premature or preterm; some full-term babies are classified as low birth weight. In general, a baby's risk factors increase as its period of gestation and weight decrease. A short gestation period or low birth weight is one of the leading causes of **infant mortality.** These babies die before the age of 1 year. Despite declines in infant mortality over the last decades, the U.S. infant mortality rate ranks highest of industrial countries (see Figure 2.4). In the United States, infant mortality rates are almost twice as high for black infants (13.8 deaths per 1,000 live births) as for Hispanic and white infants (U.S. Department of Health and Human Services, 2000). The statistics are difficult to accept when the United States has one of the most advanced medical systems in the world.

Babies who weigh less than 5.5 pounds or 2,500 grams are low birth weight.

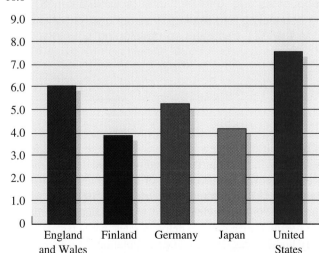

FIGURE 2.4

Cross-national Comparisons of Infant Mortality Rates per 1,000 Live Births

SOURCE: U.S. Department of Health and Human Services, 2000.

Focus on Research

Recent statistics indicate that over 1 million children under the age of 15 are living with HIV/AIDS, and approximately 3.2 million children have died from the virus or associated causes. It is also estimated that 7,000 young people between the ages of 10 and 24 become infected with HIV every day—five new cases per minute. More than 95 percent of all HIV-infected people live in developing countries. The United States has a relatively small percentage of the world's children living with HIV/AIDS. The latest available data, which were compiled in 1996, indicated that HIV was the seventh leading cause of death for U.S. children through age 14.

How is HIV transmitted to infants? Nearly 90 percent of infections worldwide occur during pregnancy or birth. Although the precise mechanism is not yet known, scientists believe HIV may be transmitted when the mother's blood enters the fetal circulation or when the infant is exposed to the mucous lining during the birth process. The risk of maternal-infant transmission is significantly increased if the mother has advanced HIV disease. The disease also may be transmitted from a nursing mother to her infant. In developing countries, approximately one-third to one-half of HIV infections occur through breast feeding. Before blood was routinely screened for HIV in 1995, some infants were infected with AIDS through blood transfusions or blood products contaminated with HIV.

What can be done to stop the transmission of AIDS to infants? The best way to prevent pediatric HIV infections is to prevent AIDS in adults or to prevent pregnancies in HIV-infected women. Unfortunately, HIV has a long incubation period (up to 10 years or more) during which mothers can transmit the disease without knowing they were infected. If HIV is detected through screening, it is possible to reduce the risk of mother-infant transmission through the use of the drug AZT. A landmark study in 1994 showed that AZT can reduce the transmission of HIV from 25 percent to 8 percent (Center for Disease Control, 1994). In this study, AZT was given to the mother in the second or third trimester and through delivery, and the infants were treated for 6 weeks following birth. The AZT produced no serious side effects in the mothers and infants. The use of AZT has dramatically reduced the incidence of perinatal AIDS in the United States and Europe. However, this treatment is not available to developing countries due to its high cost (approximately $1,000 per pregnancy, not counting counseling and testing). International organizations are studying ways to provide the AZT treatment to developing countries at lower costs.

SOURCE: National Institutes of Health, 2000.

It is also interesting to note that the United States has one of the highest low-birth-weight rates among many industrialized countries, including Canada, Germany, France, Japan, Sweden, and Norway. Moreover, the proportion of U.S. babies born at low birth weight is at its highest level since 1976 (Children's Defense Fund, 1999). As with infant mortality rates, preterm and low-birth-weight deliveries vary by the infant's ethnic background. Asian populations have the lowest preterm delivery rates, while Hispanic and Native Americans have slightly higher rates than do white populations. African Americans have the highest rates of preterm and low-birth-weight deliveries of any major ethnic group in the United States (U.S. Department of Health and Human Services, 2000). African American babies are twice as likely as white or Asian babies to be born preterm, to be born low birth weight, and to die at birth (Shiono & Behrman, 1995).

What are the causes of prematurity and low birth weight? The causes of prematurity are not well understood. In some cases, problems with the placenta or cervix are associated with a premature birth. In the third trimester, toxemia (characterized by water retention, high blood pressure, and urine in the blood) can also lead to a premature birth.

The causes of low birth weight are much clearer. The most common and direct cause is poor nutrition. Within the United States, the rates of low birth weight are higher in some areas than in others. In the District of Columbia, for example, rates of low-birth-weight births are around 13 percent for all ethnic groups, whereas 5.5 percent babies born in Oregon are of low birth weight (Children's Defense Fund, 2000).

Another common cause of low birth weight is poor prenatal care. Mothers who receive no prenatal care are three times more likely to produce low-birth-weight babies than mothers who receive care in the first trimester. As with proper nutrition, access to prenatal care is related to socioeconomic status. Low-income mothers are less likely to receive prenatal care in the first months of pregnancy than higher-income mothers. Since 1991 access to prenatal care has been improving in the United States (see Figure 2.5). Other factors that can increase the risk of low birth weight are substance abuse (including smoking cigarettes, drinking alcohol, and using drugs), maternal age (see Figure 2.6), multiple pregnancies, short time between pregnancies, and the mother's general health condition.

Through the use of modern medical technology, many preterm and low-birth-weight babies survive, but they are at risk for developing a number of complications. Birth weight is the most reliable predictor of infant survival and healthy development. A low birth weight is associated with an increased risk for infections, cerebral palsy, visual impairments, brain damage, and lung and liver disease. As they enter school, children born with a low birth weight are more likely than children of normal birth weight to have mild learning disabilities, attention problems, poor concentration, language delays, and asthma. Low-birth-weight infants are three to five more times more likely to be placed into special education classes or retained in school (Hack, Klein, & Taylor, 1995).

As a nation, we spend about $15 billion per year on neonatal intensive care. We seem to focus more on keeping low-birth-weight babies alive than on preventing this problem. It is estimated that for every dollar we spend on prenatal care, we could save $3.00 in postnatal

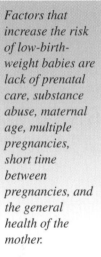

Factors that increase the risk of low-birth-weight babies are lack of prenatal care, substance abuse, maternal age, multiple pregnancies, short time between pregnancies, and the general health of the mother.

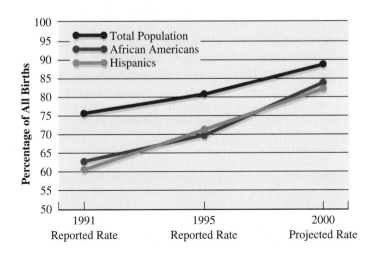

FIGURE 2.5

Progress in Prenatal Care During First Three Months of Pregnancy

SOURCE: Children's Defense Fund (1998).

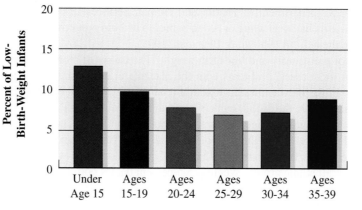

FIGURE 2.6

Percent of Low-Birth-Weight Infants as Percentage of All Infants Born in the United States, by Mother's Age

SOURCE: U.S. Department of Health and Human Services, 2000.

Maternal age is a contributing factor to low birth weight. A higher percent of low-birth-weight infants are born to mothers under the age of 19.

intensive care and more than $4.60 in long-term health costs for low-birth-weight or preterm babies (Lu, Lin, Prietto, & Garite, 2000). Other recommendations for preventing low-birth-weight and preterm births are described in the Focus on Research box.

Brain Development

The brain of a human being is the largest among land mammals relative to body size. It is believed that humans are eight times as "brainy" as the average mammal living today (Jerison, 1973). The human brain is not fully mature until early adulthood, and scientists believe this lengthy period for brain development enables humans to acquire thought processes and skills not found in other animal species. The largest part of the human brain, and the last to develop, is the frontal lobe or cerebral cortex, shown in Figure 2.7, which controls higher cognitive abilities such as reasoning and speech.

Brain development is a fascinating and very active area of study. With the sophisticated technology for studying the human brain available today, scientists are making important discoveries about brain development, and many ideas about brain development are open for discussion and debate. As we will see, one issue of debate concerns whether or not there is a "critical period" for children's cognitive, language, social, and emotional development. As recently as 1980, scientists believed that the structure of the brain, and its development, were genetically determined. In the last several years, however, scientists discovered that early experiences play a powerful role in brain development, physically determining how the brain becomes "wired." Some 10 billion nerve cells form connections after birth, and new evidence suggests that brain development occurs well into the adolescent years. In this section, we explore changes in the brain from infancy through adolescence. We also discuss the role of environmental experiences in brain development. The Focus on Teaching box on p. 77 discusses the implications of this research for educators.

The largest part of the brain, and the last to develop, is the cerebral cortex, which controls thought and consciousness.

Changes in the Brain

The central nervous system is made up of the brain, the spinal cord, and nerve cells, and it controls almost every aspect of human functioning. At the center of this sophisticated control system are billions of long thin cells called **neurons,** which are formed during the first

Focus on Research

Reducing the Risk of Low-Birth-Weight and Preterm Births

Three major factors that raise the risk of low-birth-weight and preterm births are cigarette smoking during pregnancy, low maternal weight gain, and low prepregnancy weight. These factors account for nearly two-thirds of delayed growth in infants (Shiono & Behrman, 1995). Although access to prenatal care can reduce the rates of preterm and low-birth-weight deliveries, this effort alone is not enough. Prenatal care is too late to address the problem of low prepregnancy weight, and few prenatal programs include intensive services to help pregnant women stop smoking. Smoking is a strong addiction, and it is difficult to stop at will. Only 9 to 27 percent of women who participate in smoking cessation programs while pregnant are able to quit. The nicotine patch or gum is successful in helping smokers quit but cannot be used during pregnancy.

To prevent low-birth-weight and preterm births experts recommend the following:

- Programs that prevent young women from starting to smoke.

- New and innovative ways to help women stop smoking during pregnancy.

- Health insurance packages that include smoking cessation programs.

- Increased access to prenatal care, and improvement in its quality and effectiveness.

- Comprehensive health programs for women that include prepregnancy counseling.

Although the data are not conclusive, federal programs aimed at reducing the effects of poverty, such as the Special Supplement Food Program for Women, Infants, and Children (WIC), have been helpful in improving maternal weight gain.

SOURCE: Adapted from Shiono & Behrman, 1995.

---

5 months of gestation. Neurons differ from other body cells because they are not closely packed together. There are tiny gaps between neurons, known as **synapses,** where fibers from different neurons come close together but do not touch. Neurons release chemicals, called **neurotransmitters,** that cross over these gaps to communicate with other neurons (see Figure 2.8).

When a sound or image enters the senses, it is transmitted to the brain as an electrical impulse. It then travels to a region of the brain where it is interpreted and recorded by a set of neurons. The more often this same set of neurons is used due to frequent exposure to the same stimuli, the more likely a particular sound or image will be stored in long-term memory. Every memory we have is made up of thousands of these neural connections.

Research on early brain development suggests that during the early months and years of life, the brain is growing at an unprecedented rate, not to be matched in later years

The central nervous system— the brain, the spinal cord, and nerves—control almost every aspect of human functioning.

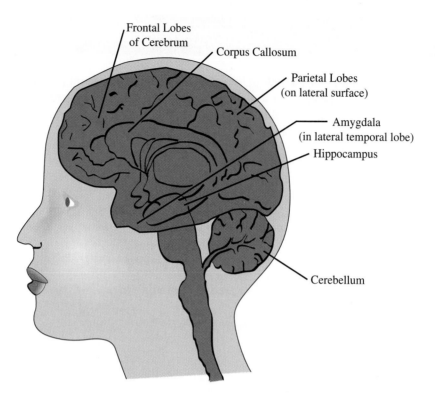

FIGURE 2.7

*Left Side of
the Human Brain*

Different parts of the brain have different functions

- The hippocampus makes it possible to recall recent experience and new information

- The amygdala directs our emotional responses

- The frontal lobes of the cerebrum allow us to solve problems, plan ahead, understand the behavior of others, and restrain our impulses

- The parietal areas control hearing, speech, and language

- The cerebellum regulates balance, body movements, coordination, and the muscles used in speaking

- The corpus callosum passes information from one side of the brain to the other

The strength of connections between neurons is largely determined by experience.

(Thompson, 1998). At birth, each neuron has approximately 2,500 synapses, and as many as 15,000 two years later (Nash, 1997). Brain development after birth involves two important changes. First, the number and length of neural fibers that connect different neurons and nerve cells (dendrites and axons) increase. Figure 2.9 shows the growth of these fibers during the first 2 years of life. The dark spots are the neurons, and the thin lines are the dendrites and the axons that connect the cells. These connections allow brain cells to communicate with one another. Humans are born with more neurons than they need. It is believed that connections between neurons are formed each second during the first few months of life. Half of the neurons produced during prenatal development die because they fail to link to other neurons. As we will learn, the strength of connections between neurons is largely determined by activity or experience.

The second major change is the process of **myelination,** whereby the neurons and dendrites become coated with a fatty substance called myelin. Myelination enables neural

Focus on Teaching

New research on early brain development has been the feature of numerous books, journals, magazines, and newspapers. A 1997 White House Conference called "Early Learning and the Brain" released a report detailing the importance of early brain development for child care and other social programs. Impressed by new research suggesting that classical music can improve academic learning, the former governor of Georgia, Zel Miller, convinced state legislatures to fund a program to give every newborn in the state a classical tape. Following Georgia's lead, Florida politicians proposed that child care centers receiving state funds should be required to play classical music. And in a book written for teachers, David Soussa (1995) describes how the typical classroom favors learners who are left-hemispheric dominant. Because males are believed to be right-hemispheric dominant, they are at a disadvantage in this learning environment. Sousa argues that teachers need to give equal time to activities that involve the right hemisphere of learning.

Are these educational practices justified on the basis of brain research? In a recent article, John Bruer reports that there is little scientific evidence to support these practices. Early research suggested that the young brain is more active than the adolescent and adult brain, but it is not clear that high brain activity means greater efficiency and depth of learning (Bruer, 1999, p. 656). As mentioned earlier, the brain continues to develop into adolescence, and a good deal of research is still needed to establish the influence of early brain development on later learning. Similarly, studies of brain functioning suggest that *both* hemispheres are involved in many cognitive activities. According to Bruer (1999), "The fundamental problem with the right-brain versus left-brain claims that one finds in the educational literature is that they rely on our intuitions and folk theories about the brain, rather than on what brain science is actually able to tell us" (p. 653).

Although research on early brain development and hemispheric lateralization is controversial, it is important to note that researchers have learned a great deal about what promotes healthy brain development. We know that poor nutrition and toxic substances can harm early brain development. Poverty can have both direct and indirect effects on brain development. Parents and caregivers are also an important source of stimulation and support for early brain development. We know, too, that infants and young children need opportunities to explore, experiment, and play in ways that are natural to them. These early attempts at learning need to be supplemented with age-appropriate stimulation of thinking, reasoning, and problem-solving abilities as new brain processes emerge in later development. Without this continued support for brain development, early gains may be gone. In an article about the social policy implications of brain research, Ross Thompson (1998) writes, "The mysteries of brain development are not understanding its unfolding growth (researchers learn more each day) or knowing how to promote brain development. The mystery is why, as a wise society, we do not invest more in creating the conditions that support the development of healthy minds" (p. 8).

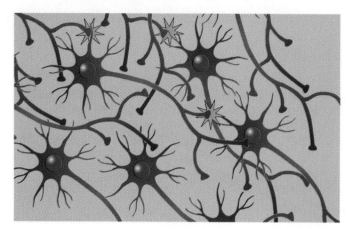

FIGURE 2.8

What Is a Neuron?

Nerve cells, or neurons, transmit information throughout the brain in the form of electrical impulses. When an impulse moves through a neuron, the cell releases neurotransmitters into the synapses to communicate with other neurons.

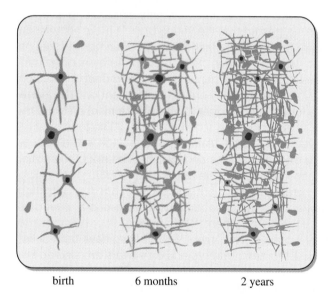

birth   6 months   2 years

FIGURE 2.9

Early Brain Development

SOURCE: After Conel (1959).

impulses to travel faster. The changes occur rapidly in the first few years, but the process of myelination in the frontal cortex can continue into adulthood. Over the course of early development, neurons become increasingly selective and respond only to certain neurotransmitters.

Although brain growth is most rapid early in development, the brain continues to develop into childhood and adolescence. In fact, researchers have made several new discoveries about the teen brain (see Focus on Research). As we will learn in Chapters 3 and 4, more complex thought processes emerge in childhood and adolescence. These cognitive abilities include problem solving, strategic planning, emotion management, and searching the memory for information and events. Many of these more sophisticated thought processes are located in the cerebral cortex, which develops more slowly than other areas of the brain (see Figure 2.7).

Myelination enables neural messages to travel faster through the brain.

Focus on Research

The Teen Brain

Much of the recent research on brain development has focused on the first 3 years of life. Recently, however, new discoveries have been made about brain development in adolescence. Contrary to the idea that the brain reaches maturity by puberty, researchers at UCLA's Lab of Neuro Imaging have discovered that the frontal lobes undergo significant changes between the ages of 10 and 12. These areas of the brain are responsible for executive functions such as judgment, self-control, emotional regulation, and planning. Additionally, researchers have discovered that temporal lobes, which are responsible for language as well as emotional control, do not fully mature until the age of 16. Together, recent research suggests that the brain undergoes many more changes in the second decade of life than originally thought. Whereas brain development early on is mainly directed by parents and caregivers, teenagers have more independence and freedom to create their own worlds. As a member of the UCLA team explained, "Teens thus have the power to determine their own brain development, to determine which connections survive and which don't. Whether they do art, or music, or sports, or videogames, the brain is figuring out what it needs to survive and adapting according" (Begley, 2000, p. 59).

The brain is a living organ, and, like other biological systems, it cannot develop without adequate nutrition and protection from dangerous or toxic substances. The effects of undernutrition (lack of sufficient protein and other nutrients) on the developing brain have been studied for several decades. This research has shown that the timing of nutritional deprivation is important. In the first trimester of pregnancy, poor nutrition can negatively affect the production of neurons, whereas deprivation in late pregnancy affects the maturation of neurons. Additionally, specific nutritional deficiency, such as insufficient folic acid, can cause fetal brain damage. After birth, the developing brain is most vulnerable to nutritional deprivation within the first 2 to 3 years of life. The earlier and longer that malnutrition occurs, the greater effect on the brain (National Research Council, 2000). Similarly, the brain is most vulnerable to drugs, diseases, viruses, and other toxic substances while it is undergoing rapid growth.

However, it is important to keep in mind that the immature brain has considerable flexibility. Research suggests that it can recover from early damage or defects when periods of deprivation are followed by adequate nutrition and environmental stimulation. In Chapter 4, we will look at the success of early intervention programs in reducing the long-term impact of poverty on children's intellectual development.

The brain is a living organ, and it cannot develop without proper nutrition and protection from toxic substances.

Brain Development and Experience

Genetics largely influence the timing of brain development, but research from the past 5 years suggests that experience plays a more important role in shaping brain development than was previously thought (Gopnik, Metzoff, & Kuhl, 1999; National Research Council, 2000; Thompson, 1998). Stimulation or input from the environment is important for increasing and maintaining connections between neurons. As one group of researchers described it:

> Many species seem to have evolved such that the genes need only roughly outline the pattern of neural connectivity in a sensory system, leaving more specific details to be determined through the organism's interactions with its environment. (Greenough, Black, & Wallace, 1987, p. 543)

Scientists believe that the brain is programmed to receive certain inputs and stimulation early in development.

Scientists believe that the nervous system fine-tunes itself during the course of development. Neurons are programmed to receive certain input or stimulation during the period in which the formation of synapses are at a peak; that is, certain environmental stimulation is expected (Greenough et al., 1987). Neurons that receive this stimulation from the environment form connections, whereas those that fail to receive the appropriate input or stimulation fade and die off. For example, a baby born with cataracts will become permanently and irrevocably blind if the condition is not treated within the first 6 months of the infant's life. The region of the brain controlling movement is also highly sensitive to input during the first 2 years. If movement is restricted, it could inhibit the formation of connections. Thus, early experiences are believed to be crucial to the wiring of the young brain.

However, the idea that there is a "critical period" for brain development is an issue of considerable debate. Some researchers have interpreted new research on early brain development in terms of a "windows of opportunity" metaphor. The developing brain is primed to receive certain stimulation by a particular time, and this stimulation is necessary for continued normal development. If this stimulation is not received, the window "closes." To date, much of the research in support of a critical period perspective is drawn from animal research. For example, when 1-month-old kittens are deprived of light for 3 or 4 days, the visual center of their brains begin to deteriorate. If kept in the dark for the first 2 months of life, damage to the kittens' eyesight could be permanent (Hubel & Wiesel, 1970). Studies have also shown that rats raised with toys and other stimuli grow 25 percent more synapses than rats deprived of such stimuli (Greenough et al., 1987). And rats reared with more visual stimulation have better developed visual cortexes than rats that had little to see (Black & Greenough, 1986).

Although such research with animals suggests there is a critical period for brain development, it is not clear if the brain circuitry of humans operates the same way. Neuroscientists do not yet know the range of typical early experiences that are necessary for early brain growth in humans. The exposure to light and sound is best understood at this time. However, movement, touch, and other sensory experiences may be important as well. A recent National Research Council report, *From Neurons to Neighborhoods* (NRC, 2000), offers the following conclusion about the role of early experience in brain development:

> Scientists are far from linking specific types or amounts of experiences to the developing structure or neurochemistry of the immature human brain, and conversely, from understanding how early brain development affects the ways in which young children process the abundance of information and experiences that their environment presents to them. Answers to questions about when during development particular experiences must occur and when, in fact, timing is important and when it is not also lie, to a large extent, beyond the boundaries of current knowledge. (p. 194)

Just as neuroscientists are providing important insights into early brain development, other research findings indicate that there is a considerable degree of flexibility and plasticity in the human brain, especially in the early years of development. **Plasticity** refers to the ability of the brain to change. A lack of stimulation may slow the development of brain connections and delay the appearance of some abilities, but later stimulation can compensate for the experience of early deprivation to some extent. For example, a child who spent the first 4 years of life in a body cast will eventually learn to walk and run but not as smoothly as a child who was able to move during those years. Similarly, children who learn a second language before the age of 10 can generally speak it without an accent, but older learners are unlikely to speak another language like a native, unless it is very similar to their first language. In the latter case, existing circuits may facilitate the learning of language sounds.

As suggested earlier, it is commonly believed that the brain is most open to change during the early years of development. Neurons that are not stimulated during the peak of synapse formation may be lost forever. However, new research suggests that the brain may retain some of its ability to change and adapt well into old age (Golden, 1994). The plasticity to form new neural connections may decline, but it does not totally disappear. Some evidence suggests that the brain works like a muscle: If it is well exercised, dendrites continue to grow. This research is opening new possibilities for the treatment of strokes, head and spinal cord injuries, and Alzheimer's disease. It may be possible to "teach an old dog new tricks," but most theorists believe that the plasticity and adaptability of a child's brain is unparalleled in the life span (Golden, 1994).

Plasticity, which refers to the ability of the brain to change, gradually diminishes over time.

Brain Organization and Specialization

The human brain is a highly specialized organ. Our brain is more specialized than the brain of any other mammal living today. The cerebrum of the human brain is divided into two halves by a deep fissure creating what are known as the left and right hemispheres. Researchers have known for some time that the left hemisphere controls the right side of the body, and the right hemisphere controls the left side. Each hemisphere also performs different cognitive functions. In adults, the left hemisphere largely controls verbal abilities (spoken and written language) and positive emotion, whereas the right hemisphere processes visual and spatial information as well as negative emotions, such as distress (Springer & Deutsch, 1993). John Bruer (1999) describes the left hemisphere as a serial processor that processes information in a sequential, analytical manner, whereas the right hemisphere is a parallel processor that processes information in terms of patterns and images. Some popular writers describe the "left brain" as more logical, and the "right brain" as more creative and intuitive.

The brain's left hemisphere controls the right side of the body and language processes; the right hemisphere controls the left side and spatial, visual, and social-emotional cues.

Specialization of the two hemispheres is known as **brain lateralization.** It is believed that the two hemispheres may begin to specialize in their function by age 3, but researchers are still debating this point. Some researchers argue that lateralization of the brain begins before birth; whereas others argue that this process of lateralization is not complete until adolescence. There is evidence to support both arguments.

Studies of brain damage have been informative in understanding brain organization and specialization. If damage occurs in one of the hemispheres before the age of 1, the other hemisphere will take over the damaged side's function, but the child will not develop the same level of functioning as a normal child who did not experience brain damage. In addition, early research suggested that children who are less than 5 years old recovered more fully and quickly from brain damage to the left hemisphere than adults (Lenneberg, 1967). For example, a recent study showed that preschool children with a wide variety

Studies of brain injuries provide valuable information about specialized brain functions.

of brain injuries from the first year of life showed milder language and spatial skill deficits than did brain-injured adults. By age 5, the children's cognitive impairments had largely disappeared (Stiles, Bates, Thai, Trauner, & Reilly, 1999). It is believed that children are better able to make a fuller recovery because they are able to shift their language processing over to the right hemisphere. Adults, however, have more of their neurons committed to specialized functions, so they are not able to take over functions in the damaged regions. This argument fits with the research we discussed earlier on declines in brain plasticity.

However, new evidence has raised some important questions about the timing of brain lateralization. First, evidence suggests that brain lateralization may occur before birth when the fetal testes begin to produce testosterone. The larger amounts of testosterone in the male's fetal environment may predispose male babies toward greater specialization of cognitive functioning from birth. In addition, 2-month-old infants of both sexes respond more to sounds heard through their right ear than their left ear. By 2 years of age, children begin to show hand preferences, which may be related to one hemisphere's becoming more dominant than the other.

Recent research also suggests that both cerebral hemispheres influence more aspects of cognitive functioning than was previously thought. In a reading task, for example, the left hemisphere comprehends syntax and grammar, but the right hemisphere is better at figuring out a story's meaning and purpose. Both sides of the brain must work together to perform this activity. Brain scanning technology has shown that electrical impulses are passed between the two hemispheres during a reading task. It is believed that many other cognitive activities involve the use of both hemispheres. Much of the research that is currently taking place involves how the two sides of the brain interact and function together (Bruer, 1999; Caine & Caine, 1994).

There is no strong evidence that links learning styles to brain functioning.

Is there a relationship between hemispheric specialization and learning disabilities? About 60 years ago, Orton (1937) suggested that incomplete dominance of the left hemisphere leads to writing and reading disorders. Since then, considerable research has examined the role that "abnormal" patterns of hemispheric specialization might play in the explanation of learning disabilities. Some research evidence suggests that children with reading problems do not show normal lateralization patterns (Baringa, 1996). In general, however, the neurological basis of learning disabilities is not well understood at this time.

Another common misconception is the presumed relationship between brain functioning and cognitive styles. As suggested earlier, some popular writers have argued that the left and right hemispheres of the brain process information very differently. Information processing of the left hemisphere is analytical, rational, sequential, and logical, whereas the right hemisphere is believed to be more intuitive, holistic, and emotional. Although individuals may process information in these different ways, these preferences are not necessarily tied to brain organization. At present, there is no strong scientific evidence to categorize individual differences in learning styles according to left- and right-brain hemispheric specialization (Hiscock & Kinbourne, 1987).

Perceptual development involves the processing of sensory information by the brain.

Perceptual Development

Perceptual development involves the processing of sensory information by the brain. As we just learned, the areas of the brain that interpret and respond to visual or auditory stimulation develop rapidly during the first 2 years of life. Developmentalists now believe that an infant's perceptual abilities are more advanced than was originally assumed. In this section, we explore the development of children's ability to process sensory information. As you will see, an infant quickly develops the perceptual abilities it needs to receive stimulation from the environment and to form emotional attachments.

Visual Perception

A newborn infant will gaze at an object and track it to keep it in view. However, a newborn's visual acuity (sharpness of the image) is not the same as an adult's. Infants are born legally blind, unable to see more than 7 to 8 inches in front of their faces, which is about the distance to the mother's face when a baby is nursing. A newborn infant is able to see at 20 feet what a person with perfect vision can see at 500 feet (Aslin, Jurczyk, & Posoni, 1998). As discussed earlier, the brain region that controls vision is highly sensitive to environmental stimulation and input in the early months of development. Visual acuity improves dramatically during these months, so that infants achieve adult like levels of vision by 12 months.

Depth perception develops after 6 months, when babies begin to move around on their own. Figure 2.10 shows the visual cliff experiment that is used to test children's depth perception (Gibson & Walk, 1960). A plate glass covers the surface of a platform to give the illusion of a dropoff. Babies who are crawling will not cross the plate glass, whereas precrawling babies will not show the same apprehension when placed on the glass. It is believed that the experience of falling and getting hurt facilitates the development of depth perception. Precrawling babies who can move around in their walkers seem to show a fear of depths as well. In short, movement (motor development) may facilitate the development of depth perception, which enables infants to move around more adaptively in a three-dimensional world.

Through a technique called the *habituation* procedure, researchers have learned a great deal about the type of visual stimulation infants prefer. Research in the 1960s revealed that infants preferred to look at stimulus displays that are novel and complex. When exposed to new sights, sounds, smells, and tastes, infants display an *orienting response*. They become quiet and attentive, and their breathing and heart rate may even slow. **Habituation** is the decrease in an infant's response to a stimulus after repeated exposure to it. For example, the infant may stop sucking a pacifier when there is a new person or new sound in the room. Using the habituation procedure, researchers can determine what stimuli are interesting and new to infants. They have learned that infants prefer human faces to other patterned stimuli.

FIGURE 2.10
Visual Cliff Experiment
SOURCE: Mark Richards/Photo Edit.

Infants prefer stimuli that are novel and complex to that which is familiar, and they prefer human faces over other forms of patterned stimuli.

When gazing at a face, an infant tends to focus his or her attention on the eyes and facial expression, which provides important information about danger or safety in their surroundings.

By the time children enter school, they are able to systematically scan and attend to stimuli for short periods of time. At this point, they begin to exert voluntary control over their attentional processes. Developmental changes in attentional processes will be discussed again in Chapter 4.

Auditory Perception

What can a newborn hear? When are children able to discriminate sounds? Unlike vision, auditory perception is fairly well developed at birth. There is growing evidence that fetuses react to sound by the sixth or seventh month of prenatal development (Aslin et al., 1998). Three-day-old infants show a preference for familiar rather than unfamiliar voices, which suggests that they prefer sounds they may have heard while still in the womb. In a classic study, mothers read Dr. Seuss's *The Cat in the Hat* to their unborn children. After birth, these children responded more favorably to the book that had been read to them prenatally than to an unfamiliar book (DeCasper & Spence, 1986).

In addition to remembering familiar sounds, newborns are quite adept at discriminating between sounds. For example, young infants are able to discriminate between the sounds of *pah* and *bah*. This early ability to make subtle discriminations between sounds prepares an infant to learn the sounds of his or her language. By the time they say their first words, 2-year-old infants produce only the sounds of their native language. Auditory perception develops rapidly during infancy, but it does not reach adult levels until the elementary school years (Mauer & Mauer, 1988).

Taste, Smell, and Touch

Babies seem to be born with a "sweet tooth." They prefer sweet fluids to other tastes, and they dislike sour and bitter tastes. One interpretation of newborns' preference for sweet tastes is that they are naturally attracted to their mother's milk, which tends to have a sweeter taste than cow's milk. A preference for sweet tastes does not mean that infants should regularly drink sugar water. There is some evidence to suggest that feeding patterns in the first few years have long-term effects. For example, infants who are frequently fed sweet liquids in the first years show a preference for these liquids at age 2 (Beauchamp & Moran, 1985).

The sense of smell is also present at birth. Newborns turn away from smells like rotten eggs or ammonia, and they smile when exposed to the smell of bananas. It is believed that the sense of smell may play an important role in bonding. Researchers have shown that breast-fed babies can recognize their own mothers' smells as opposed to the smells of other lactating mothers (Cernoch & Porter, 1985). Mothers are also able to recognize the smell of their 1- or 2-day old infants (Porter, Cernoch, & McLaughlin, 1983).

Newborns are responsive to touch. If you touch a newborn's cheek it will begin to suck. This response is an automatic reflex, and one of several reflexes that enable babies to interact with their environment. Researchers also believe that touch is important for brain development. In animals, the sensation of touch releases certain body chemicals that are necessary for physical growth. For example, the licking of a mother rat influences the setting of her pups' heart rate, temperature, growth immune system, and other physiological states. When deprived of this licking, the pups fail to grow normally.

Human touch may have the same effect on the infant's development. Studies of babies who are born prematurely support this suggestion. A preterm baby is generally placed in a plexiglass-enclosed box, called an isolette, so that the air temperature of the baby's environment can be carefully controlled. Human contact is limited because of possible infection. If preterm infants must be fed through stomach tubes, they do not receive the tactile stimulation babies normally experience during feedings. Research has shown that when preterm infants are massaged gently several times a day, they tend to grow faster than babies who do not receive this stimulation. At the end of 1 year, the massaged babies were also more advanced in motor development than the other babies (Field et al., 1986).

Research on **infant attachment** also supports the importance of human contact. Attachment is the process by which infants form strong, affectional ties with their caregivers. Generally this process begins to take place within the first 6 months of age, such that babies begin to show a preference for the people they want to be near, especially in times of stress, by 7 or 8 months. Babies who are cuddled, hugged, and handled tenderly and carefully tend to form more secure attachments with their caregivers. As will be discussed in Chapter 7, this attachment process is important for developing a basic sense of trust.

If infants can respond favorably to touch, then it is not surprising that they can also feel pain. Young infants respond to injections and circumcision by fussing and crying. Doctors no longer think that infants can be treated as if they are insensitive to pain. There is no evidence, however, that the pain experienced in routine medical care has any long-term effects on physical or emotional development.

Implications for Educators

Knowledge of children's perceptual development has important implications for educators. It suggests that the developing child is attracted to stimuli that are novel and complex. Babies are attracted to colorful mobiles and patterned displays. Preschool children are attracted to picture books and enjoy finding figures of animals and other familiar objects that are hidden in larger visual displays. Older children are also attracted to colorful and stimulating displays. Walk down any elementary school hallway, and you will see art displays and samples of children's writing. It is always striking how most high school classrooms lack visual displays or attractive decorations when compared with the elementary or preschool classroom. Look around your college classroom and you will find the same. An attractive and changing classroom environment can hold the attention of learners.

It is also important for educators to understand how visual and auditory perception develops and what factors can indicate atypical development. Children and adolescents with learning disabilities may exhibit problems with auditory and visual discrimination tasks. For example, it may be difficult for a ninth grader to remember visual images and symbols, and a fourth grader may reverse letters, such as seeing and writing the letter *b* for *d*. Children with learning disabilities may also have difficult hearing the difference between words that sound alike, such as *fit* and *fib*. In Chapter 5, we will learn that the ability to hear individual letter sounds (phonemic awareness) plays a crucial role in the development of children's reading abilities. Early intervention programs for children with special learning needs generally include activities that help to strengthen perceptual abilities. We will discuss other approaches for assisting students with special learning needs in Chapter 6.

Motor Development

When are children able to walk, hold a pencil, or hit a baseball? Motor development involves children's increasing ability to move and control their body movements. In the following sections, we explore developmental changes in children's reflexes, gross motor skills, and fine motor skills.

Infant attachment, the process of forming strong affectional ties to a caregiver, is nurtured by cuddling and hugging during the early months and is important for producing a basic sense of trust.

Children are attracted to colorful and stimulating displays in the classroom.

Table 2.5	Examples of Infant Reflexes	
Reflex	**Description**	**Function**
Eye blink	Infant closes eyes with bright light or noise near eyes	Protects infant from strong stimulation
Rooting	Head turns toward source when stroked on cheek near mouth	Helps infant find nipple
Moro*	Infant attempts to cling when startled	May have helped animal ancestor cling to mother
Palmer grasp*	Spontaneous grasp when object placed in palm	Prepares infant for voluntary grasping
Stepping*	Infant lifts one foot after another when held to permit feet to touch flat surface	Prepares infant for voluntary walking
Babinski reflex*	Toes fan out and curl if sole of foot is stroked	Unknown

*Reflex disappears within first 6 months.

Newborn Reflexes

A newborn infant's movements are mainly due to innate reflexes. Sneezing, blinking, and gagging are examples of reflexes that are not consciously produced by the infant. Some of these reflexes are evident before birth. For example, sonograms show the developing infant hiccuping or sucking. Table 2.5 lists other examples of newborn reflexes that are present at birth. Some of these responses have a protective or survival function. Crying enables the baby to signal distress, gagging prevents choking, and sucking enables infants to nurse right after birth. Some reflexes, such as blinking and gagging, are evident throughout the life span. Other reflexes, however, are present for a few months and then disappear at predictable times. These responses reappear later in development, but they are then under the voluntary control of the child. At birth, physicians routinely check an infant's reflexes. If a certain reflex is missing or present for a longer time than it should be, it may signal a neurological problem.

Early motor development, the ability to move and control bodily movements, consists mainly of innate reflex movements such as blinking, sucking, grasping, and crying.

Development of Gross Motor Skills

Gross motor skills involve the movement of the head, body, legs, arms, and large muscles. The Focus on Development box on page 88 presents the sequence of development in this area. Remember that every child follows a universal as well as a unique timetable of development.

Perhaps the most significant change for children and their parents is the emergence of locomotion skills. Once infants can move about on their own, their environment greatly expands. Crawling generally appears around 8 to 10 months. By 13 months, some infants are able to climb up stair steps, but coming back down is a different matter. The appearance of crawling places new demands on parents, such as removing fragile objects from surfaces the child can reach, covering electrical outlets, securing cupboards with baby locks, and closing off stairways. Most parents "baby proof" their home by the time their baby is 6 months old, if not sooner.

Between 10 and 15 months, children begin to walk. Because their head and trunk are larger than their legs, they walk with their legs apart and toes pointed inward for balance. Children are affectionately called toddlers at this age because their steps are short and uncertain, and they toddle from side to side. As their bodies lengthen and become less top-heavy between the ages of 4 and 7, their walk begins to resemble that of an adult. By age 3, children can run, jump, and ride a tricycle.

During the preschool years, children's muscles grow stronger, and their physical coordination improves. Now they can throw a ball without losing their balance, hop on one foot, and run more smoothly. By age 5, most children can catch a ball with two hands, turn somersaults, and skip. Children's running, jumping, throwing, and coordination continues to improve in middle childhood. If you observe a group of late elementary school children playing on the playground, you will see fancy footwork in skip rope or hopscotch; games of dodgeball, kickball, or softball; or activities requiring a great deal of agility and balance,

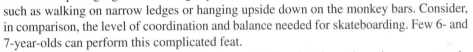

Gross motor skills involve moving the head, body, legs, arms, and large muscles, whereas fine motor skills involve small body movements necessary for working with a puzzle, drawing, or using scissors.

As this high school student is demonstrating, motor skills, coordination, and balance are well developed by adolescence.
SOURCE: Jim Bounds/News & Observer.

such as walking on narrow ledges or hanging upside down on the monkey bars. Consider, in comparison, the level of coordination and balance needed for skateboarding. Few 6- and 7-year-olds can perform this complicated feat.

The effective performance of some motor activities also depends on improvements in certain cognitive skills. To hit a ball, for example, a child must choose the appropriate time to swing the bat. The child must judge the speed of the ball, formulate an appropriate response, and allow time for the plan of action to reach their muscles (Cratty, 1986). Young elementary school children usually swing the ball too early or too late. For this reason, T-ball, a modified version of baseball using a pitching machine, may be more appropriate for younger elementary school children than baseball. Similarly, kickball should precede instruction in soccer, basketball, or football (Thomas, 1984).

Development of Fine Motor Skills

The advent of walking in the second year frees up the hands for the development of **fine motor skills,** the skills that involve small body movements. Activities such as pouring milk, cutting food with a knife and fork, drawing, assembling a puzzle, writing, working at a computer, and playing a musical instrument all involve fine muscle coordination and control. As with gross motor skills, this development is a continuous and gradual process. The development of fine motor skills also follows a universal sequence, but each child has his or her own individual timetable.

Reaching and grasping are among the first fine motor movements to appear. Around 5 months, an infant is able to grasp and hold objects, but hand and eye coordination is very

Once the pincer grasp develops, the child's ability to manipulate small objects expands.

Focus on Development

Sequence of Motor Skills Development

Age	Description of Skill
Birth to 6 months	Exhibits many reflexes Reaches for objects Rolls from front to back Holds head up when on stomach
6 to 12 months	Demonstrates fewer reflexes Sits up Creeps and crawls Stands holding on Pincer grasp emerges
12 to 18 months	Begins to walk Climbs up stairs
18 to 24 months	Begins to run Shows hand preference Turns pages one at a time Can stack 4 to 6 blocks Gains control over bowels
24 to 36 months	Jumps Begins to ride tricycle Can kick a ball forward Can throw a ball with two hands Gains control over bladder

limited. The infant can hold a bottle with two hands but may have difficulty guiding it to his or her mouth. This type of coordination must wait for myelination of those areas of the brain that coordinate eye and hand movements. By the end of the first year the pincer grasp appears. The infant can use the thumb and index finger to pick up small objects, such as blocks, buttons, or puzzle pieces. Once the **pincer grasp** develops, the infant's ability to manipulate objects greatly expands. By age 2, infants can turn knobs and faucets and play with screw-type toys. The ability to assemble simple puzzles and to hold large crayons, paintbrushes, or marker pens develops during the preschool years (ages 3 to 5).

By age 5 or 6, most children are able to copy simple geometric shapes, manipulate buttons and zippers, and, perhaps, tie their own shoes. They can also print the alphabet, the letters in their name, and numbers from 1 to 10 with reasonable clarity, although writing tends to be quite large and not well organized on the paper. When children first begin to write, they reverse many letters (e.g., *b* and *d* or *w* and *m*). These letter reversals are normal and generally disappear by the age of 8 or 9. Children generally master uppercase letters first, because vertical and horizontal movements are easier to control. By age 7, children begin to form letters of uniform height and space and to use lowercase. These improvements indicate that they are ready to master cursive writing.

3 to 4 years	Masters running
	Walks upstairs alternating steps
	Can button large buttons
	Can catch large ball
	Holds pencil between thumb and first two fingers
4 to 5 years	Can dress self
	Walks downstairs alternating steps
	Can gallop
	Can cut on straight line with scissors
	Can thread beads, but not needle
	Can walk across balance beam
	Begins to hold writing tool in finger grip
5 to 6 years	Can button small buttons
	Can hop 8 to 10 steps on one foot
	Can connect zipper on a coat
	Might be able to tie shoes
	Plays ball games
6 to 7 years	Can skip 12 or more times
	Can ride a bicycle
	Can throw ball in adult manner
8 years and onward	Skips freely
	Rides bike easily
	Writes individual letters

SOURCE: After Thomas (1984).

Between the ages of 10 and 12, children begin to show manipulative skills similar to those of adults. They can perform crafts, type at a keyboard, play musical instruments, and work puzzles with tiny little pieces almost as well as any adult.

When do children begin to show a preference for using their right or left hand? **Hand dominance** does not generally appear until age 5 or later. Most toddlers begin to show a preference for one hand while performing an activity such as reaching, but they can perform most activities with either hand. By age 5, more than 90 percent of all children show a hand preference, but they can still be taught to use their nonpreferred hand. In the past, lefties were encouraged to use their right hands by misguided parents and teachers who believed that not using the right hand was a handicap. Researchers now believe that brain specialization and lateralization leads to handedness. A strong hand preference reflects the greater capacity of one side of the brain to carry out a skilled motor action. For right-handed children, the left side of the brain is the dominant cerebral hemisphere. Once brain specialization becomes firmly established, it is more difficult for children to use their nonpreferred hand for writing, painting, and so on. It is interesting that most left-handed people are ambidextrous; that is, they can perform some activities as skillfully with their left as with their right hand. Moreover, contrary to past beliefs, there is some evidence to

Hand dominance, believed to be related to brain lateralization, generally does not appear until age 5.

suggest that left-handed and ambidextrous people tend to have superior verbal and mathematical abilities (Benbow, 1986).

Gender Differences in Motor Development

Girls tend to walk earlier than boys because the female skeleton is slightly more mature at birth. By the early childhood years, however, boys outperform girls on most gross motor tasks, such as jumping, kicking, and throwing. Girls, on the other hand, tend to have better flexibility, balance, foot locomotion, and small muscle coordination (Roberton, 1984). Differences begin to appear in preschool and extend into middle childhood and beyond.

What explains these differences? Some of the sex differences may be attributable to differences in body size. However, boys do not gain superiority in physical and muscular strength until after puberty. Many researchers believe that the environment plays a large role in the development of boys' and girls' gross motor skills. From an early age, boys are encouraged to run, jump, climb, and engage in rough-and-tumble play more than girls. Parents also hold higher expectations for boys' than girls' athletic performance, and their children internalize these messages about their abilities (Eccles & Harold, 1991). As early as kindergarten, girls report that they have less ability at sports than do their male classmates. Also, elementary school girls perceive physical activities, such as sports, as more appropriate for boys than girls (Pellet & Harrison, 1992). By sixth grade, girls are less likely than boys to devote time to sports or athletic activities (Eccles & Harold, 1991). Theorists believe that gender differences in gross motor skills are likely to disappear with the greater participation of girls in sports and athletics during childhood and adolescence. Gender differences in some motor skills seem to be more related to practice, experience, and interest than to innate differences (Roberton, 1984).

Gender differences in motor development begin to appear in preschool, with boys excelling in gross motor activities and girls in fine motor activities.

Schools and Motor Development

Children or adolescents with poor motor skills may avoid physical activities and become sedentary. We will learn later how low physical activity is an important contributor to childhood obesity. A young person's motor skills may also influence their peer relations and choices of activities. Youngsters who are skilled may be asked by their peers to participate in games, sports, and other physical activities. Peer relations have an important influence on feelings of self-esteem and self-worth. Finally, physical activity is associated with children's abilities to concentrate on cognitively demanding tasks.

How can schools help facilitate the development of motor skills? Play and physical activity is the medium by which children and adolescents develop their physical abilities. Early childhood teachers need to provide ample opportunities for children to engage in large motor activities, such as running, riding tricycles, climbing, block building, jumping, and so on. The National Association for the Education of Young Children (NAEYC) recommends that programs for toddlers and preschoolers provide daily indoor and outdoor activities that exercise children's large muscles (Bredekamp, 1997). Most preschools and kindergartens have areas for children to engage in large motor activities. These areas need to be well supervised to prevent injuries and accidents. It is also important that the preschool classroom provide activities that will develop fine motor skills, such as sand play, drawing, painting, playing with puzzles, play dough, and so on.

Play and physical activity are important for the development of motor skills.

As children move into the elementary school years, they are better able to sit and attend for longer periods of time. However, periods of concentrated work need to be distributed over the course of a school day. In Japanese and Taiwanese schools, primary grade children have

SOURCE: Bill Wittman.

Regular breaks for physical activity and social interactions can help improve attention and concentration during classroom activities.

a 10- to 15-minute break from classwork every hour or so (Stevenson & Lee, 1990). Research has shown that regular breaks for physical activity and social interactions can increase rather than decrease young elementary schoolchildren's attention to cognitive demanding tasks (Pellegrini, Huberty, & Jones, 1995; Pellegrini & Smith, 1998). Even older children and young adolescents are not able to sit and concentrate for long periods of time. They also need plenty of opportunities to stretch, move their bodies, and engage in social interactions.

As we will learn later, childhood obesity has been on the rise for the last 15 years. One of the contributing factors to this increase is the lack of regular physical activity. A 1996 report indicated that 60 percent of Americans do not exercise regularly, despite a national health campaign to raise public awareness about the many health benefits associated with physical activity (Center for Disease Control, 1996). Even fewer adolescents exercise on a regular basis. In 1999, 53 percent of eighth graders and 45 percent of twelfth graders report that they exercise on a regular basis. Also, boys report consistently exercising or participating in sports more often than girls (Bachman, Johnston, & O'Malley, 1999).

Safety Concerns

As motor skills develop and children begin to spend more time away from the careful supervision of parents, the incidence of accidental injuries rises. As stated earlier, elementary schoolchildren are still acquiring the cognitive abilities they need to make judgments of speed and timing. Every day more than 39,000 children are injured seriously enough to require medical treatment, totaling more than 14 million each year. Among children 14 and under, treatment for injury is the second leading cause of visits to hospital emergency rooms (Safekids, 1999). In fact, accidents are the number-one cause of childhood death in the United States. The average child has twice the chance of dying an accidental death before the age of 10 than dying from a disease.

Play, which is the medium by which children develop their motor skills, needs to be supervised in the early years because of the high incidence of childhood injuries.

For this reason, parents and children need information on how to prevent childhood injuries. Many elementary schools now provide classes on bicycle safety as part of the physical education program. The use of reflectors on bikes and helmets can substantially reduce a large proportion of the bicycle-related deaths that occur each year. Children and adolescents should also be required to wear helmets and protective gear for roller skating and skateboarding. This simple precaution can reduce the risk of a head injury by 85 percent (Safe Kids, 1991).

Sports Participation

Another major area of concern is the effect of children's participation in organized sports. There are now baseball, soccer, and football leagues for children as young as 4 and 5 years old. Although these activities provide children an opportunity to develop their motor skills, to learn how to be a team player, and to cope with failure, far too many children are pushed into competitive sports before their motor skills have significantly matured. One result is that some children lose interest in athletic activities at an early age. Some experts argue that the most appropriate time for the introduction of team sports is when children are able to engage in cooperative play about the age of 6 or 7. Furthermore, some children are seriously injured when they play sports before they are physically ready. For these reasons, most physical education programs in the elementary grades are replacing competitive sports with ones that encourage children to be physically active but not competitive.

Experts believe that children should not participate in organized team sports before the ages of 6 or 7.

There is still some debate concerning the effects of interscholastic or intramural sports participation for older children and adolescents. Many parents and teachers worry that athletics can take time away from studying and other extracurricular pursuits. However, most studies reveal that the effects of sports participation on academic achievement is either slight or negligible (Buoye, 1998). In fact, there is growing evidence that athletic participation can have many positive benefits for students. For example, two large-scale national studies (*High School and Beyond* and the *National Educational Longitudinal Study of 1988*) reported positive relations between sports participation and academic achievement for high school students (Bouye, 1998; Marsh, 1993). Findings also suggested that relations are stronger for individual sports (swimming, track, wrestling, etc.) than for team sports (basketball, football, and baseball), after controlling for individual characteristics (e.g., ethnicity, socioeconomic status, gender) and previous achievement.

Other studies suggest that the benefits of sports participation may extend beyond academics for samples of female and minority students. In a review of research on athletic experiences of ethnically diverse girls, Jeanne Weiler (1998) reported positive benefits for self-esteem, confidence, and career aspirations. Girls who participated in sports also had a lower risk for dropping out of school and lower rates of sexual activity and pregnancy.

Studies of minority youths have not consistently found positive relations between sports participation and school achievement.

Similarly, studies of minority youth suggest that high school sports participation can lead to increased self-confidence, peer popularity, and school engagement (Jordon, 1999; Merrill & Sabo, 1992). Participation in multiracial teams can also facilitate positive cross-ethnic relations within schools (Slavin & Madden, 1979). However, it is important to note that studies of minority youth have not consistently reported positive effects for various measures of school achievement. Barring socioeconomic differences, these results raise the possibility that minority athletes are not receiving the same level of academic challenge and support as their white peers. Researchers speculate that stereotypes about the intellectual abilities of different minority groups as well as athletes ("dumb jocks") may doubly shortchange minority athletes in the classroom (Melnick & Sabo, 1992, p. 290).

Physical Growth

Changes in Weight and Height

The average infant weighs approximately 7.5 pounds at birth. Consequently, infancy is characterized by rapid growth. During the first year, an infant's weight will triple, to 20 to 24 pounds, and the baby will grow to 20 to 30 inches. The infant's physical growth follows two basic principles. First, growth is characterized by a **cephalocaudal** pattern. It starts at the head and proceeds downward; thus, the infant's brain, neck, and trunk develop before the legs. Second, growth is also characterized by a **proximal-distal** pattern, in which development begins in the center and proceeds outward. Accordingly, the organs develop before the arms or hands. Weight gain slows in the second year, but the infant will continue to add inches. By the end of the second year, infants are 50 percent of their adult height, but only one-fourth their adult weight (Tanner, 1978). At birth, the infant's head is surprisingly large relative to other parts of the body. As the infant's height increases, the head decreases in its proportion to the overall body.

By the end of the second year, infants achieve 50 percent of their adult height but only 25 percent of their adult weight.

Physical growth slows down during the preschool and elementary school years. Between ages 2 and 5, most children gain about 6 or 7 pounds per year. Preschoolers also gain about 2 to 4 inches per year. This pattern continues until puberty, so that children who are entering adolescence are about twice as heavy and a foot taller than they were as preschoolers. Elementary schoolchildren tend to look much thinner than younger children because of their added height.

It is interesting to note that the average American is growing taller today. By 1977, the average American had gained 2.5 to 3 inches in height since the early eighteenth century, and it is believed that this trend is continuing. Also, it appears that young people are attaining their adult height at an earlier age than before. One hundred years ago people did not reach their adult height until their early or mid-20s. Today, many 16- or 17-year olds are taller than their parents. This shift in normative patterns of development is called a **secular trend.** Historical changes in growth patterns are due to improved nutrition and health conditions. We will learn that a secular trend also characterizes the onset of puberty.

Variations in Physical Size

Heredity plays a very important role in determining a child's shape and size. From the age of 2 years on, the parents' heights are good predictors of their children's heights. Ethnic background as well tends to be a good predictor of physical size. In general, children from North America, northern Europe, and Africa are the tallest in the world. Children from South America and Asia tend to be smaller. Within the United States, African American children tend to be taller than children

During the preschool years, children gain between 2 to 4 inches in height each year.

SOURCE: Rachel Epstein/Photo Edit.

Chapter 2   Physical Development

of European, Asian, or Hispanic descent. Also, girls tend to be slightly taller than boys from age 2 until about 9, when boys catch up. However, weight and muscle mass are about the same for boys and girls before puberty. As suggested earlier, with equal training and experience, girls can be as good athletes as boys in the elementary school years.

Unfortunately, variations in physical size can lead some children to be judged as less mature than other children. For example, younger children, who tend to be physically small relative to their classmates, are more likely than older children in the same grade to be retained in elementary school, because they are perceived as less mature. Achievement and adjustment problems can also emerge when children and adolescents are too physically mature for their grade level. As mentioned earlier, these young people are likely to seek out older friends who are more mature.

Physical attractiveness is another factor that can influence our judgments of other people. Adults tend to assume more positive attributes and characteristics (e.g., intelligence, leadership ability, social competence) to physically attractive than to unattractive children. Studies of children reveal the same patterns (Langlois & Stephen, 1981). Children prefer attractive peers and find unattractive peers unacceptable. One study showed that even preschool children rated attractive peers as friendlier, smarter, and better behaved than less attractive peers (Langlois & Stephen, 1981). Moreover, research on young children reveals that being attractive is more important for girls' than boys' acceptance by their peers (Vaughn & Langlois, 1983). Even more disturbing, a recent study revealed that girls who were judged by their peers and teachers as unattractive in middle school received lower grades, and 5 years later were more likely to drop out of school and to become teenage mothers than were attractive girls (Cairns & Cairns, 1994). This research raises important concerns about the effects of physical attractiveness on interpersonal relations in the classroom. It is important to recognize how cultural stereotypes of physical attractiveness may be shaping the way we evaluate and relate to children.

Onset of Puberty

Puberty refers to the period in which a young person becomes capable of sexual reproduction. This period of development involves many physical changes that typically stretch out for many years. The changes include: (a) a rapid acceleration in growth; (b) the development of primary sex characteristics; (c) development of secondary sex characteristics; (d) changes in body composition; and (e) changes in circulatory and respiratory systems.

What Causes Puberty to Begin?

To parents, and the teens themselves, puberty may seem to come rapidly, but it is actually a slow and gradual process. Puberty is activated by changes in the level of sex hormones—**androgens** and **estrogens.** Although we generally associate androgens with male characteristics and estrogens with female characteristics, both hormones are produced and present in both sexes. The level of sex hormones, and hormones in general, is controlled by the **pituitary gland,** which is under the control of the **hypothalamus** at the base of the brain. The pituitary gland is like a master hormone-secreting gland, whereas the hypothalamus is like a thermostat monitoring and regulating levels of hormones in the body.

Prior to puberty, the hypothalamus is "set" to maintain low levels of sex hormones circulating in the body. However, the hypothalamus appears to lose some of its sensitivity to sex hormones at puberty. The cause of this change is not well understood (Grumbach, Roth, Kaplan, & Kelch, 1974), but it triggers the pituitary gland to secrete hormones that cause

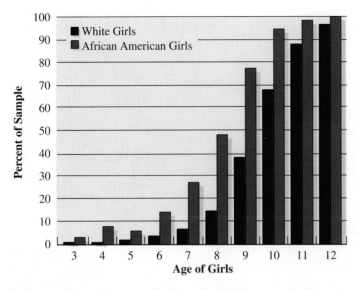

FIGURE 2.11

*Ethnic Differences
in Onset of Puberty*

SOURCE: After Herman-
Giddens et al. (1997).

By 8 years of age, 15 percent of white girls and 48 percent of African American girls have started to develop breasts and/or pubic hair.

the adrenal glands and gonads (testes in males and ovaries in females) to increase the concentration of sex hormones—estrogen in females and testosterone in males. The rate of increase is sex specific. At puberty, the production of estrogen is much higher in females (8 times the level of childhood) than males, whereas the production of testosterone is much higher in males (18 times the level of childhood) (Malina & Bouchard, 1991).

In both male and female adolescents, changes in levels of sex hormones stimulate the development of primary and secondary sex characteristics. **Primary sex characteristics** involve changes in the gonads (testes and ovaries) and the development of eggs and sperm. **Secondary sex characteristics** involve changes in genitals and breasts, and the growth of facial, pubic, and body hair. In females, **estrogen** is crucial to the maturation of the reproductive system, including the ovaries, fallopian tubes, and uterus. It is also involved in breast development and in the onset of ovulation and menstruation. In males, **testosterone** affects the development of the penis, testes, and other organs of the reproductive system.

When Does Puberty Begin?

There is considerable variability in the onset of puberty. Developmental norms published in the early 1970s indicated that the average age of onset was 10 to 12 years for girls and 12 to 14 years for boys (Tanner, 1972). These norms, however, were established based on a small sample of children growing up in British orphanages during the 1960s. For girls, puberty may have been delayed due to poor nutrition. Moreover, children of different ethnic and racial backgrounds were not studied at this time.

There is considerable variability in the onset of puberty.

A recent large U.S. study examined the onset of puberty in 17, 077 girls, aged 3 to 12 years (Herman-Giddens et al., 1997). This study defined the onset of puberty as the development of breasts and/or public hair. As Figure 2.11 shows, girls can begin puberty well before the age of 10. In fact, 15 percent of white girls and 48 percent of African American girls had started puberty by age 8. Although signs of physical maturity can begin well before the age of 10, the average age of onset of menstruation has changed little since the 1960s. For white girls, the average is 12.8 years; it is 6 months earlier for African American girls.

SOURCE: News & Observer

Because girls begin puberty earlier than boys, school dances are a little awkward.

Ethnic differences in the onset of puberty are not well understood at this time. Researchers believe that diet, genetics, environment, and even latitude may play a role. Nevertheless, it is important for educators to remember that it is not "abnormal" for girls to show signs of puberty in the middle to late elementary school years. The early onset of puberty raises some interesting questions concerning a preteen's ability to understand and cope with these changes. As we will discuss later, early maturation can have negative consequences for girls.

It is also important to point out that some adolescents may start and finish their pubertal changes before their peers of the same sex even begin their changes. As we will learn later, adolescents can experience adjustment problems if they begin puberty much earlier or later than their peers. As shown in the Focus on Development box, developmental norms based on Tanner's research indicated that the sequence of change was different for females and males. Therefore, we will consider each sex separately.

As discussed, the first sign of puberty in girls is the elevation of the breast or the appearance of pubic hair. During the middle stages of puberty, girls experience a height spurt. At the peak of puberty, girls grow about 3.5 inches per year and add another foot or so to their height before the end of the growth spurt. Most of their physical growth occurs in their torso, rather than their legs. **Menarche,** the beginning of the menstrual cycle, is generally the last physical change to occur in puberty. Hence it is wrong to assume that the beginning of the menstrual cycle marks the beginning of puberty in girls. Many other important changes have already occurred.

On the average, boys begin puberty 2 years later than girls. This 2-year difference can explain some of the tension in gender relations among young adolescents. The first signs of puberty in males are changes in their genitalia, accompanied by the appearance of pubic hair. Approximately 1 year later, the growth spurt begins. Next come changes in the size of the penis, development of facial and body hair, and a gradual lowering of the voice.

Focus on Development

Sequence of Change at Puberty

	Girls		Boys	
Age	**Characteristics**	**Age**	**Characteristics**	
8 to 13	Growth of breasts	10 to 13.5	Growth of testes	
8 to 14	Growth of pubic hair	10 to 15	Growth of public hair	
9.5 to 14.5	Height spurt	11 to 16	Height spurt	
10 to 16.5	Menarche	11 to 14.5	Growth of penis, change of voice, facial hair	

SOURCE: After Tanner (1978).

We have focused so far on the pubertal changes associated with sexual reproduction. Clearly, adolescents are concerned with these changes as well, but there are many other physical changes taking place in the adolescent body. The growth spurt is accompanied by increases in muscle mass and body fat, adding weight to the adolescent body. In general, muscle tissue grows faster in boys than in girls. Body fat increases for both males and females, but the rate of fat accumulation is greater and faster for girls, especially during the period just before the onset of puberty. By the end of adolescence, boys have a higher muscle-to-fat ratio (3:1) than do girls (5:4). The rapid increase in body fat often causes girls to become overly concerned about their weight, especially in a society that values thinness. In extreme cases, this concern can take the form of excessive dieting and bulimia or anorexia nervosa. We will discuss the development of eating disorders in a later section.

Among other things, pubertal changes involve rapid growth spurts, the appearance of sexual maturity, and increased muscle mass and fat.

As the adolescent body grows, there are also changes in the size and capacity of the heart and lungs. The magnitude of changes is greater in males than in females. Compared with girls, boys have greater physical strength, higher blood hemoglobin, more red blood cells, better exercise tolerance, and greater ability for neutralizing the chemical products of muscular exercise (e.g., lactic acid) by the end of adolescence (Peterson & Taylor, 1980). These factors may help explain sex differences in athletic ability in late adolescence, but biological differences are only part of the story. Differences in diet and exercise also play a role (Smoll & Schutz, 1990).

In summary, puberty is a dramatic period of physical development, second only to infancy. It involves changes in weight, height, and secondary sex characteristics. It also affects almost every vital organ, including, as we learned earlier, the brain. Research in the last decade also suggests that puberty can affect the sleep patterns of adolescents. The Focus on Research box describes this research and its educational implications.

Psychological Impact of Puberty

For adolescents, puberty involves more than just physical changes. Puberty often leads to changes in adolescents' self-image, self-confidence, family relations, moods, relations

Focus on Research

Do Adolescents Need More Sleep?

Any parent can describe the difficulty of waking a sleepy teenager to catch an early morning bus or a carpool ride. First-period high school teachers often find themselves in front of a group of teenagers nodding off to sleep. Many people attribute adolescents' sleep deprivation to a busy social life, to late nights of listening to music, or to lax parents who do not enforce a regular bedtime. However, researchers have discovered there is more to the story.

Sleep patterns change fundamentally at the transition to adolescence. Adolescents tend to go to bed later, and their natural time to fall asleep is around 11 P.M. Adolescents also tend to sleep less as they mature, but sleep requirements do not decline in adolescence. It is estimated that adolescents need at least $8\frac{1}{4}$ hours of sleep to function adequately, or $9\frac{1}{4}$ hours to maintain optimal alertness during the day (Carskadon, 1999). Developmental changes in sleep patterns are found not only in North America but also in Australia, Europe, and South America. Many researchers believe that internal changes in the circadian timing system may delay the timing of sleep behavior in adolescents (Carskadon, 1999). Controlled by light signals, circadian rhythms are synchronized to a 24-hour day and function as an internal biological clock to control wake and sleep cycles.

Changes in adolescents' sleep cycles raise some interesting questions for schools. In most communities, high schools have the earliest starting times, followed by middle schools, then elementary schools. Younger children tend to go to school later. The transition to high school can require a change in starting time from 8:30 A.M. to 7:30 A.M. Some high schools begin as early as 7:15 A.M. These early starting times may be "out of sync" with adolescents' sleeping patterns. Even with a regular bedtime of 11 P.M., most adolescents average only 6 to 7 hours of sleep on school nights.

Sleep deficits increase daytime sleepiness and decrease alertness. One study showed that it is possible for a small group of tenth grade students to fall asleep in an average of 3.4 minutes when tested at 8:30 A.M. (Carskadon, 1999). This same pattern was found in patients with the sleep disorder called narcolepsy! Insufficient sleep is associated with memory lapses, attention deficits, depressed moods, irritability, and slow reaction times (Dahl, 1999). Sleep deprivation can also undermine adolescents' abilities to perform complex cognitive tasks, such as those involving abstract reasoning. These conditions are not optimal for learning.

Educators rarely consider these biological changes in sleep patterns when formulating school policies. Generally, school schedules are based on bus schedules, sports programs, and so on.

However, sleep researchers are encouraging schools to adjust their starting times to accommodate the biological needs of sleepy adolescents.

with the opposite sex, and many other behaviors. The ways in which adolescents react to puberty is a complicated story. The nature and timing of pubertal changes seem to be important in predicting the effects of puberty, but young people's reactions to puberty are also shaped by the larger society. Consider the ways in which adolescents are portrayed in the media. They are often depicted as sex-crazed, rebellious, troubled, indecisive, moody, and so on. You have to look long and hard to find a positive image of adolescents in the media. These images reflect cultural stereotypes, and they not only shape the way adult society reacts to young people, but also influence the adolescents themselves.

Adolescence has been called the "gangly years" (Petersen, 1987). An adolescent's body seems to be all out of proportion. In the early stages of puberty, feet, hands, and even legs can appear out of proportion to the adolescent's torso. This is, in fact, the case. Parts of the adolescent's body are maturing at different rates. In general, the hands and feet will grow before the torso and shoulders. Variations in growth can lead to feelings of clumsiness and awkwardness, which can negatively affect an adolescent's self-image until some kind of balance is restored.

Adolescents are often portrayed as moody. They can be happy and friendly one moment, and angry or sad the next. Many adults attribute the emotional fluctuations to "raging hormones." A recent review of this research suggested that adolescents may experience intense mood swings, but the links between hormones and moods are *not* particularly strong (Buchanan, Eccles, & Becker, 1992). It is difficult to identify one single source for these mood changes, because adolescents are experiencing so many changes (physical development, school transitions, new cognitive abilities), as well as increased concentrations of hormones at the same time (Buchanan et al., 1992).

There is some evidence to suggest that the rapid increase of hormones in the early stages of puberty can lead to increased irritability, impulsivity, aggression (in boys), and depression (in girls), but these effects are generally moderated by environmental events. For example, increases in hormonal levels in early adolescence may lead to depressed moods in girls, but stressful events such as problems with friends, school, and family members play a much more influential role in explaining the development of depression in adolescent girls (Brooks-Gunn & Warren, 1989). The adolescent's social setting also plays a role in his or her moodiness. Over the course of a day, most adolescents go through many mood changes (Csikszentmihalyi & Larson, 1984). They are happy at lunch, excited with friends, bored in school, and angry if treated unfairly by a teacher. In other words, their moods fluctuate as they change activities. Because adolescents change activities and settings more frequently than adults do, this may account for their greater moodiness.

Adolescents are also viewed as rebellious and uncontrollable. Is there research evidence to support this view of adolescents? Most studies find some disruption in the parent and child relationship during puberty (Buchanan et al., 1992). As children enter adolescence, they report fewer positive feelings toward their parents, less communication with their parents, and more conflict on a daily basis. For example, a recent study showed that early menarche was associated with more conflict with mothers and with more family stress in late childhood (Kim & Smith, 1998). Conflict tends to be greater among adolescents and their mothers (Paikoff & Brooks-Gunn, 1991), perhaps because they spend more time together. The intensity and frequency of conflict appear to be greatest at the peak of puberty.

Because there is a great deal of individual variation in puberty, the increased conflict is not related to age per se. Most theorists believe that this increased conflict stems from the adolescent's need for more independence and for a greater say in family decisions. If parents are not able to relinquish some of their control, this could lead to rebellious behavior. It is safe to say that in most families, the onset of puberty brings about some imbalance in the parent and child relationship. Rebellious behavior is more common among parents and adolescents who have a history of conflict. When there are positive parent-child relations, balance is usually restored as parents and their adolescents renegotiate roles, rules, and expectations. The implications for teachers are clear. Teachers of adolescents can also expect more conflict if they are not willing or able to allow students to have some independence or control in the classroom.

Young people are affected by the nature and timing of their pubertal changes as well as by the expectations that society has for them during this period.

The psychological impact of puberty (moodiness and rebelliousness) is due to a variety of influences, such as hormones, social setting, stress level, and autonomy level.

Teachers of adolescents can expect conflict if they do not allow students to have some independence or control in the classroom.

Effects of Early and Late Physical Maturity

As mentioned earlier, there is considerable individual variability in the onset of puberty. Some youngsters can begin puberty at age 7 or 8, whereas others may not begin puberty until age 14 or 15. Although adjusting to adolescence can be difficult for most adolescents, it is particularly stressful for young people who mature earlier or later than their peers. Adolescents are very much aware of whether or not they are early or late for their age. Interestingly, adolescents' *perceptions* of themselves as early or late have a stronger impact on their reactions than the actual timing of puberty (Dubas, Graber, & Peterson, 1991).

The effects of early and late physical maturation are different for girls and boys. Early maturity in girls is particularly problematic, because the average girl matures 2 years earlier than boys. Consequently, an early-maturing girl is out of sync with both male and female agemates.

Early physical maturity in girls can have some positive consequences, but it also poses some risks. Initially, early maturity can enhance girls' peer relations, popularity, and social competence (Simmons, Byth, & McKinny, 1983). Early-maturing girls are also less dependent on parents than their late-maturing peers (Simmons & Blyth, 1987). However, early maturity in girls can lead to a number of emotional difficulties, including low self-esteem, poor self-image, depression, anxiety, and eating disorders (Aro & Taipale, 1987; Ge, Conger, & Elder, 1996; Simmons & Blyth, 1987). Early-maturing girls are also more likely to engage in deviant behavior, to have problems in school, and to experience early sexual intercourse (Caspi & Moffitt, 1991; Magnusson, Stattin, & Allen, 1986). These problem behaviors are more likely to occur in girls with a prior history of difficulties (Caspi & Moffitt, 1991). Additionally, the negative effects of early maturity are accentuated when combined with other significant transitions such as a change in schools, a geographical move, or a family divorce or remarriage (Simmons & Blyth, 1987).

What explains the negative consequences of early maturity for girls? The lowered self-esteem of early-maturing girls may be related to their body types. Early-maturing girls tend to be heavier than their girlish, late-maturing peers. As a result, their bodies no longer fit the current feminine ideal of thinness that our culture so highly values. Early-maturing girls are also more likely to associate with older peers, which can lead them to engage in actions they are not emotionally prepared to handle, such as early dating and sexual activity, drinking, and deviant behaviors. School involvement tends to be lower among early-maturing girls who have older friends, begin to date early, and engage in early sexual activity (Magnusson et al., 1985). Early-maturing girls who choose not to associate with older peers or engage in these behaviors are less likely to experience long-term social adjustment problems. Thus, the effects of early maturity are partly due to the company girls choose to keep.

What about boys? Is early maturity also associated with negative consequences for boys? Studies conducted some years ago revealed that early maturity has many positive consequences for boys. During high school, early-maturing boys are more self-assured, more popular, and more likely to be chosen as leaders than late-maturing boys (Mussen & Jones, 1957). Early-maturing boys tend to have more favorable self-images, fewer psychological problems, and higher peer popularity than late-maturing boys (Graber, Lewinsohn, Seeley, & Brooks-Gunn, 1997). As with girls, cultural ideals play an important role in how early-maturing boys react to their physical changes. Their physical appearance is moving closer to the cultural ideal of a tall, muscular male body. In contrast to girls, then, an early-maturing boy is more likely to react positively to his physical changes.

However, like their female counterparts, early-maturing boys who choose to affiliate or "hang out" with older peers are at greater risk for engaging in deviant or antisocial activities (Anderson & Magnusson, 1990; Duncan, Ritter, Dornbusch, Gross, & Carlsmith, 1985;

Early maturity, influenced by social and cultural context, often has negative effects on girls but positive effects on boys.

Silbereisen, Petersen, Albrecht, & Kracke, 1989). For example, studies in the United States and Europe show that early-maturing boys who develop friendships with older peers are more likely to be truant, to experiment with drugs and alcohol, to have school problems, and to engage in early sexual activities (Magnusson et al., 1985).

Other data reveal that late maturity in boys may be advantageous for some reasons. At age 30, early-maturing males tend to be more conforming, more traditional in their gender role, and less creative than their late-maturing male peers (Livson & Peskin, 1980). It is believed that early-maturing males are pushed into adult roles before they have an opportunity to experiment with different roles and identities. In a way, the greater adjustment problems early-maturing males face in adolescence may lead them to develop coping skills that are useful in adulthood.

As implied in this discussion, the effects of early and late maturity are influenced by a young person's social and cultural context. A New Zealand study revealed that the effects of early maturity in girls are less likely to be found when girls attend single-sex, instead of coeducational, schools (Caspi, Lyman, Moffitt, & Silva, 1993). Similarly, the effects of early maturity are different for girls depending on whether they are attending an elementary or middle school, with early-maturing girls experiencing more difficulty in middle school because they are experiencing multiple transitions (Blyth, Simmons, & Zakin, 1985). Coeducational and middle schools also increase the opportunities of early-maturing girls to engage in deviant behavior. Additionally, the effects of early and late maturity would have less impact on both sexes if our society did not place such a high premium on physical appearance and attractiveness. Parents and teachers can help young people make the transition to adolescence by preparing them for the changes that will take place (e.g., many children go through a "chubby" phase just before their height spurt) and by diminishing the importance of physical appearance. It is important to help young people recognize that individuals have many qualities that make them special, unique, and attractive.

Special Health Concerns

In this last section, we examine several health problems that can occur in childhood or adolescence. As you know, young people today face a number of risks and challenges including drug use, early sexual experimentation, and AIDS, to name just a few. Figure 2.12 presents a portrait of the health of young adolescents in the early twenty-first century. From this figure, it is easy to conclude that many young people are indeed in jeopardy. However, it is important to remember that the problems documented here do not include a majority of adolescents. Although their numbers are growing, only a minority of youths find it difficult to make a healthy transition into adulthood.

We turn now to four major health issues facing young people: eating disorders, substance abuse, adolescent sexuality and pregnancy, and depression and suicide. These health problems were selected because schools can play an important role in prevention and intervention efforts. The Focus on Research box describes how a sense of school connection can help protect adolescents from harm.

Eating Disorders

As we have seen, there is considerable individual variation in young people's height and weight during childhood and adolescence. Although most youngsters are able to maintain a weight within the normal range for their height, some children and adolescents may

- In 1999, approximately 17 percent of adolescents have no health care coverage.

- In 1999, more than one-third of high school students reported smoking cigarettes in the last 30 days, and about one-half reported alcohol use. Almost half of high school students have tried marijuana.

- In 1999, 33 percent of female students and 45 percent of male students have had sexual intercourse by ninth grade.

- In 1997/1998, more than 900,000 adolescents became parents, and 493,600 babies were born to adolescents 13 to19 years of age.

- In 1999, 25 percent of female adolescents and 14 percent of male adolescents in grades 9 to 12 seriously considered or attempted suicide.

- In 1999, 6 percent of female and 29 percent of male high school students reported carrying a gun or other weapon in the last 30 days.

- During the period 1992 to 1997, an average of 3.4 million adolescents, ages 12 to 19 years, were reported to be victims of violent crime.

- In 1996/1997, about 19,000 adolescents died each year. The two leading causes of death were motor vehicle injuries and firearm injuries.

- In 1999, youth homicide rates for black males age 15 to 24 years are eight times the rate for white males.

FIGURE 2.12

Portrait of Adolescents Today

SOURCE: Adapted from Center for Disease Control, 2000.

develop eating disorders that have serious physical and psychological implications. In this section, we briefly consider the causes and consequences of three different types of eating disorders: obesity, anorexia, and bulimia nervosa.

Obesity

In the last 30 years, Americans have become increasingly preoccupied with their weight. At the same time, the percentage of young people who are overweight has more than doubled in the last 30 years (see Figure 2.13). Between 10 and 15 percent of young people aged 6 to17 years are overweight today (Centers for Disease Control, 2000). Not only is childhood obesity on the rise, but it is also occurring at a younger and younger age. The number of 4- and 5-year-olds who are overweight has almost doubled in the past 20 years, from 5.8 percent to 10 percent (Damon Institute, 1999). Obesity is the most common eating disorder among young people today.

Obesity is defined as a greater than 20 percent increase over average body weight for the child's age, sex, and body build (Behrman & Kliegman, 1990). Because childhood obesity has increased so rapidly in the last 30 years, we know the problem is not simply genetic: The gene pool has not changed rapidly during the course of this epidemic. A number of factors contribute to childhood obesity including heredity, unhealthy diet, lack of exercise and, in some cases, abnormal metabolism or family trauma. There is growing recognition that television watching is also associated with weight problems. While watching

Focus on Research

Protecting Adolescents from Harm

Numerous studies have documented the various conditions that can lead to health-compromising behaviors in adolescents. Some health risk behaviors (cigarette smoking, alcohol use, weapon-related violence, etc.) appear to be disproportionately high among adolescents of color, lower-income adolescents, and those living in single-parent homes. In addition, low grades, low self-esteem, having repeated a grade in school, and working 20 or more hours per week are all positively associated with risky behaviors in adolescents. Consistent with research on early maturity, being "out of sync" with peers can also place young people at risk. Both male and female adolescents who perceive themselves as looking *older* than their peers initiate sexual intercourse at a younger age, and they have a higher likelihood of using cigarettes, alcohol, and marijuana. They are also more likely to participate in violence and to experience emotional distress, including suicide ideation, than adolescents who view themselves as age-appropriate. Interestingly, these patterns were found for those adolescents who perceived themselves as looking older, not younger, than their agemates (Resnick et al., 1997).

Having identified important risk factors, researchers are now turning to the home, school, and individual characteristics that help protect young people from harm. Results from the *National Longitudinal Study of Adolescent Health* (Resnick et al., 1997) showed that one of the significant protective factors for adolescents is their sense of connection to parents, families, or other caring adults. Adolescents who feel loved and wanted by family members are less likely to engage in risky behaviors. The importance that adolescents place on prayer and religion is also a significant protective factor in their lives.

More importantly for educators, the adolescents' sense of school connectedness functions as an important protective factor in their lives. *School connectedness* was defined as the degree to which adolescents (a) feel their teachers treat students fairly; (b) feel close to people at school, and (c) feel part of their school. Other studies of adolescents also show that participation in school activities and academic achievement can reduce risky behaviors (Cairns & Cairns, 1994; Eccles & Barber, 1999; Mahoney, 2000; Steinberg, 1996). Using a national data set, one group of researchers found that after controlling for race and poverty status, tenth graders who reported spending *no* time in school-sponsored activities were 49 percent more likely to use drugs, 37 percent more likely to become teen parents, and 35 percent more likely to have smoked cigarettes compared to students who spend 1 to 4 hours weekly in extracurricular activities (Zill, Nord, & Loomis, 1995). However, involvement in school activities may not lower rates of binge drinking (Eccles & Barber, 1999).

Studies of risk and protective factors in adolescents' lives underscore the need for school environments that enhance young people's ability to cope with difficult and challenging circumstances in their lives. This capacity is known as **resiliency**. Schools that help adolescents develop their talents and a positive identity, that provide opportunities for meaningful participation, and that promote caring relationships among students and teachers are resiliency-building environments (Henderson & Milstein, 1996). It is important for schools to focus on adolescents' well-being and healthy development, rather than on problem behaviors.

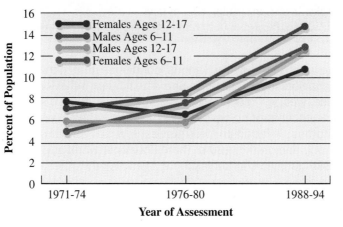

FIGURE 2.13

Percent of
Overweight Youths
in the United States,
by Age and Gender
SOURCE: U.S.
Department of Health and
Human Services (2000).

Overweight is defined as body mass index (BMI) at or above sex- or age-specific 95th percentile BMI cutoffs for children ages 6–11 and for adolescents ages 12–17.

television, children see a steady stream of junk food commercials, eat more snacks, and burn fewer calories (Gortmaker, Dietz, & Chueng, 1990). In fact, some evidence suggests that television viewing places children in a relaxed state, which lowers their metabolism below the normal level (Kleseges, 1993). Many of these same factors contribute to obesity in adulthood as well.

The rise in childhood obesity is also attributed to low physical activity. As we learned earlier, American children spend far less time in physical activity at school than children in other countries. A 1997 survey of adolescents indicated that more than 36 percent did not regularly participate in any rigorous physical activity. Approximately 51 percent were not enrolled in physical education classes, and daily participation in physical education classes had dropped from 42 percent in 1991 to 27 percent in 1997 (Centers for Disease Control, 2000).

Obesity, a greater
than 20 percent
increase over
average body
weight for a
child's age, sex,
and body build,
often leads to
low self-esteem,
depression, and
behavioral
problems.

Obesity has serious consequences for children and adolescents. It is associated with respiratory and orthopedic problems as well as diabetes. Childhood obesity can also result in increased blood pressure and high cholesterol, which are risk factors for cardiovascular disease in adults. Recent studies reveal that cardiovascular disease can be detected as early as age 8 (Harrell et al., 1996). Because of societal definitions of attractiveness, obese children and adolescents also experience teasing, ridicule, and rejection from peers. As a result, they can develop low self-esteem, depression, and behavioral problems (Strauss, Smith, & Forehand, 1985). Childhood obesity becomes a vicious cycle in which low self-esteem and social isolation contribute to overeating, keeping the young person overweight.

Without treatment, most obese children and adolescents will become obese adults. The metabolic changes that come with obesity make it more difficult to lose weight later (Centers for Disease Control, 2000). The most successful treatment programs are family-based interventions that focus on encouraging healthy eating habits and increasing physical activity for both parents and children. Interventions should begin early before unhealthy eating habits are established. Approximately 40 percent of obese 7-year-olds are likely to become obese adults, but 70 percent of overweight adolescents will continue to be overweight in adulthood (Kolata, 1986). Severe or crash dieting while a young body is still growing can be dangerous, and adults should discourage children's attempts in this regard.

Because young people spend so much time at school, schools also play an important role in improving students' eating habits and in promoting physical activity. Teachers can assist families in their weight-management efforts by encouraging healthy eating habits, eliminating junk food snacks, increasing children's physical activity, discouraging name calling and teasing, and reducing stereotypes of overweight people. Schools can also sponsor walking or biking groups for children and their families.

Anorexia and Bulimia Nervosa

At the other end of the continuum are youngsters who are seriously underweight. The eating disorder **anorexia nervosa** mainly affects adolescent girls between the ages of 14 and 18. Girls with this disorder lose between 25 percent and 50 percent of their body weight through excessive dieting and exercise. A large number of anorexic girls will also develop **bulimia nervosa,** an eating disorder in which one goes on an eating binge and then vomits or uses laxatives as a way of purging the body. Whereas anorexia nervosa is common among adolescent girls, bulimia tends to be common among older teens and young adults. It is estimated that anorexia affects from 0.5 to 1 percent of teenage and young women, and bulimia from 1 to 3 percent (U.S. Centers for Disease Control, 2000). Women are 8 to 10 times more likely to suffer from anorexia or bulimia than are men.

Anorexia nervosa and bulimia nervosa are common among adolescent girls and young adults.

As with obesity, anorexia and bulimia result from a complex interplay of many different factors including biological changes, familial relations, and the larger society (Manley, Rickson, & Standeven, 2000). As you know, physical attractiveness and self-esteem are strongly linked in childhood and adolescence, especially for girls. For many girls and women, it is extremely difficult to meet society's definition of physical attractiveness. Female models, often considered to have the ideal body type, are 9 percent taller and 16 percent thinner than the average woman (Wolf, 1991). Even the most well-adjusted female will have difficulty meeting this standard. Unfortunately, girls who are at most risk for eating problems are those who most often accept society's definition of the ideal female body. For example, white adolescent girls are more likely to be dissatisfied with their bodies than African American girls, who are less likely to define beauty in terms of the size of a woman's waistline. African American girls believe it is better to be a little overweight than underweight (Ingrassia, 1995; Becker, Yanek, Koffman, & Bronner, 1999). Another characteristic of anorexics is that they are typically perfectionists who are model students with high standards for their behavior and performance. Unlike anorexics, who tend to be highly controlled, bulimic young women are impulsive and perceive themselves as out of control. Bulimics are also at greater risk than anorexics for developing substance abuse problems.

Both anorexia and bulimia, if left untreated, have serious consequences. Each is a compulsive disorder that begins as a strategy to control weight but then takes on a life of its own. Anorexia can result in malnutrition, stunted growth, hair loss, disruption of the menstrual cycle, and extreme sensitivity to the cold. Nearly 20 percent of anorexic girls inadvertently starve themselves to death. Bulimia can result in malnutrition, dental problems, and electrolytic imbalances that can trigger heart attacks as well as cause life-threatening damage to the throat and stomach. Both disorders can be associated with low self-esteem and depression.

Treatment of anorexia and bulimia requires professional help. Teachers who are concerned about a student should consult with a health professional at their school (nurse, social worker, psychologist, or counselor) to obtain information about the referral process. The Focus on Teaching box includes some strategies teachers may use if they suspect one of their students has an eating disorder that has not yet been diagnosed.

Treatment of anorexia and bulimia may be lengthy and difficult for both the students and their families. Generally, treatment involves a combination of individual and family therapy. Girls with these disorders tend to have a distorted view of their body image. Anorexics believe they are too fat, even when they are visibly underweight, and they do not

Helping Students with Eating Disorders

If teachers suspect that a student may have an eating disorder, but he or she has not been diagnosed, they should consider the following strategies:

- Express concern to the student and a willingness to help, while still respecting his or her need for autonomy and privacy.

- Do not force the student to eat.

- Find out where to go for support, and encourage the student to seek help.

- Observe, describe, and document eating behaviors of concern across times and across settings.

- Consult with the school-based team regarding referral to other experienced professionals for a thorough assessment.

SOURCE: Manly, Rickson, & Standeven, 2000.

believe their eating habits are abnormal. Bulimics are generally aware of their abnormal eating patterns, but they lack the ability to control their impulses. Consequently, bulimia is generally easier to treat than anorexia through family and individual therapy. Anorexia generally requires hospitalization as the initial step. Medical treatment must be accompanied by family therapy focused on changing parent-child interactions and expectations.

Substance Abuse

It is commonly believed that drug problems among young people are at an epidemic level in the United States. Research on substance abuse among young people has focused on the use of alcohol, cigarettes, inhalants (glue and paint thinner), and illegal drugs such as marijuana, amphetamines, LSD, and cocaine. During the 1980s, substance abuse was the focus of considerable public attention. From 1975 to the early 1990s, there were significant declines in use of cigarettes, alcohol, stimulants, and marijuana. However, researchers believe that these patterns are beginning to reverse themselves. As Figure 2.14 shows, the use of illicit drugs (e.g., marijuana, hallucinogens, cocaine, heroin, etc.) increased among adolescents from the early to the mid 1990s. In 1998, it began to show a downturn (Johnston, O'Malley, & Bachman, 2000). **Substance abuse** is defined as frequent or excessive use of a drug. Rates of substance abuse depend on the substance. The three most commonly used substances are cigarettes, alcohol, and marijuana.

Cigarette smoking is one of the most preventable causes of death in the United States. Research evidence suggests that those individuals who initiate smoking in adolescence have a high likelihood of continuing to smoke into adulthood (U.S. Department of Health & Human Services, 1999). Additionally, youths who smoke are more likely to drink alcohol and use illicit drugs than their nonsmoking peers. Daily smoking among high school

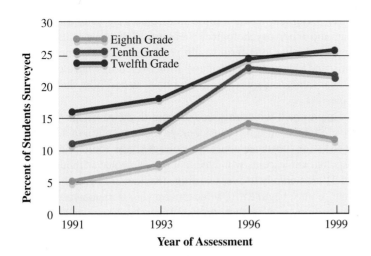

FIGURE 2.14

Percent of High School Students Reporting Use of Any Illicit Drug in Previous 30 Days

SOURCE: After Johnston, O'Malley, and Bachman (2000).

Use of any illicit drug includes marijuana, hallucinogens, cocaine, heroin, stimulants, tranquilizers (not under doctor's orders), and so on.

students has been increasing steadily through the 1990s, and smoking is most prevalent among white adolescents. Between 1992 and 1997, the percentage of high school seniors who reported smoking on a daily basis increased from 17 percent to 25 percent. Approximately 9 percent of eighth graders and 16 percent of tenth graders reported smoking on a daily basis. It is estimated that currently there are 4 million underaged smokers in the United States (Children's Defense Fund, 2000). This figure does not include young people who use smokeless tobacco. Almost 90 percent of adults who die from smoking-related illnesses started smoking as teens.

Daily cigarette smoking is on the rise among adolescents today, and it is most prevalent among white teens.

Along with cigarette smoking, there have been dramatic increases in young people's use of marijuana, and it is the most commonly used illicit drug. The number of high school seniors who have smoked marijuana has risen from 12 percent in 1992 to 23 percent in 1998. There has also been a rise in the use of marijuana among eighth- and tenth-grade students (U.S. Department of Health & Human Services, 1999). The use of other illegal drugs is less frequent. In 1999, 17 percent of high school seniors had tried amphetamines, 14 percent had tried hallucinogens (e.g., LSD), and 10 percent had tried cocaine (Johnston et al., 2000).

Alcohol use among adolescents is also of considerable concern. In 1999, 51 percent of high school seniors reported using alcohol at least once in the last week, and 31 percent reported engaging in **binge drinking** (drinking five or more alcoholic drinks in a row) during the past two weeks (Johnston et al., 2000). Additionally, this study indicated that one-half of the eighth-grade students surveyed had tried alcohol, and one-fourth had been drunk. An earlier study of youth risk behaviors indicated that 40 percent of adolescents in grades 9 through 12 reported within the last month they had either driven after drinking alcohol or had ridden with a driver who had been drinking alcohol (U.S. Department of Health & Human Services, 1999).

Drug and alcohol abuse in adolescence is associated with poor school achievement, as well as depression, chronic fatigue, and other psychological problems.

As mentioned, substance abuse is associated with many different problems, and the consequences become more severe with greater use. It is important to distinguish between occasional experimentation and frequent use. Most young people will experiment with alcohol, cigarettes, and perhaps other drugs. Drug use becomes problematic when it is frequent and excessive. Young people who abuse drugs or alcohol are more likely to experience problems in school. In fact, dramatic changes in school performance are often a symptom of substance abuse. Drug and alcohol abuse is associated with loss of sleep, chronic fatigue, depression, and other psychological problems. Substance abusers also place themselves at risk for developing long-term health problems, such as cancer, heart disease, respiratory problems, and kidney or liver damage. Moreover, drugs and alcohol are often implicated in fatal or near-fatal accidents (e.g., automobile crashes, falls, and drownings) involving young people.

Most young people first experiment with drugs and alcohol in their teenage years, so childhood and adolescence are important times to encourage the prevention of substance abuse. One of the greatest risks for substance abuse in adolescence or adulthood is early exposure. Research suggests that adolescents who have not experimented with alcohol or marijuana before the age of 21 are unlikely to ever use drugs (Kandel & Logan, 1984). Efforts to prevent substance abuse must begin early, while children are in elementary school, and most drug prevention programs are, in fact, provided in school settings (Dryfoos, 1990). Research suggests that the risk of substance abuse for a student who attends a school in which illegal drugs are kept, used, or sold is at twice the risk of a student in a drug-free school. According to a national survey, only 44 percent of teens say they attend a drug-free school, and 40 percent say the drug situation is getting worse in their schools (National Center on Addiction and Substance Abuse, 1999).

Efforts to prevent substance abuse need to start in late elementary school, and continue on an annual basis through the middle and high school years.

Most prevention programs have targeted the "gateway" drugs—alcohol, tobacco, and marijuana. Project Dare (Drug Awareness Resistance Education) is a popular school-based program that focuses on teaching students to resist peer pressure and that educates young people about the health dangers of substance use. It is also clear that efforts to keep schools free of drugs can reduce the rates of substance abuse among young people. However, there is growing recognition that a variety of strategies are needed. The most successful programs are ones that are not only implemented in the schools but also involve the adolescents' peers, parents, and community. Efforts to prevent substance abuse must also start early, perhaps in late elementary school, and continue on an annual basis through the middle and high school years.

Adolescent Sexuality and Pregnancy

As a consequence of popular culture and society's relaxed attitudes about sexuality, many researchers believe that young people are dealing with sexual issues at a younger age than ever before. A recent 1999 survey of students indicated that approximately 40 percent of ninth graders nationwide report having had sexual intercourse, and this figure rises with each grade. By the twelfth grade, 65 percent of teens report having had sexual intercourse. Males are more sexually active than females at each of the grade levels surveyed (U.S. Department of Health and Human Services, 2000). There are also ethnic differences in young people's sexual behavior, as shown in Figure 2.15. A higher percent of African American and Hispanic adolescents are sexually active than white adolescents. Additionally, 24 percent of African American adolescents report having had intercourse by age 13, compared with 9 percent of Latinos and 6 percent of whites (Centers for Disease Control, 1999). Research also indicates that 19 percent of students in grades 9 to 12 have already had sexual intercourse with four or more partners (Warren, Harris, & Kann, 1995). Without a doubt, sex is very much a part of the adolescent experience.

The consequences of adolescent sexuality are well known. Compared with adults, adolescents are at a higher risk for acquiring sexually transmitted diseases (STDs). The most common STDs are chlamydia, gonorrhea, and herpes simplex. Both chlamydia and gonorrhea can be treated with antibiotics, but left untreated these diseases can lead to serious health problems including infertility. There is no known cure for herpes simplex, and this disease results in sores, blisters, fever, headaches, and fatigue that can last for up to four days. This disease is also highly infectious. Overall, approximately two-thirds of all STDs occur in people under the age of 15 (Carroll & Wolpe, 1996). The risk of infection from human immunodeficiency virus (HIV), which leads to AIDS, is also substantial in adolescence, because teens are more likely to engage in risky behaviors associated with this disease, such as unprotected intercourse, multiple sex partners, and intravenous drugs.

To date, however, the problem that has received the most attention is adolescent pregnancy. Pregnancy rates have declined for women between the ages of 15 and 19 years by 15 percent since 1991, when teen pregnancy rates had reached their peak. However, more than 900,000 adolescents become pregnant each year. The United States now has the highest rate of teenage pregnancy in the industrialized world. In the mid 1990s, rates were twice as high as in England or Canada, and eight times as high as in Japan (Singh & Darroch, 2000). In the United States, teen pregnancy rates vary by ethnic background. In 1996, pregnancy rates were more than twice as high among non-Hispanic blacks and Hispanic teens as among non-Hispanic white teens (U.S. Department of Health and Human Services, 1999).

Along with pregnancy rates, teenage birth rates have been steadily declining and have fallen 18 percent since 1991. In 1997 and 1998, there were approximately a half million births to adolescents 13 to 19 years of age. This figure represented 13 percent of the births for each year (U.S. Department of Health and Human Services, 1999). Teenage parenthood has adverse effects on the life chances of young people and their babies. Teenage mothers are likely to drop out of high school, and almost half will never finish. Because only a small percentage of teenage mothers marry and stay married to the child's father, many women must rely on public assistance. Early childbearing is one of the strongest factors associated with poverty and welfare dependency.

Babies born to adolescent mothers are likely to be low-birth-weight babies due to poor nutrition or poor prenatal care. As discussed previously, these babies will experience many difficulties in early infancy. By the preschool and elementary years, learning and psychosocial problems are generally evident in the offspring of teenage mothers. In adolescence,

Sexually transmitted diseases and pregnancy are consequences of adolescent sexual practices.

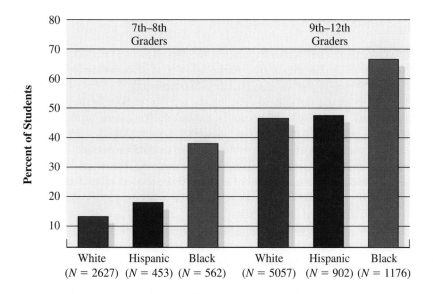

FIGURE 2.15

Percent of U.S. Adolescents Reporting Sexual Intercourse

SOURCE: Adapted from Blum et al. (2000).

children of teenage mothers have more achievement and discipline problems than children of older mothers do. Many of these problems are attributed to the low socioeconomic and educational levels of the teenage mothers. Unfortunately, poor academic achievement, discipline problems, and low socioeconomic status place the girls of teenage mothers at risk for an early pregnancy, and the cycle repeats itself.

The leading causes of adolescent pregnancies are lack of sex education and lack of reliable contraceptives.

Experts agree that the leading causes of adolescent pregnancies are lack of sex education and lack of access to reliable contraceptives. School-based efforts to prevent adolescent pregnancies have been disappointing at best. If taught at the secondary level, these programs are too late. Moreover, most sex education programs focus on the biological aspects of sex and ignore the emotional and ethical issues involved. A national survey revealed that 86 percent of the public school districts that have a policy to teach sex education require educators to teach abstinence as the preferred or only option outside of marriage (Alan Guttmacher Institute, 1999). Such programs provide little protection for those adolescents already engaged in sexual activity. Additionally, most school-based sex education programs totally ignore the needs of homosexual youths, who have one of the highest rates of suicide among adolescents.

There are a number of ways schools can improve their sex education programs. First, it is important to recognize that most teenage pregnancies are unintended and unwanted. Second, efforts to increase young people's knowledge about sex, contraceptives, pregnancy, and sexually transmitted diseases must begin early. Some parents and policy makers are reluctant to provide this information because they fear it will encourage sexual promiscuity. In fact, research shows that increasing a young person's knowledge about sexual matters can lead to fewer unwanted pregnancies. Furthermore, sex education programs should be designed to teach decision-making skills and interpersonal assertiveness (e.g., how to say "no" under peer pressure). The most successful adolescent pregnancy prevention programs combine education about sexuality with school-based health clinics, where students can obtain contraceptives and learn to use them effectively (Children's Defense Fund, 1996). This last recommendation is perhaps the most controversial of all, but the one with the greatest impact.

Depression and Suicide

Depression is an affective disorder characterized by such disturbances as inability to concentrate, feelings of helplessness, sleep problems, inactivity or overactivity, lack of motivation, and inability to have fun.

Although many children and adolescents experience feelings of sadness and loneliness, a small number suffer from chronic depression. **Depression** is an affective disorder that is characterized by disturbances in cognitive and behavioral functioning. Common symptoms of childhood depression are the inability to concentrate, feelings of hopelessness, weight changes, sleep problems, inactivity or overactivity, slowed thinking, lack of motivation, low energy and fatigue, inability to have fun, and thoughts of death (American Psychiatric Association, 1994). Depression is often difficult to diagnose in children because sleep disturbances and appetite changes are relatively frequent for this group. However, most clinicians and researchers believe that some form of childhood depression exists, even if it is difficult to diagnose. If any of the symptoms discussed here persist longer than 2 or 3 weeks, the child should be referred for professional help.

Some researchers have also argued that depressive disorders are not possible until adolescence, when children are cognitively able to reflect on their inner thoughts and feelings. Consistent with this view, depression is twice as frequent in adolescence as in childhood (Compas, Ey, & Grant, 1993). Approximately 20 percent to 25 percent of adolescents report mild feelings of depression, and 4 percent are severely depressed (National Institutes of Mental Health, 2000). By adolescence, depression is more common among girls than boys. Researchers believe that the higher rates of depression in girls is mostly due to gender-role expectations. Interestingly, girls with a highly feminine gender-role identity are more likely to experience depression than are those with a masculine or androgynous gender role identity (Petersen, Compas, Brooks-Gunn, Stemmler, Ey, & Grant, 1993). Another explanation for the gender difference in depression is that girls are more likely than boys to experience multiple transitions (changes in body, family, school, etc.) early in adolescence, when they have less-effective coping strategies. In *Reviving Ophelia*, Mary Pipher (1994), a clinical psychologist who works with teenage girls, writes, "Girls are under more stress in the 1990s; they have less varied and effective coping skills to deal with that stress, and they have fewer internal and external resources on which to rely" (p. 158). She observes that young women often deal with this pain by harming themselves through self-mutilation (e.g., burning, cutting, or piercing themselves), which has been on the rise in recent years.

Approximately 20 percent to 25 percent of adolescents report mild feelings of depression; 5 percent are severely depressed.

Like other health concerns discussed in this section, depression has serious consequences. It is associated with poor school achievement, substance abuse, juvenile delinquency, anxiety and eating disorders, and suicidal ideation. Without treatment, depressed children and adolescents have a high likelihood of becoming depressed adults.

In extreme cases, depression can lead to suicide. It is estimated that six children and youths a day commit suicide (Children's Defense Fund, 2000). In 1999, 25 percent of female adolescents and 14 percent of male adolescents in grades 9 to 12 had seriously considered attempting suicide, according to the Youth Risk Surveillance Study by the Centers for Disease Control and Prevention (Centers for Disease Control, 1999). Suicide is close behind homicide as the second leading cause of death among young people. Rates of adolescent suicide are higher among Native Americans than other ethnic groups. Also, homosexual youths are at greater risk than heterosexual youths for suicide (Remafedi, 1999). Whereas girls make more suicide attempts than boys, more boys die in suicide attempts, because they use more effective methods for taking their lives (e.g., hanging or gunshot).

What can cause a young person to take his or her life? Several factors increase the risk of suicide in young people. As mentioned previously, depression and substance abuse are associated with an increased risk. Other risk factors are family stress, parental rejection, and family disruption. A family history that includes psychiatric or depressive disorders is also a risk factor. Sadly, access to a firearm is associated with an increased risk. Some researchers believe that increases in adolescent suicide rates can be partly attributed to the increased availability of firearms in the last 20 years. Additionally, adolescents who have attempted suicide once are at risk for attempting it again (Garland & Zigler, 1993).

Contrary to popular belief, suicide is rarely an impulsive reaction to a distressing event, such as a divorce or a romantic breakup. Young people who take their lives generally first make appeals for support from friends, family, and teachers. There are also several early signs that should not be ignored. Suicidal teens may give away their prized possessions, say good-bye to friends, show disregard for their personal safety, and become preoccupied with death. Some reports suggest that adolescents may be absent from school for long periods of time before they commit suicide (Hawton, 1986; cited in Garland & Zigler, 1993). Several risk factors associated with adolescent suicide are summarized in Figure 2.16. Most schools now provide group counseling when a student in a school has committed suicide. Through group discussions, school officials hope to reduce the risk of cluster suicides, which involve an unusually high number of suicides within a particular geographic location or time period. There is a higher risk of cluster suicides among young people.

Schools can play a role in preventing adolescent suicide through programs that promote social competence, problem-solving skills, stress management, and mental health education.

A teacher may be one of a few people in a child's life who can recognize or respond to these appeals for help. If you suspect a young person is contemplating suicide, you should take the person seriously. Ask direct questions (Are you planning to hurt yourself? How will you do it?) in a calm manner. Encourage the young person to talk about his or her feel-

- Sudden decline in school attendance and achievement, especially in above-average students

- History of substance abuse, conduct problems, or affective disorders

- Poor coping skills and deficits in interpersonal skills

- Family turmoil and instability

- History of sexual abuse

- A humiliating or shameful event, such as an arrest, breakup of romantic relationship, or school or work failure

- Access to firearms

- Exposure to suicidal behavior

- Feelings of hopelessness and preoccupation with death

FIGURE 2.16

Risk Factors of Adolescent Suicide

SOURCE: After Garland & Zigler (1993).

ings and listen carefully. You should then contact a health professional in your school (school nurse, guidance counselor, or social worker) who can provide further assistance. Most communities also have crisis hot lines that can provide professional help. It is important that you assist the young person in getting professional help. Thoughts or attempts of suicide may be a trial run for the real thing.

Although our discussion of depression and suicide has focused on individual treatment, researchers believe that schools can play a much larger role in preventing these problems. Programs that promote social competence, problem-solving skill training, coping strategies for stress, and basic mental health education may provide the best prevention of all. According to Ann Garland and Edward Zigler (1993), "These types of programs are truly primary prevention and would address many of the current social problems" (p. 177).

Chapter Summary

www.mhhe.com/meece

Prenatal Development

- Developmental processes begin at the moment of human conception. The period from conception to birth is called prenatal development. This period of development is mainly directed by genetic influences and follows a universal pattern.

- Genes and chromosomes are the basic building blocks of human life. Each cell contains 23 pairs of chromosomes, which are composed of DNA structures containing thousands of genes. Most human traits are caused by dominant genes, but some characteristics are also caused by recessive genes. Many human characteristics are polygenetic, meaning they result from the combination of more than one gene.

- The twenty-third chromosome determines the sex of the child. Females have two X chromosomes, whereas males have one X and one Y chromosome. Traits carried on the sex chromosome are called sex-linked characteristics. Males have a higher likelihood of baldness, blindness, and hemophilia, because these traits are carried on the female X chromosome, and there is no corresponding dominant gene on the Y chromosome.

- Every person is a carrier of at least 20 genes that can produce genetic disorders and diseases. Most genetic disorders are caused by recessive genes. Common genetic disorders include hemophilia, sickle-cell anemia, PKU, muscular dystrophy, congenital diabetes, and cystic fibrosis. Some genetic disorders are caused by abnormal chromosomes. Down syndrome and fragile-X syndrome are two conditions caused by an extra or a damaged chromosome. Both conditions affect the mental and physical development of the child.

- The genes a person inherits from both parents determine the person's genotype for a particular trait. The expression of these traits is called a phenotype. The person's genotype and phenotype can differ when the genotype includes a dominant and recessive gene. The environment can also affect the expression of a particular genotype. If the environment does not facilitate the expression of a particular trait (e.g., high intelligence) then the genotype and phenotype will differ. The concept of reaction range defines the degree to which the environment can affect the expression of genes.

- Prenatal development is divided into three major stages. During the germinal period (first 2 weeks after conception), the fertilized egg travels down the fallopian tube and attaches itself to the uterine wall. In the embryonic period (weeks 2 to 8), all the basic structures of the child-to-be are formed. This prenatal stage is particularly vulnerable to environmental agents because of the rapid development of new organs and systems. During the fetal period (8 weeks to birth), the fetus increases in size and weight. Most babies are born between 38 and 42 weeks.

- Although prenatal development is mainly guided by genetic influences, exposure to dangerous environmental agents or conditions can disrupt this process. Alcohol, nicotine, drugs, radiation, and environmental pollutants can have a negative effect on prenatal development and must be avoided during pregnancy. The fetus is most vulnerable to environmental influences in the early stages of pregnancy when body structures and major organs are developing.

- A premature birth or low birth weight are risk factors in a child's development. Premature births and low birth weights are caused by poor nutrition, poor prenatal care, and environmental agents such as nicotine, alcohol, and drugs. In elementary school, children with a low birth weight are more likely than children of normal birth weight to have mild learning disabilities, attention problems, poor concentration, language delays, and asthma.

Brain Development

- The human brain is not fully mature until early adulthood. Brain development after birth involves increases in the number and length of neural fibers that connect nerve cells, and deposits of a fatty substance (myelin) on neural fibers which enables impulses to travel faster through the brain. Areas of the brain are programmed to receive certain environmental stimulation. Neurons that receive this

113

stimulation form connections, whereas those that do not receive the appropriate stimulation fade and die off.

- The human brain is most open to change in early development. It loses some of its plasticity once the two hemispheres of the brain begin to specialize. This specialization is known as lateralization. The left hemisphere of the brain controls language processes, whereas the right hemisphere processes visual and spatial information. Researchers have not found a link between hemispheric specialization and learning disabilities or cognitive styles.

- The infant brain quickly develops the perceptual abilities it needs to process and interpret information from the five senses. Babies achieve adult levels of vision by 12 months and prefer visual stimulation that is complex and novel, which stimulates their cognitive development. Auditory perception is quite developed at birth, and newborns are quite adept at discriminating different human sounds. Babies also show preferences for certain smells and tastes, and they respond to touch and pain.

Motor Development

- Motor development involves children's increasing ability to move and to control their body movements. A newborn's movements are mainly due to innate reflexes, such as sucking, choking, and grasping. Gross motor skills that involve the movement of head, body, legs, and arms develop first. Most infants begin to walk between 8 and 10 months. By the time they enter school, children can ride bikes, skip, catch a ball with two hands, and play kickball. Fine motor skills develop in the preschool years. By age 5 or 6, children can copy simple geometric shapes, button their shirts, tie their shoes, and print numbers and letters. Manipulative skills are not fully developed until around the age of 10 or 12. Gender differences in gross and fine motor skills are evident in childhood due to differences in socialization experiences.

- Play is the medium by which children develop their motor skills. Preschool and young elementary schoolchildren need daily activities that exercise their large muscles and help develop their fine motor skills. Older elementary children are able to sit for longer periods of time, but they also need frequent periods of activity. As motor skills are developing, children's play activities need careful supervision. Accidents are the number-one cause of childhood deaths.

Physical Growth

- Infancy is characterized by a rapid period of growth. In the elementary school years, physical growth slows down, although children continue to gradually add weight and height to their bodies. In general, African American children tend to be taller than children of European, Asian, or Hispanic descent. There are few gender differences in physical size until adolescence.

- Children's physical size and attractiveness can influence how they are perceived by others. Children who are small for their age tend to be judged as less mature and competent than children of average height. Children and adults attribute more positive attributes and characteristics to physically attractive than unattractive children. Children who are physically attractive also have more positive peer relations.

- Puberty begins between the ages of 10 and 12 for girls and 12 and 14 years for boys. Within each sex, there is considerable individual variability in the timing of puberty, but the sequence of change is universal. The changes that occur in puberty primarily prepare the body for sexual reproduction, but the development of secondary characteristics is only one of many changes that are taking place. There are changes in the skeleton, muscles, and vital organs.

- Puberty can pose adjustment problems for adolescents. It often leads to changes in the adolescent's self-image, self-confidence, social relations, moods, and so on. Parts of the body mature at different rates, which can make adolescents feel clumsy and awkward. Adolescents are moody, but there is little evidence to suggest that their mood swings are caused by "raging hormones." The moods of adolescents fluctuate as they change social settings. There is more conflict between children and adults at puberty, but the conflict dissipates as the different parties renegotiate roles, rules, and expectations. Adolescents are more likely to rebel when parents are too controlling and unable to adjust their expectations.

- Early and late maturity have different effects for girls than for boys. Early maturity in girls can lead to low self-esteem, depression, anxiety, and eating disorders. If early-maturing girls seek out the company of older peers, it can also lead to risk behaviors such as drinking, early sexual activity, and delinquency. Early-maturing boys tend to have the advantage in terms of their self-esteem, popularity, and leadership skills. However, if they associate with older peers, they may also be at risk for engaging in deviant or antisocial behavior. In general, recent studies suggest that late-maturing boys and girls experience fewer adjustment problems in the long run than do early maturers.

Special Health Concerns

- Young people, especially adolescents, face more health risks than ever before. In the last 20 years, the health of young people has declined by 50 percent, due to poverty. Most young people are able to make a healthy transition to adulthood, but the numbers of young people who are at risk for serious health problems are increasing.

- Obesity is the most common eating disorder. It is estimated that 11 percent of youths are overweight. A number of factors contribute to childhood obesity, including heredity, an unhealthy diet, lack of physical activity, and television viewing. Obese children experience peer rejection, low self-esteem, and other behavioral problems. They also have a high likelihood of becoming obese adolescents and adults. Schools can help obese children by encouraging healthy eating habits, eliminating junk food, increasing physical activity, and reducing stereotypes of overweight people.

- Anorexia and bulimia nervosa affects 3 percent of adolescent and young women. The girls who are most at risk for these eating disorders are those who have accepted society's definition of feminine attractiveness. Both anorexia and bulimia are associated with low self-esteem and depression and can be life-threatening if left untreated. Medical treatment is generally accompanied by family therapy focused on changing parent-child interactions and expectations.

- The four most frequently abused substances among young people today are tobacco, alcohol, marijuana, and inhalants. Young people who abuse alcohol and drugs experience problems in school as well as psychological and health problems. Childhood and adolescence is an important time for the prevention of substance abuse. The most successful prevention programs educate young people about the risk of drug use but also promote interpersonal skills and self-esteem.

- Sex is very much a part of the adolescent experience. Adolescents begin to experiment with their sexuality earlier than ever before. By age 16, one-third or more of young people have already had sexual intercourse. By age 20, 1 out of 4 young people will have contracted a sexually transmitted disease, and 1 out of 3 teenage girls will have become pregnant. The leading causes of these problems are lack of sex education and lack of access to contraceptives. Sex education through the schools has had little effect. Most schools do not teach sex education until it is too late, and most programs do not provide information or access to contraceptives. Furthermore, few programs teach young people the decision-making or inter-personal skills they need to assert themselves in sexual matters.

- A small number of children and adolescents suffer from chronic depression. The symptoms are inability to concentrate, changes in weight, sleep problems, lack of motivation and energy, feelings of hopelessness, and thoughts of death. Depression is more prevalent in adolescents than children, due to the adolescent's ability to be self-reflective and self-critical. Depression is also more common in girls than in boys during adolescence. In extreme cases, depression can increase a young person's risk of suicide, which is now the second leading cause of death among young people. Researchers believe that schools must play a larger role in preventing these problems. Prevention efforts should focus on improving social skills, teaching stress management strategies, and promoting basic mental health.

Key Terms

anorexia nervosa (105)	dizygotic twins (62)	low-birth weight (71)	polygenetic traits (61)
brain lateralization (81)	Down syndrome (64)	menarche (96)	proximal-distal pattern (93)
bulimia nervosa (105)	fine motor skills (87)	mitosis (67)	puberty (94)
cephalocaudal pattern (93)	fragile-X syndrome (64)	monozygotic twins (62)	reaction range (66)
chromosomes (61)	genotype (65)	myelination (76)	resiliency (103)
depression (110)	gross motor skills (86)	neurons (74)	secular trend (93)
	habituation (83)	obesity (102)	teratogen (69)
		phenotype (65)	

Activities

1. Observe three different age groups (e.g., kindergarten, third-grade, and fifth-grade) playing outside at a local school. Use the following checklist to record the various motor skills exhibited by each age group. After collecting your observations, describe the age differences you observed. Give specific examples of behaviors you observed to support your assessment of each age group. Were most of the students "on time" in their motor development, according to the information in Focus on Development on page 88? Were some students more or less advanced for their age group? Did you observe any gender differences in students' motor skills? How would you account for these gender differences?

Motor Skill Checklist

Age _____

Skill _____

a. Runs well

_____

b. Climbs well

_____

c. Shows good balance

_____

d. Hops on one foot

_____

e. Skips well

_____

f. Gallops

_____

g. Climbs alternating feet

_____

h. Kicks ball well

_____

i. Throws ball well

_____

j. Catches ball well

_____

2. Design an outside play area for elementary schoolchildren to promote the development of gross motor skills. Your design should include play equipment for younger as well as older children. In designing your play area, be sure to consider safety and supervision concerns.

3. As you know, society's definitions of physical attractiveness affect the way variations in children's physical size are perceived. For this activity, choose a particular age group and observe the social interactions of students who are either tall or short for their age. Observe how these children are treated by others as well as what personality characteristics they exhibit (e.g., leadership abilities, shyness, impulsiveness, etc.). After collecting your observations, analyze the patterns you observed. Were tall and/or short students treated differently? What personality characteristics did they exhibit? Were there gender differences in the patterns you observed? How do your observations help you understand the ways cultural stereotypes of physical attractiveness may shape the way people evaluate and relate to children?

4. Interview three girls and three boys who are between 13 and 16 years old. Ask them to respond to the following questions:

   a. What do you think is your best feature?

   b. What do others tell you is your best feature?

   c. What do you think is your worst feature?

   d. What would you like to change about yourself?

   Following the interviews, analyze the students' responses for themes about their body image. Do girls or boys have a more positive body image? Do girls' responses show a preoccupation with weight? What concerns do the boys express about their body image? How do your results compare with the research on the psychological impact of puberty?

Chapter 3

Cognitive Development: Piaget's and Vygotsky's Theories

Teacher: Can someone tell me whether the water today boiled more or less quickly than before?

Student: More quickly.

Teacher: Why? Who has some ideas?

Student: Particles are more separated.

Teacher: Okay; let's think about density. Is tap water more or less dense than boiled water? What happens to water when it boils?

Student: There are bubbles.

Student: It evaporates.

Teacher: Is the water turning into gas?

Student: Yes.

Teacher: Would that make the water more or less dense?

Student: Less dense.

Teacher: Okay; think about two pots of beans. If you have one pot with just a little bit of beans and a pot with a lot of beans, which pot would take longer to boil?

Student: The pot with a lot of beans.

Teacher: Why?

Student: It's more dense.

Teacher: Okay; let's talk about temperature. At what temperature did the tap water boil? What about the already boiled

Chapter opener photo: Photo Disc.

> *water? What did you see? Maybe we first need to come to some consensus about boiling. Who can give me a definition?*

Student: *When the water starts to bubble.*

Student: *When there is steam.*

Teacher: *Okay; if we get steam, what is the boiling water doing? Is it changing states?*

Student: *It's changing into gas.*

Teacher: *Okay; now did the boiling occur at a higher or lower temperature with the already boiled water?*

Student: *Higher.*

Teacher: *Who can tell me why?*

Student: *It's less dense.*

Teacher: *Why?*

Student: *It's got less stuff in it.*

Teacher: *Okay; can anyone give us a general rule about the relationship between density and boiling?*

Student: *The less dense the solution, the longer it takes to boil.*

Teacher: *Good. Now let's think about some other solutions. What about salt water?*

Student: *It's more dense.*

Teacher: *What about alcohol?*

Student: *It's less dense.*

Teacher: *Which would take longer to boil—alcohol or salt water?*

Student: *Alcohol, because it's less dense.*

Teacher: *Good. We'll talk about the experiment some more tomorrow. It's time to change classes.*

This conversation is from a sixth-grade science class. The students have just completed an experiment in which they observed and recorded the temperature of and the time it took to boil a solution of previously boiled water. The teacher expected the students to compare these data with the information they collected from a similar experiment with tap water. At the end of an activity, the teacher and students discuss the results together.

Do you think the students demonstrate a good understanding of the experiment at the beginning of discussion? Not really. Although the students make some very good observations about the experiment, few are able to give a scientific explanation for what they observed. The teacher and students *construct* this understanding jointly. The teacher does not give the students the answers but helps the students think through the experiment by posing questions, linking new information to familiar experiences, giving feedback, and so forth. We will learn that this teacher is providing a *scaffold* to guide the students' thinking. By the end of the discussion, the teacher and students have come to a shared understanding of the experiment, and the students are able to apply this learning to new problems (e.g., What about alcohol and salt water?).

This science teacher is using what is known as a **constructivist approach.** The simple proposition underlying this approach is that children must construct their own understandings of the world in which they live. Knowledge is not something teachers can directly transmit to learners. The information must be mentally acted on, manipulated, and transformed in order to have meaning for the learner. However, as the example illustrates, the teacher helps guide this knowledge construction process through focusing attention, posing questions, and stretching children's thinking. The teacher's role is to help students rethink their ideas by asking questions they would not generally think about on their own. According to a constructivist point of view, learning involves structural changes in the way children think about their world.

Constructivism is the basis for many current reforms in education. Both the National Council for Teachers of Mathematics and the National Science Teachers Association have called for classrooms where problem-solving, "hands-on" experimentation, concept development, logical reasoning, and authentic learning are emphasized. Similarly, advocates of whole language approaches to reading and language arts also stress the importance of authentic learning in which students are immersed in a language-rich environment in meaningful and productive ways.

In this chapter, we examine the developmental theories that provide the developmental foundations for a constructivist approach to learning. Constructivism is theoretically grounded in the developmental research of Piaget and Vygotsky. Piaget's theory can help teachers understand how children reason or think about their world at different ages. Vygotsky's theory can help teachers understand the social processes that influence the development of children's intellectual abilities. Both theories have important implications for teaching.

> *Following the constructivist view of learning, children build their own knowledge of the world from interactions with their environment, and teachers help guide this knowledge construction process by focusing attention, posing questions, and stretching children's thinking.*

Piaget's Theory of Cognitive Development

Jean Piaget had a major impact on the way we think about children's development. Before Piaget's theory was introduced, children were generally thought of as passive organisms who were shaped and molded by their environment. Piaget taught us that children act as "little scientists," trying to make sense of their world. They have their own logic and ways of knowing, which follow predictable patterns of development as children biologically mature and interact with the world. By forming mental representations of their world, children are able to act on and influence their environment as much as their environment influences them.

Piaget was born in Switzerland in 1896. As a child, he was extremely bright and inquisitive. By the age of 10, he published his first scientific paper; he received his first job as a curator of the mollusk collection at the Geneva museum by the age of 15. He received his Ph.D. in natural sciences 6 years later. Piaget continued to develop his scholarship in many areas, including sociology, religion, and philosophy. While studying philosophy, he became intrigued with epistemology, or how knowledge is obtained. This question led him to study philosophy and psychology at the Sorbonne, where he met Theodore Simon, who, at the time, was developing the first intelligence test for children. Simon persuaded Piaget to assist him in collecting age norms for his test items. It was through this work that Piaget began to explore children's reasoning processes. He became intrigued with the fact that individual children often had very different reasons for the answers they chose. For example, two children might say a tree is alive but explain their answers differently. One child

> *Piaget taught us that children actively seek knowledge through their interactions with the environment and that they have their own logic and ways of knowing that evolve over time.*

may say it is alive because it moves, while another may say it's alive because it makes seeds. Through a set of procedures, which became known as the *clinical interview method* (see Chapter 1, pp. 48–49), Piaget explored the reasoning processes underlying children's correct and incorrect answers. His fascination with children's knowledge acquisition processes helped sustain a 60-year career in child development research. By the end of his career, Piaget had published more than 40 books and 200 articles on child psychology.

Piaget was an early constructivist theorist in psychology. He believed that children actively construct their own knowledge of the environment using what they already know to interpret new events and objects. Piaget's research focused primarily on how children acquire knowledge as they develop. That is, he was not so interested in *what* children know as he was in *how* they thought about problems and solutions. He believed cognitive development involved changes in a child's ability to reason about his or her world.

Key Concepts in Piaget's Theory

Cognitive Stages

Piaget divided cognitive development into four major stages, each stage representing a transformation into a more complex and abstract way of knowing.

Piaget was a stage theorist who divided cognitive development into four major stages: sensorimotor, preoperations, concrete operations, and formal operations. At each stage of development, children's thinking is assumed to be *qualitatively* different from their thinking at other stages. According to Piaget, cognitive development involved not simply quantitative changes in facts and skills but rather major transformations in the way children organize knowledge. Once children have entered a new cognitive stage they do not revert to an earlier form of reasoning or functioning.

Piaget proposed that cognitive development occurs in an invariant sequence. That is, all children proceed through the four stages of cognitive development in the same sequence. It is not possible to skip or miss a stage. Piaget's stages are generally related to specific age ranges, but there is a great deal of individual and cultural variation in the amount of time children may spend in a particular stage. We will examine the cognitive characteristics of each stage in a later section.

Development as Changes in Knowledge Structures

Schemes are sets of physical actions, mental operations, concepts, or theories people use to acquire information about their world.

Piaget believed that everyone, even infants, begin to organize their knowledge of the world into what he called *schemata* or *schemes*. **Schemes** are sets of physical actions, mental operations, concepts, or theories people use to organize and to acquire information about their world. Young children primarily know their world through physical actions they can perform, whereas older children and adults can perform mental operations and use symbol systems (e.g., language) to acquire knowledge about their world. As children progress through Piaget's stages, they become increasingly able to use complex and abstract schemes for organizing knowledge. Cognitive development involves not just the construction of new schemes, but the reorganization and differentiation of existing schemes.

Piaget distinguished between three types of knowledge. **Physical knowledge** is knowing the attributes of objects such as their number, color, size, and shape. Other examples of physical knowledge may include the observations that some objects roll and other do not, that some objects float and others do not, or that length of string can effect how fast objects on a pendulum move back and forth. Physical knowledge is acquired by acting on objects, experimenting, and observing reactions.

Logico-mathematical knowledge involves the mental construction of relationships. For example, logico-mathematical knowledge involves the understanding that a certain number of objects (which can be observed and counted) also represent a more abstract concept such as number. The number "eight" is an abstract concept that cannot be derived from experience. Also, groups of 10 objects can make up larger numbers such as 50 or 100. Logico-mathematical knowledge is also evident in the understanding that a mathematical problem such as 4 + 4 can also be represented by 2 + 2 + 2 + 2. Whereas physical knowledge is derived from observing and experimenting, logico-mathematical knowledge involves mental constructions or a **reflective abstraction.** Figure 3.1 shows children's representation of the number "eight" in Piaget's theory. In this example, the eight apples, tallies, and circles are concrete and observable (physical knowledge), but the number "eight" is a form of logico-mathematical knowledge because it is a construction that needs to constructed by the child from social knowledge. Unlike tallies and pictures that children can use to express their understanding of eight, the spoken word or sign for eight is taught (Kamii, 2000).

In this way, Piaget's theory also recognized the importance of **social knowledge** that is derived in part through interactions with others. Examples of this form of knowledge are mathematical words and signs (e.g., "+" for addition), languages, musical notations, as well as social and moral conventions, such as turn taking in conversations, ways of initiating interactions, how to play a game, or how to respond to another person in distress.

Physical knowledge is derived from observing and experimenting, but logico-mathematical knowledge involves mental constructions or abstractions.

Principles of Development

Organization and Adaptation   In Piaget's theory two basic principles guide children's intellectual development. The first of these principles is **organization,** which Piaget believed is an innate predisposition in all species. As children mature, they integrate simple physical patterns or mental schemes into more complex systems. The second guiding principle is **adaptation.** According to Piaget, all organisms are born with the ability to adapt their mental structures or behavior to fit environmental demands.

Assimilation and Accommodation   Piaget used the terms *assimilation* and *accommodation* to describe how children adapt to their environment. Through the process of **assimilation**

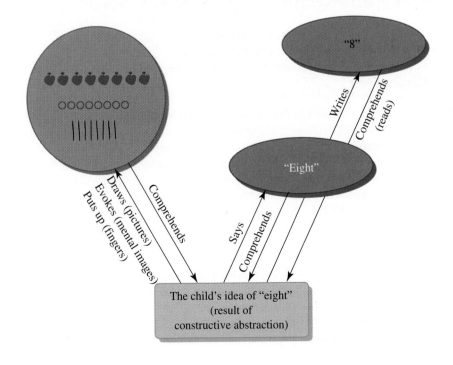

FIGURE 3.1

A Child's Representation of "Eight" in Piaget's Theory
SOURCE: After Kamii (2000)

children mold new information to fit their existing schemes. For example, a young child who has never seen a donkey may refer to it as a pony with long ears. Assimilation is not a passive process; it often involves actively modifying or transforming new information to make it fit prior knowledge. When this new information is consistent with what the child already knows, a state of equilibrium or balance is achieved. All the pieces of information fit together. When new information does not fit into an existing scheme, the child may alter his or her old way of thinking or acting to fit the new information. The process of changing existing schemata is called **accommodation.** In the example given here, the child may form a new scheme when he or she learns that the animal was not a pony but a donkey. Accommodation is most likely to occur when the information is only slightly discrepant with the child's existing schemes. If the information is too discrepant, accommodation may not be possible, because the child does not have any mental structures for interpreting this information. According to Piaget, the processes of assimilation and accommodation are closely intertwined and explain changes in cognition throughout the life span.

Can you think of an example of assimilation and accommodation from your own learning experiences? As you are reading this material, you should be using what you already know about children's development to make sense of the new information. However, you may need to adjust some of your ideas as you acquire new information. For example, you may have learned elsewhere that infants are incapable of symbolic thought. As you will see, Piaget's theory teaches us that a form of symbolic thought begins to emerge during the second year. Therefore, in order to develop a more sophisticated understanding of infancy, you would need to change your existing knowledge of infant development to incorporate (accommodate) this new information.

Development Processes

If cognitive development represents changes in children's cognitive structures or schemata, what causes those developmental changes? As an interactional theorist, Piaget viewed development as a complex interaction of innate and environmental factors. According to Piaget, the following four factors contribute to children's cognitive development:

- Maturation of inherited physical structures
- Physical experiences with the environment
- Social transmission of information and knowledge
- Equilibration

Equilibration is a unique concept in Piaget's theory that refers to our innate tendency to keep our cognitive structures in balance. Piaget maintained that states of disequilibrium or imbalance are so intrinsically dissatisfying that people are compelled to alter their cognitive structures in order to restore balance. Equilibration is thus a form of self-regulation in Piaget's theory. By altering and adjusting our cognitive structures we maintain organization and stability in our environment. We also reach a higher level of cognitive functioning as a result of this equilibration process.

Stages of Cognitive Development

Piaget proposed that cognitive development followed an invariant sequence from infancy through adolescence. The four stages of development are: (1) sensorimotor stage (birth to 2 years); preoperational stage (2 to 7 years); (3) concrete operational stage (7 to 11 years); and (4) formal operational stage (11 years through adulthood). The Focus on Development summarizes characteristics of each stage. As we will discuss later, child development

Assimilation is the process of actively molding new information to fit existing schemes; accommodation is the process of changing existing schemes to fit new, discrepant information.

Equilibration is the innate tendency to keep one's cognitive structures in balance using the processes of assimilation and accommodation.

Focus on Development

Stages in Piaget's Theory of Cognitive Development

Stage	Age	Characteristics
Sensorimotor		
The Active Child	Birth to 2 Years	Infants develop goal-directed behavior, means-ends thinking, and object permanence.
Preoperations		
The Intuitive Child	2 to 7 Years	Children can use symbols and words to think. Intuitive problem solving, but thinking limited by rigidity, centration, and egocentrism.
Concrete Operations		
The Practical Child	7 to 11 Years	Children develop logical operations for seriation, classification, and conservation. Thinking tied to real events and objects.
Formal Operations		
The Reflective Child	11 to 12 Years and Onward	Children develop abstract systems of thought that allow them to use propositional logic, scientific reasoning, and proportional reasoning.

researchers today question several aspects of Piaget's theory. For instance, questions have been raised about the ages associated with each stage. We will learn that children may be able to perform some cognitive operations earlier or later than Piaget originally proposed. Theorists have also raised questions about the stagelike nature of children's thinking. When children are making a transition into a new stage, they often exhibit characteristics of the new and old stage at the same time. We will first discuss the four stages, then consider the limitations of Piaget's theory.

Sensorimotor Stage (Birth to 2 Years)

During the **sensorimotor stage,** children acquire schemes for two basic competencies: (1) goal-directed behavior and (2) object permanence. Piaget regarded these schemes as the building blocks of symbolic thinking and human intelligence.

Development of Goal-Directed Behavior One defining characteristic of the sensorimotor period is an infant's clear progression toward goal-directed actions. At birth, a child's behavior is largely controlled by reflexes. Babies are born with the ability to suck, grasp, cry, and move their bodies, which allows them to assimilate physical experiences. For example, a young child learns to differentiate hard from soft objects by sucking on them.

According to Piaget, children acquire the competencies of goal-related behavior and object permanence during the sensorimotor period.

Infants learn through acting on objects. By simply changing the position of the rattle, this infant is experimenting with cause-and-effect relations.

Within the first few months, new behaviors are added. Thumb-sucking, for instance, is a chance occurrence that, once discovered, is repeated over and over, because it is a pleasant sensation for the baby. It is initiated by the child with a specific goal in mind. Piaget referred to this set of intentional or goal-directed actions as **circular reactions.**

By the end of the first year, a child begins to anticipate events and combines previously acquired behaviors to achieve those goals. At this point, infants are no longer repeating accidental events but are initiating and selecting a sequence of actions to obtain a specific goal. Piaget first observed this sequence of behavior when he placed his 10-month-old son's favorite toy under a pillow. His son paused, batted the pillow away, and grabbed the toy. He combined several actions to get what he wanted.

At the end of the sensorimotor period, children begin to experiment with new ways of accomplishing their goals when a problem cannot be solved with existing schemata (such as looking, reaching, and grasping). If, for example, a child's toy is out of reach under the sofa, the child may crawl around to the back of the sofa to retrieve it. Rather than continuing to apply existing schemata, the child is now able to mentally construct new solutions to problems. For Piaget, the invention of new problem-solving methods marked the beginning of truly intelligent behavior. Although children continue to solve problems through trial and error for many more years, some of this experimentation can now be carried out internally through mental representation of action sequences and goals.

Development of Object Permanence

Another important development that occurs in the sensorimotor period is object permanence. **Object permanence** involves the knowledge that objects continue to exist even when they can no longer be seen or acted on. As adults, we know a missing shoe continues to exist even though we cannot see it. We search the closet, check under the bed, and finally find it under the sofa in the living room. Young infants act differently when objects disappear from their sight. They act as though the object no longer exists.

A child's concept of object permanence can be studied in a number of different ways. As described here, one way is to hide a child's favorite toy under a pillow or blanket while the child watches. Young infants (1 to 4 months) may visually track the object to the spot where it disappears but show no awareness of the object once it is no longer visible. Piaget explained that at this age, objects have no reality or existence for children unless directly perceived. Because the child's only way of knowing objects is through their reflexive actions, an object no longer exists if it cannot be sucked, grasped, or seen. In other words, the child is not yet able to form a mental representation of this object.

Object permanence involves the knowledge that objects continue to exist even when they are out of sight.

The first glimmer of object permanence emerges around 4 to 8 months. The child will now search for an object if it is partially visible but needs some perceptual cue to remember the object continues to exist. Between 8 and 12 months, a child's behavior indicates that he or she understands an object continues to exist even though it cannot be seen. Children will now actively search for hidden objects by combining several sensorimotor schemes, such as looking, crawling, and reaching, into goal-directed actions.

Some researchers have questioned Piaget's findings on object permanence (Baillargeon, Spelke, & Wasserman, 1985; Flavell, 1985). Recent evidence suggests that a mental representation of objects may appear as early as 3 and 4 months. Other researchers claim that babies may understand that objects are permanent, but may lack the memory skills to remember the location of the object or the motor skills to carry out the actions needed to find the object. Nevertheless, most theorists agree that the ability to construct mental images of objects within the first year of development is a significant achievement. From this point on, children's intellectual development is influenced more by mental representations than by sensorimotor activities.

Preoperational Stage (2 to 7 Years)

The ability to think about objects, events, or people in their absence marks the beginning of the preoperational stage. From 2 to 7 years old, children demonstrate an increased ability to use symbols—gestures, words, numbers, and images—to represent real objects in their environment. They can now think and behave in ways that were not possible before. They can use words to communicate, use numbers to count objects, engage in make-believe play, and express their ideas about the world through drawings.

SOURCE: LWA/Dann Tardif/The Stock Market.

During the preschool years, pretend play represents real events in children's lives.

Although the ability to represent objects and events symbolically is a significant advance, preoperational thinking is limited in a number of ways. Piaget used the term **preoperational stage** because preschool children lack the ability to do some of the logical operations he observed in older children. Before examining the limitations of preoperational thinking, let's consider the important cognitive advances of this stage.

Semiotic or representational thinking is the ability to use words to stand for (symbolize) an object that is not present or events not directly experienced.

Representational Thinking   During the preoperational stage, children can use symbols as a tool to think about their environment. The ability to use a word (e.g., *cookies, milk*) to stand for a real object that is not present is called **symbolic** or **representational thinking.** Piaget suggested that one of the earliest forms of representational thinking was deferred imitation, which first appears toward the end of the sensorimotor period. **Deferred imitation** refers to the ability to repeat a simple sequence of actions or sounds several hours or days after they were originally produced. Piaget (1962) observed the following example of deferred imitation with his daughter:

> Jacqueline (1 year, 4 months) has a visit from a 1.5-year-old boy whom she used to see from time to time, and who, in the course of the afternoon, got into a terrible temper. He screamed as he tried to get out of the playpen and pushed it backward, stamping his feet. Jacqueline stood watching him in amazement, never having witnessed such a scene before. The next day, she herself screamed in her playpen and tried to move it, stamping her feet lightly several times in succession. (p. 62)

The ability to repeat a sequence of actions or sounds several hours or days after they were originally made is called deferred imitation.

Several new examples of representational thinking appear during the preoperational stage. The preschool years are often considered the "golden age" of symbolic play (Singer & Singer, 1976). Symbolic play begins with simple sequences of behavior using real objects, such as pretending to drink from a cup or to eat with a spoonlike object. By 4 years of age, children can invent their own props, make up a story line, and assume various social roles. Consider how these 4-year-olds are learning to negotiate social relationships in the following example of pretend play from Vivian Gussin Paley's (1988) *Bad Guys Don't Have Birthdays:*

Barney:	Keep makin' gold. You're the walkout guards and the goldmakers. Don't forget, I'm the guard that controls the guns.
Frederick:	But we control the guns when you sleep.
Barney:	No. You make the gold and I control the guns. Anyway, I'm not sleeping, because there's bad guys coming. Calling all guards! Stuart get on. You wanna be a guard? Bad guys! They see the ship because it's already in the sun.
Mollie:	No bad guys, Barney, the baby is sleeping.
Barney:	There hasta be bad guys, Mollie. We gots the cannons.
Mollie:	You can't shoot when the baby is sleeping.
Barney:	Who's the baby? We didn't say a baby.
Mollie:	It's Christopher. Come on, baby Starlite. Lie down over here.
Barney:	Say no, Christopher. You can be the Boy Scout brother. Say no, say no.
Christopher:	I gotta shoot bad guys for awhile, okay, Mollie? (p. 19)

Should Superheros Be Banned from the Classroom?

Children's involvement in superhero play is a growing concern of teachers and parents. Many believe that permitting children to play Ninja Turtles, Power Rangers, and Buzz Light Year can increase young children's aggressive tendencies. In Chapter 8, we will discuss the influence of television violence on the development of aggression in children. For the most part, this research suggests that the effects of television violence are not straightforward. Research also suggests that superhero play makes up less than 5 percent of play time in early childhood settings, and generally only a few children, mostly boys, engage in this type of play (Boyd, 1997). Studies further suggest that teachers and children often have differing perspectives on superhero play. Teachers tend to see these behaviors as "aggressive," whereas children see them as playful. Interviews with preschool teachers reveal that superhero play is often equated with adolescent violence and gang activity. However, there is no evidence connecting superhero play to violent behavior in later development. Furthermore, researchers argue that fantasy play may help children to work through issues related to power and control (Carlsson-Paige & Levin, 1991). Banning superhero play from the classroom or playground can send the message to children that they need to hide their interests from adults, and teachers may lose an opportunity to help children express concerns about power and control. This is not to say that educators should not help children learn from their superhero friends. There are resources available to help teachers support and use superhero play effectively in their classroom (see Greenberg, 1995; Gronlund, 1992; Levin, 1994).

For the most part, children's pretend play reflects real events in their lives (e.g., playing house, going to the store, going on a trip), but pretend play involving fantasy and superhero characters is very appealing to young children as well. As discussed in the Focus on Teaching box, many parents and educators have become vocal opponents of superhero play in the classroom. However, many experts believe that pretend play is important for the development of children's language, cognitive, and social skills. It also helps to foster their creativity and imagination.

Piaget believed that the development of representational thinking enables children to acquire language. The preschool years are a period of rapid language development, with most children saying their first words around their second birthday and increasing their vocabulary to approximately 2,000 words by the age of 4. We will discuss language development in detail in Chapter 5; for now, it is important to understand its connection to representational thinking. When babies first begin to talk, they use words that refer to ongoing activities and events and immediately present desires. During the preoperational period, children begin to use words in a truly representational way. Rather than focusing exclusively on ongoing activities or immediate desires, children begin to use words to stand for absent objects and past events (Ginsburg & Opper, 1988). In other words, children use words to refer to events they are not experiencing directly. Piaget believed that representational thinking facilitates the rapid development of language in the preoperational period. That is, thinking precedes language development in Piaget's view.

In Piaget's view, the development of representational thinking allows children to acquire language.

During the preoperational period, children also begin to represent their world through pictures and images, leading some experts to refer to children's art as the "silent language." By studying children's art, we can learn much about their thinking and feelings. For example, 2- and 3-year-old children, when asked what they are drawing or painting, are likely to respond, "I'm just drawing." By age 3 or 4, however, children begin to combine marks to make squares, crosses, circles, and other geometric shapes. Children enter the representational stage of drawing around the age of 4 or 5. They draw houses, animals, people, cartoon characters, and other objects. Their figures may represent real objects in their environment or fantasy characters they have heard about or seen. The Focus on Development box shows this developmental progression in children's drawings. As they develop, children add more and more detail to their drawings, including words that tell the story line. By the time they enter kindergarten, some children can write their own names. Now, printed words as well as pictures can stand for a real object in a child's environment.

Number Concepts   Along with an increased ability to use words and images as symbols, children begin to use numbers as a tool for thinking during the preschool years. Piaget argued that children do not acquire a true concept of numbers until the concrete operational stage when they begin to understand serial and hierarchical relations. However, recent research has indicated that some basic number principles begin to appear during preoperations. Research by Rochel Gelman and her associates (Gelman & Gallistel, 1978; Gelman & Meck, 1983) suggests that some 4-year-olds can understand the following basic principles of counting: (a) any array of items can be counted; (b) each item should be counted only once; (c) numbers should be assigned in the same order; (d) the order in which objects are counted is irrelevant; and (e) the last spoken number word is the number of items in that set. Preschool children also have some basic understanding of number relationships. Most 3- and 4-year-olds, for example, know that 3 is more than 2. In addition, preschool children seem to have an intuitive understanding of addition and subtraction.

Although preschoolers are beginning to understand basic number concepts, it is important to keep in mind that they will make plenty of counting errors. They may skip numbers (e.g., 1, 2, 3, 5), miss items while counting, and so on. In addition, most preschool and early elementary children have difficulty counting large groups of disorganized items (Baroody, 1987). It is also difficult for preschool children to count beyond 10 in English, because the teen-number words do not follow their 1 to 10 counterparts. Learning to count beyond 10 is easier for children who speak Japanese, Chinese, or Korean (see Focus on Research on page 132).

Intuitive Theories   Young children are known for their curiosity and inquisitiveness. During the preschool years, children begin to form **intuitive theories** about natural phenomena. Piaget (1951) interviewed young children to find out how they explained events, such as the origins of trees, the movement of clouds, the beginning of the sun and moon, and the concept of life. He found that young children's conceptions of the world are characterized by **animism**; that is, they do not distinguish between animate (living) and inanimate (mechanical) objects, and they attribute intentional states and human characteristics to inanimate objects. For example, a 3-year-old may say that the sun is hot because it wants to keep people warm or that trees lose their leaves because they want to change the way they look. Rocks, trees, fires, rivers, cars, and bicycles are all judged to have lifelike characteristics because they move. The following example illustrates this animistic thinking, according to Piaget:

Preoperational children have an animistic conception of the world; they do not distinguish between animate and inanimate objects.

> Zimm (7 years, 9 months; child's responses in italics). Is a cat alive? *Yes.* A snail? *Yes.* A table? *No.* Why not? *It can't move.* Is a bicycle alive? *Yes.* Why? *It can go.* Is a cloud alive? *Yes.* Why? *It sometimes moves.* Is water alive? *Yes, it moves.* Is it alive when it does not

Focus on Development

Developmental Progression of Children's Drawings

Level of Development	Age Range	Characteristics
Placement stage	Age 32 months	 (scribbles)
Basic shapes	Age 42 months	 (circle)
Design stage	Age 40 and 47 months	 (combination design)
Pictorial stage	Age 45 months	 (sun)
Pictorial stage	Age 48 to 60 months	 (humans)

SOURCE: After Kellogg (1970).

move? *Yes.* Is a bicycle alive when it isn't moving? *Yes, it's alive, even when it doesn't move.* Is a lamp alive? *Yes, it shines.* Is the moon alive? *Yes, sometimes it hides behind the mountains.* (Piaget 1951, p. 199)

In constructing their beliefs, children draw on their own personal experiences and observations. The term *intuitive* is often applied to the preoperational stage, because the child's reasoning is based on immediate experiences.

Basic number concepts begin to emerge during the preschool years.

Focus on Research

Learning Place Value: Does Language Make a Difference?

International comparisons of mathematics achievement consistently show large differences in favor of Asian students. Research studies have shown that the superior performance of Asian students in abstract counting and in understanding place value may already be apparent by the first grade. Differences in children's understanding of number concepts may be due to differences in the number words. In most languages, the numbers 1 to 10 are arbitrary, and the numbers after 20 have a regular pattern (twenty-one, thirty-two, etc). English, French, and Swedish children have a difficult time learning the number words from 11 to 20, because the teen-numbers do not match their 1 to 10 counterparts. In Japanese, the numbers from 11 to 20 follow a regular pattern, and they are composed of "ten" plus the single number. For example, in Japanese the number 10 is *juu* and the number 2 is *ni*. The word for twelve is *juu-ni* ("ten-two"). The number words for 11 to 20 also follow this pattern in Chinese and Korean.

Do the number words for 11 to 20 give Asian children an advantage in learning to count? Studies show no differences in children's counting performance through the age of 3 when learning is focused on acquiring the first 10 number words. However, around the time children begin to learn the teen words large differences appear. Learning to count beyond 10 is considerably easier for children who speak some Chinese, Japanese, or Korean because the number words for 11 to 20 follow a regular pattern (e.g., "ten-one," "ten-two," etc.). In addition, studies reveal that Asian children have less difficulty than U.S. children in understanding place value because the number names in their languages explicitly state each number's composition ("ten-five"). By the time Asian children are 6 years old, they have little difficulty making models of multidigits using 10 blocks and units. For example, they can represent the number 54 with 5 ten blocks and 4 unit blocks. In contrast, U.S. children showed a preference for representing whole numbers in terms of individual units rather than units of 10. Asian number words may help children in those countries to learn place value at a younger age than U.S. children who, even by the third grade, have difficulty identifying correctly the value of numerals in different positions (e.g., in the one place, tens place, and hundreds place).

This research has important implications for education. To help children acquire a sense of number and place value, teachers might use counting words that resemble Asian languages, such "ten-one," "ten-two," "ten-three" as a different way of saying *eleven, twelve,* and *thirteen.* Children also need opportunities to work with math manipulatives that provide opportunities to organize large numbers of items into units of 10s.

SOURCE: Adapted from Miura, Okamoto, Kim, Steere, & Fayol (1993).

However, recent studies reveal that children's intuitive understandings of their physical and biological concepts are a little more sophisticated than Piaget believed. In the area of physics, research suggests that young children have a naive understanding of atomic theory of matter—objects are composed of tiny bits of matter (Carey, 1991). Four-year-olds understand that you cannot pour water into a box that is already filled with a steel block.

- Sugar ceases to exist when placed in water.

- Clouds or the earth's shadow causes the phases of the moon.

- Plants get their food from the soil.

- Light travels farther at night than in the day.

- Shadows are made out of matter.

- Heavier objects fall faster.

- Electric current is used in a light bulb.

- The world is flat.

- Coldness causes rust.

- If you add warm water to an equal amount of warm water, you get water that is twice as warm.

FIGURE 3.2

Elementary School Students' Naive Conceptions in Science

SOURCES: After Driver, Guesne, & Tiberghien (1985) and Hyde & Bizar (1989).

Preschoolers can also attribute the snuffing out of a candle to a fan that was turned on rather than one turned off. Other research suggests that preschool children have also developed concepts about the earth's shape, the movement of the planets, and so on. Along these same lines, toddlers and preschoolers have acquired some rudimentary biological conceptions as well. Preschool children can distinguish inanimate from living objects, contrary to Piaget's suggestion, and they are beginning to develop an understanding of biological properties. Recent research suggests that preschool children recognize that plants, like people, can grow, heal, and decompose (Wellman & Gelman, 1998). Preschool children also have a rudimentary understanding of inheritance. They expect, for example, that animals of the same family share certain physical properties. Additionally, they understand that an infant calf that comes from a cow will grow up "to moo" and "to have a straight tail," even if it is raised among pigs.

However, young children have many misconceptions of their intuitive physical and biological worlds that can have a lasting influence on their learning. When children are presented factual information in school this information is often assimilated into the naive or commonsense theories they have already formed about the world. For example, Eaton, Anderson, & Smith (1984) found that after 6 weeks of science lessons on light and vision, most of the fifth graders in their study held onto their naive conceptions: We see things because light shines on them and brightens them. According to these researchers, the teachers seemed to do everything right in presenting scientific explanations, but they did not directly confront their students' naive conceptions of light. Figure 3.2 lists other examples of children's naive theories in science. These schemes for explaining natural events may persist, unless children's naive conceptions are confronted directly.

Just as children begin to develop theories of the external world during the preoperational period, they also begin to develop theories about the internal world of the mind. Piaget (1963) proposed that children confuse mental and real events. This confusion was most evident when children were asked to explain the origins of dreams (e.g., Where do dreams come from?). For preoperational thinkers, dreams are external events that can be seen by other people. Piaget used the term **realism** to describe the young child's tendency to confuse physical and psychological events.

Preschool children understand that the mind can think, remember, and dream.

Current research indicates that preschoolers' knowledge of the mind is more sophisticated than Piaget originally suggested (Wellman & Gelman, 1998). According to Henry Wellman (1990), most 3-year-olds understand that internal wishes and desires can cause a person to act a certain way. Most 3- to 5-year-olds also know it's not possible to touch or eat cookies that are in a person's dreams, and they know dreams can be about impossible events, such as a dog flying (Wellman & Estes, 1986). When asked to name things the mind can do, 4- and 5-year-olds say that the mind can think, remember, and dream. By this age, children can also distinguish between their own knowledge and that of others (Wellman, 1990).

Although children are beginning to develop a theory of mind in the preoperational stage, they have a very limited understanding of thinking processes and memory. Preschool children, for example, believe they can remember everything they see and hear. Between the ages of 8 and 10, children begin to acquire what is known as *metacognitive knowledge*. **Metacognition** is "thinking about thinking," and it plays a very important role in children's cognitive development during the middle childhood years. We will discuss how metacognition influences children's cognitive development when we explore information processing theories.

Preoperational thinking is limited because it is egocentric, rigid, and centered on only one aspect of a stimulus.

Limitations of Preoperational Thinking   So far we have discussed the important advances in children's thinking during the preoperational period. Let's turn to some of the limitations of preoperational thinking. The three main cognitive limitations of this stage are egocentrism, centration, and rigidity of thinking.

Egocentrism refers to the tendency to "perceive, understand, and interpret the world in terms of the self" (Miller, 1993, p. 53). This egocentrism is particularly evident in the conversations of preschoolers. Because young children are unable to take the perspective of others, they make little effort to modify their speech for the listener. Three-year-olds seem to have what are called **collective monologues,** in which their remarks to each other are unrelated. By 4 and 5 years of age, children begin to show some ability to adjust their communication to the perspective of their listeners.

Piaget & Inhelder (1956) used the famous mountain task to study the egocentrism of young children. A model of a landscape containing three mountains was placed on top of a table with four chairs arranged around the table. For the study, a child sat in one chair and was asked to choose from a group of drawings the one that best described how the mountains might look to a person sitting in another chair. This study found that most children under the age of 7 or 8 picked the drawing that showed how the mountains looked to them, not how the mountain might look to someone sitting in another chair.

Some researchers have claimed that the mountain task is not a fair test of children's perspective-taking abilities. To do this task, children must be able to rotate objects in a spatial arrangement. When a simplified form of this task is used, preschoolers seem to be less egocentric than Piaget claimed. For example, most 3-year-olds understand that if a picture of an object is held vertically facing them, they can see the depicted object, but someone sitting opposite them cannot, as Figure 3.3 shows. This later research suggests that an understanding that two people can have different perspectives of the same object develops between the ages of 3 and 4 (Flavell, 1985).

Another limitation of preoperational thinking is *centration*. **Centration** means that young children tend to focus or center their attention on only one aspect of a stimulus. Other features of the stimulus are ignored. As will be discussed later, centration explains why children have difficulty performing conservation tasks. Suppose you show a 4-year-old two identical glasses containing the same amount of water and then pour the contents

Which child can see the cat?

FIGURE 3.3

Perspective-Taking Task

of one glass into a tall, thin glass. When asked, "Which glass has more?" the child will focus on the height of the water and choose the taller glass. Other dimensions of the glass, such as its width, will be ignored.

This example illustrates another limitation of preoperational thought. Young children's thinking tends to be very rigid. In the previous example, the child is focusing on "before" and "after" states rather than the transformation process. With development, children's thinking becomes less rigid, and they begin to consider how transformations (pouring the contents of one glass into another glass) can be reversed. The ability to mentally reverse operations is a characteristic of the next stage of cognitive development known as *concrete operations.*

Until children have developed some mental operations, such as reversibility, they tend to base their judgments of quantity on perceptual appearances rather than reality. If a glass looks like it has more water, young children assume it has more. Flavell and his associates (Flavell, Green, & Flavell, 1986) studied children's understanding of appearances and reality. They found that the ability to distinguish appearance from reality develops between the ages of 3 and 5. When 3-year-olds are shown a sponge that looks like a rock, they believe it really is a rock. If a cloth smells like an orange, then it is an orange. This tendency to confuse reality and appearances is what makes Halloween a scary event for most 3-year-olds and some 4-year-olds. If a person looks like a monster, then that person must be a monster! By age 5, most children begin to distinguish between appearances and reality.

Concrete Operational Stage (7 to 11 Years)

In the elementary years, children begin to use mental operations and logic to think about events and objects in their environment. For example, if asked to arrange a set of five sticks according to size, concrete operational thinkers can mentally compare the objects and then draw logical inferences about the correct order without physically performing the actions. This ability to use logic and mental operations allows concrete operational children to approach problems more systematically than a preoperational child.

According to Piaget, there are several advances in children's thinking during the **concrete operational** stage. First, their thinking appears to be less rigid and more flexible. The child understands that operations can be mentally reversed or negated. That is, you can

The ability to think logically and perform mental operations allows concrete operational children to approach problems more systematically than preoperational children.

During concrete operations, children begin to sort, organize, and classify objects according to
common attributes.

change a stimulus, such as the water poured into the thin beaker, back to its original state
by reversing the action. Along these same lines, the child's thinking appears to be less centrated and egocentric. The grade school child can attend to several characteristics of a stimulus at the same time. Rather than focusing exclusively on static states, the child is now
able to make inferences about the nature of transformations. Finally, concrete operational
thinkers no longer base their judgments on the appearances of things.

Let's take a closer look at the three types of mental operations or schemes children use
to organize and make sense of their world during concrete operations: seriation, classification, and conservation.

*Seriation, a
mental operation
that appears in
the concrete
operations stage,
involves the
ability to order
objects in a
logical
progression.*

Seriation   Seriation involves the ability to order objects in a logical progression, such as
from shortest to tallest. **Seriation** is important for understanding the concepts of numbers,
time, and measurement. For example, most preschoolers have a limited concept of time. In
their minds, 2 minutes is the same as 20 minutes or 200 minutes. In contrast, elementary
schoolchildren can order concepts of time in terms of increasing or decreasing quantity. For
them, 20 minutes is fewer than 200 minutes, but more than 2 minutes.

In one of his experiments, Piaget asked children to order a series of sticks like the ones
shown in Figure 3.4. At ages 3 and 4, children can find the longest and shortest sticks. They
seem to understand the **logical rule of progressive change**—that is, items can be ordered
in terms of increasing and decreasing size—but they have difficulty constructing an ordered sequence of three or more sticks. To succeed at this task, the children must perform
two mental operations simultaneously. They must select the appropriate stick by thinking
about how long or short it is in relation to the sticks already used as well as to those that remain. Preschool children are unable to perform this task because they focus on one dimension at a time (i.e., their thinking is centrated). The ability to coordinate two pieces of

Can you put these sticks in order from shortest to longest?

In concrete operations, children can order a series of sticks according to size.

FIGURE 3.4

Seriation Task

information simultaneously develops gradually during the early elementary years, when children's thinking begins to be characterized less by centration.

In order to solve seriation problems, children must also apply the **logical rule of transitivity.** Part of the problem for young elementary children is that they do not understand that objects in the middle of a series are both shorter and longer than others. Older children can mentally construct relations among objects. They can infer the relationship between two objects by knowing its relationship to a third. For example, if they know stick A is shorter than stick B, and stick B is shorter than stick C, then A must be shorter than C. This answer is a logical deduction based on the rule of transitivity (A > B and B > C, thus A > C). According to Piaget's theory, an understanding of transitivity is acquired between the ages of 7 and 11.

Classification　In addition to seriation, Piaget believed that classification skills are central to the development of concrete operations. **Classification** is another way children can impose order on their environment by grouping things and ideas according to common elements. Classification is a skill that begins to emerge in early childhood. Toddlers and preschoolers can generally group objects according to a single dimension, such as size or color. However, it is not until the concrete operational period that children classify objects according to multiple dimensions or understand relations between classes of objects. Piaget described two different types of classification systems that develop during middle childhood as matrix and hierarchical classification.

Matrix classification involves classifying items by two or more attributes, as shown in Figure 3.5. We already know that preschool children can group objects according to single dimensions. What would happen, however, if you gave a group of children objects of different shapes *and* colors to sort? Piaget found that young preschool children sort things correctly along one dimension, either shape or size. A slightly more advanced preschool child might then subdivide each of the color groups along the second dimension. This behavior suggests that children are in a transition stage. They *notice* more than one dimension but are unable to coordinate this information. By age 8 or 9, children will demonstrate the ability to sort objects using two dimensions simultaneously.

Piaget believed that centration places a greater constraint on younger than on older children's classification skills. Young children tend to group things based on their similarities; differences between objects are typically ignored. Older children are able to consider how objects may be similar and different at the same time. The ability to classify objects according to two dimensions also requires *reversibility* in thinking. This ability to mentally reverse an operation allows a child to first classify an object by one dimension (color) and then reclassify it by a second attribute (shape or size). Older elementary school children are able to handle this problem, because they are becoming more flexible in their thinking.

During the later elementary school years, children also begin to use **hierarchical classification** systems for imposing order on their environment. Such classification systems are

Piaget believed classification skills are central to the development of concrete operations.

Matrix classification involves sorting items by two or more attributes; hierarchical classification involves understanding the ways in which parts are related to the whole.

FIGURE 3.5

Matrix Classification Task

What is the color and what is the shape of the missing object?

used to organize information about geology, biology, astronomy, history, physics, music, and so forth. By sixth grade, for instance, children are expected to know that all matter is composed of molecules, and each molecule is made up of atoms, which carry different units of protons, electrons, and neutrons. The child must also be able to reason about hierarchical relations in order to understand number concepts. For example, the number 5 is part of a set that also includes the numbers preceding it (1, 2, 3, and 4). The number 1 can be divided into several different parts (halves, quarters, tenths, etc.), and the number 100 is made up of 10 groups of tens. During the concrete operational stage, children begin to understand hierarchical relations.

The standard test for assessing children's understanding of hierarchies is the *class inclusion* task. A child is shown pictures of two different animals, say three dogs and seven cats, and then asked, "Are there more cats or more animals?" (see Figure 3.6). Most 5- and 6-year-olds say there are more cats. They typically compare the subclasses (dogs and cats) and do not grasp that they make up a larger class (animals). To answer correctly, children have to think about the subsets in relation to the whole. Around the age of 8 or 9, children begin to base their responses on the **logical rule of class inclusion.** They now understand that a total collection of items must be larger than any one of its subparts and use this logical operation to organize information in class inclusion problems. Before children have acquired an understanding of class inclusion, they may have difficulty understanding part-whole relations in math, science, reading, and many other subjects.

Conservation involves the understanding that an entity remains the same despite superficial changes in its form or physical appearance.

Conservation   According to Piaget's theory, the ability to reason about conservation problems was the major hallmark of the concrete operational stage. **Conservation** involves the understanding that an entity remains the same despite superficial changes in its form or physical appearance. During the concrete operational stage, children no longer base their reasoning on the physical appearance of objects. They recognize that a transformed object may seem to have more or less of the quantity in question, but it may not. In other words, appearances can be misleading.

Piaget examined children's understanding of five types of conservation: number, liquid, substance (mass), length, and volume. Examples of these conservation tasks are shown in the Focus on Development box on page 140. Although these tasks differ with respect to the dimension that is to be conserved, the basic paradigm is the same. In general, a child is

FIGURE 3.6

*Are There More
Cats or Animals?*

Preschool children respond that there are more cats, because they compare the two groups. They do not understand that each group also belongs to a larger class (animals).

shown two identical sets of objects, such as identical rows of coins, identical amounts of clay, or identical glasses of water. After the child agrees that the objects are the same, one object is transformed in a way that changes its appearance but not the basic dimension of interest. For example, in the conservation-of-number task, one row of coins is shortened or lengthened. The child is allowed to observe this transformation. The child is then asked to state whether the dimension of interest (quantity, mass, area, etc.) is still the same.

Children who have entered the concrete operational stage will reply that the set of objects is still the same. One object may look bigger, longer, or heavier, but the two objects are really the same. According to Piaget, children use three basic mental operations to perform conservation tasks: **negation, compensation,** and **identity.** These mental operations are reflected in the ways an 8-year-old might explain why the amount of water in two different glasses remained the same:

> "You could pour it back and it will be the same." *(negation)*

> "The water goes up higher, but the glass is skinnier." *(compensation)*

> "You just poured it, nothing was added or taken away." *(identity)* (Miller, 1993, p. 57)

Between the ages of 7 and 11, children acquire the mental operations needed to think about the transformations represented in conservation problems. When children can reason logically about number, mass, and volume without being confused by physical appearances, they are capable of *reflective abstraction.* They can separate the invariant characteristics of stimuli (e.g., weight, number, volume) from how the object may appear to them.

The acquisition of the mental operations used to perform conservation tasks does not take place at the same time in all areas. Children's understanding of conservation problems

Focus on Development

Children's Understanding of Conservation Problems

CONSERVATION SKILL	BASIC PRINCIPLE	TEST FOR CONSERVATION SKILLS	
		Step 1	Step 2
Number (Ages 5 to 7)	The number of units in a collection remains unchanged even though the units are rearranged in space.	Two rows of pennies arranged in one-to-one correspondence	One of the rows elongated or contracted
Substances (Ages 7 to 8)	The amount of a malleable, plastic-like material remains unchanged regardless of the shape it assumes.	Modeling clay in two balls of the same size	One of the balls rolled into a long, narrow shape
Length (Ages 7 to 8)	The length of a line or an object from one end to the other end remains unchanged regardless of how it is rearranged in space or changed in shape.	Strips of cloth placed in a straight line	Strips of cloth placed in altered shapes
Area (Ages 8 to 9)	The total amount of surface covered by a set of plane figures remains unchanged regardless of the position of the figures.	Square units placed on top of each other	Square unit rearranged
Weight (Ages 9 to 10)	The heaviness of an object remains unchanged regardless of the shape that it assumes.	Units placed on top of each other	Units placed side by side
Volume (Ages 12 to 14)	The space occupied by an object remains unchanged regardless of a change in its shape.	Displacement of water by object placed vertically in the water	Displacement of water by object placed horizontally in the water

SOURCE: After Vander Zanden (1993).

follows a developmental sequence (see Focus on Development). Children generally acquire the ability to conserve numbers between the ages of 5 and 7. The ability to conserve area and weight develops between the ages of 8 and 10. Most children are unable to perform conservation of volume tasks until 10 or 11 years. Piaget referred to this inconsistency of children's thinking within a stage as **horizontal decalage.**

Formal Operational Stage (11 to 12 Years and Onward)

Having the ability to handle problems like seriation, classification, and conservation, children from about 11- or 12-years-old begin to develop a coherent system of formal logic. By the end of the concrete operational period, they have the cognitive tools for solving many types of logical problems, for understanding conceptual relations among mathematical operations (e.g., $15 + 8 = 10 + 13$), and for ordering and classifying bodies of knowledge. During adolescence, the mental operations that emerged in previous stages are organized into a more elaborate system of logic and abstract ideas.

As children enter the formal operations stage, their thinking begins to differentiate between the real (concrete) and the possible (abstract).

The most important change that occurs during the formal operations stage is that children's thinking shifts from the *real* to the *possible* (Flavell, 1985). Older elementary schoolchildren can reason logically but only about people, places, and things that are tangible and concrete. In contrast, adolescents can think about things they have never experienced (e.g., When you read this story, try to imagine what it might have been like to be a slave in the 1850s.); they can generate ideas about events that never happened (e.g., What would Europe be like today if Germany had won World War II?); and they can make predictions about hypothetical or future events (e.g., Suppose the federal government passed a bill to ban the death penalty. What would happen to the crime rate?). Older adolescents can discuss complex social and political issues involving abstract ideas such as human rights, equality, and justice. They can also reason about proportional relations and analogies, solve algebraic equations and geometric proofs, and analyze the inherent validity of an argument.

The ability to think abstractly and reflectively is called formal operations.

The ability to think abstractly and reflectively occurs during the **formal operational** stage. In the following sections, we look at four key characteristics of formal operational thinking: propositional logic, scientific reasoning, combinatorial reasoning, and reasoning about probabilities and proportions.

Propositional Logic   Adult mental operations correspond to a certain type of logical operation called *propositional logic,* which Piaget believed was central to formal operational thinking. **Propositional logic** involves the ability to draw a logical inference based on the relationship between two statements or premises. In everyday language, propositional logic can be expressed in a series of if/then statements. Consider the following example:

> If babies are older than adults;
> And babies are older than children;
> Then adults are older than children.

The *conclusion* is factually correct but invalid, because it *does not follow* from the information that preceded it. David Moshman and Bridget Franks (1986) found that elementary schoolchildren tend to evaluate the above conclusion on the basis of its factual truth rather than the validity of the argument. As children enter formal operations, however, they begin to consider the inherent validity of the argument, regardless of its factual truth. The conclusion may be factually correct, but some adolescents would question the validity of the argument.

Propositional logic is more concerned with the logical relationship between two statements or premises than with their accuracy or truth.

For formal operational thinkers, the validity of the argument has to do more with the way the statements are related than with the truthfulness of the content. According to Piaget, formal operational reasoning involves thinking about the logical relationships among propositions. Formal operational thinkers seem to understand that logical arguments have a "disembodied, passionless life of their own, at least in principle" (Flavell, 1985, p. 101).

Many types of problem-solving situations involve the use of propositional logic. Solving algebra problems, for example, involves the ability to think about propositional statements (e.g., $x + 2y = 11$; if $y = 1$, then $x = $ _____?). Propositional logic is also essential for reasoning about scientific problems, such as determining how to classify an animal or plant (e.g., If all mammals nurse their young and this animal nurses its young, then it must be a mammal.).

Good writers, lawyers, politicians, and teachers use propositional logic when they want to argue a point. When adolescents acquire this ability, be prepared. They not only become more argumentative, but also better arguers. They can find the fallacies in your logic and come back with the appropriate counterargument.

Scientific Reasoning   As adolescents develop their use of propositional logic, they approach problems in a more systematic manner. They can form hypotheses, determine how to test each one against the facts, and rule out those that prove to be wrong. Piaget called the ability to generate and test hypotheses in a logical and systematic manner **hypothetico-deductive thinking.**

To study the development of this type of thinking, Piaget used the pendulum task shown in Figure 3.7. In this experiment, a child is given a rod from which strings of different lengths are suspended. Different size weights can be easily attached to each string. The child is shown how the pendulum works, and then asked which of four factors—length of string, weight of object, force of push, or height of drop—is responsible for the speed at which the pendulum swings. They are allowed to experiment with the apparatus before stating their answer.

SOURCE: Cleve Bryant/Photo Edit.

As adolescents acquire formal logic, they become more skilled at debating issues, such as why they deserve a higher grade on a test.

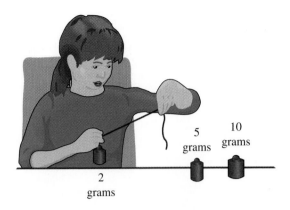

What makes the pendulum swing faster? The four factors involved are the length of the string, the weight of the pendulum, the height from which the pendulum is released, and the force with which the pendulum is pushed.

FIGURE 3.7
Pendulum Task

What do you think the correct answer is? How would you approach this problem? The first step is to generate a hypothesis or make a prediction. Concrete operational thinkers are able to use this problem-solving strategy. The next step involves testing the hypothesis. This step generally separates the concrete from the formal operational thinker. The trick is to change one of the problem's factors or variables while holding all others constant. Concrete operational thinkers often get off to a good start but fail to test all possible combinations. They may also change more than one variable at the same time (e.g., the string and the weight). Because they do not approach the problem systematically, concrete operational thinkers often draw the wrong conclusion when there are multiple variables to consider. In contrast, the formal operational thinker typically thinks about all possible combinations of variables. In this example, there are 16 different combinations that should be considered to draw the correct conclusion. The correct answer, of course, is the length of string. *A short string makes the pendulum go faster, regardless of all other factors.*

> *Hypothetico-deductive thinking is the ability to generate and test hypotheses in a logical and systematic manner.*

Combinatorial Reasoning   Another characteristic of formal operations is the ability to think about multiple causes. Suppose you give elementary and secondary students four plastic chips of different colors and ask them to put the chips together in as many different ways as possible. Children are likely to combine only two chips at the same time. Few will be able to do this task in any systematic way. Adolescents, on the other hand, may develop a way of representing all the possible combinations, including combinations of three and four chips. They are also more likely than children to produce these combinations systematically. This process is known as **combinatorial reasoning.**

Piaget and Inhelder (1956) used a chemistry experiment to study children's and adolescents' ability to use combinatorial logic. Figure 3.8 shows this experiment, in which children must combine liquids from different bottles to create a yellow solution. When the liquids from two bottles are combined with the g liquid, the solution turns yellow. Liquid from one of the bottles has no effect, and liquid from a fourth bottle can turn the solution clear. Concrete operational children generally take a drop of liquid from each of the four bottles and combine it with the g liquid one by one. If nothing happens, they think they have exhausted all possibilities. If they are told to combine liquids, they may do so but not in a systematic way. Formal operational thinkers go beyond testing each liquid one at a

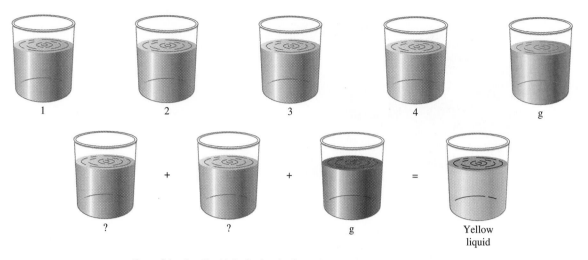

Two of the clear liquids in the four beakers when combined with liquid g produce a yellow solution. How would you solve this problem?

FIGURE 3.8 *Chemistry Task*

time. They combine the liquids systematically (1 + 2 + g, 1 + 3 + g, 1 + 4 + g, etc.), until they find the combination that turns the solution yellow when g is added. Some adolescents may even go on to speculate about which liquids would combine to turn the solution clear again.

Reasoning about Probabilities and Proportions Elementary-aged children generally have a limited understanding of probability. Piaget's theory helps to explain why. Figure 3.9 shows a bubble gum machine with 30 red balls and 50 yellow balls. If a child inserts a coin into the machine, which color gumball is most likely to come out? A concrete operational thinker is likely to say "yellow," because there are more yellow than red balls. This child focuses on the absolute difference between the two quantities. Formal operational thinkers will mentally represent the problem differently. They will think about the problem in terms of the ratio of red to yellow balls. Adolescents are more likely to say that the child has a higher likelihood of getting a yellow ball, because there is a higher proportion of yellows to reds. A ratio is not something a person can see; it is an inferred relationship between two quantities. This example illustrates how concrete and formal thinkers may answer a question the same way, but they use a qualitatively different system of logic.

Some theorists contend that Piaget's research may have overestimated the ability of adolescents to reason about proportions. There is some evidence to suggest that even adults may not use a proportional reasoning strategy when solving practical problems. In one study, researchers asked 50 women in a supermarket to judge which of two sizes of the same product was a better buy (Capon & Kuhn, 1979). One bottle of garlic powder contained 1.25 ounces and sold for 41 cents, whereas the second bottle contained 2.37 ounces and sold for 77 cents. The women were given pencil and paper and told to justify their responses. The most direct way to do this problem is to compute the price of garlic powder per ounce for each bottle, and then compare the amounts. This strategy involves reasoning about proportions, which, according to Piaget's theory, is a characteristic of formal operations. Capon and Kuhn's supermarket study reported that fewer than 30 percent of the women used a proportional reasoning strategy when comparing products. Most used a

If you insert a coin, which color
gumball is most likely to come out?

FIGURE 3.9
Ratio Task

subtraction strategy, and justified their response by saying, "With the bigger one you get 32 more ounces for 36 more cents." Others just relied on previous experience and justified their choices by simply saying, "The bigger one is always better or cheaper." This study concluded that many adults may be unable to use formal operations when solving real world problems.

This finding will not surprise most high school teachers. Most know that their students have difficulty with tasks involving more abstract forms of reasoning. It is estimated that only 30 percent to 40 percent of high school students in American schools can solve formal operational tasks (Keating, 1990). The development of formal operations is greatly influenced by cultural expectations and experiences. Formal operational thinking is more prevalent in societies that emphasize mathematical and technical skills. Even within scientifically oriented countries like the United States, some groups of students have greater experience with mathematical and scientific thinking than others.

Limitations of Piaget's Theory

Piaget's theory is one of the most widely cited and discussed theories of cognitive development. Piaget helped to alter the course of research on children's development. Once researchers viewed development through Piaget's eyes, they could no longer see a child as a passive organism molded and shaped by the environment (Miller, 1993). Although Piagetian research continues to influence the way we think about children, in recent years his theory has generated substantial controversy and criticism. Questions have been raised about (a) his research methods; (b) the stagelike nature of children's thinking; (c) the adequacy of the equilibration models for explaining developmental changes; and (d) the universality of Piaget's stages (Flavell, 1985; Miller, 1993).

Concerns about Research Methods   Many contemporary theorists believe that Piaget underestimated younger children's abilities due to the research methods he used. As stated earlier, the tasks he used were highly complex and cognitively demanding, many requiring sophisticated verbal skills. Critics have argued that children may have the ability to perform

Focus on Research

Magic Mice Experiment

Rochel Gelman (1972) designed a simple task to study young children's ability to conserve number. In Gelman's experiment, 3-year-olds were shown two different plates. One plate contained three toy mice and the other plate contained two mice. The children were told to pick the "winner" plate and the "loser" plate. Children consistently identified the plate with three mice as the "winner." After children demonstrated they could correctly identify the winner and loser plates, the experimenter "magically" changed the winner plate by taking away the middle mouse or by pushing the mice closer together. When the children viewed the plates again, they acted surprised. Some asked where the missing mouse had gone. More important, they defined the winner plate by the number of mice on it rather than by the length of the row. When the three mice in the row were pushed together, they still called it the winner. Gelman's magic mice study showed that children can conserve number much earlier than Piaget claimed.

Piaget's theories are not without criticism: some question his theory of invariant stages, others point out his lack of attention to the cultural context in which thinking skills develop, and others feel his equilibration view of developmental change is inadequate.

problems at higher cognitive levels but may lack the verbal skills to demonstrate their competence. Thus, when nonverbal measures are used to test for the presence or absence of key concepts, the results differ from those reported by Piaget. In the infancy section, for example, we discussed recent research suggesting that object permanence may appear earlier than Piaget claimed. We also reviewed research suggesting that 3- and 4-year-old children can perform simple visual perspective-taking tasks (see section on egocentrism). In another experiment, Rochel Gelman (1972) found that 3-year-olds were able to understand number conservation tasks when more familiar language and a small number of objects were used. A description of this experiment appears in the Focus on Research box. This study supports contemporary theorists' suggestions that children's cognitive abilities in both infancy and childhood were underestimated by Piaget (Gelman & Baillargeon, 1983).

Concerns about the Nature of Development   Piaget has received the most criticism for his ideas about the qualitative nature of cognitive development. Some theorists have questioned that changes in children's cognitive systems are as "fundamental, momentous, qualitative, and stagelike as Piaget suggested" (Flavell, 1985, p. 82). Researchers have also argued that the equilibration model is inadequate for explaining advances in cognitive development. There are no precise statements as to what cognitive activities actually take place during the process of assimilation, accommodation, and equilibration (Flavell, 1985; Miller, 1993; Siegler, 1991).

Considerable research now suggests that stagelike changes in children's thinking appears to be causally linked to more gradual and quantitative sorts of changes in children's attentional and memory capacities. This research suggests that young children may be unable to perform some Piagetian tasks because they fail to attend to the relevant dimensions, to encode the appropriate information, to relate information to existing knowledge, to retrieve the appropriate solution from memory, and so forth (Siegler, 1991). When young children are trained to use these cognitive processes more effectively, age differences in children's performances on Piagetian tasks begin to disappear. For example, nonconservers as young as 4 years old can perform conservation tasks when they are trained to attend to the relevant dimensions (Gelman, 1969). Other research suggests that concrete

Focus on Development

Stages in Case's Theory of Cognitive Development

Stage	Age Range (approx.)	Characteristics
Sensory motor control structures	Birth to $1\frac{1}{2}$ years	Mental representations are linked to physical movements.
Relational control structures	11/2 to 5 years	Children can detect and coordinate relations along one dimension among objects, events, or people. For example, weight is viewed as bipolar—heavy and light.
Dimensional control structures	5 to 11 years	Children can extract the dimensions of significance in the physical and social world. They can compare two dimensions (e.g., height and width) in a quantitative way.
Abstract control structures	11 to $18\frac{1}{2}$ years	Children acquire abstract systems of thought that allow them to use proportional reasoning, solve verbal analogy problems, and infer psychological traits in other people.

SOURCE: After Miller (1993).

operational children can be trained to solve formal operational problems (Siegler, Robinson, Liebert, & Liebert, 1973). However, this learning may not transfer to other types of formal operational tasks.

Although training studies call into question the qualitative nature of developmental changes, the issue of stages in children's cognitive development remains controversial (Flavell, 1985). Some theorists contend that a stage theory of cognitive development may still be viable (Case, 1985). **Neo-Piagetian theories** have attempted to add greater specificity to developmental changes, while maintaining the basic assumptions of Piaget's theory (e.g., knowledge is actively constructed, cognitive changes are stagelike, etc.). These theories have begun to look at the role of children's information processing capabilities in explaining structural changes in children's thinking. The Focus on Development box presents Robbie Case's cognitive development model. This model links structural changes (movement from stage to stage) to the development of cognitive strategies and memory processes. Case's theory is just one of many that attempt to integrate Piagetian and information processing theories (see also Fisher, 1980).

Concerns about the Universality of Piaget's Stages   An additional issue of concern for contemporary theorists is the universality of Piaget's stages. As stated earlier, it is estimated that only a small minority of adolescents reach Piaget's formal operational stage. The

Focus on Research

A group of British and Brazilian researchers studied the computational skills of 9- to 15-year-old street vendors in Brazil. In many Brazilian towns, it is common for younger sons and daughters of street vendors to help their parents at the market. Adolescents may develop their own businesses to sell roasted peanuts, popcorn, coconut milk, or corn on the cob. These researchers found that children and adolescents develop sophisticated arithmetic skills in the context of buying and selling, but they are unable to perform the same mathematical operations when they were presented out of context. For example, a typical interview with a 12-year-old street vendor in the market might go like this (Carraher, Carraher, & Schlieman, 1985):

Customer: How much is one coconut?

Child: 35 cruzerios.

Customer: I would like ten. How much is that?

Child: (pause) Three will be 105, with three more, that will be 210. (pause) I need four more. That is…(pause) 315. I think it is 350.

After the interviewers posed a number of such questions, the children were given a paper and pencil and asked to solve identical problems. For example, they were asked: $35 \times 10 = $ _____? The math operation that was performed on the street was also represented in a word problem: Each banana costs 12 cruzerios. Mary bought 10 bananas. How much did she pay altogether?

The results of this interesting study showed that when mathematical problems were embedded in real life contexts (e.g., buying and selling), they were solved at a much higher rate than the same problem presented out of context. Children correctly answered the context-specific question 98 percent of the time. When the same operation was embedded in a word problem, children correctly solved the problem 73 percent of the time. In contrast, children correctly solved the mathematical operation with no context 37 percent of the time.

The results of this study show that context can have an important influence on whether or not children are able to use their existing mathematical knowledge. The children in this study were unable to use the computational strategies they used while selling on the streets for solving problems in school-type situations. This study raises questions about teaching mathematics as a set of conventions and routines that are divorced from children's daily problem-solving activities.

development of formal operations seems to be influenced by cultural expectations and experiences. Some theorists claim that Piaget's research did not adequately consider the role of culture in the development of thinking skills. Compare Capon and Kuhn's supermarket study with the study described in the Focus on Research box. In this study, 10- to

12-year-old vendors in Brazil had very little difficulty making large number computations when selling on the street but were unable to perform similar operations when asked to read multidigit numerals in written form. The results of cross-cultural studies underscore the importance of considering the cultural context in which thinking skills develop (Rogoff, 1990).

Conclusions about Piaget's Theory   Despite the criticisms discussed here, most theorists believe that Piaget captured many of the major trends in children's thinking (Flavell, 1985). Most preschool children are unable to consider more than one dimension of a stimulus object, to think about relations, or to take the perspective of another person. Older elementary school children can think logically about relations, perform mental operations, and reflect on their own thinking processes, but they are unable to solve hypothetical problems in their heads or to approach problems in a systematic way, especially when multiple steps are involved. Adolescents are better able to use complex symbol systems, to analyze the inherent logic of an argument, and to draw inferences from multiple pieces of evidence, even when there is some conflicting information. Simply put, Piaget taught us that children do not see and think about the world as adults do.

Piaget taught us that children do not see and think about the world as adults do.

Educational Implications of Piaget's Theory

Much of Piaget's research focused on children's development of logical, scientific, and mathematical concepts. Although Piaget reflected on the general educational implications of his research, he refrained from making specific educational recommendations. Nevertheless, Piaget's research on children's intellectual development inspired major curriculum reforms during the 1960s and 1970s. Piaget's theory of cognitive development had a major impact on preschool education (DeVries, 1990). The National Association of Young Children (NAEYC) developed and published teaching guidelines that incorporated Piaget's ideas about children's development (Bredekamp & Copple, 1997). Piaget's theory also serves as the theoretical rationale for constructivist, discovery, inquiry, and problem-oriented teaching approaches in today's classrooms. The Focus on Research box describes a constructivist approach to teaching and learning mathematics that incorporates learning principles from Piaget's theory. In this section, we discuss the implications of this theory for teaching.

Piaget believed "learning how to learn" should be the major focus of education and also that children must construct their own knowledge from interactions with their environment.

Focus on Cognitive Processes

One of the most important contributions of Piaget's work concerns the purposes and goals of education. Piaget was critical of educational approaches that emphasized the transmission and memorization of ready-made information. Such approaches, he argued, discourage children from learning to think for themselves and from developing confidence in their own thinking processes. In Piaget's view, "learning how to learn" should serve as the major focus of education, so that children can become creative, inventive, and independent thinkers. Education should "form not furnish" children's minds (Piaget, 1969, pp. 69–70).

Focus on Exploration

The second most important contribution of Piaget's research is the idea that knowledge is constructed from the child's own physical and mental activities. Piaget (1964) taught us that knowledge is not something that can simply be given to children.

Focus on Research

Learning and Teaching Mathematics: A Constructivist Approach

Piaget was very critical of the teaching of mathematics. In his view, mathematics was being taught as a set of ready-made rules and formulas. When math is taught this way, children acquire very little understanding of mathematical concepts and rules. As a result, they are unable to explain problem solutions. When asked, for example, to explain why they do the steps of a long-division problem, most fourth graders reply, "I don't know, my teacher told me to do it this way."

Terry Wood, Paul Cobb, and Erna Yackel (1992) developed a set of mathematical activities for second-grade children that were based on constructivist principles of teaching and learning. These activities were subsequently used in ten second-grade classrooms for a full year. The mathematical activities could be solved in a variety of ways. The children worked on the problem in pairs so that they could share ideas, justify answers, and resolve conflicting points of view. As children worked on problems collaboratively, the teacher observed and listened. When appropriate, the teacher intervened to offer suggestions to challenge ideas and to probe the children's thinking. Small-group work was then followed by a whole-class discussion. In this setting, children explained and shared their problem solutions. The goal of this whole-class discussion was to construct some shared meaning of the mathematical problem and its solution. The following excerpt illustrates how the class developed a "shared" understanding of commutativity:

Teacher: Okay. Can we stop a minute boys? I think we have all agreed on something that I want to get clear. We all agree that 3 times 6 is 18?

Children: Yes.

Teacher: And we agree 6 times 3 is 18?

Children: No. No. Yes. (Children begin to talk.)

SOURCE: From Sullivan Palincsar & Brown (1984).

> Knowledge is not a copy of reality. To know an object, to know an event, is not simply to look at it and make a mental copy or image of it. To know an object is to act on it. To know is to modify, to transform the object, and to understand the process of this transformation, and as a consequence to understand the way the object is constructed. (p. 8)

Piaget's theory of intellectual development has also greatly influenced mathematics and science education. Current reform efforts in these areas are guided by constructivist views of teaching and learning that are based in part on Piaget's theory. Consistent with Piaget's views, the new curriculum standards in mathematics and science education emphasize that knowledge is not simply transmitted. Students must have opportunities to experiment, to question, and to create their own meaning through their own physical and mental activities. The curriculum standards also emphasize the important role of peer interactions in children's cognitive development. Students need opportunities to share, discuss, and argue different points of view. Moreover, reform efforts in mathematics and science emphasize the role of teachers in choosing appropriate learning activities, guiding learning, and

Matt: But I will count on my fingers. (He goes to front.) Watch. 6 plus 6 is 12.

Teacher: Let's listen.

Matt: So that's two (holds up two fingers for the two 6s) and then adds 6 more on. Six (putting his thumb up then pausing to think) 12–13, 14, 15, 16, 17, 18 (counts on, using his other hand).

Teacher: Okay we have agreed on that, haven't we?

Children: Yeah.

Teacher: We've agreed that 3 times 6 is 18 and that 6 times 3 is 18, so is it possible to switch them around and still come up with the same answer?

Children: Yes.

Teacher: I think we have pretty much agreed on that, haven't we?

Children: Yes.

At the end of the school year, researchers assessed how well children in the problem-oriented mathematics curriculum performed on a standardized achievement test (Wood, Cobb, & Yackel, 1992). When compared with children who had traditional textbook instruction in mathematics, children in the problem-oriented classes did just as well on computational tests, but they scored higher on tests that measured mathematical concepts and applications. In addition, children in the problem-oriented classes were more likely to report that understanding and collaboration leads to success in mathematics, whereas children in the traditionally taught mathematics classes reported that success depended on conforming to the ideas of others, being neat, and working quietly.

stimulating children's reasoning processes. The Focus on Teaching box presents a high school biology lesson that incorporates Piaget's principles of learning.

Focus on Social Interactions

Another important contribution of Piaget's research to education concerns the role of social interactions in children's cognitive development. Piaget (1976) emphasized, "No real intellectual activity can be carried out in the form of experimental actions and spontaneous investigations without free collaboration among individuals, that is to say, among students" (pp. 107–108). For younger children, social interactions play an important role in the reduction of egocentrism. For older children, especially adolescents, interactions with peers and adults are a natural source of cognitive conflict. Through interacting with others, children clarify their views, obtain conflicting opinions, and reconcile their ideas with those of others. The equilibration processes described previously are often set into motion when children do not agree with one another.

Focus on Teaching

Learning Genetics Through Inquiry

Mrs. Johnson is planning a semester unit on how traits are inherited from one generation to the next. She believes that many important learning goals of her school's science program can be met in this unit. Mrs. Johnson wants to provide students with opportunities to understand basic principles of transmission genetics. She also wants them to appreciate how using a *mental model* is useful for understanding. She wants her students to engage in and learn the processes of inquiry as they develop their mental models, and she also wants them to understand the effect of transmission genetics on their lives and on society.

Selecting an appropriate computer program to simulate genetic events is important, because simulation will be key. In reviewing several programs, she noted several common features. Each simulation allows students to select parental phenotypes and make crosses. Offspring are produced quickly by all programs. The student will be able to simulate many generations of crosses in a single class period.

All the programs are open-ended—no answer books are provided to check answers. All the programs allow students to begin with data and to construct a model of elements and processes of an inheritance program. Students will work in teams to develop their inheritance models. Mrs. Johnson also plans to obtain reprints of Mendel's original article for students to read early in the unit. In addition to using the simulations and reading, Mrs. Johnson wants her students to be working with living organisms. She has ordered yeast strains, fruit flies, and Fast Plants. She has prepared units in genetics using each of these organisms and has adapted the units to meet the needs of the students. As the unit progresses, a genetics counselor from a local hospital will talk to the class about common genetic disorders and how such disorders are diagnosed and treated.

For the final project, each student will become an "expert" in one inherited disorder and prepare a report that discusses its inheritance pattern, symptoms, frequency, and effects. Students will present their findings as a poster, presentation, or report to be shared with their classmates and parents. Mrs. Johnson has also actively gathered information from organizations, such as March of Dimes, so students, if they choose, can become involved in service organizations focused on a particular genetic disorder.

SOURCE: From National Academy of Sciences (1996).

Social interactions can also help children develop an awareness and understanding of others. Teachers and parents can facilitate perspective-taking skills by asking children to explain how they feel when they are hurt or injured by another child. When negotiating conflict, adults can help children generate and evaluate different solutions to problems. Role taking and simulation activities are also helpful for helping children understand the perspective of others. Children's literature may be helpful as well. Adults can ask children how different characters feel about different events or to act out how a character may be feeling. Discussion and reading groups for adolescents can help them to understand that others may have feelings like them.

The Importance of Play

Piaget's theory also emphasizes the important role of play in children's development. Play is a natural way for children to learn. It is through play that children learn about the world and how to master the environment. Play is also an important window into children's cognitive and social development. Researchers indicate that forms of children's play follow Piaget's stages of cognitive development. Infants play by exploring and manipulating objects, such as shaking a rattle or kicking a mobile in their crib. Preschoolers engage in pretend, sociodramatic or fantasy play, such a pretending to be a firefighter or going on a trip. Children in the primary grades engage in a good deal of fantasy play, but as they cognitively mature they begin to prefer organized games with rules. By late childhood, children have moved away from dramatic play to games that are group oriented. Play may involve organized sports, board games, or simply hanging out with friends and listening to music.

Although children's play is often not taken seriously by adults, it has many important benefits. In infancy, play can stimulate brain development and provide the foundation for understanding causality. Through symbolic play, children express and represent their ideas, thoughts, and feelings. Play also helps to develop abstract thinking, problem solving, perspective taking, and persistence. In addition to supporting cognitive development, play has many important benefits for children's language, social, emotional, and physical development. As Maria Montessori so wisely observed, "Play is the child's work."

The Role of Learning

Although Piaget's ideas about development have influenced educational theory, there is one dimension of his theory that remains controversial. Piaget (1964) argued that "learning is subordinated to development and not vice-versa" (p. 17). Piaget's theory represents a fundamental departure from the view that learning can stimulate development. Behaviorists such as Edward Thorndike and B. F. Skinner, for example, assert that learning new information or skills can result in higher levels of cognitive functioning. As will be discussed presently, Vygotsky (1978) also proposed that "properly organized learning results in mental development and sets in motion a variety of developmental processes that would be impossible apart from learning" (p. 90). For Piaget, the stage of development limits what children can learn and how they learn. It is not possible to accelerate development through learning experiences. The following statement (Duckworth, 1964) makes this point very clear.

Unlike most of his contemporaries, Piaget believed that development controls learning more than learning controls development.

> The goal in education is not to increase the amount of knowledge, but to create the possibilities for the child to invent and to discover. When we teach too fast, we keep the child from inventing and discovering himself....Teaching means creating the situations where [mental] structures can be discovered; it does not mean transmitting structures which may be assimilated at nothing other than the verbal level (p. 3).

Unfortunately, Piaget's view on the relationship of development to learning is often interpreted to mean that the teaching of certain skills and subjects should be delayed until the child is "mentally ready." It is important to keep in mind that Piaget recognized social interactions as a factor that stimulated children's development. Piaget's point was that external stimulation of thinking can only succeed if it provokes the child to engage in assimilation and accommodation processes. It is the child's own efforts to resolve a conflict that takes him or her to a new level of cognitive functioning. Children can certainly memorize that $2 + 18 = 20$, but do they really understand that the 1 in 18 stands for ten? The Focus on Research box describes how teaching simple algorithms like "carrying" and

Focus on Research

For 20 years, Constance Kamii has observed children doing math lessons in the early primary grades. Her book *Young Children Reinvent Arithmetic* (Kamii, 2000) uses Piaget's theory to explain how children acquire number concepts. Consistent with a constructivist approach, Kamii believes that mathematical knowledge is *"constructed (created) by each child from within, in interaction with the environment"* (Kamii, 2000, p. 3). Kamii's research has shown that teaching children algorithms can "unteach" place value. This conclusion is based on interviews with three classes of second graders. One of the teachers taught algorithms (i.e., carrying and borrowing), but two did not. At the end of the school year, children were asked to solve the following problem without paper or pencil: $7 + 52 + 186 =$ _____. Children in the no-algorithm classes produced the highest number of correct answers (45 percent), and the algorithm classes produced the lowest number (12 percent). By analyzing children's *incorrect* answers, Kamii began to see the harmful effects of algorithms. Children in the algorithm classes gave answers that were not reasonable (e.g., 29, 30, 198, 938, 989, etc.) in relation to the addends given. Kamii explained that answers in the 900s were obtained by adding 7 to the 1 of 186, and carrying one from another column. Answers smaller than 186 were obtained by adding all the digits as one: $7 + 5 + 2 + 1 + 8 + 6$. In contrast, incorrect answers in the no-algorithm classes were reasonable. The children in these classes began by adding 50 to 180, then adding the 1s. They appeared to be using good number sense (i.e., the answer could not be smaller than one of the addends).

Kamii argues that encouraging young children to use algorithms to solve arithmetic problems can prevent them from developing number sense. It encourages them to give up their thinking about numbers. Adults understand that the 5 in 52 stands for 50, but children who are still acquiring a sense of place value think that the 5 means five. In this way, algorithms can "unteach" place value. Kamii has developed a series of videotapes for teaching numerical concepts using Piaget's theory:

Kamii, C. (1989). *Double-column addition: A teacher uses Piaget's theory.* [videotape]. New York: Teachers College Press.

Kamii, C. (1990). *Multidigit division. Two teachers using Piaget's theory.* [videotape]. New York: Teachers College Press.

Kamii, C. & Clark, F. B. (2000). *First graders dividing 62 by 5.* [videotape]. New York: Teachers College Press.

SOURCE: After Kamii (2000).

"borrowing" while children are acquiring an understanding of place value can undermine the development of their numerical reasoning.

According to Piaget, a better approach would be to ensure that students have numerous opportunities to group and count objects before problems are presented in a symbolic or abstract form. The task for teachers is to probe their students' current level of understanding and to determine the prerequisite experiences students need to move to a higher level of understanding. This interpretation implies that teachers should not simply wait until children are "mentally ready" to learn. They should adjust their instructional tactics to meet the levels of cognitive development they encounter.

Vygotsky's Theory of Cognitive Development

Lev Vygotsky (1896–1934) was a major figure in Russian psychology. Vygotsky provided a theory of children's development that was greatly influenced by the historical events of his time. Following the Russian Revolution in 1917, leaders of the new Soviet society emphasized the role of each person in transforming society through labor and education. Vygotsky constructed a psychological theory of development that fit the view of this new Soviet state.

Vygotsky's theory stresses relations between the individual and society. He asserted that it is not possible to understand a child's development without some understanding of the culture in which the child is raised. Vygotsky believed that an individual's thinking patterns are not due to innate factors but are products of cultural institutions and social activities. Adult society has a responsibility to share its collective knowledge with younger and less advanced members in order to promote intellectual development. Through social activities, children learn to incorporate cultural tools such as language, counting systems, writing, art, and other social inventions into their thinking. Cognitive development occurs as children internalize the products of their social interactions. According to Vygotsky's theory, both the history of the child's culture and the history of the child's own experiences are important for understanding cognitive development. This tenet in Vygotsky's theory represents a cultural-historical view of children's development.

Vygotsky's career as a psychologist was brief, due to his premature death at age 38 from tuberculosis. During his 10-year career, however, Vygotsky wrote more than 100 books and articles. His most influential book, *Thought and Language,* was not published until the year of his death. From 1936 to 1956, Vygotsky's work was banned in the Soviet Union, because it contained references to Western psychologists. Consequently, Vygotsky's work did not become widely available to researchers until the 1960s, almost 30 years after his death.

In the last two decades, Vygotsky's influence on developmental psychology has steadily grown. His views regarding the social context of learning also have a major impact on educational practices today. In the next sections, we consider the major contributions of Vygotsky's theory for understanding children's cognitive development and learning in the classroom.

Key Concepts in Vygotsky's Theory

Social Origins of Thought

Vygotsky is considered one of the earliest critics of Piaget's theory of cognitive development. In Vygotsky's view, knowledge is not individually constructed, as Piaget proposed, but socially *coconstructed* between people as they interact. Social interactions with more knowledgeable peers and adults provide the main vehicles for intellectual development. For Vygotsky, knowledge is not located in the environment nor in the child. Rather, it is situated in a particular social or cultural context. In other words, Vygotsky believed that

Vygotsky did not believe that knowledge is individually constructed, as Piaget proposed, but that it is coconstructed between people as they interact.

individual mental processes, such as remembering, problem solving, or planning, have a social origin (Wertsch & Tulviste, 1992).

According to Vygotsky, children are born with elementary mental abilities such as perception, attention, and memory. As they interact with more knowledgeable peers and adults, these "innate" abilities are transformed into higher mental functions. More specifically, Vygotsky believed that cognitive development involves the internalization of functions that first occur on what he called a *social plane*. **Internalization** refers to the process of constructing an internal representation of external physical actions or mental operations. James Wertsch (1985) described Vygotsky's ideas about the social origins of cognition in this way:

> An important point to note about Vygotsky's ideas on the social origins of cognition is that it is at this point that he uses the notion of *internalization*. He is not simply claiming that social interaction leads to the development of the child's abilities in problem solving, memory, etc.; rather, he is saying that the *very means* (especially speech) used in social interactions are taken over by the individual child and internalized. Thus, Vygotsky is making a very strong statement here about internalization and the social foundations of cognition. (p. 146; italics added)

Internalization refers to the process of forming a mental representation of external physical actions or mental operations.

A good example of this internalization process may be observed when an adult reads to a young child. For instance, a parent may point to objects on a page and count off "one," "two," "three," and so forth. The next time this parent and child read the book together, the child may point to the pictures and try to count the objects on his or her own. A very young child will have difficulty remembering the order of number tags, so the parent is likely to say the number words too. In the Vygotskian sense, the child is internalizing a way of using numbers to give meaning to a set of objects. When children begin to count off objects in the absence of a parent's prompts or assistance, then they have truly made this external operation their own. The counting operation has become a part of the children's own internal organization, and it is carried out without the support of others.

Tools for Thought

Technical tools are used to change objects or to gain mastery over the environment; psychological tools are used to organize or to control thought and behavior.

Similar to Piaget's way of thinking, Vygotsky defined cognitive development in terms of qualitative changes in children's thinking processes. However, he described these developmental changes in terms of the technical and psychological tools children use to make sense of their world. Technical tools are generally used to change objects or to gain mastery over the environment, whereas psychological tools are used to organize or control thought and behavior.

In the example described previously, the child is learning to use a counting system as a way of ordering objects. Numbers, words, and other symbol systems are different examples of psychological tools. Other examples include systems of logic, social norms and conventions, theoretical concepts, maps, literary forms, or drawings. Some examples of technical tools include pencil and paper, protractors, machines, scales, hammers, and so on. According to Vygotsky, every culture has its own set of technical and psychological tools that are passed on to children through social interactions. These cultural tools in turn shape the mind.

What are some ways children's thinking is molded by society? In the early 1900s, for instance, mothers taught their daughters to churn butter and to weave cloth by the time they reached puberty. Few young women today learn these skills. Before the availability of inexpensive calculators, students of all ages were required to memorize arithmetic facts, including square roots of numbers. Most schools today allow students to use calculators in mathematics and science classes. Currently, another technological tool, the computer, is becoming more and more common in classroom and home environments. It is interesting to consider how computers are influencing the way children and adolescents think.

Language and Development

For Vygotsky, language is the most important psychological tool influencing children's cognitive development. In Vygotsky's (1962) words, "The child's intellectual development is contingent on mastering the social means of thought, that is, language" (p. 24). He identified three different stages in children's use of language: social, egocentric, and inner speech.

In the first stage, **social speech,** language is used primarily for communicative functions. Thought and language have separate functions. Children enter the next stage of development, **egocentric speech,** when they begin to use speech to regulate their behavior and thinking. For example, many 5- and 6-year-old children talk aloud to themselves as they work on various tasks. Because children are not trying to communicate with others, these self-verbalizations are viewed as private rather than social speech. At this point in development, speech begins to serve an intellectual as well as communicative function. Berk and Garvin (1984) observed the following examples of *private speech* in an Appalachian mission school for low-income children aged 5 to 10 years old.

> [Student] O. Sits down at the art table and says to himself, "I want to draw something. Let's see. I need a big piece of paper. I want to draw my cat."

> [Student] C., working in her arithmetic workbook says out loud to no one in particular, "Six." Then counting on her fingers she continues, "Seven, eight, nine, ten. It's ten, it's ten. The answer's ten." (p. 277)

In Vygotsky's last stage of speech development, **inner speech,** children internalize egocentric speech. They use language internally to guide their thinking and behavior. At this stage, children can think about problem solutions and action sequences by manipulating language "in their heads."

Zone of Proximal Development

One of the most important contributions of Vygotsky's theory to psychology and education is the *zone of proximal development.* Vygotsky (1978) was interested in children's *potential* for intellectual growth rather than their *actual* level of development. The **zone of proximal development** includes those functions that are in the process of developing but not yet fully developed.

> The zone of proximal development defines those functions that have not yet matured but are in the process of maturation, functions that will mature tomorrow but are currently in an embryonic state. These functions could be termed the "buds" or "flowers" of development rather than the "fruits" of development. The actual development level characterizes mental development retrospectively, while the zone of proximal development characterizes mental development prospectively. (pp. 86–87)

In practice, the zone of proximal development represents the gap between what children can do on their own and what they can do with the assistance of others, as illustrated in Figure 3.10. For example, a 6-year-old might have difficulty assembling a model airplane alone, but with the assistance and guidance of an older, more experienced sibling, the child can successfully complete the task.

Vygotsky identified three stages—social, egocentric, and inner speech—in a child's use of language.

Vygotsky's zone of proximal development is the gap between cognitive activities children can do on their own and what they can do with the assistance of others.

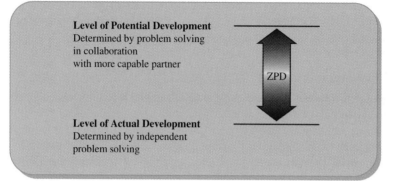

FIGURE 3.10

Zone of Proximal Development

SOURCE: After Hamilton & Ghatala (1994).

In the example presented at the beginning of the chapter about boiling tap water, the students are acquiring a more sophisticated understanding of their science experiment with the teacher's guidance. Note that the teacher is not telling students what they should learn from the experiment. He is guiding their thinking through the use of questions (What happens when the water is boiled?) and prompts (Think about density.). At the end of the discussion, the students can use what they learned from the experiment to make hypotheses about other liquids. As a result, the students are thinking about the experiment at a level that was not evident when they were carrying out the experiment on their own.

Vygotsky assumed that interactions with adults and peers in the zone of proximal development help children to move to a higher level of functioning. We will examine how adults can help "build scaffolds" for children when we consider the educational implications of Vygotsky's theory.

Contrasts Between Piaget's and Vygotsky's Theories

There are several important differences in the basic assumptions of Vygotsky's and Piaget's theories. Both theorists agree that knowledge must be mentally constructed by the child, but Vygotsky placed a much stronger emphasis on the role of social interactions in this construction process. To Vygotsky, the construction of knowledge is not an individual process. Rather, it is primarily a social process in which higher mental functions are products of socially mediated activity. Collaborative learning and problem solving are the main vehicles of cognitive change.

Compared with Piaget, Vygotsky also placed a stronger emphasis on culture in shaping children's cognitive development. As children develop, they learn to use tools for thought that are valued by their culture. There are no universal patterns of development because cultures emphasize different kinds of tools, intellectual skills, and social conventions. The intellectual skills needed for survival in a highly technical society differ from those needed for survival in a largely agrarian society.

Another important difference between Piaget's and Vygotsky's views concerns the importance placed on learning. As we know, Piaget believed that cognitive development limits what children are capable of learning from social experiences. It is not possible to accelerate development through learning experiences. Although Vygotsky (1978) agreed that learning is not the same as development, he argued that "learning is a necessary and universal aspect of the process of developing culturally organized, specifically human, psychological functions" (p. 90). Vygotsky believed instruction (both formal and informal) by more knowledgeable peers or adults is at the heart of cognitive development. Vygotsky believed that learning precedes development.

In addition, Vygotsky's zone of proximal development offers a very different view of readiness than the one provided by Piaget's theory. According to Piaget, children's readiness for learning is defined by their existing level of competence and knowledge. If a teacher attempts to teach a concept or operation before a child is mentally ready, it can result in what Piaget called "empty learning." In contrast, Vygotsky (1978) argued that instruction should be directed toward children's potential level of development, the level of competence they can demonstrate with the assistance and guidance of others. In his words, "The only 'good learning' is that which is in advance of the child's development" (p. 89).

Finally, Vygotsky and Piaget had very different opinions about the role of language in development. In Piaget's view, the egocentric speech of young children reflects the child's inability to take the perspective of others. It plays no useful role in their development. Thinking processes develop from children's actions on objects, not from talking. Vygotsky, on the other hand, thought that egocentric speech is an extremely important developmental phenomenon. He believed that egocentric speech helps children organize and regulate their thinking. When children talk to themselves, they are trying to solve problems and think on their own. According to Vygotsky, egocentric speech, or private speech, is the means by which children move from being regulated by others (other-regulated) to being regulated by their own thinking processes (self-regulated). Egocentric speech has both an intellectual and a self-regulatory function for young children.

> *Vygotsky believed that learning precedes development and is the product of social interactions shaped by one's cultural tools.*

Limitations of Vygotsky's Theory

Vygotsky's theory helps us to understand the how cognition and learning is a social collaborative process with others (Rogoff, 1998). This theory represents a radical departure from Piaget's view that cognition is an individual activity, and, as described below, it has important implications for education. Nevertheless, Vygotsky's theory has some important limitations that need to be considered. First, Vygotsky's theory places much less emphasis on physical maturation or innate biological processes than most other developmental theories. We have learned that development involves a complex interaction of genetic and environment influences. Additionally, little attention was given to what is meant by learning and development in this perspective. In Vygotsky's view, development involves changes in the child's participation in social activities; however, the cognitive processes that enable this transformation to occur have not been clearly specified. For example, what cognitive changes enable the child to move from an assisted reader to an independent reader? As discussed in Chapter 5, this transformation involves attention and memory processes, as well as social interactions that support reading efforts.

Educational Contributions of Vygotsky's Theory

Vygotsky regarded education as central to the development of children (Moll, 1990). In the introduction to Vygotsky's *Thought and Language* (1962), Jerome Bruner wrote, "Vygotsky's conception of development is at the same time a theory of education" (p. v). Although seven of Vygotsky's first eight writings in psychology (written between 1922 and 1926) addressed educational issues, his work is only beginning to have a significant impact on education in the United States (Moll, 1990; Newman, Griffin, & Cole, 1989; Tharp & Gallimore, 1989). This section examines the educational implications and applications of Vygotsky's theory.

The Role of Private Speech

In Vygotsky's theory, **private speech** serves an important self-regulatory function. It is the means by which children guide their own thinking and behavior. Children engage in overt self-regulatory speech before they use covert, inner speech. As children make this transition in the early grades, they need learning activities that permit them to talk aloud as they are solving problems and completing tasks.

In Vygotsky's theory, egocentric speech is the means by which children move from being regulated by others to being self-regulated by their own thinking.

Observations of children in classroom settings provide clear support for Vygotsky's claim that private speech plays an important role in learning. For example, Berk and Garvin (1984) observed the frequency and variety of private speech among 5- to 10-year-olds in a school setting. They observed an average of 30 private utterances per hour. Interestingly, there were no age differences in the quantity of private speech observed, and, for all age groups, private speech increased when students completed cognitively demanding tasks without an adult present. In another study, Berk (1986) observed the frequency of private speech in first- and third-grade mathematics classes. She reported that nearly 98 percent of the children talked aloud to themselves as they worked on math problems. Furthermore, this task-related private speech was positively related to mathematics achievement in the early grades.

As children mature, task-related vocalizations are gradually transformed into quiet whispers until they are internalized as inner speech. Private speech in the form of self-guiding statements or reading aloud declines by the age of 10. However, some studies suggest that older students can continue to benefit from the use of self-instructional strategies, especially if they lack an ability to regulate their behavior or thinking.

Donald Meichenbaum's (1977) program of **cognitive behavior modification** uses self-regulatory speech to help children control and regulate their behavior. Children are taught self-regulatory strategies that can be used as a verbal tool to inhibit impulses, control frustration, and promote reflection. The training program generally begins with an adult performing a task while talking aloud *(cognitive modeling)*. Next, a child performs the same task under the guidance of an adult who encourages the child to talk aloud as he or she works on the task *(overt guidance)* and reinforces the child for using the modeled strategies. When children in this program become proficient in the use of cognitive strategies and overt self-instructions, they are encouraged to perform the task while guiding their behavior by way of whispering the instructions to themselves *(faded self-guidance)* or by internal speech *(covert self-instruction)*. Following is an example of a training protocol for a line drawing task that was first modeled by an adult and eventually used by a child (Meichenbaum & Goodman, 1971):

> Okay, what is it that I have to do? You want me to copy the picture with the different lines. I have to go carefully and slowly. Okay, draw the line down, down, good; then to the right, that's it; now down some more and to the left. Good. I'm doing fine so far. Remember, go slowly. Now back up again. No, I was supposed to go down. That's okay. Just erase the line carefully. . . . Good. Even if I make an error I can go on slowly and carefully. I have to go down now. Finished. I did it! (p. 117)

Self-instructional training has been used successfully to improve self-management skills and self-control in impulsive and aggressive children (Manning, 1988; Camp, Blom, Hebert, & van Doornick, 1977; Neilens & Israel, 1981). These techniques also show promise for improving children's writing skills, reading comprehension, and mathematics achievement (Harris & Graham, 1985; Meichenbaum & Asarno, 1978; Schunk & Cox, 1986). In sum, considerable research suggests that private speech is a valuable tool for learning. Because private speech is important for the development of self-regulatory processes, teachers need to model self-instructional strategies and to encourage students' use of task-related verbalizations when they are having difficulty in the classroom.

The Importance of Adult Guidance and Scaffolding

Vygotsky's theory emphasized the critical role of adults in guiding and supporting children's intellectual development. Through the social guidance provided by others, children can function at a higher level of development, their zone of proximal development. Several researchers have studied the processes by which adults guide children's participation in the zone of proximal development. We will examine two different but closely related conceptions of this social process—guided participation and scaffolding.

Barbara Rogoff (1990) used the term **guided participation** to describe the mutual involvement between children and their social partners in collective activities. Guided participation has three phases: choosing and structuring activities to fit the skills and interests of children; supporting and monitoring children's participation in activities; and adjusting the level of support provided as children begin to perform the activity independently. The goal of guided participation is to transfer responsibility for the task from the skilled partner to the child.

Rogoff and her colleagues (1984) observed many examples of guided participation in a study of mothers assisting 6- and 9-year-old children to perform two different classification tasks in the laboratory. The tasks resembled either a home activity (i.e., sorting food items onto shelves) or a school activity (i.e., sorting photographs of objects into abstract categories). The mothers used a variety of techniques to guide their child's participation in these activities. For example, some mothers connected the food sorting task to putting groceries away at home. Other mothers used subtle gestures (pointing, looking, etc.) and verbal cues to guide their child's participation.

Most significantly, Rogoff and her colleagues found that mothers adjusted their level of support according to their perceptions of the child's ability to handle the task. For example, mothers of 6-year-olds provided more formal instruction in the school task than mothers of 8-year-olds. Age differences in the level of support provided by mothers were less evident in the more familiar home task. In addition, as the children showed they could handle more of the task on their own, the mothers provided less instruction, but when the children began to make errors, this instructional support reappeared. This sensitive adjustment of support is perhaps the most significant aspect of guided participation, because it enables the child to gradually assume more responsibility for managing the activity.

Rogoff's notion of guided participation is closely related to the concept of *scaffolding*. Jerome Bruner and his associates (Wood, Bruner, & Ross, 1976) introduced this term before Vygotsky's work was widely known in the United States. Similar to guided participation, **scaffolding** refers to the process by which adults provide support to a child who is learning to master a task or problem. When adults scaffold a task or problem, they perform or direct those elements of the task that are beyond the child's ability.

Scaffolding can take the form of verbal or physical assistance. For example, a father who is building a birdhouse with his 7-year-old daughter might help guide her hands while she saws and nails the pieces of wood. The daughter is not yet able to perform these activities on her own, but with her father's assistance, she can participate meaningfully in the activity. At a later point, the father may assist his daughter in another woodworking task by providing verbal reminders ("Remember how I taught you to hold the hammer.") or by providing feedback ("This piece of wood needs to be sanded some more before you paint it."). With practice and time, the daughter will learn to perform woodworking activities more and more independently.

Guided participation and scaffolding both involve adults' helping children perform some task they could not perform without help and then gradually withdrawing help as the children become more proficient.

Vygotsky's theory of development emphasized the importance of adults in guiding and supporting children's learning. Less guidance is needed as children learn to perform activities on their own.

In a classic study, Wood, Bruner, and Ross (1976) studied an adult's role in helping a child move from joint to independent problem solving. Female tutors, who were given no special training, were asked to build a pyramid from interlocking wooden blocks with 3-, 4-, and 5-year-old children. By observing this joint problem-solving activity, the researchers identified six important elements of the scaffolding process. These are shown in Figure 3.11.

In summary, the concepts of guided participation and scaffolding were both inspired by Vygotsky's theory of development. Both processes are powerful teaching tools at home and school. In the classroom, these processes can take the form of demonstrating skills; leading students through the steps of a complicated problem; breaking a complex task into sub-tasks; doing part of the problem as a group; asking questions to help students diagnose errors; and providing detailed feedback (Rosenshine & Meister, 1992). Keep in mind, however, that teachers need to gradually pass more and more control of the activity to the child. By relinquishing control, the teacher enables the child to engage in independent and self-regulated learning.

Reciprocal Teaching

One of the best applications of Vygotsky's theory is the **reciprocal teaching** model developed by Annemarie Palincsar and Ann Brown (1984). The model was originally designed to help poor readers acquire comprehension skills. In this program, teachers and students take turns being the discussion leader. Through collaborative learning dialogues, children learn how to regulate their own reading comprehension. The reciprocal teaching procedure has been used successfully with both elementary and secondary school students.

The program starts out with adults or teachers serving as the leaders and modeling how to lead the discussion. The leader is responsible for asking questions that require students to summarize material, detect inconsistencies, and make predictions about what will

1. **Recruitment.** The adult elicits the child's interest in accomplishing the intended goal of the activity. This function is particularly important for learners who are not able to keep the goal in mind.

2. **Demonstrating solutions.** The adult demonstrates or models a more appropriate form of a solution than was originally performed by the child. Children are much more likely to perform those acts they can already do.

3. **Simplifying the task.** The adult breaks the task into a set of subroutines that the child can successfully complete on his or her own.

4. **Maintaining participation.** The adult provides encouragement and keeps the student oriented toward the goal of the activity.

5. **Providing feedback.** The adult provides feedback that identifies discrepancies between what the student is doing and what is required to successfully complete the task.

6. **Controlling frustration.** The adult helps control frustration and risk in finding problem solutions.

FIGURE 3.11

Elements of the Scaffolding Process

SOURCE: After Wood, Bruner, & Ross (1976).

happen next. Students carry out simpler aspects of the task while observing and learning from the adult. As the students develop their comprehension skills, the teacher increases his or her demands, requiring students to participate at slightly more challenging levels. Eventually, students assume the leader's position, and the teacher acts more as a coach than as a model. During the course of training, student questions become more and more sophisticated. The Focus on Research box compares the quality of reciprocal teaching dialogue on day 3 and day 13 of the program.

Palincsar and Brown's instructional program incorporates several features of Vygotsky's theory. First, group discussions allow less competent students to perform at levels slightly above their current level of competence or at their zone of proximal development. Second, the learning situation is carefully scaffolded by the adult. The teacher continues to push for deeper understanding and to provide instructional support for less able students but then "fades into the background when students demonstrate they can take over" (Brown & Campione, 1990, p. 119). Finally, the meaning of the text is socially negotiated and constructed in the context of group discussions.

Studies reported by Palincsar and Brown (1984) indicate that the reciprocal teaching procedure leads to substantial improvements in seventh-grade students' comprehension skills. Additionally, the students maintained the effects of the program for at least 8 weeks. Even more important, the training generalized to other subject areas. The students who participated in the program showed a better understanding of science and social studies materials they read in their classroom. Thus, the internalization of strategies learned in the reciprocal teaching program allowed students to better monitor and regulate their comprehension in other learning situations as well.

The Role of Peer Interactions

Both Piaget and Vygotsky emphasized the importance of peers in children's cognitive development. Following Piaget's theory, children can influence each other's cognitive development when they say or do something that is in conflict with the other child's thinking. Cognitive conflict leads children to restructure their thinking *(accommodate)* in order to restore a balance *(equilibration)*. By comparison, researchers examining peer interactions from a Vygotskian perspective have argued that children influence each other's development

Focus on Research

Day 3

TEXT (read silently):

Can Snakes Sting with their Tongues? No—snakes' tongues are completely harmless. They're used for feeling things and for sharpening the snakes' sense of smell. Although snakes can smell in the usual way, the tongue flickering in the air picks up tiny particles of matter. These particles are deposited in two tiny cavities at the base of the nostrils to increase the snake's ability to smell.

1. A: Do snakes' tongues sting?

2. K: Sometimes.

3. A: Correct. This paragraph is about do snakes sting with their tongue, and different ways that the tongue is used for and the senses of smell.

4. T: Are there any questions?

5. C: Snakes' tongues don't sting.

6. T: Beautiful! I thought, boy, I must have been doing some fast reading there because I missed that point. A, could you ask your question again?

7. A: Do snakes' tongues really sting?

8. T: Now, A, since you have asked the question, can you find in that paragraph where the question is answered?

9. A: No, snakes' tongues are completely harmless.

10. T: So we'll try again. Can you generate another question that you think a teacher might ask?

11. A: What are the tongues used for?

12. T: Good!

through the process of collaboration (Tudge & Rogoff, 1989). The following example illustrates how one student can help guide the thinking of another student while working on a lever task in fifth-grade science.

Hank: Ready? Do you want to hold the lever?

Lester: Yeah.

Day 13

TEXT (read silently):

The second oldest form of salt production is mining. Unlike early methods that made the work extremely dangerous and difficult, today's methods use special machinery, and salt mining is easier and safer. The old expression "back to the salt mine" no longer applies.

1. L: Name two words that often describe mining salt in the old days.

2. K: Back to the salt mines?

3. L: No. Angela?

4. A: Dangerous and difficult.

5. L: Correct. This paragraph is about comparing the old mining of salt and today's mining of salt.

6. T: Beautiful.

7. L: I have a prediction to make.

8. T: Good.

9. L: I think it might tell when salt was first discovered, well, it might tell what salt is made of and how it's made.

10. T: O.K. Can we have another leader?

L = Indicates discussion leader

T = Indicates adult teacher

A, B, C, K, and L are seventh-grade students with reading comprehension skills 2 years below grade level.

SOURCE: After Palincsar & Brown (1984).

Hank: Now, let's wait a sec. Let's make sure that we're setting everything up right. Now, that [spring scale] goes on the 4 and the block goes on 5. [Lester begins adjusting the scale.]

Hank: I'll tell you when it's level. You just have to pull. You have to pull real hard. OK. A little bit more, pull a little bit more. OK, stop. You got it. Great. (Jones & Carter, 1994, pp. 613–614)

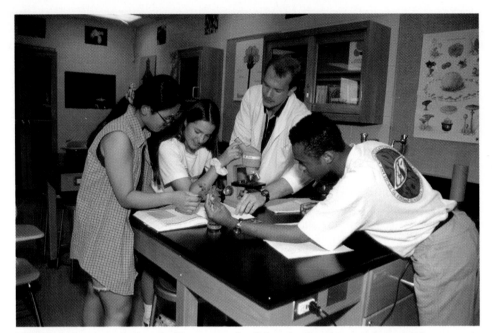

SOURCE: Bill Whitman.

Vygotsky's theory emphasizes the importance of collaborative learning experiences with peers.

From a Vygotskian perspective, collaborative problem solving among peers offers some of the same experiences for children as adult-child interactions. When children work jointly on problems, they must come to some mutual understanding of the problem, procedures, and solution. Children use speech to guide each other's activities, and these social interactions are gradually internalized as tools for regulating independent problem-solving efforts in the future.

To study the processes by which peers influence learning and development, Jonathan Tudge (1993) paired nonconservers with conservers on a mathematical balance beam problem. The results showed that the less competent partner improved significantly on the balance beam task when paired with a peer who could reason about the problem at a more advanced level. This study also suggested that the less competent partner needed to adopt the reasoning of the more competent partner while performing the task. That is, mere exposure to a higher level of thinking did not lead to improvements in the less competent partner's use of problem-solving rules. Of even greater importance was the finding that there were some circumstances under which children's thinking may be adversely affected by a peer. This decline is most likely to occur when children are not provided any feedback after working on a problem or when they are not confident about their reasoning. Under these conditions, children's thinking may be negatively influenced by social interactions that are slightly behind their current level of thinking (Tudge, 1993).

Although Tudge's study provides support for Vygotsky's ideas about the cognitive benefits of peer interactions, it also suggests that teachers need to carefully structure the conditions under which children work together. In a review of Vygotskian research related to the effects of peer interactions on development, Tudge and Rogoff (1989) conclude:

> **1.** Young children may show limited cognitive benefits from peer interactions, because they are unable to provide each other the type of scaffolded assistance or guidance that older children and adults can provide.

Piaget believed peer interaction stimulates thinking by creating cognitive conflict situations; Vygotsky believed peer interaction stimulates thinking through cognitive cooperation.

Applying Piaget's and Vygotsky's Theories in the Classroom

Applications of Piaget's Theory

- Provide opportunities for students to communicate through symbols—art, writing, drama, mathematical formulas, and so on.
- Provide a range of "real world" experiences to serve as foundations for building new concepts, and provide opportunities for children to choose activities of interest to them.
- For young learners, use concrete objects, visual aids, and other teaching tools (videotapes, geoboards, unifix cubes) for teaching abstract and unfamiliar concepts.
- Provide opportunities for students to explore, experiment, apply knowledge, and to engage in "hands on" learning.
- Ask students to explain their reasoning and help them to find inconsistencies. Suggest alternative explanations to consider.
- Provide opportunities for students to express opinions, discuss, debate, and receive feedback from peers.

Applications of Vygotsky's Theory

- Use guided participation in which students can be apprentices in learning. Use modeling and verbal cues to guide students' learning, gradually giving the students more responsibility for carrying out the learning activity on their own.
- Model "thinking aloud" when problem solving with students, and encourage students to "talk themselves" through challenging problems.
- Provide opportunities for students to collaborate on learning activities together. Peers are important role models for problem solving, and learning is facilitated when there are opportunities to explain ideas and resolve controversies with other students. Interactions with equal or more skilled peers have the most positive benefits.
- Direct learning and assessment toward students' *zone of proximal development*. By providing sufficient instructional supports (cues, suggestions, assistance), help students perform challenging tasks. Gradually withdraw the support when they are able to perform the task on their own.

2. Adult-child interactions may be more beneficial than peer interactions when children are first learning new skills or concepts.
3. Peer interactions are most effective when partners must achieve a shared understanding of a topic or problem and work toward a shared goal.

Putting Piaget's and Vygotsky's Theories Together

We have examined important distinctions between Piaget's and Vygotsky's theories; now it is time to consider some common themes in this last section. As we have discussed, both theories serve as the foundation for constructivist approaches in education. Piaget and Vygotsky both believed that cognitive development involved changes in children's abilities to represent knowledge in terms of more abstract forms such as symbols, logical rules, principles, concepts, and so forth. Both theorists also emphasize that children are not passive recipients of knowledge. Piaget focused on how children constructed knowledge by ordering, transforming, and reorganizing existing knowledge, whereas Vygotsky described how children constructed internal representations of mental operations learned through social interactions with adults and peers. Finally, both theories maintain that teachers serve as important organizers, stimulators, guides, and supporters of learning. The Focus on Teaching box on the previous page summarizes some ways the two theories can be applied in the classroom.

Chapter Summary

www.mhhe.com/meece

Constructive Approaches to Education

- Piaget's and Vygotsky's theories of cognitive development provide the psychological foundations for constructivist approaches to teaching and learning. Constructivists believe that children must form their own understanding of the world in which they live. Adults help guide this knowledge construction process by providing structure and support.

- Both Piaget's and Vygotsky's theories of cognitive development are concerned with qualitative changes in children's thinking. Piaget argued that cognitive development involved major transformations in the way knowledge is organized. Vygotsky believed that cognitive development represented changes in the cultural tools children use to make sense of their world.

Piaget's Theory of Cognitive Development

- Piaget proposed that two basic principles guide children's intellectual development: organization and adaptation. As children mature, their knowledge schemes are integrated and reorganized into more complex systems that are better adapted to their environment. Adaptation of knowledge schemes occurs through the process of assimilation and accommodation. Through the process of assimilation, children mold information to fit existing knowledge structures. Through the process of accommodation, children change their schemes to restore a state of equilibrium. The process of assimilation and accommodation explains changes in cognition at all ages.

- Piaget proposed that development follows an invariant sequence. The early childhood years are characterized by two stages. During the sensorimotor period (birth to 2 years), children acquire schemes for goal-directed behavior and object permanence. In the preoperational stage (2 to 7 years), children begin to use words, numbers, gestures, and images to represent objects in their environment. Children also begin to form intuitive theories to explain events in their environment that can have a lasting influence on learning. The major limitations of preoperational thinking are egocentrism, centration, and rigidity of thinking.

- The elementary and secondary school years are characterized by two additional stages. During the concrete operational stage (7 to 11 years), children begin to use mental operations to think about events and objects in their environment. The mental operations that appear in this stage are classification, seriation, and conservation. These mental operations can only be applied to concrete stimuli that are present in the child's environment. In the last stage of cognitive development, formal operations (11 years to adult), adolescents and adults can think about abstract objects, events, and concepts. They develop the ability to use propositional logic, inductive and deductive logic, and combinatorial reasoning. Formal operational thinkers are also able to reflect on their own thinking processes.

- Piaget's theory has generated a lot of controversy and criticism. Concerns have been raised about Piaget's research methods, the adequacy of the equilibration model for explaining developmental changes, and the universality of Piaget's stages. Nevertheless, Piaget's research provides a rich description of children's thinking at different ages.

- Neo-Piagetian theories have attempted to add greater specificity to Piaget's theory, while maintaining its basic assumptions that cognitive development is qualitative and stagelike. Neo-Piagetian theorists examine the role of children's information processing capabilities in explaining developmental changes.

- Piaget's theory has inspired major curriculum reforms, and it continues to have an important influence on education practice today. Among Piaget's major contributions to education are the ideas that (a) knowledge must be actively constructed by the child; (b) educators should help children learn how to learn; (c) learning activities should be matched to the child's level of conceptual development; and (d) peer interactions play an important role in the child's cognitive development. Piaget's theory also emphasizes the role of teachers in the learning process as organizers, collaborators, stimulators, and guides.

Vygotsky's Theory of Cognitive Development

- When compared with Piaget, Vygotsky places a stronger emphasis on social interactions. Knowledge is not individually constructed, but coconstructed between two people. Remembering, problem solving, planning, and abstract thinking have a social origin.

- In Vygotsky's theory, elementary cognitive functions are transformed into higher mental functions through interactions with more knowledgeable adults and peers. Internalization refers to the process of constructing an internal (cognitive) representation of physical actions or mental operations that first occur in social interactions. Through internalizing elements of social interactions, children develop ways of regulating their own behavior and thinking.

- Vygotsky described developmental changes in children's thinking in terms of the cultural tools they use to make sense of their world. Technical tools are generally used to change objects or to gain mastery over the environment, whereas psychological tools are used to organize behavior or thought. In Vygotsky's view, society shapes the child's mind through the transmission of tools that are appropriate for functioning in that culture. The history of both the culture and the child's experiences are important for understanding cognitive development.

- Vygotsky believed that language was the most important psychological tool that influences children's cognitive development. He identified three different stages in children's use of language. At first, language is primarily used for communication (social speech). Next, children begin to use egocentric or private speech to regulate their own thinking. Talking aloud or whispering while performing a task are forms of private speech. In the last stage of language development, children use inner speech (verbal thoughts) to guide their thinking and actions.

- Vygotsky used the term *zone of proximal development* to refer to the difference between what children can do on their own and with the assistance of others. If an adult or peer carefully provides an appropriate level of support and guidance, children are generally able to perform at a higher level than they can perform on their own. Vygotsky assumed that interactions with adults and peers in the zone of proximal development help children move to higher levels of mental functioning.

Putting Piaget's and Vygotsky's Theories Together

- There are several important distinctions between Piaget's and Vygotsky's theories. The most important ones for educators concern the role of language and learning in development. Whereas Piaget believed that egocentric speech plays no useful function in young children's development, Vygotsky argued that egocentric speech is the means by which children organize and regulate their thoughts and actions. With regard to learning, Piaget claimed that development limits what children are capable of learning from social experiences. For Vygotsky, instruction by more knowledgeable peers or adults is at the heart of cognitive development.

- Vygotsky's writings are beginning to have a major impact on education in the United States. Among the major educational contributions of Vygotsky's theory are the role of private speech in cognitive development, the importance of guided participation and scaffolding, and the role of peer interactions in cognitive development. Palincsar and Brown developed the reciprocal teaching procedure that incorporates several features of Vygotsky's theory. This procedure has been used successfully with elementary and secondary students.

Key Terms

accommodation (p. 124)

adaptation (p. 123)

animism (p. 130)

assimilation (p. 123)

circular reactions (p. 126)

centration (p. 134)

cognitive behavior modification (p. 160)

collective monologues (p. 134)

combinatorial reasoning (p. 143)

concrete operations (p. 135)

conservation (p. 138)

constructivist approach (p. 121)

egocentricism (p. 134)

egocentric speech (p. 157)

equilibration (p. 124)

formal operations (p. 141)

guided participation (p. 161)

hierarchical classification (p. 137)

horizontal decalage (p. 141)

hypothetico-deductive thinking (p. 142)

internalization (p. 156)

logico-mathematical knowledge (p. 122)

matrix classification (p. 137)

metacognition (p. 134)

object permanence (p. 126)

physical knowledge (p. 122)

preoperational stage (p. 128)

propositional logic (p. 141)

realism (p. 134)

reciprocal teaching (p. 162)

reflective abstraction (p. 123)

representational thinking (p. 128)

schemes (p. 122)

sensorimotor stage (p. 125)

seriation (p. 136)

social knowledge (p. 123)

social speech (p. 157)

zone of proximal development (p. 157)

Activities

1. Piaget used many different tasks to study children's logic while performing operations such as seriation, classification, and conservation. The purpose of this activity is to examine how elementary school children of different ages perform Piagetian tasks. Three simple tasks are described below. Using these tasks, individually test two kindergartners and two third graders, and then compare their responses. Be sure to ask children to explain their responses, to get at their logic and reasoning. If you do these activities at school, you will need the teacher's permission. After collecting your data, answer the following questions: (a) Which tasks were the kindergarten and third-grade children able to solve correctly? (b) How do the kindergarten children's responses reflect the limitations of preoperational thinking? (c) What types of cognitive operations did the third-grade students use in solving the problems? (d) How did your observations help you understand Piaget's theory of cognitive development?

Task 1: Seriation

Use 5 to 10 sticks or strips of paper that vary in length from 1 to 10 inches. Begin by asking students to place 3 sticks in order, then 5 sticks, and add 2 more sticks until the student is unable to perform the task. Be sure to mix up the sticks each time, and record the students' responses.

Task 2: Conservation of Number

Use 12 coins of the same denomination (all pennies or dimes). Place 6 coins in one row about a half inch apart, and place the other 6 coins below the first row. Ask the students if the number of coins in each row is the same or different, and then ask, "How do you know?" Next, spread out the coins in the first row, so that each coin is several inches from the others. Ask the students again if the number of coins in each row is the same or different. Again ask, "How do know?" and record the students' responses.

Task 3: Multiple Classification

Cut out geometric shapes (triangles, squares, and circles) from red, blue, and yellow construction paper (3 colors per shape). Ask the students to sort the cutouts that go together into different piles. Record how the students sort the cutouts. Now, ask the students if there is another way the cutouts can be sorted, and record how they do the second sort.

2. Observe two or three small groups of children working on a common task. Record the way in which the children help one another to perform the task. After completing your observations, answer the following questions.

   a. Did you see evidence of the students directing, monitoring, or assisting one another?

   b. How did the children negotiate roles? Did one student assume responsibility for leading the activity?

   c. Did you see evidence of scaffolding by the children or teacher? If so, describe some examples of this scaffolding.

   d. How did this activity help you understand Vygotsky's concept of the zone of proximal development?

3. Obtain permission to observe an elementary or secondary classroom (any subject) in a local school. Observe three to four lessons in each classroom, and identify the questions or problems that pose difficulty for the students. Describe the problems in your observational notes. After collecting your observations, use Piaget's theory of

cognitive development to analyze the problems students encountered in their lessons. Use the following questions to analyze your notes.

a. How are the problems related to limitations in the students' concrete or formal operational thinking?

b. What type of instructional support or scaffolding was available to help students when they were having difficulty?

c. How did this observation help you understand different aspects of concrete or formal operational thinking?

4. To assess students' formal operational thinking, individually test two middle school students and two high school students using the Piagetian tasks described below. Be sure to use mixed-gender groups at each level. Ask students to think aloud as they do the problems, and record their responses. If you do these tasks in a local school, you will need the teacher's permission. After collecting your data, answer the following questions:

a. How did the students approach each task? Did they have a systematic plan that considered all possible solutions or combinations. In task 1, did they systematically manipulate each variable and test its effect?

b. What differences did you observe between the responses of the younger and older adolescents? Did you see evidence of formal operational reasoning in either group, both groups, or neither group of adolescents? Do your observations support Piaget's theory?

c. Did you find evidence of gender differences in students' responses? How would you account for these findings?

Task 1: Pendulum Problem

For this task, you will need three different lengths of string and four different weights that can be attached to the string. Instruct your students to experiment with the string and weights in order to determine which variable(s) makes the pendulum go faster or slower. They should consider four variables: the length of the string, the different weights, the force of the initial push, and the height at which they let go of the pendulum.

Task 2: Sandwich Combinations

For this task, you need to write on a piece of paper four different breads (white, rye, sourdough, and wheat), four different meats (ham, beef, turkey, and salami), and four different spreads (mayonnaise, mustard, butter, and ketchup). For each sandwich, they can only use one bread, one meat, and one spread. Ask your students to figure out how many different sandwich combinations they can make. The students may want to use pencil and paper for this task.

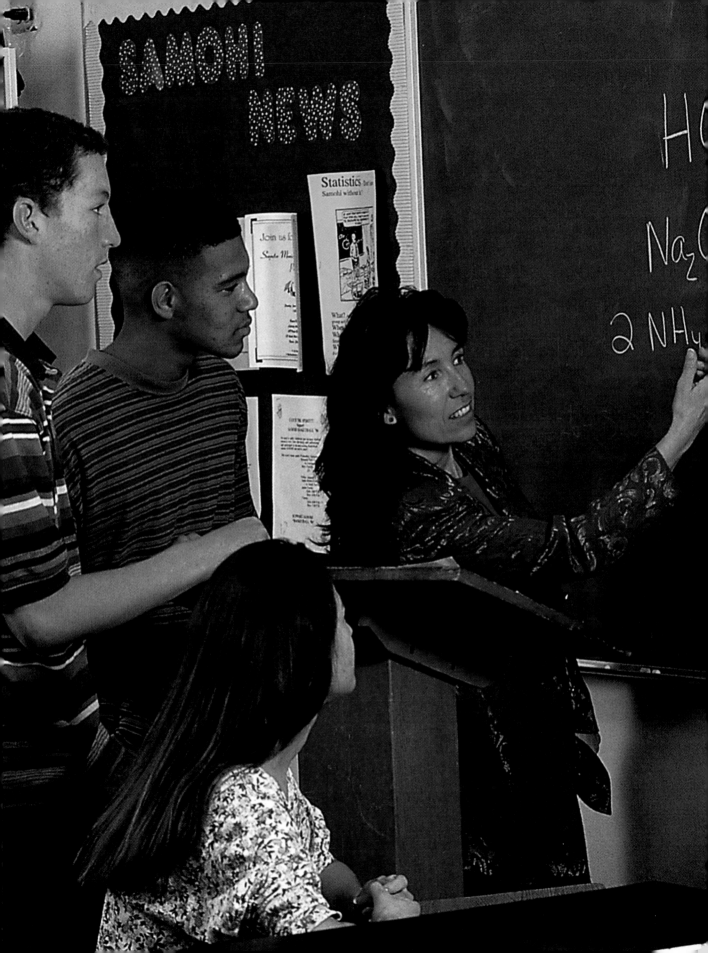

Chapter 4

Cognitive Development: Information Processing and Intelligence Theories

Mr. Johnson is a high school teacher at a local private school for girls. He has taught for 6 years and prefers to teach lower-ability students. In the following interview, Mr. Johnson (MJ) discusses his approach to teaching mathematics with a student intern (S):

MJ: I think of myself as a high school teacher who teaches mathematics rather than as a mathematics teacher who teaches high school. Because I work with students who are not very good in mathematics, I work very hard getting them to break down problems into smaller steps and to see overlaps between different types of problems. I want them to understand the structure of lessons and problems. I also want them to work on their skills for getting support, such as using the textbook, seeing the teacher outside of class, using other students to get help, and learning to formulate good questions. So I am trying to get my students to pay attention to their own learning and thought processes.

S: How much variability do you see in your students' mathematics abilities?

MJ: Within any one classroom, my students range from very high to average ability, but it is possible to teach to that range of students. I find ways to encourage both low- and high-ability students to participate in the lesson.

Chapter opener photo: David Young-Wolff/PhotoEdit, Inc.

S: *Is it hard for you to teach this way?*

MJ: *It took a fair amount of trial and error on my part. As a beginning teacher, I spent most of my time just talking at the class. With time, I learned how to get students actively involved in the lesson and this made learning more interesting and enjoyable for everyone.*

S: *What do you think explains the variation in your students' abilities?*

MJ: *One of my students has low ability for mathematics, which is complicated by a learning disability. I came to this conclusion after talking to her parents and looking at her record. Physical structures, like the two sides of the equal sign, are very hard for her, because she cannot hold onto that separation very well. This student has good parental support and good academic support in terms of extra work outside the classroom but has found mathematics very frustrating and difficult since late elementary school. The better students in my classes tend to have an overall sense of self-confidence, which distinguishes them from the average students. They are more willing to try out their own ideas. It seems to me that over the course of their lives, they have gotten more confirmation for trying out new ideas, so they keep doing it. For these students, I see some combination of natural ability and encouragement from the environment.*

Mr. Johnson typifies many teachers. He wants his students to develop some conceptual understanding of mathematics and to acquire the learning strategies they need to become ongoing, independent learners. He also realizes that students have different strengths and weaknesses and that his lessons need to accommodate a wide range of abilities. As the interview suggests, he believes that variations in students' mathematical abilities are due to a combination of innate and environmental influences.

How do students become independent learners? How are individual differences in students' mental abilities assessed? Are some students naturally more able than others? If not, what explains variations in children's cognitive development? These questions are the focus of this chapter. We will examine the contributions of information processing and intelligence theories to research on children's development. If you recall, neither Piaget nor Vygotsky provided a fine-grain analysis of a child's cognitive system. The two theories described in this chapter help specify the cognitive processes and mental abilities children use to make sense of their world.

The chapter begins with a discussion of information processing theories. This perspective focuses on developmental changes in children's attention, memory, problem-solving skills, and knowledge base. As students progress in school, greater demands are placed on them to remember large amounts of information, to recall it quickly and effortlessly, and to learn independently. Information processing theories can help teachers understand the limitations and constraints of a child's information processing system. It can also help teachers identify learning difficulties that involve problems in attention, memory, and information retrieval.

Information Processing Theories

In the last 30 years, information processing theories have become the leading strategy for studying children's cognitive development (Klahr & MacWhinney, 1998). These theories claim that cognitive development involves changes in content, structure, and processing of information. This approach to studying cognition was greatly influenced by advances in computer technology in the early 1960s. With the invention of digital computers, psychologists began to view the human mind as a symbol-manipulating system. Like computers, people must manipulate symbols and transform inputs into outputs. Both computers and people are limited with regard to the amount of information they can attend to, process, and act on at one time.

Cognitive theorists describe human information processing in terms of computer models: symbol input, processing, and output.

Key Concepts in Information Processing Theory

Components of the Information Processing System

Information processing theorists focus on the flow of information through the cognitive system. The basic structures and processes included in most information processing models were described in Chapter 1. The information processing system begins with inputs into the cognitive system from any of the sense modalities, such as the ears, the eyes, and the fingers. This information is stored for a very brief period of time—only a few milliseconds—in what are called **sensory registers.** There is a separate sensory register for each sense. Information will be lost from the system unless it is recognized or interpreted. We often use previously learned information to interpret or make sense of sensory inputs.

Once information is interpreted, it passes into **short-term memory,** a component of the information processing system that holds information while we consciously work on it some more. The fact that information in short-term memory is consciously manipulated in some way has led some researchers to refer to this structure as **working memory.** Adults can store a limited amount of information, perhaps five to nine pieces of information, for 15 to 30 seconds in short-term memory. Because short-term memory has a limited capacity, a person must perform certain cognitive operations on new information in order to remember it for a longer period of time. For example, we can generally remember a phone number for more than 30 seconds if we repeat it over and over. We may be able to remember this information still longer if we can form a mental image of it or relate it to existing information, such as the year of an important event or a birthday.

The basic components of the information processing system include a series of sensory registers, a short-term or working memory, and a long-term memory.

Information that is transformed or organized in some way moves into **long-term memory.** This component of the cognitive system has a large capacity and presumably stores information indefinitely. During retrieval, information from long-term memory and the sensory registers may be brought together in working memory to perform various cognitive and problem-solving activities. For example, an adolescent may recall previous car problems as he or she attempts to diagnose a strange engine noise.

An alternative model is the level-of-processing theory. Rather than focusing on different types of memory stores (sensory registers, short-term memory, long-term memory), this theory proposes that differences in the level or amount of information processing determines how long and how well it will be remembered (Craik & Lockart, 1972). When information is processed at the shallow level, little mental energy is expended and, consequently, it will be remembered for only a short time. Skimming or repeating information is an example of shallow processing. In contrast, when considerable mental effort is expended organizing or altering information in a way that makes it more meaningful, it is processed at a deeper level and is generally remembered longer. Organizing information

The level-of-processing theory of cognition proposes that what is stored in memory is determined by the amount of mental effort expended and by the kinds of operations applied to it.

into categories or separating it into manageable chunks as we do with phone numbers is an example of deep processing. According to the level-of-processing model, what is stored in memory is determined by the amount of mental effort expended and by the kinds of operations applied to it.

How Is Information Stored in Memory?

We have some long-term memories that are vivid, rich, and detailed, and other memories that seem more factual or impersonal. **Episodic memory** includes events or information that is personal or autobiographical, such as a friend's birth date, a first date, or a childhood memory. It also stores information about the place, time, and order of events. **Semantic memory** is where information, skills, and concepts of a general nature are stored, such as words to a particular song, grammar rules, historical dates, and so on. Much of what is learned in school is stored in semantic memory.

Researchers also believe that information is stored in both visual and verbal forms. Concrete objects such as a flower, table, or state map can be stored as an image. Abstract concepts such as democracy, honor, injustice, or laws of physics are stored as verbal codes. Knowledge can also be stored in both verbal and visual forms. For example, you probably picture your grandmother as well as describe her verbally. Some researchers argue that information encoded both verbally and visually is easier to learn and to remember (Mayer & Sims, 1994). It is also believed that people have a preferred mode of visual or verbal storage (Paivio, 1971). Some of my students, for example, need a visual representation of a concept (e.g., zone of proximal development) before they can understand it. This research emphasizes the need to use both visual images and verbal explanations when teaching new or complex material.

Both visual and verbal information can be stored in memory.

Additionally, researchers believe that information is stored in the form of connected networks (Anderson, 1995). Borrowing a term from Piaget's theory, these organizational structures are called **schemas** or **schemata.** In these networks of information, there are central ideas (or nodes) that connect many related facts or ideas into a meaningful system. We have schemas for organizing vast amounts of information (e.g., branches of the federal government). In educational settings, these organizational structures are sometimes called concept maps. We also have organizational structures for remembering sequences of events (e.g., greeting a new person, reading or writing a story, ordering food at a restaurant). These structures are called event schemas or **scripts.** Later, we will discuss how children form scripts for daily routines at a fairly young age.

As you know, we have a limited capacity for remembering vast amounts of information. Schemas help us to use our cognitive resources more efficiently. A schema alerts us to relevant information. For example, a story schema would alert students to look for the setting, the primary characters, and the plot. Schemas also cue learners as to what to expect in a certain situation. Adults are less fearful of thunder than young children because they have a schema for what causes thunder. Schemas also help us to encode and to organize information in meaningful ways. We will learn that organizational strategies aid in the long-term retention and recall of information. In information processing theories, meaningful learning takes place when students can incorporate new information into an existing schemata or when a new schema is formed based on an existing one. For example, a student may use his or her understanding of the U.S. Congress to understand different forms of government.

Developmental Processes

The digit-span task is widely used to estimate children's information processing capacities. An adult reads a random set of numbers (e.g., 7-2-10-8-1-3-9) to the child at a rate of one per second. The child is then asked to repeat the sequence in the same order. Depending on

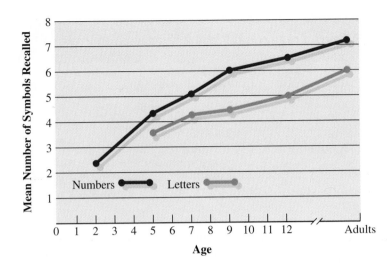

FIGURE 4.1

Improvement with Age in Memory Span for Numbers and Letters

SOURCE: After Dempster (1981).

the child's age, the adult would begin with a three-digit sequence and add a digit until the child's limit is reached. Figure 4.1 shows how children's improvement on the digit-span task improves with age. The average 5-year-old can repeat about four digits, whereas the average 12-year-old can repeat six or seven digits.

What explains this improvement? Does the physical size of children's storage structures expand so they can store more information? Using the computer analogy, the hypothesis implies that cognitive development represents improvements in children's "hardware." That is, children acquire a larger and faster central processing unit. A second hypothesis is that older children have developed better procedures for processing and storing information. In computer terminology, they acquire more sophisticated "software" to run the information processing system.

Although theorists are not yet able to rule out biological explanations, most of the research in the last 20 years has focused on developmental changes in the strategies and knowledge children apply to information. The following sections examine developmental changes in attention, memory, content knowledge, metacognition, and learning strategies. The Focus on Development box summarizes the development changes that take place in three aspects of the information processing system.

Development of Attention

A child's ability to attend to a learning task is often used as an indicator of cognitive maturity. Several school readiness tests, for example, contain items to assess children's attention. Teachers often believe that many children's learning and behavioral problems result from poor attention as suggested by comments such as, "She's easily distracted," "He won't pay attention," "She has

Young children are able to attend to puzzle tasks that are highly engaging.

SOURCE: James L. Shaffer.

Focus on Development

Developmental Changes in Components of Information Processing System

Source of Development	Early Childhood	Middle Childhood	Adolescence
Attention processes	Focus on salient features of objects. Experience difficulty distinguishing relevant irrelevant information.	Selective attention develops. Focus on central information. Gradual automatization of basic skills and information.	Ability to divide attention between more than one activity at the same time. Strategic use of attention strategies.
Memory processes	Use memory scripts and simple rudimentary strategies.	Acquisition and increasing use of organization and rehearsal strategies.	Use elaboration strategies and more strategic use of memory strategies. Able to retrieve information from memory with fewer prompts.
Metacognition	Little knowledge of learning and memory processes.	Understand that memory is limited. Begin to use strategies to increase comprehension and retention of information.	Better able to reflect on learning processes and to effectively apply metacognitive knowledge.

a short attention span." In some instances, teachers may suspect a student has a serious attentional problem that needs remediation or treatment. It is estimated that 3 percent to 5 percent of school-age children have some type of serious attentional disorder (see Chapter 6). These students display poor concentration, low sustained attention, and problems with inhibiting impulses compared to other children of the same age and sex. Therefore, it is important to understand how various attentional processes develop.

What Is Good Attention?   A good place to begin is to consider what is meant by good attention. Is it simply the ability to stay focused on the task at hand? Early theories defined attention in terms of a general mental capacity of the child (Gibson & Rader, 1979). The term *attention span* is often used in this regard.

Studies indicate that attention span increases during the preschool years (Ruff, Capozzoli, & Weissberg, 1998). For example, as shown in Figure 4.2, research on the television program

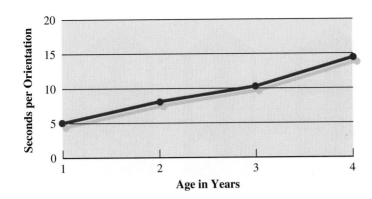

FIGURE 4.2

Attention to Sesame Street

SOURCE: After Anderson & Levin (1976).

Sesame Street has revealed significant improvements in children's attention from 1 to 4 years of age (Anderson & Levin, 1976). This research further suggests that children's attention is highly variable. That is, children's attention to *Sesame Street* was greater in the presence of some program features (e.g., women, puppets, and animation) and lower in the presence of others (e.g., adult men, animals, and still drawings). In addition, children were less attentive when attractive toys were placed in the room or the program content was too abstract. The research on *Sesame Street* illustrates how difficult it is to draw any firm conclusions about how long children can attend at a given age, because so much depends on the nature of the stimulus object, the child's physical and motivational state, and the surrounding circumstances.

Current research no longer defines attention as a general mental capacity but, rather, as a set of behaviors and processes. Good attention involves perceiving what is relevant to the task at hand (Gibson & Radar, 1979). From this perspective, it would be a mistake to define attention solely as some mental capacity of the child. Attention involves "extracting information from ongoing events in an active, selective, and economical way" (Gibson & Radar, 1979, p. 3).

As discussed in Chapter 2, most of a child's basic cognitive processes are well in place by early childhood. From this point onward, developmental changes primarily involve learning how to make better and more efficient use of existing perceptual and attentional processes. Some of the more important changes include the ability to make fine discriminations between stimulus objects, the development of automaticity and selective attention, and the ability to exert control over attentional processes. Consistent with the definition of attention presented here, most learners are able to deploy their attention in a planned, strategic, and efficient manner by adolescence.

Attentional Bias and Preferences   In Chapter 2, we discussed how various physical and psychological factors influence what attracts and maintains an infant's attention for short periods of time. Preschool and early elementary schoolchildren also appear to have certain attentional biases and preferences. Some features of an object, such as its size, shape, or color, attract children's attention more than others (Odom & Guzman, 1972). Younger children are also more likely than older children to attend to the holistic similarity of objects (Flavell, 1985). That is, they are more likely to attend to how objects are similar overall rather than to attend to their distinctive features. For example, the letters F and E, or D and O may look holistically similar and may appear to preschool and kindergarten children as the same letter symbol.

In order to learn numbers and letters, children must be able to compare symbols in terms of their similarities and differences. Older children are better able to discriminate between letters, because they can visually scan material more systematically. Figure 4.3 shows a set

> *Current research no longer defines attention as a general mental capacity but as a set of behaviors and processes used to extract information from ongoing events.*

> *Young children tend to focus on how objects are similar rather than different.*

FIGURE 4.3

Developmental Changes in Scanning Strategies

SOURCE: After Vurpillot (1968).

The process of focusing attention on task-relevant information and ignoring irrelevant information is called selective attention.

of pictures used to study children's visual scanning. Elaine Vurpillot (1968) asked 4- and 8-year-olds to determine whether or not the house on the left was identical to the one on the right. Using a camera to record children's eye movements during the task, this study showed that older children more often looked back and forth between corresponding windows in the two houses and more often proceeded down a column or across a row within a house. In other words, they systematically analyzed the pair of houses. The 4-year-olds, in contrast, were more likely to state their answers after viewing only about half the windows in the two houses. In short, young children's visual exploration of stimulus objects was much more haphazard.

Automaticity and Selective Attention   Automaticity is another factor that plays an important role in the development of children's attentional processes. **Automaticity** is defined as the "gradual elimination of attention in the processing of information" (La Berge, 1975, p. 58). As children gain experience with certain objects and problem-solving tasks, less effort is needed in the early stages of information processing. For example, experienced readers can recognize letters and words with very little mental effort. Decoding skills have been mastered and can be performed without thinking. When is the last time you had to decode a word, to sound out letters, or figure out the meaning of a word? If you have ever tried to learn a foreign language, you can appreciate the demands placed on children's attentional processes during the early stages of reading. It involves effort and hard work, and it is difficult to do for long periods of time. As children gain experience and acquire knowledge, fewer cognitive resources are expended in the picking up of information.

Around the age of 10, children also become better able to focus their attention on task-relevant information and to ignore irrelevant information. This process is called **selective attention.** Similar to the development of automaticity, this developmental change allows children to use their limited cognitive resources more efficiently. Researchers use what are known as incidental learning tasks to study the development of selective attention in children (Hagen & Hale, 1973; Miller & Weiss, 1981). In these studies, children are typically shown pictures with pairs of objects, such as a familiar animal paired with a common household object. The child is then told he or she will be asked to recall one member of each pair later on (e.g., the animals). The animals, then, are the central learning stimuli, and the other item in each pair serves as the incidental learning stimulus. Because the child's attentional capacity is limited, the most efficient way to approach the task is to attend only to the animals (the central learning stimuli) and to ignore information that is not relevant to the task. After each picture is presented, the child is asked first to recall the central stimuli (e.g., the animal in the pair). The experimenter then asks the child to recall the information he or she was suppose to ignore (i.e., the incidental objects).

SOURCE: Chris Seward/News & Observer.

During the elementary school years, children gain more control over attentional processes needed for independent learning activities in the classroom.

Figure 4.4 on page 184 shows the general pattern of findings from studies of children's selective attention. As you can see, the processing of relevant information continues to improve well into the high school years, whereas decreases in incidental learning do not occur until about the age of 11 or 12. These studies show that older children devote a higher proportion of their processing capacity to relevant material, whereas younger children do not effectively filter out irrelevant and distracting information. Compared with older children, young children spend more of their mental effort attending to irrelevant information rather than concentrating on the central features of the lesson.

With the development of selective attention, the older child is gaining more voluntary control over his or her attentional processes. Like adults, they can consciously force themselves to focus on certain stimuli and to ignore distracting stimuli. Older children are also better able than younger children to broaden or narrow their attention according to the task demands (Flavell, 1985). Because different learning tasks may require different attentional strategies, this flexibility is advantageous for learning.

Memory Processes

According to information processing theories, only a small amount of information can be kept in working memory at any one time. For young children, it may be difficult to engage in complex learning activities because the task itself overloads their memory capacities. Learning to read, for example, is a highly complex cognitive activity. As mentioned earlier, children must remember the distinctive feature of each letter and associate it with a specific sound. To make sense of this information, children must associate letter patterns with other information stored in memory. Ever greater demands are placed on children's memory processes as they progress in school. To perform successfully on an essay test, for instance, high school students must be able to recall and hold in working memory letter formations, correct spellings, rules of grammar and punctuation, and content knowledge.

Memory processes begin to develop within a few days of birth.

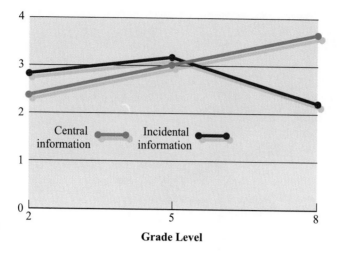

FIGURE 4.4

Recall of Central and Incidental Information, Selective Attention Task

SOURCE: After Miller & Weiss (1981).

Memory scripts are familiar patterns of behavior or familiar sequences of events that children store in a single network.

Memory development is at present one of the more active areas of research in developmental psychology. As with attention, memory processes begin to develop early in infancy. Within a few days of birth, breast-fed infants can recognize the smell of their mother's breast milk. This rather amazing feat implies that infants must have some way of storing the smell of their mothers' breast milk in order to recall it. Memory processes are also involved in forming emotional attachments to people. Without some ability to form a mental image of a caregiver, infants would not show signs of distress or cry when their mother or father leaves the room. Similarly, looking for hidden objects involves memory processes. In order to search for a ball that has rolled under a chair, a young toddler must have some mental image of that object after it disappears. By 5 months of age, infants can recognize previously seen stimulus material (objects, faces, numbers, shapes, etc.) as long as 2 weeks after the material was first presented.

Memory Scripts   Memory processes continue to improve through the preschool years. Young children often store information in the form of a script. These **memory scripts** are mental representations of frequently repeated events in children's everyday life (Nelson & Hudson, 1988). Two- and 3-year-olds can easily recall the sequence of events in familiar routines such as eating breakfast, brushing their teeth, and getting ready for bed (Wellman, 1988). For example, a script for going to a restaurant might include driving to the restaurant, waiting to be seated, ordering food, waiting for food, eating, and paying for the food as you leave. Events are recalled in a very logical and orderly sequence. For children, these scripts help to increase the predictability of events in their world. When scripts are violated, young children may become upset and confused. Children's scripts provide interesting insights into how information is organized and remembered early in development. By the end of the preschool years, children can recall familiar stories, experiences, and events that are of interest to them as well as most adults (Flavell, 1985; Miller, 1993).

Memory encoding strategies include rehearsal, organization, and elaboration.

Memory Encoding Strategies   During the preschool and early elementary years, children begin to use memory strategies to encode or place into memory information that is abstract, unfamiliar, or not meaningful. To store this type of information, a child must do something special to the material in order to remember it (Miller, 1993). What children do is apply some type of **memory strategy.** Suppose you were asked to remember the following list of items. What would you do?

apple	chair	goat
dog	potato	table
orange	lamp	bird
bed	cat	cabbage

Some people may repeat the items over and over again. This memory strategy is known as *rehearsal*. Others will try to group together the items into meaningful categories such as food, animals, and furniture. Researchers refer to this memory strategy as *organization*. Another group of people will try to construct a mental image of the items. This memory strategy is an example of *elaboration*. In terms of the levels of processing model described earlier, rehearsal is an example of shallow processing, whereas both organization and elaboration involve a deeper processing of information.

Rehearsal strategies, the first kind of memory strategy to appear, are generally used when verbatim recall of information is required (Siegler, 1998). Research indicates that children younger than 6 or 7 years use rehearsal strategies less often than older children. In a classic study, John Flavell and his colleagues (Flavell, Beach, & Chinsky, 1966) showed that 10 percent of kindergartners, 60 percent of second graders, and 85 percent of fifth graders used a verbal rehearsal strategy in performing a memory task. A later study indicated that children who spontaneously rehearsed the information to be remembered recalled more of the items after a planned delay than those who did not (Keeney, Cannizzo, & Flavell, 1967). The second study also showed that nonrehearsers could be taught to rehearse with a minimum of instruction and that using this strategy increased their level of recall to that of the spontaneous rehearsers.

Developmental changes in children's use of **organizational strategies** parallels those found in research on rehearsal strategies. These memory strategies entail grouping items or information into a form that is easier to remember. In the classroom, organizational strategies can take several different forms including organizing ideas into an outline, searching for relationships between ideas, identifying the main ideas in a segment of text, and grouping items into categories. In general, these strategies enhance memory and understanding, because children are actively transforming the learning material in some way that is meaningful to them. In Piagetian terms, they are *assimilating* the information. Children younger than 6 years old use organizational strategies less frequently than 9- and 10-year-olds do. Because organizational strategies are more complex than rehearsal strategies, they generally emerge later in development (Siegler, 1991).

Elaboration strategies involve adding to the information to make it more meaningful and easier to store. For example, one fourth-grade teacher uses the image of a hamburger to help students remember the components of a good paragraph. Figure 4.5 illustrates this mental image. Other examples of elaboration strategies include relating information to existing knowledge, translating information into one's own words, providing concrete examples of abstract concepts, and summarizing the main ideas of a story or chapter. Compared with rehearsal and organizational strategies, the spontaneous use of elaboration strategies appears much later in development. Studies indicate that elaboration strategies are primarily used by older elementary school children and adolescents.

Memory Retrieval Strategies The research we have reviewed so far has focused on the strategies children and adolescents use to move information into short- or long-term memory. How is information retrieved from memory? Are there developmental differences in the types of strategies children use to retrieve information from their memory? Researchers distinguish between recognition and recall tasks.

Rehearsal involves repeating information over and over and is the first memory strategy to appear in young children.

Organizational strategies involve grouping items or information into easier-to-remember forms, such as categories or outlines.

Elaboration strategies involve adding to or elaborating on the information to be remembered in order to make it more meaningful.

Retrieval strategies refer to mental operations used to recover information from memory.

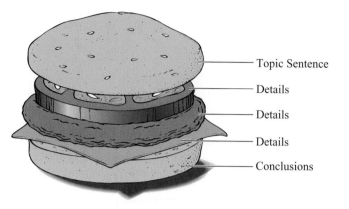

Topic Sentence

Details

Details

Details

Conclusions

FIGURE 4.5

Hamburger-Helper Paragraph

Recognition memory tasks involve recognizing a stimulus as something you have seen, heard, or somehow experienced before. The stimulus itself triggers the recall of this "memory." To some extent, a multiple-choice test assesses recognition memory. You might not be able to freely recall the answer to a specific question, but you are likely to recognize it when you see it. Seeing the answer triggers the retrieval of this information from memory. **Recall memory** tasks involve retrieval of information without any cues or prompts to aid the recall process. This form of memory is generally assessed on an essay test. In general, memory tasks that involve the free recall of information involve more mental effort and cognitive resources than do recognition tasks.

Whereas encoding strategies move information from sensory registers into different memory stores, **retrieval strategies** refer to the cognitive operations a learner might use to recover information from memory (Flavell, 1985). Like the strategies children use to encode information (rehearsal, organization, and elaboration), retrieval strategies vary in complexity and sophistication. One of the simplest forms of a retrieval strategy is not to give up efforts to recall information just because it does not immediately come to mind (Flavell, 1985). Research suggests that older children tend to be more exhaustive in their memory searches, whereas younger children may give up the search after only a few items are retrieved (Flavell, 1985).

In addition, older children tend to be more systematic and deliberate in their memory searches than younger children are. For example, A. Keniston and J. Flavell (1979) asked subjects from grades 1, 3, 7, and college to write down on a small card each alphabet letter the experimenter named. After 20 letters were written down in a random order, the cards were taken away and the subject was asked to write down the same letters on a large sheet of paper. The most effective memory strategy is to go through the alphabet in one's head and write down the letters you recognize from before. This simple strategy changes a difficult free-recall task into an easy recognition task. The researchers found that older children were more likely to use this retrieval strategy spontaneously. Younger children could use the strategy when they were told to do so, but they did not think of it on their own.

Summary of Memory Development   Much of what develops in the area of memory consists of learning to encode and retrieve information more selectively, deliberately, systematically, and flexibly, depending on the task at hand. Some theorists say that children become more strategic learners; that is, they use cognitive strategies to enhance their learning, with age and experience (Paris, Lipson, & Wixson, 1983). Children aged 10 to 12 are more likely to remember information because they organize and elaborate the information in ways that make it personally meaningful. Older children are also better able to conduct thorough searches of their memory, and they can recall information with fewer prompts and cues. In fact, some theorists claim that improvements in memory during childhood are more the result of effective retrieval than of encoding skills (Flavell, 1985).

Role of Prior Knowledge

Older children certainly know more about their world than younger children. What role does a child's existing knowledge play in the development of the information processing system? In general, the more that children know about a particular topic, the easier it is for them to interpret and store related information in a meaningful and memorable way (Flavell & Wellman, 1977).

The more prior knowledge one has about some topic, the easier it is to recognize and store related information in a meaningful way.

In a classic study, Michelene Chi (1978) demonstrated the effects of knowledge on memory processes by studying adult's and children's recall of chess pieces. This study had an interesting twist. The researcher recruited six children from the third to eighth grades who had participated in chess tournaments and six adults who knew how to play chess but were not good at the game. She then showed both groups a picture of a chessboard with pieces arranged as they might appear during an actual game. She also administered a standard test of digit span (see Figure 4.6). When asked to reconstruct chess pieces from memory, the child experts recalled more pieces than the adults who were novices at the game. However, as expected, the adults outperformed the children on the digit-span test. Chi's findings illustrate the influence of prior knowledge on memory. If children are highly knowledgeable in a certain area, their memory capacities may equal or even surpass those of less knowledgeable adults.

Chi's study was one of many **expert versus novice studies.** Researchers have compared the thinking and problem-solving processes of experts and novices in tennis, soccer, and physics. Regardless of the domain or the participants' ages, more knowledgeable individuals are better able than novices to group or organize information in meaningful patterns. For example, research on both children (Chi, 1978) and adults (Chase & Simon, 1973) has shown that chess experts organize chess pieces into familiar patterns, whereas novices tend to remember the location of individual pieces. In addition, experts tend to relate facts and information to higher-level concepts more than novices do (Chi, Feltovich, & Glaser, 1981). Expert and novice studies suggest that advances in children's thinking processes are explained by quantitative changes in knowledge as well as by qualitative changes in how knowledge is structured and organized.

Cognitive functioning is explained by quantitative changes in children's knowledge as well as by qualitative changes in how knowledge is structured and organized.

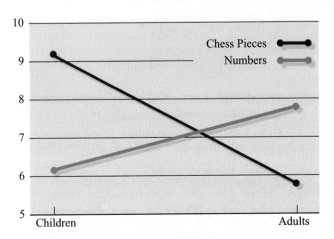

FIGURE 4.6

Children's and Adults' Recall of Numbers and Chess Pieces
SOURCE: After Chi (1978).

Children's performances on memory tasks are influenced by their knowledge base.

Evidence suggests that even young children can have highly integrated knowledge structures for topics of great interest to them. Chi and Koeske (1983) studied how one 4-year-old boy organized his knowledge of dinosaurs. While most children are fascinated with dinosaurs, this child knew the names of more than 40 dinosaurs. However, he seemed to know more about some dinosaurs than others. By asking the boy a series of questions on six separate occasions, the researchers were able to "map" his knowledge of dinosaurs. Figure 4.7 presents a graphic representation of the findings.

As shown here, the boy seemed to know more about armored dinosaurs than giant plant eaters. Notice the difference in the number of characteristics and links between pairs of dinosaurs on the left and right sides of the figure. The lines indicate which pairs were linked in the child's memory. On all six recall tasks, for instance, the child mentioned stegosaur and triceratops together in a consecutive order, prompting the conclusion that he had better recall of the armored dinosaurs, because they were closely linked in his knowledge network. Recalling one of the dinosaurs facilitated the recall of others associated with it.

To summarize, children's prior knowledge can influence memory processes in a number of different ways. As children acquire knowledge, they are better able to identify relevant information and to organize it in meaningful ways. Improvements in children's memory processes may also reflect changes in the number and strength of connections between ideas and concepts in children's memory stores. Having a more highly integrated or structured knowledge base results in faster processing of information, more effective use of deep processing strategies, and more efficient use of cognitive resources (Alexander, 1996; Bjorklund, Muir-Broaddus, & Schneider, 1990).

Metacognition

Metacognition refers to children's knowledge and understanding of their own mental capabilities and thinking processes.

As we discussed in Chapter 3, **metacognition** refers to children's knowledge and understanding of their own cognitive capabilities and thinking processes. With age and experience, children acquire knowledge of how tasks, strategies, and learner characteristics affect recall and learning (Flavell, 1985). Children use this metacognitive knowledge to choose more effective memory and learning strategies. For this reason, developmental changes in children's metacognition play an important role in school learning.

Much of a child's knowledge about cognition is acquired between the ages of 5 and 10 (Siegler, 1998). Preschool and kindergarten children tend to believe they cannot forget things they see or hear, whereas children beyond age 6 know they can forget (Kreutzer, Leonard, & Flavell, 1975). When asked how many of 10 items they can remember, young children believe they can remember all 10. The responses of older children suggest they view their memory capabilities as more limited. Further, older elementary schoolchildren understand reasonably well that relearning something is easier than learning it for the first time (Kreutzer et al., 1975) and that the longer one studies something the longer it will be remembered (Yussen & Bird, 1979).

More important, there are age-related improvements in children's knowledge of how a particular learning strategy can enhance recall or comprehension. In an early interview study, M. Kruetzer, C. Leonard, and J. Flavell (1975) asked elementary schoolchildren to describe some different ways they could remember to take their ice skates to school the next morning. Older children were able to think of more things they could do to remember than younger children. Interestingly, the most commonly mentioned strategies were external aids, such as asking their mothers to remind them or writing themselves a note.

Scott Paris, Marjorie Lipson, and Karen Wixon (1983) offer a more complicated view of strategy knowledge. They describe developmental changes in children's *declarative, procedural,* and *conditional knowledge* about learning strategies. That is, as children

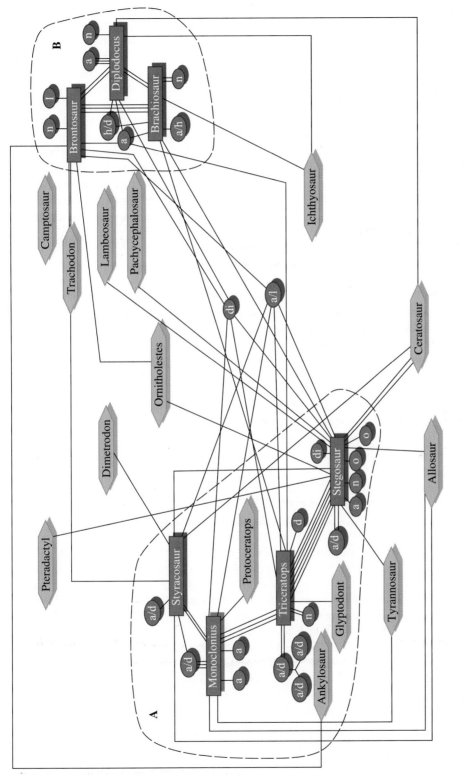

This concept map represents an 8-year-old's knowledge of dinosaurs. Dinosaurs in Group A are armored, whereas the ones in Group B are plant eaters. Multiple lines between dinosaurs indicate that the names are closely linked in the child's semantic network. The small letters indicate what the child knows about the dinosaur: appearance (a), defense mechanism (d), diet (di), nickname (n), habitat (h), and locomotion (l).

FIGURE 4.7 *Child's Concept Map of Dinosaurs*

SOURCE: After Chi & Koeske (1983).

develop they learn not only what strategies are available to help them **(declarative knowl-edge)** but also how they should be applied **(procedural knowledge)** and why they are ef-fective in specific situations **(conditional knowledge).** Scott Paris and Peter Winograd (1990) maintain that young children may know what strategies to use but lack knowledge of how to apply the strategy in various situations or how to evaluate its effectiveness.

In summary, there are several age-related changes in metacognitive knowledge that can affect how children approach learning tasks. As children develop, they acquire a greater un-derstanding that there are limits to what can be remembered (person knowledge), that some learning tasks require more cognitive effort than others (task knowledge), and that certain strategies can aid the recall of information (strategy knowledge). Generally, this "knowing how to know" begins to appear during the preschool years, but it is slow to develop, be-cause it requires the ability to consider one's own cognitive processes as objects of thought and reflection (Flavell & Wellman, 1977). It is also believed that age-related improvements in metacognition may be due to the large amount of information older children and adoles-cents are expected to remember in school (Siegler, 1998).

Self-Regulated Learning

Self-regulated learning involves abilities such as planning, setting goals, organizing, self-monitoring, and self-evaluation.

With the development of metacognitive knowledge, children begin to regulate and control their own learning activities. Some theorists refer to this process as **self-regulated learning** (Paris & Winograd, 1990; Zimmerman, 1990). According to Barry Zimmerman (1990), self-regulated learners can "plan, set goals, organize, self-monitor, and self-evaluate at various points during the process of knowledge acquisition" (pp. 4–5). The ability to learn indepen-dently is important for children's success in school. By high school, students spend a good deal of class time learning from textbooks, listening to lectures, and studying on their own.

When are students able to regulate and control their own learning? Research suggests that the answer to this question depends on the learning task and the students' prior knowl-edge (Brown, Bransford, Ferrara, & Campione, 1983). However, there are some clear de-velopmental trends in students' use of planning, monitoring, and evaluation strategies in learning situations.

Much research has focused on the strategies students use while studying and reading on their own. Between the fifth and eighth grades, children show a significant increase in their reported use of planning, sequencing, and goal-setting strategies (Zimmerman & Martinez-Pons, 1990). Additional evidence suggests that elementary and middle school students tend to use passive rather than active strategies for remembering text (Brown & Smiley, 1978). For example, when given extra time to study, younger students favor rereading the learning material, whereas high school students tend to take notes or underline passages. Further-more, when asked to summarize or outline text, elementary and middle school students tend to copy words verbatim rather than connecting ideas, arranging information by topic clus-ters, or stating information in their own words (Brown et al., 1983). Most students are not able to adequately summarize a typical fifth-grade text until well into the high school years.

Comprehension monitoring is an essential component of self-regulated learning. Skilled learners monitor their comprehension as they study or read and take corrective action when they fail to comprehend (Brown et al., 1983). Elementary schoolchildren tend to under-estimate their level of mastery on learning tasks and how much time they need to study in order to achieve mastery (Pressley & Ghatala, 1990). In addition, elementary school chil-dren are less likely than older students to monitor their comprehension while reading. If a younger reader can decode and make sense of individual words, he or she continues reading (Baker & Brown, 1984). Older students are better able to detect inconsistencies and confu-sion when they read. When comprehension falters, they adjust their strategies accordingly.

For example, they may reread confusing passages, look up a word in the dictionary, look for meaning in the surrounding context, or slow down until comprehension is restored. These comprehension-monitoring skills continue to develop well into adolescence.

Implications of Information Processing Theories for Teaching

Before discussing the specific implications of information processing research for educational practices, it is important to point out what this approach shares in common with Piaget's and Vygotsky's theories of cognitive development. First, all three views emphasize that learners must play an active role in the learning process. In information processing approaches, this activity involves selectively attending, interpreting, and organizing information; using cognitive strategies; and building webs of connected knowledge. Like Piaget and Vygotsky, information processing theorists also emphasize that learning is the construction of meaning. Students come to the classroom with a range of experiences, beliefs, skills, and concepts, and this prior knowledge plays a role in how new information is interpreted, organized, and remembered. Finally, "learning how to learn" is central to the development of cognition. In information processing theory, this process involves becoming a strategic learner, critical thinker, and skilled problem solver.

Having identified some common themes across different theories of cognitive development, what are the specific implications of information processing research for educational practices? The Focus on Teaching box summarizes several ways information processing theory can be applied in the classroom.

In order to increase alertness and attentiveness, it is important to create a classroom environment that is secure, attractive, novel, and stimulating. Posing unexpected problems, changing the displays on bulletin boards, and introducing variety into the schedule can capture students' attention. As we learned in Chapter 2, it is difficult for students of all ages to maintain high levels of concentration. Physical movement and activity can help increase students' concentration (Pellegrini et al., 1995).

The findings from research on the development of selective attention suggests that young elementary school students may have difficulty differentiating relevant from irrelevant information. They may also have difficulty when tasks require a shift in attention—say, from a central idea to peripheral topics or from a broad to a narrow focus. In such situations, teachers will need to help students focus their attention on the most relevant features of learning tasks. When complex or unfamiliar learning tasks are introduced, even high school students may experience difficulty identifying the significant features that require special attention. Some discussion of the activity beforehand may guide students' attention to relevant aspects of the task. Outlines and study guides may also help cue students' attention, as can the use of advance organizers that connect new information to students' prior knowledge. For younger students, it may be important to color-code or highlight important information. For example, a new letter or number symbol can be highlighted or can be written in a different color to cue attention. Additionally, teachers can use questions and feedback to help students stay focused on relevant aspects of the learning task.

Research on the development of memory processes offers additional suggestions for educational practices. It is important for teachers to recognize that students, especially younger ones, are limited in terms of the amount of verbal or visual information they can process. Most of the memory strategies we discussed do not develop until after the age of 5. However, younger children form scripts to help them remember routines and expectations. Songs and fingerplays can also help young children remember important information such as numbers or letters. These activities are a form of rehearsal.

Focus on Teaching

Applying Information Processing Theories in the Classroom

Attention Strategies

Introduce learning material by relating information to students' interests or by asking questions to stimulate interest.

Use novelty, variety, and unexpected problems to capture students' attention, but minimize unnecessary distractions.

Provide opportunities for physical movement and activity to help increase students' concentration.

Help students identify salient dimensions, main ideas, or key features of information.

Use questions, outlines, study guides, and visual aids to help cue attention and keep students focused.

Use instructional methods and formats that will hold students' interests.

Recognize developmental and individual differences in attention, and adjust assignments accordingly.

Memory Strategies

For young learners, use charts, visual aids, songs to help children remember routines or basic information like numbers and letters.

Present information in an organized way and cue important information to be remembered.

Help students relate information to what they already know. Model strategies for organizing and retrieving information.

Encourage students to use concept maps, outlines, or pictures to help them organize information in ways that are meaningful.

Encourage students to use elaboration strategies such as teaching information to a peer, relating it to their own experiences, or applying it to real-life situations.

Ask students to help review and summarize information in lessons. Review key concepts or information regularly.

When students experience difficulty remembering information, provide retrieval cues that relate information to what the student already knows.

Self-Regulated Learning

Provide opportunities for students to set their own goals, and monitor their progress toward those goals.

Model and help students learn strategies for focusing and controlling attention.

Help students learn strategies such as outlining, summarizing, making concept maps, and connecting ideas.

Encourage students to monitor and check their comprehension as they read and learn.

Model and teach strategies students can use when they experience difficulty, such as rereading the directions, dividing problems into smaller tasks, trying different strategies, seeking help from books, and seeking assistance from others.

For older learners, provide assignments that require independent learning, and provide the necessary guidance for students to complete them on their own.

192

As with brain development, the principle of "use it or lose it" applies to memory processes. Practice and use increases the strength of a particular memory record, and it facilitates the process of automaticity. For example, in the next chapter, we will learn that when children begin to recognize many words on sight, they are on their way toward becoming a fluent reader. Similarly, "expert" physicists can easily recognize and encode technical terms that most of us could not interpret or comprehend without a great deal of cognitive effort. Accordingly, students need opportunities to practice newly learned material to increase both its strength and familiarity in memory.

Does this suggestion mean that students should simply memorize facts and information? The current thinking on this question is that some information (e.g., letter sounds, sight words, addition facts, multiplication tables, etc.) needs to be readily accessed with minimal effort to enable higher levels of cognitive processing. For example, solving long division problems takes more cognitive effort when students have not learned simple multiplication facts. The problem can be solved, but similar to the reading example given earlier, most of the student's thinking processes are focused on doing multiplication, rather than understanding the concept of long division. The same applies to more complex tasks such as writing. As I finish this paragraph, for instance, I am not thinking about how to spell familiar words or where to place my fingers on the keyboard. My thinking is focused on what I am trying to communicate.

Because memory capacities are limited, it is also important for teachers to help children organize their learning experiences. To help students separate essential from nonessential details, teachers need to introduce lessons with a set of guiding questions or goals. In other words, teachers need to provide a "road map" for the lesson to help students sequence and organize the learning material. Teachers also need to help students make connections between new information and what they already know. Through questioning, teachers can help students retrieve information that is relevant for understanding the new material.

Additionally, research on memory suggests that teachers need to promote the deep processing of information. Deep processing is facilitated by the use of organizational and elaboration strategies that involve transforming the learning material in meaningful ways. Examples of organizational strategies are clustering information into categories, identifying relationships between ideas or concepts, or connecting information to existing knowledge. Concept maps like the one shown in Figure 4.8 are often used to help students organize information in terms of meaningful categories. Outlines are another way students can organize knowledge into meaningful categories. It is important to point out that when students do their own organization, it has a stronger effect on recall than when teachers provide that organization (McDaniel, Waddill, & Einstein, 1988). Elaboration strategies involve imposing meaning on learning material. Organizing information into meaningful categories can aid in that process, but elaboration can take other forms as well. It can include restating new material in one's own words, explaining or teaching the material to someone else, creating a visual or mental image of the material, or applying information to real-world situations. The use of journals in which students can draw or write about what they are learning can help in the deep processing of learning material.

As you know, the development of metacognition enables learners to regulate and control their learning or to become self-regulated learners. Numerous classroom-based programs have been developed to train students in metacognitive skills and cognitive strategies. Instructional programs have focused on the development of planning, organization, and comprehension strategies. Research suggests that explicit strategy instruction can be beneficial for less-advanced learners (Schunk, 2000). However, explicit strategy instruction is most beneficial when students also learn when and how to use the strategy effectively and why the strategy is helpful. In other words, explicit strategy instruction is

Explicit strategy instruction— emphasizing what, when, why, and how to use a specific cognitive strategy— increases the likelihood that children will use a strategy in a variety of situations after training ends.

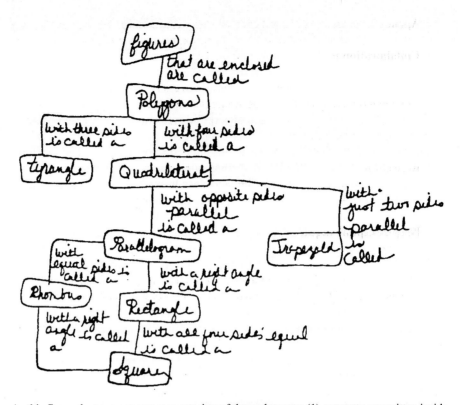

FIGURE 4.8

A Fourth Grader's Map of Geometric Concepts

SOURCE: After Baroody & Bartels (2000).

As this figure shows, a concept map consists of three elements: (1) concepts are written inside loops, boxes, rectangles, or other shapes; (2) linking lines show connections between concepts; and (3) linking phrases describe the relationship between concepts. Concept-mapping can promote meaningful learning in the classroom because the process enables students to actively construct relationships between concepts. To correctly place a trapezoid in the above figure, students must recognize that a trapezoid is a four-sided shape and, thus, a type of quadrilateral.

most beneficial to learners after the instructional program ends, when it emphasizes *what, when, why,* and *how.* Research also suggests that interventions of this type need a good deal of scaffolded instruction to ensure that internalization of the strategy takes place.

Research on the development of basic cognitive processes is having a major impact on education today. Research on the development of attention and memory can help teachers diagnose learning problems. As will be discussed in Chapter 6, students with learning disabilities often experience problems with attention and memory. Researchers draw on information processing theories to develop classroom interventions or accommodations for these students. Additionally, information processing approaches have been used to design instructional interventions to help children with poor reading or writing skills (Pressley, Harris, & Guthrie, 1992).

Many theorists believe that educators need to go beyond the teaching of specific skills to developing a culture of thinking and learning in the classroom (Bruner, 1996; Perkins, 1992; Tishman, Perkins, & Jay, 1995). An excellent illustration is the **community of learners** approach. Ann Brown and Joe Compione (1994) blended social constructivist and information processing views of cognitive development to help create a school environment "where children learn to think deeply about serious matters" (Brown, 1997, p. 399). A community of learners is structured around several key learning principles (Brown, 1997):

- **Agency** Both teachers and learners routinely engage in the search for meaning and understanding. The *strategic* nature of learning is emphasized.
- **Collaboration** Both teachers and students must share in developing and sustaining the community of learning. Teachers help guide students to deeper levels of understanding, but learning is a shared and joint activity. Cooperative and collaborative learning among students is also commonplace. These activities not only have an important learning function (children share their expertise and take responsibility for their learning), but also strengthen the collaborative structures of the classroom.
- **Reflection** The classroom is designed to stimulate active exchange of ideas and discourse. Students are encouraged to ask themselves, "Do I understand?" or to say, "That doesn't make sense to me." Discussion, analysis, and critique are all valued practices in this community.
- **Deep discipline inquiry** Students engage in disciplined inquiry on a central theme that can sustain in-depth research over time. Students need opportunities to reason about serious matters at the upper limits of their capabilities. Deep discipline inquiry involves reasoning with research and evidence, seeking expert advice, and sharing results and ideas with others.

Every classroom has a culture of some sort. The classroom culture influences the ways students and teachers interact and their shared understanding of what is valued and acceptable. In a community of learners, learning is negotiated and shared as a way of life.

Intelligence Theories and Cognitive Development

So far our discussion of cognitive development has focused on cognitive differences among different age levels. It is important to keep in mind that there is a wide range of variation in children's cognitive abilities within a particular age group. In any third-grade classroom, for example, there will be children reading at a fourth- or fifth-grade level as well as children who are just starting to read on their own. What might explain these cognitive differences within an age group? Do some children simply have more innate ability for learning than others? Are these differences related to children's early learning experiences? How might differences in children's home environment contribute to their cognitive development?

In this section, we discuss how researchers assess and explain individual differences in cognitive development. Central to this discussion is the question of how much heredity and environment each contribute to individual differences in intelligence. This question has been hotly debated for decades, and it continues to be a subject of much controversy. In 1994, the publication of *The Bell Curve* by Richard Herrnstein and Charles Murray sparked considerable debate, because the authors claimed that social problems such as high school dropout, teenage pregnancy, infant mortality, unemployment, crime, poverty, and even "broken homes" were a function of innate intelligence. Because research on heredity and intelligence is so extensive, we will limit our discussion of individual differences in cognitive development to the following questions:

- How are individual differences in cognitive development measured?
- How is intelligence defined?

- How does the environment influence intellectual development?
- What can parents do to enhance their child's intellectual development?
- How do schools influence children's intellectual development?

Key Concepts in Intelligence Theories

Assessing Cognitive Differences

The most common methods of assessing individual differences in cognitive development is to use standardized tests of intelligence and academic achievement.

The most common methods of assessing individual differences in cognitive development are **standardized tests of intelligence** and academic achievement. These tests yield scores that provide an index of the person's intellectual performance relative to other people of the same chronological age. The use of standardized tests of intelligence to study individual differences in cognitive development is known as the *psychometric approach*. If you recall, Piaget focused on individual differences in the quality of children's thinking. Information processing theorists focus on individual differences in children's attentional processes, encoding and retrieving strategies, and metacognitive knowledge. In contrast, psychometricians focus on what and how much children know. They argue that individual differences in cognitive development can be measured and quantified through the use of standardized tests.

Alfred Binet, a French psychologist, published the first intelligence test in 1904. Binet claimed that a person's intellectual ability could be inferred from his or her performance on a series of cognitive tasks. Binet and his student Theodore Simon assembled a series of cognitive tasks that measured such things as memory for numbers, attention, reading comprehension, mathematics reasoning and computation skills, and general information (knowledge of numbers, days of the week, coins, etc.). The tasks were graded in difficulty and linked to chronological age.

SOURCE: Chris Seward/News & Observer.

An important issue of debate is when schools should begin testing children. Should chhildren in the early elementary grades take standardized tests?

Binet and Simon developed their measure as a practical device for identifying children who needed special help in school (Gould, 1981). They were responsible for introducing the concept of mental age (MA). This score represents the number of test items a child gets correct, which is then compared with the average number of items children of the same age get correct. A 10-year-old who can answer as many answers correctly as the average 12-year-old has a mental age of 12. Later, a German psychologist, William Stern, introduced the **intelligence quotient (IQ),** which represents a score obtained by dividing a child's mental age score by the child's chronological age (CA) and multiplying by 100 (e.g., IQ = MA/CA = 100). If a child has a score of 100, his or her performance is average for that age. Scores above 100 indicate that a child is above average for that age, whereas scores below 100 indicate that a child is below average.

Conceptions of Intelligence

Despite the fact that IQ tests have been around for nearly 100 years, there is no widely accepted definition of intelligence (Neisser et al., 1996). Because Binet and Simon's IQ test yielded a single score, this assessment procedure is assumed to represent a unitary conception of intelligence. That is, intelligence is considered to be a general cognitive ability. As you will see, many intelligence tests are based on this unitary conception of intelligence. However, this view of intelligence is beginning to lose ground to a more multidimensional conception in which intelligence is defined in terms of several different mental abilities or intellectual competencies.

Before we discuss different conceptions of intelligence, it is important to distinguish between intelligence tests and **achievement tests.** Intelligence tests are thought to measure a child's ability to learn or to apply information in new ways. These tests assess learning that results from a wide variety of experiences. Most intelligence tests are individually administered by a trained examiner. Two of the most widely used intelligence tests will be described in the following section. An achievement test, on the other hand, is designed to measure what children have gained from instruction at home or at school. Test items stress the mastery of factual information. These tests are generally group administered by teachers, and they provide a way of comparing children in different instructional programs or tracking children's academic progress over time. Examples of widely used achievement tests are the *California Achievement Test, Metropolitan Achievement Test, California Test of Basic Skills, Iowa Test of Basic Skills,* and *National Assessment Educational Progress.* Although intelligence tests and achievement tests are generally viewed as distinct assessment instruments, we will point out some overlap between them.

Intelligence tests are thought to measure a child's potential to learn or to apply information in new ways, whereas achievement tests are designed to measure what children have already gained from instruction at home or at school.

Single-Factor Conceptions of Intelligence   Traditional approaches to intelligence testing define intelligence as a single ability or capacity. Lewis Terman of Stanford University, who was responsible for bringing Binet and Simon's testing methods to the United States, defined intelligence as an ability to think in abstract terms. He translated and revised Binet's test, then standardized it on a large sample of children and adults. The revised test, called the *Stanford-Binet Intelligence Scale,* was first published in 1916, and it became the standard for IQ tests (Gould, 1981). Terman and his followers argued that a **general intelligence,** called g, underlies all cognitive functioning. Someone with a high score on Terman's test is expected to do well on all intellectual tasks.

The *Stanford-Binet Intelligence Scale* (Thorndike, Hagen, & Sattler, 1986) is the most widely used intelligence test for children between the ages of 2 and 18. The Stanford-Binet test measures visual reasoning, quantitative reasoning, short-term memory, and abstract visual reasoning. Rather than a single score, the scale now yields four scores, as well as a

Single-factor conceptions of intelligence postulate a general intellectual factor, called g, that underlies all forms of intellectual functioning.

Multiple-factor conceptions of intelligence attest to multidimensional and independent skills that can be measured.

composite score for the test as a whole. See Figure 4.9 for a description of the subtests in the revised Stanford-Binet test.

Another widely used test is the *Wechsler Intelligence Scale for Children—Third Edition* (WISC—III) (Wechsler, 1991) for children between the ages of 8 and 18. The design of this scale was influenced by the Stanford-Binet, but it places less emphasis on children's verbal skills. The WISC—III contains 10 subtests divided into two separate scales. The verbal scales assess vocabulary, digit-span memory, general comprehension, basic facts, and arithmetic knowledge and reasoning. The performance scales, on the other hand, measure spatial orientation, perceptual abilities, and problem-solving skills that are thought to be less dependent on verbal skills, formal education, and other cultural factors. Wechsler's scale thus yields a separate score for verbal and performance IQ as well as a full-scale IQ based on the combined scores.

Although the WISC—III yields two separate IQ scores, Wechsler defined intelligence as a unitary construct. It is "the aggregate or global capacity of the individual to act purposively, to think rationally, and to deal effectively with his environment" (Wechsler, 1958, p. 7). The WISC—III is valuable for diagnostic purposes because it distinguishes between a child's verbal and performance abilities. A child who does well on the performance scale but poorly on the verbal scale may have poor language skills. Conversely, a child who performs well on the verbal scale but poorly on the performance scale may have perceptual or spatial orientation problems.

The Stanford-Binet Intelligence Test and WISC—III are the most reliable, best validated, and most widely used intelligence tests we have today. Both tests are individually administered by a trained examiner. Scores on these tests are viewed as an estimate of general intelligence or g. Other tests that yield a single IQ-like score are the *Lorge-Thorndike Intelligence Test*, the *Raven's Progressive Matrices*, the *Otis Lennon Mental Ability Scale*, and the *Peabody Picture Vocabulary Test (Revised)*. There are also intelligence tests for infants and young children. The best-known scale is the *Bayley Scale of Infant Development* (Bayley, 1969). This scale assesses the motor and mental development of infants of 2 to 30 months old. It yields a score called the Bayley Mental Development Index (MDI).

Multiple-Factor Conceptions of Intelligence   Many researchers have questioned the idea that intelligence represents a single cognitive ability. As stated earlier, some psychologists view intelligence as multidimensional, representing several independent and potentially measurable skills.

More than 70 years ago, Charles Spearman (1927) argued that intelligence represents a g or general factor and a number of s or specific ability factors. In 1938, Louis Thurston suggested that intelligence was composed of seven separate skills that included perceptual speed, numerical facility, word fluency, inductive reasoning, and memory. Later, J. P. Guildford (1967) concluded that intelligence consists of 120 different factors, and he developed a test to assess 75 of these.

Research in the 1970s proposed that there are basically two kinds of intelligence, known as crystallized intelligence and fluid intelligence (Catell, 1971). **Crystallized intelligence** is assessed by measures of word fluency, general information, and vocabulary and verbal comprehension. In contrast, **fluid intelligence** involves speed of information processing, memory processes, ability to detect relationships, and other abstract thinking skills. Research suggests that fluid intelligence improves until the early adult years, then slowly declines, whereas crystallized intelligence continues to improve well into the adult years (Horn, 1985).

The question of whether intelligence represents a general capability or multiple abilities remains unresolved today. In 1985, Robert Sternberg introduced the **triarchic model of intelligence.** He defined intelligence as "mental activity directed toward purposive adaptation to, and selection and shaping of, real world environment relevant to one's life" (p. 45).

Verbal Reasoning

Vocabulary (14 pictures, 32 words)

The child is asked to identify pictures and give an oral definition of written words.

Comprehension (42 questions)

The child is asked to identify body parts (e.g., foot, nose, etc.) and to answer questions involving social comprehension (e.g., What does a nurse do?)

Absurdities (32 items)

The child is asked to identify the incongruity in pictures (e.g., writing with a spoon, a person riding a bike with one wheel missing, etc.).

Verbal Relations (18 items)

The child is asked to determine how the first three items are alike but different from the fourth item.

Abstract/Visual Reasoning

Pattern Analysis (42 items)

The child is asked to complete a form and to reproduce stimulus designs that are shown on cards using two, three, four, six, and nine blocks.

Copying (28 items)

The task is to reproduce designs with blocks or to copy simple and complex geometric designs (e.g., lines, squares, circles) that are shown on cards.

Matrices (26 items)

The child is asked to select the object, design, or letter that best completes the matrix.

Paper Folding and Cutting (18 items)

The child is asked to select the picture that shows how a folded and cut piece of paper may look unfolded.

Quantitative Reasoning

Quantitative Problems (40 questions)

The child is asked to solve quantitative problems.

Number Series (26 items)

The child is asked to predict the next two numbers in a series.

Equation Building (18 items)

The child is asked to arrange numbers and mathematical signs into an equation.

Short-Term Memory

Bead Memory (42 items)

The child is asked to reproduce bead patterns by finding them in photograph or placing beads on a stick.

Memory for Sentences (42 items)

The child is asked to repeat successively longer sentences.

Memory for Digits (26 items)

The child is asked to repeat a 14-digit series in a forward sequence and a 12-digit series in a backward sequence.

Memory for Objects (14 items)

The child is asked to recall pictured objects in the exact sequence in which they are shown.

FIGURE 4.9

Subtest Descriptions of the Stanford-Binet Intelligence Scale, 4th Ed.

SOURCE: After Sattler (1988).

- Recognizing and defining the nature of a problem

- Deciding on the processes needed to solve the problem

- Sequencing the processes into an optimal strategy

- Deciding on how to represent problem information

- Allocating mental and physical resources to the problem

- Monitoring and evaluating one's solution processing

- Responding adequately to external feedback

- Encoding stimulus elements effectively

- Inferring relations between stimulus elements

- Mapping relations between relations

- Applying old relations to new situations

- Comparing stimulus elements

- Responding effectively to novel kinds of tasks and situations

- Effectively automizing information processing

- Adapting effectively to the environment in which one resides

- Selecting environments as needed to achieve a better fit of one's abilities and interests to the environment

- Shaping environments to increase one's effective use of one's abilities and interests

FIGURE 4.10

Principal Characteristics of Intelligent Behavior
SOURCE: After Sternberg (1984).

According to Sternberg's theory, there are three major components of intelligent behavior. The first component, **componential intelligence,** draws heavily on information processing theory. It involves such skills as the ability to allocate mental resources, to encode and store information, to plan and monitor, to identify problems, and to acquire new knowledge. The second component, **experiential intelligence,** involves the ability to cope with new situations in an effective, efficient, and insightful manner. Experiential intelligence is involved in diagnosing why a computer program might not run. The third component of Sternberg's model is called **contextual intelligence.** It involves the ability to adapt to a changing environment or, more importantly, to shape that environment to capitalize on one's abilities or skills. In Sternberg's view, this component of intelligence involves the application of intelligence to everyday problems, or what he called **practical intelligence.** An intelligent person, according to Sternberg, is one who can use his or her skills effectively in a particular environment. Above Figure 4.10 lists what Sternberg saw as the principal abilities that underlie intelligent behavior. At present, however, there are few standardized measures that assess these components of intelligence.

| Table 4.1 | | Gardner's Eight Intelligences |

Intelligence	End States	Core Components
Logical-mathematical	Scientist Mathematician	Sensitivity to and capacity to discern logical or numerical patterns; ability to handle long chains of reasoning
Linguistic	Poet Journalist	Sensitivity to sounds, rhythms, and meaning of words; sensitivity to the different functions of language
Musical	Composer Musician	Abilities to produce and appreciate rhythm, pitch, and timbre; appreciation of different forms of musical expressiveness
Spatial	Navigator Sculptor	Capacities to perceive the visual-spatial world accurately and to perform transformations on one's initial perceptions
Bodily kinesthetic	Dancer Athlete	Abilities to control one's body movements and to handle objects skillfully
Interpersonal	Therapist Salesperson	Capacities to discern and respond appropriately to the moods, temperaments, motivations, and desires of other people
Intrapersonal	Person with detailed, accurate self-knowledge	Access to one's own feelings and the ability to discriminate among them to guide behavior; knowledge of one's own strengths, weaknesses, desires, and intelligences
Naturalistic	Botanist Farmer Veterinarian	Ability to discriminate among living things (plants, animals) as well as demonstrate a sensitivity toward other features of the natural world (e.g., rocks, cloud formations, etc.)

SOURCE: After Gardner & Hatch (1989); Checkley (1997).

Multiple Intelligences Another multiple-factor view of intelligence is Howard Gardner's (1999) theory of **multiple intelligences.** Like Sternberg, Gardner questions traditional measures of intelligence that are narrow in their focus. Gardner proposed that there are at least eight different types of intelligences, and possibly more. He further suggests that each intelligence has its own form of perception, memory, and learning. Gardner believes that each intelligence has a unique developmental history, and it may be governed by a distinct region of the brain. He also believes that cultural values, historical changes, and learning opportunities have a great influence on the abilities of individuals to develop and to express their intellectual strengths. In Gardner's view, we are currently entering a new century in which people need to be adept at manipulating symbols and adapting to change. At the turn of the twentieth century, a naturalist intelligence was critical for an economy dependent on farming, fishing, and hunting.

Table 4.1 presents the eight intelligences identified by Gardner. Linguistic, logical-mathematical, and spatial intelligences are generally assessed by traditional measures of intelligence. Gardner argues that people also show special abilities in bodily kinesthetic, interpersonal, intrapersonal, and naturalistic domains. For example, dancers and athletes generally have a great ability to move their bodies through space (bodily kinesthetic intelligence); good teachers, social workers, and psychotherapists seem particularly adept at understanding the feelings, motives, and moods of others (interpersonal intelligence). Veterinarians, botanists, and farmers are skilled in observing, understanding, and appreciating the natural world, or what Gardner calls naturalistic intelligence. It is also possible for individuals to show strengths in two or more areas. Novelists, for example, generally make use of heightened linguistic and interpersonal intelligences.

Gardner's ideas about multiple intelligences are being applied in many schools and classrooms today. His theory has helped teachers to understand that there are different ways of being "smart" and that it is important to foster all kinds of intelligences, not just verbal or mathematical abilities. According to Gardner, teachers should follow the Chinese adage "Let a hundred flowers bloom" (Gardner, 1999, p. 89).

Summary

As you can see, there is no one definition of intelligence. Most intelligence tests today yield more than one score, so it is possible to compare children's intellectual functioning across different domains. These profiles are useful for assessing a child's intellectual strengths and weaknesses. For the most part, the tests used in schools today emphasize children's linguistic, mathematical, and analytical abilities. They reflect the type of intellectual abilities our culture values. Multifaceted views of intelligence offer new ways of conceptualizing children's intellectual abilities. It is hoped that such views will help educators see intelligent behavior in all children in one form or another. The important point to remember is that different students show intelligence in different ways.

Developmental Changes in Intelligence

Interpreting an IQ Score

Whether an IQ test yields one or several scores, it is assumed that these scores represent some estimate of a child's cognitive ability relative to other children of the same age. As mentioned earlier, an IQ score is the ratio of the child's mental age to chronological age. Most intelligence tests today use a scoring procedure that results in a deviation IQ score. These scores have a mean of 100 points and a standard deviation of 15 or 16 points, depending on the test. A **standard deviation** is a measure of the average amount scores vary from the mean. The smaller the standard deviation, the more scores cluster around the mean. Deviation IQ scores are based on a normal distribution or bell curve, like the one shown in Figure 4.11. The mean is at the midpoint of this distribution, and 95 percent of all scores are within two standard deviation units above or below the mean (i.e., between 70 and 130).

Using the deviation IQ score procedure, children with raw scores that match the average for their age group receive an IQ score of 100. Half of the children (50 percent) score below 100, and half score above 100. On the WISC—III, children with raw scores one standard deviation (15 points) above the mean receive an IQ score of 115. These children perform better than 84 percent of children their age. In contrast, 84 percent of same-aged children perform better than children with an IQ score of 85, one standard deviation (15 points) below the mean. In a normal distribution, most children's scores fall within one standard deviation above or below the mean (between 85 and 115 on the WISC—III). Very few children will have scores more than two standard deviations from the mean.

The question of whether intelligence represents a general capability or multiple abilities remains unsolved, but it is important to remember that individual students show intelligence in different ways.

Most intelligence tests today use a deviation IQ score in which half the children have scores above 100 and half below 100.

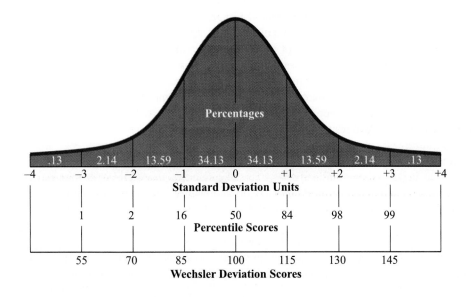

FIGURE 4.11

The Normal Curve and Selected Scores

Factors That Threaten the Validity of IQ Scores

The validity of a test has to do with the degree the test accurately measures what it is intended to measure. For example, does the Stanford-Binet Intelligence Scale provide an accurate measure of the child's aptitude for learning? Is this measure equally valid for all children? What if a child comes from a cultural or language background in which standard English is not spoken or school achievement is not valued? Some people have argued that mental tests are inevitably biased in favor of the mainstream culture which, in turn, leads to the overrepresentation of minority children in special education classes. After a widely publicized court case in 1979, *Larry P. v. Pikes,* the California State Department of Education issued a directive to prohibit the use of IQ tests in the assessment of minority children referred for special education placement.

Critics of IQ tests maintain that they are not culture free; that is, they are inevitably biased in favor of people from the mainstream culture.

The most vocal critics have argued that intelligence tests are biased against anyone who does not come from white, Anglo-American, middle-class, English-speaking families. To perform well on an IQ test, they claim, children must have a good deal of familiarity with middle-class culture and good-standard English verbal skills. As we will see, African American, Latino, and poor children generally do not perform as well on standardized tests as white middle-class children. Stephen Ceci (1990) argued that many children who perform poorly on traditional IQ tests may demonstrate more sophisticated cognitive abilities in more familiar domains. Tests such as the *Kaufman Assessment Battery* (Kaufman & Kaufman, 1983) have been developed to minimize cultural bias. On these tests, gaps in the performances of white and minority children are considerably smaller. Therefore, teachers should use caution when traditional IQ measures are employed to assess children from different socioeconomic, cultural, and language backgrounds.

What Do IQ Tests Predict?

An IQ test is alleged to predict everything from mental health to job performance (Ceci, 1991). Some psychologists have claimed that intelligence tests have even helped to win wars (Gould, 1981). However, for a number of researchers, IQ scores are simply viewed as relatively good predictors of success in school, at least in American culture (Ceci, 1991, Ceci & Williams, 1997).

If you recall, Binet originally developed the intelligence test to identify children who needed special assistance in school. Binet claimed that IQ scores derived from his measure should not be viewed as an estimate of the child's inherent intellectual capacity (Gould, 1981). Unfortunately, Binet's ideas were largely ignored by early American psychologists who favored a hereditarian view of intelligence. Terman, for example, viewed his test as a measure of innate intellectual functioning that was independent of environmental experiences. If Terman's ideas were correct, then children's IQ scores would not be affected by schooling. The evidence does not support this claim.

Intelligence test scores are best thought of as an indicator of how well children will do in school and should not be thought of as measures of innate ability or creativity.

Studies repeatedly show that IQ scores are correlated with various measures of school achievement (Ceci, 1990, 1991; Ceci & Williams, 1997). Children with higher IQ scores typically do better on standardized tests of academic achievement, have higher school grades, and complete more years of school. Correlations between IQ scores and measures of school achievement are in the range of 0.40 to 0.60, not a perfect correlation but certainly a substantial one. Because these are correlational data, they should not be interpreted to mean that intelligence causes a child to do well or poorly in school. In fact, considerable evidence suggests that schooling plays an important causal role in the development of intelligence, at least as it is currently defined and assessed (Ceci, 1990). We will discuss this evidence later on.

To summarize, a child's IQ score is best thought of as an indicator of how well that child will do in school. Under optimal testing conditions, an intelligence test can help diagnose learning problems or areas in which children need special instructional assistance. Intelligence tests are not measures of innate ability, creativity, or even complex reasoning (Ceci, 1991). Furthermore, IQ scores are not very good predictors of occupational success, social success, mental health, or personality. An IQ score provides information about what intelligence tests were originally intended to measure, namely a child's ability to perform in school.

Stability and Change in Intelligence

How much does a child's IQ score change during development? If we know a child's IQ score at age 5, how well can we predict his or her score at age 15 or 18? Will a bright kindergartener be at the top of her class when he or she graduates from high school? Questions concerning the **stability of IQ** have been of interest to psychologists for some time (Bloom, 1964; Jones & Bayley, 1941; McCall, Applebaum, & Hagarty, 1973) because it sheds light on the nature–nurture issue. If IQ scores are relatively stable over time, then the environment is presumed to have little influence on intellectual development. If, however, IQ scores vary a great deal from infancy to adulthood, then the environment must play a more significant role than heredity.

Beginning at about age 7, childhood IQ scores are reasonably good predictors of adult IQ.

What can childhood IQ scores tell us about adult intelligence? Table 4.2 shows correlations of IQ scores for the same individuals at different ages. Higher correlations indicate more stability in children's IQ scores. During infancy and early childhood, there is little stability in children's IQ scores as measured by traditional tests. As children get older, the stability of IQ scores increases, as indicated by the higher correlations. It is generally believed that IQ scores begin to stabilize during the middle childhood years. From the age of 7 onward, childhood IQ scores are reasonably good predictors of adult IQ. For example, the correlation between IQ scores at ages 10 and 14 years is around 0.86. Increases in stability are most likely due to the increasing similarity of test items as children get older.

It is important to remember that a child's IQ score is always tied to chronological age. A child with an IQ of 110 at age 7 is very likely to have an IQ around 110 at age 10. Stability in IQ scores refers to the relative constancy of a child's rank within a particular age

Age at Retest (years)	Age at First Test (years)			
	2	7	10	14
7	0.46			
10	0.37	0.77		
14	0.28	0.75	0.86	
18	0.31	0.71	0.73	0.76

Table 4.2   Stability of IQ Scores

SOURCE: After Jensen (1973).

group. As children mature, they pass more items on an intelligence test (i.e., they get smarter), but their scores remain fairly constant unless their intellectual development is delayed or accelerated in some way relative to their age group. Evidence suggests that some children's IQ scores can vary as much as 20 to 30 points from age 2 to 17 (McCall, Applebaum, & Hagarty, 1973). Furthermore, there are individual differences in these patterns of IQ change. While some children show steady increases, others show increases at certain ages and then declines later in development.

Are IQ scores fixed at birth? On the basis of the evidence so far, the answer to this question is not straightforward. On the one hand, research suggests that IQ scores are fairly stable from middle childhood onward (Kopp & McCall, 1982). On the other hand, there seems to be considerable individual variation in the degree to which IQ scores fluctuate from infancy to adulthood. Currently, most researchers believe that individual differences in these patterns of change are related to aspects of a child's home or school environment. The next section examines some of these influences more closely.

Genetic and Environmental Influences on Intelligence

Genetic Influences on Intelligence

Studies of biological twins are a valuable source of information concerning how genetic and environmental factors influence intelligence. In Chapter 2, you learned that monozygotic twins have the same genotype, whereas dizygotic twins are born from two separate eggs fertilized at the same time by different sperm. Researchers compare these two different sets of twins to estimate the heritability of intelligence. **Heritability** refers to "the proportion of observed variance for a behavior that can be ascribed to genetic differences among individuals in a particular population" (Plomin, 1989). The key word in this definition is *population*. A heritability index is a statistic that applies to a population, rather than a trait or an individual (e.g., She inherited her mathematical abilities from her mother.).

What can twin studies tell us about the heritability of intelligence? Recent data suggest that 50 percent of the variation in intelligence within a population can be attributed to genetic differences between people (Plomin, 1990). Table 4.3 presents findings from two different studies. As you move down the table, individuals differ with regard to genetic similarity. The correlation between IQ scores for monozygotic twins is around 0.86,

Table 4.3	Average Correlations of IQ Scores in Familial Studies	
	Bouchard & McGrue (1981)	**Plomin & DeFries (1980)**
Monozygotic twins reared in same home environment	0.86	0.87
Monozygotic twins reared in different home environments	0.72	—
Dizygotic twins reared in same home environment	0.60	0.62
Parent and child living in same home environment	0.42	0.32
Biological siblings reared in same home environment	0.47	0.30

SOURCES: After Bouchard & McGue (1981) and Plomin & DeFries (1980).

whereas the correlation for dizygotic twins is around 0.60. Note that the correlation between IQ scores for monozygotic twins reared apart (0.72) is higher than that for dizygotic twins reared together (0.60). When monozygotic twins are reared apart they are generally adopted shortly after birth. Because the monozygotic twins are raised in different environments, this finding offers strong support for the genetic position. The twins did not share the same environment, hence any similarity in their intelligence must be due to their similar genotypes.

Sandra Scarr and her associates (Scarr, 1996; Scarr & McCartney, 1983) have developed a model of gene-environmental relations that is useful for understanding the results of twin studies. As described in Table 4.4, there are three types of genotype-environment effects. At a young age, two processes are operating. The first is called a *passive* gene-environment effect. Parents pass on their genes to their offspring and provide an environment for development that is influenced by their own heredity. In this case, it is difficult to disentangle the influence of nature and nurture because the parents' genes are correlated with the child's, as well as with the rearing environment. However, the genotype of children begin to mold the environment through a second gene-environment effect called *evocative*. Different genotypes evoke different reactions for the social and physical environment. A happy baby elicits more positive responses than a temperamental or passive one. Similarly a very verbal preschooler elicits more social interactions with adults and peers than a shy preschooler. The responses these different children receive from their environment shapes their development in ways that correlate with their genotype. For example, the shy child has fewer opportunities to develop social skills. At older ages, an *active* gene-environment effect emerges when children begin to choose friends and activities that fit their genetic tendencies. For example, the shy child may choose to spend time in solitary activities that again limit his or her opportunities to develop social skills. This tendency to choose an environment that complements our heredity is know as **niche-picking** (Scarr & McCartney, 1983). Thus, with age, genetic factors become more important in development because they shape the environments we create for ourselves.

Twin studies provide interesting insights into the role of genetic and environmental factors in development but need to be interpreted with caution.

Table 4.4	Types of Genes → Environment Effects
Passive	Parents pass on their genes to their children and provide an environment based on a shared genetic heredity. For example, parents of a child with high verbal abilities are likely to create a literacy-rich environment. Parents' and children's genes are correlated early in development.
Evocative	Children's genotypes (i.e., temperament, verbal abilities, sex, etc.) evoke different reactions and responses from their environment. Children play a role in shaping and creating their environments. For example, a happy child is likely to evoke positive responses from caregivers, which reinforces a pleasant disposition.
Active	With maturity, children and adolescents choose environments that complement and fit their genetic tendencies. For example, a highly social adolescent is likely to choose friends who are outgoing and enjoy social activities.

SOURCE: After Scarr & McCartney (1983).

Returning to the twin studies, these different types of gene-environment effects help to explain why identical twins are more alike than fraternal twins, even when they are raised by adopted parents. Due to a shared heredity, identical twins are likely to evoke similar responses from their different environments. Similarly, when given an opportunity to choose activities and experiences, they are likely to make similar choices. Numerous stories have been written about identical twins raised apart and later reunited who find out they have similar jobs, hobbies, food preferences, and even spouses. According to Scarr and McCartney's model, differences in development would occur when the choices of one or both twins were restricted so that similar choices could not be made.

Although twin studies are interesting and informative, the data must be interpreted cautiously. Some critics have argued that twin studies do not provide unconfounded estimates of genetic influences. It is assumed that monozygotic twins reared apart experience very different environments, but, in reality, these environments may be quite similar. Adoption criteria dictate certain housing conditions and standards of care. Most adopted children are raised by upper-middle-class families and attend schools during their formative years. Also, as Scarr and McCartney (1983) point out, the child's genotype can shape that environment. Again, it is difficult to disentangle genetic and environmental influences.

Additionally, it must be emphasized that heritability estimates computed on one population cannot be generalized to other populations. Over 20 years ago, Arthur Jensen (1973) sparked a fierce debate when he interpreted data from twin studies as indicating that intelligence was 80 percent hereditary. Jensen further argued that genetic differences explained racial differences in IQ scores. These claims appeared again more recently in *The Bell Curve*, by Herrnstein and Murray (1994). This explanation of racial differences can be criticized for a number of reasons including the cultural bias of IQ tests and unitary versus fixed conceptions of intelligence. More pertinent to our discussion is the misuse of heritability estimates. Conclusions about the genetic basis of racial differences in IQ scores are drawn from twin studies of mostly white children. *A heritability index is limited to the population from which it is derived and to the range of environments found in that sample.* Heritability in other populations depends on the variability of genotypes and environments in that population.

Currently, most theorists believe that genetic factors establish the upper and lower limits, or reaction range (see Chapter 2), of intellectual development. For the most part, intelligence is malleable, and the reaction range defines the degree to which the environment can affect intellectual development. The environment has a stronger influence on children with high intellectual potential but a limited effect on those with low intellectual potential. As the next section will show, educational experiences at home and at school play an important role in the formation, maintenance, and modification of children's intellectual development.

Environmental Influences on Intelligence

Few child development researchers today question the influence of the environment on children's intellectual development. As we learned in Chapter 2, the lack of adequate nutrition and exposure to toxic substances can have a negative effect on early brain development. Also, according to Scarr and McCartney's model, children's intellectual development is most strongly influenced by the home environment during infancy and early childhood when they are under the direct influence of parents. As children mature, schools and peers also begin to play a role in their intellectual socialization. In this section, we examine the influence of the home environment and schooling experiences on children's intellectual development.

Children's intellectual development is strongly influenced by the home environment during infancy and early childhood.

The Home Environment and Early Intellectual Development   We have already discussed how IQ scores begin to stabilize by late childhood. For this reason, numerous studies have focused on the influence of learning experiences in the early childhood years, when parents can have a substantial impact on their children's intellectual development. Many of these studies have used the Home Observation for Measurement of the Environment (HOME) scale developed by Betty Caldwell and Robert Bradley (1978) to characterize the quality of a child's early learning environment. Categories from the HOME scale assess such things as the mother's responsiveness, discipline style, and involvement with the child; the organization of the environment; the availability of appropriate learning materials, and the opportunity for daily stimulation.

Research suggests that parents can have a positive influence on their child's early development if they provide a stimulating and encouraging home environment.

Studies indicate that each of the HOME categories relate positively to children's IQ scores from 6 months to 5 years (Bradley & Caldwell, 1984). Two subscales in particular show consistent and strong relations to IQ scores. Children whose mothers are more responsive and regularly provide stimulating learning activities have scored higher on IQ measures. Figure 4.12 shows mean IQ scores from 1 to 3 years for children whose home environments received high and low ratings. Note that children's early experiences are not only related to their level of IQ but also to changes in their IQ over time. These findings have now been replicated across six different longitudinal studies, in which the HOME scale was used to study a combined sample of 931 children and their families (Bradley et al., 1989).

In summary numerous studies have examined the effects of home and family influences on children's early cognitive development. The findings are fairly consistent across studies and suggest that parents have a positive influence on their child's early intellectual development when they provide appropriate play and learning materials; encourage exploration and stimulate curiosity; and create a warm, responsive, and supportive environment (Belsky, 1981; Baharudin & Luster, 1998).

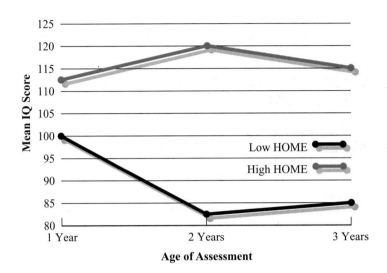
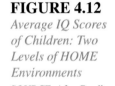

FIGURE 4.12

Average IQ Scores of Children: Two Levels of HOME Environments

SOURCE: After Bradley (1989).

Parenting Behavior and Later Intellectual Development   Research examining the influence of the home environment on early cognitive development is primarily concerned with the factors responsible for the establishment of intellectual competence (Bjorklund, 1995). How can parents help to maintain the benefits of early learning experiences? What can research tell us about the effects of the home environment and parenting practices on children's later intellectual development?

In an early study, Robert McCall and his colleagues (1973) examined changes in children's IQ scores over a 15-year period. This study found patterns of IQ change from ages 2 to 17 that were explained by different types of parenting behavior. In general, children who showed the highest overall IQ levels and the greatest increase in IQ scores between the ages 3 and 12 had parents who were described as "accelerating." These parents attempted to accelerate and stimulate their child's mental and physical development but did so "in a context of moderate structure and discipline" (p. 67). These effects could not be explained by differences in parents' educational levels. Beginning with adolescence, however, there were declines in the IQ scores of these children. This early study seems to support the idea that parents may have less influence on children's intellectual development as they grow older and develop interests outside the home.

Recent studies of adolescents, however, suggest that parenting behavior can affect cognitive functioning well beyond childhood. In general, school achievement is positively related to adolescents' reports of more authoritative parenting styles (Dornbusch, Ritter, Liderman, Roberts, & Fraleigh, 1987; Steinberg, Lamborn, Dornbusch, & Darling, 1992). Authoritative parents are characterized as having high levels of warmth, acceptance, and responsiveness but as setting reasonable expectations for their children and firmly enforcing rules. Authoritative parents also tend to be highly involved in their adolescents' schooling, which studies have shown can have an added influence on school achievement. In contrast, children of authoritarian and permissive parents do not perform as well in school. Chapter 9 provides a more detailed discussion of parenting styles and their relation to different aspects of development.

Although research evidence strongly suggests that the home and family play an important role in the establishment and maintenance of children's intellectual abilities, a few unresolved issues need further discussion. First, much of the research on the home environment and parenting practices has focused on interactions between the mother and child. Researchers have only recently begun to study the effects of fathers on children's abilities (see Chapter 9). Second, it is important to keep in mind that measures of home environment are not totally free of genetic influences. As discussed earlier, parents with a high IQ may provide a better organized environment or more stimulating learning materials. Similarly, a child's genetic characteristics, such as alertness or temperament, may elicit different reactions from the environment. For example, some children may be more responsive to intellectual stimulation than others, thereby reinforcing parental efforts to provide such stimulation. It is important to remember that children affect their environment as much as their environment affects them. The research on parent-child relations underscores the point made earlier that it is nearly impossible to separate genetic and environmental influences.

Furthermore, researchers have only recently begun to examine the validity of home and family findings for different ethnic and socioeconomic groups. For the most part, the general patterns discussed earlier hold up across socioeconomic groups, but there are some important ethnic differences. In adolescent studies, measures of authoritative parenting have a stronger influence for Anglo-Americans and Mexican Americans than they do for Asian and African Americans (Steinberg, Dornbusch, & Brown, 1992). As Robert Bradley and his colleagues (1989) explained, "Parents from different cultural groups not only parent differently, but the 'effect' of particular parent behaviors may vary across different ethnic groups as well" (p. 233). Others have speculated that peer norms and values may explain the lack of influence of parenting practices on school achievement for some minority students (Steinberg, Dornbusch, & Brown, 1992). We discuss the influence of peers in later chapters.

The Effects of Early Intervention   We have discussed how intellectual competence is established and maintained through early experiences in the home. We now turn to research concerning the degree to which children's intellectual development can be modified through early intervention. It is clear that an appropriate level of stimulation, structure, and support is important for optimal intellectual development. Many factors associated with poverty, such as poor nutrition, low maternal education, unemployment, inadequate living conditions, limited educational opportunities, and poor health can all raise the risk of poor intellectual development (Sameroff, Seifer, Barocas, Zax, & Greenspan, 1987). Is it possible to reverse, or at least offset, the negative effects of a poor home environment on children's intellectual development?

During the 1960s, a number of compensatory educational programs were implemented to offset the negative effects of poverty on children's intellectual development. One of the best-known efforts is Project Head Start, a federally funded program for children from low-income families. Established in 1965, Head Start programs provided preschool children with intensive educational experiences, as well as social, medical, and nutritional services. Most of the programs also include a parent education and involvement component. Head Start began as a summer program, grew into a full-year program for 4-year-olds, then continued as Project Follow Through, a compensatory education program for the first three years of elementary school (Oden, Schweinhart, & Weikart, 2000).

Early evaluations of Head Start indicated that almost all programs were able to produce short-term gains in IQ scores. A study of 14 projects showed an IQ increase of approximately 7.42 points (Lazar, Darlington, Murray, Royce, & Snipper, 1982). During kindergarten and first grade, children who attended Head Start performed better on measures of cognitive development than comparable groups of children who had not attended Head Start programs. However, Head Start children lost their advantage as they grew older. By ages 10 and 17, few significant differences were found in the IQ scores of children who did or did not participate. Additionally, evaluations of Project Follow Through showed no

Although high-quality preschool education programs have not produced long-term gains on intelligence tests, they have produced long-term gains in school performance.

enduring changes in IQ scores for its participants. Thus, initial studies concluded that there were no lasting changes in IQ test scores associated with participation in any compensatory education program.

Despite these early findings, researchers and educators were not willing to dismiss the potential benefits of early intervention for economically disadvantaged children. A survey of 14 longitudinal studies of children who participated in Head Start programs during the 1960s reported several positive but delayed effects of the intervention (Lazar et al., 1982). As compared with comparable groups of children who did not participate in the program, Head Start graduates scored higher on reading and mathematics achievement tests in elementary school, and they were less likely to be retained a grade or to receive special education services. Moreover, as teenagers, Head Start participants were less likely to drop out of high school and were more likely to attend college than those who did not participate. In view of this later evidence, researchers now believe that high-quality preschool educational programs, such as Head Start, have long-term effects such as increases in achievement, socialization, motivation, and parental involvement in school. However, the data on raising scores in IQ tests is less clear (Barnett, 1998). The Focus on Research box describes a highly successful early childhood program for low-income children, the High/Scope Perry Preschool Project, that has documented effects well into adulthood.

SOURCE: Cindy Charles/Photo Edit.

Head Start programs for 3- and 4-year-old children can have a lasting influence on development.

Although most Head Start programs typically enroll 3- or 4-year-old children, a few intervention programs have focused on infants (Garber; 1988; Ramey & Campbell, 1984). One of the most successful intervention programs for infants was the Carolina Abecedarian Project, in which participants began before they were 3 months old and continued to the age of 8 (Ramey & Campbell, 1991). The children who participated in this program were judged to be a serious risk for school failure on the basis of family income, maternal IQ and educational level, a history of poor school achievement among older siblings, and other family problems. Participants were randomly assigned to a treatment or control group. The intervention, which enrolled four cohorts of children between 1972 and 1977, occurred in two phases. For the first 5 years, children in the treatment group attended a full-time day care program that promoted the development of motor, cognitive, language, and social skills. When children entered elementary school, a parent education component was implemented to increase parental involvement in the children's education at school.

Evaluations of the Carolina Abecedarian Project were done on a regular basis. Figure 4.13 shows that children who participated in the intervention began to outperform control children on standardized tests of mental abilities after the first year. All children showed a decline in their mental abilities between infancy and age 8, but the decline for the control group was much more significant and substantial. Children in the treatment group maintained their advantage in IQ through preschool and elementary school. At age 12, children in the treatment group were achieving better in school, especially in the areas of reading, writing, and general knowledge, and achievement differences favoring the treatment group

Focus on Research

The High/Scope Perry Preschool Project

Since the early 1960s researchers have been following 123 children who participated in the High/Scope Perry Preschool Project at the ages of 3 or 4. All of the children were African American and were from the same neighborhood in Ypsilanti, Michigan. The mothers of these children had completed an average of 9.5 years of school, and half were on welfare at the onset of the program. The children were randomly assigned to two different groups at the beginning of the project. One group served as the control, and these children did not receive the preschool program. The other group received a high-quality early childhood program based on the child development principles of Jean Piaget. It included activities and social interactions that promoted children's active, constructivist learning and development (Hohmann & Weikart, 1995). The program consisted of 2.5 hours of preschool experience, 5 days a week for 7.5 months over a 2-year period. Teachers also visited each mother and child at home for 90 minutes per week during the school year. Both groups were assessed annually from ages 3 to 11, at ages 14 to 15, at age 19, and at age 27. During the school years, information was collected on school achievement, special education placement, attitudes, classroom behavior, and self-reported delinquency. For the adult assessments, information was collected on years of school completed, employment, public assistance, and criminal records.

Longitudinal data collected over 25 years revealed that the High/Scope program improved children's school achievement, reduced their years in special education placement and compensatory education programs, and increased their graduation rates and years of school completed. Compared with the control group, program participants had lower rates of self-reported delinquency at age 14, and they were less likely to be chronic juvenile offenders at age 19. The latest assessment at age 27 noted these differences favoring the preschool participants:

FIGURE 4.13

IQ Scores of Children in the Carolina Abecedarian Project

SOURCE: After Ramey & Campbell (1991).

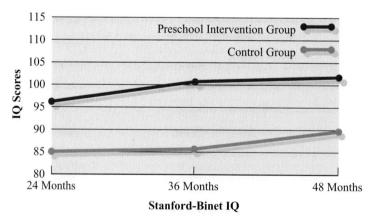

were still evident at age 15 and 21 (Campbell, 2000; Campbell & Ramey, 1993). Interestingly, evaluations of this project showed that school-age interventions alone were not associated with enhanced school achievement or IQ scores. Rather, the low-income children in this project seemed to benefit the most from the preschool phase.

212

- Higher monthly earnings

- Higher percentages of home ownership

- Higher levels of schooling completed

- Lower numbers receiving public assistance

- Fewer arrests

Given these long-term benefits, it is estimated that a high-quality early childhood program, like the Perry Preschool Project, can save taxpayers $7.16 for every $1.00 invested, due to savings in special education and remediation programs and welfare assistance, as well as gains in economic productivity. *Quality* in this preschool program was defined by the following dimensions:

- A developmentally appropriate, active learning curriculum

- Systematic and ongoing staff development, training, and supervision

- A strong parent involvement and inclusion components

- A reasonable child-adult ratio, appropriate assessment procedures, and supportive administration

SOURCE: Oden, Schweinhart, & Weikart (2000); Scheinhart & Weikart (1993).

In summary, outcomes from carefully designed early intervention programs suggest that it is possible to modify the course of intellectual development for low-income children. The results of the Carolina Abecedarian Project further suggest that earlier and longer treatments may have more powerful and longer lasting influences on intellectual development than preschool or school-age interventions (Campbell, Helms, Sparling, & Ramey, 1998; Ramey & Campbell, 1991).

Schooling Influences on Intellectual Development

How important is schooling for children's intellectual development? In Chapter 1, we discussed the ways formal schooling can shape young children's reasoning and thinking abilities. However, we have just seen that the cognitive benefits of early intervention may not extend into the school years. Does schooling have only a limited impact on older children's intellectual development, as these findings seem to suggest?

The available evidence suggests that children's educational experiences affect their intellectual development well beyond infancy and early childhood. In a recent review article, Ceci (1991) organized and presented several different types of evidence to support this claim.

- There are strong correlations between IQ and years of school completed. After controlling for socioeconomic status and other background variables, this correlation ranges between 0.60 and 0.80. Individuals who stay in school longer have higher IQ scores.
- Children who are truant or frequently absent from school have lower IQ scores than children who attend school regularly.
- A South African study showed that children experience a 5-point deficit in IQ scores for every year their schooling is delayed.
- A Swedish study of high school dropouts and graduates indicated that there was a loss of 1.8 IQ points for each year of high school that was not completed.
- Children experience a small but substantial decline in IQ scores over the summer months, with low-income children showing the largest decline, possibly because their summer activities do not resemble those found in school. Children who engage in schoollike activities over the summer do not show the June to September IQ drop.
- A study of African American children who migrated from poor, segregated schools in Georgia to better quality schools in Philadelphia between World Wars I and II showed that children gained about one-half an IQ point for each year they attended the northern school.

Some of the strongest evidence of the impact of schooling on children's intellectual development can be found in studies that use the cut-off method to study early cognitive development (see Chapter 1). If intellectual development is mostly controlled by maturational or biological processes, then we would expect to find children's IQ scores to be influenced more by age than by years of schooling. If you recall, studies show that first-grade children with early birthdates (before the cut-off date for school entry) perform better than their slightly younger peers who had started school one year later.

Children who start school earlier, remain in school longer, and attend higher-quality schools generally perform better on IQ tests.

To summarize, a number of studies emphasize the important influence of schools on children's intellectual development. Children who start school earlier, remain in school longer, and attend higher-quality schools generally perform better on IQ tests. Because much of the data cited in this section are from correlational studies, it is not possible to draw firm conclusions about cause-and-effect relations. It is suggested here that the quantity and quality of school leads to increases in IQ. Of course, it is equally possible that genetically intelligent people are encouraged to start school earlier, remain in school longer, and attend better schools. However, Ceci (1990) argued that schooling is most likely to influence children's performance on IQ tests, because schools teach the information and various perceptual, memory, and problem-solving skills that are needed to perform well on IQ tests. In other words, aspects of intelligence are learned at school.

Group Differences in Cognitive Abilities

Standardized tests of intelligence and academic achievement are often used to examine group differences in cognitive abilities. This section examines recent research on ethnic and gender differences in intellectual abilities. We will also briefly discuss some possible explanations for the differences that are reported. Although many studies report ethnic and gender differences in children's standardized test scores, there is little conclusive evidence for a genetic explanation. Most researchers believe that ethnic and gender variations in intellectual abilities are due largely to socialization experiences and cultural conditions.

SOURCE: Frank
Siteman/Stock Boston.

The school population is becoming more and more ethnically diverse. Ethnic differences in achievement are found as early as first grade.

Racial and Ethnic Differences

Differences in IQ and Standardized Test Scores

The word *race* is used to refer to a group of people such as African Americans, Asians, or whites "who share biologically transmitted traits that are defined as socially significant," such as skin color or hair texture (Macionis, 1991, p. 308). Ethnicity, on the other hand, refers to a group of people who share a common nationality, cultural heritage, and language, such as Japanese, Chinese, Cuban, or Mexican. As discussed in Chapter 1, the ethnic and racial composition of American schools is rapidly changing. Over two-thirds of the students enrolled in United States public schools are likely to be a member of an ethnic minority group by the year 2010. The changing racial and ethnic backgrounds of America's schoolchildren will have profound implications for education in the future. Research indicates children from different ethnic and racial groups score significantly lower on virtually every test of cognitive ability than do their non-Hispanic, white classmates. The major exceptions to this pattern are Asian American children, who tend to perform better on tests of quantitative abilities than white children.

Most of the early research focused on racial differences in IQ and achievement test scores. Differences in IQ scores are found as early as World War I when tests were administered to military personnel. In general, performance gaps between whites and blacks on IQ tests are approximately 15 points, or one standard deviation unit. IQ gaps are generally smaller between white and Hispanic populations (Williams & Ceci, 1997). It is important to note here the overlaps in score distributions, despite the 15-point performance gap. Differences in IQ scores are found by age 3 and remain constant until adulthood (Brody, 1992). Similarly, gaps in achievement test scores show little change from first to twelfth grade (Jencks & Phillips, 1998).

Some evidence suggests that the black-white performance gap is narrowing. According to several reviews (Jones, 1984; Jencks & Phillips, 1998; Williams & Ceci, 1997), reading

It is likely that ethnic and gender variations in intellectual abilities are caused largely by socialization experiences and cultural conditions.

Table 4.5	Ethnic Group Differences in Proficiency Levels for Reading, Mathematics, and Science: 1999 National Assessment of Educational Progress		
	Age 9	**Age 13**	**Age 17**
Reading			
Whites	221	267	295
Blacks	186	238	264
Hispanics	193	244	271
Total	212	259	288
Mathematics			
Whites	239	283	315
Blacks	211	251	283
Hispanics	213	259	293
Total	232	276	308
Science			
Whites	240	266	306
Blacks	199	227	254
Hispanics	206	227	276
Total	229	256	295

Note: Scores on each subtest of the National Assessment of Educational Process range from 0 to 400. A mean score of 250 indicates that the student can perform basic operations in that area.

SOURCE: National Center for Educational Statistics (2000c).

and mathematics performance measured by the National Assessment of Educational Progress showed a decline in the white-black difference from 1971 to 1980 at each age of assessment (9, 13, and 17 years). Some estimates indicate that the gaps had narrowed by 25 to 50 percent depending on subject area and grade level (Williams & Ceci, 1997). This decline is due to rises in the average level of performance by African American students. The verbal and quantitative subtests of the Scholastic Aptitude Test (SAT), which is taken by college-bound high school seniors, also shows a decline in the white-black gap over the last 25 years. In this case, declines are due to decreases in the performance of white students and increases in the performance of African American students.

Unfortunately, recent evidence suggests that this convergence in test scores did not continue through the 1980s and 1990s. Table 4.5 shows eighth-grade results from the 1999 National Assessment of Educational Progress by race or ethnicity. For both mathematics and reading, achievement gaps have widened somewhat. Overall, the average mathematics scores of 17-year-old African Americans are about the same as those of 13-year-old white students (NCES, 2000). In science, achievement gaps are considerably larger, and there has not been much change in the size of the achievement gap from the early 1980s.

The major exception to the achievement patterns of ethnic minority students are Asian Americans, who generally outperform Anglo-American classmates on tests of mathematical reasoning, spatial abilities, and numerical skills (Sue & Okazaki, 1990). Achievement gaps

Focus on Research

Ethnic differences in educational achievement and school success are well documented. One of the most interesting findings in this research literature is the relatively high academic performance of some Asian American groups during the last 40 years (Chen & Stevenson, 1995; Sue & Okazaki, 1990; Okagaki & Frensch, 1998). On the average, Asian Americans perform better in U.S. schools than do African Americans and Hispanic Americans, even though they experience racial prejudice and discrimination (Sue & Okazaki, 1990). For college-bound students, the grade point averages of Asian Americans is often higher than that of Anglo-Americans. Moreover, the superior performances of Asian American students emerges during the transition to junior high school, when most students' grades decline (Fulgini, 1994).

What explains the exceptional achievement of Asian American students in U.S. schools? There is no evidence that these differences are explained by genetic or socioeconomic factors (Sue & Okazaki, 1990). Much of the evidence instead suggests that the values and child-rearing practices of Asian families play a very important role. Compared to other ethnic groups, Asian parents are more likely to believe that success in life is associated with educational achievement (Ritter & Dornbusch, 1989; Okagaki & Frensch, 1998). In addition, Asian parents teach their children that success is in their own hands. All children can succeed in school if they work hard (Chen & Stevenson, 1995; Stevenson & Stigler, 1992). More important, Asian parents emphasize a family-based orientation to achievement. Achievement is viewed as a way to repay one's parents for their sacrifices (Slaughter-Defoe, Nakagawa, Takanishi, & Johnson, 1990).

As a result of socialization practices at home, Asian American students value school achievement, and they worry about the possible negative consequences of not doing well in terms of their parents' disappointment and future occupational choices (Steinberg, Dornbusch, & Brown, 1992). In fact, some evidence suggests that a fear of failure may be an important motivating factor for Asian American students (Eaton & Dembo, 1997). They also spend more time on homework and significantly less time socializing and watching television than other students (Caplan, Choy, & Whitemore, 1992; Fuligini & Stevenson, 1995). Additionally, Asian American students tend to believe that the only way they can succeed in mainstream American society is through educational achievement, and they pay less of a price for their superior performance than other ethnic groups in terms of depression, anxiety, or stress (Crystal et al., 1994). In contrast, African American and Hispanic American students tend to believe that educational achievement will have less occupational payoff for them within a prejudiced society (Ogbu, 1978).

on IQ tests are approximately one-fifth of a standard deviation unit, or 3 to 4 IQ points (Williams & Ceci, 1997). Even children of Southeast Asian boat people, who arrive at school with little knowledge of English and Western culture, are able to excel in mathematics within a short period of time (Caplan, Choy, & Whitmore, 1992). The Focus on Research box describes some of the factors that contribute to the high academic achievement of Asian American students.

One of the major shortcomings of research on racial and ethnic differences in cognitive abilities is that it fails to examine differences within ethnic groups. There are often wide differences within as well as between ethnic groups. For example, there are differences in the achievement levels of Chinese Americans, Filipino Americans, and Vietnamese Americans that are masked when students are treated as one homogeneous group of Asian Americans. In addition, research indicates that recent immigrants tend to achieve better in school than American-born ethnic minority students (Spencer & Dornbusch, 1990). Girls perform better on tests of cognitive abilities than boys in some ethnic groups. Also, few studies have disentangled social class and ethnic differences. Middle-class African American students perform better on cognitive tests than their lower-class peers.

Possible Explanations

Scientists have not yet identified the genes that affect cognitive abilities. Without direct genetic evidence, it is difficult to make a strong case for innate differences. Most researchers believe that ethnic differences in intellectual performance are greatly influenced by social and economic factors. As described in Chapter 1, a disproportionate number of African American and Hispanic American children are from low-income families. Poor children experience a number of conditions that can negatively affect their cognitive development, such as poor nutrition, inadequate health care, overcrowded living conditions, low parental education, and chronic stress. Poor children also receive a poorer quality of education because they attend schools in poor communities. When differences in children's socioeconomic background are controlled, performance gaps on IQ and achievement tests narrow, but do not totally disappear (Suzuki & Valencia, 1997).

Because most schools reflect a white middle-class culture, ethnic minority children experience a number of problems when they enter school. Non-English-speaking children struggle the most, because they must master a new language before they can fully participate in learning activities in most schools. Even if children speak English, they may use speech patterns of a particular ethnic, social, or regional group, called social dialects, that white teachers find unacceptable. Because some dialects are viewed as linguistically inferior to more standard speech patterns, a dialect can affect teachers' judgments of children's abilities, their learning potential, and how they should be grouped for instruction (Harrison, 1985). Teachers who expect problems with children on the basis of judgments of their dialects are more likely to treat these children differently in the classroom, which may, in turn, influence children's feelings of competence, self-worth, and motivation to learn.

The way teachers ask questions in school can also cause problems for children who are not from the dominant culture. According to Shirley Brice Heath (1983), parents in some African American communities do not ask questions that have an obvious answer unless the child is being disciplined. Additionally, children are taught not to ask or answer personal questions. In school, however, teachers often ask "known-answer" questions ("What color is your shirt?") and personal questions ("Where does your mother work?"). When African American children take a long time to respond, teachers infer that they have a hearing or comprehension problem: "I would almost think some of them have a hearing problem; it is as though they don't hear me ask a question. I get blank stares to my questions" (pp. 107–108).

There are many other examples of cultural differences in behaviors and customs that can influence an ethnic minority child's success in school. In many cultures, group achievement is valued over individual success. Children of these cultures (e.g., Native American, Mexican American, Asian American) may resist competing with others for grades and other incentives that are used to motivate and reward students in school. They may also feel uncomfortable when their individual achievements are publicly recognized. Certain Native

American communities do not express feelings through facial expressions or maintain eye contact in verbal exchanges with adults. These cultural differences can lead to adjustment and achievement problems for ethnic minority students if the behaviors are interpreted as unacceptable, inappropriate, or "odd" by teachers or peers.

The achievement problems of racial and ethnic minority students are compounded by a school's **ability grouping** or **tracking** systems. In elementary school, children are generally grouped according to their ability for reading and mathematics. Frequently this ability grouping occurs within the classroom, but some elementary schools may assign students to classes based on their achievement levels. This process is known as between-class ability grouping or tracking. Most high schools have college preparatory, general, or vocational tracks. In general, students who are placed in low-ability groups during elementary school remain in those tracks through high school. Research indicates that a disproportionate number of ethnic minority students, not including Asian Americans, are placed in lower-ability groups or classes. Considerable evidence suggests that ability grouping and tracking systems can severely limit minority children's learning and achievement opportunities for the following reasons (Oakes, 1995; Oakes & Stuart, 1998):

> *Cultural differences, if interpreted as unacceptable or "odd" by mainstream teachers, can lead to adjustment and achievement problems for ethnic minority students.*

- There are clear differences in the quality of instruction across ability groups. Teachers of low-ability classes place little emphasis on problem-solving and inquiry skills. Compared to higher-ability classes, there is a stronger emphasis on rote memorization, basic skills, and remediation in low-ability classes. Teaching for higher-order thinking is more likely to occur in high-ability than low-ability classes.
- Students in low-ability classes are often taught by less-experienced teachers.
- Students in low-ability classes are likely to be perceived as slow and incompetent, which can lower self-esteem and motivation.
- Tracking systems determine the courses students can take in high school, which, in turn, affects students' eligibility for college.

On the basis of this evidence, it is not surprising that ability grouping and tracking tend to accentuate rather than diminish preexisiting ability differences among racial or ethnic groups. Unfortunately, it appears that students inside or outside the mainstream culture who need the most help and encouragement in school are often assigned to classes where instruction is likely to be the poorest and the least motivating.

> *Children from nonmainstream cultures are often placed in lower-ability groups, which limits their educational opportunities.*

To summarize, most theorists believe that the underachievement of ethnic minority students in American schools is due to a combination of social and economic factors. A disproportionate number of ethnic minority students are from low-income families and attend schools in poor communities. At school, ethnic minority students experience adjustment and academic problems due to the white middle-class culture of their schools. Their problems are further complicated by ability and tracking systems that can severely restrict learning opportunities and educational aspirations. Creating a positive learning environment for students of all racial and ethnic backgrounds will involve changes in the curriculum, the organization and culture of schools, the attitudes and beliefs of school staff, and the way students are currently taught and evaluated. We will discuss some strategies for achieving these objectives at the end of the chapter.

Performance Differences Between Genders

Look inside any high school physics or calculus class today, and you are likely to find more boys than girls present. At the lower grade levels, more boys than girls are diagnosed as having reading problems and are placed in the low reading groups. Most people argue that these performance differences simply reflect innate mental abilities. Boys are thought to be good at spatial and mathematical tasks, whereas girls are assumed to have good verbal skills. Are there differences in the cognitive abilities of women and men? If so, when do these differences in cognitive abilities appear in development? Because most standardized IQ tests are constructed to remove gender bias, most studies report no overall differences in IQ scores (Brody, 1992). Gender-related differences in scores are limited to specific skill areas. Early studies reported a small female advantage on tests of verbal abilities and a male advantage on tests of spatial skills and mathematical abilities (Maccoby & Jacklin, 1974). Current research indicates that there are also significant differences in students' science abilities along gender lines.

Verbal Abilities

In their classic book *The Psychology of Sex Differences,* Eleanor Maccoby and Carolyn Jacklin (1974) wrote, "Female superiority on verbal tasks has been one of the most solidly established generalizations of the field of sex differences" (p. 74). Verbal tasks can include anything from speech fluency to reading comprehension. Consistent with Maccoby and Jacklin's assertion, studies published before 1973 reveal a minor female advantage of approximately one-fifth a standard deviation on verbal assessments (Hyde & Linn, 1988). Since 1974, however, the male-female discrepancy has declined to about one-tenth a standard deviation, indicating no reliable gender difference in verbal abilities. Moreover, there is little variation in gender effects across different age groups. Thus, most researchers now believe there is a negligible difference in verbal abilities between sexes (Caplan, 1999; Hedges & Nowell, 1995; Hyde & Linn, 1988).

Spatial Abilities

Spatial skills are believed to contribute to gender-specific abilities in mathematics and science performance (Linn & Hyde, 1989). Examples of spatial problem-solving tasks include identifying hidden objects embedded in a complex design, the ability to rotate two- or three-dimensional objects in space, and the ability to reason about spatially presented information. Research in this area, however, yields no clear pattern of findings with regard to gender differences. In a 1985 review, Marcia Linn and Anne Petersen (1985) reviewed 127 gender effects in spatial abilities. Their analysis revealed that performance differences favoring males was most measurable for tasks that involved mental rotation of two- or three-dimensional objects. (A mental rotation task is shown in Figure 4.14.) A 1995 review of gender differences in spatial abilities report similar findings (Voyer, Voyer, & Bryden, 1995). Some studies report gender differences in spatial abilities before adolescence. However, the evidence also suggested that the magnitude of the discrepancy for some spatial tests has declined from one-third to one-tenth a standard deviation since 1974. Researchers argue that a gender effect of this magnitude can be eliminated by instructional intervention. Furthermore, there is little evidence to support the assertion that students' abilities to perform mental rotation tasks are related to their mathematics and science performance (Linn & Hyde, 1989).

Mathematical Abilities

Differences measured between genders in students' mathematics abilities depend on a student's age and the type of test used (Hyde, Fennema, & Lamon, 1990). During elementary and middle school, girls generally out perform boys on tests of computational skills. No gender-attributable differences in students' algebra and basic mathematics knowledge

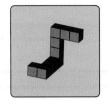

Standard

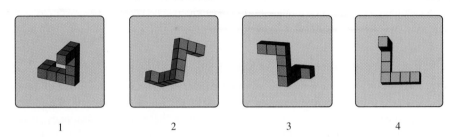

1   2   3   4

A mental rotation item. Respondents are asked to identify the two responses that show
the standard in a different orientation.

FIGURE 4.14

*Example of a Mental
Rotation Task*

SOURCE: After Linn &
Peterson (1985).

have been measured. Among high school students, boys score slightly higher on tests of mathematics reasoning and problem solving (primarily word problems). However, on most standardized tests of mathematics achievement for older adolescents and young adults, the gender gap is closing. For example, data from the 1999 National Assessment of Educational Progress (NAEP) showed no significant gender differences in mathematics performance at ages 9, 13, or 17 (NCES, 2000b). Many early studies of mathematics achievement revealed differences of 0.30 to 0.50 standard deviation, whereas recent national studies reveal differences of less than 0.15 standard deviation (Hedges & Nowell, 1995; Linn & Hyde, 1989). Among mathematically gifted students, however, tests show large differences between female and male performances, especially for the SAT—M. Some researchers, however, attribute this anomaly to the content and format of the SAT—M, which tends to favor males (Linn & Hyde, 1989). It is interesting to note here that girls receive higher grades than boys in mathematics from grade school through college (Adelman, 1991; Kimball, 1989).

Even within mathematically gifted populations, where boys generally out perform girls on standardized achievement tests, girls receive higher math grades. Female superiority in math grades is often overlooked in mathematical ability research (Halpern, 1997).

Science Abilities

Differences by gender in students' science abilities are not consistent across age groups and content areas. On general

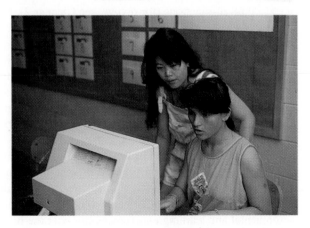

Research suggests that girls approach computers as a tool, whereas boys approach them as toys.

SOURCE: James L. Shaffer.

tests of science achievement, there are few gender-related performance differences at the elementary school level. Differences in science abilities between girls and boys begin to occur in middle school and increase as students progress in school. By high school, studies reveal gender differences of about one-third of a standard deviation, and the magnitude of this difference depends on the content area. Gender differences are more evident in the physical sciences, whereas no gender differences in achievement are found for the biological sciences (Hyde & McKinley, 1997). Recent NAEP data indicate a narrowing of the gender gap in science achievement since the 1980s (NCES, 2000). However other evidence indicates that men outnumber women by a margin of 7 to 1 among individuals who do perform extremely well (top 5 percent) on standardized tests of science achievement (Hedges & Nowell, 1995).

Conclusions About Gender Differences

In most academic areas, gender differences are declining, and some experts predict that they will disappear altogether in the next decade.

It is difficult to draw any firm conclusions about gender differences in cognitive abilities. Measurable ability differences between sexes depend on the age of the subjects, the content area, and the type of cognitive measure used. In most areas, these ability differences are declining. Although this section's focus has been on performance differences between boys and girls, it is important to keep in mind the considerable overlap in all students' abilities. Some girls can out perform the majority of boys on mathematical tasks, and some boys can do better than most girls on verbal tasks. Most researchers view girls and boys as more similar than different in their cognitive abilities. As one researcher put it, "We can predict very little about an individual's mental abilities based on his or her sex" (Kimura, 1989).

Possible Explanations

Biological Explanations   Researchers who favor biological explanations point to hormone levels and brain organization. There is growing evidence that hormone levels can influence women's and men's performance on cognitive tasks. Recent evidence suggests that women's abilities to perform certain cognitive or motor tasks fluctuates over their menstrual cycle. Similarly, men's performance on visual-spatial tasks fluctuates with daily variations in testosterone. Also, studies show that testosterone treatment for men with low levels of this hormone can improve their spatial performance (Halpern, 1997).

The biological explanation of gender-based differences in cognitive functioning fails to explain why differences are not evident during early development.

Another popular theory states that the female brain is less lateralized than the male brain. By *lateralized,* researchers mean that each of the two cerebral hemispheres performs a special set of functions (for review, see Chapter 2). New technologies have enabled researchers to perform brain scans while men and women are performing different cognitive tasks. By monitoring changes in the blood flow to different areas of the brain, researchers have found that women tend to use both sides of the brain while performing spelling and mental rotation tasks. Men, on the other hand, primarily use their left hemisphere for spelling tasks and their right hemisphere for spatial tasks. It is believed that this lateralization in brain functioning enables men to perform highly specialized visual-spatial tasks better. Currently, however, there is not agreement among researchers on this assertion (Halpern, 1997).

The search for biological causes to explain gender differences in cognitive functioning is likely to continue for some time. At present, the influence of hormonal levels and brain lateralization on cognitive functioning is not well understood. Even if there are innate causes to explain gender differences in cognitive functioning, the influence at birth of environmental and learning experiences can alter the brain's biochemistry and physiology. Perhaps the strongest evidence against the biological argument is that gender-related performance differences in some spatial perception tasks can be eliminated through instructional intervention (Conner, Shackman, & Serbin, 1978). More important, if biological factors were the strongest influence on ability, we would expect to see gender differences in children's cognitive abilities early in development, which is not the case. Linn and Petersen's (1985) review of a decade of possible biological influence on spatial abilities concluded that there is "no noncontroversial evidence for genetic explanations of gender differences in cognitive and psychosocial factors" (p. 53).

Environmental Explanations   Researchers who favor environmental explanations focus on the socialization experiences of boys and girls in a number of different contexts. In Chapter 7, we will discuss research on sex-role socialization, the process by which children acquire the knowledge, skills, and traits appropriate for their gender. In the home, this socialization begins early and takes a number of different forms. From an early age, boys and girls have opportunities to learn gender-appropriate skills and traits. Traditionally, parents tended to buy trucks, hammers, and blocks for their sons and stuffed animals, dolls, and kitchen toys for their daughters. American parents react more positively when children play with sex-typed toys or engage in gender-appropriate behaviors. For example, parents respond more positively when their sons rather than their daughters play with cars and trucks. They also respond more negatively to daughters than to sons who demand attention or take toys away from other children (Fagot & Kavanaugh, 1991). Collectively, studies of children's early socialization into gender roles indicate that boys are encouraged to engage in activities that help develop spatial skills, mathematical reasoning, and problem solving, whereas girls are encouraged to develop their verbal and interpersonal skills (Lytton & Romney, 1991). We will touch on gender-role socialization within the family again in Chapter 7 including the family conditions that lead children to develop less sex-stereotypic attitudes.

Sex-role socialization is the process by which children acquire the knowledge, skills, and traits considered appropriate for their gender.

Along these same lines, American parents also communicate different expectations for achievement to their sons and daughters. For example, Anglo-American parents expect their sons more than their daughters to attain an advanced graduate degree (Adelman, 1991). Studies of high school students also reveal that Anglo-American parents are more likely to encourage their sons rather than their daughters to take advanced high school courses in mathematics, chemistry, and physics (Eccles, Jacobs, & Harold, 1991). Gender differences in parental expectations for their sons' and daughters' achievement in mathematics and reading are found as early as the first grade (Lummis & Stevenson, 1990).

It is clear that gender socialization begins at home. What role might schools play in this process? Unfortunately, much evidence suggests that schools serve to reinforce or strengthen gender differences in students' skills and interests (Meece, 1987). Two major reports, *How Schools Shortchange Girls* (AAUW, 1992) and *Failing at Fairness: How Schools Cheat Girls* (Sadker & Sadker, 1995), identified ways in which schools help to reproduce gender inequities in society.

Evidence suggests that schools serve to reinforce or strengthen gender differences in students' skills and interests.

- Women constitute a majority of classroom teachers, but they are underrepresented in administrative positions. Also, a higher number of men than women teach advanced mathematics and science classes in high school. Such staffing patterns teach students who can lead and who is good at math or science.
- Masculine images and interests continue to be overrepresented in curriculum materials, particularly in mathematics and science. A male bias is also evident in computer programs and testing materials.
- Boys receive considerably more attention than girls in the classroom, which reinforces a perception of male dominance and importance. High-ability girls receive the least amount of attention of all groups.

- When asking complex, abstract, or open-ended questions, teachers call on boys more frequently than girls. They also wait longer for boys than girls to answer questions and provide more detailed feedback to boys than to girls. These differences are most pronounced in mathematics and science classes.
- Approximately 90 percent of the criticism girls receive for school work is directed at the intellectual quality of their work, compared with 50 percent for boys. When boys are criticized, they are often told their poor performance is due to lack of effort. Girls are less likely to receive this message from teachers.
- When classes are divided into ability groups, boys with high mathematics achievement scores are more likely than girls with similar scores to be assigned to high-ability groups.
- When boys and girls work on projects together, girls are more likely to watch and listen while boys perform the activity.
- Girls respond more favorably to a cooperative rather than competitive classroom environment, but few classrooms emphasize cooperation and collaborative efforts.
- Student reports of sexual harassment are increasing. In most cases, boys are harassing girls, which can affect girls' participation in class, school attendance, and study habits.

As this analysis indicates, sex-role messages pervade almost every aspect of children's schooling experiences. A recent analysis of post-1992 studies reveals that gender-differentiated behaviors continue to be perpetuated and reinforced in school settings (AAUW, 1998).

It is important to point out that gender differences in teachers' behaviors may be due to how boys and girls behave in the classroom. As discussed earlier in this chapter, people evoke certain reactions from their environment. Boys may be called on more frequently than girls, because they are more active or assertive. Despite the source of these exchanges in the classroom, the result is that as young women progress in school they are less likely than men to take advanced courses in mathematics and science. Research also indicates that when differences in course enrollment patterns are controlled, gender differences in mathematics achievement in late adolescence and young adulthood decrease substantially or disappear altogether (Adelman, 1991; Oakes, 1990).

What Can Schools Do?

By the year 2020, two-thirds of the workforce will be made up of women and ethnic minorities, a fact that makes it imperative that schools provide an equal education for all children.

By the year 2020, two-thirds of our workforce will be made up of women and ethnic minorities. Clearly, schools need to make a better effort to create learning environments that provide equal resources, encouragement, and opportunities to girls and boys of all backgrounds. The subtle and not-so-subtle messages women and minorities receive in school about their abilities and future careers must be changed.

Most teacher preparation programs now offer courses on multicultural education. According to James Banks (1994), multicultural education has two important goals: (1) to increase educational equality and opportunity for all students, regardless of their culture, race, ethnicity, gender, religion, social class, or exceptionality; and (2) to promote positive intergroup attitudes and values, so that all students can function more effectively in a pluralistic society and an international community. To achieve these objectives, multicultural education will need to go beyond the study of Native American cultures at Thanksgiving or celebrations of Black History Month, Cinco de Mayo, and Women's History Week. Creating culturally compatible schools will involve radical changes in the curriculum materials, the organization of schools, the attitudes and beliefs of school staff,

Focus on Teaching

1. Teachers and school administrators have expectations for all students and positive attitudes toward them. They also respond to them in positive and caring ways.

2. The formalized curriculum reflects the experiences, cultures, and perspectives of a range of cultural and ethnic groups as well as of both genders.

3. Teaching styles match the learning, cultural, and motivational styles of the students.

4. Teachers and administrators show respect for the students' first language and dialects.

5. Instructional materials used in the school show events, situations, and concepts from the perspectives of a range of cultural, ethnic, and racial groups.

6. Assessment and testing procedures used in the school are culturally sensitive and result in students of color being represented proportionately in classes for the gifted and talented.

7. The school culture reflects cultural and ethnic diversity.

8. School counselors have high expectations for students from different racial, ethnic, and language groups and help all students to set and to realize positive career goals.

SOURCE: After Banks (1994).

the school culture, and the ways students are currently taught and assessed. The Focus on Teaching box lists eight characteristics of multicultural schools identified by Banks (1994).

Television, Computers, and Children's Learning

Over the last 50 years, televisions, radios, videos, CD players, and computers have become a central feature of children's lives. By the time young people reach their eighteenth birthday, they will have watched at least 15,000 hours of television (Minow & LaMay, 1995). This figure does not include the time they have spent watching videos, playing video games, or surfing the Internet. Sixty percent of American homes with children between the ages of 8 and 17 have computers, and most of these computers are connected to the

It is estimated that young people watch 15,000 hours of television by their eighteenth birthdays.

Internet (Turrow, 1999). Household surveys also reveal that children as young as 2 are using the computer for 27 minutes per day (Woodward & Gridina, 2000).

Concerns about the effect of technology on children's development date back to the early 1900s, when motion pictures were first introduced (see Watella & Jennings, 2000). This technological innovation was soon labeled as immoral for exposing children to "scenes of violence and debauchery" (Wartella & Jennings, 2000, p. 32). A 1929 study of more than 10,000 children's movie-watching habits in Chicago indicated that they were often exposed to content well beyond their years (Mitchell, 1929; as cited in Watella & Jennings, 2000). By 1931, national organizations were calling for federal legislation to regulate motion pictures. The introduction of radios in the 1920s was met with similar opposition from religious and education groups. Although radio was federally regulated from the beginning, it was soon attacked for its treatment of crime and violence and charged with contributing to juvenile delinquency. Studies in the 1940s revealed that radio had a wide range of effects on children's development, but these effects were modified by family circumstances and the child's level of development (Wartella & Jennings, 2000). Television was introduced in 1948, and Congress was holding hearings on its possible effects on juvenile delinquency and crime as early as 1955.

For the most part, this early research focused on the effects of different technological innovations on children's attitudes, values, and social behavior. Although much attention is still focused on the negative socializing influence of mass media (see Huston & Wright, 1998), researchers have also begun to focus on the role of technology in children's cognitive development. Much of the research to date focuses on television, but there is now a growing body of research examining the effects of computer technology on children's learning in and outside of school. In the following sections, we will consider the effects of television and computers on young people's learning and school achievement.

Television: The 15,000-Hour Curriculum

Young people spend as much time in front of the television as they do in school. On a school day, they watch an average of 3 hours of television per day. Television viewing increases to 6 to 8 hours per day on weeks and holidays. As Figure 4.15 shows, younger

FIGURE 4.15

Percent of Students Who Reported Watching 6 or More Hours of Television per Day

SOURCE: U.S. Department of Health and Human Services (2000).

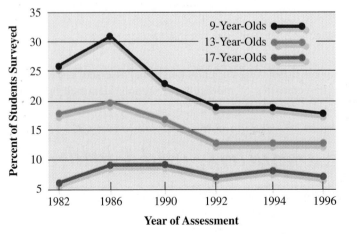

Children watch an average of 3 hours of television per day. Younger children watch more television than do adolescents.

children watch more television than adolescents do, and boys watch more television than girls do. Also, poor children of all ethnic backgrounds watch more television than do children from more affluent homes. Although there are many good television shows for young people, such as *Sesame Street, The Magic Bus,* and *The Puzzle Place,* children more often watch noneducational programs or adult programs.

Since the introduction of television, concerns have been raised about its potential effects on children's intellectual development. When children are "glued" to the television for 3 to 4 hours per day, it may leave less time for other activities. We have already discussed how television viewing may contribute to childhood obesity. There is also some evidence that television displaces leisure reading, but this association is not straightforward nor consistently found across studies (Huston & Wright, 1998). For example, one longitudinal study showed that television displaced reading as children moved from grade 3 to grade 5, but for older children, an increase in reading resulted in a decrease in television viewing (Ritchie, Price, & Roberts, 1987). Similarly, there is no strong evidence indicating that television viewing reduces time for homework (Huston & Wright, 1998).

Although many educators and parents believe that television viewing can negatively affect school achievement, this pattern is most consistently found in young people who are heavy viewers (Neuman, 1988; Williams, Haertel, Walberg, & Haertal, 1982). Among eighth and twelfth graders, for example, television was negatively related to achievement for teens who exceeded 30 hours of television viewing per week (Porter, 1987). When specific academic skills are examined, television viewing is negatively related to early reading skills, but the effect is weak and not found in older students (Huston & Wright, 1998). It is also important to point out that television viewing does not appear to negatively affect older children's attention span, creativity, or imagination. Several studies have examined these effects and found no conclusive evidence to support this claim (Huston & Wright, 1998).

Other evidence suggests that high-quality programs can have positive academic benefits for all children but especially for low-income children. *Sesame Street* is a prime example. Repeated evaluations of this program have shown that it has positive effects on children's school readiness, academic skills, and school adjustment. In a group of 2- to 5-year-olds who watched this program, improvements were found in vocabulary size, letter recognition, and math skills. These effects were not otherwise related to parent's education, income level, language spoken at home (English versus Spanish), or the overall quality of the home environment (Huston & Wright, 1998). Thus, these studies suggest that television can be an effective teacher when programs are well designed for young children. Children can learn literacy and numeracy skills, as well as information about science, geography, and history.

In summary, there is little doubt that television is a part of young people's daily life. To date, there is only weak evidence that television displaces school-related activities (homework and reading) or negatively affects children's reading, attention span, or school achievement when differences in family characteristics and the home environment are controlled. Television's positive or negative effects depend on the amount of time young people spend in front of the television, as well as on the content of the program. High-quality television programs can have positive benefits. Unfortunately, less than high quality television often presents a social world that includes violence, stereotyped images, and frightening events. It is estimated that the average preschool child, who is still learning to distinguish reality from fantasy, witnesses 600 violent acts per week on television (Minow & LaMay, 1995). Studies also reveal that nearly 30 percent of the interactions in shows most popular among adolescents contain statements related to sexuality (Ward, 1995). In Chapter 8, we will discuss the potential effects of television on social concepts and aggression.

High-quality educational programs designed for children can have positive effects on early reading and math skills and on school adjustment.

Computers and Children's Learning

Like television, the use of computers is rapidly becoming a routine part of children's lives. Among households with children ages 2 to 17, home computer ownership went from 48 percent in 1996 to 70 percent in 2000 (Woodward & Gridina, 2000). Surveys also revealed that nearly twice that number of children have access to computers at school (Becker, 2000). As with other technological innovations, researchers are interested in the effects of computers on children's activities and development. What are the potential educational benefits or risks of this form of mass media? In this section, we will consider how computers are changing what and how children learn. We will begin with a discussion of who has access to computers, then turn to their influence on learning and school achievement. Research is also beginning to identify the impact of computers on children's social development and emotional well-being (Watella & Jennings, 2000), but discussion of this research is beyond the scope of this chapter.

Access to Computers

One issue of concern is *who* has access to computers. It is generally believed that there is a growing digital divide separating children from different socioeconomic groups in the United States. On the whole, surveys reveal that children between the ages of 2 and 17 spend approximately 1.5 hours per day using the computer or playing video games (Becker, 2000). When this figure is added to hours of television viewing, children with access to computers or video games are spending, on average, 4 to 5 hours per day in front of a television screen or a computer monitor (Stranger & Gridina, 1999). However, as shown in Figure 4.16, children's access to computers at home is greatly influenced by family income. In 1997, only 15 percent of low-income students in grades 7 to 12 had access to a home computer, compared with 78 percent of high-income students (NCES, 1998). There are also significant socioeconomic differences in the quality of children's computer access. Children from more affluent homes are more likely than lower-income children to have access to computers that have a CD-ROM drive, a printer, and a modem for Internet access (Becker, 2000).

FIGURE 4.16

Increases in Students' (Grades 7 to 12) Access to Home Computers

SOURCE: National Center of Educational Statistics (1998).

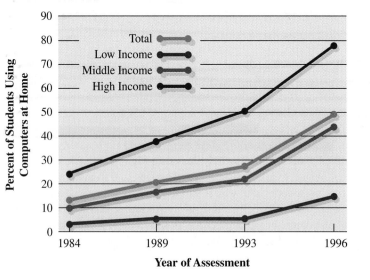

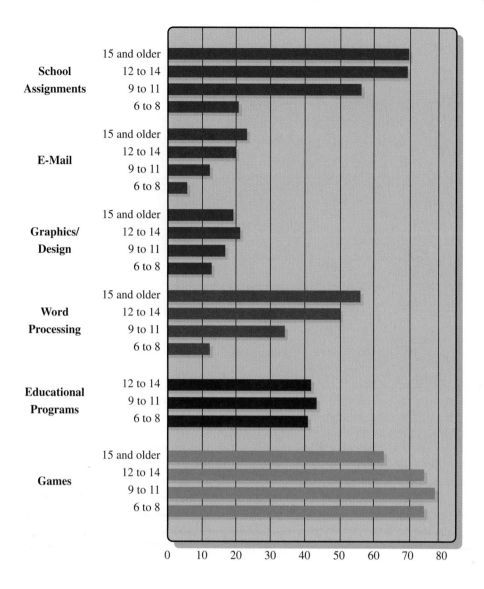

FIGURE 4.17

Percentage of Children with Home Computers Reported to Use Different Types of Software, by Age Group (1997)

SOURCE: Data analyzed from the U.S. Census Bureau's Current Population Survey of U.S. Households (October 1997 supplement).

How do young people use their home computers? Household surveys indicate that home computers are used for both school-related and recreational purposes. Figure 4.17 shows age differences in how young people use their home computers. As shown here, students' use of home computers for school assignments, electronic mail, and word processing increases with age. There is a higher use of computers at home when parents or siblings have computer experience and when students have access to computers at school. Children from higher socioeconomic backgrounds use a broader range of computer applications than lower-income children, even when parents have the same level of work-based experiences with computers (Becker, 2000). Although concerns have been expressed about gender differences in computer literacy, a 1997 study found similar patterns of home computer use by boys and girls (Becker, 2000). There were only small differences in the use of computer games (75 percent for boys and 68 percent for girls) and for word processing (36 percent for boys and 41 percent for girls). As the array of computer applications increases, gender differences in home computer use are expected to decrease.

Schools are equalizing low- and high-income students' access to computers, but disparities remain in the quality of equipment and software.

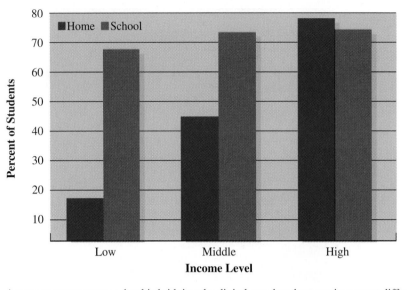

FIGURE 4.18

Differences in Students' (Grades 7 to 12) Access to Computers at Home and School

SOURCE: National Center of Educational Statistics (1998).

Access to computers at school is bridging the digital gap, but there are important differences in the quality of computer equipment found in schools serving low- and high-income students.

For many young people, school provides the greatest access to computers. As shown in Figure 4.18, a greater number of children and adolescents have access to computers at school than at home, especially among lower-income groups. Since the 1980s, the number of computers in American schools has grown steadily. Whereas half of schools nationwide had no computer in 1983, all schools were equipped with at least one computer by 1998 (Becker, 2000). Additionally, students in low-income schools are equally likely to have access to computers as students in high-income schools (see Figure 4.18). However there are important differences in the availability of high-quality computer equipment, sophisticated software, and high-speed Internet access. When these factors are taken into account, schools with the highest proportion of students from low-income families are 1 to 2 years behind middle-income schools, and even farther behind schools serving high-income families (Becker, 2000).

Effects of Computers on Learning and School Achievement

Although computers are more widely used by young people today than ever before, it is not clear that this technological innovation is making them "smarter" (Subrahmanyam, Kraut, Greenfield, & Cross, 2000). Let's first consider the use of home computers. As Figure 4.17 showed, young people use different computer applications, but computer games in particular are designed in ways that emphasize *visual* rather than *verbal* information processing. If related to spatial problem-solving skills, such programs should be beneficial for more abstract forms of mathematics but few studies have examined this possible link.

A few studies indicate that computer use at home can enhance school achievement (Subrahmanyam et al., 2000). However, as we know, children's access to, and use of, computers are tied to their parents' income levels. Studies have not adequately controlled for these influences. With this caveat in mind, one longitudinal study that tracked seventh through twelfth graders showed that students with computers at home had higher grade point averages (GPAs) and, more specifically, better grades in English and mathematics than those students without access to a home computer. Among those students who reported at least 10 hours of computer use during the year for activities unrelated to a class, a positive relation was found for overall grades, for math and English grades, and for scores on a test of scientific knowledge (Subrahmanyam et al., 2000).

How is access to computers at school influencing learning? Computer technology today clearly has the potential to change the way young people learn in school. Students can now participate in real-life expeditions to Mars, rain forests, archeological digs, coral reefs, or jungles. The Global Learning and Observations to Benefit the Environment (GLOBE) program, introduced by Vice President Gore in 1992, connected more than 3,800 schools around the world to scientists studying the environment. Teachers and students collected environmental data in their local areas and worked with scientists to analyze environmental problems (Gore, 1992). Computer programs like ThinkerTools enables middle-school students to visualize the concepts of velocity and acceleration (White, 1993), and computer software is available to help students visualize and explore geometric and algebraic concepts online. There are also computer tools that enable students to choreograph plays and to examine cultural artifacts from ancient civilizations. Interactive storybooks are available to help first-graders learn basic reading skills, and various multimedia applications exist to provide opportunities for older students to actively construct presentations that reflect their knowledge and understanding of a particular subject matter or topic. Lastly, computer technology is providing new ways for children with special needs to learn in the regular classroom environment (Roshelle, Pea, Hoadley, Gordin, & Means, 2000).

Computer programs that have the greatest impact on students' learning use constructivist approaches and emphasize higher-order thinking skills.

Although these computer applications have the potential to enhance students' learning, information on their effectiveness is fairly limited. Much of the research to date has focused on math and science, and on middle and high school students. In general, the strongest evidence for positive effects are computer applications that use a constructivist approach and that emphasize conceptual understanding and higher-order thinking skills. One nationwide study, for example, showed that highly interactive software that promotes active engagement and participation was more effective than drill-and-practice software in increasing mathematics achievement in fourth- and eighth-graders (Weglinsky, 1998). However, software applications that emphasized repetitive skill practice improved students' performance on basic skill tests (Kulik, 1994).

As with any curriculum innovation, the positive benefits of computer technology for student learning are influenced by many different factors, including teacher training, administrative support, state and local curriculum standards, and assessment procedures. Clearly students' experiences with computers outside of school will play a role as well. For this reason, socioeconomic factors cannot be dismissed. As discussed, children from different socioeconomic backgrounds do not have equal access to computers and sophisticated software at home. It is not clear that schools can address these disparities. Low-income children are likely to attend schools with fewer resources to purchase the computer equipment needed to run highly interactive software. As discussed, many more schools in low- than in high-income areas have outdated computer equipment and have limited high-speed access to the Internet. Additionally, computers in low- and high-income schools tend to be used for different purposes. A 1998 nationwide survey of teachers indicated that lower-income students used computer applications for remediation or practicing skills, whereas higher-income students used computer applications for research, analyses, and written expression (Becker, 2000). For this reason, experts have argued that economic disparities in students' access to enriched learning opportunities with technology are increasing (Shields & Behrman, 2000).

Chapter Summary

www.mhhe.com/meece

Information Processing Theories

- Information processing and intelligence theories help specify the cognitive processes and mental abilities that change with development. Information processing theories focus on developmental changes in children's abilities to encode, store, and retrieve information, whereas intelligence theories focus on individual differences in children's cognitive abilities within age groups.

- According to information processing theorists, important developmental changes occur in children's attentional processes, memory strategies, content knowledge, and metacognitive knowledge. As children mature, they become more selective and efficient in their use of attentional, memory, and learning strategies. As a result, they can remember larger amounts of information for longer periods of time.

- Attention is a process of perceiving or extracting what is relevant for the task at home. As children develop, they acquire the ability to make fine discriminations between stimulus objects, to deploy their attention selectively and strategically, and to exert control over their attentional processes.

Developmental Changes in Cognitive Processes

- Memory processes are evident early in development. By the preschool years, children can recall familiar stories, experiences, routines, and events. During the early and late elementary years, children begin to use memory strategies to encode information that is unfamiliar. Rehearsal strategies appear first, followed by organization and elaboration strategies.

- Researchers distinguish between recognition and recall memory. Recognition memory involves recognizing a stimulus, whereas recall memory involves remembering that stimulus without information, prompts, or cues to aid its recall. With development, children can recall information with fewer prompts or cues. They can also search their memory in a more systematic, selective, and strategic manner.

- Children's existing knowledge can influence attentional and memory processes. Expert versus novice studies indicate that a highly integrated knowledge base results in faster processing of information, more effective use of encoding strategies, and more efficient use of cognitive resources.

- Metacognition refers to children's knowledge and understanding of their own thinking processes. As children develop, they acquire a greater understanding that there are limits to what can be remembered, some learning tasks require more cognitive effort than others, and certain strategies can aid the recall of information. Children use this knowledge to choose more effective memory and learning strategies.

- Age-related changes in metacognitive knowledge also facilitates the development of self-regulated learning. Self-regulated learners can plan, organize, monitor, and evaluate their own learning activities. Evidence indicates that children show a significant increase in their use of self-regulated learning strategies between the fifth and eighth grades. However, study strategies, such as comprehension and monitoring, continue to develop well into adolescence.

- Although there are many ways teachers can facilitate the development of information processing skills in the classroom, research suggests that strategy instruction is very infrequent. Teachers need to make a greater effort to teach specific cognitive strategies, to provide information concerning their usefulness in learning, and to suggest when strategies may be useful for other learning situations.

Individual Differences in Cognitive Abilities

- There is considerable variability in children's cognitive abilities within any age group. Standardized tests of intelligence or achievement are used to assess individual differences in cognitive development. Intelligence tests are thought to measure a child's ability to use information in new ways or potential to learn, whereas achievement tests measure what children have gained from instruction at home or school.

- There is no agreed-on definition of intelligence. Some theorists have argued that intelligence represents a general or global intellectual capacity, whereas others have argued that intelligence represents several independent skills or abilities. Most intelligence tests used today yield a profile of a child's intellectual abilities.

- An IQ score represents an estimate of a child's cognitive abilities relative to other children of the same age. Most IQ tests have a mean of 100 points. A standard deviation is a measure of the average amount scores vary from the mean. In a normal distribution, most children's scores fall within one standard deviation above or below the mean.

- IQ tests are not equally valid for all children. To perform well on traditional measures of intelligence, children must have a good deal of familiarity with middle-class culture and good verbal skills. Caution should be used when these tests are employed to assess children from different ethnic, socioeconomic, and language backgrounds.

- As children develop, the stability of their IQ scores increases. By middle childhood, IQ scores are reasonably good predictors of adult IQ. However, the IQ scores of some children can fluctuate as much as 20 to 30 points between the ages of 2 and 17.

Genetic and Environmental Influences on Intelligence

- Studies of biological twins are an important source of information concerning the influence of genetic and environmental factors on intelligence. For the most part, these studies reveal that approximately 50 percent of the variation in intelligence within a population can be attributed to genetic influences. However, it is very difficult to separate genetic and environmental influences. Most researchers focus on how genetic and environmental factors interact to influence intellectual development. Genes may set the upper and lower limits for intellectual development, but the environment may explain variations in development within that range.

- Several aspects of the home environment can influence early intellectual development. Research indicates that parents can have a positive influence on their children's cognitive development when they provide appropriate stimulation and play materials; encourage exploration and stimulate curiosity; and create a warm, supportive, and responsive environment. Later in children's development, parents not only must provide a stimulating and encouraging home environment but also must take an active role in the child's schooling. The validity of this research for different ethnic and socioeconomic groups is currently being examined.

- Early intervention can help offset the negative effects of a poor home environment. Head Start children are more likely to make significant gains in IQ, to score high on academic achievement tests, to remain on grade level, to graduate from high school, and to attend college than comparable groups of children who did not attend Head Start programs. Evidence suggests that earlier and longer interventions may have a stronger impact on children's intellectual functioning, but these programs are costly and not widely available.

- Formal schooling is another important aspect of the environment that influences children's intellectual development. Children who start school earlier, remain in school longer, and attend higher-quality schools have higher IQ scores. Theorists argue that schooling influences IQ scores because schools teach the type of information and skills children need to perform well on intelligence tests. Because IQ tests are strongly influenced by schooling experiences, some researchers question the use of IQ tests as a measure of innate intellectual functioning.

Racial and Cultural Differences in Cognitive Abilities

- Research shows that children from different ethnic and racial groups, with the exception of Asian-Americans, score significantly lower than Anglo-American children on virtually every measure of cognitive ability. Some evidence suggests that ethnic differences in achievement are narrowing, but they remain large.

- Most researchers believe that ethnic differences in students' IQ and achievement test scores are due to social and economic factors. When differences in socioeconomic background are controlled, performance gaps narrow but do not completely disappear. Some factors that contribute to the lower performance of ethnic minorities on mental tests include language or dialect differences, a school culture that favors white, middle-class students, and tracking systems that limit minority children's learning and achievement opportunities in school.

Gender Differences in Cognitive Abilities

- Gender differences in students' cognitive abilities are less evident today than 20 years ago. Differences are small for tests of verbal, visual-spatial, and mathematical abilities, but remain large for tests of scientific skills. Most researchers view girls and boys as more similar than different in their cognitive abilities.

- Efforts to explain gender differences in cognitive abilities focus on biological and environmental influences. The influence of hormones and brain organization on cognitive functioning is not well understood. Therefore, most researchers focus on differences in children's socialization experiences. There is considerable evidence that boys and girls are treated differently and encouraged to pursue different activities at home. Research has also documented the numerous ways boys and girls are treated differently at school. Schools tend to reproduce gender inequities in society.

- Schools need to make a better effort to create learning environments that provide equal resources, encouragement, and opportunities for boys and girls of all backgrounds. Multicultural education programs are designed to promote equal educational opportunities and to increase positive intergroup attitudes and values. Creating a positive learning environment for all students will involve radical changes in curriculum materials, the organization and culture of schools, the attitudes and beliefs of school staff, and the ways students are currently taught and assessed.

Television, Computers, and Children's Learning

- On average, children watch 3 to 4 hours of television per day. Younger children watch more television than adolescents do, and boys watch more television than girls do.

- There is no strong evidence that television displaces reading or homework time.

- The effects of television viewing depend on the amount of viewing time and content. When children watch more than 30 hours of television per week, it can have a negative impact on school achievement.

- High-quality television programs for children can have positive effects on early math and reading skills, as well as school readiness and adjustment.

- Computers are becoming a routine part of children's lives, but access to high-quality computers and software is tied to family income.

- Students' use of computers for school-related purposes increases with age. There are similar patterns of computer use for girls and boys today.

- Research on the effects of computers on students' learning is fairly limited. Computer programs tend to have the greatest impact when they use a constructivist approach and emphasize high-order thinking skills.

Key Terms

ability grouping (p. 219)

automaticity (p. 182)

componential intelligence (p. 200)

contextual intelligence (p. 200)

elaboration strategies (p. 185)

episodic memory (p. 178)

experiential intelligence (p. 200)

expert versus novice studies (p. 187)

fluid intelligence (p. 198)

heritability (p. 205)

intelligence quotient (IQ) (p. 197)

long-term memory (p. 177)

memory retrieval strategies (p. 184)

memory scripts (p. 194)

multiple intelligences (p. 201)

niche-picking (p. 206)

organizational strategies (p. 185)

practical intelligence (p. 200)

recall memory (p. 186)

recognition memory (p. 186)

rehearsal strategies (p. 185)

retrieval strategies (p. 186)

selective attention (p. 182)

self-regulated learning (p. 190)

semantic memory (p. 172)

sensory registers (p. 177)

short-term memory (p. 177)

spatial skills (p. 220)

stability of IQ (p. 204)

tracking (p. 219)

triarchic model of intelligence (p. 198)

Activities

1. A digit-span test is often used to assess children's memory processes. Using the list of digits below, test four individuals of different ages (a 4-, 7-, 12-, and 20-year-old). Present each digit approximately 1 second apart. Start with line 1, and work your way up until the person recalls less than half the list. For each list, record the number of digits the person recalled correctly. If you interview children at school, you will need the permission of the teacher. In analyzing your data, consider the following questions:

(a) Were there age differences in memory span? What was the nature of the differences observed? (b) What accounts for these differences? What else might account for the differences? (c) How does this exercise help you to understand developmental changes in memory?

Digit-Span Test Number Correct

1. 3
2. 5 - 9
3. 1 - 6 - 8
4. 2 - 4 - 7 - 0
5. 3 - 9 - 4 - 1 - 8
6. 9 - 4 - 3 - 7 - 8 - 5
7. 1 - 2 - 6 - 3 - 7 - 9 - 0
8. 7 - 5 - 1 - 8 - 6 - 2 - 4 - 9

2. Study skills increase with age. For this activity, interview an upper-elementary student, a middle-school student, and a high school student about their study skills. Ask each student the following questions:

a. Tell me about the last test you had in this class.

b. How well did you do on the test?

c. Did you do anything special to prepare for the test?

d. If you got stuck on a problem or question, what did you do?

e. Did you do anything special before you turned in your test?

After collecting your interview data, compare the responses of your students. Were there age differences in the types of strategies students use in preparing for a test, getting unstuck, or reviewing their test? What was the nature of these differences? What might explain these differences? How did this exercise help you to understand developmental changes in learning strategies?

3. Observe two lessons (any subject) in two classrooms at different grade levels (e.g., a fifth and a seventh grade). While observing each lesson, record the following:

a. Describe any teacher instruction related to a specific strategy students can use to complete the assignment. Examples might include: read the directions carefully, think about a prior assignment, use a particular reading or mathematical skill, use aides or resources in the classroom, ask a friend for assistance, check over answers, make a plan, organize thoughts, take some notes, etc.

b. Describe the teacher's rationale for using the strategy (i.e., what was it supposed to accomplish?).

c. Describe what the teacher said or did to remind students to use the strategy. After collecting your observation data, answer the following questions:

• What type of strategy instruction did each teacher provide?

• How did the strategy instruction differ across subject areas or grade levels?

• How often did the teacher provide a rationale for using a particular strategy?

• How did this exercise help you understand the ways teachers can facilitate the development of learning strategies in the classroom?

4. Racial or gender biases in curriculum materials can affect students' learning. For this activity, analyze two current textbooks (any subject or grade level) for social stereotypes. First, examine the degree to which women and minorities are represented in the texts you selected. Who are the main characters? Who do you see in the

pictures? Next, analyze the characteristics of the women and minorities. Are the men strong and active and the women weak and passive? Are ethnic minorities depicted as leaders and competent? Describe the roles and occupations of the characters. In your opinion, are these texts appealing to females and minorities? Do they strengthen or weaken social stereotypes? What would you do as a teacher to counteract racial or gender stereotypes in curriculum materials?

5. Review computer software for different age groups (preschool, elementary, etc.). Analyze the software in terms of its ability to support the cognitive skills that are emerging at that point in development. To what extent does each program emphasize drill-and-practice versus problem solving? Examine the programs for their attractiveness to different gender and ethnic groups. Which of the computer software programs would you recommend to teachers? Include a rationale for your explanation.

Chapter 5

Language and Literacy Development

As part of a thematic literature unit on "bears," a group of first graders is preparing to stage a performance of "Goldilocks and the Three Bears." The children in this class attend an inner-city elementary school where 80 percent of the students are minorities, mostly African American. One of the children preparing for the play is a boy named Pha, from Laos, who entered school in September, at which time he did not speak any English at all. This morning Pha joins a group of children making masks for the characters in the play. When the play begins, he will perform the role of the baby bear.

Pha performed wonderfully as Baby Bear. When he discovered that somebody had eaten his porridge, he noted with much surprise, "Somebody ate my soup!" And when he found that his chair was broken, he shouted indignantly, "Somebody broke my chair." And in the final episode of the play, when the bears find Goldilocks in bed, Pha was the first to make the discovery and exclaimed, "Somebody's in my bed, AND THERE SHE BE!" (Vacca & Vacca, 1991, pp. 3–4)

Chapter opener photo: Richard Hutchings/Photo Researchers, Inc.

A s this scenario illustrates, children use language to express themselves creatively, to engage others in social settings, to make meaning, and to become members of a social group. Language mediates and facilitates mental growth, but it also builds social relationships. Even though Pha's English is limited, he is able to fully participate in this literacy event, because his language and actions are not isolated but occur in a supportive context. The story of "Goldilocks and the Three Bears" is predictable, with many repetitive words and phrases, which helps Pha understand the story's meaning. When he is speaking and acting, he responds to the words and behaviors of others. Pha's limited proficiency in English does not allow him to interact on his own, but he succeeds brilliantly when engaged in the group process of the performance. Producing this play enhanced language development and literacy, not only for Pha, who gained valuable practice with English, but for all the children participating.

What Is Literacy?

Language is a socially constructed symbolic system in which either sounds or written symbols are used to represent objects, actions, and ideas.

Literacy is the ability to read and write a variety of texts for different purposes.

Most commonly, we think of literacy as the ability to read and write. Being able to read print and to produce written words are regarded by our culture as important skills. Often whether a person can work productively in society depends on his proficiency with reading and writing. Why are reading and writing so valuable? We know that in young children language develops alongside cognition, each process mutually enhancing the other. **Language,** on the other hand, is a symbolic system: a series of sounds in which the words *freedom, ball,* and *Mommy* can represent an idea, an object, a person. Such symbolic representation eventually becomes the medium through which we think. Imagine what it would be like to think without language. Is that even possible?

In this text, we define **literacy** as constructed meaning—meaning created through the interaction of reader or writer and written text (Hiebert, 1991). In short, literacy can be thought of as a set of language-based skills that allows us to comprehend a text, whether the newspaper or a classic novel. In addition, to function in our increasingly complex society, individuals must develop critical literacy, the ability to use written language to solve problems and to communicate (Calfee, 1994). But is literacy limited only to printed texts? With the advent of electronic technology, including computers and video capabilities, our culture's conception of what it means to be literate has expanded. In an essay entitled "Rethinking Literacy," Elliot Eisner (1991) pointed out that literacy now extends beyond print to include other systems for constructing meaning and communicating with others: "Literacy is not limited to text…[but] relates to the ability to construe meaning, in any of the forms used in the culture to create and convey meaning" (p. 125). Multiple literacies, those associated with music, visual images, dance and theater, as well as computers and other technological literacies, all depend on the mind's ability to use symbols to represent and to communicate about thoughts or experiences.

Although spoken language is crucial for the development of cognition, written language provides additional benefits for thought. Writing enables us to fix ideas permanently to a printed page, or onto a computer file, so that we don't have to rely on memory alone. Being able to read and write enables people to communicate with each other across space and time. With the use of technologies such as electronic mail, the amount of information that can be produced and exchanged by written (visual) forms far exceeds that which is possible when spoken language is the only available medium. The term *literate thinking* has been coined to describe "the ability to think and reason like a literate person, *within a particular society*" (Langer, 1991, p. 11). In order to participate fully, individuals need to develop ways of thinking (such as analysis and synthesis) that are associated with the uses of literacy in their particular culture.

But no single culture is monolithic or uniform. Rather, individuals belong to various subcultures, which means that several literacies are being learned, practiced, and enjoyed at any one time. For example, the children performing "The Three Bears" have created a production based on a written story. Thus, they are internalizing the qualities of a good story, but they are also learning the importance of visual dramatics, using a dialect of English to enhance their performance.

In this chapter, we will discuss the role of language in child development, including cognitive as well as social dimensions. Can a child develop emotionally or intellectually without language? How does language affect human development? Although psychologists have devised different theories about the relationship between language and cognition, all agree that language is a medium for thinking and learning, because it is a system for representing or symbolizing our experiences. However, languages are social systems fundamentally. Everyone who learns and speaks the English language agrees that the sound of *cat* [kaet], for instance, means a small furry house pet. From a social perspective, this shared knowledge enables communication: We describe experiences, exchange information, make plans, discuss ideas, create stories, and build personal bonds through conversational routines.

In every culture, language is fundamental. Increasingly, it is common for a culture to be multilingual—in which people speak two or more languages. As we have discussed, approximately 8.5 percent of all school-aged children speak a language other than English at home (National Center for Education Statistics, 2000). Instead of being English-dominant, these and many other children in the next generation will grow up bilingual. In addition to being multilingual, children will increasingly develop in an environment with multiple literacies. Because of the complexity of learning several languages and literacies, the process of language acquisition and development will become more extended, beginning with speech in infancy, but growing to include multiple forms of language and literacy throughout adolescence.

By first grade, children have a great deal of experience and skill in using spoken language. They understand and appreciate the values of written language, particularly from their encounters with picture books and with the print that saturates their environment. While children will continue to develop and refine speaking skills once they enter school, it is in the area of literacy (reading and writing) that children will change most dramatically.

Some Basic Principles of Language Development

Language takes on several forms and comes in many varieties, such as the English spoken in the South, Black English dialects, and the abstract writing of legal documents. However, to understand how all forms of language develop, we need to remember a few basic concepts.

1. ***Language is a social phenomenon.*** People living together have devised ways of interacting and communicating with each other. Children acquire whatever language or languages they hear spoken around them. The need to communicate—as when a hungry baby cries—is the primary force behind language acquisition. As children grow, they will need to learn a variety of language forms, such as slang terms particular to their peer group, the features of formal expository writing, oral storytelling styles, and creative

The need to communicate within a social context is the force behind language acquisition.

Before children begin to talk, they use gestures to communicate.

SOURCE: Robert Ginn/Photo Edit.

genres, such as poetry and fiction, in order to participate fully in society.

2. ***Children acquire language without direct instruction and within a short span of time.*** By the age of 7, most children have learned about 90 percent of all the language structures used by adults in their society (Daniels, 1985). They can ask questions, form negative sentences, choose appropriate pronouns, and produce complex sentence structures such as relative clauses. Besides structural knowledge, children also learn how to use language more broadly. They can conduct conversations, adjusting their language to fit their audience, such as an adult would with a 2-year-old, and can invent jokes and play word games.

   As children grow older, they begin to combine the structure they have learned in order to communicate more complex ideas, they gain proficiency with written language, and they acquire grace and skill in using language in a wide variety of social settings.

3. ***All languages are symbol systems with socially constructed rules for combining sounds into words, for making meaning with words, and for arranging words into sentences.*** Children actively construct these unconscious rules through observation and hypothesis testing (Clark & Clark, 1977). They observe others and form an idea about how to express something, test their idea by speaking, and modify the end result as needed. For instance, a child might infer that adding the sound of /s/ to a word means "more than one" as in *cats*. When the child produces a non-standard form like "mouses," the child is testing out a hypothesis about how to make a plural noun. Eventually, through practice, the child will modify the rule to account for exceptions in English, producing *mice* as the plural form of *mouse*. Remember that a child is learning to speak by participating in social exchanges. The social context in which language is learned supports the child in producing not only well-formed utterances but also ones that are appropriate in a given situation (Elliot, 1981).

4. ***Because language is so complex, children cannot learn the system all at once.*** Instead, they go through stages in which they work on learning a few things at a time, for instance, putting two words together meaningfully. When a young girl says, "Mommy sock," she is not producing a random string of words. Because her sentence is not grammatical, the child depends on the skills of her mother to interpret her words. Using feedback from her mother or other adults, she gradually begins to produce sentences that approximate more closely the qualities of adult language.

5. ***Language is linked to identity.*** Through language we are able to interact with others and to make sense of the world. This process allows us to develop a sense of self, to convey our private thoughts, and to share our experiences with others. The earliest efforts at symbolic formation—a child's first scribble presented to his mother, a nonsense song performed by a 2-year-old to entertain a visitor—are a child's way of establishing

a sense of self in relation to others (Dyson, 1993). Our native language, with its speech and interactional patterns, connects us to our family and community, and in the process becomes a basic part of our inner selves. Language is central to our personality, "an expression and mirror of what we are and wish to be, . . . as integral to each of us as our bodies and our brains" (Daniels, 1985, p. 32).

6. ***Language abilities grow by using language in meaningful contexts.*** Children learn to talk by talking with others who delight in listening. This holds true not only for spoken language but also for promoting children's acquisition of literacy. Typically, spoken language is learned in home settings, whereas reading and writing are taught to children in school settings. However, just as children learned to speak because they want to interact with others, to express their thoughts and desires, so too must communication be the motivating force behind reading and writing. Too often schools teach these language skills to children using artificial tasks. For instance, a teacher may ask children to write a short paragraph describing a favorite toy. If the audience is the teacher, and if the real reason to write is only to complete the assignment, then the true purpose of writing (authentic communication) has been distorted. Instead of writing to share some personally meaningful thoughts—a central purpose of written language—children write in school mainly to demonstrate mastery for a teacher. Such tasks are often what constitute literacy instruction in school. James Britton, a British educator, calls such artificial tasks "dummy runs." He argues that children need authentic, real-life, socially meaningful reasons to speak and write. Language (speaking, reading, writing) helps children to make sense of the world. Children "must *practise* language in the sense in which a doctor 'practises' medicine, . . . and *not* in the sense in which a juggler 'practises' a new trick" (Britton, 1970, p. 130). Recall that both Piaget and Vygotsky emphasize the fact that learning is most likely to occur in meaningful contexts (see Chapter 3).

> *Language acquisition occurs best in contexts that are personally meaningful to a child and thereby stimulate a desire to communicate.*

Language Development and Teaching

Teachers who understand the way language develops initially can provide a better and more natural language learning environment. This holds true for both acquiring written and extending spoken language abilities. However, the relationships between these language processes are complex: Do children acquire speech or are they biologically hardwired for language? If speaking develops without formal instruction, why doesn't reading and writing develop similarly? Will every child in a literate culture learn to read and write? What determines who becomes literate? Does a child who is bilingual learn differently than one who is monolingual? We will explore these issues in this chapter.

Contrasting Views on Language Development

Most children learn to speak a language without direct instruction during the first few years of life. Language enables human beings to represent objects and actions, to understand and discuss abstract ideas, to invent stories, and to exchange complex information. Many cultures develop a way of writing their language. Having a written form of language allows a culture to develop new ways of communicating, which would not be possible if only spoken language were used. Writing adds permanence to language. With writing, very long texts can be created and preserved, and texts can be repeatedly read and referenced in order to make decisions or to think through an issue. In addition, writing allows for consistency; anyone who is able to read a particular text reads exactly the same words as any other reader.

In cultures that have writing systems, children must learn to read and write their language as well as to speak it. However, these language forms develop quite differently in individuals. Spoken language is primary; all individuals (apart from those with severe impairments) learn to speak their language, but not everyone becomes literate. It is remarkable that learning to speak a language happens to everyone, whereas learning to read or write occurs only when individuals are taught these skills. In addition, children all over the world go through similar stages in acquiring spoken language. Furthermore, they appear to pay attention to certain generalizations and to ignore irregularities no matter what language (or languages) they are learning. How can we account for the universal ability of all children to learn language? And, furthermore, how do they manage it?

Various answers have been proposed. Many parents believe that their children learn language by imitating the words and sentences they hear. In addition, parents believe that reinforcing the "correct" parts of children's utterances leads to development. Yet other adults notice, often with great concern, that children create their own ways of speaking, experimenting with tenses, endings, and word order, which often do not resemble adult speech.

Although there are competing theories for *how* children develop language, we do know *what* children learn when they develop language. Learning a language is basically learning grammar. **Grammar** is not a set of prescriptions such as "don't end sentences with a preposition," but rather is "the set of rules that describe how to structure language" (Moskowitz, 1985, p. 47). Grammatical rules extend from the simplest level of combining sounds to the complex level of extended conversation. For example, word order is one rule of grammar. Speakers of English produce sentences that consist typically of a subject, a verb, and an object, put together in that order: "Carmen hit the ball." Speakers may not be conscious of these rules, but they can easily recognize a sentence that does not follow this pattern. If someone said, "Carmen the ball hit," an English speaker would be able to change the word order to make the sentence grammatically correct, although he or she may not be able to explain the underlying rule. All languages, and all dialects, have rules that control the major components of language—*phonology, semantics, syntax, pragmatics,* and *lexicon.* Figure 5.1 lists these rules.

All individuals, except those with severe disabilities, learn to speak their language, but literacy— learning to read and write—must be taught.

All languages and dialects have rules that control their major components: phonology, semantics, syntax, pragmatics, and lexicon.

Theories of Language Development

Because language is so closely tied to thinking, theories of human development have also been used to describe language development. One issue we have considered in earlier chapters is the extent to which mental development depends on internal or external factors—the nature versus nurture controversy. Similarly, theories of language acquisition involve the same debate. Do children have an innate predisposition to learn language? Is language structure—the ability to produce and understand sentences—actually built into the brain? Or is language simply a special form of behavior that children learn through their parents? In order to answer these questions, we will turn our attention to what we know about human development and how different theories may illuminate our understanding of language development.

Several theories of cognitive development were discussed in Chapter 1. Our first perspective held that development occurs naturally as the result of simple biological *matura-*

- **Phonology**   The sounds of a language, the rules for combining them to make words, along with stress and intonation patterns. The word *bat* consists of three sounds, two consonant sounds /b/ and /t/ connected with the vowel sound /ae/. The word *basket* has two syllables; the first syllable is stressed.
- **Semantics**   The meaning of words. Only certain strings of sounds are meaningful. Combining the sounds /r/, /t/, /a/ makes the words *art* and *rat*, but *tra* or *rta* are meaningless. Individual words carry meaning, and words can be combined into meaningful sentences, for example, "Is that picture of a rat really art?" However, words are related in complex networks and have special properties. Although both *rat* and *art* are nouns, they cannot change position and make a meaningful sentence: "Is that picture of an art really a rat?"
- **Syntax**   The way words are combined to form phrases and sentences in a language. To form a statement in English, words are arranged in the order of subject, verb, object: "The tornado destroyed the house." Syntax also determines the form of other kinds of sentences, such as questions: "What destroyed that house?" or "How did that house get destroyed?"
- **Pragmatics**   The strategies for using language appropriately in different contexts. Turn-taking rules is one strategy speakers have for structuring speech and for managing social interaction. Interrupting a speaker too soon is a pragmatic violation. Introducing topics into conversation as well as knowing how to structure a formal argument in writing constitute pragmatic knowledge.
- **Lexicon**   Vocabulary; all the words in a language for objects, qualities, actions, and events, ideas, or states of mind: *flowers, unique, running, marathon, democracy, blissful.*

FIGURE 5.1

The Major Components of Language

tion, and follows a predetermined biological timetable. Second, we examined how development is shaped by the environment, a *behaviorist* perspective. Third, we discussed how development results from an *interaction* between innate and environmental factors, with the child as an active participant. Fourth, from a *contextual* perspective, we saw how both child and environment are malleable and undergoing constant change. As you read the following section, think about which perspective on language development you find most compelling.

Does Language Depend Entirely on Nurture?

Believing that the mind is a blank slate at birth, behaviorists like B. F. Skinner (1957) attribute language development totally to environmental factors. Learning to understand and speak a language depends on the way adults nurture children. Since languages vary so considerably in sound and structure, behaviorists argue that there cannot be any innate mental program general enough to allow children to learn languages as different as Swahili and French without difficulty. Instead, behaviorists believe that language learning depends on mechanisms, such as imitation, and on operant conditioning. It is the positive and negative reinforcements that follow from one's responses to external stimuli that shape the development of language (Staats, 1968).

Here is a possible behaviorist scenario: A babbling child might produce a wide array of random sounds. Gradually, the range of sounds is reduced and shaped through adults' responses. For instance, English-speaking parents react positively to any babbling that sounds like *da da da* and *ma ma ma* for obvious reasons. Thus, the theory suggests that children learn appropriate sounds and words in reaction to their parents' reinforcement.

But what about learning how to put a sentence together or to express happiness in words? Except for very few formulas—"How are you?"—most sentences that people say are unique in terms of structure. In the course of a single day, it would be extremely unusual for any two people to use exactly the same words when speaking. Reinforcement does not account for the fact that speakers produce novel sentences, sentences they have neither said before nor heard uttered. A child could conceivably learn the words *ball* and *go* through imitation and constant parental reinforcement, but there is no way conditioning can explain the moment when the child says, "Go ball" (meaning "Go and get the ball" or "I'm going to go and get the ball"), or "Ball go" (meaning, "Look at the ball going!"). For one thing, a child would never hear a parent say either of these two-word sentences. The child who produces "Go ball" is in the process of learning how to make a grammatical sentence. However, behaviorist theory cannot explain such inductive learning.

Is Language Biologically Programmed?

No matter what the culture, children begin to learn language around the same time—between 18 and 28 months—all over the world. Some theorists believe that biological maturation is the only way to account for such regularity in the onset of language (Lenneberg, 1967). Furthermore, any language is an extremely complicated system, which consists of sets of overlapping and interrelated rules. It is not clear just how children go about learning anything this complex, especially when the underlying structures of language are not taught directly to children.

So far, no research has revealed definitively the procedure by which children discover grammatical rules. Therefore, some linguists believe that an innate genetic component provides children with a chunk of the necessary grammar. If grammar is built-in, then it is simply activated as the child matures. In addition, not only does language emerge at a certain time, it also develops in a regular sequence with identifiable milestones. This aspect of language development is also considered a feature of general biological development (Aitchison, 1985). Thus, the basis for language exists within the child for biological theorists.

Chomsky's View   The linguist Noam Chomsky (1957, 1965) has generated the most complete theory to describe the role of innate knowledge in language acquisition. Chomsky believes that there are universal qualities common to all languages, for instance, ways of making statements and questions, the ability to refer to past time, and ways to form negatives. Therefore, these universal qualities of language must reflect the universal, inborn, character of the human mind. In fact, Chomsky has hypothesized that children are born with a **language acquisition device (LAD),** which is programmed to recognize the universal rules that underlie all languages. Although the child does not have a fully formed language at birth, as the child matures, the LAD is activated, enabling the child to develop more and more complex language structures until they reach adult levels of ability.

Searching for linguistic universals is one method of investigating the universal nature of the mind (Chomsky, 1986). Chomsky believes that particular qualities of the human mind dictate *operating principles* that all languages must follow. One such principle is called *structure-dependency.* For example, many grammatical rules depend on the fact that sentences have structure, in English and in any other language. We know that questions and

Behaviorists believe that language is a learned phenomenon based on operant conditioning within particular cultures; maturationists believe language is the unfolding of an innate biological program that everyone is "hardwired" to develop.

statements are constructed differently. Someone might state, "I'm going to the store now," while a person out of earshot might inquire, "Are you going to the store now?" The words in a statement have to be reordered and adjusted to form a question. The auxiliary *am* not only is transformed to *are* to agree with the new subject *you,* but it also has to be moved to the front of the sentence. What Chomsky has suggested is that children approach the job of learning language *expecting* that language will have structure, a particular order, and regularity. This prior readiness and expectancy are possible only if the principle of structure dependency is already part of the child's mental makeup.

For Chomsky and others who work within this theoretical framework, the core of **syntax** or language structure of all languages is inherited. The environment plays almost no role in the innate structural theories of language development. Experience only determines *which* language a child will speak. Whatever language a child hears, whether it be Chinese or Mohawk, will be the one the child learns. Furthermore, all languages are equally learnable from a child's point of view.

Not everyone is convinced by Chomsky's work. Biological theories are difficult to investigate, since we have no direct way of studying the physical makeup and physiological functioning of the brain. No one can prove or disprove genetic principles. However, it is also true that linguists cannot explain definitively how children learn language. But the absence of an adequate theory to provide an alternative explanation of language development simply means more research is needed. It does not mean that Chomsky's proposals concerning innate characteristics or genetic hardwiring are true (Hockett, 1968). Chomsky's theory has several deficits. It cannot explain basic processes, such as how children acquire word meaning, or the mechanism by which the language acquisition device is triggered.

Chomsky theorized that all languages are structured around a set of biologically programmed core principles, so his is a maturationist view of language development.

Does Language Emerge from the Interaction of Mind and Environment?

Piaget's View Arguing for a middle ground, interactional theorists such as Piaget insist that both nature and nurture contribute something to intellectual growth and language development. The child actively participates in constructing the interactions that occur between internal states and external environmental conditions. Piaget's views on language development are colored by his primary concern with understanding the developing mind of the child, as suggested by his book *The Language and Thought of the Child* (1926). Given this predisposition, it is predictable that Piaget would assume that symbolic thought is a precondition for language acquisition. During infancy, as sensorimotor schemas appear, a child is able to think symbolically. Only then is it possible for the child to understand that language functions as a system of symbols. Words can represent objects, actions, or abstract ideas; *bottle* or the more likely *baba* is a sound-symbol that represents the desired object.

Since language depends on thought, it follows in Piaget's theory that early speech will share some of the characteristics of early thought. Although a child realizes by the end of the sensorimotor period that he or she is part of a world but has a separate self, the child's thoughts are egocentric, centered on the self. Likewise, Piaget noted that much of children's language (even for the kindergarten children he studied) had nothing to do with communication and served no obvious social function. Instead, such verbalizing mirrored the child's thinking. Piaget called instances of this kind of egocentric speech—talking in the presence of others without expecting interaction or comprehension—*collective monologues.* Here is part of an exchange between two preschool children that resembles two parallel monologues rather than conversational interaction.

Jenny: They wiggle sideways when they kiss.

Chris: (Vaguely) What?

Jenny: My bunny slippers. They are brown and red and sort of yellow and white. And they have eyes and years and these noses that wiggle sideways when they kiss.

Chris: I have a piece of sugar in a red piece of paper. I'm gonna eat it but maybe it's for a horse.

Jenny: We bought them. My Mommy did. We couldn't find the old ones. These are like the old ones. They were not in the trunk.

Chris: Can't eat the piece of sugar, not unless you take the paper off.

Jenny: And we found Mother Lamb. Oh, she was in Poughkeepsie in the trunk in the house in the woods where Mrs. Tiddywinkle lives.

Chris: Do I like sugar? I do, and so do horses.

Jenny: I play with my bunnies. They are real. We play in the woods. They have eyes. We all go in the woods. My teddy bear and the bunnies and the duck, to visit Mrs. Tiddywinkle. We play and play.

Chris: I guess I'll eat my sugar at lunch time. I can get more for the horses. Besides, I don't have no horses now. (Stone & Church, 1957, pp. 146–147)

To account for such egocentric language, Piaget looked for a cognitive explanation instead of considering social factors. He proposed that this kind of *egocentric speech* reflects the thinking characteristic of young children at the preoperational stage of development (see Chapter 3). At later stages of development, as Piaget observed, these monologues would eventually become dialogues, since children by then would be developmentally able to take the perspective of their listeners into consideration.

To summarize, Piaget's cognitive approach emphasizes that internal structures are fundamental but not completely deterministic. Language is not a direct result of an innate characteristic but is an ability related to cognitive maturation. Piaget's theory is interactional; there are many factors—social, linguistic, cognitive—that affect the course of development. Furthermore, these factors interact with and mutually depend on each other as well as being reciprocal. In other words, Piaget (1954) claimed that advances in language growth are constrained by cognition, but at the same time he recognized that cognitive development alone is not sufficient to ensure language development. In reacting to Chomsky's theory during a debate in 1957, Piaget asserted that the complex structures of language are not necessarily innate or learned. Instead, linguistic structures emerge as a result of the continuing interaction between a child's inner intellectual functioning and the outer social and linguistic environments. However, Piaget left the nature of this interaction unexplored, perhaps because he was more interested in how children arrive at an understanding of their physical world than of their language development.

Piaget has been criticized for underestimating social factors in development, especially the role that parents, caregivers, siblings, and other people have in affecting a child's cognitive and linguistic development. Piaget's work depicts the child acting independently to figure out the surrounding world. Other theorists believe that the child never interacts alone, but always in concert with others. Development in language and thought depends on

Piaget viewed language development as the interaction of both innate and environmental factors, with a child's natural curiosity guiding much of this interaction.

a child's working collaboratively with other people to explore the physical and social worlds (Elliot, 1981). The possibility that intelligence may have a social origin was not something that Piaget explored. However, other researchers have attempted to study the issue of social interaction, which has led them to reinterpret some of Piaget's classic experiments (Karmiloff-Smith, 1979). Piaget used an interview method in which he relied on children's verbal responses to a set of questions as well as on informal conversation about the materials or activity at hand. It turns out that changing the way questions are worded strongly affects children's abilities to answer the questions (Sinha & Walkerdine, 1978). These findings suggest that language and cognition are deeply intertwined; language does not simply reflect the mind's functioning in any clear manner, as Piaget believed.

Does Language Development Depend on Social Interaction?

Vygotsky's View   Although Piaget felt that development involved a child's environment, he envisioned each child individually constructing a worldview based on the interaction between internal mental and external physical experiences. Piaget's theory downplays the fact that language is essentially social, and that children learn about the world in the company of others. For Vygotsky (1987), however, the social environment and surrounding culture are critical factors that motivate children's development in all areas, including the realm of language.

Vygotsky believed that thought and language originate independently but that sometime in early childhood, the two processes merge. Neither language nor thought is predominant. In addition, Vygotsky emphasized that children are born into a social community, cared for by others, and connected to the world through linguistic interactions. Psychological functions emerge in children as they interact with adults who nurture and support their efforts.

In his theory of language development, Vygotsky asserts that communicative speech develops before verbal thought. During the child's first two years, language and thought have independent origins. For example, children's babbling is essential to language development but does not seem critical for cognitive development. As children engage in communication, this "social speech" as Vygotsky called it, becomes "speech on its way inward." It is the precursor to verbal thought. When social speech becomes internal dialogue, a child develops what Vygotsky calls inner speech, which is the earliest form of thought mediated by language (see Chapter 3). Social speech precedes the development of inner speech; therefore Vygotsky (1962) believed that thought, in the form of inner speech, has a social origin: "Thought development is determined by language, i.e., by the linguistic tools of thought and by the sociocultural experience of the child" (p. 51).

Vygotsky's observation that language is first used by a child to communicate, and that thought emerges from internalized social speech, is the reverse of Piaget's theory. Piaget proposed that thought preceded language and that language development depended on the child's reaching new levels of cognitive development. But Vygotsky imagines the relationship between language and thought as dynamic and volatile. As language and thought develop in the child, the relationship between these two processes changes constantly. For about the first two years of life, language and thought develop independently, as parallel processes. But language gradually merges with thought around the age of 2, and this combination creates a unique and powerful medium. With language, individuals can internally represent objects, actions, and relationships as private thoughts and then communicate these thoughts to others. Perception, memory, and problem solving are all mental processes that depend on internalized language. One important aspect of development for Vygotsky was children's growing ability to control and direct their own behavior (see Chapter 3).

Vygotsky believed that language first appears as communicative speech and that thought gradually emerges from the process of internalizing this social speech.

Language helps children to control present action, but they can also use language to plan, order, and to some degree control their actions in the future as well (Vygotsky, 1978).

It is important to remember Vygotsky believed that young children are capable of social and intellectual cooperation to a greater degree than Piaget ever thought was possible. Individuals are part of a community in which knowledge and practices are guided by social conventions; indeed, language itself is an agreed-on set of conventions. Vygotsky's theory of language development assumes that individuals and their thoughts are not independent of their culture but are formed through social interactions shaped by a particular culture (Vygotsky, 1978).

Reconciling Different Points of View

We have discussed several different ways of understanding language as it relates to cognition. Most psychologists agree that language and thought are two distinct processes, yet they are inseparable from one another. One primary distinction between theories is the degree to which biological factors (nature) versus social factors (nurture) account for language development, as shown in Table 5.1. Chomsky proposed that LAD enables children to develop language. Piaget and Vygotsky, on the other hand, emphasized interactions between children's developing language and thought systems and their environment. Neither nature nor nurture alone can fully explain how children acquire language. No matter how we account for the origins of language acquisition, the fact remains that language exists within a social community. Becoming a competent speaker or writer depends on the amount and quality of experience individuals have in using language to communicate.

Learning to Communicate

Children learn the language that they hear spoken around them. However, only being able to hear a language is not sufficient. For instance, listening to a TV will not enable a child to learn language. Being able to interact with other people who offer immediate responses is essential to language development. So-called wild children, or children who grow up in total isolation from language and normal human interaction, do not learn language. Furthermore, no matter what a child's cultural heritage may be, he or she will acquire the lan-

Table 5.1		Different Perspectives of Language Development
Perspective	**Theorist**	**Major Causal Factor**
Behaviorist	Skinner	Language development is completely environmental
Innatist	Chomsky	Language structure depends on innate, biological characteristics of the human mind
Interactionist (cognitive)	Piaget	Language results from interaction between cognitive and environmental factors
Interactionist (contextual)	Vygotsky	Language is constructed within a particular sociocultural context, depending on cognitive and environmental factors

guage spoken by people in the immediate community. A child born of Chinese parents but adopted in infancy by English-speaking Americans will grow up speaking English.

Language Learning Methods

In learning language, children must make sense of the sounds, gestures, and intonation patterns their parents direct toward them. When Jessie's father leans over the crib, he is already talking to his daughter. As he leans to pick her up, he accompanies his actions with words, repeating important ones such as *bottle,* and naming himself and his child.

> Daddy's going to pick Jessie up.
> Does Jessie need a bottle?
> Oh yeah, Jessie needs a bottle.
> Here! U—p we go.
> Daddy's getting the bottle.

In order to respond, or to express a desire, Jessie needs to analyze the stream of speech in the surrounding world and select pieces to learn—those sounds that will grab her parents' attention and communicate her intentions. Parents do a good job of helping their children by emphasizing important words, speaking in a high-pitched intonation, and using many repetitions. This type of child-directed speech is sometimes known as **motherese,** or more appropriately in this time of joint child-rearing, *parentese* or caretaker speech, which is described in the Focus on Research box.

As Jessie's father is speaking, she must sift through a tremendous number of sounds in order to identify a word such as *bottle* and know that it signifies a particular object. Once the child recognizes a meaningful sound, she then must discover a way of making the sound that approximates *bottle* and of saying it with a particular kind of emphasis. And all this must happen while her parents are present to hear her request. Learning to say a single word at the right moment is the result of a great deal of analysis and construction on the child's part. We will examine several methods by which children accomplish this tremendous task.

Learning to say a single word at the right moment is the result of a great deal of analysis and then construction on the child's part.

Learning by Imitation

Parents interact verbally with their infants from the moment of birth. Words, sentences, and sounds function to entertain the child and to convey parental love and care. In talking to children, adults will often repeat their utterance. "Look at the bear. Here! See the bear. Look at the bear." The child reacts to these repetitions by looking at the bear, or smiling at the parent, or reaching for the bear, or by making sounds or even a word. The child does not respond by saying, "Look at the bear" or by imitating adult language.

In fact, children don't seem capable of repeating adult structures. In many language acquisition studies children are asked to imitate adult speech. The next example shows what happened in one project as a 2-year-old girl tries to reproduce an adult's sentence.

> *Adult:* The owl who eats candy runs fast.
>
> The man who I saw yesterday got wet.
>
> *Child:* (2 years, 4 months)
>
> Owl eat a candy and he run fast.
>
> I saw the man and he run fast. (Slobin & Welsh, 1973 p. 494)

Focus on Research

Parentese or Caretaker Speech

Parents modify the language directed toward their infants from birth. Such behavior appears to facilitate children's language development by simplifying language structure. While looking at a baby, adults will make high-pitched cooing sounds, which both simplifies and stresses particular speech sounds. This type of child-directed speech is widespread. Researchers found that adults in general, including nurses in hospital neonatal units (Rheingold & Joseph, 1977), not just parents, modify their speech for infants. Parentese, especially cooing, repetition, and simplification, has been documented in 14 different languages. In experimental studies in which children are exposed to different speech sounds, linguistic and nonlinguistic, they consistently prefer parentese over regular speech (Friedlander, 1970; Rileigh, 1973), and infants respond even more eagerly to the voice of their own mother compared with other female voices (DeCasper, 1980). *Baby talk,* or special vocabulary words we use with children, is considered an aspect of parentese. Words such as *tummy* for *stomach, choo-choo* for *train, doggie* for *dog,* and *bye-bye* for *goodbye* are examples of baby talk in which sounds are simplified and repeated (Snow & Ferguson, 1977). The most pervasive feature of caretaker speech is simpler syntax. As soon as children get beyond babbling and begin to produce words, adults will adjust their language. They will produce shorter, simpler sentences, use fewer complex verb forms, emphasize content words such as nouns and adjectives, as well as ask more questions. It is not entirely clear how such speech modifications facilitate child language acquisition, but its prevalence suggests it does play an important role. Some studies (Snow, 1977; Seitz & Stewart, 1975) suggest that specific features of parentese are constructed jointly between parent and child. The important point is that adults modify the language environment systematically to make language acquisition easier for children.

Although the child clearly comprehends what the adult means, she cannot reproduce the adult's structure. Instead she breaks the information up into two separate parts and links the information together with *and.* For imitation to be a strategy by which to learn language, children would have to be able to imitate structures more complex than what they can already produce. The previous example demonstrates that children do not imitate structures they do not already know (Ervin-Tripp, 1964). But while imitation is not used to learn syntax, children do imitate words. Therefore, imitation does play some role in language acquisition, especially in learning first words. But imitation is not the primary way that language develops.

Learning by Reinforcement

As described earlier, behaviorists believe that children learn language through systematic reinforcement. Children learn a language because adults provide positive feedback supporting the child when he or she produces a grammatically correct utterance, but responding negatively when the child says something ill-formed. This theory depends on the premise that adults pay attention to *how* children are speaking rather than to *what* they are saying. Review the following exchange between parent and 4-year-old daughter in which the parent tries to call attention to the verb form. The child, on the other hand, believes reasonably that the adult is questioning her about the event she is discussing.

Child: My teacher holded the baby rabbits and we patted them.

Adult: Did you say your teacher held the baby rabbits?

Child: Yes.

Adult: What did you say she did?

Child: She holded the baby rabbits and we patted them.

Adult: Did you say she held them tightly?

Child: No, she holded them loosely. (Cazden, 1972, p. 92)

Correcting the *form* of children's speech is quite ineffective, as this example illustrates. Whether or not they realize it, parents spend most of their time encouraging children to talk by coconstructing the content of these conversations. The parent may ask questions or add a detail to a child's story. Adults rarely correct the structure of children's speech, although they may occasionally comment on the meaning or truthfulness of what children say, and they sometimes model correct pronunciation (Clark & Clark, 1977). However, adults do reinforce children's active attempts to participate in conversation. By reinforcing participation, especially in early language development, adults encourage and reward children's efforts to learn language.

The following exchange between mother and daughter is typical of how adults interpret the meaning of a child's utterance, while ignoring the issue of grammatical structure.

Eve: Have that?

Mother: No, you may not have it.

Eve: Mom, where my tapioca?

Mother: It's getting cool. You'll have it in just a minute.

Eve: Let me have it.

Mother: Would you like to have your lunch right now?

Eve: Yeah. My tapioca cool?

Mother: Yes, it's cool.

Eve: You gonna watch me eat my lunch?

Mother: Yeah, I'm gonna watch you eat your lunch.

Eve: I eating it.

Mother: I know you are.

Eve: It time Sarah take a nap.

Mother: It's time for Sarah to have some milk, yeah. And then she's gonna take a nap and you're gonna take a nap.

Eve: And you?

Mother: And me too, yeah. (Bellugi, 1970, p. 33)

Thus, language development cannot be entirely accounted for by positive or negative reinforcement. First of all, adults do not commonly focus on the structure of a child's language. Second, when adults do attempt negative reinforcement, the child may not even be conscious of the particular structure the adult is correcting. In short, adult disapproval usually fails to have any effect on a young child's utterance (Brown, Cazden, & Bellugi, 1969).

Learning by Constructing Rules

Children learn language through imitation, reinforcement, and hypothesis testing.

Neither imitation nor reinforcement can account for the kind of language that Eve produces while she is speaking with her mother. At one point Eve comments, "I eating it." Among the many other things she is learning about English, Eve is at present working on verb forms and tenses. Since these forms are complex in English, Eve constructs her own way of describing present action, which leaves out the auxiliary verb *am.* Such a strategy is common among children at similar stages of language development. The important point is that Eve is making guesses about how the system works and testing out these hypotheses. A hypothesis-testing theory is powerful enough to explain three important features of language development: the rapid growth children make, the consistent patterns they produce that are not like adult structures, and the fact that learning occurs without direct instruction and in diverse circumstances that vary considerably from one child to another.

We can observe children actively constructing rules for speaking by paying attention to the way they monitor themselves and experiment with structural forms:

Laura (aged 2 years, 2 months):	Her want some more.
	Her want some more candy.
	Let's dooz this.
	Let's do this.
	Let's do this puzzle. (Laura adds nouns— *candy* and *puzzle.*) (Moskowitz, 1985, p. 59)

Older children continue to monitor and experiment to achieve new forms:

Jamie (aged 6 years, 3 months):	Who do you think is the importantest kid in the world except me?
Mother:	What did you say, Jamie?
Jamie:	Who do you think is the specialest kid in the world not counting me?
Jamie (aged 6 years, 10 months):	I figured something you might like out.
Mother:	What did you say?
Jamie:	I figured out something you might like. (Moskowitz, 1985, p. 59)

Children learn grammar—phonology, syntax, semantics, lexicon, and pragmatics—by breaking each system down into its smallest part and then developing rules for combining the parts. In the first two years, a child spends much time taking apart the sound system and learning sound combinations that make words. After words, children focus on structures, combining words into sentences of various kinds to communicate their intentions.

Children are very methodical language learners. The most general rules are hypothesized first; then newer rules are added to increase precision. For instance, learning word order in English—subject, verb, object—is a more general rule than learning how to produce a present or past tense verb. Generally children will deal with clear-cut issues first and sort out the details later. When it comes to language, children are very inventive, as we saw in Eve's conversation. They are adept at circumventing the difficult parts of the language system while still managing to communicate.

The Critical Period Theory of Language Acquisition

In this discussion, we have assumed that every child, apart from those who suffer extreme disabilities, develops language. But do children have to be exposed to language from birth in order to learn it? Is there a critical age by which children must have acquired language if they are to learn it at all? Or is the brain so malleable and resilient that language can be acquired at any age, even if the child has been deprived and isolated from human contact for many years?

One theorist, E. H. Lenneberg (1967, 1969), believes that language has a biological basis; there is a *critical period* in infancy when particular neurological faculties develop, which allows the child to learn language. The **critical period hypothesis** suggests that if certain internal or external conditions related to language development are missing, then a child will never be able to acquire language.

Since human interaction is necessary for children to develop language during the first 2 years of life, the critical period hypothesis predicts that extensive social deprivation will prevent language development. As evidence, Lenneberg points to the fact that around 18 months of age the two hemispheres of the brain begin to specialize. Each hemisphere functions to control different areas of human activity. In most people, language functions are located in the left hemisphere. But the brain is somewhat plastic, and studies of brain injuries suggest that if damage occurs in one hemisphere, in some cases the undamaged hemisphere can control new functions. But after puberty, Lenneberg noted the brain loses plasticity, because its special functions become permanent. He believed that if language is not a part of the brain's functions by this time, it never will be.

In those few cases we know of where children have endured severe isolation, their development has been retarded in all areas—cognitive, social, linguistic (Itard, 1962). Once development has been arrested, can it be restarted? Can developmentally delayed children catch up once they are no longer isolated? There is no straightforward answer to this question. Language development depends in part on the age and condition of the child at the time of isolation, the length and intensity of the deprivation, and other biological factors, such as adequate food for brain growth. Much of what we know about this topic has been learned from the case mentioned in Chapter 1 of a girl named Genie, who, for the first 14 years of her life, lived confined to a small, dark room with virtually no human contact. (For Genie's story, see Curtiss, 1977.)

Although she was 14 years old when first exposed to it, Genie did make some progress in acquiring language. However, scientists believe that she was using her right brain for language processing, which is atypical. She learned fairly quickly how to produce short sentences, but her grammar never developed much beyond the linguistic capacities of a 2½-year-old child. In contrast, her vocabulary was larger and more sophisticated than that of a young child, which indicates that her cognition developed faster than her linguistic abilities. Since Genie never developed language completely, Susan Curtiss (1977) concluded that, contrary to Lenneberg's theory, *some* degree of language acquisition is possible after the critical period.

Children learn language methodically, beginning with broad, general rules and then adding new, specific rules for greater precision.

The critical period hypothesis suggests that if certain internal or external conditions related to language development are missing (e.g., social interaction), a child will never be able to acquire language.

To summarize, children learn language through a variety of methods. Learning a language means learning the rules for sound combinations, word meanings, sentence structure, and interaction patterns. Imitation of adult speech does not play a significant role in language acquisition. Children must hear adults speaking language in order to acquire language, but their early attempts at speaking are not imitations of adult patterns. Reinforcement plays a role in language acquisition, but it is children's efforts to learn and to interact with other speakers that are reinforced. Adults reinforce children's global language behavior; specific grammatical structures are not learned through reinforcement. Children construct the rules of their grammar by generating a series of hypotheses about how sounds blend to form words, or how words join together into phrases. They test these preliminary ideas about language by speaking and receiving feedback about meaning from other speakers. Adults support children's efforts by responding to the content and meaning of what they say, by asking questions to encourage speech, and by modeling adult forms of the language.

Early Stages of Language Acquisition

Historically, language has been studied by developmental psychologists mainly because of its role in an individual's cognitive and social development. But during the 1960s, researchers became interested in studying child language for opposite reasons, on account of its universal qualities. Language was something that everyone learned in the same way. In learning to speak, children who were acquiring the same language made identical mistakes and consistently learned some structures before others. The early stages of language acquisition are shown in the Focus on Development box.

One and Two Words

Before they know a single word, children are communicating. Babies vocalize, changing tone and volume to convey their needs—cooing to express pleasure at seeing a parent or crying over an empty stomach. Babies babble, repeating speech sounds individually or producing long stretches of sound that seem oddly like the intonation patterns of the language spoken around them.

Around age 1, children begin to exhibit representational thinking through the use of single words, such as ball, dada, and mama.

Sometime around their first birthday, most children begin to say single words, or what adults take to be words (Bates, 1976). First words commonly refer to concrete objects in the child's world: *ball, dada, kitty, juice.* This is not surprising, since at this age children are in the sensorimotor stage of development in which concrete knowledge is being developed (Piaget, 1952). By the time children are saying their first words, they have acquired object permanence (see Chapter 3). They understand that when a ball rolls behind a chair, it may be out of sight, but it still exists even though hidden by the chair. Children also understand something about tools—for instance, pulling the blanket closer to grab the bear resting on it—and about symbolic play—using a spoon to feed their bear some applesauce. All these abilities (object permanence, tool use, symbolic play) require the child to represent experience in some other form. Words provide such symbols. Piaget maintained that representational thinking is an important precondition for language development.

Although children may have fewer than a dozen words in their speaking vocabulary, they are able to use intonation, gesture, and facial expressions to impart an entire sentence's worth of meaning into a single word. **Holophrases** are single words intended to convey more complex meaning. A child may say *truck* and mean, "There's a truck" or "Give me

Focus on Development

Early Stages of Language Acquisition

Age	Developmental Milestone
Birth to 6 months	Cries and coos (open vowel sounds)
	Recognizes human voices
	Responds well to high-pitched, melodic vocalizations
	Can distinguish *d* from *b*
	Varies cries to signal pain and distress
6 to 12 months	Begins babbling (vowel-constant sounds)
	Imitates voice patterns and sounds
	Uses voice to get attention
	Says first words
	Waves bye-bye
	Understands more words than can say
12 to 18 months	Uses holophrases
	Uses gestures to convey meaning
	Shakes head to mean "no"
	Understands simple commands
	Begins to use me, you, I
18 to 24 months	Uses two-word phrases ("Mommy go")
	Refers to self by name
	Uses telegraphic speech
	Uses correct word order
	Knows 50 words
24 to 36 months	Begins to use word endings
	Uses three-word sentences
	Enjoys songs, rhymes, and rhythms
	Uses simple pronouns
	Continues to expand vocabulary
	Telegraphic speech declines
	Uses strategies to begin conversations
	Uses adjectives and adverbs
	Speaking vocabulary may reach 200 words
	Can articulate *m, n, f, p, t, d, w*

SOURCES: National Center for Infants, Toddlers, and Families (1995); National Institutes of Mental Health (1995).

the truck" or "I hear the garbage truck" or "The truck is driving down the road." Children understand many of the functions of full sentences, and by using one word they may extend a greeting, identify an object, make a request or demand, issue a protest, or ask a question. They are trying to convey the meaning of a whole sentence in a single word. Adults help by interpreting children's utterances and making appropriate verbal and physical responses. Adults can foster children's development through verbal interactions like the following.

Child: Spoon!

Adult: Down! It fell down, didn't it? Did the spoon make a noise? That was loud!

Within a few months of saying their first words, children begin combining words into two-word utterances. Although there is a great deal of variation among children, two-word utterances appear on average at 18 months of age. The progression from one- to two-word combinations is so predictable and stable that psychologists have hypothesized a cognitive limit to explain the two-word condition.

Remember that children are not trying to reproduce adult sentences, which are far longer than two words, but are simply trying to communicate. In a sense, each child is constructing his or her own system, based on the language input the child is receiving from other speakers. Look at the list of 2-year-old Kendall's utterances as shown in Figure 5.2.

Two words are better than one, because children may talk about more than one role or action at a time. There are many possible variations. For instance, "Kimmy bike," or naming the experiencer and the object, is just as likely as the reverse "Bike Kimmy." Another child may name the object and then the place, "Pillow here," or the opposite, "There doggie" (Braine, 1976). These patterns are unpredictable, which demonstrates that children are constructing language individually.

Children's first words are concerned with semantics, not with grammatical structure.

Sometimes, children's two-word phrases like "Mommy go" look like adult syntax, but most linguists reject this interpretation. The flexibility in children's two-word combinations shows that they are focusing on meaning (semantics) not on structure (syntax). Not only do children learn words *(dog, cat, shoe, go, up, no)*, they also categorize words (action, location, actor). Their concept of a cat, for instance, includes the notion of a living creature capable of action in a way that a shoe is not.

Many Words

One word, two words, . . . three words? On the basis of their first utterances, it is tempting to conclude that children will keep adding a word at a time to their sentence length. But two-word combinations are the foundation for future sentences with any number of words, not just three.

FIGURE 5.2

Two-Word Utterances

Verb and agent:	"Kendall swim."
Verb and goal:	"Writing book."
Verb and location:	"Sit pool."
Experiencer and object:	"Kimmy bike."
Location and object:	"Pillow here."
Verb and object:	"Shoe off."

SOURCE: Bowerman (1973).

Language development is extremely consistent: All children learn a small set of single words first; then as they learn more words, they combine them into two-word utterances; then they begin producing multiple-word utterances with great speed, huge variety, and little regularity from child to child. Two strategies children appear to use are to combine smaller sequences and to embed one sequence inside another. For instance, knowing the two expressions, "Kendall swim" (agent and verb) and "sit pool" (verb and location), a child may be able to create, "Kendall swim pool." Sometimes this phase is called **telegraphic speech.** As the example shows, early telegraphic speech is typically a short, simple sentence, with primarily content words. Linking words such as *in* are omitted.

Although this expression seems rudimentary, children are acquiring new words and new functions and combining expressions so quickly that they soon begin producing complex utterances as Andrew demonstrates:

Andrew (2 years, 8 months):   What he can ride in?

He not taking the walls down.

I want to open it.

Although not perfectly grammatical, Andrew is able to produce a question and indicate a negative state. Both forms are quite complex in English and, in acquiring them, children follow regular patterns. (Both these forms have been extensively studied; see Klima & Bellugi [1966] on questions and Bloom [1970] on negatives.)

Around 3 years old, children start to produce more complex sentences.

Complement: "I want to go out."
Relative: "The ones you've got are bigger."
Adverbial (Subordination):   "I was crying when my Mommy goed away."
(Clark & Clark, 1977, p. 359)

Generally, once past the two-word phase, children expand both the structure and function of their basic language system. Structurally, word endings such as *-ed* begin to appear as in, "He kicked Teddy" and possessive forms develop, as in, "My dog's bone is gone." In addition to these small refinements, children grow functionally. Part of communicating effectively entails learning how to interact with listeners in increasingly sophisticated ways. For instance, 4-year-olds know that using a hedge rather than making a direct assertion will foster cooperation. Instead of saying, "That piece fits here," the child may opt to say, "*I think* that piece fits here" (Gelman & Shatz, 1976). Children are learning language on all fronts at once—not only are they improving their syntax and acquiring new vocabulary, they are also learning to argue with their peers and to solicit help from adults when they need it.

Children's Language after Age Five

The early stages of language acquisition have been well studied, perhaps because of children's dramatic progress in the first few years of life. For parents, no other time is as heartening as the day their child speaks the first word, or invents a name for a sibling whose own name is unpronounceable (*Rainman* for *Raymond*). Although older children's language development has been less studied, there is still a great deal that children learn about language during the school years. At 5 and 6 years old, their progress in acquiring vocabulary or in syntax may be less spectacular, but the pragmatic structures and strategies children are perfecting are vital for their later competence as adult speakers and writers. In fact, developing **communicative competence,** or learning to use language in an appropriate manner, that is, knowing what words and structures to use on what occasion, is the major area of linguistic growth during childhood, through adolescence, and continuing into adulthood (Hymes, 1974).

At 5 years old, children do not make the phonological or syntactic errors typical of 3-year-olds. In English, they can distinguish between verbs that have a special form for the past tense (I *run;* I *ran*) and those that take the common *-ed* form (I *walk;* I *walked*). Preschool-aged children know how to produce a variety of complex sentences in which two or more clauses are combined, as in the following adverbial clause example: "I ran away *when the big dog came into the yard.*" Along with syntax, children's vocabularies are also expanding rapidly. By age 5 or 6, children have a vocabulary of approximately 15,000 words (Pinker, 1994). Learning new words or extending their understanding of what a word means is a constant process. Understanding words that refer to locations, such as *beside* or *between,* is difficult conceptually, and children begin to use them reliably at about the age of 5.

In addition to sentence structure (syntax) and word meaning (semantics), school-age children's progress in social (pragmatic) uses of language develops rapidly. They are learning to engage in more sustained and effective interchanges with others. Around age 5, their delight at jokes and riddles, rhymes, and silly sounds becomes contagious. Around age 7, a child who can create a joke will have learned an important social skill, earning the respect and attention of peers. Knowing how to interrupt politely in a conversation, the rules for arguing, strategies for storytelling, and other forms of public discourse are all important parts of children's developing communicative competence.

Language into Adolescence

Once children reach middle childhood, the sound, meaning, and grammatical systems are well developed apart from a few, less commonly used forms in speech, such as relative clauses and passive sentences. Now that they have mastered the basics, older children focus their energies on learning how to use language, greatly expanding their range of language registers (formal and informal speech) and styles (narrative, argumentative, etc.) in both speaking and writing. In addition, school has a major impact in fostering this flexibility as well as teaching specialized knowledge about written styles.

Temperamentally, any adolescent can be volatile, moody, exuberant, and restless, sometimes withdrawn but socially preoccupied with peers and dismissive of adults as authorities. At this age, teenagers use language to express their deepest emotions and thoughts. In her work teaching middle school, Nancie Atwell (1987) reported that poetry is a mode most often chosen by her eighth graders because it allows them to give shape and voice to their inner experiences. This attraction to poetry and other techniques used in creative writing, such as parody and sarcasm, is not surprising. Around the age of 11 or 12, children pass another linguistic benchmark when they perceive that meaning is multidimensional: Words have both literal and metaphoric definitions. Remember that young children make literal interpretations of words or texts. Fairy tales are simply entertaining and engrossing stories to an elementary-school child whose thinking is very concrete. But older children develop the ability to make complex interpretations of texts. Fairy tales convey morals and messages that a middle-school child can articulate. Language takes on an entirely new dimension for creative expression and comprehension once the child understands how figurative language, such as metaphor, conveys meaning. Their cognitive and linguistic abilities complement each other. Adolescent students can view a film and afterward argue about its sym-

Communicative competence, or learning to use language in an appropriate manner, is the major area of linguistic growth from childhood through adolescence.

SOURCE: Michael Newman/Photo Edit.

Drama and theater provide adolescents opportunities to experiment with many different language forms and linguistic styles.

bolism; they are apt to see patterns and to assess motives in events that previously had seemed straightforward. Linguistic styles proliferate at this age, especially those associated with humor: puns, quips, nonsequiturs, jokes, ad-libs, double entendres, caricatures, and imitations are common fare.

By adolescence, students are extremely skilled at adapting their language to different situations. This flexibility serves two purposes: as a creative outlet and as social currency. The way we speak both reflects our individual personalities and conveys information about our relationships with other people. Imagine the conversational variety in these contexts: a 15-year-old on the phone with a close friend, a last-minute discussion between a coach and her basketball players before a big game, the small talk among a group of boys sitting on the school steps, a teenager asking to use the family car on a Saturday night. What might be some of the factors shaping speech? What social relations underlie each discourse style? Language addressed to adults will be more formal and polite compared with peers. Formality of language in tone and structure is further heightened in school contexts versus home settings. Language between peers of the same gender may be more casual and telegraphic compared with mixed-gender conversations. Language between members of an established social group, like a neighborhood gang, may contain many special words or expressions, whose meanings are unintelligible to outsiders. Slang, or language used in casual settings to establish group solidarity and to signal group membership, is a prototypical practice during adolescence precisely because peer group socialization is so important at this age. The Focus on Research box provides more information about the function of teenage slang.

Thus, language development through adolescence entails expanding communicative competence, since grammatical development is fairly complete. Individuals develop a repertoire of styles suited to a social context and the other participants. This ability includes knowing when and how to speak, being sensitive to appropriate topics, and adjusting style, vocabulary, and politeness levels to match the age and gender of other speakers.

During adolescence, students learn to communicate in figurative as well as literal ways and to adjust their use of language to a variety of social contexts.

Focus on Research

Teenagers are preoccupied with social relationships. They become acutely aware of their relations with others, particularly with their peers. Because language is a flexible system for communicating and representing individual identity, speaking styles, like clothing choices, are important emblems of teenage life. Peer-group membership is often signaled by a distinctive style or special vocabulary, especially *slang*. Slang consists of words or expressions that develop in special contexts and have particular meanings. Typically, slang is used in casual settings and is created by in-groups to include some and exclude others. Teenagers generate slang expressions that their parents, for instance, might not understand at first and would certainly never use. Every teenage generation has its own slang terms, many of which become widespread, such as *cool,* whereas other slang is very specialized, perhaps extending no farther than a single high school group or region. For example, *Valspeak* is a kind of teenage slang originated by affluent California girls from the San Fernando Valley region north of Los Angeles during the early 1980s. Expressions such as *awesome* (good), *bag your face* (to disagree), *mondo* (very), *tubular* (very good), and *grody* (unspeakably awful) are part of the valley girl vocabulary. You might recognize or even use some of these words, which shows how slang expressions transcend their original groups and disperse through communities and even nations.

Schools are fertile breeding grounds for slang words and expressions, as well as for other stylistic dialects such as rap songs or preppy talk. Such language serves important social functions, creating ties and relationships, and should not be discouraged by parents or teachers just because it is not standard English. However, some slang words, terms, and expressions are offensive and objectionable; teachers need to use the same judgment about allowing these terms to be used publicly as they would other language, such as obscenities, in their classroom and community. Slang is also creative work; many new words are added to English every year through the ingenuity and cleverness of the teenage mind. The following words, now perfectly acceptable, began as slang: *freshman, mob, dwindle,* and *glib.*

For a class project, ask students to make up a list of any slang terms they know associated with a sport they play, a club or group they belong to, or a particular field of interest, such as computers. Students can then compare lists with both members in the same group and different groups. They can account for differences and similarities as well as make some generalizations about why slang exists.

Learning Two Languages

For many adults, learning to speak a second language may be regarded as an extremely difficult if not impossible task. Whether it is a college student eager to learn a foreign language for studying abroad or an adult emigrating to a new country, acquiring another language is a formidable experience. However, when we think about children learning a second language, we assume they will learn faster and more easily than any adult. A woman laments, "Oh, if only I had learned Russian from my grandmother when I was 3."

Or the hopeful wish of immigrant parents for their child, "He'll learn English when he goes to school." What accounts for this attitude? Is it true that children have special advantages over adults? How do children learn a second language?

Some children learn two languages from the beginning of language acquisition, whereas other children may not begin to acquire a second language until they enter school. If a child is born into a family and community in which several languages are flourishing, chances are the child will grow up **bilingual,** speaking two languages, or **multilingual,** speaking more than two. Remember that a child needs more than exposure to learn a language, including a second language. Just because English-speaking Canadian children can watch and listen to French TV or radio does not mean they will learn French. Interaction with other speakers for the purpose of communicating in the target language is necessary for second-language acquisition. Amazingly enough, children seem equipped to learn multiple languages simultaneously if the environment is sufficiently rich to provide the necessary linguistic interactions.

For children who are **simultaneous bilinguals,** learning several languages at the same time, their pattern of acquisition is fairly clear. At first, a child acts as if he or she is learning one language system, even though the child is being exposed to several languages. The child constructs a single system made up of combinations of features—sounds and words—from both languages. This period, called **mixed speech,** lasts until the child is about 2 years old (Imedadze, 1978). Remember that most 2-year-olds have not acquired much syntax, so combining features of two languages is not problematic. Sometimes the bilingual child will use a word from each language in producing a two-word utterance (Volterra & Taeschner, 1978) or even put a word ending from one language onto the main word of the other language (Burling, 1959). Some children know how to name an object in both languages. For instance, an 11-month-old girl with an Israeli mother and British father regularly said the word *parpar,* which means butterfly in Hebrew. She understood that the English word *butterfly* meant the same creature and could easily point to the right picture when asked in English by her father to find the butterfly in a book. But she consistently used the Hebrew word in speaking.

During the next stage, children begin to discriminate between the two languages. They start by separating the words of each language, and then they combine them according to the syntax of each language. They no longer include words from different languages in the same utterance, and they demonstrate an ability to translate from one language to another. Some studies have found that around the age of 4, children who are simultaneous bilinguals have fully separated the two languages (Volterra & Taeschner, 1978). For a child to remain bilingual, both languages have to be in constant use throughout childhood. For most people, a language disappears if it is not actively used.

A common concern about childhood bilingualism is that it may delay children's cognitive and language development. Early research indicated that bilingual immigrant children performed more poorly on various measures of intelligence than their monolingual peers (Diaz, 1983). However, this research failed to take into account socioeconomic differences in the samples studied. More carefully controlled studies reveal that experience with two language systems can enhance mental flexibility, concept formation, and metalinguistic abilities (National Research Council, 1998). Additionally, children's use of their native language does not impede the acquisition of English (August & Hakuta, 1997).

We sometimes assume that children learn a second language easily simply because they are children and are predisposed to learn language. Children do seem to have an early predisposition to learn a *first* language, but it is not clear that age correlates with learning a *second* language. As we discussed earlier, research on whether or not there is a critical

Interactive communication with other speakers in a natural social context provides the best setting for learning a second language.

period for language acquisition has not proved conclusive. Even if there is a critical period for learning a first language, it does not mean there is one for a second language.

How long does it take for children to acquire a second language? The answer to this question depends on the child's age, home environment, and schooling conditions, as well as the definition of proficiency used. Studies of students with limited English proficiency in the United States have shown that it can take 1 to 3 years to acquire oral communication skills. However, it may take 6 to 10 years to acquire a level of English proficiency necessary for learning core subjects in school (Garcia, 2000).

Second-language learning is a complex process that is influenced by many different factors. Because of more advanced cognitive skills, older children acquire a second language at a more rapid rate than do younger children (Garcia, 2000; National Research Council, 1998). Some experts also believe that second-language acquisition is faster and easier, when children have mastered basic grammar structures of their first language. Thus, continued development of children's first language is important for the acquisition of a second language (National Research Council, 1998).

If older children and even adults have difficulty learning a second language, the fault may be not with age or the nature of the mind but rather with the kinds of experiences or the environment in which the second language is being learned. It is much easier for someone at any age to learn a language if they are surrounded by native speakers in a natural social context and experience the need to communicate themselves. Adult instruction in a foreign language, which typically occurs in classrooms, is not often characterized by any of these conditions. Language is not easily learned in restricted situations with minimal interaction between students; it is learned through meaningful interactions with other speakers.

Remember Pha, the 6-year-old from Laos who is learning English by immersion into an American classroom? At this time in American history, there are thousands of individuals like Pha who live in the United States but do not yet speak English. While the majority are Spanish speakers, there are large numbers of Hmong, Chinese, and Vietnamese speakers (see Chapter 1). Many of these individuals will become bilingual. If a person learns English but retains his or her native language, we call this situation **successive bilingualism**. If a person already speaks one language, the stages of development in another language will be completely different. Both babbling and one- and then two-word utterances are unique features of early childhood development and will not occur when a school-age child or adult acquires a second language.

However, it is very possible Pha may not retain his native language after being acclimated into American culture. At present, he is a bilingual learner, but depending on the kind of education he receives, he may or may not grow up to be bilingual. In this section, we have learned how bilinguals *acquire* several languages. In the final section of this chapter, the subject of bilingual education is discussed in greater detail.

Fostering Language Development

Children do not learn language on their own. From the first moment, language is social: the mother looks into a child's eyes and pronounces her name. Granting that humans are predisposed to learn language, we also know that language development is fostered by adults and by environments that encourage communication.

First, adults assume that children will learn language. They act as if children are participants in the language game immediately. This assumption—that their children have intentions and are communicating—helps children to focus on sounds and to recognize that language is an important part of life.

Adding a second language to a previously learned first language is referred to as successive bilingualism.

Second, adults and children are partners in creating meaning and cooperate in constructing language (Ochs, Schieffelin, & Platt, 1979). A child may only need to point to a favorite toy car before the adult provides a long dialogue about it.

Third, adult speakers structure a child's environment so that learning can occur more easily (Snow, 1986). They fill the world with talk. Even when a child is too young to make sounds, adults are constantly addressing their child. Adults focus on the concrete. While a child is eating, the father may point to the picture of the baby on a cereal box, allow the baby to touch the box, all the while producing a stream of talk that ensures that the child is making connections between words and things.

Some parents may also alter their intonation, adding stress and often using a higher pitch when speaking, to gain the child's attention. Middle-class American parents sometimes keep sentences short and simple, they repeat themselves endlessly, and often use a higher proportion of questions and imperatives than is typical in their everyday conversation. Some of these features are culture specific (Heath, 1983). For example, some cultures use strategies other than pitch for gaining attention. Gender plays a role, too. Mothers tend to ask more questions of their children than fathers do. But most cultures have standard strategies adults use to create a positive learning environment for their children.

Fourth, learning language is motivated by the desire to communicate and to engage others in the community. Conversational exchanges are embedded in natural contexts and are part of ongoing social action. Children's experiences with language are authentic acts of communication; they speak when they have something to say to an interested listener. The importance of authentic situations to ensure language learning and development at every age from infancy through adulthood cannot be overemphasized.

Literacy Development

In our society children are exposed to print from birth. Although children develop spoken language before they learn to read or write, they are nevertheless learning about written language from the start. A 2-year-old girl at the grocery store can recognize a box of Cheerios, her favorite cereal, demonstrating that she understands the concept of visual representation, that symbols can stand for things. On a long car trip, a 3-year-old boy shouts to his parents when he spots the "big 6" logo advertising their motel (and the pool that accompanies it). He knows that print carries meaning.

Both spoken and written language are symbol systems, but each form is represented differently, speech as sound and writing as visual marks. Thus, each system has unique features that children must master. In addition, writing serves different purposes than speech in our culture. Figuring out the written system and the special functions of writing begins as soon as children are exposed to print. Early experiences may include looking at picture books, examining a blanket or favorite toy covered in letters, listening and interacting while an adult reads aloud, or scribbling on paper and telling a story. Early childhood educators once believed that young children needed to know letter names or sound–letter relationships before they were ready to read and write. But researchers and teachers now recognize that children who pretend they are reading or writing understand a great deal about literacy. For instance, long before children can translate written letters to words, they learn the basic concept that print carries meaning. This is a sign of **emergent literacy**. It is important to realize that certain concepts and behaviors, such as when children pretend they are translating words to print, are the basis for children's literacy when they actually do begin to read and write (Teale & Sulzby, 1986).

Even though children master spoken language before reading and writing, the notion of emergent literacy holds that both spoken and written language are learned from birth.

Emergent Reading and Writing

To learn to read and write, children must discover the *purposes* for print, the details of the *visual symbol system,* the *arbitrary conventions* for making letters and texts, and the *characteristics of different texts*—the differences between stories, letters, or grocery lists. Four-year-old Nora holds a book on her lap ready to read. She points to the cover of *Allison's Zinnia,* by Anita Lobel (1990). Pointing to the author's name and dragging her finger across the cover from left to right, Nora pronounces in an exaggerated voice "A—lli—son's Zi—ni—a." Her mother removes her daughter's finger from the author's name and places it on the first letter of the title. Her mother reads, "Allison's Zinnia" while sliding Nora's finger under the letters. Then she says, "Allison's Zinnia! See Allison begins with A."

Learning to read and write involves discovering the purposes for print, the details and conventions of the visual symbol system, and the characteristics of different kinds of text.

As a 4-year-old, Nora can make broad distinctions about print. She can identify writing or printed text from everything else on the page, such as a drawing or a picture. She points to the letters on the cover when she says the title, not to the large picture that occupies most of the cover. Nora also knows that the language found in books is special since she speaks with a loud and dramatic tone, one she doesn't adopt in a casual conversation. In addition, she is aware that print is read from left to right, as her finger sweep suggests. Her mother fosters her literacy knowledge, in particular by matching the printed to the spoken word as she helps the child point to *Allison.* Furthermore, her mother reinforces letter recognition and models a reading strategy by telling her to look at the first letter of a word: "Allison begins with A." So even though Nora is not able to read the print yet, she is certainly an emergent reader.

The concept of emergent literacy was first introduced in the early 1980s. This conception of literacy development represented a move away from the now outdated **reading readiness approach,** which emphasized a set of skills children needed to master before beginning formal reading instruction (Whitehurst & Lonigan, 1998). Emergent literacy encompasses the time from birth to age 5 or 6, and it consists of a set of "skills, knowledge, and attitudes that are presumed to be developmental precursors of reading and writing" (Whitehurst & Lonigan, 1998, p. 849). Examples of early literacy skills include letter recognition, knowledge of letter sounds, awareness of print conventions (e.g., direction and sequence of print, difference between book covers and pages, etc.), and interest in print and books. Researchers who study emergent literacy have uncovered interesting links between children's early literacy experiences (storybook reading, dramatic play, exposure to print, etc.) and later reading and writing achievement. Figure 5.3 summarizes key elements of the emergent literacy perspective.

Recognizing Print

Through repeated exposures to a story read aloud, young children quickly understand that what an adult reader says is determined by the print in the book. Two-year-olds will object when a parent misreads a word or skips a line in a favorite story. Often they are capable of providing the appropriate word or sentence, or indeed of "reading" the entire book from memory. Jacob, a 2-year-old whose mother was distracted momentarily pushed at the book impatiently and commanded that his mother "Go . . . do it . . . make the book say it." He demonstrates through his behavior his knowledge that the words are fixed in the book and that his mother knows the magic to get the book talking.

Around the age of 3 children can readily distinguish writing from other visual marks. How do children make these distinctions? In one study, children ages 3 to 6½ were shown cards on which various combinations of letters, pictures, doodles, and numbers were

The following findings from research on children's literacy development are central to the emergent literacy perspective:

1. Literacy development begins long before children start formal instruction. Children use legitimate reading and writing behaviors in the informal settings of home and community.

2. Literacy development is appropriate to describe what was called reading readiness. The child develops as a reader and writer. The notion of reading preceding writing, or vice versa, is a misconception. Listening, speaking, reading, and writing abilities develop concurrently and interrelatedly, rather than sequentially.

3. Literacy develops in real-life settings for real-life activities in order to "get things done." Therefore, the functions of literacy are as integral a part of learning about writing and reading during early childhood as the forms of literacy.

4. Children are doing critical cognitive work in literacy development during the years from birth to 6.

5. Children learn written language through active engagement with their world. They interact socially with adults in writing and reading situations, they explore print on their own, and they profit from modeling of literacy by significant adults, particularly their parents.

6. Although children's learning about literacy can be described in terms of generalized stages, children can pass through these stages in a variety of ways and at different ages.

SOURCE: Teale & Sulzby, 1986.

FIGURE 5.3

Elements of the Emergent Literacy Perspective

printed (Lavine, 1977). They were asked to make two piles of cards: writing in one pile and other nonwriting marks in another. Cards with writing were correctly identified by 80 percent of the 3-year-olds, 90 percent of the 4-year-olds, and 96 percent of the 5-year-olds. Those children who did not yet recognize letters paid attention to several features of print in order to make their decisions. *Linearity, the way print is arranged in rows*, and variety, different shapes in the row, were two salient traits. Children who recognized letters already used that knowledge to distinguish between marks on the page and real writing.

Our understanding of children's literacy learning was greatly enhanced when three researchers, Jerome Harste, Virginia Woodward, and Carolyn Burke (1984), reported their study of preschool children's knowledge of written language. They worked with 3- to 6-year-old children; boys and girls in high-, middle-, and low-SES classes; blacks and whites, small town and urban inner-city families. They examined children's interactions with print found in the environment—such as store signs or logos, children's scribbling, their encounters with picture books—and they observed children in experimental as well as natural settings. Their work, reported in *Language Stories and Literacy Lessons,* provides an account of what preschoolers know about literacy and what experiences foster literacy development. In one part of their study, 3-year-olds were asked both to write and to draw. They found that all children could produce "systematic and organized" marks that distinguished writing from drawing (p. 18). Terry, one 3-year-old, consistently made linear marks to indicate writing, particularly writing his name, while his drawing marks were global and circular. The researchers concluded that Terry was demonstrating, "both in form and in process, the stuff of real literacy, being invented from the inside out" (p. 18).

Interviews with kindergarten-age children reveal that by this age they can identify different kinds of reading materials and tell why people read them. In one study, 5-year-olds were shown a variety of reading materials, including picture books, magazines, calendars, and TV schedules (Weiss & Hagen, 1988). Most children in the study were able to recognize and discuss the function of different kinds of print. All except 1 of the 110 children interviewed could explain the purpose for reading storybooks, and more than 95 percent of the children understood the functions of newspapers and the telephone book. Other materials, such as shopping lists, magazines, directions, and TV guides, were recognized by about 80 percent of the children. Such knowledge arises out of children's experiences with print in their everyday life.

Through play and experimentation with print, children discover that a relationship exists among print, sound, and meaning.

Sounds and Letters

A baby's fist waving in the air was considered by Vygotsky (1978) as a precursor of writing: "Gestures . . . are writing in the air, and written signs frequently are simply gestures that have been fixed" (p. 106). When materials for marking are available, the gestures descend from the air onto a surface. Children persist in making marks and leaving visual traces, whether it is making ketchup circles on their high chair tray, using crayons on paper, or leaving finger trails in sand. These scribbles have meaning for the child who produces them whether or not an adult understands the representation.

As soon as a child realizes that writing exists—that special marks carry meaning—then the child will probably begin thinking about the connection between speaking and writing. Through play and experimentation with print as well as exposure to books and print in the environment, the child will discover print, sound, and meaning relationships.

Because written English is an **alphabetic system,** children learn that single shapes are letters and eventually that letters are linked to specific sounds. Other written systems, for example, Chinese, are based on an **ideographic system,** in which each character, or ideograph, in the script represents the meaning of an individual word. But whatever the visual system, children must learn to recognize its features and eventually to produce the script themselves.

Children's concern with meaningful communication leads them to learn words before they learn the meaningless sound parts of words, such as letters or syllables.

Just as children learn the mapping principles between sound and meaning when learning to speak, so too they must learn the intricacies of linking letters to sounds and the combinations of letters into words. The ability to connect the distinctive sounds, or phonemes, in words to letters is called **phonemic awareness** (Perfetti, Beck, & Hughes, 1985; Juell, Griffith, & Gough, 1986). However, such awareness does not develop easily. Children are aware of words—because a word carries meaning—long before they are self-conscious about parts of words, such as a single sound or letter. In speech, children aim to produce words even in the earliest stage, when they have only a few sounds. Paying attention to single sounds is not a process children need in order to understand spoken language (Menyuk, 1976). In learning to read and write, a child must map sounds to letters, a tremendously difficult process. For instance, the word *bat* contains three sounds (phonemes). A child learning to write *bat* has to segment the meaningful syllable *bat* into three meaningless sound

SOURCE: Michael Newman/Photo Edit.

What are young children learning when they help to write stories?

parts /b/, /a/, and /t/. Furthermore, individual sounds are shaped by the surrounding sound context. Think about the word *bar*. Although only one letter is changed, the sound of /a/ is completely different in this new word. Children who speak English have difficulty matching sounds to letters because their language lacks one-to-one correspondence between sound and spelling. English has 26 letters, but the same sound may be represented by different combinations of letters such as the /f/ sound in words *phone* and *fix*. There are occasions when some letters represent no sound at all as the *gh* in *thought*. Or when the same letter sounds differently depending on its placement as the *c* in *cat* or *science*. All of these English-specific issues must be untangled by a beginning writer.

Researchers have discovered that children's ability to distinguish individual phonemes is an accurate predictor of reading success (Adams, 1990; Snow, Burns, & Griffin, 1998; Whitehurst & Lonigan, 1998). Phonemic awareness appears to have a stronger influence on the acquisition of reading skills than measures of intelligence, memory, and even social class (Whitehurst & Lonigan, 1998). Hearing individual sounds is something all speaking children can do. English speakers have many similar sounding words—such as *bat, rat, hat, sat*—the difference between them being a single sound. But it is not just *hearing* sounds that creates phonemic awareness; rather it is the ability to be *self-conscious* about these sounds. This ability to think and talk about language is called **metalinguistic awareness**. In other words, a child who can identify the first sound as making the difference between the words *rat* and *bat* understands a great deal about sound/print relationships.

Nora, the emergent reader we met earlier, will often "read" to her father familiar books she has memorized. Sometimes she will run her finger under the words as she "reads," imitating her parents' reading behavior. But she speaks much faster than her hand moves. In reading the title of the story "Daddy, Can You Play with Me?" she finishes speaking before her finger reaches the last word. Eventually she will begin to wonder about this mismatch, and with more experience or explanation from her parent, she will eventually understand that letters represent individual sounds and not syllables.

The Alphabet

In addition to matching sounds to letters, children also have to recognize and distinguish the letters of the English alphabet. In Chapter 4, we discussed how young children have difficulty focusing on the *distinctive features* of an object. Regarding the alphabet, children must not only learn the distinctive features of the letters but also develop the mental and perceptual processes of comparing differences between letters. For adults as well as for children, focusing on how things are different is probably more difficult and less practiced than thinking about how things are alike. Nevertheless, spoken and written language systems rely on distinctive features. The sounds of /p/ and /b/ are similar but not identical. The words *pack* and *back* when spoken aloud are only minimally distinct.

In learning the letters of the alphabet, however, children begin with similarities and ignore differences. When Matthew looked at his name, printed MATTHEW, he thought that the *M* and the *W* were the same letter, with one just upside down. After all, one cognitive principle he has learned is that even if an object is turned upside down, it remains the same thing. His toy car is still a car whether it is rolling on its wheels down the hallway, or lying on its side after a crash with the wall. Eventually with experience (for example, his teachers call the letter at the end of his name a *W*), Matthew learns that orientation in space is a distinctive feature of written letters but not of three dimensional objects.

The issue of spatial orientation may take children a while to sort out. It is common for children to write mirror images of letters and words as easily as the proper orientation. Figure 5.4 shows how Marin, a 4-year-old, writes her name as a mirror image. Such reversals may persist in the writing of 6- and 7-year-olds but will gradually disappear. In a print-rich culture such as ours, most children by the age of 5 can recognize and name the uppercase letters of the alphabet.

FIGURE 5.4

Four-Year-Old Marin Writes Her Name in Mirror Image

Learning the Conventions of Print

Language works as a form of communication because speakers agree about the way the system functions. These agreements are arbitrary. For instance, the particular combination of sounds /h/ /a/ /t/ for *hat* is not universal but was simply designated sometime in the past to mean a head covering. Likewise, grammatical rules are conventions. Speakers decided that a typical English sentence consists of a subject, verb, and object, as in, "Ralph ate the tomato." Both spoken and written forms of language have particular conventions, a kind of etiquette for performance. In conversation, speakers learn to signal the end of a turn, and to begin a new turn. Likewise, in writing, words must be spelled consistently by all writers in order to facilitate reading.

Literate adults may not be aware of how many conventions children must learn. For example, reading and writing progresses from left to right, not top to bottom or right to left. At the end of a line of text, the eyes return to the left side and begin scanning to the right. Words are separated by blank spaces. Margins and indentations mark paragraphs and story boundaries. Also a new reader has to notice the structural category of the sentence, a unit marked by punctuation and capitalization. In writing, sentences are well formed and grammatically complete. Written sentences are very different from the most common structures in spoken language, in which the clause or the phrase is the more basic structure. Along with new structures, new vocabulary and concepts have to be learned—*letter, word, sentence, paragraph, period*—in order for literacy learning to progress. Children must also learn how these individual structures, such as letters and words, are related. In a way, learning the conventions of writing is like solving a hierarchical classification problem, which we discussed in Chapter 3.

Both spoken and written language systems are based on a host of arbitrary conventions that must be learned before children can become literate.

Conventions of Stories

Besides conventions of print format, children also must learn the various patterns of discourse forms, such as narratives. Telling stories is a common event in speaking, and there is a broad range of story-telling styles with flexible conventions. Although there is great variety in written stories as well, writers have developed more rigid conventions for narratives, such as the opening formula "Once upon a time . . ." or the way action or sound must be described in a dialogue, "Hiding behind a bush, Jack whispered to Megan, 'Hurry up and find the flashlight.'" Specific detail, complete sentences, and a formal tone are characteristics of written stories.

How do preschool children learn these conventions? Long before children can read and write, they are absorbing these written conventions through exposure to books when adults read stories aloud. Around the age of 3, children are sensitive to story markers, such as using a formulaic beginning and ending and employing the past tense to signal time shifts (Applebee, 1978). Gradually their stories become more complex and involve settings, themes, and actions that may be invented or beyond the scope of concrete experience. Children around the age of 5 or 6 are telling stories that are true narratives built around an elaborated theme with developed characters, contain some kind of action or main event, and typically end with a clear resolution to the situation. The following story, told by a 5-year-old, exhibits narrative traits very clearly.

Children typically learn the conventions of a language system by exposure to books read aloud to them by adults.

> There was a boy named Johnny Hong Kong and finally he grew up and went to school and after that all he ever did was sit all day and think. He hardly even went to the bathroom. And he thought every day and every thought he thought up his head got bigger and bigger. One day it got so big he had to go and live up in the attic with trunks and winter clothes. So his mother bought some gold fish and let them live in his head—he swallowed them—and

every time he thought, a fish would eat it up until he was even so he never thought again, and he felt much better.

—Tracy H., 5 years, 8 months
(Applebee, 1978, p. 66)

Tracy's narrative is quite sophisticated. Not only does she create the story's plot, but she uses connecting words such as *then, finally,* and *so* to link events in the story and provide time sequencing. These connectives show that the child is able to coordinate several cognitive and social factors that are characteristic of narratives (Peterson & McCabe, 1991).

Although preschool children cannot typically write their own stories, dictated narratives reveal their awareness of literate practices. The more experience they have with translations from sound to print, the easier it is for them to learn to read and write. Because they can create a narrative, they will approach reading a story with a narrative frame in mind. Having expectations about how stories proceed or being able to make predictions about characters or events greatly improves listening and reading comprehension.

Social Influences on Emergent Literacy

A literate environment is one in which children encounter print with authentic purposes and adults value and participate in reading and writing themselves.

In a print-rich culture, literacy learning begins at birth. Children learn about reading and writing through social and linguistic interactions with others in their world. Researchers who have studied early readers and writers report that the strongest correlating factor is the nature of the home environment (Bus, van Ijzendoorn, Pellegrini, 1995; Yaden et al., 1999; Whitehurst & Lonigan, 1998; Teale, 1978). A large body of research suggests that children who are poor readers in the early elementary grades generally lack early literacy experiences at home (Beals & Detemple, 1993; Purcell-Gates, 1995; Shapiro, 1995).

There is a strong link between children's play experiences and emergent literacy (Yaden et al., 1999). As we discussed in Chapter 3, dramatic play is an important arena for the development of representational and language skills. Children often incorporate story characters and scripts into their play. These dramatic reenactments have a positive effect on story comprehension in kindergarten and first grade (Pellegrini & Galda, 1993; Yaden et al., 1999).

Additionally, children who learn to read early have many easy reading materials at home and often are frequent visitors to the local library. Parents or caregivers of early readers read aloud to their children and talk with them about books and print on a daily basis. Shared book reading provides a rich source of information and opportunities to learn new vocabulary (DeLoache & DeMendoza, 1987; Pellegrini, Brody, & Sigel, 1985). One study showed that 5 percent of daily speech for 2-year-olds occurred in the context of storytime (Wells, 1985). Also, parents or caregivers who read themselves are modeling such behavior for their children, demonstrating that reading is purposeful and pleasurable. Early readers are early writers as well. Preschool children engage in scribbling, drawing, making letters as well as letter-like shapes, copying words, writing their names, and other simple words. A literate environment, whether it is a child care facility, a nursery school, or the home, is one in which children encounter print with authentic purposes and where adults value and participate in reading and writing themselves.

The relationship between phonemic awareness (sound and letter relationships) and reading ability is mutually enhancing, although one skill is not a prerequisite for the other. Children as young as 3 years old can exhibit signs of phonemic awareness, but it is much more common in 6-year-olds (Read, 1975). Phonemic awareness can be developed in a variety of ways: exposing children to sets of regular patterned words, repeated readings of familiar books with predictable sound patterns, direct phonics instruction, wordplay involving rhyming games, and experimenting with writing. It is not clear from the research that any

One of the strongest influences on children's early literacy development is the home environment.

one approach to developing phonemic awareness is sufficient or effective (Mason & Allen, 1986). Providing a range of opportunities geared to children's needs is best.

However, being able to discriminate phonemes is not a necessary or sufficient condition for learning to read (Perfetti, Beck, & Hughes, 1985). On the other hand, being self-conscious about language definitely aids children in literacy learning. When a child says, "Hey, *cat* sounds like *bat*," the child is demonstrating metalinguistic awareness. Research has shown that being self-conscious about language can be enhanced simply by having more interactive experiences with print, which is good news for parents and teachers. Such awareness is not determined by reaching a particular point in children's cognitive development (Templeton & Spivey, 1980).

The Focus on Development box summarizes developmental accomplishments in a child's journey to becoming a reader and writer. This process depends heavily on social context. Frequent access to and enjoyment of a range of literacy activities, including large-print books, picture books, and books children make themselves through dictation, help literacy develop for all children. Early literacy development also depends on how parents and caregivers help children to construct meaning from their emergent reading and writing.

As we will discuss in Chapter 9, increasing numbers of young children are spending time in either a preschool or a day care setting. Preschool teachers and child care providers, therefore, play an increasingly important role in promoting early literacy development. The Focus on Teaching box describes ways of promoting children's literacy development in the preschool or day care setting.

Learning to Read

By the time children enter school, many are well on their way to becoming proficient readers and writers. However, between 25 percent and 40 percent of children in the United States encounter series roadblocks on the way to becoming fluent and proficient readers

Focus on Development

Developmental Milestones of Early Literacy

Birth to Three Years

- Recognizes specific books by cover.

- Pretends to read books.

- Understands that books are handled in specific ways.

- Enters into book-sharing routines with primary caregivers.

- Play vocalizations gives way to rhyming language, nonsense word-play, and so forth.

- Labels objects in books.

- Comments on characters in books.

- May begin attending to specific print such as letters in names.

- Uses increasingly purposive scribbling.

- Occasionally seems to distinguish between drawing and writing.

- Produces some letter like forms and scribbles.

Three to Four Years

- Knows that alphabet letters are a special category of visual graphics that can be individually named.

(Snow et al., 1998). The latest National Assessment of Educational Progress (NAEP) indicated that less than one-third of our nation's students are proficient readers by fourth grade, and only 33 percent are proficient readers by Grade 8 (Donahue, Voelkl, Campbell, & Mazzeo, 1999). There are also large gaps in students' reading proficiency related to gender, race/ethnicity, parental education, and socioeconomic status. For a large number of students, the quality of reading instruction at school will determine their level of reading proficiency. The Focus on Development box on page 280 describes the development of children's reading and writing skills in the early elementary years, and what teachers can do to support this development.

A Beginning Reader

Seven-year-old Kevin sits with his father on the couch. He is reading the story "Pecos Bill," by Ariane Dewey (1983), aloud to his father.

- Recognizes local environmental print.

- Knows that it is the print that is read in stories.

- Understands that different text forms are used for different functions of print (e.g., lists for groceries).

- Pays attention to separable and repeating sounds in language (e.g., Peter, Peter, Pumpkin Eater, Peter Eater).

- Is sensitive to some sequences in stories.

- Shows an interest in books and reading.

- When being read a story, connects information and events to life experiences.

- Questions and comments demonstrate understanding of literal meaning of story being told.

- Can identify 10 alphabet letters, especially those from own name.

- Writes (scribbles) messages as part of playful activity.

SOURCE: Adapted from Snow, Burns, & Griffin (1998).

Kevin:	Bill [pause] guh—guh—guh—[he stops, wiggles, sighs].
Father:	Grabbed.
Kevin:	Grabbed hold of the rat . . . rattler. The s—nake (pause) fff—fight hard . . . fighted . . . [pause] fought hard. He squeezed all the pppp—pa—h! [he yells and throws down the book].
Father:	Poison. Come on. Calm down. It's poison.
Kevin:	Poison out of the snake. I . . . I'm beat. [he repeats the phrase, this time with intonation that signals dialogue in the story] "I'm beat," The s—n . . . uh . . . rattler finally hissed.

[*Story Text:* Bill grabbed hold of the rattler. The snake fought hard, but Bill fought harder. He squeezed all the poison out of the snake. "I'm beat," the rattler finally hissed. Bill coiled the snake up and put it over his shoulder.]

Promoting Literacy Development in Early Childhood Settings

Creating a Literate Environment

Young children's learning environment should be rich in print. Children are more likely to become readers and writers when they repeatedly encounter print. A *literate* classroom offers numerous opportunities for children to make use of print and practice their emerging literacy skills.

- Enable children to have access to age-appropriate, high-quality books. The class reading area should be well stocked with books, poems, and magazines. Displaying books on open shelves increases their accessibility. Books for infants and toddlers need to be sturdy and washable. Stiff cardboard is easier for young children to handle.

- Provide many types of books including picture books, nature books, counting books, alphabet books, wordless words, and books written by the children themselves.

- Read to children daily and invite them to help choose the books.

- Prepare cozy places where children can sit and enjoy reading a book, perhaps with a friend, a stuffed animal, or a doll.

- Enable print to be visible throughout the classroom on signs, labels, alphabet letters, name tags, posters, songs, fingerplays, lists, magnetic letters, and alphabet blocks.

Oral Language Activities

Children learn vocabulary and language structures through conversations with teachers and peers. A rich vocabulary and knowledge of language structures helps with reading later on.

- Make time each day for individual conversations with children. One of the most effective ways to engage children in conversation is by joining in on their play.

- Share with children events in your own life, and encourage them to talk about their personal experiences.

- Use high-quality books to engage children in conversations.

Sociodramatic Play

Through sociodramatic play, children use language to plan, organize, negotiate, and carry out the "script" of their play. Sociodramatic play involves representational thinking (letting one object stand for another), which is important in understanding abstract symbol systems.

- Include in every early childhood setting materials and spaces geared toward fantasy and creative play, such as an art center, a puppet center, a store, a nature center, a woodworking area, a housekeeping center, or an office.

- Equip play spaces with written materials that can be incorporated into children's play. Menus, catalogs, calendars, phone books, travel brochures, maps, food packages, and so forth can help children feel like readers.

- Make available writing materials for dramatic play. Children can make lists for grocery shopping in the house area, write on deposit slips for the bank, and write letters to take to the post office.

Listening Skills

The ability to hear different speech patterns and sound discriminations is essential for learning to read.

- Provide opportunities to listen to books on tapes.

- Use songs, finger plays, poetry, and stories with rhyming words.

- "Simon Says" requires children to listen to sequences of directions to play.

Phonemic Awareness

During the preschool years, children need to acquire an ability to think about the sounds of spoken words, independent of their meaning. It is important to help children understand the smallest meaningful units or phonemes that make up spoken words (phonemic awareness).

- Repeat readings of the same text to enable children to hear sound patterns.

- Isolate the beginning sound of words by asking children to say the sounds they hear.

- Play games that involve grouping objects by ending or beginning sounds.

Promoting Literacy Development in Early Childhood Settings

- Search for objects in the room that begin or end with the same sound.

- Read books with predictable rhyming patterns and ask children to provide a new rhyming word (Dr. Suess books are good for this purpose.)

- Sing rhyming chants and songs.

- Clap or tap out the syllables of a word

Letter and Word Connections

To read and write, children need to distinguish letters and to connect letters to sounds.

- Provide access to letters in many different forms: alphabet blocks, wall charts, magnetic letters, letter puzzles, and so forth.

- Begin to point out distinctions between such letters as *C* and *G, b* and *d,* and *p* and *b.*

- When reading to children, point out that a sentence has many words starting with the letter *s.* Ask children to point out the words.

- When writing for children, sound out words and show them the letters for the sounds.

- When writing group stories, highlight words (e.g., *and, can, the*) that are repeated in sentences.

Reading, for Kevin, is a language process, a cognitive process, and, perhaps most important, a social process. Kevin is intent on figuring out the meaning in the story, but he cannot automatically decode or transform the written symbols into words. Because the difficult words interrupt the flow of the story, Kevin is frustrated. Nevertheless, Kevin can read the majority of the words he encounters, and with support from his father, he is able to finish reading several pages of the book. What skills has Kevin developed to become a reader? What strategies does he rely on while he is reading? What factors enable Kevin to persist with the difficult task of learning to read?

Reading involves transforming written symbols into words and combining words into phrases and sentences. As we discussed earlier, preschool children may recognize the alphabet and also know about the relationships between sounds and letters. Whereas such knowledge is essential for learning to read, it doesn't enable a child to read.

Print Awareness and Writing

Through early writing experiences, young children begin to learn many key concepts such as the function of print, uses of print, conventions of print, and phonological awareness.

- Provide access to a variety of paper, writing utensils, and materials for book making.

- Equip the art area with a variety of colored pencils, markers, pens, and paper of different sizes.

- Establish a separate writing area for children to scribble and pretend to write.

- Enable plenty of opportunities to dictate letters and stories and to have them read back to them.

- Invite children to dictate the daily schedule or menu for lunch.

- Encourage children to be "print detectives" and figure out what the words on a sign or box may say.

- When reading to children, point to the text and show children how print is read on a page (left to right, top to bottom). Also draw attention to breaks between words, uppercase and lowercase letters, and punctuation marks.

SOURCES: National Research Council (1999), Neuman, Copple, & Bredekamp (2000).

Kevin uses phonemic information—the sounds he associates with *r* and *s*—as he encounters the words *rattler* and then *snake*. But is knowledge of letters and sounds all there is to reading? Definitely not. Kevin would not have recognized either of these words if it had been isolated on a card, out of the context of the story. He is intent, first and foremost, on the meaning of the story. Having heard several versions of the tale of Pecos Bill, Kevin brings background knowledge and a set of expectations to the task of reading. Knowing about cowboys and the danger that comes from tangling with snakes helps him decode the words.

Kenneth Goodman (1976) claimed:

> Reading is a psycholinguistic guessing game. It involves an interaction between thought and language. Efficient reading does not result from precise perception and identification

279

Focus on Development

Development of Reading and Writing, Grades 1 to 3

What Children Can Do	What Teachers Can Do	What Parents and Family Members Can Do
Grade 1		
Read and retell familiar stories	Support the development of vocabulary by reading daily to the children, transcribing their language, and selecting materials that expand children's knowledge and language development	Talk about favorite storybooks
Use strategies (rereading, predicting, questioning, contextualizing) when comprehension breaks down		Read to children and encourage them to read to you
Use reading and writing for various purposes on their own initiative	Model strategies and provide practice for identifying unknown words	Suggest that children write to friends and relatives
Read orally with reasonable fluency	Give children opportunities for independent reading and writing practice	Bring to a parent-teacher's conference evidence of what your child can do in writing and reading
Use letter-sound associations, word parts, and context to identify new words	Read, write, and discuss a range of different text types (poems, informational books)	Encourage children to share what they have learned about their writing and reading
Identify an increasing number of words by sight	Introduce new words and teach strategies for learning to spell new words	
Sound out and represent all substantial sounds in spelling a word	Demonstrate and model strategies to use when comprehension breaks down	
Write about topics that are personally meaningful	Help children build lists of commonly used words from their writing and reading	
Attempt to use some punctuation and capitalization		

of all elements, but from skill in selecting the fewest, most productive cues necessary to produce guesses (about meaning) which are right the first time. (p. 498)

Kevin demonstrates that "guessing" is a critical part of the reading process. When Kevin encounters *fought,* he first says *fight,* then self-corrects to *fought* when the verb's tense does not match up with others previously encountered in this story. Thus, getting to meaning involves paying attention to word meaning and sentence structure while simultaneously

What Children Can Do	What Teachers Can Do	What Parents and Family Members Can Do
Grade 2	Create a climate that fosters analytic, evaluative, and reflective thinking	Continue to read to children and encourage them to read to you
Read with greater fluency		
Use strategies more efficiently (rereading, questioning, and so on) when comprehension breaks down	Teach children to write in multiple forms (stories, information, poems)	Engage children in activities that require reading and writing
	Ensure that children read a range of texts for a variety of purposes	Become involved in school activities
Use word identification strategies with greater facility to unlock unknown words	Teach revising, editing, and proofreading skills	Show children your interest in their learning by displaying their written work
Identify an increasing number of words by sight	Teach strategies for spelling new and difficult words	Visit the library regularly
Write about a range of topics to suit different audiences	Model enjoyment of reading	Support your child's specific hobby or interest with reading materials and references
Use common letter patterns and critical features to spell words		
Punctuate simple sentences correctly and proofread their own work		
Spend time reading daily and use reading to research topics		

scanning a line of text and discriminating letter and word shapes. While Kevin is emotionally involved with the character and events in the story, at another level he is interacting with his father. Thus, a beginning reader has many different sources of information available, any one of which the child may draw on to keep reading (Stanovitch, 1986).

When Kevin becomes frustrated, he continues to read because his father encourages him to persist. Motivation and support from an adult reader may be the most critical factor in helping children become readers. The point of reading aloud is not so much to demonstrate

Focus on Development (continued)

What Children Can Do	What Teachers Can Do	What Parents and Family Members Can Do
Grade 3	Provide opportunities daily for children to read, examine, and critically evaluate narrative and expository texts	Continue to support children's learning and interest by visiting the library and bookstores with them
Read fluently and enjoy reading		
Use a range of strategies when drawing meaning from the text	Continue to create a climate that fosters critical reading and personal response	Find ways to highlight children's progress in reading and writing
Use word identification strategies appropriately and automatically when encountering unknown words	Teach children to examine ideas in texts	Stay in regular contact with your child's teachers about activities and progress in reading and writing
Recognize and discuss elements of different text structures	Encourage children to use writing as a tool for thinking and learning	Encourage children to use and enjoy print for many purposes (such as recipes, directions, games, and sports)
Make critical connections between texts	Extend children's knowledge of the correct use of writing conventions	
Write expressively in many different forms (stories, poems, reports)	Emphasize the importance of correct spelling in finished written products	Build a love of language in all its forms and engage children in conversation
Use a rich variety of vocabulary and sentences appropriate to text forms	Create a climate that engages all children as a community of literacy learners	
Revise and edit their own writing during and after composing		SOURCE: After Neuman, Copple, Bredekamp (2000).
Spell words correctly in final writing drafts		

Beginning readers need adult motivation and support to persist in the trial-and-error process of learning to read.

that Kevin can read but for both "readers" to discover what happens to Pecos Bill. Father and son will discuss the adventure either during the reading or afterward in conversation. They are participating in a *transaction of meaning,* a relationship between the text, its author, and the readers (Rosenblatt, 1988).

Components of the Reading Process

Reading is a complex process during which the reader is translating the printed code into words, comprehending and predicting meaning, and interacting emotionally with the characters or events of the story. We will discuss each of these components separately, but it is critical to remember that these processes occur simultaneously while someone is reading.

Decoding Text

Decoding is the process that readers use to determine the oral equivalent of written words. When Kevin reads the sentence "Bill grabbed hold of the rattler," what knowledge is important? Context knowledge, phonic knowledge, and sight word knowledge are all used by readers while they are decoding. When Kevin reads the word *Bill*, he is using **context knowledge**—the surrounding text and his background knowledge—to identify the word. He knows from the title of the story that the main character is named *Bill*. But the second word, *grabbed,* is not as predictable. When he makes the sound "guh—guh—guh," Kevin is using **phonic knowledge,** or what he knows about sound-letter relationships. But phonic knowledge in English is complicated, since one letter may be pronounced several different ways. Also, phonic knowledge includes information about how the sounds of several letters blend together, for instance, the /g/ and /r/ make a fluid sound /gr/, which is much different from the "guh—guh—guh" that Kevin made.

When Kevin pauses for several seconds, his father supplies the word *grabbed.* Neither context nor phonic knowledge was strong enough to help Kevin with this difficult word. **Sight word knowledge** is the other strategy readers use to decode. In fact, mature readers decode most words automatically, without consciously thinking about other decoding strategies. In contrast, beginning readers have little or no sight word knowledge, but it will develop as their experience with reading increases.

Learning sight words is made easier by the fact that a small set of words appears frequently in standard English writing. If a reader knows by sight from 200 to 400 of the most frequently occurring words, then it is possible to recognize between 50 percent and 65 percent of the words in almost any reading passage (Harris & Sipay, 1990). In addition, with enough reading experience, readers will automatically recognize words that at first they must figure out using context or phonic knowledge (Stahl, 1992).

Reading specialists have identified a limited number of words that are most helpful for beginning readers to know by sight: high-frequency words such as *is, the, to, she,* and simple words with familiar meanings such as *car, come, pool, food*. Also, words that are hard to recognize by relying on phonic knowledge, such as *said, poison, one, gone* will have to be learned as sight words, since the sound-letter relationships of these words are unreliable.

Understanding Text

Although decoding is a necessary part of the reading process, the purpose of reading is to construct meaning. Comprehension depends on the reader's ability to use syntactic, semantic, and pragmatic information in order to make sense of text. **Comprehension** is an active process in which readers strive to construct a meaningful message from text. The interactions among reader, writer, and text help readers make meaning. Many factors shape a reader's interpretation: prior knowledge of a subject; attitudes or feelings toward the characters, events, or ideas in the text; and situational knowledge. Kevin knows that the snake is speaking in the dialogue, "I'm beat." On the basis of this knowledge, he predicts *snake* as part of the next phrase "the rattler finally hissed." When he reads, "The s—n . . . uh . . . rattler . . . ," his prediction makes sense, but something else doesn't fit. As Kevin's eye tracks the text, his decoding knowledge comes into play. Before he completes the word *snake,* he self-corrects by substituting the synonym *rattler,* which matches the written text. Thus, reading comprehension depends on both the content

Decoding is the process of using context knowledge, phonic knowledge, and sight-word knowledge to identify an unknown word.

Comprehension is the ultimate goal of reading and depends on the readers' ability to use syntactic, semantic, and pragmatic information when processing text.

knowledge a reader brings to the text and his decoding knowledge and skills (Anderson, Hiebert, Scott, & Wilkinson, 1985).

Becoming a Fluent Reader

Children who become fluent readers have mastered three important skills. They can identify printed words using connections between spellings and sounds. They can also use previous knowledge and comprehension strategies to read for meaning. Moreover, gaining fluency also involves rapid and automatic word recognition. In Chapter 4 we discussed the concept of automaticity. When children can automatically recognize words, it frees up more of their working memory for comprehending the meaning of the text. Figure 5.5 lists a set of characteristics that a successful reader is likely to exhibit by the end of the third grade. This summary presupposes appropriate support for literacy development at home and at school.

The *America Reads Challenge* listed a set of characteristics of successful readers at each developmental level. The checkpoints for third graders included:

- They are fluent and strategic.

- They relate what they read to what they already know.

- They monitor their comprehension.

- They learn new vocabulary from context.

- They figure out unfamiliar words with word analysis skills including phonics and context clues.

- They understand literary elements as events, characters, and settings, and they compare these elements across books.

- They recognize themes.

- They understand how genres such as fables, nonfiction, and poetry differ and can write examples of each.

- They are motivated to read.

- They have favorite authors and types of books.

- They read widely in diverse types of materials.

- They talk and write about what they read.

FIGURE 5.5

Characteristics of Successful Readers

Approaches to Teaching Reading

No matter what beginning-reading program teachers use, children must learn how the written code works and how to construct meaning from print. Reading research conducted during the 1970s produced three theories about how to teach reading: a *skills-based approach*, a *holistic or whole language approach*, and a *balanced approach* that combines elements of the other two. These three perspectives are reflected in the following definition, "Reading is a complex skill, a holistic act," published in the influential national report "Becoming a Nation of Readers" (Anderson et al., 1985, p. 7). Although there are many people who favor either a skills-based or holistic approach, a greater number of teachers are currently adopting a more comprehensive, integrated approach to teaching reading.

Skills-Based Approach

Some beginning-reading programs focus on a sequence of reading skills that children must acquire. Typically, these skills are taught directly by the teacher using an explicit, often deductive, method. Easier skills, such as *word attack strategies* based on phonics, are taught before harder skills, such as techniques for identifying the main ideas in informational articles. Usually, such programs are organized around a basal reading series, a collection of stories accompanied by worksheets and designed to follow a set sequence of skills. **Direct instruction,** in which the teacher explains, demonstrates, and then provides supervised student practice, is the most common instructional method. Often, skills are taught in isolation rather than in conjunction with reading stories or articles. When children do read texts, reading experience is thought of as an opportunity to practice new reading skills.

The skills-based approach, especially the widespread reliance on basal reading programs, has dominated reading instruction in American schools for several decades (Harste, 1989). Because reading is such a complex process, many people believed children would learn more easily if the process were broken up into small parts: words, letters, sounds. Once children learned these individual components, they could be combined and, when added together, would result in reading.

Holistic Approaches

In the early 1980s, researchers and educators began to challenge the part-to-whole logic that is central to a specific skills approach (Clay, 1980; Goodman, 1986). When language is splintered into small parts, they said, its essential ingredient, meaning making, is lost. Consequently, the act of reading becomes even more difficult for children. To remedy this situation, an alternative philosophy emerged, which centered on meaning making and the need to communicate through language. These researchers believed language must remain whole if meaningful interaction and communication are to occur. The term **whole language** was promoted by Ken and Yetta Goodman to describe this perspective (1979, 1986, 1992).

Several beliefs are central to a whole language approach (Freppon & Heading, 1996). First, the purpose of language is to create and share meaning. Second, language is language, regardless of whether it is spoken or written; the same conditions that foster the acquisition of speaking work with writing. Third, language is best learned by using it in a

> The skills-based approach to reading instruction focuses on learning a carefully sequenced set of skills that are often taught in isolation from one another or in conjunction with artificially created text.

social context for authentic purposes. As Goodman (1986) put it: "Why do people create and learn written language? They need it! How do they learn it? The same way they learn oral language, but using it in authentic literacy events that meet their needs" (p. 24). Teachers who adopt this broad philosophy must translate it by designing specific practices in their classrooms. Therefore, no two whole language classrooms look alike.

In the whole language approach, students are thought to develop specific reading abilities inductively, based on extensive and varied experiences with print. Literature-based reading programs promote this kind of learning (Cullinan, 1987, 1992). On the basis of interest, children choose fiction or nonfiction books of all genres to read. They may participate in book groups, or they may even write their own books. These various activities occur voluntarily and collectively, fostering a community of readers in the classroom.

Another underlying assumption of the holistic approach is the idea that spoken and written language abilities develop similarly (Weaver & Schonhoff, 1984). In other words, those factors that help children acquire spoken language are also critical in their acquisition of literacy. If children learn to speak by interacting with others in meaningful contexts, then they will need the same kind of social experiences when they are learning to read and write. Therefore, teachers should provide a context in which children have a functional need to communicate. Children should be surrounded by peers and adults who are actively engaged in authentic speaking, writing, and reading activities.

The concept of whole language has proven to be a fertile and dynamic catalyst in the field of literacy education. It has led to new teaching methods and encouraged evaluation and revision in reading curriculum and materials. However, declining achievement test scores in schools where whole language approaches were heavily used raised questions about this approach. Research indicates that children from low socioeconomic backgrounds in kindergarten through the third grade benefited more from basal instruction than from whole language instruction. Perhaps most important, the notion of whole language continues to generate heated debate about how children, especially children from diverse populations, become literate. Lisa Delpit, author of *Other People's Children*, shared this observation about whole language instruction:

> In California I saw a Black child who was in a class where the kids were supposed to read a piece of literature and then respond to it. The child clearly couldn't read the selection. When asked about the situation, the teacher said, "Oh, he can't read it, but he'll get it in the discussion." Perhaps it's good that he will be able to get it in the discussion, but at the same time nobody is spending time teaching him what he also needs to learn—how to read for himself. Sometimes we have the best intentions but actually end up holding beliefs that result in lower expectations for certain students. (1991, pp. 544–545)

Balanced Approaches

Many teachers find that adhering too closely to either a skills-based or a whole language approach may be too inflexible for teaching diverse groups of students. For instance, constant attention to skills instruction bore some students. If children can already segment phonemes, why teach it? Instead of reading self-selected texts, children are forced to complete skills worksheets. On the other hand, the emphasis on self-directed learning in whole language programs may overwhelm those students who thrive on structure and guided instruction, or who need direct instruction in reading skills. If children are unable to hear sounds in words, it is urgent that teachers help them acquire those skills.

The holistic approach to reading instruction doesn't attempt to teach isolated skills but concentrates instead on reading self-selected texts or stories for authentic purposes; it sees comprehension as a unified process that can't be broken down into separate skills.

A *balanced approach* to teaching reading is based on the assumptions that children need to be engaged in meaningful and functional literacy activities and that they need to learn specific reading skills in the process (Pressley, 1998). Balanced reading instruction combines whole language and phonics approaches. Many reading theorists argue that phonics is an important part of the reading process. The question is no longer whether phonics should be taught but *how* it can be integrated into reading programs that emphasize literature, composition, inquiry, and other process-centered instruction that are common to whole language classrooms (Freppon & Heading, 1996). The Focus on Teaching box describes a first-grade phonics lesson embedded in the morning message. Teachers who take an integrated approach provide many authentic experiences with reading and writing, but they also use systematic direct instruction in reading skills and strategies when necessary (Spiegel, 1992).

In summary, the most successful reading teachers incorporate methods from different approaches to address the literacy needs of their students. The classrooms of effective first-grade teachers are characterized by the following (Pressley, Wharton-McDonald, Allington, Block, Morrow, 1998, p. iv):

- High academic engagement
- Excellent classroom management
- Positive reinforcement and cooperation
- Explicit teaching of skills
- An emphasis on literature
- Much reading and writing
- Matching of task demands to student competence
- Encouragement of student self-regulation
- Strong cross-curricular connections

Keeping Young People Engaged in Reading

The focus in the early grades is clearly *learning to read*. What happens after children have mastered the basics of reading? How do children make the shift to *reading for learning*? Clearly the amount of time young people spend reading is important for further development of their reading competencies. However, you will be surprised how little students engage in reading after the early years of school. The National Assessment of Educational Progress (NAEP) has shown that leisure reading is associated with reading achievement. Figure 5.6 shows the percent of students, ages 9, 13, and 17 years, who report reading for fun on a daily basis. Whereas over half of 9-year-olds read for fun regularly, this figure drops to less than one-quarter of the 17-year-olds. Most surprisingly, the 1996 National Assessment of Educational Progress indicated that adolescents reported reading fewer than 5 pages per day in school or for homework. As one reading researcher stated, "If they don't read much, how are they ever gonna get good?"(Allington, 1977).

How can we help young people stay engaged in reading? Many of the same principles discussed earlier apply here. Students of all ages need a literacy-rich environment, with plenty of opportunities to read independently and with others. It is important for young people to have a variety of reading materials to select from: paperbacks, magazines, poetry, textbooks, and so on. They need access to these materials for self-selected reading on their own. They also need meaningful reading materials related to their interests and cultural

Using Embedded Phonics

Ms. Brown started the language arts lesson with a morning message, using yesterday's target pattern, —am. She wrote, "Sam will be 15 years young on tuesday" Then she asked the children to help her edit the message. They changed "young" to "old" and pointed out that Sam will be 7, not 15. With prompting, they agreed to capitalize the *t* in "Tuesday" and to add a period at the end of the sentence.

Ms. Brown's targeted spelling pattern for the day was —*ap*. She introduced this pattern through shared reading of a big book. During this shared reading the teacher pointed to each word of the big book as she read the story, occasionally checking the understanding of the 22 children seated cross-legged in front of her by asking a question about the story. When she came to a word containing the target pattern, *tap*, she stopped reading the story, wrote "tap" on the blackboard and asked the children what word family "tap" belonged to. Then Ms. Brown asked what other words belonged to the *ap* word family. She asked the children to spell these words to her as she wrote them on the board. The children had trouble with the *l* in *slap* so Ms. Brown had the children stretch out the sounds so that the letter /l/ was apparent.

After writing these words on the blackboard, Ms. Brown sent all but eight of the students to their seats. A strip of construction paper and a pile of alphabet letters from a bag of cereal were placed at each seat. Students were instructed to glue the letters *ap* on the construction paper and make new words by adding letters to the front. One student made *pay* and was not corrected because the teacher was busy working with the group of eight. When students were finished with this seat work, they were told to read independently a book of their choice.

Ms. Brown worked with the group of eight by writing yesterday's spelling pattern, *am,* on a slate board. She elicited words with this pattern in it—*clam, slam, ram*—and wrote them down. She checked their understanding of *ram* by asking a student to use it in a sentence. Then she passed out copies of a book to each child that had the word *family* in it. The children were familiar with the story and read along with the teacher in choral reading. When they had finished, she gave them each a laminated tag board mat and laminated letters. She asked them to write some words with the *am* pattern while she listened to one of the children read. As he read, Ms. Brown kept a record of his reading miscues, prompting him to use context cues to guess the meaning of the unknown words. Finally Ms. Brown introduced a new book to the children that contained the spelling pattern of the day, *ap*. She previewed each page, eliciting prior knowledge from the students by asking them to expand on their interpretations of illustrations. Then she put the book in a plastic bag for each child to take home and practice reading with a partner.

With 30 minutes left for language arts, Ms. Brown began a process writing workshop on Thanksgiving activities. Students brainstormed about Thanksgiving activities while the teacher wrote down sentences that expressed their ideas. If previously taught spelling patterns appeared, she pointed them out. Once the brainstorming was complete, students wrote about their favorite Thanksgiving activity.

SOURCE: Adapted from Snow, Burns, & Griffin (1998).

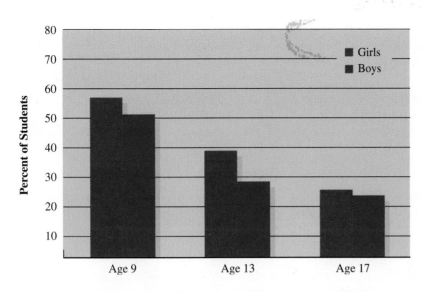

FIGURE 5.6

Percent of Children and Adolescents Who Read for Fun Daily

SOURCE: U.S. Department of Health and Human Services (2000).

During adolescence young people spend less time reading for fun on a daily basis.

background. Reading needs to be integrated into all curriculum areas, and the use of writing should be used to support reading development.

Supporting and fostering students' motivation to read is important to keep students engaged in reading. Research shows that students who are higher in intrinsic motivation read much more than students low in motivation (Wigfield & Guthrie, 1977). Some studies show that intrinsic motivation for reading declines over the elementary years (see Wigfield, 2000). Teachers need to model positive attitudes toward reading and to share favorite stories and books. Some teachers help facilitate after-school book clubs to enrich students' literacy experiences.

Like younger learners, older students need explicit instruction in comprehension strategies, especially as they begin to handle more complex and technical material. Studies reveal that abstract, specialized, and technical reading material decreases reading fluency, even for good readers (Chall, Jacobs & Baldwin, 1990). The International Reading Association recommends that content area teachers in the middle and secondary grades work with reading specialists to more effectively support the development of advanced reading strategies. By modeling effective reading strategies, teachers can help students maintain confidence in their reading abilities, which is strongly related to reading motivation and achievement (Wigfield, 2000).

Just as young students need special attention when they are experiencing reading difficulty, so do older students. As we discussed, national assessments indicate that only 6 percent of adolescents become advanced readers, and over 70 percent read at basic levels. These young people need services to address their reading difficulties. Figure 5.7 presents several recommendations of the International Reading Association's Commission on Adolescent Literacy.

Learning to Write

Each morning in first grade, Kevin goes to his cubby, pulls out his journal, and starts writing. This daily writing, along with many other opportunities for composing at home and school, allows Kevin a chance to express his ideas and experiences in written form. Since

These elementary school students are enjoying a special reading time together.

he is not yet proficient with spelling, he experiments as he tries to represent words with letters, as you can see in Figure 5.8.

When children spell words in unconventional ways they are using **invented spelling,** and these attempts should not be regarded as errors to be corrected with beginning writers (Chomsky, 1970). Instead, invented spelling is a positive sign that Kevin is consciously analyzing speech sounds and print. In his journal, he spells *presidents* as *Prds,* and *shark* as *srck.* When children are learning to write, ideas are more important than correct spelling. Invented spelling increases children's fluency and makes it easier for them to compose (Sowers, 1982). Contrary to the fears of many parents, it does not interfere with reading development or inhibit the development of conventional spelling. Each time children use invented spelling, they are experimenting with sound–letter relationships as well as grappling with the unpredictable aspects of English spelling. Reading specialists agree that teachers and parents should support children's use of invented spelling, recognizing that it is a transitional phase in a developmental process (Vacca, Vacca, & Grove, 1995; Leu & Kinzer, 1995). Language learners need freedom to experiment and construct the rules for any language system, whether it is sentence structure or conventional spelling (Henderson, 1990).

Remember that children are not learning to spell in a vacuum but in a literate environment. Teachers and parents can foster spelling development. The more children read or are exposed to printed words, the faster their approximate spellings will become conventional. Frequent writing experiences, including daily journals, ensure ample opportunity for practice and feedback. In addition, an effective spelling program teaches strategies that help children notice the generalities and patterns inherent in English (Cunningham, 1995).

Children use systematic strategies in learning to spell (Read, 1975; Gentry, 1982), going through several stages of development, as listed in the Focus on Development box. Most children master the mechanics of writing slowly and unevenly. Since children are coordinating cognitive and physical processes simultaneously, their progress may fluctuate (Graves, 1979). Focusing on the meaning of what children write instead of being

- Provide tutorial reading instruction that is part of a comprehensive program connected with subject matter.

- Assess students' reading and writing—and enable students to assess their own abilities in these areas—to plan instruction, foster individuals' control of their literacy, and immediately support learners when progress diminishes.

- Teach vocabulary, fluency, comprehension, and study strategies tailored to individuals' competencies.

- Relate literacy practices to life management issues, such as exploring careers, examining individual's roles in society, setting goals, managing time and stress, and resolving conflict.

- Offer reading programs that recognize potentially limiting forces such as work schedules, family responsibilities, and peer pressures.

SOURCE: After International Reading Association (1999).

5-04-93

Last night I read in the newspaper. We read about presidents.

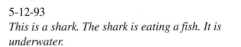

5-12-93

This is a shark. The shark is eating a fish. It is underwater.

FIGURE 5.8

First Grader Kevin's Journal Entries with Invented Spelling

Focus on Development

The Stages of Spelling Development

- **Prephonemic spelling.** One early spelling is to represent a word by writing only one or two consonants, usually the initial or final consonant such as "K" for "sink," or "RT" for "rabbit."
- **Phonemic spelling.** Vowels appear along with consonants. Children attempt to match more of the sounds they hear with letters, although they still focus on beginning and ending sounds: "OEN" for "ocean," or "JRAS" for "dress."
- **Transitional spelling.** With more exposure to written English, children rely less on the one-to-one correspondence strategy. They look for letter patterns or chunks common in English such as consonant-vowel-consonant patterns: "CEAP" for "keep," or "YESDDAY" for "yesterday."
- **Conventional spelling.** By 8 or 9, children spell many words according to conventional patterns, although they are not completely accurate spellers. One child showed this spelling progression: btPba, MTR, MMOSTR, MONSTUR, MONSTER.

SOURCE: After Gentry (1982).

excessively concerned with mechanics is the best way of encouraging young writers (Moffett, 1968).

Writing as Composing

Becoming a writer involves physical development and control, for holding a pencil and forming letters and words, as well as for learning conventions, such as spelling and punctuation. But the essence of writing development is learning to compose, to make meaning with printed text. There are many different reasons for writing, and a variety of genres unique to written language: stories, letters, arguments and other forms of expository writing, poetry, journals, and news writing. Teaching students to produce these diverse forms of text, each one with a special purpose, will be the ongoing goal of writing instruction from the early grades, through middle and high school, and into college.

A writer's task entails having a reason to communicate, planning content, producing some writing, and revising to fit the needs and interests of the intended audience. Composing is a complex process in which writers coordinate content and structure, while shaping language to accommodate the needs of their audience. The components of the writing process include *planning* (rehearsing), *drafting* (getting it down), *revising* (making changes to accommodate the reader or purpose), *editing* (attending to conventions and correctness), and *publishing* (making it public). Although we can refer to distinct parts of the writing process, writers do not experience them in any set progression, nor do they necessarily occur one at a time. Many writers are planning, drafting, and revising simultaneously. Neither do these processes proceed in a linear fashion; rather, the writing process is recursive. For example, while drafting, a writer may reread an earlier sentence and revise it before proceeding.

The components of the writing process include planning, drafting, revising, editing, and publishing.

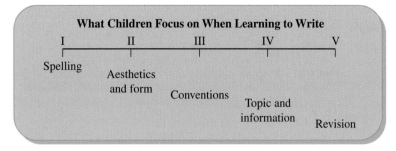

FIGURE 5.9

Developmental Order of Writing Concepts

SOURCE: Graves (1983).

Of course, inexperienced writers do not learn all the parts at once; instead, they become conscious of certain issues at particular times in their writing development. After 2 years of studying teachers and children in one elementary school, Donald Graves (1983) discovered that there was a general order in which children practiced and understood writing concepts, which is shown in Figure 5.9.

At first, writers are concerned with the mechanical and physical qualities of making words on a page, such as forming letters. Only later do they turn their attention to composing, focusing on issues of content and audience.

Revision and Audience

Young writers have no difficulty in finding something to say but spend much energy producing the physical marks on paper. Once the act of writing becomes easier, children become conscious of communicating with an audience. Graves (1983) reported that sometime around grades 3 and 4, children become less egocentric about their writing. That is, they no longer assume that everyone is interested in their message and become increasingly concerned about their readers' reactions. Once this happens, children are likely to begin revising their texts to match audience needs and interests.

Revision is a doubly difficult task since it requires the writer to step back from the text and think about it abstractly. The revision process also entails imagining what the needs and interests of one's readers might be. Writing programs that incorporate extensive peer review and group conferencing facilitate the development of revising abilities. Both elementary and high school students are better able to identify problems in papers written by other students than in their own work (Bartlett, 1982). Peer review develops this critical ability. Direct feedback from a peer or teacher also eliminates some of the difficulty inherent in writing to an imagined audience.

Syntax in Writing

Children's language development during the school years is generally marked with increased proficiency in using complex syntax, more variety in sentence structure, and longer sentences in both speaking and writing (Loban, 1976). This development is particularly critical for learning to write, since the grammatical structures typical of written language differ considerably from those used in speaking. For instance, someone telling a story aloud would use many short clauses linked together by coordinators such as *and, so,* or *but.*

> I was sitting around reading the newspaper, and I heard this scratching noise, over and over, and I just didn't want to get up, but I keep hearing it, so I went and checked to see if the cat wanted to come in, but no cat, so I sat down and started reading again.

Someone writing the same story would create discrete sentences, embed one sentence in another, and use more adjectives and adverbs.

> It was a little after five, on a rainy night. Not having had a minute to rest all day, I was savoring the soft cushions of my favorite chair and reading the evening paper. "How perfect," I thought, until a persistent and irritating scratching sound interrupted me. "Was it the cat?" I wondered, debating about whether to abandon my peace and quiet.

This example shows clearly that writing is not simply spoken language written down. Although beginning writers, between the ages of 6 and 8, rely on spoken language patterns, they gradually adapt their language to reflect the patterns and genres associated with writing (Kress, 1982). A 7-year-old wrote this story:

> Scruffy
>
> On Saturday My Dog got run over and the driver did not stop. The dog's name was scruffy and he died and then we buried him. (Kress, 1982, p. 55)

The next excerpt was written by a 12-year-old. Notice the differences in sentence structure, word choice, and genre compared with the story above.

> Beaked Whales
>
> The Beaked Whales live out in mid-ocean, where the tasty squid are found. Squid, it seems, provide most of their meals. Men do not know much about their family because even the scientists who study whales have seen very few Beaked Whales. Generally members of this family have long, narrow snouts, or "beaks." (Kress, 1982, p. 113)

By middle school, children are writing expository texts (descriptive and informational writing) in addition to the narratives (stories) usually adopted by beginning writers. The sentences produced by 12-year-olds are precise, detailed, and condensed, demonstrating more syntactic and cognitive complexity than those written by younger children.

The writing of high school students reflects the same trend toward syntactic complexity. The following excerpt from a narrative by a 17-year-old demonstrates the carefully constructed and formal sentence structure typical of written texts.

> The chain of events leading to the appearance of the black shoes on the street had begun about four hours earlier. A young lady, Mary Vincent, had bought the flats at an auction late that night. Fortunately they were a little too big, for when she was suddenly dragged into a car by a couple of kidnappers, the shoes remained on the street. The crooks, being in a hurry, did not stop to pick up the flats even after they noticed Mary's stocking feet. (Loban, 1976, p. 115)

A longitudinal study of students' language from kindergarten through grade 12 showed that as children grow older they write longer clauses and embed dependent clauses more often (Loban, 1976). In particular, clauses are more complex because of changes in noun phrases found in the subjects and objects, including objects of prepositions (Hunt, 1977). For example, the subject noun phrase in this sentence written by a 17-year-old contains 15 words:

[subject noun phrase]

The chain of events leading to the appearance of the black shoes on the street

[verb phrase with prepositional phrase]

had begun about four hours earlier.

However, age alone cannot account for complicated syntax of teenage writers. Particular written genres, particularly expository forms, require grammatical complexity. For instance, tenth-grade writers in another study produced longer clauses when writing arguments than narratives (Crowhurst & Piche, 1979). Syntactic complexity is a function of the kinds of writing older students produce in the school context, along with changes in their thinking processes.

Form and Function

As children grow older, written language development evolves in two dimensions: expanding the variety of writing forms or styles and writing for more abstract purposes. In a literate culture, developing communicative competence includes knowing how to communicate effectively in writing in many contexts, but especially in school. Writing in the classroom serves several functions. Often, writing is used by students to learn academic content such as taking notes, writing book reports, and writing research papers. Sometimes students are asked to write in order to demonstrate what they have learned, as in the case of essay tests in a history class. In other instances, writing fosters particular kinds of thinking skills, such as analysis and interpretation, which a student would use in writing a critique of a literary work. Another function of writing is as an outlet for expression, a way for individuals to communicate ideas, emotions, and experiences, both in and outside of school. As children mature throughout middle and high school, their needs and desires change. As a result, new forms become common practices. Middle- and high-school-aged students begin to keep diaries and journals, write letters to friends, and fill notebooks with poetry. High school newspapers and literary magazines flourish as students write to serve many different social needs. It is important to remember that children learn the language forms and functions that are practiced and therefore valued by the local culture of the home, the school, the neighborhood. Not every community values language and literacy in the same way (Heath, 1983), nor are there equitable opportunities for individuals to engage in literate practices. The way we use language is also related to social factors, such as family income level, ethnic group identity, and geographical factors, as detailed in the Focus on Research box.

Once students reach high school, expository writing, especially arguments and analysis, will be dominant. In order to write well, older students' language must become more complex and abstract. A student in the middle grades may be quite comfortable producing a narrative that centers around a plot but more than likely will struggle when writing an argument that entails the use of supporting evidence. Beginning in middle school but carrying on through the upper grades, teachers will focus on teaching written genres that have fairly abstract functions, including arguments, analysis, and problem solving. In writing a persuasive essay, a writer must coordinate several variables: producing a coherent and convincing argument, marshaling effective evidence, relating to the audience, and using a formal style. A successful essay depends on sentence and paragraph structure that is tightly structured and planned. This kind of organizational planning is difficult for high school students. However, the latest National Assessment of Educational Progress (NAEP) study revealed that more middle and high school students are engaging in prewriting activities, such as outlining, listing ideas, or taking notes than in earlier assessments. Results also suggest that adolescents who use prewriting activities had higher test scores than those students who did not use any visible planning (Greenwald, Persky, Campbell, & Mazzeo, 1999).

As children progress through school, their syntax becomes more complex and they learn that written syntax has a different and more precise set of rules than spoken syntax.

School-based writing teaches students the many purposes of writing, such as recording information, demonstrating learning, developing or analyzing persuasive arguments, and creative expression.

Focus on Research

In 1980, Shirley Brice Heath published the results of a 10-year-long qualitative study of how spoken and written language is used for different purposes in two distinct but neighboring communities. Her research demonstrated that literacy practices in the home and community that matched those found in school enabled children to be successful. She studied adults' and children's language development at home and in school in two communities in the Carolina Piedmont from the late 1960s to the late 1970s. One town, Roadville, is a white working-class community in which families have worked for four generations in the textile mills. The other town, Trackton, is a black working-class community in which families are currently working in the mills but whose previous generations once farmed the land. This work, *Ways with Words: Language, Life and Work in Communities and Classrooms,* provides startling and fascinating documentation about how language is intimately connected to race, class, gender, and culture.

She discovered that historical segregation meant that each community built separate and different religious institutions, ways of communicating, worldviews, and patterns of social relations. Consequently, the way language is used to worship, for social control, and in asserting identities is distinctive to Trackton and Roadville. Both communities are literate, but each has its own traditions. Heath found that Roadville residents used writing only when they were required to; writing is seen "as an occasional necessary tool—to aid their memory, to help them buy and sell things, and sometimes to keep them in touch with family and friends" (p. 231). On the other hand, reading is considered a good thing, and residents collect reading materials for themselves and their children.

In Trackton, reading is not recognized as a special activity. Reading materials do not accumulate but are read and discarded. Reading is considered an aspect of everyday social interaction. "Trackton residents read aloud to anyone who

Obviously, the intellectual demands are much greater in producing expository writing than they are with narrative genres. High school writers' abilities to produce argumentative writing reflects their cognitive capacities, but such tasks can also encourage intellectual development. Russell Durst (1987) found that students who were asked to analyze a history passage did more complex thinking than those who were asked only to summarize the passage. Thus, certain kinds of writing assignments are more beneficial than others. Teachers who assign analytic writing can help students build their intellectual as well as communicative abilities.

In an extensive and now classic study of the writing abilities of children ages 11 to 18, James Britton and his colleagues (1975) discovered that the context of school exerts a tremendous influence on how children develop as writers. (Although they studied British schools, Applebee [1981] extended these findings to American schools.) Britton and his research team categorized students' writing as personal (expressive), poetic (literary), or transactional (expository). They also identified the intended audience in each case. After analyzing more than 2,000 writing samples, they reported that 63 percent of all student writing is expository in nature. Furthermore, as students move through the upper grades, they are given less and less opportunity to produce literary (short stories, poetry) or personal writing. In addition, they found that 92 percent of all writing is produced for the wants to listen on the plaza, report what they have read, ask for interpretations of the written materials by the group, and enjoy the stories which invariably ensue from a report of something read." The meaning of any written materials is not interpreted individually but constructed jointly. A resident of Trackton focuses on the content of the text: "What does it say about me, or someone or something I know, and what do I do?" (p. 232).

Because of the way literacy is practiced in each community, children from Roadville and Trackton arrive at school with different ideas about writing and printed text. Trackton's children have extensive experience with the shape and style of print found on signs, cans, and in newspapers but usually are not accustomed to formal sessions devoted to reading stories. In Roadville, children are more likely to have had books read to them at bedtime and sessions with coloring books around the kitchen table. When children from both communities arrive at school, their patterns of socialization around literacy lead to very different outcomes. School is a place where structure, lessons, and clear knowledge boundaries are emphasized. Roadville children are familiar with this kind of world; what happens at home is not all that different from at school. But the children from Trackton are used to negotiating meaning together, to engaging in dramatic speaking styles, and to learning by observing and imitation, all behaviors that diverge from school values. Consequently, it is harder for the Trackton children to succeed in school and dropout rates are high, whereas the Roadville children feel more comfortable, completing high school at a higher rate. Because of her findings, Heath believes that schools must be sensitive to the literate cultures children bring with them. Teachers must be able to build cultural bridges between home and school and to link ways of being literate in school, at work, or in the home.

teacher as audience, with 49 percent being written for the sole purpose of evaluation by the teacher.

Schools, then, have a tremendous impact on how children learn to write and what styles or genres they develop proficiently. Writing ability is tied to specific uses of writing in the home, school, and larger social settings. Despite an increased national focus on writing instruction, there has been little change in students' writing proficiency levels since 1984, when the NAEP first included a writing assessment for students at grades 4, 8, and 11. The latest NAEP data reveal that fewer than one-quarter of students at each grade level reach a proficient level. And only 1 percent reach an advanced level (Greenwald et al., 1999). Writing at this level is characterized by clear, complete, and detailed responses to assignments that are well organized and coherent.

To develop writers at all grade levels, two elements are essential. First, writing must be used for authentic purposes. In the larger culture, writing is used by individuals as creative expression (fiction, poetry, drama), as a means of learning (note taking, summarizing, listing), and as communication of information, thoughts, ideas (essays, newspapers, scientific studies, etc.). In school students develop as writers when they use writing purposefully, instead of writing only to be graded. Students who write short stories that are then published in their classroom and read by their classmates as literature experience what it feels like to be writers.

They are invested in how their readers react to or interpret their work. Having readers in addition to their teacher is one way of ensuring that students write for an authentic purpose.

Second, the more students write, the more developed their writing abilities become. Early national assessments indicated that the typical high school student was producing one substantial piece of writing per month (Applebee, Langer, & Mullis, 1986). Similarly, recent evidence from the NAEP indicates that students are not asked to write multiple drafts of a paper on a regular basis. However, eighth- and twelfth-grade students had higher average writing scale scores when their teachers always asked them to write more than one draft (Greenwald et al., 1999).

Not only is practice essential, but writing in a variety of genres and styles for a range of different audiences is especially important. Outside school we use writing to accomplish many goals: to communicate, to organize, to record information, to entertain, to learn new ideas, to think. Students need experience with a range of writing genres so that they can function better in school and later in real life. However, high school students write less than younger students in all subject areas except English (Applebee et al., 1986). As a remedy, many teachers now endorse **writing across the curriculum** programs in which writing is incorporated into all subject areas from music to mathematics (Maxwell, 1996). The Focus on Teaching box lists different ways teachers can encourage student writing in meaningful ways.

To enhance writing development it is important to recall the process by which children develop spoken language. The need to communicate, an environment rich in social interchange, available and experienced adults, and hour upon hour of practice are all essential to language development. Writing, however, is more difficult and less practiced in everyday life than speaking, so teachers need to provide extra support to help students' abilities to grow. Therefore, writers need instruction and practice in the process of writing. Process-oriented teachers build in more exercises for prewriting and drafting. They use a workshop approach in which students receive regular conferences and feedback from peers as well as the teacher while they are revising their work. Although writing is a different mode from speaking, the same basic social factors are involved in all language development.

Literacy Development in the Classroom

Millions of adults in America are functionally illiterate; that is, they are not able to read and write well enough to carry out many basic tasks of modern life.

Although we live in a literate culture, there are millions of adults in America who are not **functionally literate.** Such individuals are not able to read or write well enough to negotiate daily life. Many cannot use a phone directory, complete a job application form, or read a newspaper. The most comprehensive report, *Adult Illiteracy in the United States* (Hunter & Harman, 1979), found that well over a third of the adult population has difficulties in the area of literacy. Using the figures from this report, Jonathan Kozol in *Illiterate America* (1985) estimates that 60 million Americans are functionally illiterate. A joint report issued by the U.S. Department of Labor and the U.S. Department of Education warned that by the year 2000, individuals old enough to work would not be able to compete in the marketplace because they lacked basic literacy skills (1988). Computer literacy is necessary to hold a job whether one is a clerk in an auto parts store or a personnel director for a large corporation. Bus drivers need to read street signs and city maps; assembly-line workers must read directions and interpret diagrams projected onto computer screens at their workstations. Most important, literacy is critical to democracy. To be functioning citizens, everyone must be able to read a newspaper and interpret the television news and other media in order to remain informed enough to vote thoughtfully and otherwise participate in a democratic society.

What can teachers do to ensure that every student has the best possible chance of becoming literate? Reading and writing development can be fostered in students from kindergarten through grade 12 by (a) creating language-rich classroom environments; (b)

Focus on Teaching

Journals or diaries
Fiction
   Fantasy
   Historical
   Adventure
   Science fiction
   Choose-your-own-adventure
   Children's books
Picture books
Dictionaries
Fact books
How-to books
Biographies
Letters to real or imaginary people
Dialogues and conversations
Thumbnail sketches
   People
   Places
   Important concepts
   Historical events
Requests
Applications and resumes
Research reports
Science
   Observations
   Notebooks
   Lab reports
   Hypotheses
Interviews (real or imaginary)
Photos and captions
Recipes
Catalogs
Obituaries, epitaphs, eulogies

Memos
Poems
Scripts
   Plays
   Radio
   Television
Prophecies, predictions, visions
Newspaper writing
   Articles
   Editorials
   Features
   Advertisements
Proposals
   Social programs
   Grants
   Research
   Construction
Position papers and responses
Reviews
   Books
   Movies and TV
   Recordings
   Performances
Math
   Word problems
   Problem solutions
   Practical applications
Cartoons
Debates
Songs and rap
Games and puzzles
Posters, displays, collages
Instructions or directions

SOURCE: After Tchudi & Yates (1983).

focusing on meaning and communication as the main purpose for literacy; (c) encouraging social interaction and collaboration; (d) providing explicit instruction in reading and writing strategies; and (e) using formative assessment keyed to individual growth in literacy.

A classroom environment that promotes literacy provides students with many opportunities to interact with print and nonprint sources. Listening to stories, giving oral readings of drama and poetry, reading books and magazines, viewing and discussing films and videos, and sharing book experiences are significant activities for all grade levels. Some of the books and stories children are reading should be ones they themselves have written. Publication of student writing in the classroom is vital, since student writers can experience how to produce for a real audience. Sharing student writing creates a community of writers and reinforces the notion that literacy is a part of everyone's everyday life in school.

Language predominates in an effective classroom, and opportunities for students to practice all modes of communication are essential. Children who are talking, reading, listening, and writing in alternating and sustained contexts are learning. Talk is especially critical in promoting concept development, developing interactional skills, and sharing knowledge in general (Wells, 1986). After all, literacy is socially constructed; individuals interacting with others is the wellspring of all language systems.

Creating and communicating meaning are the main purposes of literacy. Therefore, teachers must provide literacy activities and assignments that are both intrinsically satisfying and authentic acts of communication. Allowing children to choose their own reading materials from a wide array of styles, genres, and topics will support their individual interests. Mandated reading, which requires that every person in the class read exactly the same material in lockstep fashion, prevents individual development. Teachers should avoid practices that *confine* literacy, such as the exclusive use of basal readers in the lower grades and required reading lists of a handful of classic texts in high school English classes. Using an approach such as the reading and writing workshop promoted by Nancie Atwell (1987) that stresses the qualities of choice, ownership, and response will ensure student engagement in reading and writing experiences that are meaningful to them.

Classrooms in which collaboration is the norm will naturally reinforce the idea that literacy is socially constructed. Classroom structures should encourage collaboration in which there are many chances for students to read, write, talk, and respond to one another. One common practice is the use of literature circles, in which students group themselves around a topic, a theme, or an individual text to read and then discuss or even write about their reactions (Harste, Short, & Burke, 1988). Books are chosen by the students, and the questions they bring to the group are student generated. Students are trained to play different roles in their circle including that of discussion leader. The teacher arranges the classroom space and materials and facilitates the groups to foster this kind of student-centered literacy.

Social interaction in the form of response and feedback is essential for developing writers and supporting the writing process, especially during the stages of drafting and revising. Frequent teacher and peer conferences are useful for supporting developing writers. Students and teachers must be trained in order for the conferences to be effective, but both types of conferences are relatively easy to learn. Guidelines for peer and teacher conferencing are available for primary-grade children (Graves, 1983), middle-grade students (Atwell, 1987), and high school students (Spear, 1988; Murray, 1985).

Additionally, as we already discussed, it is important to provide explicit instruction to help students develop their reading and writing competencies. This instruction should occur within the context of meaningful learning activities. For example, teachers can teach comprehension strategies while reading storybooks. Children can be asked to retell parts of the story, predict events in the story, or make up a conclusion. Reading and writing skills need to be taught, but not in isolation.

Teachers can promote literacy by creating language-rich environments; focusing on meaningful communication as the main goal of literacy; encouraging social interaction and collaboration; and providing ongoing, informal assessment of students' literacy growth.

Assessment of students' progress should be ongoing, occurring during the time students are actually engaged in a literacy task. By observing and interacting with students as they are reading or writing, teachers can keep anecdotal records of each child's developing skills, difficulties, progress, changes, and goals. *Kidwatching* is a term devised to capture the teacher's powerful role in observing children as they develop as language users (Goodman, 1978). This kind of formative assessment will ensure that teachers are intervening and instructing exactly when and where individual students need it most. Since literacy is fundamental to educational achievement, it is imperative that children learn to read and write in the first few years of school. Primary grade teachers undertake the formidable task of teaching children to read and also bear the burden of assessing those children who are not making sufficient progress. Because future learning and self-sufficiency depends so heavily on printed text, it is important to intervene early in the literacy acquisition process if children are failing to learn to read. The Focus on Research box describes two promising intervention programs for elementary school students.

Evaluation is not the sole responsibility of teachers. Students can profit directly from reflecting on, assessing, and evaluating their own work, even in the early elementary grades, but certainly during the middle and high school years. Not only can students report on what they have learned or enjoyed, but teachers can encourage them to notice their processes and strategies while reading and writing. Keeping journals on their reading or writing process and building portfolios are both tools for keeping track of what students are reading or writing as well as for building in reflection and self-consciousness about each student's literacy development. A portfolio typically consists of a collection of a student's work over a period of time. Students select specific items for their portfolio that, in their opinion, represent their best work. By asking students to compile their own portfolios, teachers are encouraging students to make judgments about the nature and quality of their work. Portfolios can be open-ended, consisting of a wide variety of artifacts, such as a finished essay including the prewriting and drafts that led up to the final product, a videotape of the student's shared book performance, parts of a journal, notes from peer-writing conferences, story maps or other graphics, and taped oral readings. To encourage collaboration, teachers can work with students in devising the contents of a portfolio as well as in setting up criteria for evaluating its contents (Valencia, 1990; Wolfe, 1989).

Cultural Influences on Language Development

Americans think of their country as diverse, where many subcultures coexist and interact. All individuals vary along the lines of race, economics, and cultural heritage. People identify themselves variously as members of a family, a neighborhood, and a community. Language is one way that individual and community identities are created, maintained, and signaled to others. A person's language, dialect, or manner of speaking reflects features of their social, economic, and cultural background. Because language is so variable and plastic, it can be shaped by speakers to reflect a particular group identity. A language community can be identified in many ways: by pronunciation, such as /cah/ for *car* (New England area); by a dialect, such as the use of *be* as in "He be here" (Africanized English); or by linguistic fluency in several languages (a child who speaks Mandarin at home but English in school).

> *A dialect is a variation of a single language spoken by members of a speech community; an accent involves the way certain sounds are pronounced.*

Dialects

Every person who speaks English speaks in a distinctive dialect and with an accent (Shuy, 1967). This is true whether one's family arrived from Scotland in the 1700s, from Africa in

Focus on Research

Reading Recovery is a program for low-achieving readers developed by the child psychologist Marie Clay, during the 1960s in New Zealand. Her research showed that once children were "recovered," about 85 percent continued reading and rarely needed any further special support. The program came to the United States in 1985 through The Ohio State University; 5 years later, sixteen states and one Canadian province had established training programs for Reading Recovery teachers.

The program provides short but concentrated periods of individual instruction on a daily basis for about 15 weeks. Success rates are high, with between 70 percent and 80 percent of all children reading at the level of their peers by the end of the instructional period. The philosophy behind Reading Recovery ensures that teachers focus on where a child is and then builds on existing strengths, while guiding the child through reading a series of whole, predictable texts and writing self-generated sentences.

Each 30-minute session is carefully structured around each child's responses. The lessons consist in reading and rereading "little books" along with sentence writing. First, a student begins by reading a familiar short book with bright illustrations and very predictable language. While the child is reading, the teacher will keep a running record of the oral reading, noting any strategies the child is using or ignoring. The teacher will introduce a new book, looking at the pictures and asking the child to make predictions about story. They will read the new book together, and the teacher will remind the child of word attack strategies—such as checking the beginning or final letters in a word. Or the teacher will direct the child's attention to the story content, adding context to help with word identification and comprehension. Next, the student may dictate, then write a sentence message. Often the sentence is written on tag board and cut up into individual words that are then reassembled into a sentence. Sometimes games using sight words such as *the* or *they* are played. The lessons move very quickly, and teacher and student work intensely together on a series of manageable high-success tasks. Most important, the teacher notices and comments on the student's behavior. The goal is to move children toward independence.

However, not all children succeed in Reading Recovery. The program is intense but fairly brief, and it is very expensive to staff. Research has shown that if a child is not succeeding during the 15 weeks, then he or she will not profit from the program. Alternative instruction will be necessary.

the 1800s, or from Vietnam in the 1900s. A **dialect** is a variation of a single language spoken by members of a speech community, whereas an *accent* refers to the way certain sounds are pronounced. Why do we have so many varieties of English? The answer is personal. Since language feels so basic to our identities, we usually maintain the distinct qualities of our home language even after moving away from our family and community.

However, the language variations in the United States today have created major problems for educators. For one thing, the language of instruction in schools, sometimes called **standard American English (SAE),** is often not the dialect of English spoken in children's

Success for All is a prevention and early intervention program designed to restructure elementary schools so that all children are successful in reading, writing, and language arts. This program began as a partnership between educational researchers at Johns Hopkins University and the Baltimore City Public Schools, and it is now used in some 300 schools around the country. It has a companion program, *Roots and Wings*, that focuses on mathematics, science, and social studies.

Success for All is comprehensive and intensive in its approach. Prekindergarten and kindergarten classes include shared reading, telling and dramatizing stories, thematic interdisciplinary units, and a focus on letters and the sounds of words. In the first grade, students receive *Reading Roots,* a reading program that combines phonics with the use of meaningful texts. Reading tutors are a prominent feature of the reading program. Students who experience difficulty with reading receive daily 20 minutes of one-on-one tutoring from certified teachers, many of them trained as reading specialists or special educators. Teachers and tutors communicate regularly to maintain continuity for the child. When students attain a second-grade reading level, the focus shifts to vocabulary building, decoding practice, and comprehension strategy instruction (predicting and summarizing sequences).

At every grade level, children's literature is included, and students have opportunities to discuss the meaning of the story with their classmates to develop their knowledge of story structure, as well as listening and speaking vocabulary. In addition, there is a family support team at every school, which develops programs to encourage family involvement in school programs and offers parents' strategies for helping their children at home. The team also addresses issues related to health services, attendance, and behavior problems.

Early evaluations indicated that the program helped to boost reading achievement in the first through third grades. Participants continued to outperform a comparison group of children from fourth grade through middle school. The program also helped to reduce special education placements, and the program benefited those with low ability as well as more capable students. Program adaptations for Spanish bilingual and English language learners are also showing success. Research is continuing to monitor the effectiveness of the program across different school sites.

SOURCES: Pennell, Deford, & Lyons (1988); Slavin (1996); Slavin et al. (1996).

speech communities. No matter the source of variation—whether children come from inner cities or rural settings, from insulated, culturally distinct communities such as Cuban Miami, or from newly immigrated families from Haiti—they are likely to speak a dialect of English significantly different from that studied at school. In the future, language variation in America will only increase, not diminish. In contrast, our schools are at present oriented to one standard form of English. This situation frustrates teachers and children alike who must struggle to find ways of communicating across a wide variety of language or dialect differences. Educational reform is needed in all areas. The curriculum, the materials, and the teaching methods of our schools currently are not flexible enough to accommodate the linguistic diversity of the children now attending them (Langer, 1991).

During the 1960s, differences between home and school language were blamed for many children's failures in school. For example, terms such as *culturally deprived* and *language deficient* were often used to describe children who spoke a recognizable dialect such as Black English that differed from the SAE dialect expected in school. Intensive research in the area of language variation has shown that learning is not inhibited by a person's dialect (Shuy, 1980; Smith, 1975). Dialects differ from one another, but all are rule-bound, conventional ways of speaking. Every dialect is fully capable of allowing all human experiences or thoughts to be expressed. A dialect such as Black English, for instance, is not an impoverished language form, nor is it a sloppy or ungrammatical second cousin to other English dialects (Labov, 1972; Smitherman, 1985).

Linguistically, all dialects are equally valid, but socially, not all dialects are equally valued. Dialects spoken by dominant social groups are regarded more highly than those adopted by groups with less economic or political power. The most valued dialect in America, standard American English, is the variety spoken in the Northeast and Midwest. Other distinctive dialects exist in the South, in Appalachia, in New England, in the Southwest, and on the West Coast. Black English is spoken by some but not all African Americans; it is also spoken by some European Americans, Hispanic Americans, and Asian Americans. Hispanic and Asian American dialects may not be closely tied to geographic areas but rather to cultural communities throughout the United States.

However, standard American English is the language of schooling. If children are to succeed in school today, they must learn and use standard English no matter what their home dialect is. This presents a dilemma for children and teachers alike. How are children to learn standard English if it is not their home dialect? Should a standard dialect replace a home dialect? Should teachers reject children and their school work if they speak and write in a dialect other than standard English? These questions cannot be answered easily, but there are several principles to keep in mind. Above all, children's home dialects should be respected, since a person's identity and sense of self are intertwined with their language patterns. Instead of rejecting a child's home dialect, a teacher can help *add* standard English to the child's linguistic repertoire. Children who speak several varieties of English are said to be **bidialectal**, which helps individuals function effectively in different social settings.

Dialects in the Classroom

As the diversity of students increases, educators should expect to hear many different dialects in their classroom. It is important to remember that language develops with use. Allowing children to speak and interact at school in their home dialect or language will increase their general fluency with language and thereby develop their communication skills. In addition, the teacher can encourage competency in standard dialect by making it clear to children that acquiring a new dialect is important and by instructing them in its conventions (Delpit, 1988). For example, teachers can ask children to write two versions of the same story on facing pages, one in standard dialect and the other in a different dialect (Leu & Kinzer, 1995). All children, no matter which one was their home dialect, would become conscious of the differences between the two versions, and teachers will have the opportunity to value each dialect for its communicative effectiveness.

Additionally, teachers should *model* the standard English dialect used in school. Constantly intervening and correcting children's language will not promote their development of the dominant dialect. Remember that the child learning to speak does not benefit from a parent's correction of form. The child intuitively constructs the grammatical system by analyzing the language patterns he or she hears and then interacting in real exchanges. Chil-

Linguistically, all dialects are equally valid ways of representing the world, but socially, all dialects are not equally valued and, consequently, speakers of nonmainstream dialects often face discrimination.

Children can learn new languages or dialects by being exposed to the target language and by frequent interaction where they feel comfortable making mistakes.

dren learn new languages or new dialects by being exposed to the target language and by frequent, meaningful interactions where they feel comfortable making mistakes. If teachers focus on correcting nonstandard speech, they will succeed in silencing children rather than in promoting their language development.

Instead of form, teachers should focus on a child's message, providing a response that models the appropriate form (Galda, Cullinan, & Strickland, 1993). For example, if a student says, "My papa, he goed to the store," a teacher might reply, "Your papa went to the store? Why did he go to the store?" This strategy reinforces the child's success in communicating while simultaneously allowing the child to hear the appropriate verb form. Eventually, with enough exposure to alternative forms and with frequent interaction in nonthreatening, purposeful settings, children will acquire the dialect of school language (Delpit, 1990).

Language and Culture

Language varieties reflect cultural patterns and values. One dialect or language differs from another not only in terms of grammar but also in speaking styles and interaction patterns. Children behave, learn, and interact according to the values and worldviews of their culture. Thus, culture influences school achievement. In particular, there is great variability in how different cultures imagine, cultivate, and value literacy (Laquer, 1983). If there is significant discontinuity between children's home and school environments, then children can become so confused and frustrated that they are unable to participate in learning (Sleeter & Grant, 1988). Many studies, including Shirley Brice Heath's study (1983) discussed earlier, have now documented the fact that differences in classroom and home discourse patterns adversely affect the learning of children from ethnic or minority communities (Au & Mason, 1981, 1983; Erickson & Mohatt, 1982; Philips, 1983).

How do classroom interaction patterns affect access to school knowledge? In a traditional teacher-led classroom, a whole-group lesson works only if the participants know and adhere to the rules for turn-taking. With this kind of lesson, teachers choose the subject matter and use direct instruction (telling, showing, and guided practice) to transmit information to students. Children are expected to pay attention and to sit quietly until they are asked a question. They may not call out answers but are expected to raise their hands and speak only if they are chosen to respond. This teacher-dominated interactional model does not work equally well for all students, especially for those who are unfamiliar with this discourse pattern. Students bring the distinctive discourse patterns of their homes and communities with them into the classroom. When these patterns differ from those traditionally practiced in school, children are effectively prevented from participating.

Teachers need to understand that students' ways of speaking and interacting are inherently logical no matter how different they appear from school-based patterns.

Changing Classroom Discourse and Interaction Patterns

As we discussed in Chapter 4, multicultural education involves revising school curriculums to reflect the beliefs, traditions, and contributions of all people in an ethnically diverse society. Teachers need to understand that students' ways of speaking and interacting are inherently logical no matter how different they appear from school-based patterns. By investigating children's home cultures and finding out more about typical social interaction patterns, teachers can change their classroom to accommodate a range of behaviors.

Children's verbal participation is greater when classroom discourse patterns are similar to those used in the home or community (National Research Council, 1998). In work with Hawaiian children in the Kamehameha Early Education Program, educators devised an instructional program that incorporated the *talk story,* a Hawaiian conversational form, into classroom literacy activities (Au & Kawakami, 1985; Au & Mason, 1981). A talk story is a

SOURCE: News & Observer.

One way to create a multicultural learning environment is to include reading materials written in languages other than English.

rambling personal narrative in which two or more speakers work together to create and jointly perform the story. A good storyteller in this culture is someone who can draw others into the conversation, not someone who can hold the floor independently. As compared with traditional classroom recitation, the talk story reflects cooperative rather than individualistic cultural values and depends on collaborative instead of monologic patterns of interaction. Because children were familiar with the simultaneous speaking, interruptions, and shared creation that occur during talk story, they participated more readily. Also, teachers were able to spend more time discussing content rather than managing the interaction.

The use of talk stories allowed children in this community to bridge home and school literacy more easily. Introducing the talk story as a school form of discourse not only ensured children's access to instruction but also changed the relationship between teachers and children. The teacher's talk became less privileged, and children and the teacher had more equal conversational rights (Au, 1993).

When faced with a variety of cultural patterns, teachers can also use small-group and cooperative learning formats. Reciprocal-teaching approaches, like the one discussed in Chapter 3, also change classroom discourse patterns from teacher monologues to *instructional conversations* (Palinscar & Davide, 1991). These more student-centered approaches permit freer, more open dialogues between all students and the teacher and among peers (McCollum, 1991). Such interactive learning does not occur in traditional classrooms where the teacher's role is to transmit information and the students' role is to recite correct answers.

Respecting students' ways of interacting and accepting them in the classroom help to establish a multicultural climate. But students still need to learn school-based ways of speaking in order to be successful. By providing many opportunities for interaction, during which students use familiar patterns but also are exposed to the unfamiliar school-based patterns, teachers can create a composite classroom culture (Au, 1993). Literacy learning is enhanced when old and new language patterns are integrated.

One of the most effective ways of creating a multicultural learning environment is to bring culturally diverse reading materials into the classroom, including some written in languages other than English. Education in the United States has been English language dominant despite the fact that we are a multicultural and multilingual society. However, beginning in the 1960s, different ethnic and minority groups (including Cuban refugees, Hispanic immigrants, and African Americans) struggled intensely for equal access to education with the result being the emergence of bilingual education.

Bilingual Education

As we have discussed, a growing number of students are coming to school from homes where a language other than English is spoken. When these students are not proficient in English, they need more than a culturally sensitive classroom environment. They need to acquire English as their second language in order to participate in mainstream American society. How do schools best serve these children? First, it is important to know that President Johnson signed into law the Bilingual Education Act of 1968 as Title VII of the Hawkins-Stafford Elementary and Secondary Education Act. This legislation was greatly influenced by an experimental program, funded by the Ford Foundation in 1963, to use Spanish in teaching Cuban children at the Coral Way Elementary School in Dade County, Florida. The academic success of this program spurred Hispanic groups nationwide to lobby for bilingual education programs. The Bilingual Education Act of 1968 provided guidelines for curriculum development, teacher training, and program monitoring and evaluation. The law did not stipulate that these programs needed to use the students' native language. By 1971, 30 states had legislation that allowed some type of bilingual education, and 50 states had permitted it by 1983. Although the Bilingual Act was reauthorized for funding in 1988, state legislation regarding bilingual programs has been allowed to lapse, has been repealed, has suffered budget cuts, or is undergoing review.

At issue today is how our schools can best serve students with limited proficiency in English. There are four common approaches for serving English-learning students. One method is **bilingual education**, in which at least two languages are used in basic subject areas (mathematics, social studies, science) during the first two or three years of schooling, usually a child's native language and the second language the child is acquiring. Another popular approach is **English as a second language** (ESL) programs. Students in these programs spend time in receiving special instruction in English in special classrooms, then spend most of their day in a regular classroom. A third approach is **structured immersion**, in which children receive up to a year of intensive training in English before they are placed in an English-speaking classroom. Finally, there is the **submersion** or "sink or swim" approach. In these programs, English-language learners are placed into a monolingual, English classroom without instructional support.

Although the advantages and disadvantages of each approach continue to be debated in the public policy arena, most language experts agree that some form of bilingual education is best for English-language learners. As you recall, it takes nearly 3 to 5 years to acquire oral proficiency in a language and considerably longer to gain the level of proficiency needed to learn in core subject areas (Garcia, 2000).

The most effective approaches in bilingual classrooms emphasize natural approaches to language development. Those factors that were critical in learning a first language, including active engagement, frequent experimenting, using language to communicate, and supportive adults, remain just as important in learning a second language.

Having a meaningful purpose for using language remains primary for second-language acquisition. Pha, the bilingual learner whose story introduced this chapter, exemplifies this point. He practiced English during informal conversations while planning the play and making the costumes. Later he used language to entertain others while performing as a baby bear. Talking about meaningful content is a far more effective way to practice

Effective Strategies for Teaching Linguistically Diverse Learners

- *Create truly bilingual classrooms.* Teachers provide literacy and content instruction for students in their native language while they are learning English. When children are able to learn in their native language, they are less likely to fall behind and they develop skills (e.g., decoding or comprehension skills) that can be transferred to English.
- *Incorporate dual-language strategies.* In dual-language learning environments, English-language learners learn content in their native language while learning English as a second language from English-speaking peers who are also learning a second language for enrichment. All students in this environment work toward becoming bilingual and biliterate.
- *Use integrated, whole language approaches.* Students practice English in oral and written forms in ways that are meaningful, purposeful, engaging, and enjoyable. Rote drill-and-practice typically lacks meaning for young people. They must go beyond learning the rules of grammar to using their new language in real-life situations.
- *Use subject matter to teach language.* The learning of language cannot be separated from what is being learned. When students learn language in a functional way (similar to the way they learned their first language), the process has real meaning to them. Instead of removing an English-language learner from a lesson, that student can be paired with bilingual or monolingual students in small groups.
- *Use sheltered-language strategies.* Sheltered-language strategies make use of visuals and simple language. Similar to learning a first language, context cues and simple language structures facilitate comprehension. Teachers provide many examples and hands-on activities, so students can comprehend abstract as well as concrete instructions.
- *Practice English by solving problems in cooperative groups.* English-language learners learn more by being actively engaged in cooperative

speaking a language than working on isolated-skill exercises (Allen, 1986). Furthermore, when students are engaged in successful literacy tasks, such as a class play, they are motivated to learn a new language.

Ideal classrooms provide language-rich environments in which bilingual learners are encouraged to interact with native speakers (Krashen & Terrell, 1983). Knowledge gained from frequent speaking and listening experiences will ease the transition to reading and writing. Two types of informal writing have been used successfully with bilingual students: *dialogue journals,* in which students and teachers write back and forth about everyday issues, and *literature logs,* in which students record their personal reactions to reading materials (Reyes, 1995). In addition, cooperative group activities with more casual discourse patterns are beneficial. In such settings, bilingual learners gain practice speaking, they are able to participate successfully, and, consequently, their self-esteem is promoted (Long & Porter, 1985). Most important, using diverse reading materials that reflect particular cultures or individual histories will encourage bilingual learners to draw on background knowledge, making it easier to comprehend information and to participate in discussions (Au, 1993).

learning activities. Teachers can organize classrooms into flexible, heterogeneous, cooperative learning groups composed of native and nonnative English speakers in order to provide students with opportunities to practice English in problem-solving situations.

- *Use cross-age and peer tutoring.* Use cross-age tutoring and peer tutoring to enhance literacy and language acquisition. Research shows that learning is enhanced both for those who are tutored and for the tutors themselves. In bilingual programs, roles between the tutee and tutor can be switched depending on the content of the learning activity.

- *Respect community language norms.* Teachers demonstrate respect for each student's language and do not prevent bilingual students from alternating between English and their native language (code switching) while they work together. The most important consideration in teaching is that communication is accomplished.

- *Use thematic interdisciplinary teaching.* English-language learners learn content with greater comprehension if their learning is interdisciplinary. New learning is incremental and added to a theme the students already understand. Having a base vocabulary related to the theme enables students to make connections across disciplines.

- *Use computers and peer tutors to enhance language learning.* Teachers who create situations in which two students can use a common computer enable students to learn English as a second language more readily. Working together, students can work on problems, conduct electronic searches, create multimedia presentations, write stories, make revisions, and correct vocabulary and grammar. Simple drill-and-practice that is easier for English-language learners should be avoided.

SOURCE: After Cole (1995).

Creating a Positive Classroom Environment for Linguistically Diverse Students

Despite the shifting political views on bilingual education, the fact of the matter is that there is a large and growing population of students in the United States who are entering school with limited English proficiency. Also, few teacher education programs provide the necessary training for teaching linguistically diverse students. However, numerous reports in the last several years have identified a number of school- and classroom-level practices that can enhance the achievement of these students (see National Research Council, 1998).

At the school level, exemplary programs for English-language learners have a supportive school climate. There are high achievement expectations for all students, and their cultural and linguistic backgrounds are valued. Several teachers at these schools speak more than one language, and students are encouraged to develop and maintain their native language while becoming proficient in English. Not surprisingly, there is also strong educational leadership in exemplary schools for linguistically diverse learners. School principals play a key role in making the achievement of English-language learners a high priority. There is staff

English-language learners need a supportive school environment, and different instructional approaches must be used and customized for the diversity of the students served.

309

development to help all teachers, not just language specialists, to work effectively with these students. Additionally, there is a strong schoolwide commitment to involving parents in classroom and school activities and to fostering good communication between home and school. We will discuss various parent involvement strategies in Chapter 9.

At the classroom level, there are a number of instructional strategies that can be used to raise the achievement of linguistically diverse learners. These strategies are summarized in the Focus on Teaching box. As you know, there is no *one* way to teach diverse learners. Different approaches must be used and customized for the diversity of students served and for different school conditions.

Chapter Summary

www.mhhe.com/meece

Language Development

- In everyday terms, literacy is the ability to read and write. More broadly considered, literacy means being able to communicate clearly and to think analytically when speaking, listening, reading, and writing. In our complex culture, individuals will develop a variety of technological literacies, such as computer and video literacy. Literate thinking may occur after viewing a film as well as after reading a book. In short, literacy includes communicative competence with print as well as nonprint sources.

- Children acquire spoken language without direct instruction and within a relatively short time. Around the age of 2, children begin saying individual words, then combining two words, and moving on to multiple word phrases and sentences. By the age of 7, a native speaker will know about 90 percent of the grammatical structures of English. Being social creatures, children have a natural urge to learn language in order to communicate their thoughts and desires to others.

- Language acquisition is a process that researchers cannot completely explain. Several theories have been proposed, including the behaviorist, the maturationist, and the interactionist. Although each theory has limitations, the interactionist, which combines elements of the other two, provides the most comprehensive and flexible account of how children acquire language. Interactional theory proposes that language structures evolve as a result of the interplay between a child's internal mental structures and the external social world, where interaction with others is primary.

- Children intuitively construct the rules and patterns of their language by actively testing hypotheses about the language system. The most general rules, such as word order, are the ones children generate first. Later, they experiment with more complicated elements of the language, such as tense forms, questions, and negatives.

- The critical period hypothesis suggests that if certain internal or external conditions related to language development are missing, a child will never learn language. Only weak versions of this hypothesis are supported by research. However, it is true that depriving children of human interaction and language at an early age will impair their language development. The extent of the damage varies depending on the length of time and the child's age at the time of deprivation.

- If children grow up in a family or community in which two languages are spoken, then they will likely grow up bilingual. Young children are capable of learning several languages simultaneously without confusion. It may take longer for a child to construct grammars for several languages at once, but the method of acquisition and pattern of development are exactly the same for a child learning only one language. Older children and adults learning second languages experience different patterns of acquisition.

What Is Emergent Literacy?

- Most children learn to read and write in school, usually through intentional teaching in a print-rich environment. Children are motivated to develop print literacy when they are given many opportunities to engage purposefully with texts in authentic situations. A child picks up a story to read in order to discover what happens, not because there are comprehension questions to be answered at the end.

- In a literate culture, children learn about the characteristics and processes of reading and writing from birth, a developmental process called emergent literacy. Through experience with books, preschoolers learn that print carries meaning, recognize letters and words, and can mimic true reading by reciting memorized stories.

- Children make progress with writing and reading when they develop phonemic awareness, an understanding that words contain distinctive phonemes (sounds) represented by letters. They develop self-conscious knowledge about how the print represents spoken language. Besides matching sounds to letters, children must recognize, distinguish, and produce the letters of the alphabet. Focusing on distinctive features and spatial orientation are two strategies that help children accomplish this task.

- Social context has the greatest effect on whether a person becomes a proficient reader and writer. A literate environment, whether it is in a child care facility, a nursery school, or the home, is one in which children's experiences with print are for authentic purposes and in which adults value and participate in reading and writing themselves.

Learning to Read

- Reading is a complex process during which the reader translates print into words, comprehends and predicts meaning, and interacts emotionally with the characters or events of the story. Decoding is the process of determining equivalence with written words. Comprehension is the active process of ascribing meaning to a message. Comprehension depends on the reader's ability to use syntactic, semantic, and pragmatic information in order to make sense of what is written on the page.

- Three theories of reading instruction are current. In the specific-skills approach, a teacher teaches directly various decoding and comprehension skills using an explicit, often deductive, method of instruction. These skills are often taught in isolation, separated from the actual reading of stories or articles. The holistic language approach purports that children inductively learn and develop specific reading abilities based on extensive and varied experiences with print. Children read complete texts or stories for authentic purposes. Third, the integrated approach assumes that children must be engaged in authentic (meaningful) literacy activities but also must learn specific skills. Using an integrated approach, teachers give children many authentic experiences with reading and writing, but direct instruction in reading skills and strategies is provided when necessary.

Learning to Write

- When learning to spell, children experiment with sounds and letters. Their unconventional patterns are called invented spelling and should not be regarded as errors. Invented spelling increases children's fluency, makes it easier for them to compose, and does not interfere with reading or conventional spelling development.

- The essence of becoming a writer is learning to compose. Composing is a complex process that includes planning, drafting, revising, editing, and publishing. Although the writing process can be described as having discrete parts, many writers do not experience them separately or in any set order. Children normally work on the mechanical aspects of writing before focusing on perfecting the writing process. Since revision entails considering the needs of the audience and being distanced from the text, it is the most difficult part of the process to learn. In the upper grades and high school, children become proficient with expository writing and use writing as a way of learning in the academic disciplines.

Culture and Literacy

- A person's language, dialect, or manner of speaking reflects social, economic, and cultural background. A dialect is variation of a single language spoken by members of a speech community. The language of instruction in schools, sometimes called standard American English (SAE), is often not the dialect of English spoken in children's speech communities. Instead of rejecting a child's home dialect, a teacher can help children acquire a new dialect. Being bidialectal helps individuals to function effectively in different social settings.

- Multicultural education refers to teaching that relies on culturally relevant materials and school curriculums that reflect the beliefs, traditions, and contributions of all people in an ethnically diverse society.

- Children who are able to speak, read, or write some English in addition to their native language are considered bilingual learners. Many bilingual children have limited English proficiency (LEP). Some bilingual programs are designed to move children into English-dominant classrooms, whereas other programs attempt to teach English and to maintain a home language such as Spanish. Bilingual education programs reflect multicultural awareness.

Key Terms

alphabetic system (p. 268)

bilingual (p. 263)

bilingual education (p. 307)

communicative competence (p. 260)

comprehension (p. 284)

context knowledge (p. 283)

critical period hypothesis (p. 255)

decoding (p. 283)

dialect (p. 303)

emergent literacy (p. 265)

English as a second language (ESL) (p. 307)

functionally literate (p. 248)

grammar (p. 244)

holophases (p. 256)

invented spelling (p. 290)

language (p. 240)

language acquisition device (LAD) (p. 246)

literacy (p. 240)

metalinguistic awareness (p. 269)

phonemic awareness (p. 268)

phonic knowledge (p. 283)

reading readiness approach (p. 266)

Sight word knowledge (p. 283)

simultaneous bilinguals (p. 263)

standard american english (SAE) (p. 303)
structured immersion (p. 307)

successive bilingualism (p. 264)
syntax (p. 247)
telegraphic speech (p. 259)

whole language (p. 286)
writing across the curriculum (p. 268)

Activities

1. Children's language development is supported by interaction with others, especially with parents or caregivers. Audiotape or videotape a child between the ages of 2 and 3 in a social setting for at least an hour. (Taping several shorter sessions is also an option.) Describe or analyze the following, based on your observation.

   a. The child's stage of language development, using specific examples from your data.

   b. The role of other people in structuring or shaping the child's language. Refer to a conversation or verbal interaction between the child and adult (or older child) in addressing this issue.

2. Test out your teaching intuitions by finding a child who is just learning to read (usually a first grader). Spend three half-hour sessions with the child, if possible. In the first session, design some way of assessing the child's current decoding skills. For example, does the child know letter-sound correspondences? Then plan and teach two sessions on some aspect of decoding appropriate for your child. Try varied teaching methods, such as games, big books, physical activities, language experience stories. (For teaching ideas, see *Language, Literacy, and the Child* (Galda, Cullinan, & Strickland, 1993) or *Reading and Learning to Read* (Vacca, Vacca, & Gove, 1995), or any reading methods textbook. Tape the sessions so you have a record of what you have taught. Finally, assess what the child learned, what strategy or activity proved most helpful, and your strengths as a teacher.

3. By the time students reach middle and high school, they are writing in a variety of modes as well as writing to learn in all content areas, from math to history. Conduct a survey to discover the amount and type of writing a student accomplishes in a single school day. You can approach the survey in different ways. You might shadow a student for the day, keeping track of when, what kind, in what class, and for how much time the student writes that day. Or you might prepare a questionnaire using the modes of writing found in Figure 5.9, and survey a larger sample of students from one school for a day or even for a week. You might compile your findings with other students in your college class who are conducting the same survey. Write a brief report on the nature and extent of writing required of older students. You might compare your results with those reported in Applebee (1981).

4. As children grow older, differences between their spoken and written language become more pronounced. To discover how significant these differences are, collect spoken and written language samples from a child in either middle school or high school. Tape-record a 20-minute conversation between you and the child. Prepare for the spoken session by thinking of some questions to ask, particularly ones that will elicit extended responses. You could ask the child to tell you the plot of his or her favorite movie, book, or television show, for example. For the child's written language, ask the child for permission to copy several pieces of his or her writing from school. Book reports, descriptive essays, literary analyses are all possibilities. Transcribe at least 5 minutes of the spoken session. Write a brief report comparing and contrasting the spoken and written samples, but consider sentence structure and word choice in particular.

Chapter 6

Children with Exceptional Learning Needs

I have 19 students this year. They are all so different in their behavior, their independence, their attention span, their self-control. In reading, my students probably show the most variability of all the academics. They range from nonreaders to eighth grade, and everything in between. We have four different spelling lists. One is a basic spelling list, and some of the students get this list ahead of the others, giving them more time to study. Another is the regular list. Some children pick out their own challenge words in addition to their regular list, and others use nothing but their own challenge words, choosing adult-level vocabulary. We don't use any spelling books. The lists are on the computer, and students practice spelling words from them in different activities I've planned. The activities vary; some children write out their spelling words in different colors and then make puzzles out of them. Others write stories with their spelling words in them. Others look them up in the dictionary. Some make word searches and finish other students' word searches. Spelling activities are very much open-ended, and there are always additional activities children can do for more practice.

Some are very creative writers; they even write poetry. Others favor narrative writing or factual writing, preferring nonfiction pieces. Some write original stories and adventures, getting into the characters. Still others write about their personal lives, about their pets and

Chapter opener photo: James L. Shaffer.

things like that. I do have some children dictate their stories to their writing helper. And then I have children who are writing books and publishing them, editing stories completely on their own. Some want to publish their stories, but they need help editing. A few children express their ideas through pictures, which they then label.

Some children are on grade level in math. Others are working on addition and subtraction facts under five. Some are working on carrying and borrowing, and others are doing multiplication and division. Some students use only one or two strategies for computing numbers, while others have a complex repertoire of strategies.

In language, LaToya has a very rich vocabulary, but she has difficulty producing certain speech sounds. Sam's receptive vocabulary is better than his expressive vocabulary. Most children are doing well with their fine motor and gross motor coordination. Only one student has problems in cutting and handwriting, but he loves to work in clay. Some children excel in gymnastics, but others have trouble throwing and catching a ball while they're running.

> *Interindividual variation refers to differences in developmental needs from one child to the next, while intraindividual variation refers to the unique pattern of developmental strengths and needs within a single child.*

As this partial interview of a primary-level teacher, Ms. B, indicates, a typical classroom contains children with a wide range of needs in the developmental areas. One can expect **interindividual variation,** that is, differences in developmental needs from one child to the next. Likewise, **intraindividual variation,** a unique pattern of strengths and needs related to each child's physical, cognitive, language, social, and emotional growth, is to be expected. The interindividual differences in Ms. B's class are readily apparent. However, intraindividual differences, which are not so easy to discern, are also present. Ms. B reports that Juan, whom she considers an "average" child, "is very strong in expressing himself in writing and art. He is average, I would say, in reading and math. His handwriting needs a lot of work though, and his self-concept needs work, too." Nicole, a student with specific learning disabilities, also has a pattern of intraindividual differences. "She does grade-level work in reading and spelling, but math is her area of difficulty. Her writing and language are strengths. She's also very attentive and has strong self-control, but she tends to be a bit dependent on others."

Children are classified and labeled according to their interindividual differences, then given special education (specialized instruction and settings) to fit those classifications. In Ms. B's class, 6 out of 19 students receive special services from one or more of the following: a learning disabilities specialist, a gifted specialist, a speech-language pathologist, or a psychologist.

Before we examine different categories of exceptionality, it is useful to consider a few issues that relate to categorizing or labeling. The practice of labeling has been shown to cause negative effects on children's self-esteem, peer relationships, and teacher expectations (Hobbs, 1975; Jones, 1972; Reschly, 1979). Yet without a label, children cannot receive services from special educators, such as a speech pathologist or an occupational therapist. Nor can they have access to technology and specialized equipment, such as communication boards and voice synthesizers. How ironic that under our current educational policies, children with interindividual and intraindividual needs must demonstrate that their differences require *individualized,* specialized services and support by qualifying as a member of a disability *group!* This labeling process blurs the distinction between the

> *The practice of labeling has been shown to cause negative effects on children's self-esteem, peer relationships, and teacher expectations.*

individual and the disability category. It also creates a tendency to see the individual's disability, what the person cannot do, rather than the individual's abilities.

The process of labeling and categorizing children remains controversial but unchanged. M. Stephen Lilly (1992) reports:

> Haven't the shortcomings of the [special education] system been addressed, and aren't we on the verge of implementing identification and placement protocols [procedures] that are defensible and conceptually sound? Unfortunately the answer is no. Categorical identification remains the *sine qua non* for special education services in virtually every state, and the United States Department of Education continues to require that each state report the number of students in special education by category of exceptionality each year in order to receive federal funds. (p. 87)

In this chapter, we attempt to reduce labeling stereotypes in several ways. First, we use people-first terminology, placing reference to the individual before reference to the exceptionality. (**Exceptionality** is used as an umbrella term to describe all who receive special education—children with disabilities as well as children who are gifted.) In instances where professional groups have stated strong objections to federal terminology, we use the profession's preferred term. For example, in the deaf community, researchers, educators, advocates, and those with the disability have raised objection to the federally derived term *hearing impairment*. Therefore, we use *deaf* or *hard of hearing* throughout the chapter. Figure 6.1 contains examples of appropriate terminology using people-first language, as well as some stigmatizing language to avoid.

We also seek to avoid stereotyping by stressing the fact that children with exceptionalities are more similar to their nondisabled peers than they are different from them. *Their interindividual differences emerge when they cannot meet the learning and behavioral expectations of the classroom.* Strong proponents of this view use the term **curriculum casualties**

Children with exceptionalities are more similar to their nondisabled peers than they are different from them.

Examples of Person-First Language

A student with a disability	NOT ➡	A disabled student
Children receiving special education	NOT ➡	Special education children
A man who has cerebral palsy	NOT ➡	A cerebral palsy sufferer
A child with a specific learning disability	NOT ➡	A learning disabled child
The boy with Down syndrome	NOT ➡	The Down syndrome boy
People who are physically disabled	NOT ➡	Physically disabled people
She has epilepsy	NOT ➡	She is epileptic

Avoid Using Stigmatizing Terminology (Examples)

Afflicted with . . .	Hare lip	Retardate
Crippled	Hearing Impaired	Trainable mentally retarded
Deviant	Mute	
Handicapped	Orthopedically impaired	Victimized by . . .

FIGURE 6.1

Nonstigmatizing Terminology

to illustrate that the disability does not reside within the child but is created when the child's needs clash with the expectations of the educational system (Gickling & Thompson, 1985). Third, in describing learner characteristics for each of the categories, we acknowledge that we are focusing on common needs, not intraindividual strengths and needs. Our intention is to identify shared characteristics so that we can then discuss how a teacher can provide for these differences in the classroom. "Categories are inventions for the convenience of thinking and communicating" how professionals can better address diversity (Nelson, 1993, p. 84). We remind our readers that every child, whether disabled or nondisabled, and regardless of disability category, is an individual who has a unique set of strengths and needs. The characteristics associated with a child's disability describe a mere fraction of the whole child.

This chapter begins by examining the major categories of exceptionality and the reasons for educating these children in a regular classroom. We then present some of the interindividual learner characteristics for each of the categories, followed by a discussion of the classroom teacher's role in identifying and serving all children. In the last section, we introduce some practices for teaching children with diverse needs in general classrooms and conclude with a discussion of resources that will assist teachers in working with exceptional students.

Historically, the education of children with exceptional needs has been separate from that of their nondisabled peers, and they received all or most of their instruction outside general classrooms.

Integrating Children with Special Learning Needs

Historically, children with exceptional needs have been educationally isolated from their nondisabled peers, receiving their instruction outside general classrooms. These children were considered to be the responsibility of special educators—teachers who were trained in specialized teaching strategies, diagnostic-prescriptive teaching methods, individualized instruction, and applied behavior management. A variety of separate special education settings were available for labeled students. Among these were *resource rooms,* where students were "pulled out" from the general classroom and spent part of the day so that they received small-group or individualized instruction; *separate self-contained* special education classes where children with similar exceptionalities spent the entire school day; *special schools* or centers; and *residential schools.*

During the 1980s two movements challenged the separation of special and general education. Proponents of the regular education initiative (REI) advocated that children with mild disabilities who were in pull-out programs would be better served in general classrooms with special educators entering the classroom to provide services. This approach is known as the "pull-in" approach (Lieberman, 1992). A second movement was the inclusive schools movement, which argued against residential facilities and special schools for children with severe disabilities (Lipsky & Gartner, 1992). Advocates wanted children with severe disabilities to remain in their home-school, socially integrated with their neighborhood peers. The REI proponents emphasized the academic aspect of integration, whereas inclusionists advocated its social benefits.

Current trends reflect the impact of these two movements. Over the last two decades, a dramatic shift has occurred from most restrictive settings, such as residential schools, to the least restrictive environment, the general classroom. As a result, classroom teachers are expected to teach a more diverse group of students, with a wider range of exceptionalities than ever before. Figure 6.2 presents some viewpoints about the integration of children with exceptionalities into general classrooms.

Over the last two decades, a shift has occurred in which children with mild disabilities have been moved from the more restrictive (pull-out) settings to the least restrictive (pull-in) setting, the general classroom.

Full inclusionists advocate for all children to be placed in the general classroom at their home-based school, regardless of their exceptionality.

Cathy Heizman, a parent of a child with severe disabilities:

> *On a hot sunny day in 1955, Miss Rosa Parks refused to take her place at the back of the bus in Montgomery, Alabama. That one simple act of defiance and courage changed the face of America forever. Somebody asked me once why I was so adamant about integration. "Kids with disabilities don't learn any better or any easier in an integrated class," he said. "Their education isn't any better." Maybe not. And the ride in the first seat of the bus isn't any smoother than in the back. But Miss Rosa Parks knew just how important it was to be in the front in 1955. And so do I. (Stainback & Stainback, 1992, pp. 39–40)*

Susan and William Stainback, university researchers and professors:

> *It should be noted here that when general educators (or any one else) in the mainstream of school life reject children with disabilities or fail to offer them what they need to grow and learn, it is a serious problem that this society must face up to and change. It should never be tolerated or accepted as a "reason" for maintaining segregated special classes or schools. People with disabilities, just as any other citizens, have a right to be treated with dignity and respect and offered an education geared to their needs in the mainstream of school and community life. (Stainback & Stainback, 1992, p. 34)*

Fair inclusionists advocate for choice in deciding which placement is most appropriate for each child, as determined by those who know him best—parents and teachers.

Jim Kauffman, a university researcher and professor:

> *First, I don't believe that blanket placement decisions should be made for special education categories. It was an appalling mistake to make blanket decisions to place students with disabilities in institutions and special classes. It is equally appalling and inhumane to make the blanket decision to place all students in regular classrooms. Special education is intellectually bankrupt and morally derelict to the extent that it embraces a philosophy that insists on the same placement decision for all students. Second, . . . I agree with the concepts of the least restrictive environment and a full range of alternative placements. We must take precautions not to overlook the regular classroom as a potentially appropriate placement. (Kauffman, 1994, p. 13)*

Laurence Lieberman, consultant to school systems at the national and international level:

> *The day the standard for education becomes meeting the individual needs of all children, all disabled . . . children can be in regular classrooms. This statement comes at a time when the movement in education is away from the individual and toward preservation of the system in terms of arbitrary standards and competencies and excellence of achievement in a set curriculum or course of studies. Perhaps the pendulum will swing back. It usually does. But for now, we better fight to preserve special education. (Lieberman, 1992, p. 24)*

FIGURE 6.2

Views on Integrating Children with Special Needs

Special educators and classroom teachers have become jointly responsible for the education of students with exceptionalities. Their relationship is a collaborative arrangement, with shared responsibility for meeting student needs (Will, 1986). Collaboration often occurs in the form of cooperative teaching and/or consultation. In cooperative teaching, a pair of special and general educators work together in one of three ways: team teaching, complementary instruction, or supportive learning activities (Bauwens, Hourcade, & Friend, 1989). In **team teaching,** special and general education teachers plan and implement instruction in the general classroom, working together in small- and large-group settings. For example, one teacher may be presenting to the class, while the other teacher monitors students and lends assistance to any student having difficulties. Or the class may be divided into two groups, with each teacher teaching similar skills at different levels. In effective coteaching partnerships, the general-special education teacher distinction is not present. Both teachers rotate among the children, actively supporting the learning process of all students.

Using **complementary instruction,** the roles and responsibilities of each teacher are clearly delineated. The general educator teaches academic content while the special educator teaches "academic survival skills (e.g., taking notes, identifying main ideas in reading or lectures, summarizing, and related study skills)" (Bauwens et al., 1989, p. 19). **Supportive learning activities** occur when the educators divide the academic content. The general educator is responsible for introducing and covering the basic content while the special educator provides supplementary instruction that reinforces or enriches the academic content, for example, a group project or a small-group discussion.

Collaborative consultation is another type of partnership and often accompanies cooperative teaching. In the consultative relationship, both special and general educators discuss academic and social behavioral problems in the general classroom. Together, they collaborate to meet the needs of individual students.

Who Are the Students with Exceptional Needs?

On the national level, 11 percent of the school-age population qualifies as having a disability or a limitation (U.S. Department of Education, 1999). Table 6.1 lists the disability categories identified by federal special education laws, as well as the number and percentage of students in each for the 1997–1998 school year.

As you can see, the largest number of children with disabilities have either a specific learning disability or a speech or language impairment. Together they constitute approximately 64 percent of the population receiving special education. The next-largest categories are children with mental retardation (12 percent) and children with preschool disabilities (12 percent). Since 1992 a free, appropriate public education must be made available for all 3- through 5-year-olds with disabilities.

The number of children served under the category of other health impairments has increased dramatically since 1992. This increase may be due in part to a 1991 Department of Education, Office of Special Education and Rehabilitative Services memorandum stipulating that children with attention deficit disorder (ADD) and attention deficit hyperactivity disorder (ADHD) were eligible for services under the other health-impaired category. The remaining number of children with disabilities are scattered among nine categories, representing 16 percent of the students receiving special education.

The majority of disability categories contains a relatively high number of children who participate in the general or regular classroom for a large part of their school day. Some students from every category spend large portions of the school day in the regular class. Table 6.2 lists the percentage of students ages 6 through 21 by disability and the percentage of time they receive services outside the regular class.

Table 6.1	Children with Disabilities, Ages 0 to 21, Served in Federally Supported Programs for the Disabled, 1997–1998	

Disability	Number	Percent of Identified Students
Specific learning disability	2,726,000	46.2
Speech or language impairments	1,059,000	17.9
Mental retardation	589,000	10.0
Serious emotional disturbance	453,000	7.7
Hearing impairments	69,000	1.2
Orthopedic impairments	67,000	1.1
Other health impairments	190,000	3.2
Visual impairments	25,000	0.4
Multiple disabilities	106,000	1.8
Deaf-blindness	1,000	0.0
Autism and traumatic brain injury	54,000	0.9
Developmental delay	2,000	0.0
Preschool disabled	564,000	9.6
All disabilities	5,904,000	100.0

Table 6.2	Percentage of Students Ages 6 to 21 by Disability and Percentage of Time Served Outside Regular Class, 1996		

Disability	0 to 21 Percent of the Day	21 Percent to 60 Percent of the Day	More than 60 Percent of the Day
Specific learning disabilities	43.1	38.9	17.1
Speech or language impairments	88.6	6.6	4.4
Mental retardation	10.5	28.4	54.2
Emotional disturbance	22.5	23.3	35.3
Multiple disabilities	9.5	16.6	44.4
Hearing impairments	37.6	18.4	26.6
Orthopedic impairments	41.6	20.4	30.7
Other health impairments	41.3	34.5	17.3
Visual impairments	48.3	19.3	17.6
Autism	14.3	11.7	53.1
Deaf-blindness	14.1	11.8	38.1
Traumatic brain injury	28.8	26.1	30.6
All disabilities	45.7	28.5	21.4

SOURCE: U.S. Department of Education, Office of Special Education Programs, Data Analysis System (DANS).

The majority of students with speech or language impairments spend less than 21 percent of the school day being served outside the regular class. Large numbers of students with visual impairments, specific learning disabilities, orthopedic impairments, other health impairments, and hearing impairments also spend less than 21 percent of the school day receiving services outside the regular class. In the years between 1986 and 1996, regular class placement for special needs students has increased by approximately 20 percentage points from 25 percent in 1986 to 45 percent in 1996 (U.S. Department of Education, 1998). We can expect that the current trend toward classroom integration will continue, with increasing numbers of special needs children placed in general classrooms each year.

In addition to federally funded categories, another category of exceptionality, gifted and talented, is used to describe students who receive special education. Approximately 5 percent of school-age children are classified as gifted. This category is not covered under current federal laws, yet the children get special education at the school and district levels.

Each exceptionality category has unique criteria for state and federal eligibility. In order to qualify, students complete a battery of assessments that measure cognitive abilities, academic achievement, perception, motor skills, social development, and affect or emotional behaviors. If these measures match eligibility criteria, the child becomes identified and thereby eligible for special services. Children who do not meet the specific identification criteria for any one disability category continue to struggle in the general classroom without support. They "fall through the cracks" of the educational system.

Why Integrate Children with Exceptional Needs into the General Classroom?

Recent federal laws, such as IDEA, continue to hold states accountable for providing every child with a free public education in the least restrictive setting that is appropriate to their needs.

As previously mentioned, laws have been established to identify who should be served by special education. Laws also specify the rights or procedural safeguards guaranteed to the parents and their child who is receiving special education or being considered for special education. Federal and state laws describe procedural rights related to student referral, student evaluation, program planning, student placement, and student review. Later in this chapter the role of the classroom teacher in each of these areas is described.

The most recent federal law, the **Individuals with Disabilities in Education Act** (1990), also known as IDEA, requires that every state have a plan to ensure the following nine provisions:

1. Attempts are made to identify all children between the ages of 3 and 21 who have a disability (this does not include gifted).
2. Every student with a disability is guaranteed a free, appropriate public education. This includes the provision of any related services necessary for children to develop to their maximum potential. Examples of related services are assistive technology, speech-language therapy, occupational therapy, physical therapy, and transportation.
3. Parents must give informed, written consent before their child can be evaluated, identified (labeled), or served.
4. Students receive nondiscriminatory evaluation, free of cultural or language-based bias.
5. Student information is confidential; access to student files is restricted.
6. A written **individualized education plan (IEP)** is required for every child with a disability.
7. Training is provided for teachers and other professionals who work with children with disabilities.

8. Transition services must be planned by age 16; these services must identify how the student will be prepared for adulthood, including employment, post-secondary education, vocational training, and community living.
9. Every student must be placed in the least restrictive environment appropriate to his or her needs, that is, alongside students without disabilities.

This last provision is important. For many students, the least restrictive environment is the general classroom.

The most recent legislation continues to support further integration of students with exceptionalities into the general classroom. In 1997 a number of amendments were added to IDEA. These amendments require that students with exceptionalities have access to the general education curriculum. That is, the special services they receive must not exclude them from access to the same curriculum as students in the general classroom. Also, the amendments to IDEA now require participation of general classroom teachers in the planning, implementation, and reevaluation of the individual education plan (IEP) for students with exceptionalities. This places shared responsibility for the education of students with exceptionalities on both the special and regular classroom teachers. The amendments to IDEA also call for accountability of progress of students with exceptionalities through participation in state and district assessments. Most certainly today's regular classroom teachers will need to be skilled in addressing the needs of students with exceptional needs.

Characteristics of Children with Exceptional Needs

High Prevalence Categories

Many young people exhibit some type of exceptionality requiring special services beyond the general classroom. However, children with special needs should be viewed first as children with the developmental needs that all children share, and second as children with special needs. The manifestations of exceptionalities will change as a child grows and so it is important to take a developmental perspective of students with special needs. This section focuses on exceptionalities teachers are most likely to encounter in the regular classroom (specific learning disabilities, attention deficit hyperactivity disorder, and gifted) and discusses the developmental histories and characteristics of children with these exceptionalities.

Specific Learning Disabilities

Before discussing definitions and causes of learning disabilities, it is helpful to identify what a learning disability is *not*. A learning disability is *not* due to a lack of motivation or effort on the child's part, although sometimes parents and teachers treat children with learning disabilities as if they are lazy or are not trying hard enough. A learning disability is also *not* due to poor teaching, however, students with learning disabilities may tend to fair better with certain types of teaching styles and in certain classroom settings. A learning disability is *not* due to a lack of intelligence. On the contrary, students with learning disabilities demonstrate at least average potential for learning as measured by intelligence tests. Finally, a learning disability is *not* due to any temporary causes, but persists throughout the course of development. The IDEA (1990) legislation defines a **specific learning disability** as

Specific learning disabilities is a loosely defined category that includes a wide range of students who have difficulty learning despite having average or above-average intelligence.

> A disorder in one or more of the basic psychological processes involved in understanding or in using spoken or written language, which may manifest itself in an imperfect ability to listen, think, speak, read, write, spell or to do mathematical calculations. (IDEA, Sec. 1401[a][15])

A child is *not* considered to have a learning disability if learning difficulties can be attributed to visual, hearing, or motor handicaps; mental retardation; emotional disturbance; or environmental, cultural, or economic disadvantage.

Causes of Learning Disabilities   The causes of learning disabilities are difficult to determine, and often the specific cause of a child's learning disability is unclear. However, what does seem clear is that in many cases some part of the child's brain is not functioning as it should. Various possible causes have been identified, including biological and environmental factors, and their interaction.

There is evidence that learning disabilities may be genetic, tending to run in families (Decker & DeFries, 1980; Defries, Fulker, & LaBuda, 1987; Tallal, 1988). Learning disabilities have also been attributed to prenatal factors, such as maternal consumption of alcohol while pregnant as well as maternal smoking during pregnancy. Difficulties during the birth process resulting in a prolonged birth which decreases the oxygen supply to the fetus have also been identified as possible causes of learning disabilities. Learning disabilities have also been related to premature births and mild head injuries.

Special Olympics enable children with mental disabilities to experience a sense of acccomplishment.

Home and child-rearing factors have also been identified as possible causes of learning disabilities. Polloway and Smith (1994) identified a cluster of home environmental factors that may be related to the development of learning disabilities. Some of these factors include lack of organization and structure in the home, reliance on punishment to discipline children, teenage mothers, large number of children, lack of parenting preparedness or readiness, lack of social support for the family, and so on. These factors should not be interpreted as causing learning disabilities but as related to them.

Although the exact cause of learning disabilities may not be clear, it is logical to conclude that a learning disability exists in some form before school age, at a time when such students are usually identified (Lewandowski, 1991). During infancy, problems in arousal, attention, activity

Focus on Development

Common Developmental Abnormalities Exhibited by Children
Later Diagnosed as Having a Learning Disability

Age	Common Abnormalities Exhibited
Infancy	Problems in arousal, attention, activity level, temperament, alertness, and muscle tone
6 to 24 months	Delays in motor milestones, neuromuscular integrity, and fine and gross motor skills
2 to 4 years	Speech delays, articulation problems, dysfluency, and poor phonology
4 to 6 years	Perceptual motor difficulties with skills such as drawing, cutting, and printing letters
7 to 12 years	Academic/learning problems accompanied or followed by behavior or social skill deficits that persist into adulthood

level, temperament, alertness, and tone have been noted. Between the ages of 6 and 24 months the child may exhibit delays in motor milestones, neuromuscular integrity, and fine and gross motor skill development. In the preschool years, difficulties with language development have been noted, including speech delays, articulation problems, dysfluency, and poor phonology. Between the ages of 4 and 6 years old, perceptual motor difficulties are generally exhibited in skills such as drawing, cutting, and printing letters. Between the ages of 7 and 12 years old, when most students are diagnosed as having a learning disability, academic learning problems are common. These most often occur in the form of linguistic difficulties. The Focus on Development box summarizes the developmental delays children who are later diagnosed as having a learning disability may exhibit.

Children with Learning Disabilities in the School Years Children with specific learning disabilities exhibit a wide range of academic learning problems. Some have a learning disability in only one academic area, such as reading or math. Others have difficulty in many or all academic areas. Children with specific learning disabilities also differ from one another in the level of severity. A fifth-grade student may have a mild learning disability and read at the second-grade level; or he or she may be a nonreader and have a severe learning disability that requires intensive instruction. Table 6.3 describes different academic skill disabilities. It is important to remember that because academic skills build on one another, a student may have more than one disability at the same time. For example, the ability to read and to comprehend written language will also interfere with the development of writing abilities.

Students with learning disabilities have at least average intelligence as measured by intelligence tests, yet they perform below grade level in class work and on achievement tests. This discrepancy between intelligence and achievement may occur in one or more areas:

1. Spoken language. Delays, disorders, or discrepancies in listening and speaking.

2. Written language. Difficulties with reading, writing, and spelling.

Table 6.3	Description of Various Academic Skill Disabilities
Developmental reading disability	This type of disability, also known as **dyslexia**, is quite widespread. It affects approximately 2 to 8 percent of elementary school children. Children with dyslexia have difficulty separating and distinguishing sounds in spoken words. For example, they may not be able to identify the word *sat* by sounding out the individual letters. They may also have difficulty with rhyming words, such as *ball* and *fall*. Reading disabilities are also linked to an inability to relate new words and ideas to information in memory, which makes reading comprehension difficult.
Developmental writing disability	As with reading, writing also involves various brain functions. Disabilities involving writing stem from problems with sequencing words, spelling, vocabulary, and expressive language. Children with this specific disability have difficulty composing complete, grammatical sentences.
Developmental mathematics disability	Mathematics is a complex process involving distinguishing and recognizing numbers, aligning numbers, memorizing mathematical facts, and reasoning about abstract concepts such as place value or ratios. Problems with numbers and basic concepts emerge in the early grades, whereas problems in the later grades are linked to reasoning.

SOURCE: National Institute of Mental Health (1995).

3. Arithmetic. Difficulty in performing arithmetic functions or in comprehending basic concepts.

4. Reasoning. Difficulty in organizing and integrating thoughts.

As can be seen, a vast range of learning and behavioral characteristics are manifested by students with specific learning disabilities. In addition to cognitive problems, some students with learning disabilities have trouble with perception and motor development. They may show gross motor awkwardness, poor balance, uncoordinated movement, or poor handwriting and cutting skills. Participation in competitive sports may be particularly frustrating for some of these students.

Children with specific learning disabilities often attribute their academic or social successes to factors outside of their control, a situation referred to as external locus of control.

Students with specific learning disabilities often experience social and emotional problems. Although it is not always apparent whether social and emotional problems are contributing to a student's academic difficulties, these aspects of a student's behavior usually appear to be counterproductive to learning and thus limit success (Mercer, 1991, p. 598). From what we know about the dependence of social interaction on communication skills, it is no surprise to find that some children with specific learning disabilities have problems with peers. Their unpopularity may be attributed to poor skills in interpreting social cues, problem solving in social situations, and verbal and nonverbal communication.

SOURCE: Joel Gordon.

With specialized instruction, many children with learning disabilities are able to experience academic success.

When children with specific learning disabilities succeed either academically or socially, they are likely to attribute it to factors outside of their control. This is called **external locus of control.** Students exhibiting external locus of control do not reap the positive benefits of their successes, because they do not believe their accomplishments are the result of their own abilities or efforts. Rather, they attribute them to luck, fate, or something unrelated to themselves. For example, they are likely to attribute a good grade to an easy assignment. This has direct implications for students who repeatedly experience academic failure. Over a period of time, they may apply less effort as they operate on the assumption that they are helpless to change their performance, thus perpetuating a cycle of failure. Many students lose their motivation for learning. In many cases, students avoid tasks they expect to fail. Students with specific learning disabilities tend to evaluate their cognitive abilities more negatively than children without learning disabilities, and the unrelenting process of frustration and failure can erode a child's confidence in his or her abilities and skills (Bryan, 1986; Kistner & Osborne, 1987; Vaughn & Erlbaum, 1998).

As they reach adolescence, students with specific learning disabilities continue to fall further behind in academics as their deficits "manifest themselves in more subtle or controlled ways" (Deshler, 1978, p. 68). Problems in affective development persist, namely in self-concept, motivation, and social interaction (Alley & Deshler, 1979). The adolescent's need for organization and structure intensifies as curricular demands shift from learning skills to learning content at the secondary level. Oral reading becomes more problematic than silent reading, specifically, with word substitution errors, fluency, comprehension, ignoring or misreading punctuation, lack of expression, and losing their place (Alley & Deshler, 1979). Poor silent and oral reading skills interfere with reading comprehension in all subject areas. Alley and Deshler (1979) also describe troublesome writing characteristics: a narrow word pool; frequent errors in spelling, capitalization, and punctuation; organizational problems; and poor monitoring of writing errors.

Because of their low expectations and weak sense of control, adolescents with specific learning disabilities continue to fall further behind academically and socially.

Language and Communication Disorders

Defined as impairments in the ability to use language to communicate, **communication disorders** have much higher prevalence rates than statistics indicate. Since the federal government collects and reports head counts only for the primary disability, all those who have communication as a secondary disability are excluded from the prevalence rates for communication. When secondary disabilities are taken into account, the projected estimates of school-aged children with communication disorders vary from 3 percent to 5 percent (Nelson, 1993).

Causes of Language and Communication Disorders   As was the case with specific learning disabilities, language disorders develop as a result of the interaction of various biological and environmental factors. Table 6.4 outlines the various interrelated factors associated with the development of language disorders.

The acquisition of language skills is dramatic as children move from the one- to two-word utterances of toddlerhood to putting together sentences of three or more words during the preschool years. Language development during this period is critical to later success. IDEA stipulates that any child between the ages of 3 and 5 who needs special services should receive them. Thus, it is critical to identify children whose language development is not proceeding as expected so that the appropriate services can be provided. Some criteria for referring a child for a speech/language evaluation appear in the Focus on Development box.

Although screening may occur anytime throughout childhood, prekindergarten screening is common. Schools may use the results of early language screening to recommend that children wait a year before beginning kindergarten or that they attend a language-based developmental kindergarten class. This practice is controversial. Some see this practice as leading to early ability tracking with children being placed in classes where there is a

Table 6.4	Factors Associated with Development of Childhood Language Disorders
Central factors	Specific language disability
	Mental retardation
	Autism
	Attention-deficit/hyperactivity disorder
	Acquired brain injury
	Others
Peripheral factors	Hearing impairment
	Visual impairment
	Deaf-blindness
	Physical impairment
Environmental and emotional factors	Neglect and abuse
	Behavioral and emotional development problems
Mixed factors	

SOURCE: After N. W. Nelson (1998).

Focus on Development

Potential Danger Signals for Development of Language Disorders: Ages 3 to 5

- **Limitations of language expression.** Is close to 3 years of age and produces few creative utterances that are three words or more in length.
- **Problems learning words.** Has limited receptive or expressive vocabulary and has difficulty acquiring new words to express new ideas.
- **Problems comprehending language.** Appears to rely too much on familiar contexts to understand language (shows difficulty comprehending language without gestural support or when produced by unfamiliar partners).
- **Limitations of social interaction.** Shows little interest in social interaction, except perhaps to gain adult assistance to fulfill specific desires.
- **Limitations of play.** Shows little interest in playing with peers or in combining toys and objects in imaginative symbolic play.
- **Problems learning speech.** Has difficulty pronouncing words so that they are intelligible to unfamiliar adults (perfect articulation is not expected).
- **Difficulty with strategies for learning language and using language to learn.** Demonstrates unusual learning strategies for age level, such as either too much reliance on imitation (e.g., signs of echolalia) or inability to imitate the actions of others. Shows little interest in using language to learn more about language and the world (e.g., does not ask "What's that?" questions early, or "Why?" questions, which become prevalent for most children around age 4 or 5).
- **Short attention span for language-related activities.** Shows little interest in sitting with an adult and looking at a book while naming and talking about the pictures or in communicating with peers.

SOURCE: From N. W. Nelson (1998).

weaker learning environment, lowered expectations, and segregation of children in minority groups, particularly those of low socioeconomic status. However, sometimes the added boost of a year in a language-based developmental kindergarten program can provide a child with the language skills needed to be successful.

Language and Communication Disorders in the School Years   If children have not been identified prior to elementary school, teachers become the primary source of referral. Children's language disorders, however, are not always apparent to teachers. Whereas misarticulations, pronoun substitutions, and morphological immaturies are relatively easy to identify, later forms of language development, such as more complicated syntactic structures and language comprehension, are more difficult (Nelson, 1998). Damico and Oller (1980) suggest the following criteria for identifying elementary-aged children who may need to be referred for a speech/language disorder:

- *Linguistic nonfluency.* Disruption of speech production by a disproportionately high number of repetitions, unusual pauses, and excessive use of hesitation forms.

- *Revision.* Breakup of speech production by numerous false starts or self-interruptions; multiple revisions are made as if the child keeps coming to a dead end in a maze.
- *Delays before responding.* Pauses of inordinate length following communication attempts initiated by others.
- *Nonspecific vocabulary.* The use of expressions such as *this, that, then, he,* or *over there* without making the referents clear to the listener; also, the overuse of all-purpose words such as *thing, stuff, these,* and *those.*
- *Inappropriate responses.* The child's utterances appear to indicate that the child is operating on an independent discourse agenda, not attending to the prompts or probes of the adult or others.
- *Poor topic maintenance.* Rapid and inappropriate changes in the topic without providing transitional clues to the listener.
- *Need for repetition.* Requests for multiple repetitions of an utterance without any indication of improvement in comprehension.

Language is critical in shaping cognitive development, and children with communication disorders experience many academic problems.

Because language is critical in shaping cognitive development, students with communication disorders experience numerous academic problems in school. They can experience developmental problems in any of the following cognitive areas: metacognitive skills, placing concepts in a hierarchy, problem-solving skills, word-retrieval skills, attention, memory, and performing formal operational thought in adolescence (Larson & McKinley, 1987). Speech and language problems often coexist with reading problems and adversely affect the student's ability to understand and use language in all academic subjects. A child with a receptive language problem may have difficulties with listening comprehension that are severe enough to interfere with the child's ability to acquire content information. A student could also have expressive language difficulties resulting in an inability to verbalize thoughts and knowledge either orally or in writing. Ensuing poor performance, on tests and in class, may lead to gross underestimations of the child's learning ability.

Language is also the primary vehicle for understanding oneself and others. It is not surprising that many students with communication disorders also experience social interaction problems because they do not understand or use nonverbal communication; do not adhere to conversational rules (e.g., turn-taking); cannot shift conversational style according to the social context; do not use effective listening skills; and cannot express their negative feelings in a nonabrasive manner (Larson & McKinley, 1987). During adolescence in particular, communication disorders persist across all domains, resulting in a "continuum of failure" in academics, peer relationships, and personal skills (Larson & McKinley, 1995, p. 64). The following was noted by Stephens (1985):

> There is strong evidence now . . . that many young language impaired children will continue to encounter difficulties in acquiring more advanced language skills in later years and these problems will be manifested in both social and academic realms. Thus children's understanding of figurative language affects both their ability to use slang correctly with peers and their ability to recognize metaphors that appear in language arts or English literature texts. (p. v)

For children with communication disorders, the classroom teacher and speech pathologist are responsible for developing activities that encourage communication skills in the classroom. It is essential that children use specific skills in natural settings with peers so that newly learned communication skills can *generalize;* that is, children should be able to independently apply what they learn to new situations. The classroom teacher can integrate the

SOURCE: Robin L.
Sachs/Photo Edit.

Children with communication disorders may experience problems with peer relations and social interactions.

development of learning strategies into reading, written expression, and content areas. It is also important for all who work with these children to model effective communication skills.

Attention Deficit Hyperactivity Disorder

Attention deficit hyperactivity disorder (ADHD) is a commonly diagnosed behavior disorder affecting 3 to 5 percent of school-age children (National Institutes of Health, 1998). ADHD is characterized by developmentally inappropriate levels of activity, concentration, distractibility and impulsivity. ADHD is perhaps the most frequent reason why children are referred for behavioral problems to guidance clinics. ADHD is more frequent in boys than in girls. This gender difference may be due to the fact that ADHD is more often associated with aggressive behavior in boys (Barkley, 1998).

There are many myths and misconceptions about people with ADHD. Some of these views are summarized in Table 6.5. ADHD is assumed to have a neurobiological basis, and it is diagnosed according to the criteria established by the American Psychiatric Association in the *Diagnostic Statistical Manual of Mental Disorders* (DSM–IV, 1994). As described in Figure 6.3, the DSM–IV provides indicators for each of the three major characteristics: inattention, impulsivity, and hyperactivity. These indicators need to be present before the age of 7 and in more than one setting (e.g., home, school, etc.). Also, there needs to be clear evidence of a significant impairment in academic or social functioning, and these problems are not explained by other mental disorders (e.g., mood disorder, anxiety disorder, etc.). Many children exhibit some of these behaviors at one time or another. A distinction between *expected* and *excessive* levels of attention, impulse control, and activity is made by a qualified professional, such as a child psychologist, child psychiatrist, or pediatric neurologist. A trained evaluator uses multiple measures and collects information about the child from teachers, parents, the child, and a pediatrician.

Children with attention deficit disorder tend to be abnormally inattentive, impulsive, and hyperactive, exhibiting characteristics presumed to have a neurobiological basis.

Table 6.5   Misconceptions about Attention Deficit Hyperactivity Disorder (ADHD)

Myth	Fact
All children with ADHD are hyperactive.	Some children with ADHD exhibit no hyperactivity and are classified as predominantly inattentive.
ADHD is a fad of recent times, with little to support it.	Reports of ADHD go back to the mid nineteenth century. There is now an established research base on ADHD.
ADHD is primarily the result of minimal brain injury.	In most cases, there is no evidence of brain injury or damage. Most researchers believe that ADHD is the result of neurological dysfunction, which is related to hereditary factors.
Using drugs for ADHD can easily turn children into drug abusers.	There is no evidence that the use of drugs to treat ADHD leads directly to drug abuse. However, the use of prescribed drugs needs to be carefully monitored.
Because students with ADHD react strongly to stimulation, their learning environments need to be unstructured to take advantage of their natural learning styles.	Most researchers suggest a highly structured classroom for students with ADHD, especially in the early stages of instruction.
ADHD disappears in adolescence.	Researchers now believe that childhood ADHD continues into adulthood.

SOURCE: Adapted from Hallahan & Kauffman (2000); National Institute of Mental Health (2000).

Children with ADHD do not qualify for special education simply on basis of their label. Decisions regarding educational needs and placement are made on an individual basis. Some children are found to be severely affected and are served by special education under the category of "other health impaired," because it includes "chronic or acute health problems that result in limited alertness, which adversely affects educational performance" (Fowler, 1992, p. 65). Other children with ADHD qualify for special education because they have a primary disability in one of the other categories. The numbers of children with learning disabilities (LDs) and emotional or behavioral disorders (BDs) who also have attention deficit/hyperactivity disorder is staggering—as many as 20 percent of LD and 47 percent of BD (Silver, 1990; Forness, Swanson, Cantwell, Guthrie, & Sena, 1992). Researchers in the field of giftedness have suggested that some characteristics are shared between children with ADHD and those who are gifted.

Onset of ADHD   Barkley (1998) identified a number of factors associated with the early emergence and persistence of ADHD. These factors include (1) a family history of ADHD; (2) maternal smoking and/or alcohol consumption, and poor maternal health during pregnancy; (3) single parenthood; (4) low parental educational levels; (5) poor infant health or developmental delays; (6) early emergence of high activity level and demandingness in infancy; and (7) critical/directive maternal behavior in early childhood (p. 188). In a longitudinal study of children from birth to 10 years of age, Carlson, Jacobvitz, and Sroufe (1995)

A child having problems with *inattention* often:

- Fails to give close attention to details or makes careless mistakes in schoolwork, work, or other activities

- Has difficulty sustaining attention in tasks or play activities

- Does not seem to listen when spoken to directly

- Does not follow through on instructions and fails to finish schoolwork, chores, or routines (not due to oppositional behavior or failure to understand instructions)

- Has difficulty organizing tasks or activities

- Avoids, dislikes, or is reluctant to engage in tasks that require sustained mental effort (such as schoolwork or homework)

- Loses things necessary for tasks or activities

- Is easily distracted by extraneous stimuli

- Is forgetful in daily activities (pp. 83–84)

A child with problems in *impulse control* often:

- Blurts out answers before questions have been completed

- Has difficulty awaiting his or her turn

- Interrupts or intrudes on others (e.g., butts into conversations or games) (p. 84)

A child experiencing *hyperactivity* often:

- Fidgets with hands or feet or squirms in seat

- Leaves seat in classroom or in other situations in which remaining seated is expected

- Runs about or climbs excessively in situations in which it is inappropriate (in adolescents or adults, may be limited to subjective feelings of restlessness)

- Has difficulty playing or engaging in leisure activities quietly

- Talks excessively

- Acts as if "driven by a motor" and cannot remain still (p. 84)

FIGURE 6.3

DSM Indicators of Inattention, Impulsivity, and Hyperactivity

SOURCE: DSM-IV (1994).

concluded that other than hyperactivity itself, the strongest factors associated with ADHD behaviors and the change or maintenance of those behaviors were single parenthood, level of social support for the parent, and an intrusive parenting style. Thus, it seems that a number of environmental factors may serve to maintain ADHD-type behaviors.

By the preschool years, children with ADHD present many challenges to their caregivers. Their behavior is described by parents as restless, always on the go, acting as if driven by a motor, and frequently climbing on and getting into things (Barkley, 1998). These children are more likely than typical children to suffer accidental injuries because of their impulsive behavior and thus require close monitoring and supervision. Noncompliance is common among children with ADHD, and at least 30 percent to 60 percent are actively defiant (Barkley, 1998). Mothers of children with ADHD are more likely to give far more commands, directions, criticism, supervision, and punishment than mothers of typical preschoolers (Barkley, 1998; Battle & Lacey, 1972; Campbell, 1990; Cohen & Minde, 1981, cited in Barkley, 1998). Difficulties with toilet training, sleep problems, and speech and/or motor delays that many ADHD children experience put further strain on the parents of children with ADHD. Parents of preschool ADHD children report much more stress in their life than do mothers of normal preschoolers or mothers of older ADHD children (Fischer, 1990; Mash & Johnston, 1982, 1983, cited in Barkley, 1998).

Is the prevalence of ADHD in children increasing? According to the National Institutes of Mental Health (2000) the answer to this question is not known at this time. It is clear that the number of children identified with this problem has increased over the last decade. However, this increase can be attributed to greater media interest, heightened consumer awareness, and the availability of effective treatments. Other countries are also reporting increases in the prevalence of ADHD in young people (NIMH, 2000).

ADHD in the School Years   Formal education presents a number of significant challenges to the child with ADHD. The ability to sit still, attend to instruction, inhibit impulsive behavior, and follow instructions can prove to be extremely difficult. Socially, children with ADHD find it difficult to cooperate with others, share, play well, and interact pleasantly with their peers.

Children with ADHS often experience problems with memory, problem-solving skills, metacognition regulation, and peer relations.

Children with ADHD also may experience problems similar to those experienced by children with learning disabilities. They may have cognitive difficulties associated with memory, due to deficits in attention and problem-solving skills. They also may have difficulties using inhibitory controls to lead them through cognitive problem solving, causing an underutilization of problem-solving strategies and lower metacognitive regulation. Academic achievement is adversely affected, with difficulties observable in reading, writing, and math (Evans, Pelham, & Grudberg, 1994–95). Some children exhibit one or more difficulties in psychosocial development, such as aggression, poor peer relationships, low frustration threshold, or low self-esteem (Campbell & Werry, 1986; Evans, Pelham, & Grudberg, 1994–95).

By middle childhood there is also an emerging pattern of social rejection of children with ADHD because of poor social skills. The tendency for the child with ADHD to be overly active, exhibit vocal noisiness, and to touch and manipulate objects more than is normal can be aversive to others. Because of social rejection and academic failure, many children with ADHD may develop depression and a general feeling of incompetence. Many children with ADHD will develop an accompanying psychiatric, academic, or social disorder by adolescence. According to a leading expert on ADHD, approximately 40 to 60 percent may develop oppositional defiant disorders, 25 to 40 percent may develop conduct disorder and antisocial behavior between ages 7 and 10, and 20 to 35 percent may develop a reading disorder (Barkley, 1998). A very small proportion of individuals with ADHD also

SOURCE: Ellen B. Senisl/
Photo Researchers, Inc.

Children with ADHD often need assistance in many academic areas.

have a rare disorder called Tourette's syndrome. These disorders are discussed when we examine moderate prevalent categories.

Although it is often assumed that young people will outgrow their symptoms, many do not. When compared to typical adolescents, students with ADHD were more likely to have failed a grade in school (29 percent versus 10 percent), to have been suspended (46 percent versus 15 percent), or to have been expelled from school (10 percent versus 1 percent). Levels of academic achievement as measured by standardized achievement tests were significantly below normal for adolescents with ADHD in the areas of math, reading, and spelling (Barkley, 1998). Estimates indicate that up to 80 percent of youths with ADHD will continue to display symptoms of the disorder to a significant degree during adolescence and young adulthood (Barkley, 1998); however, there is a decline in the levels of hyperactivity and improvement in ability to attend and control impulsivity (Hart, Lahey, Loeber, Applegate, & Frick, 1995). Despite these improvements, new issues arise in adolescence to further exacerbate the difficulties already being experienced. These issues include identity formation, peer group acceptance, dating, and physical development (Ross & Ross, 1976).

Children with ADHD have shown behavioral and academic improvement when a **multimodal approach** is used (Fowler, 1992). Such an approach combines educational support, psychological counseling, behavioral management at school and home, and medical management that typically involves psychostimulants, such as Ritalin, Cylert, and Dexedrine. Given the fact that many children with ADHD take medication, an accurate diagnosis is crucial. It is also crucial that the classroom teacher be informed of any medication a student is taking and be aware of possible side effects. Adjustments in dosage may be necessary when side effects adversely impair the child's performance. The use of stimulants to treat ADHD remains controversial. The Focus on Research box presents current information on the use of stimulants and their effects on children with ADHD.

Since many attention deficit disorder children take medication, it is imperative that classroom teachers be informed of such medication and be aware of possible side-effects.

Focus on Research

Are Stimulants Effective in Treating Children with ADHD?

It is natural for teachers and parents to be concerned about the effects Ritalin and other stimulants have on children. Some worry about their side effects and long-term consequences. Many parents believe that stimulant medication can lead to drug addiction and substance abuse. Another debate is whether stimulants are prescribed unnecessarily for too many children.

According to the U.S. National Institutes of Health (2000), stimulant medications are the most thoroughly studied of all drugs used to treat children with psychiatric disorders. Stimulant use in the United States has increased substantially over the last 25 years. Numerous short-term studies have established the safety and efficacy of these medications for alleviating the symptoms of ADHD. Drug treatments are most effective when combined with intensive behavioral interventions. Careful management of medication is important when treating children with ADHD. Some children may experience insomnia and decreased appetite, especially in the stages of use. Stimulant medication can also become addictive if abused by adolescents and adults.

Although little information is available on the long-term effects of stimulants, there is no evidence that careful medical use is harmful for children. When stimulant medications are taken as prescribed, they do not lead to substance abuse problems or to addiction when children are older. In fact, the evidence appears to be the opposite. Stimulants help many children to focus and to be more successful at school, home, and play. Avoiding negative experiences early in development may actually prevent addiction and other emotional problems later on. If ADHD is left untreated, young people with ADHD are a greater risk for later alcohol or substance abuse. In a study funded by the National Institutes of Mental Health and the National Institute on Drug Abuse, boys with ADHD who were treated with stimulants were less likely to abuse drugs and alcohol when they got older (NIMH, 2000).

It is important to point out that there are conflicting research findings, and more research is needed to understand the effects of stimulant medication on children. However, most experts agree that stimulant medication is an effective treatment for children with ADHD when carefully supervised and combined with intensive behavioral treatments.

SOURCE: National Institute of Mental Health (2000).

Protective Factors for Children with High-Incidence Disabilities

Thus far, our discussion of children with developmental delays and disabilities has focused on risk factors in their lives. The Focus on Development box summarizes these risk factors at different stages of development. In Chapter 2, we discussed the concept of resiliency—the ability to overcome adversity and to achieve positive outcomes. As described in the Focus on Research box on page 338, longitudinal research on children with developmental disabilities has identified several protective factors in their lives. This research has taught us many important lessons about children with high-incidence disabilities and disorders. First, the probability and severity of developmental delays and disabilities are not the same for all children. The effects of many biological risk factors (maternal smoking, premature birth, perinatal

Focus on Development

Summary of Risk Factors Associated with High-Incidence Disabilities in Children

Prenatal Period	Perinatal Period	Postnatal Period
Chromosomal abnormalities	Anoxia	Cerebral trauma
Inborn errors of metabolism	Congenital defects	Encephalitis
Harmful drugs	Disorders of delivery	Micronutrient deficiencies
Nutritional deprivation	Low birth weight	Toxic substances
Maternal infections	Infections	Family dysfunction
Metabolic disorders	Metabolic disorders	Parental mental illness
Radiation	Intracanal hemorrhage	Parental substance abuse
Toxic agents	—	Child abuse

SOURCE: Adapted from Werner (1999).

complications, etc.) diminish with the passage of time. Second, there are large individual differences among children with developmental disabilities. Developmental outcomes for most risk factors depend on the quality of care these children receive, as well as their own competencies, self-esteem, and temperamental dispositions. Most important, it emphasizes the role of teachers, psychologists, counselors, and other caring adults in the lives of these children. Supportive teachers and mentors at school can play an *enabling* role in children's lives and help reduce the negative effects of childhood disabilities and disorders.

Developmental outcomes for children with disabilities depend on the quality of care these children receive, as well as their own competencies, self-esteem, and temperamental dispositions.

Giftedness

Young people in this category have been identified for an *ability* rather than a *disability*. Many different terms are used to describe individuals who have unique talents or gifts, including genius, creative, gifted, and talented. Since 1970, the federal government has adopted five definitions of giftedness. The latest definition (1993) was as follows:

> Children and youth with outstanding talent perform or show the potential for performing at remarkable high levels of accomplishment when compared with others of their age, experience, or environment. These children or youth exhibit high performance capacity in intellectual, creative, and/or artistic areas, and unusual leadership capacity or excel in specific academic fields. They require services or activities not ordinarily provided by the schools. Outstanding talents are present in children and youth from all cultural groups, across all economic strata, and in all areas of human endeavor. (U.S. Department of Education, 1993)

Although the federal government offers a definition of giftedness to guide school practices, there is no federal law requiring specific educational services for students with special gifts or talents.

Focus on Research

Beating the Odds

One of the pioneering studies of childhood resilience was conducted by Emmy E. Werner and Ruth Smith (1982) on the Hawaiian island of Kauai. They followed the development of 698 infants from their birth in 1955 through their early thirties. Approximately half of the infants grew up in poverty, and one of six was diagnosed with a physical or mental handicap before the age of 2. By age 10, two-thirds of the high-risk infants had developed serious learning or behavioral problems. Twenty-two of these children (13 males and 9 females) had been diagnosed with a learning disability, which included ADHD in this study. By grade 12, most of this group had a history of poor academic performance and serious underachievement. At ages 17 and 18, they also scored significantly lower than their peers on measures of socialization and responsibility, achievement motivation, and self-assurance. Only one in four of the children diagnosed as learning disabled showed a more positive profile by age 18. These young people attributed their successful adaptation to the "sustained emotional support of family members, peer friends, or elders who bolstered their self-esteem" (p. 21). In contrast, most of the other teens with learning disabilities stated that special education teachers, counselors, and mental health professions were of "little help."

In the course of following these individuals into adulthood, the researchers made some interesting discoveries. By adulthood, the life course of individuals with childhood learning disabilities had significantly improved. No one was unemployed or dependent on public assistance. As adolescents, roughly two-thirds of the sample had a delinquency record or a serious mental health problem. At age 32, less than 10 percent had criminal records or persistent mental health problems. And by age 40, three out of four individuals with childhood learning disabilities were judged to be making an "adequate to good" adaptation to the demands of work, marriage, and family life (p. 21). There were several different clusters of protective factors operating in the lives of these individuals:

Gifted and talented children are identified in three ways: high IQ scores, high academic achievement, and teacher nomination.

The majority of children with special gifts and talents served in schools are the academically gifted. In most states, the criteria for **giftedness** require a minimal IQ score (usually 130) and above-average academic achievement (usually 2 years above grade level). In some states, children have been identified through nonstandardized methods, such as classroom teacher nomination and observation of outstanding skills and talents. By expanding identification practices beyond standardized intelligence and achievement tests, schools are including more children from culturally and linguistically diverse backgrounds. They are also including children with other disabilities, particularly those with learning disabilities. Some children are both gifted and learning disabled. They tend to be highly intelligent but have a specific learning disability in one academic area coupled with poor organizational skills (Van Tassel-Baska, 1992). It is estimated that approximately 3 percent to 5 percent of the school population in the United States falls into the category of gifted, but this number depends on the definition of gifted used (Hallahan & Kauffman, 2000).

Origins of Giftedness As with other types of exceptionalities, both genetic and environmental factors play a role in the development of giftedness. In a recent review of this

- Cluster 1 included temperamental characteristics of the individual that helped him or her to elicit positive responses from a variety of caring persons: parents, teachers, friends, spouses, and coworkers.

- Cluster 2 included special skills and talents as well as the motivation to use efficiently whatever abilities they had; faith that the odds could be overcome; realistic educational and vocational plans; and regular chores and domestic responsibilities assumed as children and teenagers.

- Cluster 3 included characteristics and caregiving styles of parents, especially the mother, that reflected competence and fostered self-esteem in their offspring, and structures and rules in the household that gave their children a sense of security.

- Cluster 4 consisted of supportive adults who fostered trust and acted as gatekeepers for the future. Among these "surrogate" parents were grandparents, elder mentors, youth leaders, and members of church groups.

- Cluster 5 consisted of openings of opportunities to major life transitions—from high school to the workplace, from civilian to military life, from single to married status and parenthood—that put the life trajectories of the majority of individuals with learning disabilities on the path to successful adult adaptation.

It is unfortunate that this list of protective factors does not include schooling experiences. These findings underscore the important role schools need to play in fostering self-esteem and efficacy, creating supportive relationships, engendering a sense of security and trust, developing competencies, and providing new opportunities for the future. Werner and Smith's study of Kauaian children teaches us that a substantial number of children with developmental disabilities can "beat the odds" when they have various protective factors from which they can draw.

SOURCE: Adapted from Werner (1992) and Werner & Smith (1992).

research, Ellen Winner (2000) reports that there is some evidence to suggest that children with mathematical gifts show enhanced brain activity in their left hemisphere when asked to recognize faces, a task that is typically done in the right hemisphere. Also, people who are gifted in mathematics, visual arts, and music are disportionately left-handed. Studies also show that mathematically and musically gifted individuals have a more bilateral, symmetrical brain organization than usual. Other evidence suggests that giftedness in mathematics is associated with a disproportionate incidence of language-related learning disorders and with immune disorders. Taken together, studies suggest that giftedness in some areas may be due to atypical brain organization, which may in turn be due to testosterone effects on the brain during prenatal development.

Although this evidence of biological influences cannot be dismissed, it is important to recall our discussion of variations in intellectual abilities from Chapter 4. Researchers have not yet identified the genes associated with different cognitive abilities. Some researchers have argued that individuals with special gifts and talents are not necessarily genetically endowed. There is some evidence to suggest that giftedness in any domain is due to hard work or deliberate practice. For example, studies show that expertise in piano, violin, chess, bridge, and athletics are directly related to the amount of deliberate practice (Ericsson, Krampe, & Tesch-Romer, 1993). Benjamin Bloom (1985) showed that eminent adults did not achieve their level of talent without a long intensive period of training, which often began in early childhood with supportive and encouraging caregivers. However, Bloom's account also suggests that prior to intensive training, children demonstrated an usual ability in a particular area that teachers and parents recognized as special.

As suggested, a child's skills need to be recognized and supported. Numerous studies have identified ways in which the special talents of children are nurtured by their home environment. Parents of gifted children typically have high expectations for their children and model hard work and achievement themselves (Bloom, 1985; Csikszentmihalyi, Rathunde, & Walen 1993; Gardner, 1993). They also encouraged their children to explore and provided home activities related to their child's developing talent, but teaching was informal and occurred in a variety of settings. Later on, they would seek out teachers or formal learning opportunities to further develop their child's abilities. Overall, the home environment of children with special talents is stimulating, warm, supportive, directive, and rewarding, regardless of the child's ethnic or socioeconomic backgrounds (Hallahan & Kauffman, 2000; Winner, 2000).

The home environment plays an important role in the development of special talents.

Characteristics of Children with Special Gifts and Talents   Clark (1992) compiled a list of various characteristics found in children who are academically gifted. Each child shows some but not all of the characteristics in cognition, language, and affective domains listed in Figure 6.4. Both preschool and school-age students with a special gift or talent will be more advanced in a particular area than their agemates. They can also have strong verbal skills, superior intellectual abilities, and well-developed sensory awareness. Students with special gifts and talents may also be above average in adaptive behavior, leadership skills, and self-sufficiency. They also have a deep intrinsic interest to master the domain in which they are talented, and it is difficult to tear them away from the computer, the art center, or a math book. This intense drive needs to be nurtured, not destroyed. If reasonably challenged, most students with special gifts remain interested and engaged in school.

The peer relations of academically gifted students have been an issue of some concern. Although gifted students may spend more time alone developing their talents, they report a preference for being with others and having peer contact (Csikszentmihalyi et al., 1993). Although there are exceptions, they are well liked by their peers. They are sensitive to the feelings of others and concerned about interpersonal relations and moral issues. However, students who are profoundly gifted (IQs over 180) may experience social or emotional problems. Extreme levels of giftedness can lead to social isolation. Profoundly gifted children are known to hide their talents to increase their peer popularity (Winner, 2000).

Many gifted and talented students, especially girls and minorities, hide their talents to increase peer popularity.

As they enter adolescence, students who are academically gifted have qualities that help them cope with many of the challenges presented during this developmental period. Yet, they are vulnerable to some special difficulties. The social disadvantages that result from being perceived by peers and teachers as "different" can undermine their personal growth. For example, their preference for independent learning may be misinterpreted by teachers as "oppositional" and by peers as "elitist." Ethnic minorities, particularly males, tend to be underrepresented in classes for the gifted and talented. Once placed in gifted programs or advanced placement courses, minority students risk rejection from peers of the same ethnic background, as well as from white students and teachers who do not understand them. Many African American students hide their academic abilities by being the classroom clown, suppressing effort or dropping out (Ford, 1996). Strong negative social implications have also been documented in gifted girls, who are subject to conflicting gender-role expectations and stereotypes (Kerr, Colangelo, & Gaeth, 1988). Some evidence suggests that

Cognitive Characteristics

- Extraordinary quantity of information

- Unusual retentiveness

- Advanced comprehension

- Unusually varied interests and curiosity

- Ability to generate original ideas and solutions (pp. 38–39)

Language Characteristics

- Strong verbal skills

- Highly developed receptive language and written language

- Well-developed sensory awareness

- Vulnerable to "Cartesian split," "a lack of integration between mind and body" (p. 43)

Affective Characteristics

- An evaluative approach toward self and others

- Persistent, goal-directed behavior

- Unusual sensitivity to the expectations and feelings of others

- Heightened self-awareness, accompanied by feelings of being different

- Earlier development of an inner locus of control and satisfaction

- Unusual emotional depth and intensity

- High expectations of self and others, often leading to high levels of frustration with self, others, and situations

- Advanced level of moral judgment

- Advanced cognitive and affective capacity for conceptualizing and solving social problems (pp. 40–43)

SOURCE: After Clark (1992).

FIGURE 6.4

Clark's Characteristics of Giftedness

gifted girls are more likely than their male counterparts to suffer from low self-esteem, depression, and other psychosomatic symptoms (Gross, 1993).

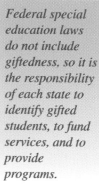

Federal special education laws do not include giftedness, so it is the responsibility of each state to identify gifted students, to fund services, and to provide programs.

Educational Concerns   As mentioned previously, the category of giftedness is unique because it is an exceptionality, not a disability. Since federal special education laws do not include giftedness, it is the responsibility of each state to identify students who are gifted and to fund services and programs for them. Currently, there is considerable debate concerning how best to serve children with special gifts and talents. One issue of concern is that most school systems focus on academically gifted and talented students. If students demonstrate superior artistic, musical, or athletic abilities, these talents tend to be nurtured and supported through existing physical education and arts programs offered by schools. When schools experience budget difficulties, these programs are generally the first ones to be "downsized" or eliminated altogether.

Most school systems do not test for academic giftedness until the third or fourth grades. Advocates of early intervention argue that preschoolers with special gifts need to receive educational programs appropriate for their abilities, especially if they are from low-income families or have disabilities (Gallagher & Gallagher, 1994). Another issue concerns testing and screening procedures. Standardized tests measure a narrow range of abilities, notably those needed to succeed in school. Teacher nominations may be biased due to cultural or gender stereotypes. As previously mentioned, ethnic minority students tend to be underrepresented in gifted programs. For example, African American students constitute 16 percent of the public school enrollment but make up only 8 percent of those enrolled in gifted programs (Hallahan & Kauffman, 2000). Girls, on the other hand, tend to be overrepresented in programs for the gifted and talented in elementary school, but underrepresented in mathematics and science courses for high-ability students at the high school or college levels

SOURCE: Jeff Greenberg/
Photo/Edit.

African American students represent 16 percent of the public school population but make up only 8 percent of those enrolled in gifted programs. Experts believe that this discrepancy is due to screening procedures and cultural stereotypes.

(Eccles, 1995). The Focus on Teaching box presents a set of multicultural and diversity issues that need to be considered in programs for academically gifted and talented students.

Once they are identified, there are a wide variety of plans for educating students with special needs and talents. Some schools offer **enrichment programs,** in which students are offered additional experiences without placing them in a higher grade. **Acceleration** is another approach that involves moving a student ahead of his or her age in one or more curriculum areas or grade levels. In some schools teachers who are certified in gifted education coteach and/or consult with classroom teachers. The Focus on Teaching box on page 346 shows various ways that content in social studies can be adjusted for middle school students who are gifted. Learning centers can be developed that include challenging, higher-order thinking skill activities. Some schools provide mentorship programs that pair a student with an adult who shares a common interest or vocation. In addition, secondary-level programs are offered in special honors courses, advanced placement classes, elective courses, and summer institutes that recruit students statewide.

Moderate Prevalence Categories

Classroom teachers can expect to have one or two children from moderate prevalence categories during their first few years in the classroom. They will encounter children classified as either having mental retardation or emotional or behavioral disorders.

Mental Retardation

Students with **mental retardation** have difficulties that occur across all areas, "learning, communication, social, academic, vocational, and independent living skills" (NICCYD, 1994c). They differ from their same-age classmates in their levels of intelligence and adaptive behavior. Adaptive behavior consists of those skills that enable a person to live an independent, socially productive life. Children with mental retardation have developmental delays in specific adaptive skills: "communication, self-care, home living, social skills, community use, self-direction, health and safety, functional academics, leisure and work" (Luckasson et al., 1992).

Students with mental retardation have difficulties that occur in all areas: learning, communication, social and vocational skills, and independent living skills.

Levels of intelligence and adaptive behavior vary, and children are usually classified as mild, moderate, or severe/profound retarded.* A child with mild mental retardation may be reading at the second-grade level and performing basic mathematical computations, whereas a child of the same age with severe/profound retardation may not be toilet-trained, may be unable to dress himself, and may use the vocabulary of a 1-year-old. Figure 6.5 contains a brief description of Reuben, an adolescent with mild retardation.

Factors Contributing to Mental Retardation Mental retardation has both genetic and environmental causes. As discussed in Chapter 2, genetic abnormalities such as Down's syndrome, fragile X syndrome, and Tay–Sachs disease result in mental retardation. Infections in the mother such as rubella (German measles), syphilis, and herpes simplex can cause mental retardation in their children. Fetal alcohol syndrome and low birth weight are also associated with mental retardation, as well as loss of oxygen during the birth process. Infections in the child, such as meningitis, encephalitis, and pediatic AIDS, are other causes of mental retardation. Additionally, poverty, family instability, and low parental education are associated with mental retardation. Currently, however, experts are able to pinpoint the causes of mental retardation in only about 10 to 15 of the cases (Hallahan & Kauffman, 2000).

*Although an alternative classification system has been proposed by Luckasson and colleagues (1992), these subclassifications are currently used in schools.

Focus on Teaching

Multicultural and Diversity Considerations in Education Programs and Services for the Gifted

1. What is the school district's philosophy of gifted education and definition of giftedness?

- In what ways are the philosophy and definition inclusive? Exclusive? To what extent are the strengths of black (and other minority) students represented in the definition?

- Does the gifted education program reflect community needs? Are students retrofitted to the program or is the program reflective of student needs?

- Have contemporary definitions of giftedness been adopted and/or modified for use with racially and culturally diverse students?

2. Is the gifted program reflective of community demographics?

- To what extent is there diversity relative to gender, race, and socioeconomic status?

- What discrepancies, if any, exist among the community, school, and gifted program demographic characteristics?

- Is there evidence of increasing diversity among professionals and students in the gifted programs?

3. Are there opportunities for continuing professional development in gifted and multicultural education?

- Are faculty and other school personnel encouraged and given opportunities by administrators to participate in workshops, conferences, university courses, and so forth? Do administrators attend such professional development training? Do personnel seek or willingly take advantage of these opportunities?

Characteristics of Children and Youths with Mental Retardation   Table 6.6 summarizes and compares the level of functioning of children classified as mildly, moderately, and severely retarded. As you can see, homogeneity within this category of exceptionality is more the exception than the rule. Since intellectual development and language development are closely related, language difficulties are found in most children with mild or moderate retardation. Other common characteristics among children with mental retardation are shared by children with other disabilities: inattention, memory problems, low self-esteem, external locus of control, and difficulties generalizing newly learned skills. Children with mental retardation also have difficulty making and keeping friends. Social problems are evident as early as preschool (Kasari & Bauminger, 1998).

- What are the indications of multicultural commitment? For instance, does a library exist for teachers and students that contains up-to-date multicultural resources (e.g., newsletters, journals, books)?

4. Are assessment practices equitable?

- Are the measures used valid and reliable for the student population?

- What biases exist relative to the selection process?

- How are instruments administered (individually or in a group)?

- Which instruments appear to be most effective at identifying the strengths of minority students?

- Is a combination of qualitative and quantitative assessment practices used? If so, is one type given preference or higher weight than the other?

- What are the primary purposes of assessment?

- Are personnel trained to administer and interpret test results?

- In what ways are students' learning styles accommodated relative to test administration and instructions?

- To what extent are students' home language, culture, and background reflected in the tests?

- Are tests biased in favor of verbal students, higher SES students, white students?

SOURCE: After Ford (1996)

Our knowledge of developmental issues in adolescents with mental retardation is minimal, because the focus has been on programming needs rather than on developmental processes (Rowitz, 1988). As a group, these adolescents need assistance in socialization, personal skills, vocational preparation, transition into the community, independent adult living, and functional math and reading skills (Drew, Hardman, & Logan, 1988).

Educational Programs for Students with Mental Retardation   Educational programs differ by the severity of the mental retardation. When children with mental retardation are placed in the regular classroom, teachers collaborate with special educators, speech language therapists, occupational and physical therapists, and vocational education teachers

Focus on Teaching

Content Adjustments for Middle School Social Studies

The student will

- Master the skills of research techniques.

- Demonstrate effective communication skills.

- Practice the art of inquiry.

- Learn to communicate effectively and respect the opinions of others.

- Gain an understanding of cause and effect and chronological development of history.

- Demonstrate knowledge of current events and how they relate to life.

- Locate and show relative positions and size of the world's countries.

- Appreciate cultural diversity through the cumulative study of peoples and lands.

- Provide for the development of human potential through goal setting.

- Prepare a research paper.

- Provide for the application of classroom-acquired information to real life.

- Enrich the social studies program through use of psychology, anthropology, sociology, and economics. (pp. 12–13)

SOURCE: From the North Carolina Department of Public Instruction (1992).

to provide support. Areas that may be in need of support are as follows (Luckasson et al., 1992):

- Functional academics (e.g., balancing a checkbook, ordering from a menu, planning a bus trip, reading signs).
- Home-living skills (e.g., laundering clothes, cooking meals).
- Self-care skills (e.g., toileting, grooming, hygiene).
- Communication—understanding and expressing verbally (e.g., sign language, spoken word, written word) and nonverbally (e.g., facial expression, touch, gestures).

Reuben Murray is a gregarious 18-year-old whose interests include weight lifting, listening to music with his friends, and "hanging out at the mall." In addition to attending high school, he has a part-time position as a bagger for a major grocery chain and participates in a monthly self-advocacy group for people with developmental disabilities.

Reuben is also a popular and frequent guest lecturer on the university circuit. Speaking to graduate-level students in the fields of special education and medicine, he readily shares his insights and experiences. During a recent presentation, when asked what makes a "good" teacher, Reuben replied, "They're the ones who help me so I can learn."

From the time he was 4 months old, Reuben has received special education services. These began with an early developmental program that focused on stimulation activities for implementation in the home. For the past few years, Reuben and his parents have been concerned with transition issues—preparing Reuben for independent living and working in the community. On graduation, one of his goals is to move from his parents' home and "live with two or three other guys." Together with The Arc, a parent-professional advocacy organization, his parents are helping him attain this goal.

Reuben has Down's syndrome, also known as Trisomy #21, a chromosomal condition that occurs in 1 of every 800 to 1,000 children who are born in our country each year. It is caused by the production of an additional #21 chromosome.

FIGURE 6.5

Reuben

Emotional and Behavioral Disorders

Children and youths with emotional and behavioral disorders are perhaps the most problematic group of exceptional learners in the classroom. The U.S. Department of Education estimates that between 1 percent and 2 percent of the school-age population exhibits serious and persistent emotional or behavioral problems (U.S. Department of Education, 1997). However, some experts believe that at least 6 percent to 10 percent of children and youths fall into this category (Kauffman, 1994). Children with emotional or behavioral disorders have difficulty in any of the following areas:

- Hyperactivity (short attention span, impulsiveness)
- Aggression/self-injurious behavior (acting out, fighting)
- Withdrawal (failure to initiate interaction with others, retreat from exchanges or social interaction, excessive fear or anxiety)
- Immaturity (inappropriate crying, temper tantrums, poor coping skills)
- Learning difficulties (academically performing below grade level) (NICCYD, 1994d, p. 1)

Most of the problems children with emotional or behavioral disorders experience are externalizing problems, such as aggression or argumentation; however, some experience internalizing problems, such as depression, anxiety, and withdrawal.

The primary characteristic of children with **emotional or behavioral disorders** is that their psychosocial development differs significantly from their same-age peers. For example, children with emotional and behavioral problems may be aggressive, defiant, withdrawn, or antisocial. All children have difficulties with their emotions and socialization at times, but these children experience them much more frequently and more intensely.

Many children with emotional and behavioral disorders have also been classified into subtypes according to diagnostic criteria in the DSM–IV (American Psychiatric Association, 1994). Figure 6.6 lists the classifications, subtypes, and major characteristics in affective, cognitive, and physical development. Remember, these characteristics are a compilation of the various intraindividual needs found in children defined by this category. Rarely will an individual exhibit most or all of the traits presented.

Table 6.6   Comparison of Levels of Retardation

Characteristics	Mild**	Moderate	Severe/Profound
I.Q.	50–70	35–50	Below 35
Mental age range*	7–11 yrs.	2–7 yrs.	6 mo.–2 yrs.
Cognitive level	Concrete operational	Preoperational	Sensory motor
Primary areas in need of support	Functional academics Communication	Home-living Self-care skills Communication	Self-care skills*** Communication

*Mental age score tells us that a child can perform tasks that most children can accomplish at a particular age level. It does not tell us anything about emotional, physical, and social needs. For example, a 12-year-old child with a mental age of 6.5 can be expected to have the potential for learning exhibited in most 6-year-olds. However, he or she will not be similar to a 6-year-old in his or her psychosocial needs, interest level, or physical development.

**The majority of children with mild mental retardation share common areas of difficulty with children with learning disabilities and emotional or behavioral disorders (Hallahan & Kauffman, 1977; Heward & Orlansky, 1988; Strichard & Gottlieb, 1982).

***Since the majority of children with severe/profound mental retardation have multiple disabilities (including significant health and physical impairments) they require intensive levels of support in these areas.

Most of the problems children with emotional and behavioral disorders experience are **externalizing problems.** Their actions are overt; they may be argumentative, aggressive, antisocial, destructive, oppositional, or verbally abusive. However, some children with emotional and behavioral disorders exhibit **internalizing problems.** Internalizing behavior problems include depression, withdrawal, anxiety, obsession (repetitive and persistent thoughts), and compulsion (repetitive, ritualistic actions). Since internalizing behaviors often go undetected, children with internalizing behavior problems are not identified as frequently as those with externalizing, disruptive, antisocial behaviors.

Contributing Factors to the Development of Emotional and Behavioral Disorders

As with other exceptionalities, there is no single cause for emotional and behavioral disorders. Contributing factors also depend on the particular disorder. Children with **schizophrenia** frequently, but not always, show signs of neurological abnormalities. **Tourette's syndrome,** which is characterized by multiple motor and verbal tics, is also related to a neurological disorder. Other emotional and behavioral disorders are more complex and may involve home, school, peer, and cultural influences, as well as biological factors, such as the child's temperament (Hallahan & Kauffman, 2000).

The home environment may also play a role in the development of emotional and behavioral disorders. As will be discussed in later chapters, parents who are lax in their discipline, inconsistent in dealing with misbehavior, or abusive tend to have children who are aggressive and antisocial. Chaotic or violent homes are particularly likely to place children at risk for emotional or behavioral problems. However, it is important to keep in mind that children with emotional or behavioral disorders may influence their parents as much as their parents influence them. Also, children react to their family environment in their own unique way. Not every child who is physically abused becomes aggressive or antisocial. Generally, parents of children with emotional and behavioral disorders want their children

Subtypes of Emotional or Behavioral Disorders	Possible Characteristics
Externalizing Disorder Subtypes	
Conduct disorders	Violation of social norms at school, at home, and in the community. Includes impulsivity; overt aggression (e.g., fighting, destructive toward property); covert antisocial acts (e.g., lying, stealing); temper tantrums; defying others; destroying property; running away from home.
Oppositional defiant disorders	Argumentative with adults; external locus of control (e.g., blames others); loses temper easily; intentionally annoys others; is verbally abusive or vindictive. Often coexists with conduct disorders.
Internalizing Disorder Subtypes	
Anxiety disorders	Social withdrawal; excessive worries; nervousness; tension; overestimation of the probability/severity of a feared event and underestimation of what self or others can do; physical discomfort (e.g., headaches, stomachaches, dizziness); self-consciousness.
Depressive disorders	Social withdrawal; poor school performance; suicidal ideation; chronic fatigue; low energy level; hopelessness; self-blame; self-dislike; excessive guilt; difficulty with concentration; depressed energy level. Often coexists with anxiety disorders in adolescents. Many of these characteristics are demonstrated by children who are anorexic or bulimic.

FIGURE 6.6

Characteristics of Subtypes of Children with Emotional or Behavioral Disorders

Source: After Coleman (1992).

to behave appropriately. It is better to provide support services than to blame parents for their child's problem.

The development of most emotional and behavioral disorders, however, involves a complex set of home, school, peer, and cultural influences, as well as the child's own biological characteristics such as temperament. One of the most common and troubling problems among school-age populations is **conduct disorders,** characterized by overt aggression, or disruptive or antisocial behavior. Some estimates suggest that between 4 percent and 10 percent of children and adolescents exhibit conduct disorders (Offord & Bennett, 1994). The Focus on Research box describes the diagnosis and development of conduct disorders in children and their long-term impact.

It is important for educators to remember that the school environment is a contributing factor in the development of emotional and behavioral disorders. Children who enter schools with a specific disorder can become better or worse depending on their school experiences. The incidence of behavioral disorders in the Kauai study more than doubled between the ages of 10 and 18 years. Discipline practices that are too lax, inconsistent, rigid, or punitive can have a negative impact. Teachers are often inadequately prepared to work with these children in their classrooms. They may reward misbehavior with special attention, which can increase the likelihood the child will misbehave again for this attention,

Focus on Research

Diagnosis and Development of Childhood Conduct Disorders

Conduct disorders are among the most common diagnoses in mental health practice, with a prevalence of 4 percent to 10 percent among children and adolescents (Offord & Bennett, 1994). In order to be diagnosed with conduct disorder, a young person must manifest at least 3 of the following 15 symptoms within the last 12 months, with at least 1 occurring within the last 6 months (American Psychological Association [APA], 1994, cited in Clarizio, 1997):

I. **Aggression:** Bullies, threatens, intimidates, starts physical fights, uses a weapon that can harm others, has been physically cruel to people or animals, has stolen while confronting a victim, has forced sex on someone.

II. **Destruction of property:** Sets fires deliberately to cause serious damage; deliberately destroys property.

III. **Lying or theft:** Breaks into other's property; often cons others, lies to get things or avoids responsibility; often steals valuables without confrontation.

IV. **Serious violation of rules:** Often stays out late at night without permission, starting before age 13; has run away from home overnight at least twice; often plays hookey from school, starting before age 13.

Even though students with a conduct disorder diagnosis often experience significant difficulties in the classroom, they are frequently ineligible for special education support. A diagnosis of conduct disorder often automatically excludes a child from special education services (Forness, Kavale, & Walker, 1999). The reason for this exclusion is that services for students with serious emotional or behavioral disorders are served under the category of serious emotional disturbance (SED). The federal regulations for identifying children as qualifying for special education services as SED stipulate that the child must have a serious emotional disturbance and not merely social maladjustment. Because social maladjustment is not further defined by federal regulations, a psychiatric diagnosis of conduct disorder is frequently considered the operational definition for social maladjustment. Also, since recent Supreme Court decisions have made it more difficult to expel or suspend students identified as eligible for special education, schools may be more hesitant to classify students identified with conduct disorder as eligible for special education services (Forness et al., 1999).

There are two types of conduct disorder, based on the age of onset. When conduct disorder is diagnosed as childhood onset, it is characterized by neuropsychological abnormalities that disrupt the normal development of language, memory, and self-control. The result is a toddler with cognitive delays and a difficult, impulsive temperament (Clarizio, 1997). When conduct disorder is diagnosed as adolescent onset, it is thought that the adolescent engages in criminal activity to satisfy the desire for adult privileges. The adolescent mimics antisocial peers' delinquent behavior as an assertion of autonomy. With increasing age and adult privileges, lawbreaking typically declines (Clarizio, 1997).

A number of factors influence the development of conduct disorder. As was noted previously, age of onset has an impact on the course of development. While childhood onset is thought to result in long-term effects on the life course, adolescent onset conduct disorder is typically relatively short (Clarizio, 1997). Conduct disorder is three to four times more common in preadolescent boys than in preadolescent girls (Zoccolillo, 1993). However, females generally exhibit lower rates of violent behavior than males, with sexual behavior more likely to be the presenting problem for females. Also, conduct disorder has a significantly later onset in girls than in boys, with the average age of onset 13 years for girls as opposed to 7 years for boys. Early maturing females are most at risk, particularly if there is poor parental supervision. There also appears to be a link between intellectual performance and the development of conduct disorder. Moffitt (1990) found only a 1-point mean deficit in IQ points between adolescent delinquents and the general population, while a 17-point deficit was found for childhood onset conduct disorder offenders.

Researchers have also identified a pattern of development of conduct disorder. It begins with family variables that lead to aggressive behavior and hostility toward authority, followed by social rejection and school failure, and finally leading to deviant peer group membership. Family variables related to the development of antisocial behavior and later delinquency include harsh and inconsistent discipline, little positive parenting, and poor parental supervision of the child. These families are also characterized by a lack of reinforcement of prosocial behaviors and effective punishment for deviant behaviors, failure to set limits, and coercive parent–child interactions (Patterson, Capaldi, & Bank, 1991; Patterson, DeBaryshe, & Ramsey, 1989). The hypothesized results of this family context are children who are noncompliant and have undercontrolled behavior. Both of these characteristics are related to academic failure and rejection by members of the normal peer group. Rejection by the normal peer group and lax parental supervision have been associated with deviant peer group identification. The peer group is thought to provide the motivation, opportunity, attitudes, rationalizations, and opportunities to engage in antisocial behavior (Patterson et al., 1989).

To return to the discussion of resiliency, studies have examined protective factors in the lives of children with behavioral disorders. By age 10, 25 of the children in the Kauai Longitudinal Study (see pages 338–339) were diagnosed by clinical psychologists and child psychiatrists as having serious behavioral disorders that interfered with their school achievement. By high school graduation, this number had grown to 70 youths. Half of the males and one-third of the females in this group had records of juvenile offenses. By age 40, a third of the individuals with behavior disorders in childhood or adolescence had continuing problems, including employment and marital difficulties. However, a greater number were in stable marriages and jobs and were responsible citizens in their community. These individuals shared many protective factors. First, most had shown normal physical development in childhood, and few suffered from childhood illness. Second, they had higher mean scores on nonverbal measures of problem-solving abilities at age 10 than did youths having difficult adulthoods. Importantly, those young people who made a successful adaptation to adulthood grew up in homes where two parents were present, and their parents provide structure and rules for them to follow. However, the most significant turning point for the majority of these individuals was developing a relationship with a supportive friend or spouse (Werner, 1999).

Focus on Teaching

What I Learned from Dominick

After six years' experience as a special education teacher and having just completed a master's degree in counseling, I felt well prepared for my next challenge as a teacher. I was hired to teach the "Crisis Class," a class of 12 students identified as having severe behavior disorders. The students in the class came from six different school districts and were placed in the crisis class when they were unsuccessful in the programs for children with behavior disorders at their school.

All was going well, and then Dominick was placed in my class. He had been placed in my class after stealing the master key to all of the lockers at his middle school. He managed to pull this off despite the fact that there was a full-time assistant assigned solely to him. The first day he was scheduled to come to my class he refused to get out of his mother's car. The next day when he did come into the classroom he informed me, "I'll come here because I have to, but you can't make me do any work." And he was right.

There was a structure in place in the class whereby students could earn privileges through work completion, compliance with rules, and progress toward individual goals. Dominick wasn't interested. His first few days resulted in little work completion and much disruption in the class. I needed a different strategy. Dominick was very vocal about the fact that he didn't belong in my class or in the school. He really didn't fit in. He was of above-average intelligence, while most of the other students had some type of learning difficulty beyond their behavior disorder. Also, his family was wealthy, and most of the other students came from families with low socioeconomic status.

One day I asked Dominick what he missed most about his old school. He told me that he had been on the tennis team at his school and had been quite good. Being a part of the tennis team was what he missed the most. This knowledge became the key to Dominick's success in my class. I told Dominick (truthfully) that I had always wanted to learn how to play tennis and asked if he would be willing to give me some pointers. He agreed.

even if it is in the form of criticism or punishment. Also, it is easy to become irritated and frustrated with these children and unintentionally model negative behaviors (rejection, hostility, etc.) that they imitate. Children with emotional or behavioral disorders often become trapped in a negative spiral interaction in the classroom (Hallahan & Kauffman, 2000). As we saw with the Kauai study, a significant turning point in the lives of individuals with behavioral disorders was when they formed a supportive and caring relationship. The Focus on Teaching box describes a special educator's efforts to help a middle school student with a conduct disorder. The next section discusses some strategies for accommodating these students in the classroom.

Children with Emotional and Behavioral Disorders in the Classroom   As a group, children with emotional and behavioral disorders often experience rejection by children in the general classroom (Hollinger, 1987). Most children with emotional and behavioral disorders exhibit a lack of social-cognitive skills through hypersensitivity to social cues, misinterpretation of these cues, and inability to understand the consequences of their actions.

The next day we both brought our tennis rackets to school. However, to be able to give me my lesson, Dominick had to earn the morning break time by completing his work and earning the required number of points on his point sheet. Dominick was successful that morning for the first time. During the morning break, we went out to the parking lot of our school and Dominick was my tennis instructor. He told me what to do and I listened and followed his instructions. For 20 minutes Dominick was in control and had the power in our relationship. He also was better at something than I was, and I demonstrated my respect for his tennis skills. This was important for Dominick. He was seeking control in his environment. Virtually all control had been taken away from him at school because of his inappropriate behavior. I believe that it had also been a long time since he had experienced a positive interaction with an authority figure in a school setting. When we returned to the classroom, he was much more willing to receive instruction from me and to comply with the classroom routines, rules, and procedures. There were still difficult days, and Dominick had not suddenly been "cured." However, we had turned a corner. By the end of the school year Dominick was being successful in my class on a regular basis. He was not yet ready to return to his old school. However, he was making positive progress, which hadn't happened in a long time.

I learned a lot from Dominick about being a teacher. He taught me the importance of getting to know my students and forming a positive relationship with them *on their terms*. I needed to explore Dominick's interests and consider what he needed from me and the class environment, as opposed to what I needed from him. I knew that he was seeking power and control, however, by talking to him I was able to find an appropriate avenue to give him control, not just of the environment but, more important, of me. It's often difficult for teachers to surrender control to students. But, when the surrendering is done appropriately, the results can be amazing.

Even when children show improvements in their social skills, their peers may continue to reject them (Zaragoza, Vaughn, & McIntosh, 1991). This continual pattern of rejection suggests that the attitudes and perceptions of children without disabilities also need to be addressed.

Most children with emotional/behavioral disorders have a low-average to average range of intelligence, although some have above-average intelligence. Approximately two-thirds have difficulties in academic areas, and the rest perform at or above grade level (Steinberg & Knitzer, 1992). Most of these children are similar to children with specific learning disabilities in that both have a pattern of poor academic performance despite an average range of cognitive ability (Scruggs & Mastropieri, 1986). The majority of children with emotional and behavioral disorders have low reading levels. Cognitive problems include lack of attention, impulsivity, and external locus of control.

Some children with emotional or behavioral disorders also exhibit difficulties in language, which could account for delays and deficiencies in psychosocial development. Language skills that may present difficulties for some children are listening comprehension, following directions, expressing thoughts and feelings, and applying rules involving morphology and syntax (Camarata, Hughes, & Ruhl, 1988).

Many children with emotional or behavioral disorders struggle during their adolescence. Low reading levels continue to plummet as they mature. In high school, they are placed in remedial or low-track classes and tend to get below-average grades (Meadows, Neel, Scott, & Parker, 1994). They are at risk for multiple forms of school failure and psychosocial difficulties including depression and suicide, failing grades, school absenteeism, poor performance on minimum competency tests, dropping out of school, substance abuse, sex-related difficulties, and delinquency (Coleman, 1992; Denny, Epstein, & Rose, 1992).

It is imperative for people who work with emotionally or behaviorally disordered children to demonstrate prosocial behaviors, such as respect for diversity, self-control when frustrated, and effective interpersonal communication skills.

For children with emotional or behavioral disorders in general classrooms, classroom teachers collaborate with special educators, speech-language pathologists, and mental health professionals in addressing three major areas: management of behavior, teaching social and communication skills, and providing academic support. While using nontraditional management methods for reducing inappropriate behaviors, educators also teach prosocial skills and make accommodations for academic performance. Some successful interventions are:

- Modifying learning tasks to ensure success
- Developing learning strategies
- Providing clear and consistent expectations with resulting rewards and consequences
- Involving students in goal-setting and self-evaluation
- Giving frequent feedback on performance
- Using cooperative learning and peer tutoring to structure peer interaction
- Teaching social problem-solving skills
- Direct teaching of prosocial communication skills.

It is essential that people who work with children with emotional or behavioral disorders model prosocial actions themselves—demonstrating respect for diversity, self-control when frustrated, and effective interpersonal communication skills. Research by Jere Brophy and his colleagues (1986) has shown that classroom teachers who are effective with aggressive-disruptive children have developed a strong sense of self-efficacy. They are confident in their own ability to change these children. Kauffman and Wong (1991) agree.

> Teachers who maintain a high sense of self-efficacy tend to perceive their students as teachable and worthy of their attention and effort regardless of their students' low abilities and slow progress. These teachers do not perceive misbehaviors as intentional or threatening to their authority, nor do they expect more instances of disruptive student behavior. Instead, they are likely to seek challenge, persist in the face of slow student progress, and maintain an attitude of tolerance toward difficult students. Their successes in the classroom increase self-efficacy, which, in turn, makes them likely to succeed. (p. 231)

Summary of Moderate-Incidence Exceptionalities   Children who are members of moderate-incidence categories of exceptionality have fairly low placement rates in the general classroom when compared to the high prevalence disabilities. Level of severity plays a major factor in determining educational placement and levels of support. Children with emotional or behavioral disorders who are either mildly disruptive or exhibit internalizing disorders and those with mild mental retardation are generally placed in classrooms for most of the school day. Some schools integrate children with more intense needs by using paraprofessionals who give them individual help in the general classroom.

Children who spend most of their day in separate special classes have opportunities to interact with peers without disabilities in two major ways: reverse mainstreaming and partial participation. In **reverse mainstreaming,** students from the general classroom spend some time in the separate special classroom, interacting with children with disabilities in learning activities. **Partial participation** is the opposite situation, in which a student from the separate special classroom spends time in the general classroom engaged in activities modified to fit his or her abilities.

Low Prevalence Categories

Classroom teachers can expect to have at least one child in the first few years of teaching who has one of the following disabilities: severe and multiple disabilities, other health impairments, deafness or hearing impairment, physical disabilities, low vision or blindness, autism, traumatic brain injury, or deaf-blindness. These categories are summarized in the following sections.

Severe and Multiple Disabilities

Children with **severe and multiple disabilities** are characterized by two factors: they have concomitant disabilities—that is, they have two or more disabilities—and the extent of their disabilities is serious. For example, a child may have severe mental retardation and blindness, or severe emotional and behavioral disorders and physical disabilities. In most cases, children with severe and multiple disabilities are severely delayed in the areas of cognition, including adaptive behavior and language, and in physical development.

Other Health Impairments

Children with **other health impairments** have physical limitations that interfere with their learning. They vary according to the type of impairment, the level of severity, and whether the condition is chronic (lifelong) or acute (life-threatening, but short-lived). IDEA defines children with health impairments as "having limited strength, vitality, or alertness, due to chronic or acute health problems such as a heart condition, tuberculosis, rheumatic fever, nephritis, asthma, sickle cell anemia, hemophilia, epilepsy, lead poisoning, leukemia, or diabetes that adversely affect a child's educational performance" (sec. 300.5(7)).

Deafness or Hearing Impairment

These two groups of children—deaf and hard of hearing—differ according to the degree of hearing loss. Children who are *hard of hearing* have sufficient hearing to enable them to understand speech; many require amplification of speech through a hearing aid. Children who are *deaf* cannot hear or understand speech. The extent of the disability is also affected by three essential factors: type of hearing loss, the age of onset, and the degree of residual (intact) hearing (Diefendorf, Leverett, & Miller, 1994).

Physical Disabilities

Many *physical disabilities* result from damage to the central nervous system, either the brain or spinal cord. The extent and localization of brain damage determines the child's cognitive, language, social, and physical functioning. Damage to the central nervous system, whether it involves the brain or spinal cord, typically results in either paralysis or muscle deficiencies. Physical disabilities are either congenital or acquired. Congenital disorders are present at birth (e.g., clubfoot, "brittle bones syndrome"). Acquired disorders are either due to disease (e.g., poliomyelitis, bone tuberculosis), accident (e.g., spinal cord injury), or unknown causes.

Reverse mainstreaming involves bringing students from the general classroom into special education settings for part of the day; partial participation involves the opposite, bringing special education students into the general classroom for part of the day.

Deaf children cannot hear or understand speech, whereas hard-of-hearing children have sufficient hearing to understand speech given some form of speech amplification.

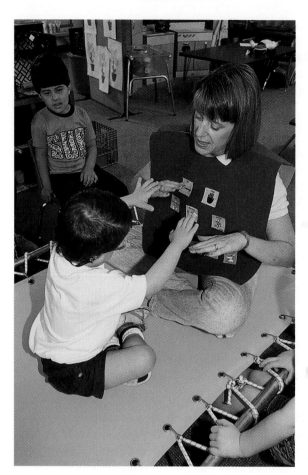

Children with severe and multiple disabilities need a highly specialized educational program.

Low Vision or Blindness

Children with *low vision* cannot read newsprint-size letters, even with corrective lenses. They do have some useful visual functioning, but they require adaptations such as optical and nonoptical aids and classroom accommodations. Children who are *blind* have either 20/200 vision (seeing at 20 feet what most people see at 200 feet), or a limited field of vision (20 degrees). These children need help in using whatever residual vision remains, while also receiving adaptations such as braille materials and/or auditory tapes.

Traumatic Brain Injury (TBI)

Traumatic brain injury is an acquired injury to the brain with either open or closed head injury that has a significant impact on learning. A child's learning difficulties may be permanent or temporary, depending on the course of recovery. Any of the following learning difficulties may be experienced by a child with TBI: "cognition; language; memory; attention; reasoning; abstract thinking; judgment; problem solving; sensory, perceptual, and motor abilities; psychosocial behavior; physical functions; information processing; and speech" (NICCYD, 1994e, p. 1). The severity and type of problem are determined by the location and extent of the brain injury.

Deaf-Blindness

Children with *deaf-blindness* have dual sensory impairments. Given the debilitating effects from hearing and vision impairments, these children have unique characteristics that separate them from those with multiple and severe disabilities. Hence, they are not categorized as severe and multiple but as deaf-blind.

The degree of integration into the general classroom depends on a child's level of cognitive development as well as the ability to communicate. For some of these children, reverse mainstreaming or partial participation will be their least restrictive environment (e.g., children with severe and multiple disabilities, deaf-blind, or low-functioning autism). For other children in low prevalence categories, the least restrictive environment will be full-time placement in the general classroom with or without a teaching assistant (e.g., children with high-functioning autism, traumatic brain injury, or health impairments).

Temple Grandin, despite a lifelong struggle with autism, earned a doctoral degree in animal science. Today she invents equipment for managing livestock and teaches at a major university. A woman of extraordinary accomplishments, she has also written several books on animal science, autism, and her own life.

Yet at 6 months old, Temple had many of the full-blown signs of autism. When held, she would stiffen and struggle to be put down. By age 2, it was clear that she was hypersensitive to taste, sound, smell, and touch. Sounds were excruciating. Wearing clothes was torture: the feel of certain fabrics was like sandpaper grating her skin. Constantly buffeted by overpowering sensations, she screamed, raged, and threw things. At other times, she found that by focusing intently and exclusively on one item—her own hand, an apple, a spinning coin, or sand sifting through her fingers—she could withdraw into a temporary haven of order and predictability.

As was customary at the time, a doctor advised that Temple be institutionalized. Her mother refused and placed her in a therapeutic program for children who were speech impaired. The classes were small and highly structured. Even though the program was not designed to treat autism, the methods worked for Temple. By age 4, she began to speak and by age 5 she was able to attend kindergarten in a regular school. Temple attributes her success to several key people in her life: her mother, who persisted in finding help; her therapist, who kept her from withdrawing into an inner world; and a high school teacher who helped transform her interest in animals into a career in animal science.

Temple's insights into the needs of animals, a strongly developed ability to think visually "in pictures," and an awareness of her own special needs led her to invent equipment that has helped both livestock and, remarkably, herself. After seeing a device used to calm cattle, she created a "squeeze machine." The machine provides self-controlled pressure that helps her relax. She finds that after using the squeeze machine, she feels less aggressive and less hypersensitive. With her love of animals and her personal sensitivity as a guide, Temple has also designed humane equipment and facilities for managing cattle that are used all over the world. Her unusually strong visual sense allows her to plan and design these complex projects in her head. She can precisely envision new, complex facilities and how various pieces of equipment fit together before she draws a blueprint.

Temple Grandin's story is a powerful affirmation that autism need not keep people from realizing their potential.

FIGURE 6.7

The Story of Temple Grandin

SOURCE: National Institute of Health, 1997.

Given the disability category and the extent of the child's needs, specialized equipment may also be crucial for the child's learning. Advances have been made in augmentative communication systems, adaptive devices, medical technology, and vision aides.

Autism

Emerging in childhood, **autism** is a neurological disorder affecting the functioning of the brain. Autism affects about one or two people in every thousand, and it is three to four times more common in boys than girls. However, girls with this disorder tend to have more severe symptoms and lower intelligence (National Institutes of Mental Health, 1997).

Autism affects a person's ability to communicate, form relationships, and respond appropriately to the environment. Children's affliction can vary from mild to severe forms of

Autism is a neurologically based disability affecting the brain. Approximately 70 percent of autistic children have some degree of mental retardation.

autism, with 70 percent having mental retardation as a concomitant disability (Mesibov, 1991). The term *high-functioning autism* is used to describe those children who are mildly affected and tend to be placed in general classrooms. Figure 6.7 on the previous page presents the story of Temple Grandin, a woman who began to show signs of autism at 6 months of age, but who earned a doctorate in animal science.

Many children with autism are highly sensitive to certain sounds, textures, tastes, and smells.

Despite the variation in abilities, intelligence, communication skills, and psychosocial development, three primary features are common to children with autism. They have deficits in communication, both verbal and nonverbal; problems with reciprocal social interactions; and a restrictive set of activities and interests. Some individuals with autism may become physically aggressive at times, and about half of all children diagnosed with autism remain mute throughout their lives (NIMH, 1997). Some children with autism are able only to parrot what they hear, a condition called *ecolahia*. As a result of brain abnormalities, many children with autism are highly attuned or even painfully sensitive to certain sounds, textures, tastes, and smells. Some children also develop fixations with specific objects, and some individuals with autism repeat certain actions over and over (i.e., flapping their hands, rocking, banging their heads). For some unexplained reason, they also like a lot of consistency in their environment, which can take the form of eating the same foods or becoming upset when a daily routine is changed.

Like the other exceptionalities discussed in this section, there is no known cure for autism. It is treated with a combination of early intervention, special education, family support, and, in some cases, medication. Intervention and educational programs can help expand these children's capacity to communicate, to learn, and to relate to others, while reducing the severity and frequency of disruptive behaviors. Many young people with autism will graduate from high school, and some, like Temple Grandin, may earn a college degree.

Identifying and Teaching Students with Exceptional Needs

An elaborate decision-making process occurs before a student can receive special education. First, a child must be identified as having an exceptional need that *cannot be met without special education support.* Such a decision cannot be made by one person or by one test. Rather, an interdisciplinary team of school professionals and the parents work together at every stage of the decision-making process. Multiple measures must be taken of classroom performance, academic achievement, and intelligence. In addition, other areas of development must be examined: perception, social behaviors, motor, affect, and communication. The classroom teacher plays a vital role in the process of identifying and serving students with exceptional needs.

Identifying students who need special education services involves five stages of decision making: prereferral, referral, evaluation, IEP development, and placement.

The Role of a Classroom Teacher

Most classrooms contain some students with identified exceptionalities as well as others who are experiencing problems that have not been identified. The classroom teacher, who is responsible for meeting the diverse needs of all students, may need to access special education for assistance and instructional support. In order to obtain these services, the classroom teacher must take an active role in the five stages of decision making: prereferral, referral, evaluation, individualized education plan (IEP) development, and placement. These stages and their corresponding responsibilities are described here. The Focus on Teaching box on page 360 provides a list of specific tasks for the classroom teacher at each stage.

In addition to these roles, secondary school (middle and high school) teachers play a crucial part in preparing their students for the transition to adult life. As we discussed in a previous section, transition services are one of the mandated provisions of IDEA. Transition services are required for students by age 16 and recommended as early as age 14. As members of the transition planning team, secondary teachers are involved in designing IEPs that specify the curricular components and modifications necessary for successful attainment of postsecondary goals. Along with the other transition team members, they share responsibility for teaching the prerequisite academic and adaptive skills. Given the poor economic and social outcomes for adolescents and adults with exceptionalities (e.g., high dropout rates and low employment rates), the need for effective transition plans and services is acute (Edgar, 1987).

We now discuss some broad recommendations for teaching children with exceptionalities, appropriate for all ages, ranging from young children to those attending high school. Many of these recommended practices—learning centers, computer-assisted instruction, and peer tutoring—were initially designed for general education students and later adapted for children with exceptional needs. Adapting these and other teaching strategies to the learning needs of an increasingly heterogeneous group of students necessitates that teachers acquire a broad repertoire of personal characteristics and professional skills. A brief review of some of the more important personal and professional competencies follows.

Teacher Competencies

What competencies are needed to teach a diverse range of students? Mercer and Mercer (1989) reviewed studies that addressed this question and identified eight principles which seemed to characterize the teaching styles of the most competent teachers. They found that most competent teachers:

- Frequently use *direct instruction;* that is, they actively lead student activities, present demonstrations, structure practice opportunities, and provide feedback
- Emphasize *academic instruction,* so that their students are actively engaged in academic tasks most of the time
- Structure activities so that students experience *high rates of success*
- Provide specific *feedback* on correct and incorrect student responses
- Create a *positive atmosphere* that recognizes student accomplishments
- Promote student *motivation* through support and encouragement
- Maintain student *attention* by redirecting them when they are off-task
- Actively *enjoy* their work and celebrate their students' success

Competent teachers need a repertoire of general teaching strategies in order to accommodate a wide range of student abilities and needs in the classroom.

In addition to these personal characteristics and professional skills, competent teachers need a repertoire of general teaching strategies that will accommodate a range of student abilities and needs in the general classroom. Some of these practices focus on teacher-directed activities, others are peer-directed, and still others are self-directed. A greater number of students with special learning needs are being educated in general education classrooms for at least half of the school day. As described in the Focus on Research box on page 362, a teacher's expertise and skills to deliver appropriate instruction for students with special learning needs can affect the degree to which these students are accepted or rejected.

Teaching and learning activities can be classified according to whether they are primarily teacher directed, peer directed, or self-directed.

Teacher-Directed Learning

Teacher-directed activities include both instructional methods and classroom accommodations that are planned and implemented by the teacher. Examples of teacher-directed

Focus on Teaching

Tasks for the Classroom Teacher During the Decision-Making Stages

Prereferral Stage

Meet with parents to discuss your concerns (document attempts to contact parents).

Identify possible modifications.

Develop a plan for implementing modifications.

Document student performance (collect samples of student work, test papers, behavioral observations, anecdotal records, etc.).

Gather information from student records (health, previous referrals/testing, attendance, grade retention).

Interview parents, previous teachers, and current professionals who work with the child.

Meet with the team to brainstorm additional modifications, evaluate effectiveness, and/or determine if special education should be considered.

Referral Stage

Provide documentation of modifications/interventions and evidence of success/failure.

Provide documentation of student strengths and needs in:

- Academics (ex: divergent thinking, problem solving, content areas, handwriting, memory, reading).

- Behavior (ex: activity level, independent skills, emotional state, self-concept, attention, peer relations).

- Communication skills (ex: language proficiency, speech articulation, written expression, oral expression, listening comprehension).

- Physical characteristics (*ex:* physical complaints, sensory impairments, fine motor and gross motor skills).

Evaluation Stage

Continue to collect samples of student work in skill areas and subjects that need attention.

Continue to record observations and anecdotes of student behavior.

Present evaluation information to team members.

Ask questions for clarification if unfamiliar terms are used, particularly professional jargon.

Ask for a written copy of the test report, if none are provided.

Collaborate with the team to determine the following:

- Does performance on standardized tests correspond to classroom performance? If no, why not? Which performance measures are more relevant and why?

- Do evaluation data match eligibility criteria?

- Will the child benefit from special education? If so, how?

IEP Stage	State the goals, objectives, modifications, and evaluation methods which pertain to the general classroom.
	Listen to each other's proposed plans and incorporate them into a written form which is a joint effort.
	Discuss how evaluation methods will correspond to grading practices.
Placement Stage	Collaborate with the team to determine the following:

- What is the least restrictive environment most appropriate for this child?

- What are the advantages/disadvantages of recommending this placement?

- What related services (speech therapy, physical therapy, etc.) are needed to support his or her learning?

- To what extent can professionals team together and provide services in the general classroom, rather than remove the child from the class? Who is responsible for which objectives?

If a "pull in" approach is used, maximize the effectiveness of both educators:

- Schedule weekly planning time when both collectively plan lessons.

- Use creative coteaching arrangements (Miller et al., 1992).

One teach–one "drift"—One person teaches while the other monitors and assists students.
Station teaching—Instructional content is divided into two parts: each person teaches his or her part to half of the class. The student groups are then rotated. Each group receives instruction from both people.
Instruct and outline—One person teaches while the other writes an outline that follows the presentation.

- Prevent communication problems by practicing effective listening skills.

If a student is not succeeding in his or her current placement despite modifications, document all intervention efforts and initiate referral procedures for possible change of placement.

SOURCE: After Schulz, Carpenter, & Turnbull (1991).

Focus on Research

Teachers' Attitudes Toward Included Students with Mild and Severe Disabilities

Over the last 10 years, the number of students with disabilities who spend at least half of the school day in a general education classroom has increased (U.S. Department of Education, 1998). Inclusion rates for students with both mild and severe disabilities are also increasing. Thus, general education teachers are assuming more and more responsibility for the education of students with disabilities.

Numerous studies indicate that positive outcomes for students with disabilities are consistently associated with inclusion (Cook, Semmel, & Gerber, 1999; Klinger, Vaughn, Hughes, Schumm, & Erlbaum, 1998; Zigmond et al., 1995). General education teachers often lack the training needed to support the learning of students with mild and severe disabilities in their classroom. Additionally, these students often experience high rates of rejection or poor acceptance by nondisabled peers (Vaughn & Erlbaum, 1999).

Recently researchers have begun to study the attitudes of teachers toward included students (Cook, 2001; Cook, Semmel, & Gerber, 1999; Cook, Tankersley, Cook, & Landrum, 2000). Early studies had identified four attitudinal categories that typify teachers descriptions and interactions with students (Brophy & Good, 1974; Good & Brophy, 1972; Silberman, 1971). Students nominated for the *attachment category* generally receive more praise, less criticism, and more process questions from their teachers than their classmates (Good & Brophy, 1972). Those students who fall into the *concern category* also receive a larger share of positive interactions in the classroom, and teachers "push them to do their best" (Good & Brophy, 1972, p. 621). In contrast, students in the *indifferent category* are often overlooked in the classroom, and they have fewer and briefer interactions with teachers than their classmates. Students in the *rejection category* have the most negative interactions with their teachers. Nominated because of attitudinal, behavioral or academic problems, these students generally receive more criticism focused on behavior and fewer instructional opportunities than other students (Good & Brophy, 1972; Silberman, 1971).

In a recent study, Bryan Cook (2001) explored teachers' attitudes of attachment, concern, indifference, and rejection in relation to students with mild and severe disabilities. Seventy elementary school teachers with included students (totaling 173) were asked to respond to the following questions: If you could keep one student another year for the sheer joy of it, whom would you pick? If you could devote all your attention to a child who concerns you a great deal, whom would you pick? If a parent were to drop by for a conference, whose child would you be least prepared to talk about? If your class was to be reduced by one child, whom would you be relieved to have removed? Teachers were asked to nominate at least three students from their classes to each category, and they

instructional methods are reciprocal instruction, scaffolding, test-teach-test-retest (mastery learning), modeling, concept attainment, direct instruction, learning centers, and computer-assisted instruction. Our discussion of teacher-directed learning will focus on how diversity can be addressed by learning centers, computer-assisted instruction, and classroom accommodations.

were asked to consider, as well, students who spent only part of their day in their classroom.

The results showed that included students were overrepresented in three attitudinal categories. The severity of disability also influenced teachers' nominations, but not as predicted. Only 12 of the 173 students were nominated for the attachment category, and a very small number of these students had severe or obvious disabilities (e.g., physical impairments, mental retardation, multiple disabilities, etc.). The remaining students were nominated for the concern (64 percent), indifferent (28 percent), and rejection (38 percent) categories. As discussed, students in the *attachment* and *concern* categories are the most likely to receive the instructional support needed to succeed in the inclusion classroom. Although a high number of included students were nominated for the concern category, it is not clear that the teachers interviewed in this study had the expertise and competencies to use their concern to create a meaningful and appropriate learning environment for these students. Cook speculates that a lack of knowledge and ability to meet the needs of students with disabilities also explained the large number of students assigned to the indifference and rejection. These students are least likely to receive the instructional support they need in the inclusive classroom. Interestingly, students with mild or hidden disabilities (e.g., specific learning disabilities) were overly represented in the indifference and rejection categories. Because these students are not physically different from nondisabled students, teachers do not adjust their expectations. When students with mild or hidden disabilities violate these expectations, teachers respond negatively because they pose unexpected instructional or classroom management problems. Cook argues that a severe and obvious disability protects children from rejection because atypical behavior and performance are anticipated and expected. In other words, there was an excuse or explanation for their behavior.

Research on teachers' attitudes toward included students has several important implications for teacher education and for educational policy. First, it is critical that general education teachers receive training in special education, applied behavioral analysis, and classroom management. Second, it is important to consider teachers' attitudes toward inclusion, as well as their training and knowledge of appropriate instructional strategies for students with mild and severe disabilities, when making placement decisions. It is also important to encourage, if not require, collaboration between general and special educators to assure that appropriate instruction is provided.

SOURCE: Bryan (2001).

Learning Centers

Learning centers provide a way to individualize instruction for all children. Traditional learning centers contain multilevel materials and activities that cover a range of objectives, skills, and interests. Their primary purpose is to teach skills acquisition. Center activities are typically described on task cards, and student progress is measured in terms of skill mastery or acquisition. These activities are beneficial for a range of learners, because they can be completed at the child's own pace and level, independent of others. The tasks generally require different modes of response, tapping a variety of learning strengths and interests. For example, a first-grade learning center on plants may have puzzles, experiments, art projects, an assortment of books, and worksheets. In addition, learning center tasks generally range from lower-order thinking (e.g., labeling the parts of a plant, identifying seeds) to higher-order thinking (e.g., comparing growth rates, evaluating the effects of sunlight).

Most learning centers focus on skill acquisition and provide a variety of ways in which children can pursue those skills on their own.

Another type of learning center is an interest development center (Burns, 1985). It is open-ended and exploratory, not driven by objectives and skills. The purpose is to "expose children to a broadened base of knowledge" and encourage them to apply research skills in pursuing their interests (p. 42). The centers contain videotapes, records, filmstrips, journals, books, audiotapes, pamphlets, and written suggestions for experimenting and exploring various topics.

Computer Technology

Teachers report that computer technology can help level the playing field for students with special learning needs in the regular classroom (Hasselbring & Glaser, 2000). In fact, for children with visual and hearing impairments, it may be the only way these children can be included in the regular classroom, unless the teacher has specialized training. For the academically gifted and talented, the Internet expands their learning opportunities well beyond the classroom walls.

Computer-assisted instruction (CAI) has been available for several years. It can be used to support the learning of children with exceptional needs in many ways: tutorial, enrichment, recording student progress, enhancing memorization skills, and supporting written expression. Although CAI has been effective in producing gains in academic achievement,

SOURCE: Stephen McBrady/Photo Edit.

Advances in technology are helping children with learning disabilities achieve success in the regular classroom.

children still require teacher monitoring while using the computer. Children can also engage in CAI activities in cooperative learning groups. Okolo, Bahr, and Rieth (1993) reviewed studies in which the effectiveness of CAI combined with cooperative learning groups was compared with CAI used individually. They found that children's academic performance increased significantly when they used CAI in the cooperative learning groups rather than individually. The researchers also noted that the students made social gains.

Computer software can also be used to support the development of various writing and language skills. Hunt-Berg, Rankin, and Beukelman (1994) described the following: speech synthesis with pronunciation editing and visual highlighting of read text; spell checking; spelling assistance that signals incorrect spellings; spelling modifications; word dictionaries, prewriting support (e.g., brainstorming activities, guidelines for specific writing styles, and outliners); grammar correction, and tutorials. Research indicates that children with disabilities related to written expression are more likely to revise and edit their work on a word processor than on handwritten drafts (Hasslebring & Glaser, 2000). Word-processing software is also beneficial for students who have difficulty writing legibly.

Hyperlinks and multimedia environments also appear to have benefits for students with special learning needs. Hyperlinks enable students to access electronically linked information with a click of a mouse. As you might expect, students with disabilities are more likely to perform electronic than text-based searches for information. With hypertext, students can click on words they do not recognize or understand and receive immediate assistance. Multimedia software can help enhance students' conceptions of ideas by using visual imagery and sound effects. These technologies are particularly effective for students with learning disabilities. Multimedia software also enables students with disabilities to collaborate on meaningful learning projects with other students. However, as we discussed in Chapter 4, these technologies are most effective when they actively engage students in the learning process.

For students with auditory, visual, or communication impairments, technology is opening new avenues for learning. Specialized technology, known as augmentative or alternative communication (ACC) devices make it possible for students with no speech or with poor speech to communicate with others. Video captioning and captioned education programs are helping students with learning disabilities read. Optical character recognition (OCR) technology can scan and read text aloud. This technology allows students with visual impairments greater access to various learning materials and to read them independently.

In sum, many many new computer technologies are now available to create new learning opportunities for students with special learning needs. However, widespread use of these technologies are limited by cost and inadequate teacher training (Hasselbring & Glaser, 2000). As recently as 1999, only 20 percent of teachers nationwide reported they were prepared to use technology in their teaching (Jerald & Orlofsky, 1999). Additionally, many school systems today must seek external funding for complex technical equipment, due to limited resources from state and federal agencies.

Classroom Accommodations

Classroom accommodations are minor modifications that can be easily implemented in the general classroom to target students' specific needs. Accommodations may target problems in learning (such as test taking, auditory perception, visual perception, fine motor skills) or problems in behavior that impede learning (such as inattention, acting inappropriately, inability to adjust to change, and lack of self-esteem).

Figure 6.8 contains a partial listing of accommodations compiled by the Alabama State Department of Education (1994) and the Montgomery County Public Schools (1992). Some common behavioral problems warrant additional accommodations. For example,

The following examples provide a partial listing of accommodations compiled by Montgomery County, Maryland, Public Schools (1992).

Children with Visual Perception Problems

- Give them the clearest copy of the dittoed worksheets. Photocopying is preferable, when available.

- Summarize the key points of your lesson at the end of the period to make sure students have recorded important material.

- Condense lengthy written directions by writing them in brief steps. Pictures or diagrams may be added to provide clarity. Allow time for students to ask questions about written directions. (p. 22)

Children with Auditory Perception Problems

- Summarize the key points of your lesson with a visual prop. For instance, after a lesson, use the overhead projector to do a simple worksheet together. This worksheet may utilize a fill-in-the-blank, true-false, or multiple choice format. Individual . . . worksheets may or may not accompany the overhead.

- Alert the students when you are giving directions by setting the stage (e.g., "This is important. I'll give you the directions now"). Additional help can be provided through alerting an individual student through eye contact, positioning toward a student, or a gentle touch.

- Allow a friend to use carbon paper to take notes . . . during a lecture. This allows the student to concentrate on listening. After the lecture, the student can add to the notes the friend took. (pp. 27–28)

Children with Fine Motor Problems

- Insist that short letters *(a,c)* take up one full space on lined paper and that tall letters *(d,h)* and long letters *(p,g)* take up two full spaces in primary.

- In math, turn lined paper vertically to help students organize math problems. This will help keep the ones, tens, and hundreds places lined up.

- Modify instructional materials that involve fine motor skills (e.g., filling in charts, maps, diagrams) by (a) using sharp, colored pencils instead of crayons or wide magic markers, (b) providing more space for color or labeling, (c) allowing extra time for completion, and (d) using

FIGURE 6.8

Classroom Accommodations

blocking technique to facilitate neatness by setting an index card at borders to prevent going out of bounds. (pp. 29–30)

Children with Organizational Problems

- Establish a standard procedure in your classroom to prevent misplacement of completed assignments. Have students place completed assignments in specific content folders, trays, or specified sections of their notebooks.

- Assist the student in making choices by gradually increasing opportunities for options. For example, offer a limited choice between two options before expecting students to decide among multiple options.

- Ask the factual questions first in a discussion. Then proceed to inferential questioning since abstract thinking is usually more difficult.

- Provide students with a study guide for novels and units. (p. 31)

Some additional accommodations are suggested by the Alabama State Department of Education (1994).

Children Who Have Difficulty Taking Tests

- Allow extra time for resting.

- When impulsivity on multiple choice tests means the student will not read all choices, have the student eliminate all incorrect responses, rather than choose one correct answer.

- Permit the student to type tests or use word processor.

- Use test format with which the student is most comfortable. Allow ample space for student response. Consider having lined answer spaces for essay or short-answer questions. (p. 12)

Children Who Are Highly Distracted

- Create a structured environment with predictable routines.

- Consider use of individual headphones to play soft music to block out other auditory directions. Introduce headphones as a privilege or pair appropriate use with reinforcement.

- Prepare a stimuli-reduced area that all students can use. (p. 13)

FIGURE 6.8

Classroom Accommodations (Continued)

some children engage in disruptive, inappropriate behavior in an attempt to obtain peer attention. In such cases, any one of a variety of accommodations may help. The teacher could avoid paying attention to (reinforcing) disruptive behavior by any of the following: attending only to the appropriate behavior; teaching conflict resolution; teaching social skills; or modeling appropriate ways to gain another's attention (Washington State Department of Public Instruction, 1994).

Transitions between activities and classes are areas of difficulty for many exceptional children.

Transitions from activity to activity and from class to class are other areas of difficulty for many children. They may spend too much time gathering and organizing their materials, or they may seem agitated during the transition. Some students have difficulty focusing their attention after the transition, whereas others may persevere on the previous task, refusing to leave it for the new task. For those students, the following accommodations are recommended (Washington State Department of Public Instruction, 1994):

- Allow students extra time to organize books and papers from their previous class before beginning the new class.
- Allow students to leave class early to go to their lockers for the next class's supplies before the hallways become a flurry of distracting activities.
- Arrange for an organized helper (peer).
- Have specific locations for all materials (pencil pouches, tabs in notebooks, etc.).
- Program students for transitions. Give advance warning of when a transition is going to take place ("Now we are completing the worksheet; next we will . . . ") and the expectations for the transition ("and you will need . . . ").
- Specifically name and display lists of materials needed until a routine is possible. List steps necessary to complete each assignment. (p. 16)

For children experiencing a low self-concept, accommodations that develop self-esteem are needed. In these cases, the teacher can do the following: plan activities that allow the student to demonstrate his or her strengths; use frequent and specific positive reinforcement (e.g., "I like the way you didn't give up, even though this task was challenging for you. You really stuck to it!"); support the student in identifying and developing interests and strengths; structure tasks for success by breaking them down into smaller, more manageable units (Washington State Department of Public Instruction, 1994).

Many local school districts and state departments of education provide extensive lists of classroom accommodations that are typically included on the child's IEP. The possibilities are virtually endless and beyond the scope of this chapter.

Peer-Directed Learning

In addition to learning from their teachers, children naturally learn from one another. Examples of ways teachers can structure student interaction are cooperative learning, peer tutoring, or a buddy system (Wood, 1993). Peer-directed learning is particularly useful for children who need to develop social skills.

Cooperative Learning

This has been the most successful and popular technique for integrating exceptional children into general classrooms. In cooperative learning, heterogeneous groups of four to six children join together to accomplish a mutual goal. Tasks are divided so that each child contributes, using a particular talent or skill to create a group product (e.g., a multimedia project on explorers, a worksheet containing mathematical computations). Students work interdependently while the teacher monitors individuals. While working together, students communicate ideas, share resources, support one another, resolve conflicts that may emerge, and evaluate each person's contribution.

Cooperative learning can be used for all academic areas and with any learner. It has been successful with every exceptionality, including with children having severe and multiple disabilities (Salisbury, Palombaro, & Hollowood, 1993) and children who are deaf-blind (Downing & Eichinger, 1990). We will discuss cooperative learning as a method for improving peer relations again in Chapter 8.

Cooperative learning is the most successful and popular technique for integrating exceptional children into the general classroom.

Peer Tutoring

Tutors may be selected from the same class (same-age), or across grade levels (cross-age). A variety of possible tutorial arrangements are possible. Children with disabilities can serve as cross-age tutors of younger children without disabilities. Children without disabilities can serve as same-age or cross-age tutors of children with disabilities. Three-way tutorials among same-age children with disabilities has been successfully used to develop reading skills (Harris & Aldridge, 1983).

Peer tutoring is not intended to supplant teacher instruction, but to supplement it. An ideal use of tutorials is to serve as practice sessions for reviewing, reinforcing, and evaluating skills and concepts that have been introduced by the teacher. Careful selection, training, and planning is required before tutorial sessions. Goals, objectives, and evaluation criteria are essential ingredients. Despite the initial time investment, many teachers find that the long-term benefits of peer tutoring are rewarding for both the tutor and tutee. "The advantages associated with peer tutoring are that it encourages social acceptance, enables explanation of assignments in student terms, increases the tutor's own learning (through teaching)" (Wood, 1993, p. 193).

Buddy System

Teachers assign a "buddy" for children who benefit from a one-on-one relationship. This could be any child, but typically buddies are used for children with emotional and behavioral disorders, sensory impairments, physical disabilities, or severe and multiple disabilities. It is essential that a buddy be given specific instructions as to the amount and type of assistance they are to provide. The purpose of a buddy is to provide assistance in learning, behavior, or general classroom functioning. For example, buddies can help by taking class notes, explaining directions for assignments, reading difficult material, offering encouragement during stressful incidents, retrieving materials, or dictating test items.

The purpose of a buddy system is to provide assistance to students who benefit from a one-on-one relationship.

Self-Directed Learning

In this section we focus on ways children can be more involved and accountable for directing their own learning. These activities teach children how to learn on their own. The purpose is to actively involve the learner, increase self-knowledge, and facilitate generalization of what has been learned. Two strategies for accomplishing this objective are learning strategies training and self-management instruction.

Self-directed learning includes both strategy instruction and self-management instruction.

Learning Strategies Training

Learning strategies are the mental schemes students use to memorize, solve problems, plan, and organize their learning. As discussed in Chapter 4, cognitive strategies that help acquire and structure information can be directly taught to children who are experiencing academic problems. Strategy training is most beneficial for adolescents who are developmentally ready to spontaneously apply the strategies they have learned (Alley & Deshler, 1979). Examples of some learning strategies are mnemonics and SQ3R.

Mnemonics (Mastropieri & Scruggs, 1994) are used to improve memory and to recall important concepts by linking unfamiliar information to familiar information. There are several different mnemonic methods, two of which are described here. Keyword mnemonics can be applied to teaching new vocabulary words. For example, to learn that dahlia is a type of flower, the word *dahlia* is first recorded to the keyword *doll*. *Doll* is a good keyword for *dahlia* because it sounds like the first part of *dahlia* and is easily pictured. The learner is then shown (or asked to imagine) a picture of the keyword and the referent interacting; in this case, the student perhaps can picture a doll sniffing a flower. It is important that the keyword be associated with the referent in the picture and not simply pictured with it. Thus, although a picture containing a doll and a flower may not be sufficient to facilitate the association, a doll sniffing, picking, or otherwise interacting with the flower is more likely to facilitate the association. Finally, the retrieval process should be explicitly described to the student: "When you hear the word *dahlia,* remember the keyword *doll,* remember the picture of the doll, and think of what else was in the picture. The doll sniffing the flower means that dahlia is a kind of flower." (pp. 172–173)

Letter strategies (Mastropieri & Scruggs, 1994) are used to recall lists or categories of information. *Acronyms* are a type of letter strategy in which each letter represents the first letter of a word in the list. An example is *homes,* an acronym for memorizing the Great Lakes: *H*uron, *O*ntario, *M*ichigan, *E*rie, and *S*uperior. Another letter strategy recommended by Mastropieri and Scruggs (1994) is making an *acrostic,* using some of the letters to form a motto or title. They use as an example, an acrostic for memorizing the planets in the solar system, "'My very educated mother just served us nine pizzas,' stands for Mercury, Venus, Earth, etc." (p. 271).

SQ3R is used to acquire study skills essential to comprehending written information. *SQ3R* is an acronym for the following 5-step process (Strichart & Mangrum, 1993):

- **Survey.** Skim the titles, headings, subheadings, subtitles, chapter introduction and summary, graphs, and figures.
- **Question.** Turn headings into questions *(who, what, where, when, why, how).* Try to answer the questions.
- **Read.** Read the content for the purpose of answering the questions, highlight the answers, and write them down.
- **Recite.** First, read the question and answer aloud. Then, read the question and state the answer without seeing it. Practice these steps a few times.
- **Review.** Practice the recitation steps every day, for at least 3 days. Practice more often if necessary.

Self-Management Instruction

Self-management instruction has been effective in improving a variety of behaviors, ranging from increasing attention (on-task behavior), to increasing accuracy of academic work, to reducing disruptive behavior. Self-management techniques are systematically taught and include the following: self-instruction, self-monitoring, and self-evaluation. **Self-instruction** teaches a child to use private speech to guide himself through a task in a step-by-step manner. Here is an example of a child with attention and impulse control problems who has been taught to apply self-management techniques while completing independent seatwork. Before using this strategy, he rushed through his work, overlooked some of the items, and produced too many errors. Now, while working at his desk, he engages in an inner dialogue:

"What is it I have to do? I have to concentrate, think only of my work. Be careful, look at one at a time. Good—I got it! Am I following my plan . . . did I look at each one? That's okay . . . even if I make an error I can back up and go slowly." (Harris, 1982, p. 6)

Self-monitoring teaches a child to record his or her performance. Using the preceding example, a child could self-monitor by checking off each worksheet item as he completed it. **Self-evaluation,** the third technique, teaches how to evaluate one's own performance. In our example, the child could tally the number of checked items as well as record the accuracy of his answers. He could compare these results to his target goal of attaining a minimum accuracy of, say, 85 percent. For additional reading, Bauer and Sapona (1991) and Savage (1991) give in-depth coverage on methods for teaching self-management skills.

Resources for Teachers

Where do teachers go for additional information and instructional support? Teachers have a variety of resources for meeting the needs of children with exceptionalities. They range from local support staff and materials within the school and school districts to state and national-level professional and parent organizations and dissemination centers.

School-Based Resources

Classroom teachers use faculty members and district support staff as consultants. These include other classroom teachers, mentor teachers, psychologists, special educators trained in

SOURCE: Ellen B. Senisl/ Photo Researchers, Inc.

Cooperative learning activities such as this one are one way of accommodating exceptional learners in the regular classroom.

a particular area (e.g., learning disabilities, mental retardation, severe disabilities, autism), speech-language pathologists, counselors, physical and occupational therapists, hearing and vision specialists, adaptive physical educators, school nurses, and social workers.

External Resources

A variety of professional and parent organizations concerned with exceptional children have been established at the state, regional, and national levels. Figure 6.9 lists their names and addresses. These addresses are for national offices, but in most cases they also have state and local affiliations. Contact the national offices for local-level affiliates. Many of these organizations offer memberships that may include journal subscriptions, newsletters, member support and information networks, publications written for educators, and professional development activities, such as workshops and conferences. Some, such as the National Library Services for the Blind and Physically Handicapped, lend instructional materials to teachers.

FIGURE 6.9

National Clearinghouses

SOURCE: From the National Information Center for Children and Youth with Disabilities (1994f).

ERIC Clearinghouse on Disabilities and Gifted Education
1920 Association Drive
Reston, VA 22091–1589
(703) 620–3660   (800) 328–0272

NICHCY (National Information Center for Children & Youth with Disabilities)
P.O. Box 1149
Washington, DC 20013–1149
(202) 416–0300   (800) 695–0285

HEATH Resource Center (National Clearinghouse on Postsecondary Education for Individuals with Disabilities)
One Dupont Circle, NW, Suite 800
Washington, DC 20036–1193
(202) 939–9320   (800) 544–3284

National Information Center on Deafness (NICD)
800 Florida Avenue, NE
Washington, DC 20002
(202) 651–5051   TTY: (202) 651–5052

National Clearinghouse on Family Support and Children's Mental Health
Portland State University
P.O. Box 751
Portland, Oregon 97207–0751
(503) 725–4040   TT: (503) 725–4165   (800) 628–1696

National Health Information Center
P.O. Box 1133
Washington, DC 20013–1133
(301) 565–4167   (800) 336–4797

DB-LINK (National Information Clearinghouse on Children Who Are Deaf-Blind)
345 North Monmouth Avenue
Monmouth, OR 97361
(503) 838–8776   TTY: (503) 838–8821

Chapter Summary

www.mhhe.com/meece

Introduction

- The typical classroom contains much interindividual and intraindividual variation among children. When interindividual differences are significant, a child is usually classified and labeled, then eligible to receive special education services.

- Labeling children is a controversial practice that tends to emphasize the *dis*ability, rather than the individual's abilities. One way to minimize negative labeling effects is to use people-first terminology. This reminds us that the person is much more than his or her disability. In other words, the disability is merely one aspect of a child's total personality.

- Currently, more children with exceptional needs are being integrated into general classrooms, with special educators entering the classroom to provide services. Special educators and classroom teachers work collaboratively, sharing responsibility for meeting student needs.

- Approximately 10 percent of this nation's school-age children have one of the following federally designated disabilities: specific learning disabilities, communication disorders, mental retardation, emotional or behavioral disorders, severe and multiple disabilities, other health impairments, deafness and hearing impairment, physical disabilities, low vision or blindness, autism, traumatic brain injury, or deaf-blindness. Two additional categories of exceptionality are served in the schools: attention deficit disorders and gifted.

- The Individuals with Disabilities in Education Act (IDEA) guarantees the rights of children with disabilities. One of the most salient rights is that they receive education in the least restrictive environment.

Characteristics of Children with Exceptional Needs

- Some common group characteristics exist for each of the disability categories, despite a range of inter- and intraindividual differences.

- Children with specific learning disabilities experience a discrepancy between intelligence and achievement. This discrepancy may occur in one or more areas: spoken language, written language, arithmetic, or reasoning. Many have difficulties with attention, memory, metacognition, and generalization. Some also have problems in perception, motor development, social interaction, and motivation.

- Children with communication disorders are delayed in either speech or language, or both. Most encounter academic problems, particularly in reading. Some children's inability to understand and use language also interferes with their social development.

- Children who are gifted and talented are either advanced in cognition and academic achievement or extremely talented and creative. Many excel in language and show some mature affective characteristics, such as leadership skills and goal-directed behavior. This category differs from the others, because it is based on children's abilities and strengths rather than on their weaknesses.

- Children with attention deficit disorders have difficulties with attention, impulse control, and activity level. Many experience problems in memory, problem solving, and academics. Some experience peer interaction difficulties, low frustration threshold, and low self-esteem.

- Children with mental retardation are low in intelligence and adaptive behavior, skills that enable a person to live independently. Most also experience significant language delays as well as inattention, memory problems, low self-esteem, external locus of control, and generalization difficulties. Their delays in cognition, adaptive behavior, and language may range from mild to severe or profound.

- Children with emotional or behavioral disorders have various difficulties in psychosocial development, either externalizing (e.g., oppositional, antisocial, aggressive) or internalizing (e.g., withdrawal, anxiety, depression) problems. Most have deficits in language and social-cognitive skills.

- Children with severe and multiple disabilities, other health impairments, deafness and hearing impairment, physical disabilities, low vision or blindness, autism, traumatic brain injury, and deaf-blindness have a range of needs scattered across the developmental domains. Many children in these categories can learn in the general classroom with the use of specialized equipment, including augmentative communication devices, adaptive devices, medical technology, and vision aides.

Identifying and Teaching Students with Exceptional Needs

- The process of identifying and serving children with exceptional needs occurs in stages, namely, prereferral, referral, evaluation, individualized education plan (IEP), placement, and review. As a member of a multidisciplinary team, a classroom teacher plays an active role throughout the decision-making process.

- In order to teach a diverse group of learners, teachers must have a repertoire of teaching strategies including learning centers, computer-assisted instruction, classroom accommodations, cooperative learning, peer tutoring, buddy systems, learning strategies training, and self-management instruction.

- Classroom teachers have access to a variety of resources and support. Within their school, they can problem-solve with colleagues in general and in special education. Many state and national professional and parent organizations offer assistance as well as clearinghouses and information centers.

Key Terms

acceleration (p. 343)

attention deficit/ hyperactivity disorder (ADHD) (p. 331)

autism (p. 357)

collaborative consultation (p. 320)

communication disorder (p. 328)

conduct disorders (p. 349)

curriculum casualties (p. 317)

dyslexia (p. 326)

emotional or behavioral disorders (p. 348)

enrichment programs (p. 343)

exceptionality (p. 317)

external locus of control (p. 327)

externalizing problems (p. 348)

giftedness (p. 338)

individualized education plan (IEP) (p. 322)

individuals with disabilities in education act (IDEA) (p. 322)

interindividual variation (p. 316)

internalizing problems (p. 348)

intraindividual variation (p. 316)

mental retardation (p. 343)

multimodal approach (p. 335)

schizophrenia (p. 348)

self-evaluation (p. 371)

self-instruction (p. 370)

self-monitoring (p. 371)

specific learning disability (p. 323)

team teaching (p. 320)

tourette's syndrome (p. 348)

Activities

1. Begin to collect printed material for a resource file on exceptional learners. To do this, contact your state department of education for manuals and handbooks concerning children with exceptional needs. Each state has information about parental rights, eligibility criteria, classroom modifications, and test modifications, as well as on other topics relevant to teachers. In addition, call or write to several national professional and parent organizations or clearinghouses (see Figure 6.9) and ask for printed material and information. If they have mailing lists, ask that your name be added for future mailings. Share the contents of your resource folder with classmates.

2. Attend the multidisciplinary team meetings for a child and keep track of the types of decisions that are made at each of the stages: prereferral, referral, evaluation, IEP development, and placement. Who were the people in attendance? What were the responsibilities of and contributions made by each person? What concerns were discussed? What decisions were made? Try to identify those things that contributed to collaboration and mutual problem solving as well as those things that detracted from group processing. Summarize your findings in a report you can share with your classmates.

3. Interview two to five teachers of different grade levels about their instructional methods and accommodations. Among the children they have taught, how many had exceptional needs, and what were they? What instructional methods have they used to meet their needs? What classroom accommodations have they implemented? What resources have they used while planning and implementing various methods and accommodations? Who have they collaborated with during this process? Compare your teachers' responses to the national prevalence rates (Table 6.1). In addition, compare their methods and accommodations to those described in the chapter.

4. Obtain a copy of the article "How Efficacious Are You?" by Holly DiBella, Elizabeth A. MacDaniel, and Regina Miller (1995). Complete the self-efficacy quiz and interpret your score according to the authors' directions. What did you learn about your belief system? Discuss what you learned with classmates.

Chapter 7

Self-Concept, Identity, and Motivation

Dear Diary,

Ever since elementary school I've been in accelerated classes. I had thought I was lucky getting the best education and the top-notch teachers. I was on the road to the brightest of the bright.

When I reached junior high, I started to realize that since I was in the accelerated program, I only knew the other accelerated kids. We didn't talk to anyone else. It was like an unspoken law. We weren't allowed to talk to the kids who weren't in the gifted program, or maybe they weren't allowed to talk with us. I knew it wasn't right, but it was all I knew. Going into high school, I was accepted into the highest academic program in my district. I thought it was a good thing, until the middle of my first semester. The work was piled over my head and I felt like I couldn't think straight. I didn't have time for anything but homework. It was hard to pay attention because my teachers talked like robots. I'm sure they were teaching me important information but by the time I got home, I couldn't remember a thing. We were assigned too many pages to read in one night and too many tests in one week. I didn't have time to actually learn. I found my way out of this program and found my way into another one at Wilson High School. I crossed my fingers, hoping this one would be better.

This new program was called Distinguished Scholars. I was given a list of qualifications that had to be met. We had to have a good grade point average, good attendance, and take more classes than the average student. It seemed tough, but I felt it was a more reachable

Chapter Opener Photo: Rudi Von Briel.

goal. I walked into this open-minded, but it wasn't the right program for me. All my teachers held their noses in the air, as if they were above the rest of the school. Looking around, I realized I was uncomfortable. The class was made up of all white wealthy kids who couldn't have more stress than planning what they were going to wear the next day. They made it clear that their race, economic state, and the classes they were taking made them popular and better than anyone else. Even though I was white, lived in the same neighborhood, and had all of the same classes, I wanted out. (The Freedom Writers, 1999)

T his diary entry of a ninth-grade student demonstrates the difficulty some students experience finding a learning community that provides the support they need to continue developing their talents. It clearly points out the important role of teachers and peers in helping students to stay motivated and interested in learning, and how schools can be stressful places for them. It also makes clear that schools teach children more than cognitive and language skills. Schools are places where children develop a sense of self-worth, identify their strengths and weaknesses, and form an identity for the future.

Schools are places where children develop a sense of self-worth, learn about emotions, identify their strengths and weaknesses, and form an identity of themselves for the future.

Schools also play an important role in the development of children's social and emotional competence. Young people who are socially and emotionally competent have a better chance of succeeding in school and in later life (Huffman, Mehlinger, & Kerivan, 2000; Pianta, Rimm-Kaufman, & Cox, 1999). They exhibit confidence, self-control, motivation, and persistence. They have a positive sense of self and plans for the future. They also have good interpersonal skills that include an ability to read social and emotional cues, to take the perspective of others, and to form positive social relations.

In this chapter, we begin to consider several important aspects of children's social and emotional development. We first discuss Erikson's theory of psychosocial development as a framework for understanding the developmental needs of young people in school settings. Next, we discuss several important foundations of children's social and emotional development—forming a secure attachment, understanding and expressing emotions, and learning self-control. In later sections we explore the development of self-concept, identity, and motivation, and what role schools play in this development.

Erikson's Theory of Psychosocial Development

Developmental psychologist Erik Erikson (1963) provided a framework for understanding children's psychological development. The Focus on Development box provides a brief overview of this stage theory. Erikson was one of the first life-span theorists, because he believed that development is a life-long process. Like Freud, he emphasized the importance of feelings and social relationships in a person's development. However, Erikson placed much more emphasis on social than biological influences in his theory. Although Erikson believed there are certain basic needs common to all people, he maintained that personal relationships and societal expectations influence the way we respond to those needs. For example, all infants must form a sense of trust for healthy development, but in some cultures infants spend as much time with substitute caregivers as with their own parents. Similarly, all children begin to "separate" from their caregivers when they become more mobile, but cultural norms may determine how much independence and freedom children are given at a young age.

Focus on Development

Erikson's Stages of Psychosocial Development

Age	Stage	Developmental Task
Birth to 1 year	Trust vs. mistrust	Children must develop a basic sense of trust or confidence that their world is predictable and safe. Their basic needs are met by sensitive and responsive caregivers.
1 to 3 years	Autonomy vs. shame and doubt	Children must develop a will of their own and sense of independence from caregivers. Their basic needs are met by caregivers who encourage independence and autonomy but do not force or shame them.
3 to 5 years	Initiative vs. guilt	Children must develop a sense of purpose and direction as their social world expands. They are asked to assume more responsibility for their actions. Their basic needs are met if caregivers do not demand too much self-control that can lead to guilt feelings when children cannot live up to parental expectations.
6 to 10 years	Industry vs. inferiority	Children must develop a capacity to work and cooperate with others as they enter school. They must direct their energies toward mastering academic skills and feeling pride in their successes. Children's basic needs are met when caregivers help them to find their special competencies.
10 to 20 years	Identity vs. role confusion	Adolescents must find out who they are, what they value, and a direction for their lives. Adolescents' basic needs are met when they are given opportunities to explore alternative options and roles for the future.
Early adulthood	Intimacy vs. isolation	Young adults must form intimate relationships with others. Intimacy involves finding oneself yet losing oneself in others. Because of early experiences, some people may not be able to form close relationships, and remain isolated from others.
Middle adulthood	Generativity vs. stagnation	Adults must find a way to give to the next generation through child rearing, caring for others, or productive work. The person who fails in these ways feels an absence of meaning in life.
Late adulthood	Integrity vs. despair	Older adults must reflect on their lives and evaluate their contributions and accomplishments and the kind of person they have been. Integrity results from feeling that life was satisfying and worth living.

Erikson believed that there were basic needs common to all people, but maintained that personal relationships and societal expectations influence how we respond to those needs.

According to Erikson's theory, children continually face new developmental tasks or issues they must somehow resolve as they mature. Erikson identified a positive and a negative outcome for each developmental stage (e.g., trust versus mistrust), and he believed that an unhealthy resolution of a particular issue could impair later development. For instance, a baby who does not develop trusting relationships during infancy may experience difficulty separating from caregivers during his or her second year. The potential for this outcome reflects Erikson's belief that the social environment largely influences how well a person's developmental needs are satisfied at each stage.

Stages of Development

Our discussion of Erikson's theory will focus mainly on the developmental stages of most concern to teachers. During infancy children must form a basic sense of trust as the foundation for later development. Children will form this trust in the first stage of development, *trust versus mistrust,* if their basic needs for food, care, and comfort are met in a sensitive and consistent manner. When children have a basic trust in their environment, they are more likely to explore and to "move away" from caregivers during the second stage of development, *autonomy versus shame and doubt.* During this stage, children require less physical contact from caregivers and begin such activities as walking, feeding, and toileting on their own. If children are unable to master some aspects of their environment or to live up to parental expectations, they may begin to doubt their ability to manage their world. In Erikson's view, infancy lays a foundation for the development of self-esteem and self-efficacy, which we will discuss later in this chapter.

During the elementary years (ages 6–12), children begin to identify their strengths and to take pleasure in their accomplishments, which Erikson called a sense of industry.

Early and middle childhood are important periods for the development of self-control, initiative, and purpose. At ages 3 to 6, children attempt to resolve the conflicts associated with Erikson's third stage, *initiative versus guilt.* Developing a sense of initiative involves the "quality of undertaking, planning, and attacking a task for the sake of being active and on the move" (Erikson, 1963, p. 255). Preschoolers are clearly on the move, but they must learn they cannot act on all their impulses. Young children must learn to balance their actions with those of others. However, if children are not allowed to take the initiative, or if they are constantly told what they do is wrong, they may develop a strong sense of guilt and avoid initiating actions on their own.

During the elementary school years, children develop what Erikson called a sense of industry. In the *industry versus inferiority* stage, children begin to identify their strengths and to take pleasure in their accomplishments. If children are not supported in their efforts, or if they are unable to live up to the expectations of others, they may develop feelings of inferiority or inadequacy. In later sections, we will learn that many children begin to develop more negative attitudes about their abilities and to experience declines in motivation as they move from childhood to adolescence.

In adolescence, young people begin forming a sense of identity as they struggle with commitment to a set of beliefs, values, and adult roles.

Perhaps Erikson's most important theoretical contribution was his view of identity development in adolescence. During adolescence, young people enter the stage of *identity versus role confusion.* Forming an **identity** involves committing oneself to a set of beliefs, values, and adult roles. Having formed a basic sense of self, Erikson believed that young people begin to struggle with such questions as Who am I? What makes me unique? What is important to me? What do I want to do with my life? Adolescents who avoid these questions experience a state of role confusion. This "identity crisis" is undoubtedly triggered by physical changes that occur during adolescence, but society also demands that adolescents behave in new ways. They must begin to be more responsible and to make decisions for themselves. In adolescence, young people must prepare for adulthood, which means figuring out what role they will play in the adult world. Although this may have seemed true when Erikson did his research in the 1940s and 1950s, more recent evidence suggests that the search for identity continues well into the adult years. Research further suggests that adolescents who commit to an identity early, without taking time to explore various options and choices, may question their commitments later on. We often make fun of adolescents who are having an identity crisis of one sort or another, but most theorists believe young people should delay making commitments to an occupation, belief system, intimate relationship, or lifestyle until they have had an opportunity to explore different perspectives and options. Some adolescents, however, are not given the opportunity to experiment with adult roles because of family expectations or economic necessity.

Limitations and Contributions of Erikson's Theory

Erikson provides a useful framework for understanding psychological development. His theory helps us to understand the importance of stable and caring relationships in early development, the need for self-sufficiency and competency in the middle childhood years, and the search for identity in adolescence. However, Erikson's theory has several limitations that need to be considered. First, his theory was based on studies of men, and the focus on identity development may come later, or take a different form, for women (Gilligan, 1982; Josselson, 1987). Moreover, Erikson's theory emphasized the importance of autonomy and independence as desirable goals for development. This view of development is deeply rooted in American individualism (Rothbaum, Weisz, Pott, Miyake, & Morelli, 2000). Not all cultures encourage the development of autonomy and individualism in their young people. For example, parents of Asian, Mexican, or African American heritage are more likely to value collectivist values such as interdependence, group solidarity, and family obligations (Phinney, Ong, Madden, 2000; Triandis, 1990, 1995). European American parents encourage less interdependence in their children than do parents in collectivist cultures (Greenfield & Crocking, 1994; Okagaki & Sternberg, 1993).

Keeping these limitations in mind, let's consider some implications of Erikson's theory for education. First, his theory makes clear that children need a secure school environment and caring relationships with adults in order to maintain the sense of trust needed for personal development. Ideally, schools should offer students opportunities to initiate new activities and to feel a sense of accomplishment from a job well done. Students also need opportunities to find their unique strengths and to develop them. More important, students need opportunities to learn about different viewpoints and career options as they begin their search for identity. Unfortunately, schools often restrict children's personal development by undermining children's sense of competency, by reinforcing cultural stereotypes, or by limiting young people's options for the future. We will discuss some of these constraints later in the chapter.

Erikson's theory helps us to understand the importance of stable and caring relationships in early development, the need for self-sufficiency and competency in middle childhood, and the search for identity in adolescence.

Schools need to offer students opportunities to initiate new activities, to find their unique strengths, and to learn about different viewpoints, cultures, and choices for the future as they begin the search for identity.

Foundations of Social and Emotional Development

Forming a Secure Attachment

Children's social and emotional development is firmly rooted in early relations with parents and other caregivers. In infancy, the term **attachment** is used to refer to the close, affective relationship formed between a child and one or more caregivers. Secure attachment

All infants form an affective relationship, or attachment, with a caregiver, but not all infants form secure attachments.

relationships enable children to develop what Erikson called a "basic sense of trust." With rare exception, infants form an attachment with a caregiver, but not all infants form secure attachments.

Many different theories have been used to explain the development of attachment relations. Psychoanalytic theorists argue that babies form attachments because caregivers satisfy certain innate needs and drives, such as the need to gain pleasure through sucking. Similarly, classical learning theorists argue that infants form attachments with caregivers because they satisfy basic needs for food. Another theory of attachment emerged from the field of animal behavior or ethology. John Bowlby (1969) argued that the formation of an affective bond between a mother and her infant served an evolutionarily adaptive function of offering protection through maintenance of proximity. A child who stayed close to his or her caregiver could more easily be monitored and rescued from peril if need be. Consequently, Bowlby's ethological theory emphasized the infant's biological predisposition to form an attachment for survival and protection, as well as early interactions between caregivers.

Variations in the Quality of Attachment Relations

Mary Ainsworth was the first developmental researcher to study differences in the quality of attachments infants form with their caregivers. She created a laboratory procedure, known as the **Strange Situation,** in which a caregiver and child experience episodes of separation and reunion. At one point in the procedure, the baby is left alone, and during another separation episode, the infant is left with a stranger. On the basis of the infant's reactions to the repeated separations and reunions, Ainsworth and her colleagues (1978) distinguished three different classifications of attachment quality.

Infants who were *securely attached* showed distress when separated from their mothers but were readily calmed and soothed by the mother's return. Securely attached infants also exhibited a willingness to use their mothers as secure bases from which they felt comfortable venturing out to explore the room in which the study took place and its contents. Secure attachment was seen in approximately 60 percent to 65 percent of American children studied.

Insecurely attached infants were divided into two subcategories on the basis of their responses to the Strange Situation. Infants classified as showing *insecure-avoidant attachment* seemed indifferent to the departure of their mothers from the room and avoided their mothers when they returned. About 20 percent of American children studied were given this classification. Another 10 percent to 15 percent were identified as having *insecure-resistant attachment*. These infants displayed high levels of distress during the separation episodes but, upon their mother's return, often responded to her with ambivalence. They alternately sought contact with her and then fought against her.

Another category of insecure attachment was identified later by other researchers (Main & Solomon, 1990). A few children showed evidence of disorientation and contradictory behavior in response to the Strange Situation. They often seemed dazed, exhibited behavioral freezing or engaged in repetitive behaviors. Their apparent confusion in these situations led to the classification of *insecure-disorganized attachment*.

Most young children form multiple attachments with both parents, siblings, and other adults with whom they have regular contact.

Although early attachment research focused on mother-infant attachments, it is important to emphasize that infants form attachments with fathers and other people with whom they have regular contact. In fact, most infants develop multiple attachments. Research suggests that infants show equal attachment to their mothers and fathers (Lamb, 1997). As children mature, they often develop attachments with siblings and peers. Studies of preschool children have shown that children experience a range of reactions when they are transferring to a new school or being left behind (Field, 1986). Reactions may include changes in eating and sleeping habits, as well as negative affect, increased irritability, and other symptoms associated with separation distress or loss.

Focus on Teaching

Teachers often assume a parental role with children. Like parent-child relationships, children's relations with teachers vary in quality. Some relationships are close and affectionate, whereas others are distant or conflictual (Howes, & Matheson, 1992; Pianta, Steinberg, & Rollins, 1995). Just as children's early attachment relations can affect later development, a growing body of research suggests that the quality of teacher-student relations can affect school adjustment and achievement.

Robert Pianta and his colleagues have studied associations between teacher-student relations and school outcomes in the school years. Using teacher reports, they found that teacher-student relations can be reliably characterized in terms of closeness, conflict, and dependency (Pianta & Steinberg, 1992; Pianta, 1994). Findings further showed that changes in teacher-student relations from year to year affected students' school adjustment. Increased conflict negatively affected school adjustment, whereas increased closeness had a positive influence. For children at high risk for grade retention or special education placement, a close teacher-student relationship functioned as a protective factor by offsetting negative consequences.

Although this research focused on the early elementary grades, students' supportive and caring relations with teachers are essential for promoting optimal development throughout the school years. Teachers who demonstrate that they care about their students are in a better position to gain cooperation from them and to maintain students' interest in learning (Midgley, Feldlaufer, & Eccles, 1989; Noddings, 1992; Phelan, Davidson, & Yu, 1998). Yet studies indicate that students may experience declines in the quality of their relationships with teachers as they progress in school, which can have a negative impact on motivation, achievement, and school engagement (Feldlaufer, Midgley, & Eccles, 1988; Midgley et al., 1989; Wentzel, 1996).

How can teachers maintain good relations with students? In a study of middle school students, Kathyrn Wentzel (1997) explored students' perceptions of caring, supportive teachers. The following dimensions characterized these teachers: (1) They cared about their own teaching and made a special effort to engage their students; (2) They recognized students' strengths and weaknesses, and treated students as individuals; and (3) They listened to students and showed an interest in their concerns. In general, teachers who support students' learning and achievement share many characteristics with nurturing and supportive parents.

There is also a growing body of research on the influence of child-teacher relations during the early school years. Research has shown that there is a moderate degree of continuity in the quality of relationships children have with caregivers at home and at school, and positive relations with teachers help to promote school adjustment (peer competencies, ability to comply with adults, ability to work independently, etc.). The Focus on Teaching box highlights this research.

What Explains Variations in Attachment Relations?

Various factors have been linked to the development of secure or insecure attachment between caregivers and their infants. Perhaps the most crucial influence arises from the pattern

383

Parental warmth and responsiveness foster positive interactions and set the stage for children to develop a sense of confidence in their relationships with caregivers.

of interactions that develops between caregiver and child. Parental warmth and responsiveness foster positive interactions and set the stage for children to develop a sense of confidence in their relationships with caregivers. Parents who are consistently available and responsive to a child's needs foster the development of secure attachment, whereas parents who are inconsistently available, unavailable, or rejecting often have insecurely attached babies (Cassidy & Berlin, 1994). These parents may have serious financial or emotional problems that make it difficult to provide for their children's needs. Changing family circumstances, such as loss of income and the experience of poverty, could undermine parenting to the point of disturbing the development of attachment (Shaw & Vondra, 1993).

Characteristics of the child must also be considered. Some babies are happy, adaptable, and calm, whereas others cry and fuss a lot, eat and sleep irregularly, and become easily distressed or upset in new situations. **Temperament** refers to the infant's characteristic style of responding to the environment. As you might imagine, caregivers are likely to experience more difficulty in forming a secure attachment with an irritable and fussy baby. However, studies show few links between infant behaviors and attachment classifications (Colin, 1996; Thompson, 1998; Vaughn et al., 1992). With good parenting skills and social support, parents can foster a secure attachment even with a temperamental baby. The Focus on Research box describes the role of temperament in children's development.

Attachment relations are also shaped by the larger cultural context. In Japan, for example, young children are rarely separated from their mothers in their first year. Japanese infants respond with more distress when placed in the Ainsworth's Strange Situation because both mothers and infants have less experience with separations and reunions. Thus, researchers have recently questioned the cross-cultural validity of the attachment theory (Rothbaum et al., 2000). Conclusions about attachment relations are primarily based on white, middle-class samples from the United States. Moreover, the assumptions underlying attachment theory reflect a Western view of children's development that defines social competence in terms of separation, self-reliance, and efficacy. Attachment relations take a different form in cultures that value relatedness more than independence (Rothbaum et al., 2000). It is important to remember these limitations as we discuss the long-term impact of attachment relations on children's development.

From early attachment relations, children begin to construct an internal model of the self and their social relationships that includes the roots of self-esteem and security.

Attachment Relations and Later Development

What implications does a child's attachment classification have for later development? It is the first affectionate relationship that children form, and attachment theorists believe it serves as an important foundation for developing the self, emotions, and morality (Thompson, 1999). From early attachment relations, children begin to construct an "internal model" of the self and their social relationships that includes the roots of self-esteem and security. Securely attached children form a model of caregivers as available and responsive, and the self as worthy of care. These beliefs and expectations are "carried forward" to future relationships with other adults and with peers and siblings.

A substantial amount of research has explored the impact of attachment on children's later development in a variety of domains. Some of the findings are summarized in the Focus on Development box on page 386. In general, secure attachment measured at one point in development tends to bode well for children's later social relationships with peers, teachers, and others, whereas children identified as insecurely attached show problems in their interpersonal skills and the quality of their social relationships.

The quality of children's attachment relations is linked to a variety of school adjustment measures, including social competence, peer popularity, and self-esteem.

It also important to note that parent-child attachment relations are also associated with the development of competencies needed for school success. Differences in curiosity, attention, problem-solving behavior, persistence, and motivation have all been linked to

Focus on Research

Temperament is what parents may mean when they say, "She has a good disposition." It includes such observable behaviors as activity level (mobility and tempo of movement), rhythmicity (extent to which bodily functions are regular and predictable), quality of moods (intensity and nature), and adaptability (ability to adapt to new situations or experiences). Recent conceptualizations have added another dimension—self-regulation—to describe the process by which infants control or inhibit their responses to stimulation (Rothbart & Bates, 1998). Individual differences in temperament emerge shortly after birth and are believed to have a biological basis. Researchers also believe that individual differences in infant temperament set the course for later emotional and personality development (Caspi, 1998; Thompson, 1999).

What are the effects of temperament on later development? In general, assessments of temperament in early infancy are not very reliable in predicting the same dimensions later in development. By the end of the first year, some short-term stability can be observed in certain characteristics such as fear, positive emotionality, and attention span (Thompson, 1999). After age 2, however, longer associations can be observed between temperament and later development. In a large longitudinal study of 800 children, Caspi and Silva (1995) found significant relations between temperament at age 3 and personality traits in adolescence. Specifically, young children who were inhibited as young children were cautious and restrained as adolescents. Some evidence also suggests that inhibited and fearful children may experience problems with social relations and with anxiety in middle childhood and adolescence (Caspi, 1998; Kagan, 1998). By contrast, those children who are impulsive, irritable, and distractible in childhood were more likely to have behavioral problems such as aggression and noncompliance (Caspi, 1998; Eisenberg & Fabes, 1998). Not all studies, however, report strong continuities between childhood temperament and adult personality (Thompson, 1999).

For now, it is important to understand that children differ in temperamental characteristics. Some children may be more predisposed than others to be sociable, emotionally expressive, reactive, and withdrawn. A child who is shy or emotionally reactive may need a little extra help in the classroom. As we have discussed previously, development is a complex interaction of genetic and environmental influences. The continuity of temperamental characteristics in children's development is significantly influenced by their interactions with caregivers (Chess & Thomas, 1977).

the quality of children's early attachments (Birch & Ladd, 1996; Pianta & Harbers, 1996; Sroufe, 1996). Measures of school adjustment (e.g., social competence, peer popularity, and self-esteem) have also been linked to the quality of children's early attachment relations (Sroufe, 1983, 1989). For example, one study showed that boys classified as insecurely attached to their mothers were rated by their teachers as less competent and as having a greater number of behavior problems than boys with secure attachments (Cohn, 1990). Thus, considerable evidence suggests that children's school experiences are more productive and positive when they have a solid base of emotional security.

Focus on Development

Attachment Classification and Later Developmental Outcomes (Ages 2 to 5)

Attachment Classification	Developmental Outcomes
Securely attached	Engages in more pretend and imaginative play
	Shows more flexibility in handling feelings
	Shows more independence and self-reliance
	Shows more enthusiasm and persistence in problem solving
	Shows greater social competence with peers and more compliance with adults
	Shows higher quality of friendships with peers
	Shows lower risk for becoming bullies or the victims of bullies
Insecurely attached	Engages in less symbolic play
	Less compliant with adults
	Less autonomous functioning
	More conflicts with friends
	Lower-quality friendships with peers
	Higher frequency of behavior problems
	Increased risk of becoming a bully or a victim of a bully

SOURCES: Jacabvitz & Sroufe (1987); Sroufe (1982); Sroufe, Fox, & Pancake (1983); Thompson (1998); Troy & Sroufe (1987).

It should be noted, however, that while many investigators in the field of attachment research assume that early attachment status exerts a long-term impact on the development of an individual, not all of the empirical evidence supports that view. In fact, attachment can change over the course of childhood with children who were once securely attached later showing insecure attachment as a result of changes in parenting or family circumstances. The opposite progression from insecure to secure attachment is also possible. For example, intervention studies have shown that providing supports for mothers and assisting them in methods for sensitively responding to the needs of their infants can foster the development of secure attachment (Lieberman, Weston, & Paul, 1991; van den Boom, 1995).

Understanding and Expressing Emotions

Young people experience different emotions at school. They feel happy with a good grade, they feel excited about a school production, they feel anxious about a test, they feel angry when teased, and so forth. As these examples imply, **emotions** are subjective reactions to events and experiences. They are generally experienced cognitively as pleasant or unpleasant, and accompanied by some form of physiological change or overt behavioral response (Izard, 1991). Emotions also function as important regulators of behavior. Anxiety or fear may lead an adolescent to avoid situations that elicit those reactions.

Parents and children first communicate with each other through emotions. An infant cries to signal hunger, discomfort, or fear, and their caregivers learn to "read" these signals as they attempt to soothe and comfort the infant. As early as 2 or 3 months, infants begin to attend to different emotional responses. Ten-week-old infants respond differently to happy, sad, and angry faces—especially when the adult's voices match the facial expressions (Walker-Andrews, 1997). When experiencing new and strange situations, a 12-month-old infant may look first at a caregiver's face before taking action. Remember the visual cliff experiment in Chapter 2? A fearful or angry look can signal a wary infant not to crawl out onto the plate glass. Studies have shown that infants' reactions to new toys or strangers are shaped by their caregivers' facial expressions (Feinman & Lewis, 1983). This process of incorporating facial cues into response sequences is known as **social referencing** (Saarni, Mumme, & Campos, 1998). It is important to note here that the baby's use of social cues for directing responses is an early form of behavioral regulation that will continue to develop.

By the end of infancy, children are able to use the emotional expressions of their caregivers to regulate their behaviors.

By the end of the second year, children show some awareness that others can have feelings different from their own. Toddlers will attempt to comfort a distressed sibling or peer. This ability to react to another person's distress is called **empathy.** Although 2-year-olds are capable of empathic responses, they may not respond or may not respond appropriately to another's distress. These responses are influenced, in part, by the infant's own attachment history. When parents are responsive to their child's distress, the child tends to be more responsive to the distress of others (Thompson, 1999).

During the preschool years, children's emotional understanding expands. With the development of language abilities, children have the capability to label their emotions. Older children spontaneously talk about simple feelings (e.g., "I so happy, Grandma"), as well as about the feelings of others (Saarni et al., 1998). At this age, children also understand that emotions are associated with the fulfillment of different desires. For example, the child understands that someone would feel sad if a favorite toy were lost or stolen (Harris, 1989).

Between the ages of 2 and 4, new emotional reactions emerge. Whereas the infant's emotional reactions were limited to expressions of fear, joy, anger, and surprise, toddlers and preschoolers can express pride, shame, guilt, or what are known as **self-conscious emotions** (Lewis, 1992). Unlike the fundamental emotions of infancy, self-conscious emotions involve an evolving sense of self. Three-year-olds who show pride in building a tall block tower by calling attention to it are making connections between their actions and feelings. As preschool children develop some understanding of standards for behavior, violations of those standards can lead to feelings of shame and guilt. Parents can tell when a child has done something wrong, such as having spilled juice on a clean shirt, from the child's distressed look or avoidance of contact. As we will discuss later, self-conscious emotions play an important role in helping children to regulate their behaviors.

Between the ages of 2 and 4, feelings of pride, shame, and guilt emerge to help children regulate their actions.

By middle childhood, children's understanding of emotions becomes more sophisticated. They understand that multiple emotions can be evoked by the same event or situation (Harter & Whitesall, 1989). For example, they feel both happy and sad on the last day of school. Like adults, they also understand how a person's personality or background can shape their emotional reactions to a situation (Gnepp & Chilamkurti, 1988). Older children are also able to better understand the causes of specific emotions ("He's mad because he wants to play outside, and his father says he has to play inside"). Additionally, school-age children have a better understanding of the social rules of displaying emotions (Gross & Harris, 1988; Saarni et al., 1998). For example, an older elementary student understands that it is not appropriate to laugh when other students make mistakes or get in trouble. With the discovery of these social conventions for expressing emotions, children come to understand that people, including themselves, can disguise their true feelings (Saarni et al., 1998).

Adolescence brings new cognitive abilities for understanding and expressing emotions. As we discussed in Chapter 3, older adolescents are able to engage in self-reflection and to think in more complex and sophisticated ways. Consider this high school student's concerns about fitting the high-achieving Asian stereotype:

> They [whites] will have stereotypes, like we're smart . . . They are so wrong, not everyone is smart. They expect you to be this and that and when you're not . . . (shook her head) And sometimes you tend to be what they expect you to be and you just lose your identity, just lose being yourself. Become part of what . . . what somebody else want[s] you to be. And it's really awkward too! When you get bad grades, people look at you really strangely because you are sort of distorting the way they see an Asian. It makes you feel really awkward if you don't fit the stereotype. (Lee, 1996, p. 59)

Although new cognitive abilities can help adolescents interpret unpleasant experiences, they are also associated with increased self-consciousness and self-criticism. Sadly, regular feelings of pride and happiness decline when students enter adolescence (Larson & Richards, 1994). Compared with younger children, adolescents report more anxiety, loneliness, moodiness, and stress (Buchanan et al., 1992; Arnett, 1999). Adolescents also find that their increased needs for independence and autonomy are in conflict with those of parents and other authority figures, which can heighten feelings of loneliness, frustration, and anger. Also, as discussed in Chapter 2, depression symptoms are more prevalent among adolescents, than younger children (Buchanan et al., 1992; Petersen et al., 1993). Thus, many adolescents will need assistance from parents, teachers, and other caring adults in coping with these challenges.

Thus far we have discussed age differences in young people's emotional development. There are also important gender and cultural differences in these patterns of development. By the preschool years, boys express more anger whereas girls express more sadness and fearfulness (Eisenberg, Martin, & Fabes, 1996). In the elementary school years, boys are less likely than girls to express feelings of hurt, distress, and sadness (Eisenberg, Schaller, Miller, Fultz, Fabes, & Shell, 1988; Fuchs & Thelen, 1988). By adolescence, however, girls report greater anxiety, worry and hopeless than do boys, which may increase their vulnerability to depression.

Cultures also differ in terms of what feelings are acceptable, and how those feelings should be expressed (Saarni et al., 1998). Emotional openness and self-assertiveness are not desirable characteristics in some cultures. It is thus important to respect cultural differences in emotional responses when working with diverse groups of students.

Developing Self-Control

Children's abilities to exercise self-control play an important role in their adaptation to school settings (Pianta, 1999). Even young kindergarten students are expected to control negative emotions, to persist at difficult and challenging activities, and to inhibit impulses. Some children are able to tolerate frustration, whereas others are quick to fly off the handle. In this section we examine the development of children's capacities for self-control. Similar to the self-regulation processes discussed in earlier chapters, the development of **self-control** involves the deliberate use of cognitive or behavioral strategies to achieve a

With the discovery of social conventions for expressing emotions, children come to understand that people, including themselves, can disguise their true feelings.

The entry into adolescence is accompanied by declines in happiness and pride, and by increases in moodiness, anxiety, stress, and loneliness.

Cultures differ in terms of what one is expected to feel, and how those emotions are expressed.

desired goal, such as reducing unpleasant emotions or redirecting inappropriate behavior. Self-control is important for establishing positive social relations, for adjusting to school life, and for learning. There is also evidence to suggest that self-control functions as a protective factor to lower adolescents' risk of alcohol and drug abuse, unsafe sex, and other health and safety problems (Resnick et al., 1997).

The capacity for self-regulation is initially shaped by early interactions between caregivers and infants. Both partners must learn to respond to each other's emotions and behaviors. At first caregivers do most of the work. They are attentive to what gestures, sounds, and actions might soothe and comfort the infant. With time, however, infants become more active players in this process. Just as waving feet and arms can cause an interesting sound or visual display (Piaget's circular reactions), babies learn that their caregivers respond differently to different gestures or cries. As these patterns are established, it is possible to observe an infant wait for a caregiver's response before reacting. By delaying their response, infants are already demonstrating an ability to regulate their reactions. What an amazing feat to accomplish in the first year!

Although babies are already learning some early lessons in self-management, important advances in self-control occur between the ages of 5 and 12. These changes are in part influenced by advances in children's abilities for remembering, representing, and generalizing behavioral standards and expectations (Thompson, 1999). During the preschool years, children demonstrate an increased ability to tolerate frustration and to delay gratification. For example, when a favorite toy is not available, older preschool children respond with less anger and frustration than younger children (Matas, Arend, & Sroufe, 1978). In a clever set of studies using marshmallows, Walter Mishel and his colleagues found that preschool and primary-school-age children were able to delay using a variety of cognitive and behavioral strategies. A follow-up study further revealed that a preschooler's ability to resist temptation predicted coping skills in adolescence. The findings are summarized in the Focus on Research box.

Important advances in children's abilities to tolerate frustration, to control impulses, and to delay gratification occur between the ages of 5 and 12.

As metacognitive and language skills develop, adolescents use more complex, diverse, and flexible methods for exercising self-control. They may cognitively reframe the problem situation, use self-talk to calm emotions, and evaluate the consequences of different responses (Campas, Connor-Smith, Saltzman, Thomsen, Wadsworth, 2001). For example, a 15-year-old girl may decide not to confront a peer who has upset her, because it might cause her to become more upset. Compared with younger students, adolescents are more likely to share feelings and to gain support from their friends. Evidence also suggests that adolescents use music and television to help them cope with negative emotions or stressful situations (Larson, 1995).

Fostering Emotional Competence in the Classroom

Children learn about the nature and expression of emotions from their day-to-day interactions with people. How parents, teachers, and other adults show emotions, teach about emotions, or react to emotional experiences are all key lessons for children. In his book *Emotional Intelligence,* Daniel Goleman (1995) proposed that emotional competence may be as important as any other type of learning that takes place in school. He calls for a "schooling of emotions" that focuses on the following emotional skills: identifying, expressing, and managing emotions; controlling impulses and delaying gratification; understanding the perspective of others; and knowing the difference between feelings and actions.

Schools teach young people important lessons for understanding, expressing, and managing emotions.

Many schools are beginning to take a more active role in children's emotional development. The diary entry at the beginning of this chapter is an example of this effort. It is from

Focus on Research

Learning to Delay Gratification

Walter Mischel and his colleagues conducted a series of studies with preschool and school-age children to trace the development of self-control strategies (e.g., Mischel, Ebbesen & Zeiss, 1972; Mischel & Moore, Mischel & Mischel, 1983). They were interested specifically in the cognitive and behavioral strategies children use to delay gratification. A standard procedure was used across the studies. Briefly, children were invited into a laboratory room at their preschool and were asked to sit at a table with a bell and reward objects (marshmallows, pretzels, or poker chips). After determining which reward was most appealing, the experimenter told the child he needed to leave the room for a few minutes and showed the child the bell to summon his return. Before leaving the room, the experimenter showed the child the reward objects—two grouped together and one apart. The experimenter then explained the delay contingency: The child can have two rewards if he waits, but one if he rings the bell first. Thus, the child would receive two marshmallows (pretzels or chips) if he exercised control by delaying gratification.

This simple procedure provided interesting insights into children's understanding of self-control strategies. Preschool children who delayed gratification used several different strategies to help them wait. They covered their eyes, talked to themselves, played games, and so on. Elementary school children also indicated that they recognized the value of strategies that cognitively transformed the marshmallows into something less tasty, like cotton balls or clouds. Even more interesting were results of a follow-up test on a subsample of the children 12 to 14 years later. Those children who had resisted temptation at age 4 were now confident, self-reliant, and able to cope with stress as adolescents (Shoda, Mishel, & Peake, 1990).

a book, *The Freedom Writers,* which was inspired by a young English teacher who used literature to help her students learn about prejudice, intolerance, racism, and respect for diversity. The book is the students' own story of this self-discovery process.

In this section we discuss some ways teachers can foster **emotional competence**—the understanding, expression, and regulation of emotions—in the classroom. Developmental research on the role of social interactions in guiding and directing the development of emotional competence is in its early stages (Denham, 1998), but several important themes have already emerged:

- Teachers need to create a caring, positive, and warm affective environment for students. A young person's emotional world is shaped by these day-to-day affective experiences.

- Teachers function as important model of how to exhibit and to express emotions. Through their own actions, teachers can help students express emotions in socially appropriate ways. Teachers can also model ways of regulating emotions, such as calming down before reacting or seeking support when stressed or frustrated.

SOURCE: Mary Kate
Denny/Photo Edit.

It is important for teachers to discuss emotions with their students. These daily interactions can help students understand and handle their emotional experiences.

- It is important for teachers to discuss emotions with their students. Emotion-related language helps to increase awareness of emotional states and the intensity of feelings. Class meetings can be used to share feelings about important events or experiences. Books, stories, plays, and films can also stimulate discussions of emotional experiences.

- Finally, explicit instruction regarding specific ways of handling emotions and stress is important. These strategies might include (a) reframing the problem situation, (b) identifying alternative actions, (c) using self-talk to calm down negative emotions, (d) seeking support and help from others, and (e) avoiding problem situations altogether.

Schools today are taking a more active role in fostering students' emotional competence.

Many of these strategies were part of a school-based prevention program, PATHS (*Pro-moting Alternative THinking*) in the Seattle public schools (Greenberg, Kusche, Cook, & Quamma, 1995). This program was designed to help elementary school children manage and express their emotions. It included a curriculum containing explicit lessons on affective states (Feelings Units), as well as instruction in recognizing the feelings of others and managing emotions. The stoplight graphic shown in Figure 7.1 was displayed in classrooms to help children bring feelings and behavior under control. Approximately 300 second and third graders completed the program, and 30 percent of the students had special learning needs. When the program was evaluated, the results showed that the program was successful in increasing children's emotional understanding and regulation (Greenberg et al., 1995). Children with behavioral problems also showed significant improvements in teacher ratings of frustration tolerance, positive peer relations, and social skills. We will examine other school-based programs for reducing aggression and antisocial behavior in the next chapter.

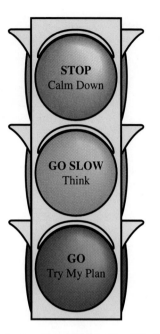

FIGURE 7.1

Control Signals Poster

SOURCE: Adapted from Weissberg, Caplan, & Bennetto (1988).

Evaluate—How Did My Plan Work?

Development of Self-Conceptions

Self-Concept and Self-Esteem

How would you describe yourself? Are you a member of a particular ethnic group? Are you strong, happy, confident, moody, shy? To what extent do you believe you are a lovable and worthy person? Answers to questions like these can tell us something about your self-concept and self-esteem. Although these two terms are frequently used interchangeably, there is an important distinction in meaning. **Self-concept** refers to the beliefs, attitudes, knowledge, and ideas people have about themselves. This self-knowledge is hierarchically organized into categories and dimensions that define the self and serve to guide behavior (Harter, 1983, 1999). For example, as will be described, adolescents have a general concept of their academic ability (e.g., "I'm a capable student") that can be broken down into different subject areas including reading, mathematics, science, and so on.

Self-esteem, on the other hand, involves an *evaluation* of our traits, abilities, and characteristics. According to one expert, self-esteem is "a personal judgment of *worthiness* that indicates the extent to which the individual believes himself to be capable, significant, successful, and worthy" (Coopersmith, 1967, p. 5; italics added). Thus, self-esteem involves a sense of self-acceptance and respect for oneself.

From an educational perspective, an important question concerns how children's self-perceptions relate to their school performance. As we will discuss later, perceptions of competence influence a student's motivation to learn. Children who perceive themselves as competent are generally more intrinsically motivated to learn than children with low-perceived competence, and they tend to choose challenging tasks, to work independently, and to persist at learning tasks (Harter & Connell, 1984). In addition to their motivational effects, self-concept and self-esteem affect children's actual achievement in school. As you would expect, children with high self-esteem and positive self-concepts tend to be more successful in school. Although associations between general measures of self-concept and

Children with high self-esteem and positive self-concepts tend to be more highly motivated and more successful in school.

academic performance tend to be moderate, they persist across gender, grade level, and socioeconomic groups (Hansford & Hattie, 1982). When domain-specific measures of self-concept and performance are used (e.g., one's self-concept of reading ability and one's grade in reading), the associations are even higher.

One issue of debate concerns the causal direction of the relation between self-concept and school achievement (Byrne, 1986; Calsyn & Kenny, 1977; Marsh, Byrne, & Yeung, 1999; Marsh & Yeung, 1997). It may be that high self-concept leads to high achievement, but the reverse could also be true: Children who do well in school generally feel better about themselves and their competence. Researchers generally believe that the relationship works both ways. For young children who are still forming their self-concept, academic performance may shape their perceptions of ability and feelings of self-worth. By middle school, however, the relationship between self-concept and school achievement becomes more complex. Students with high perceptions of ability may approach learning tasks with confidence, and success on those tasks may bolster their confidence (Bong & Clark, 1999; Marsh & Yeung, 1997; Wigfield & Karpathan, 1991). Once a child's sense of ability is firmly established, it can have a stronger influence on academic performance than objective measures of ability, such as grades and test scores (Eccles et al., 1983; Marsh, 1990; Marsh & Yeung, 1997). In other words, it is the child's *perception* of reality, rather than reality per se, that has the strongest influence on school performance.

Once a child's sense of ability is established, it can be a greater influence on academic performance than objective measures of ability, such as grades and test scores.

Developmental Changes in Self-Concept

Children begin to think of themselves as separate individuals during the toddler period. By 21 to 24 months, children can recognize themselves in the mirror, and they begin to use such words as *me, I,* and *mine* as a way of asserting their individuality. In part, behavior attributed to the "terrible twos" is an expression of the child's emerging self and individuality.

During preschool and early elementary school, children primarily describe themselves in terms of their physical characteristics, interests, actions, and other concrete labels (Harter, 1999). For example, a 4-year-old might say, "I am a boy, and I like to play with Legos." This tendency to use physical self-descriptions reflects a young child's concrete thinking abilities. That is, young children describe themselves in terms of attributes that may be physical (e.g., "I have brown

A child's sense of self begins to emerge in the toddler years.

Children first see themselves in terms of their physical characteristics, then gradually begin to see themselves in terms of psychological traits, such as kindness or friendliness.

SOURCE: Michael Newman/Photo Edit.

hair"), active (e.g., "I can count"), social (e.g., "I have a baby brother"), or psychological (e.g., "I am nice"). However, a young child's understanding of self is very limited. Children may sometimes feel mean and sometimes feel nice, but they have difficulty coordinating these two views of themselves into a unified sense of self (Harter, 1999). Also, children's self-evaluations during this period are unrealistically positive because young children have difficulty distinguishing between their real and ideal self. Because young children *want* to be smart, they often describe themselves as smart (Stipek, 1984).

During the middle childhood years (8 to 12 years old), children begin to describe themselves in terms of higher-order concepts that are based on several different features of the self. For example, a 10-year-old girl might describe herself as a good student because she reads well, gets good grades, and finishes her work on time. Whereas younger children are unable to integrate opposing attributes (e.g., mean and nice), older children are able to do so. Accordingly, their self-descriptions tend to include both positive and negative characteristics (Harter, 1999). Older children are also more likely to describe themselves in terms of interpersonal and social characteristics, such as caring, loyal, trustworthy, and so forth. These self-descriptions suggest that older children are beginning to place themselves within a social context.

Children compare themselves with others to find their unique strengths, but negative comparisons can also produce declines in self-concept and self-esteem.

Older children also understand that they may have thoughts and feelings that are hidden from others. Psychologists refer to this developmental trend as the emergence of the inner or **psychological self** (Selman, 1980). It is not until adolescence, or during the formal operational period, that children begin to describe themselves in terms of abstract values, beliefs, and attitudes (Damon & Hart, 1982; Harter, 1999). Adolescents, for example, are much more likely than younger children to describe themselves in terms of a political, religious, or sexual orientation. However, young adolescents are likely to have different conceptions of themselves in relation to parents, close friends, teachers, and so forth. Discrepancies in self-perceptions across relationships and roles can cause confusion and uncertainty. These feelings are exacerbated by the adolescent's ability to reflect on internal states. As we discussed previously, adolescents can become preoccupied with their thoughts and feelings. Cognitive advances in the late adolescent years enable young people to develop a coherent and integrated representation of the self (Harter, 1999). As described below, identity formation involves defining oneself in terms of an organized system of beliefs, goals, and values. The Focus on Development table summarizes changes in self-conceptions from early childhood through late adolescence.

Because of their greater cognitive flexibility, adolescents are much more able than young children to form a complex self-concept that includes inconsistencies in their behavior.

Along with these changes in self-conceptions, children develop a more differentiated view of the self as they mature. As early as kindergarten or first grade, children develop separate concepts of their physical, social, and cognitive abilities (Eccles, Wigfield, Harold, & Blumenfeld, 1993; Hattie & Marsh, 1996; Eccles, Wigfield, & Schiefele, 1998; Harter, 1998; Marsh, Craven, & Debus, 1991; Wigfield, Eccles, Yoon, et al., 1996). An older student's academic self-concept may be further broken down according to success in individual subject areas, such as reading, mathematics, or science. That is to say, a student may view himself or herself as good in mathematics but not musically talented. One view of a differentiated self-concept is shown in Figure 7.2. Teachers and parents need to remember that children's self-concepts vary across subject areas. They may have poor academic self-concepts in some subject areas but average or above-average self-concepts in others (Marsh, 1989).

Another important change that occurs during the school years is the use of social comparisons to evaluate oneself (Ruble, 1983). Whereas preschoolers may describe themselves in terms of actions (e.g., "I can run fast"), older children are much more likely to make comparative judgments of their abilities (e.g., "I am the fastest runner in the class"). Theorists believe that such comparisons help children to identify their unique characteristics and

Focus on Development

Developmental Changes in Self-Representations in Childhood and Adolescence

Age Period	Developmental Characteristics	Examples
Toddler and early childhood	Concrete observable characteristics focused on abilities, activities, and possessions. Isolated representations with no coordination or coherence.	I go to school. I can run fast. I have a baby sister.
Early to middle childhood	Simple links between traits; all-or-none thinking; typically positive representations.	I am nice and my teacher likes me. I am good at running and climbing.
Middle to late childhood	Trait labels that focus on abilities and interpersonal characteristics; social comparisons with peers. Integration of positive and negative characteristics.	I am good at math, but reading is hard for me. I have more friends than my sister.
Early adolescence	Integration of traits into simple abstractions. Focused on skills/attributes that influence interactions with others. All-or-none thinking. Don't detect inconsistencies between traits.	I am a pretty cheerful person, especially with my friends.
Late adolescence	Higher-order abstractions that reflect personal beliefs, values, and moral standards. More stable and balanced view of positive and negative standards.	People say I am moody. I am happy some days, but depressed sometimes. I am American, but I respect my Chinese heritage.

SOURCE: After Harter (1998).

to differentiate themselves from others. However, comparisons can also produce declines in self-concept or self-esteem when children perceive themselves as less able, less socially competent, or less attractive than their peers. As we will discuss, social comparison processes in the classroom can have a very negative effect on children's concepts of ability and on their motivation to learn.

Numerous studies report that age affects children's overall and academic self-concepts. In general, there is a decline in students' overall self-concept during late childhood and early adolescence followed by a resurgence in late adolescence and early adulthood (Eccles et al., 1993; Eccles et al., 1998; Marsh, 1989; Stipek & Mac Iver, 1989; Wigfield et al.,

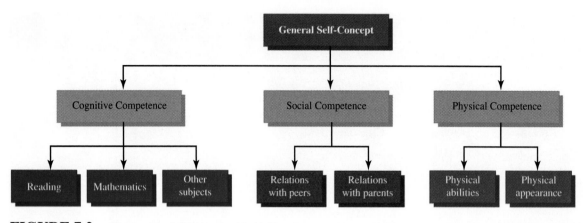

FIGURE 7.2   *Hierarchical Structure of Self-Concept*

Young children tend to overestimate their abilities, but older children gradually develop a more realistic view of their abilities built on external feedback.

Because of heightened self-consciousness in adolescence, teachers need to be careful not to single out individual students for public recognition or disciplinary actions.

1996). Similarly, researchers have found that age affects children's competence perceptions in both academic (e.g., math, reading) and nonacademic (e.g., social relations, music) domains (Eccles et al., 1993; Marsh, 1989). These declines in domain-specific perceptions, particularly for mathematics, appear to be the most acute as children enter early adolescence and often continue well into adolescence (Eccles et al., 1983; Eccles et al., 1998; Wigfield, Eccles, Mac Iver, Rueman, & Midgley, 1991).

In general, children's academic self-concepts become more accurate with age. Whereas young children are likely to overestimate their abilities in certain areas, older children have a more realistic view of their abilities. That is, their self-perceptions are more highly correlated with grades, teacher evaluations, and other external feedback (Marsh, 1989; Stipek & Mac Iver, 1989). The increasing accuracy of children's ability perceptions are related to several factors. First, as discussed, children are better able to utilize social comparison information in judging their skills and abilities by the middle childhood years. Also, age and ability stratification in school can stimulate social comparisons among children of the same age. Further, as children's cognitive abilities mature they are better able to integrate multiple sources of information about their abilities (teacher comments, grades, etc.)

Another important change in adolescents' self-perception that teachers need to consider is their increasing ability to reflect on themselves. As adolescents become more self-reflective, they develop a greater understanding of themselves. However, this self-reflective tendency among this age group often leads to an increased sense of self-consciousness, because adolescents assume that others are also observing and evaluating them. This developmental trend can often lead adolescents to dress and act like their peers, so they won't stand out from others. It can also lead adolescents to be highly critical of themselves. Because of this heightened sense of self-consciousness, teachers should take care in singling students out in public for either special recognition or disciplinary actions. It may be more appropriate to provide such feedback in private. Gradually, as an adolescent's self-concept becomes more firmly established, he or she begins to feel more secure and less self-conscious.

Developmental Trends in Self-Esteem

As we discussed, self-esteem involves an overall evaluation of one's value or worth as a person. It is often difficult for very young children to provide an assessment of their self-esteem because of various cognitive limitations. However, this limitation does not mean that young children lack a sense of self-worth. Young children display this sense of self in behavioral terms (Harter, 1990). Children who show displays of confidence, curiosity, initiative, and independence are identified by teachers as children with high self-esteem (Harter, 1990, 1999). Also, young children with high self-esteem are able to adjust to changes and transitions, to tolerate frustration, and to handle conflict.

During the early school years, children's self-esteem generally increases as they achieve success in their peer relationships and in other areas of importance to them. Theorists believe that the contributions of specific self-appraisals to overall self-worth vary according to the degree of importance or value attached to a particular attribute (Harter, 1990). This idea dates back to the writings of William James (1892) in the late nineteenth century. James believed that individuals placed a different value on success within different domains of their lives. He further proposed that individuals compare their level of competence to their aspirations for success across different domains. The degree of congruence or discongruence determines their feelings of self-worth.

According to this view, the importance of intelligence, popularity, or physical attractiveness will determine the degree to which perceived inadequacies will affect overall evaluations of self-esteem. In a study of elementary school children (grades 3 to 6), Susan Harter (1986) found that children's evaluations of global self-worth were based upon their evaluations of how competently they could perform in areas deemed important. Interestingly, children with a high self-worth discounted the importance of domains in which they were less competent. However, children with low self-worth did not use this discounting principle in the same way.

By late childhood, global measures of self-esteem also show more stability with age. Children with high self-esteem at age 8 are likely to have high self-esteem at age 10, assuming their environment and social comparison group remain fairly stable (Harter, 1983). In middle adolescence, global evaluations of self-worth also become more positive.

Young people of all ages with high self-esteem are able to adjust to changes and transitions, to tolerate frustration, and to handle conflict.

Children with high self-esteem tend to discount the importance of domains in which they are less competent.

SOURCE: Jonathan Nourok/Photo Edit.

Students with high self-esteem show pride in their schoolwork.

Increases in self-esteem may be tied to gains in personal autonomy. Older adolescents have more opportunities to choose social or academic situations that provide positive feedback about their competencies (Harter, 1999).

Although young people's self-esteem judgments may become more stable and positive with age, important changes occur as students enter adolescence. First, recall that young people's conceptions of the self become more complex and more differentiated with cognitive maturity. This same pattern applies to self-esteem. An adolescent can have high self-esteem in relation to peer popularity but low self-esteem relative to school achievement. Until late adolescence or adulthood, there can be considerable variation in self-esteem across relational contexts (family, peer, and school), as well as experiential domains such as academic subjects, athletics, and personal appearance (Harter, 1999; Hattie, 1992). Thus, it may be misleading to describe an older child's or adolescent's self-esteem as low without knowing the particular context. Consider this adolescent girl's response to the question "How much do you like yourself?"

> Well, I like some things about me, but I don't like others. I'm glad that I'm popular since I don't do as well as the really smart kids. That's OK, because if you're too smart you'll lose friends. So being smart is just not that important. Except to my parents. I feel like I am letting them down when I don't do as well as they want. But what's really important to me is how I look. If I like the way I look, then I really like the person I am. (Harter, 1990, p. 364)

Self-esteem in older children is related to conceptions of an ideal self that are formed through social experiences.

During middle childhood, children also develop the capabilities to compare their real self with a set of desired characteristics. This **ideal self** is generally constructed on the basis of social experiences. The expectations, values, and ideals of peers and adults also help to shape the content of the ideal self. When children do not measure up to their ideal self, it can lead to declines in self-esteem. A good example of this phenomenon was found in our discussion of early maturing girls in Chapter 2. As we discussed, most American girls receive consistent and clear messages that beauty is defined in terms of being "slim and trim." When early maturing girls cannot meet this cultural ideal of physical attractiveness, it leads to negative changes in self-esteem (Harter, 1993). Research shows that physical appearance is the strongest correlate of global self-worth in childhood and adolescence (DuBois, Trevendale, Burk-Braxton, Swenson, & Hardestry, 2000). These patterns were found in the United States, as well as in European and Asian countries (Harter, 1999).

School Transitions and Self-Esteem

Some adolescents, especially girls, experience significant declines in their self-esteem during school transitions.

The transition to a new school can be very stressful for many students, as we discussed previously. When students change school environments, they must adjust to new expectations and routines, as well as to unfamiliar peers and teachers. Researchers have examined how changing schools can affect students' ratings of self-esteem. In one of the first studies, Roberta Simmons and Dale Blyth (1987) compared adolescents' self-esteem in two Milwaukee public school settings. One group of students attended the same school from kindergarten to eighth grades then attended high school for four years (8–4 arrangement), and another grade, changed schools after sixth grade and ninth grade (6–3–3 arrangement). This study showed that adolescents' self-esteem ratings were affected by these different schooling arrangements, and the effects varied by gender. Figure 7.3 shows the influence of school transitions on girls' and boys' self-esteem. As you can see, girls in the 6–3–3 showed two dramatic drops in self-esteem, whereas boys showed only one

Development of Self-Conceptions

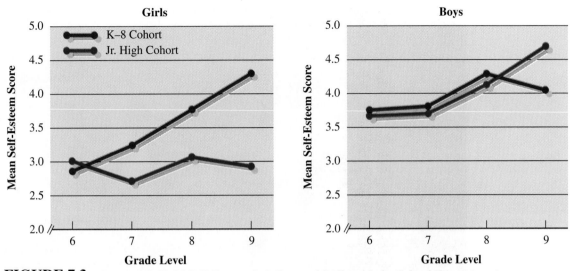

FIGURE 7.3 *Boys' and Girls' Self-Esteem Is Influenced Differently by School Transitions in Early Adolescence*

SOURCE: After Simmons & Blyth (1987).

as they entered the tenth grade. In contrast, self-esteem rises for both girls and boys in the 8–4 arrangement.

Several factors seem to explain declines in students' self-esteem as they change schools. First, youngsters experience disruptions in their social networks during the change. Second, their social status also changes, as they move from being the oldest to the youngest students in their school. Third, adolescents who change schools must adjust to new school routines and social expectations, changes that often coincide with pubertal changes, especially for girls. Junior high transitions are particularly difficult, because adolescents are beginning puberty and adjusting to a new school environment at the same time. This is not the case for adolescents who remain in the same school.

Other researchers point to the effect of changes in the quality of the school environment as adolescents make the transition to junior high schools. These schools tend to be larger, more impersonal, and less sensitive to students' developmental needs than elementary schools (Anderman & Midgley, 1996; Eccles et al., 1993; Midgley, Berman, & Hicks, 1995). Such changes can produce negative outcomes for young adolescents, especially those who are already experiencing other changes or having difficulty at school or at home (Lord, Eccles, & McCarthy, 1994). Adolescents who enter schools that are more personal and smaller in size tend to experience fewer adjustment problems. Also, adolescents who remain with a stable peer group during school transitions are less likely to experience negative changes in self-esteem, especially if the friendships are warm, supportive, and nurturing (Brendt, 1999). The Focus on Teaching box on page 401summarizes some ways that teachers can enhance self-esteem in the classroom.

In general, classrooms with high levels of cooperation, collaboration, and student autonomy tend to produce higher self-esteem among students than classrooms that are teacher-directed and competitive.

Interventions to Promote Positive Self-Esteem

Numerous programs have been developed to help children and adolescents with low self-esteem. Low levels of self-esteem are correlated with a range of problem behaviors, including poor school attendance and achievement, peer rejection, juvenile delinquency,

School transitions are often difficult for young adolescents because they must adjust to new social expectations and school routines, while adjusting to physical changes.

loneliness, depression, teenage pregnancy, social alienation, and so forth (Haney & Durak, 1998; Harter, 1990, 1999). Intervention and treatment programs in the 1960s and 1970s focused on helping young people *feel good* about themselves. However, programs that focused on affect alone had only a limited impact on measures of global self-esteem (Harter, 1999). Positive reinforcement or praise is not enough when students are still failing in areas of importance to them.

Current efforts to help students with low self-esteem are more cognitively based. For older children and adolescents, it is helpful to explore the origins of their negative self-perceptions. Some intervention programs target attributional biases that lead students to blame themselves for their inadequacies, while crediting others for their successes. When students take responsibility for their successes, it can enhance perceptions of competence in domains of importance. Another strategy is to help students focus on domains in which they display competence and discount, as much as possible, those domains in which they feel less adequate. Because not all students can excel in a particular academic area, it is important to have broad definitions of competence. Gardner's theory of multiple intelligences reminds us that there are many ways to be smart. Finally, skill development is critical for the development of self-esteem. One of the best ways to improve students' self-esteem is to teach them the knowledge and skills that will enable them to experience real success in areas that are important to them (Bednar, Wells, & Peterson, 1995).

Social support can also have a positive effect on self-esteem. As we discussed, children and adolescents with warm, responsive, and nurturing parents tend to have high levels of self-esteem. For students who are experiencing disapproval, rejection, or neglect at home, a caring adult at school or in the community can help compensate for a lack of parent support. In a study of middle school students, 60 percent reported a special adult in their lives who provided various types of social support including approval, emotional support,

One of the best ways to improve students' self-esteem is to teach them the knowledge and skills that will enable them to experience success in areas that are important to them.

Focus on Teaching

- Create an environment that is physically and psychologically safe for all students.

- Provide all students with an environment of encouragement and positive reinforcement.

- Accept and appreciate all students for their efforts as well as their accomplishments.

- Accept students as they are, and let them know it. Do not make acceptance conditional on behavior.

- Treat all students respectfully, as you would a family member.

- Accept the students' feelings, both positive and negative. Negative feelings are a normal part of life and need to be accepted.

- Avoid comparing students. Encourage students to compete against their previous levels of learning.

- Make standards of evaluation clear to students and help them learn to evaluate their own behavior.

- Make demands and challenges that are appropriate for the students' ages and abilities.

- Give students opportunities to make decisions, have responsibility, and experience feelings of competence and confidence.

- Encourage students to do as much as they can on their own.

- Attend extracurricular events that are important to the students, such as athletic games, recitals, plays, and debates.

- Avoid laughing at students, making jokes about students, or making sarcastic remarks to students.

SOURCE: After J. Canfield (1990).

advise, and help (Harter, 1999). Students reported that their special adults were teachers, counselors, coaches, ministers, relatives, parents of friends, or other adult friends. Big Sisters, Big Brothers, and other mentoring programs are also places young people can garner social support.

Identity Formation

In the previous sections, we discussed how children and adolescents form a sense of their competencies and self-worth. These developmental processes serve as the foundation for identity formation. As you recall, Erikson's theory maintains that *identity versus identity confusion* is the central issue that defines the adolescent. Young people needed to achieve a positive, coherent identity. Erikson's (1968) definition of identity was fairly broad:

> The wholeness to be achieved at this stage [adolescence] I have called a sense of inner identity. The young person, in order to experience wholeness, must feel a progressive continuity between that which he has come to be during the long years of childhood and that which he promises to become in the anticipated future; between that which he conceives himself to be and that which he perceives others to see in him and to expect of him. Individually speaking, identity includes, but is more than the sum of, all successive identifications of those earlier years when the child wanted to be, and often was forced to become, like the people he depended on. (p. 87)

For adolescents, the critical task is to select and integrate childhood identities with personal desires and societal opportunities and expectations in order to develop a sense of who they are and who they will become.

For adolescents, the critical task is to select and integrate childhood identities with personal desires and societal opportunities and expectations in order to develop a sense of who they are and who they will become. According to Erikson (1968), our identity gives a sense of inner assuredness, continuity, and direction for the future, and it involves a "series of ever narrowing personal, occupational, sexual, and ideological commitments" (p. 245).

Erikson believed that the biological and social changes that occur in adolescence lead young people to reflect on their place in society, on the ways others view them, and on their options for the future. This idea fits with what we already know about adolescents. They are growing into adult bodies and assuming greater responsibility for themselves. They also are developing the cognitive abilities to engage in introspection and to contemplate the future. However, Erikson believed that social interactions as well as the social context were critical to the formation of an identity. By interacting with others, we learn about ourselves and what we ought to be. The social environment determines what sorts of identities are possible and desirable. Over the last 30 years, for example, the career options for women have changed dramatically. Women from earlier generations defined their identities in terms of commitments to marriage and family life. Many young women today postpone marriage and parenthood to pursue a career. Over 20 years ago, Erikson (1968) commented on the "prolonged adolescent" that was becoming increasingly common in industrialized societies undergoing dramatic social and economic changes. Theorists believe that Erikson's observation applies to more young people today than ever before.

Young people who have achieved an identity are able to commit to personal, vocational, and ideological choices, and they score on measures of self-esteem and psychological well-being.

Erikson wrote extensively about identity development, using a research method called psychohistory. His most famous works of psychohistory were his psychological analyses of the developmental histories of Mohandas K. Gandhi (Erikson, 1969) and Martin Luther (Erikson, 1958). Erikson's writings inspired the research of James Marcia, who investigated identity development of young people in three areas: occupation, ideology (values and beliefs), and interpersonal relations. To determine a person's **identity status** within each domain, responses are rated on two dimensions: (1) the degree to which the person has made commitments, and (2) the degree to which the person has explored different options and alternatives.

As shown in Figure 7.4, an individual is assigned to one of four identity statuses: diffusion, moratorium, foreclosure, or achievement. Before a discussion of the characteristics of each status, it is important to point out that people do not necessarily progress through each of the categories to achieve an identity. Only one development sequence is specified. According to Erikson's theory, one must experience psychosocial moratorium before achieving an identity.

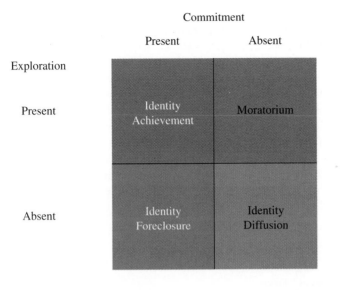

FIGURE 7.4

Categories of Identity Status
SOURCE: After Marcia (1966).

Also, it is important to point out that individuals may be at different identity statuses in forming a social, occupational, or ideological identity. For example, studies reveal that young people emerge from college with a more clearly defined set of occupational plans, but with no firm ideological commitments (Waterman, 1982). Finally, individuals may reevaluate their commitments in a particular domain, even after achieving an identity. Some of you, for example, may be studying to become a teacher as a second career.

Young people who are in the *identity diffusion* category are not actively exploring potential choices, and they are unable to make any firm commitments regarding their beliefs, social relationships, or occupational plans. This identity status is correlated with low self-esteem and low self-control. It is also associated with high anxiety and high apathy (Waterman, 1999a). Individuals with a diffused identity are at greatest risk for developing psychological problems (Meeus, Iedema, Helsen, & Vollenbergh, 1999).

Young people in *identity foreclosure* have not explored different possibilities but have nonetheless committed themselves to certain choices. This category tends to be associated with conformity, conventionality, and obedience to authority (Meeus et al., 1999). Generally, youths with a foreclosed identity have a strong attachment to their parents, and they adopt their values and guidance without going through a period of exploration. Identity foreclosure tends to be associated with high levels of psychological well-being (Meeus et al., 1999).

Young people in *identity moratorium* are actively exploring different occupational plans, ideological stances, and personal relationships, but they are not ready to make any choices or commitments. When compared with those in other statuses, individuals in moratorium status tend to score lower on measures of well-being and higher on measures of anxiety and conflict with parents, but they tend to be less rigid and authoritarian (Meeus et al., 1999; Waterman, 1999a). Theorists believe that moratorium, although necessary for achieving an identity, is closest in character to an identity crisis, and it is viewed as a transitional status rather than an endpoint for identity development.

Finally, *identity achievement* describes those young people who have engaged in exploration and who have made definite personal, vocational, or ideological choices. These individuals tend to be high in self-esteem, self-control, and self-direction (Marcia, 1980). They also tend to score high on measures of academic motivation and career maturity. Consistent with Erikson's theory, these are individuals who have achieved an identity score highest on measures of psychological well-being when compared with those in other identity statuses (Meeus et al., 1999; Waterman, 1999a). In theory, these individuals have the most favorable profile for later development.

Erikson's theory proposed that identity formation defined the period of adolescence. Do empirical studies of identity development support his claim? Although exploration may begin at this age, most studies reveal that identity development extends beyond adolescence. Figure 7.5 shows data from a study of adolescents between the ages of 10 and 18. As can be seen here, a higher proportion of high school students fall into the foreclosure and identity diffusion categories when compared with college students. These data are consistent with other studies suggesting that fewer than one-third of adolescents have achieved an overall identity by the end of high school (Meeus, 1999). Studies suggest that more identity exploration will occur during the college years, when young people have more opportunity and freedom to experiment with different social roles, occupations, and ideologies. However, studies reveal that a majority of young people have not reached identity achievement by age 21 (Waterman, 1999a).

Much of the work of identity development takes place after high school, but schools provide a safe place for exploring different identities for the future.

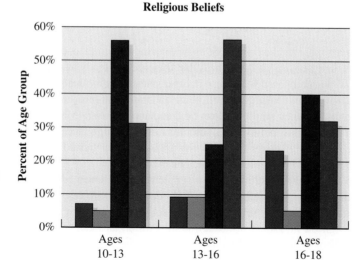

FIGURE 7.5

Percent of Children at Each Identity Status for Vocational Choices and Religious Beliefs: United States

SOURCE: After Waterman (1999).

Developing an Ethnic Identity

Ethnic identity refers to one's sense of identity concerning racial or ethnic group membership. A positively valued ethnic identity is important for a strong, positive, and stable self-identity in minority youths (Phinney & Rosenthal, 1992). An ethnic identity includes some or all of the following elements: (a) self-identification as a member of a group; (b) feelings of belonging and commitment to a group, (c) positive (or negative) attitudes toward the group; (d) a sense of shared attitudes and values, and (e) specific ethnic traditions and practices, such as language, behavior , and customs (Phinney & Rosenthal, 1992, p. 147).

Most of us in this multicultural society take pride in our ethnic heritage, whether our ancestors came from Ireland, Russia, Vietnam, Africa, Cuba, Germany, or England. Thus far, more research on the development of ethnic identity has focused on African Americans than on any other ethnic group. Moreover, few studies have differentiated among members within a particular ethnic group. For example, black youths can have either African or Caribbean ancestry, but they are generally treated as one ethnic group. Similarly Asian American youngsters come from many different countries, each with its own language, customs, and traditions. Because our society is becoming increasingly more culturally diverse, developmental researchers are focusing greater attention on the role that ethnicity plays in children's personal and emotional development.

In this section, we will examine the process of forming an ethnic identity and its important influence on self-esteem. Specifically, we will examine the following sorts of questions: When do people form an ethnic identity? What are the processes through which people form an ethnic identity? Do members of an ethnic minority group have more difficulty forming a coherent and integrated identity than those in the white majority?

A positively valued ethnic identity is important for a strong, positive, and stable self-identity in minority youths.

Developing an Awareness of Ethnic Differences

Research suggests that children begin to notice racial differences among people as early as 3 years of age. By this age, children are able to correctly identify skin color and their own race or ethnicity. Much of this research is done with doll studies, in which children are asked to choose the doll that looks like a black (or a white) child and to choose the doll that looks most like them (Clark & Clark, 1947; Katz & Zalk, 1974). By age 6, white children identify with their ethnic group with a frequency of 100 percent. In contrast, African American children of the same age identify with their ethnic group at a much lower rate, approximately 70 percent to 75 percent of the time. Research in the 1960s suggested that African American children may be less likely to identify with their own race because of the negative characteristics and attributes attributed to African Americans in our society (Greenwald & Oppenheim, 1968). However, most of these studies were conducted during the civil rights era, long before the "black is beautiful" movement. If racial identification studies were done today, African American children might identify with the correct doll at a much higher rate.

Ethnic Differences in Self-Concept and Self-Esteem

As you recall, Erikson believed that the development of a strong sense of competence and self-worth is critical for the formation of an identity in adolescence. Before we discuss how children form an ethnic identity, let's first review some of the research on ethnic differences in self-concept and self-esteem.

Racial and ethnic prejudices may make it difficult for ethnic minority children to develop positive feelings of competency and worth. As they grow older, ethnic minority children become painfully aware of how they are negatively evaluated by white society. Young people from various ethnic minority groups in the United States must contend with negative stereotypes, prejudices, and the lower social status of minorities. For this reason, early research assumed that ethnic minority children had poor self-concepts and low self-esteem because of their "inferior" status in white society.

We have already discussed that African American children are more likely to misidentify their ethnic group. Studies report similar results for Native Americans, and the selection of white dolls is presumed to indicate low self-esteem and self-hatred (Spencer & Markstrom-Adams, 1990). However, as suggested earlier, much of the research in this area is dated. In addition, few studies ask children their reasons for choosing the white doll. It has been suggested that children's doll preferences may reflect their understanding of power positions in the world around them (Spencer & Markstrom-Adams, 1990). In addition, children often make different selections when the experimenter is of the same ethnic background. For example, Native American children will choose the Native American doll if the experimenter is of the same tribe. This finding suggests that children may be choosing the doll they believe the white experimenter prefers them to choose. Furthermore, these studies assume that children are using white society as the source of information about their ethnicity. These studies tend to overestimate the influence of white prejudice on self-concepts while they disregard the role of a child's own ethnic community in mediating the effects of racial prejudice. In African American communities, for example, the church, friends, and family members are positive sources of self-concept and self-esteem, and under certain conditions, they can filter out prejudicial messages from white society (Spencer & Markstrom-Adams, 1990; Harter, 1990).

Most studies report few ethnic differences in measures of self-esteem and self-concept.

In general, studies over time report little difference in white and black youths' self-concepts and self-esteem (Graham, 1994; McAdoo, 1985; Rosenberg, 1979). Moreover, African American girls generally report higher self-esteem than white or Hispanic girls do during adolescence (AAUW, 1991). There are, however, exceptions to this pattern. African American children and adolescents tend to have higher self-esteem when they live in predominantly black neighborhoods, succeed in school, and perceive that they are held in high regard by parents and peers (Rosenberg, 1979; Luster & McAdoo, 1995). In addition, evidence suggests that success in school may be an important source of high esteem for some low-income African American children (Luster & McAdoo, 1995).

Interestingly, the school context has an important influence on the self-concepts and self-esteem of ethnic minority youth. There is some evidence to suggest that black students who attend racially integrated schools tend to report lower self-esteem than black students in racially segregated or isolated schools, at least in the South, where much of this research has been conducted (Powell, 1985). These findings have been interpreted as suggesting that African American students in racially mixed schools experience more difficulty in maintaining their own value system. In addition, racially integrated schools may foster more comparisons between different ethnic groups, which can lower the self-esteem of students who are not in the majority. White students in these schools are more likely than black students to hold positions of power and prestige (e.g., class president, homecoming queen, class valedictorian). In contrast, students in the racially segregated schools are more likely to compare themselves with members of the same ethnic group. In addition, school personnel and students are likely to have a shared value system, which may further a sense of psychological and community cohesion in the school (Harter, 1990).

The Process of Forming an Ethnic Identity

Although recent research suggests that most ethnic minority children do not suffer from low self-esteem and negative self-concepts (Spencer & Markstrom-Adams, 1990), the process of forming an identity may be particularly complicated and painful for them.

Minority youth must confront conflicting values between the larger society and their own culture, as when Native American students are expected to maintain eye contact with authority figures at school. In addition, curriculum materials continue to project stereotypical images of minority groups (e.g., Native Americans live in teepees, wear feather head-dresses, and shoot bows and arrows) that they internalize.

In the traditional "melting pot" ideal of American culture, ethnic minorities become a part of the majority culture, whereas more recent immigrant parents often want their children to maintain the traditions and language of their culture of origin. A recent study showed that immigrant parents placed more emphasis on family obligations and responsibilities than did their adolescents, especially if their sons or daughters were born in the United States (Phinney et al., 2000).

Ethnic minority youths must often live between two cultures in some satisfactory way. Some may respond by rejecting their own ethnic heritage. For example, one study showed that Asian American adolescents were more likely than African Americans and Hispanics to hold negative attitudes toward their own cultural group (Phinney, 1993). Perhaps the strong emphasis placed on achievement and conformity in Asian American families clashes with the adolescent ideal of freedom and self-expression. An added complication is that ethnic minority youths may be rejected by their own ethnic group if they associate or identify too closely with the majority culture. For example, black students who "act white" are called "oreos," or some other pejorative term. In this example, an African American high school student explains his ambivalence toward his academic success:

Ethnic minority youths may be rejected by their ethnic group if they associate or identify too closely with the majority culture.

> Because they think people won't like think, if they are smart. Like my French teacher was saying—well, my—she said—she was saying that I'm good and everything, right?—in class, around her, want everybody to act like me. And I tried to say "NO! Don't say *that!*", you know, 'cause I know people get mad at me and stuff. (Fordham, 1988, p. 77)

Some researchers believe that African Americans and Latin Americans often hide their abilities and underachieve in school so they are not perceived as acting white by their ethnic group (Fordham & Ogbu, 1986; Fordham, 1996). Thus, identity formation for ethnic minorities involves finding the right balance between their own ethnic background and the dominant culture. The complexity of this process is illustrated in the following remarks of an African American adolescent who was bused into a school that was 95 percent white:

> I don't consider myself to be a minority because my [white] friends, they don't even consider or even look at me being a different color; just being a regular, being like them. They [other bused students] prefer to be Black, they want to hang around with the Blacks, they don't want nothing to do with the Whites. . . . I'm not like that . . . I attend the ski club and I asked if anyone else wanted to get into it, and you have seen their faces, it was hysterical. What is this kid talking about, the ski club? It's a bunch of "honkies" going to be there. (Miller, 1989, p. 181)

An ethnic identity begins to emerge in adolescence when young people have the cognitive abilities to consider issues related to prejudice and racism, and to reflect on their own personal belief systems and values.

The work of forming an ethnic identity generally begins in adolescence, when young people have the cognitive abilities to consider issues related to prejudice and racism and to reflect on their own personal belief systems and values. Ethnic identity, like any other self-concept factor, takes time to discover and involves experimentation with different possibilities. It is not unusual for minority adolescents to experience some type of identity crisis in which they question how they feel about their ethnic identity. This "crisis" is often triggered by an event that causes feelings of humiliation, inferiority, or rejection (Cross, 1991). In Malcom X's autobiography, for example, he attributed the beginning of his search for his

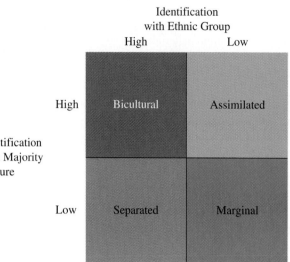

FIGURE 7.6

Ethnic Identity Status

SOURCE: After Phinney & Devich-Navarro (1997).

ethnic identity to the day he was told by his high school counselor that he should become a carpenter rather than a lawyer, because carpentry was better suited to his race.

In the process of forming an ethnic identity, youths generally go from the extreme of total assimilation to that of separation before reaching a personal solution. Jean Phinney (Phinney, 1990, 1993; Phinney & Devich-Navalino, 1997; Phinney & Rosenthal, 1992) has examined how minority youths resolve their identity issues. As shown in Figure 7.6, this research identified four different patterns. *Assimilation* involves adopting the norms, attitudes, and behaviors of the dominant culture and rejecting those of one's own ethnic group. For example, many second-generation immigrants no longer view themselves as English or German, but as American. *Marginality* involves living within the dominant culture but remaining estranged or alienated from it. This person does not feel he or she belongs to either culture. A third approach is *separation.* These minority youths reject the dominant culture and only associate with their own cultural or racial group. Finally, *biculturalism* involves maintaining ties to both cultures and developing a bicultural identity. A bicultural identity enables ethnic minorities to go back and forth between the ethnic and dominant culture, and alternate identities as appropriate for the situation. One Chinese American adolescent described her bicultural identity this way: "I feel like I am an American, but I respect my Chinese heritage" (Phinney & Rosenthal, 1982, p. 165).

There is some suggestion that achieving an ethnic identity is more closely tied to self-esteem for minority youths than for white youths (Phinney & Rosenthal, 1992). In an early study, Phinney (1989) found that African American, Asian American, and Mexican American adolescents who have made greater progress toward resolving issues related to their ethnic identity also reported higher levels of self-esteem. To achieve a positive and secure ethnic identity, minority youths must successfully cope with discrimination, stereotypes, and cultural conflicts. Unfortunately, far too many ethnic minority adolescents find it difficult to forge a strong identity. Instead, they develop what is called a *negative identity.* They reject the values of the dominant culture as well as their own. For example, a Mexican American adolescent who gave up on school was asked to describe what it means to be a successful adult. He replied, "being on the streets" and "knowing what was happening." He mentioned his uncle, the leader of a local gang, as an example (Matute-Bianche, 1986, pp. 250–251).

When minority youths develop a negative identity, they reject the values of the dominant culture as well as their own.

Schooling and Ethnic Identity

What can schools do to help students resolve their ethnic identity conflicts? As we discussed in Chapter 4, it is important for schools to actively embrace multicultural education. Schools are most helpful to students if the schools respect the cultural heritage of all who attend them. This does not mean, as stated previously, that schools can simply institute international festivals or observe ethnic holidays, such as Rosh Hashanah. Every effort must be made to reduce ethnic stereotyping and to incorporate on a daily basis a sharing of the wealth of diverse ethnic cultural specifics—foods, songs, traditions, and histories. Schools can arrange to provide successful role models for ethnic minority children. Most important, teachers should not tolerate the lack of interest expressed by many white students and their parents in learning about their own ethnic origins. That is to say, teachers need to help all students better understand their own ethnic heritage. For example, what were the circumstances that caused their ancestors to come to the United States? How were their ancestors treated when they first arrived here? What was America like then? If they experienced hardships, how did they overcome them? Not every white American came over on the *Mayflower,* as some elementary social studies texts lead children to believe. When majority youths are more knowledgeable of their own ethnic identity, they are less likely to hold stereotypes of ethnic minorities (Banks, 1994). Teachers must make every effort to help *all* students understand the diverse and pluralistic nature of American society.

Gender-Role Conceptions

Gender is a key component of the self, and it can strongly influence our sense of self-esteem. In this section, we examine how children form **gender-role conceptions,** that is, the images we have of ourselves as males and females. Do you view yourself as sensitive, emotional, and dependent? If so, then your self-image conforms to what society defines as feminine. If you describe yourself as independent, assertive, and strong, then your self-image is consistent with the masculine ideal. Gender conceptions are important for understanding not only the self but the behavior of others. As they grow up, children use information from parents, peers, school, and the media to form theories for how men and women should behave. When certain children fail to act in a gender-typical fashion, they may be rejected or reprimanded by adults or peers (e.g., "Boys don't play with dolls!").

Developmental Trends

Children's understanding of gender categories begins early in development. They demonstrate the ability to understand labels associated with sex (e.g., he or she) by age 30 months (Huston, 1983; Ruble & Martin, 1998). In making these distinctions, young children draw heavily on hair cues. People with long, curly hair, for instance, are perceived as female. By age 3, most children understand that they are a boy or a girl, and they have already begun to show gender-related preferences for toys and activities. Characteristically in American society, boys prefer trucks and blocks, and girls prefer soft, cuddly toys. Boys also engage in more rough-and-tumble play than do girls (Maccoby, 1998). At this young age, children already seem to be imitating the gender-typed behaviors and attitudes being modeled by the adults, peers, and television characters in their environment. The term *gender-typed* means that children are exhibiting a behavior that is culturally defined as appropriate for their sex. The stereotypic views of what it means to be masculine and feminine in our society are listed in Table 7.1.

Although 2- and 3-year-olds can exhibit gender-stereotypic behaviors, they have not yet acquired an understanding of **gender constancy.** Young children believe that it is possible

By age 3, children are already imitating gender-typed behavior, that is, behavior that is culturally defined as appropriate for their sex.

Table 7.1	Stereotypes of Feminine and Masculine Traits
Feminine Traits	**Masculine Traits**
Affectionate	Aggressive
Sensitive	Ambitious
Passive	Dominant
Emotional	Rational
Cooperative	Competitive
Dependent	Independent
Weak	Strong
Gentle	Tough
Fearful	Courageous

As children develop a gender-role concept, they are beginning to acquire an understanding of what it means to be a boy or a girl, and they begin attending to same-sex models.

to change one's gender by dressing or acting differently. If you recall, children have difficulty distinguishing between appearances and reality at a young age (see Chapter 3). If a person wears a rabbit costume on Halloween, he or she must be a rabbit. Similarly, young children believe that boys can become girls by wearing dresses, and girls can become boys by cutting their hair short. Boys can grow up to be mommies, and girls can become daddies, or so their thinking goes. Around the age of 4 or 5, most children acquire an understanding of gender constancy, an understanding that gender is permanent and unchangeable. Having developed a sense of gender constancy, children begin to develop a *gender-role concept.* That is, they begin to acquire an a understanding of what it means to be a boy or a girl. Boys selectively attend to male models, and girls pay closer attention to females. In other words, gender becomes a useful category for making sense of the social world. Cognitive theorists use the term **gender schema** to refer to children's knowledge of gender.

Preschool-aged children generally have a well-developed gender schema, which they use to process information. When new information does not fit the expectations of their existing schema, they transform it so that it will fit. In one study, for example, preschoolers watched videotapes of girls playing with trucks and boys playing with dolls. Several days later they were asked to recall what they saw on the videotape. The children were more likely to say that the boys were playing with trucks and the girls were playing with the dolls (Liben & Signorella, 1993). Because children begin very early to process information according to their gender schemata, it is often difficult to change sex-role stereotypes by exposing them to a few nontraditional situations (e.g., women firefighters or male nurses). Young children stubbornly cling to their gender-role concepts, because gender helps them to organize and understand themselves and others.

Boys' interests in masculine activities increase with age, but girls' interests in feminine activities decline and shift to more masculine interests, which are more highly valued by society.

During early childhood, there is a marked increase in gender-typed behavior. At this age, children believe that gender norms are "immutable, inflexible, and morally right" (Huston, 1983, p. 403). Both boys and girls prefer gender-typed activities and objects over neutral ones by age 3 or 4 (Ruble & Martin, 1998). Studies also suggest that preschool children react negatively when peers engage in cross-gender activities (Bussey & Bandura, 1999). For example, they disapprove of boys playing with dolls and girls playing with trucks. Studies of preschool children also show that they prefer to play with same-sex friends because they share the same interests and interact in a similar way. For example, Maccoby (1998) suggests that girls prefer the company of other girls, because boys play too rough. Girls also find it difficult to influence boys. In Maccoby's view, it is the girls who stop playing with the boys. This gender segregation in peer groups further strengthens gender-typed behaviors and attitudes, as children have fewer opportunities to learn cross-gender behaviors. Research suggests that gender is more important than race or age when it comes to choosing friends (Maccoby, 1998).

Gender differences in children's interests and activities persist well into adolescence. Girls and boys show different preferences for television shows and videos (Huston & Wright, 1999). Girls spend more time on indoor tasks and chores, whereas boys spend more time outdoors (Huston, Carpenter, Atwater, & Johnson, 1986; Timmer, Eccles, & O'Brien, 1985). In adolescence, girls report spending more time on personal care, socializing, and shopping, whereas boys devote more time to sports activities (Timmer et al., 1985). A recent report also raised issues concerning gender differences in adolescent's use of computer technology (American Association of University Women, 2000).

With cognitive maturity, children's gender-role conceptions become more flexible. Older children and adolescents are more likely than younger children to understand that people can have both masculine and feminine traits. This blend of masculinity and femininity is known as **androgyny.** Children and adolescents who are androgynous are less likely to exhibit gender-stereotypic behaviors and attitudes. They can be assertive or sensitive, passive or active, depending on the situation. People with androgynous gender-role conceptions tend to have high self-esteem, coping skills, and life satisfaction (Huston, 1983). For this reason, many child psychologists suggest that parents, teachers, and others should encourage children to develop androgynous gender-role conceptions.

Androgynous people are those who have both masculine and feminine traits, and they tend to have high self-esteem, coping skills, and life satisfaction.

Gender Differences in Self-Perceptions

The gender-role conceptions children learn can shape their feelings of competency and self-esteem. Different competency perceptions are evident among boys and girls by early elementary school (Eccles et al., 1993) and become more marked as students get older (Eccles et al., 1983; Eccles, Wigfield, & Schiefele, 1998; Harter, 1982; Marsh, 1989; Wigfield et al., 1991). Students' self-concepts reflect traditional sex-role stereotypes. In general, boys tend to have higher self-concepts regarding their physical ability, appearance, and math ability, whereas girls perceive themselves as more competent in reading, verbal skills, and social relationships (Eccles et al., 1983; Eccles et al., 1998; Marsh, 1989). When a general measure of academic self-concept is used, gender differences are less evident.

It is interesting that self-concept differences between adolescent boys and girls sometimes persist even though their ability differences are negligible. For example, from elementary school through college, girls have lower math self-concepts than boys, even though they generally perform equally well if not better than boys in this subject. Ability perceptions also help explain why girls strive harder to achieve in domains that use their verbal and interpersonal skills (e.g., nursing, library science, teaching, and law), and boys strive to achieve in stereotypically masculine areas (e.g., science, engineering, mechanics, and athletics) (Eccles, 1987).

Most studies also report gender differences in children's self-esteem, with boys reporting more positive feelings about themselves than girls. Differences in self-esteem begin to appear in middle childhood and are most evident in early adolescence when young people are adjusting to changes in their physical appearances and social environment (Marsh, 1989). In a recent survey, 3,000 schoolchildren from across the country were asked how often they felt happy with the way they were (American Association of University Women, 1991). In elementary school, 69 percent of the boys and 60 percent of the girls responded

Both boys and girls experience a decline in self-esteem as they enter adolescence, but girls experience a more severe decline.

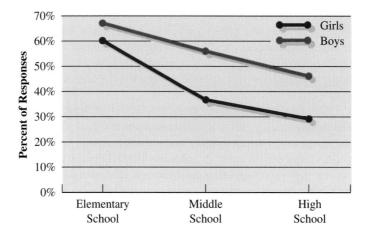

FIGURE 7.7

Developmental and Gender Differences in Self-Esteem

SOURCE: After AAUW (1992).

"always true." By high school, 60 percent of the boys responded this way. However, the figures went from 60 percent to 29 percent for girls. Figure 7.7 shows these trends.

Although the AAUW study (1992) and subsequent reports (Pipher, 1994; Orenstein, 1994) gained a good deal of media attention, a recent analysis of 174 samples concluded that gender differences in self-esteem were rather small in size (Kling, Hyde, Showers, & Buswell, 1999). Larger differences were found with age but did not go above one-third of a standard deviation unit, which is not considered a large effect. Furthermore, Kristen Kling and her colleagues (1999) concluded that gender differences in self-esteem were most pronounced in white samples. No significant overall gender effect was found for black samples (Kling et al., 1999).

What explains these patterns of gender differences? Many factors undoubtedly play a role. Recall that adolescent girls generally begin puberty earlier than boys, and, consequently, are more likely than boys to experience multiple transitions (e.g., changes in physical appearance, school settings, and social expectations) at a time when they have fewer coping strategies. Remember, too, that early maturing girls tend to be shorter and heavier than late maturers. The physical appearance of these girls is far from the present tall and slender "ideal" female body portrayed in the media, and the one they prefer. Research has shown that adolescent girls tend to prefer a body that is thinner than their own, whereas boys prefer a body that is larger than their own (Cohn et al., 1987). As a result, girls who deviate from this ideal standard tend to have a poorer self-image. Researchers believe that girls—especially white girls—are more vulnerable to disturbances in self-esteem at puberty because they place more importance on this ideal of physical attractiveness than boys do (Simmons & Blyth, 1987). Evidence suggests that cultural pressures toward female thinness have intensified in the last decade (Kling et al., 1999).

Theorists also believe that cultural stereotypes play an important role in the development of girls' and boys' self-perceptions. As you will see, children begin to learn gender stereotypes at a very early age. Because "male" skills and traits tend to be more highly valued in patriarchal societies, girls who conform to traditional female stereotypes are at a greater risk for feelings of inferiority and low self-esteem. In support of this claim, research indicates that girls who view themselves as mathematically competent, a presumed masculine trait, report higher levels of self-esteem during the transition to adolescence (Wigfield et al., 1991). Other studies indicate that both male and female adolescents who have an androgynous gender-role orientation tend to report higher levels of self-esteem (Dusek, 1987; Lundy & Rosenberg, 1987) and higher levels of identity development (Orlofsky, 1977). In the next section, we examine the effects of socialization experiences on children's gender-role conceptions.

Gender-Role Socialization

Gender-role socialization is the process by which children learn the attitudes and behavior that society defines as appropriate for their gender. As we have seen, children have already learned a great deal about gender roles before they enter school. Theorists believe that the process of gender-role socialization begins right at birth, and then intensifies in adolescence, when young people begin to prepare for their adult roles (Hill & Lynch, 1983; Huston & Alvarez, 1990). Parents, peers, schools, and the mass media all play a role in shaping children's role conceptions (Bussey & Bandura, 1999; Ruble & Martin, 1999). We briefly discuss each of these socialization influences.

Parents are extremely influential socializers of gender roles. From an early age, parents view their sons and daughters differently. They describe their newborn daughters as softer, cuter, and more delicate than their newborn sons. Baby girls are dressed in pink, dresses, lace tights, and patent-leather shoes, whereas baby boys wear blue, trousers, T-shirts, and sneakers. Even the bedrooms of infant boys and girls are decorated differently. Parents also treat their infant sons and daughters differently. They generally play in a more nurturing way with their daughters and engage in more gross motor play with their sons. Mothers are more likely to encourage autonomy and independence in their sons than in their daughters (Pomerantz & Ruble, 1998). Fathers are more likely than mothers to play with their children in a sex-stereotypic fashion, and boys receive more criticism for cross-gender behavior (e.g., playing with dolls) than girls do (Ruble & Martin, 1998).

Children also observe many examples of sex-stereotypic behavior in the home. Although gender roles are changing, the average child is still more likely to observe his or her mother cooking, cleaning, and caring for children. Fathers are observed fixing things, mowing the lawn, and driving the car. Similarly, when children are asked to do chores, girls wash the dishes and help clean the house, whereas boys mow the lawn, take out the garbage, and shovel snow (Goodnow, 1988). The average child is also likely to observe their mothers working in traditionally "female" jobs (teaching, nursing, sales, clerical positions) and their fathers working in traditionally "male" jobs (business, trades, engineering).

Parents also hold gender-stereotypic beliefs about their children's competencies. The

SOURCE: James L. Shaffer.

Schools are important arenas for learning and expressing gender-role behaviors. Unfortunately, schools often reinforce sex-role stereotypes.

Gender-role socialization is the process by which children learn society's norms for acceptable and unacceptable behavior.

research of Jacquelynne Eccles and her colleagues (Eccles, 1993, 1994; Eccles & Harold, 1991; Eccles et al., 1998; Jacobs & Eccles, 1992; Yee & Eccles, 1988) has shown that parents generally subscribe to the cultural stereotype that boys are naturally better at mathematics than are girls. For example, parents of boys rated natural ability as an important reason for their son's successes in mathematics, whereas parents of girls rated effort as important (Yee & Eccles, 1989). These differences were found even when the boys and girls had equivalent abilities in mathematics. Research further suggests that parents' stereotypic beliefs have an important influence on their development of their children's achievement beliefs and self-perceptions (Alexander & Entwisle, 1988; Eccles-Parsons, Adler, & Kaczala, 1982; Jacobs & Eccles, 1992; Eccles et al., 1998; Phillips, 1987).

Not all families, however, encourage or reinforce gender-typed behavior. Parents who make a conscious effort to avoid gender-stereotypic behaviors have less gender-typed children (Weisner & Wilson-Mitchell, 1990). One study showed that fathers' involvement in child care at home was associated with adolescents' approval of nontraditional roles for themselves (Williams, Radin, & Allegro (1992). Girls without brothers or only one brother tend to have less traditional attitudes toward gender roles (Hertsgaard & Light, 1984; Levy, 1989). Additionally, adolescents of both genders in two-parent families report less traditional gender-role attitudes when their mothers are employed outside the home (Hoffman, 1989; Huston & Alvarez, 1990; Lerner, 1994).

Parents', peers', and teachers' stereotypic beliefs have an important influence on the development of children's achievement beliefs and interests.

As children grow older, they begin to spend more time with other children. The peer group is one of the most important social contexts for the socialization of gender-role behaviors and attitudes (Bussey & Bandura, 1999; Maccoby, 1998; Martin & Ruble, 1998). In fact, some experts contend that the peer group is the primary sex-role socializing agent in development (Leaper, 1994; Maccoby, 1998). By age 3, same-sex peers positively reinforce one another for showing "gender-appropriate" behavior. Preschool children who play with toys associated with the opposite sex are often ignored or teased by their peers (Fagot, 1985; Langlois & Down, 1980). Boys are particularly intolerant of other boys who engage in cross-gender play. They often voice their disapproval using expressions like, "Stop acting like a girl," or "That's for girls." Although children spend most of their time in sex-segregated peer groups, they become more tolerant of sex-role transgressions in middle childhood (Stoddart & Turiel, 1985). However, conformity to gender-role conventions becomes important again in early adolescence. Early-adolescent girls feel less free to experiment with male sex-typed activities than they did in middle childhood (Huston & Alvarez, 1990). This intensification of gender-role socialization within the peer group is partly due to dating pressures and greater cross-sex interactions. Young adolescents conform to cultural ideals of femininity and masculinity as a way of increasing their sexual attractiveness (Crockett, 1990). By late adolescence, these factors are less important, but deviation from sex-typed norms can still lead to poor peer acceptance (Huston & Alvarez, 1990).

The mass media are another source of sex-role stereotypes. Although music, rock videos, films, books, and magazines are all popular forms of entertainment for children and adolescents, the effects of television on gender-role behaviors and attitudes have received the most attention (Huston & Wright, 1998). Young people spend 3 to 4 hours a day watching television (Roberts, Foehr, Rideout, & Brodie, 1999), and what they view is highly gender stereotypic (Calvert & Huston, 1987; Martin & Ruble, 1998). Children's programs tend to present more gender-stereotyped images than do adult programs. Cartoon and educational programs tend to be dominated by male characters such as Big Bird, Barney, and Spiderman. A recent study of commercials during children's programs also showed that boys appeared in greater numbers, assumed more active roles, and acted more aggressively than girls did (Browne, 1998). Media for adolescents are also highly stereotypic in their portrayal of women and men. For example, music videos are dominated by men, and women are generally portrayed as sexual and subservient (Gow, 1996; Sommers-Flanagan et al., 1993). As you might imagine, exposure to highly stereotypic messages on television can increase a young person's sex-typed beliefs and behaviors (Huston & Alvarez, 1990).

When children enter school, they encounter stereotypic curriculum materials, extracurricular activities, and staffing patterns (Bussey & Bandura, 1999; Meece, 1987; Ruble & Martin, 1998). It is estimated that 90 percent of students' learning time in school involves textbooks, films, videotapes, cassette tapes, and computer software, most of which continue to portray stereotypic images of men and women. Gender-related staffing patterns also characterize most elementary and secondary schools. Women teach young children, manage the library, put on Band-Aids, and prepare food, while men manage the school and staff, teach mathematics and science, fix things, and drive buses.

At school, boys and girls are encouraged to participate in activities that reinforce gender-role stereotypes. Boys are more likely to take calculus, computer, and chemistry classes, participate in contact sports, and lead the student council. In contrast, girls are expected to excel in reading, writing, and foreign languages, to participate in the performing arts (orchestra, chorus, drama club, etc.), and to cheer for male sports teams. Numerous studies have also shown that boys and girls are treated differently in the classroom (AAUW, 1992). For example, as discussed in Chapter 4, boys receive more attention and praise for correct answers and high levels of achievement. School counselors may support and encourage boys' interests in the scientific and technological fields, but may steer young women away from those fields (Betz & Fitzgerald, 1987). Gender-biased interaction patterns not only communicate different expectations of performance but also convey different views of boys' and girls' abilities.

> *Gender-role socialization begins with parents, who often encourage sex-stereotypic behavior, which continues in school as children encounter sex-stereotypic curriculum materials, teaching practices, and extracurricular activities.*

To summarize, children begin to learn gender-role stereotypes early in life. At home, boys and girls are encouraged to engage in sex-typed activities, and they can observe many examples of sex-stereotypic behaviors. The peer group and mass media continue this socialization process by perpetuating and reinforcing sex-role stereotypes of male and female behavior. Schools also play a significant role in the development of children's gender-role conceptions, and they have been slow in adapting to changes in the social roles of men and women. As a result, schools may be exposing children and adolescents to "masculine and feminine images that are even more rigid and more polarized than those currently held by the wider society" (Meece, 1987, p. 67). For this reason, it is important that teachers make a special effort to reduce gender bias and to treat *all* students equitably.

Development of Achievement Motivation

Many teachers report that motivating students to learn is one of their most difficult problems. Some students are clearly self-motivated, but others show very little interest in learning, gaining new skills, or improving their abilities. Far too many students do not develop their academic abilities or talents simply because they lack the desire to do so. By adolescence, poor motivation is one of the chief contributors to the problem of student underachievement.

Definitions of Achievement Motivation

Before exploring changes in children's motivation during the school years, we must first define what is meant by **achievement motivation.** The Latin root of the term *motivation* is the verb *movere,* which means *to move.* Achievement motivation theorists try to explain

SOURCE: David Young-Wolff/Photo Edit.

In late childhood and beyond, peers have an important influence on students' motivation to learn in school.

Theorists disagree about the precise nature of achievement motivation, which has been defined as an enduring psychological need, an environmentally activated state, and a set of cognitions and beliefs.

what initiates, sustains, and terminates behavior in achievement situations (Pontrich & Schunk, 1996). Unfortunately, there are numerous definitions of achievement motivation that involve defining it as an enduring psychological need, an environmentally activated state, and a set of cognitions and beliefs.

Motivation as a Psychological Need

Some motivation theorists focus on internal mechanisms, such as psychological needs. A need is an internal tension or conflict that leads a person to engage in goal-directed behavior. People have physiological, social, and psychological needs that can influence their behavior. If you recall, Erikson proposed that children have needs for security, autonomy, competence, and identity that can influence their behavior throughout childhood and adolescence.

Maslow's hierarchy of human needs is one of the best-known theories of motivation. Maslow (1970) proposed that people have lower- and higher-order needs. He conceptualized a hierarchy of human needs arranged according to the following priorities:

- Physiological needs (hunger, thirst, sleep)
- Safety needs (freedom from physical or psychological harm)
- Love needs (acceptance and affection from parents, friends, etc.)
- Esteem needs (confidence in one's abilities, mastery of environment)
- Self-actualization needs (self-expression, creativity, curiosity, harmony with the environment).

Maslow argued that lower-order needs (physiological, safety, love) must be satisfied before higher-order needs can be pursued and expressed. If children come to school hungry, sick, or tired, they will have little interest in learning or developing their competencies.

Similarly, it is difficult for children to learn if they do not feel safe or accepted at school. Maslow's theory is helpful in understanding why some children may not be motivated to develop their competencies, to try new things, or to express their creative abilities.

John Atkinson (1964) proposed that people differ in their *need to achieve,* that is, in their desire to excel in achievement situations. Other theorists have emphasized children's needs for competence and autonomy. For example, Robert White (1959) believed that such behaviors as mastery, exploration, and play were a result of a child's inherent need to deal competently with his or her environment. White labeled this disposition *effectance motivation.* He believed that this psychological need propels individuals to engage in activities from which they could derive a sense of personal mastery or competency. White believed that effectance motivation explains behaviors as diverse as a toddler learning to walk to an adolescent mastering calculus. Similarly, Edward Deci and Richard Ryan (1985) emphasized students' psychological needs for autonomy and self-determination. Like White, they believe that children strive to be causal agents in their environments.

Children's needs for competence, autonomy, and mastery serve as the foundation for the development of intrinsic motivation. When students are intrinsically motivated to learn, they enjoy learning for the sake of learning. **Intrinsic motivation** arises from internal sources such as curiosity, interest, enjoyment, and innate strivings for mastery and growth. A student who spends hours reading a book because it is enjoyable or interesting is intrinsically motivated. The student does not need external pressures or incentives to do this task. **Extrinsic motivation,** on the other hand, arises from external contingencies. The student engages in a particular task to get a reward, to earn a high grade, to fulfill a requirement, to please someone, and so forth. When classroom activities are undertaken for these purposes, learning becomes a means to an end. The student perceives his or her behavior as controlled by external rather than internal causes, which can reduce feelings of competence and self-determination. Early studies imply that individuals are either intrinsically or extrinsically motivated to learn. However, current research suggests that for any given activity, one or both orientations may be at work (Harter, Whitesall, & Kowalksi, 1992).

Motivation as a Situational State

Other theorists conceptualize motivation as a state that is highly influenced by a particular situation. These theories focus on the *incentive* and *reinforcement* conditions within the learning situation. According to this perspective, differences in achievement motivation are explained by an individual's reinforcement history and by reward contingencies in the present situation. There is no need to consider inner thoughts, feelings, or psychological needs. Attempts to improve student motivation involve providing the appropriate rewards and incentives. Interestingly, a recent study revealed that beginning teachers generally use rewards and punishments to motivate students (Newby, 1991). More than half of their motivation strategies involved some type of external reinforcer (e.g., extra recess time, stickers, loss of privileges). Strategies that involved increasing the perceived relevance of an activity or the student's confidence to accomplish the activity occurred in less than 7 percent of the observations.

Behavioral theorists study the external incentives and reinforcements that are built into a situation.

Motivation as a Set of Cognitions and Beliefs

In recent research, theorists have defined motivation as a set of cognitive beliefs and processes that are shaped both by early learning experiences and by the immediate learning situation. One cognitive model of motivation stresses the importance of students' achievement expectations and values. According to expectancy-value theories of motivation, students are more motivated to engage in learning activities when they *expect* and *want* to succeed. In other words, students ask themselves: "Am I able to do this task? Why should I want to do this task?" Numerous studies have shown that students' expectations and values are strongly related to a wide range of achievement behaviors, including task choice, persistence, and performance (Eccles-Parsons et al., 1983; Eccles et al., 1983; Eccles et al., 1998; Feather, 1982; Wigfield, 1994).

Another theory of motivation emphasizes the critical role of students' self-efficacy beliefs. **Self-efficacy** is defined as people's judgment of their ability to perform a task given the skills they possess and the circumstances they face (Bandura, 1986). Research suggests that self-efficacy beliefs can affect people's choice of activities, their effort, and their persistence (Bandura, 1986; Pajares, 1996; Schunk, 1991). Students who have a low sense of efficacy for accomplishing a task may avoid it, whereas those who feel capable will more readily engage in the task and persist at it longer. Students with a higher sense of efficacy are also more likely to use self-regulating learning strategies (Pintrich & Schrauben, 1992). Self-efficacy theory is very similar to expectancy-value theory because both theories emphasize the critical role of a person's judgment of his or her capabilities.

Attributional processes are believed to play an important role in the formation of expectancy and efficacy beliefs. *Attribution theories* of motivation examine how individuals interpret their successes and failures in achievement situations (Weiner, 1986). When students attribute their successes or failures to stable factors, they will expect their future performance to be similar to their current performance. If, for example, a student attributes a success (or failure) to ability, then he or she can expect to succeed (or fail) at similar tasks in the future. However, if the student attributes successes or failures to unstable factors, such as effort or luck, then the student's current performance may not be a good indicator of their future performance. To maintain high expectations for success, most motivation theorists believe that students should attribute their successes to high ability and attribute their failures to lack of effort (Eccles et al., 1983; Weiner, 1986).

Theories of intrinsic and extrinsic motivation also have a cognitive component. As stated previously, some motivation theorists claim that humans have a psychological need to feel self-determining or autonomous (Deci & Ryan, 1985). These theorists argue that people analyze their achievement activities in terms of the locus of causality. That is, people are intrinsically motivated when they perceive themselves as the causes of their behavior. By contrast, people are extrinsically motivated when the locus of causality is external. They perceive themselves as behaving a certain way to please others, to obtain a reward, or to avoid negative consequences. In this theory, perceptions of causality are critical for understanding achievement motivation. Activities are more intrinsically motivating when students believe they are choosing to engage in the activity by their own volition. In a later section, we will discuss the effects of rewards, incentives, and punishment on students' intrinsic motivation to learn.

Expectancy-value, self-efficacy, attribution, and intrinsic motivation theories all belong to a cognitive tradition in motivation research, because they emphasize cognitive beliefs and processes. Another theory that fits within this cognitive tradition is goal theory. *Goal theories of motivation* emphasize students' *reasons* for choosing, performing, and persisting at various achievement activities. For example, one student may spend an extra hour each night studying algebra because she wants to understand how to solve structural equations, whereas another student may study an extra hour because he wants the best grade in the class. Both of these students are motivated to study, but for different reasons.

Goal theorists have identified two types of goal orientations that influence students' achievement efforts. Distinctions between these two types of goals are quite similar to the internal and external sources of motivation described earlier. Students with an intrinsic goal orientation engage in learning activities because they want to learn something new, to develop their skills, or to master an activity. They are guided by what are called *task-oriented*

Self-efficacy is defined as people's judgment of their ability to perform a task given the skills they possess and the circumstances they face.

Attribution theories of motivation examine how individuals interpret their successes and failures in achievement situations.

Goal theories of motivation emphasize students' reasons for choosing, performing, and persisting at various achievement activities.

Focus on Research

What causes students to develop a sense of mastery or helplessness in academic situations? In a study of fifth-grade students, Elliot and Dweck (1988) demonstrated that patterns of learned helplessness were elicited by different learning conditions. When the benefits of learning were emphasized by the experimenter (e.g., "Doing this puzzle will sharpen your mind"), students demonstrated a *mastery-oriented* learning pattern. When they experienced difficulty or failure, they responded by trying different problem-solving strategies, concentrating harder, and staying focused on the task. In contrast, when students were told their performance would be filmed and judged by "experts," they demonstrated a *learned helpless* pattern, especially if they lacked confidence in their ability to perform the task. When these students experienced difficulty or failure, they responded by using less effective problem-solving strategies, giving up attempts to find more effective ways of solving the problem, expressing negative affect toward the task (e.g., "I'm going to hate this part"), and blaming themselves for failure ("I'm not good at this" or "I'm confused"). These students essentially perceived their learning problems as insurmountable and stopped trying, even though they had previously solved similar problems. Teachers can reduce learned helplessness by refraining from public forms of evaluation, by reducing testing pressures, and by providing specific feedback concerning how students can improve.

goals or *learning-oriented goals* (Nicholls, 1984; Dweck & Elliot, 1983). Task mastery is the desired goal. In contrast, students with an *extrinsic* goal orientation engage in learning activities because they want to get a good grade, to please others, to obtain a reward, or to avoid punishment. They are guided by goals that are extrinsic to the learning task. These students derive satisfaction from external rewards and incentives, regardless of what is learned.

If students must compete with others for grades and recognition, this condition can evoke an orientation in which students focus on their ability to perform or to compete. These students adopt what are called *performance-oriented goals* or *ego-oriented goals* (Dweck & Elliot, 1983; Nicholls, 1984). Under these conditions, students feel successful when they receive the best grade or do well with little effort, because it implies high ability. Students with performance-oriented motivation patterns are more interested in immediate rewards than long-term learning.

Both learning- and performance-oriented students are willing to complete learning activities, but research has shown that there are important differences in the ways they approach and respond to those activities. As described in the Focus on Research box above, a learning-oriented focus is associated with a *mastery-oriented* problem-solving approach, whereas students who focus on their ability to perform show a **learned helpless** pattern. Other differences in students' achievement behavior include the following.

- Students who focus on intrinsic goals prefer challenging activities over easy tasks, because they can learn from them. (Elliot & Dweck, 1988; Ames & Archer, 1988)

- With a learning-oriented focus, students are more likely to seek instrumental forms of help (e.g., asking for hints, examples, and information) that allow them to continue working on their own. When students are focused on performance goals, they prefer a

Students whose goal is task mastery (intrinsic orientation) are guided by what are called task-oriented or learning-oriented goals. Students who focus on their ability to perform or to compete (extrinsic orientation) adopt performance-oriented or ego-oriented goals.

419

Focus on Research

The "Hidden Costs" of Rewards

Lepper, Greene, and Nisbett (1973) studied the effects of rewards on preschool children. The children were first given an opportunity to draw with magic markers. After how long each child played with the magic markers was recorded, one group of children received a reward for playing with the markers and another group received no reward. The reward was a big red ribbon with a gold star, and a piece of paper with their name on it. The children were then given another opportunity to play with the magic markers. Interestingly, the children who had received the reward did not spend as much time playing with the magic markers as the children who were not given the reward did. Moreover, the quality of the rewarded children's pictures declined once the reward was withdrawn. The researchers concluded that rewards can undermine intrinsic motivation, because children are less likely to approach or choose similar activities if they do not expect to be rewarded. That is, children come to believe that they are engaging in the task not because it is interesting or they can learn something but because they are being rewarded. Extrinsic incentives or rewards work best when (a) students show little or no initial interest in learning; (b) they are contingent on a particular level of mastery or attainment of certain goals; (c) they are achievable by all students; and (d) they are not used to control students' behavior.

more passive form of help seeking, such as having someone solve the problems for them. (Arbreton & Roesner, 1993)

- With an intrinsic, learning-oriented focus, students tend to use active learning strategies that enhance conceptual understanding (e.g., reviewing material, focusing attention, setting goals, checking comprehension, and relating new information to existing information). Conversely, extrinsic goals are associated with short-term or superficial learning strategies, such as simply memorizing or rehearsing information. (Ames & Archer, 1988; Graham & Golan, 1991; Meece, Blumenfeld, & Hoyle, 1988; Nolen, 1988)

- Students who focus on their ability to perform show poor recall of information when the learning tasks require deeper levels of information processing. (Benware & Deci, 1984; Graham & Golan, 1991)

Why do learning and performance goals elicit these different learning patterns? Learning goals create a task focus in which students attend to the *quality* of their performance and the effort needed to succeed. Conversely, when one is focused on external rewards (praise and grades), attention is drawn away from how to do the task and focused on its rewards. When students must compete with others for rewards or grades, they may become anxious about their ability to perform and about how they will be evaluated by others. This anxiety and worry can undermine students' concentration and impair their problem solving.

Conclusions about Motivation Theories

Motivation researchers define *motivation* in many different ways. Early theories focused on innate needs, such as the need to achieve or competence needs. Behavioral theories focused on how rewards and incentives influenced motivation. This theory of motivation is still widely applied in classrooms today. Unfortunately, research has shown that rewards and incentives can undermine students' intrinsic motivation to learn. The Focus on Research box on the previous page describes an early study of the hidden costs of rewards on student motivation.

Most contemporary theories of motivation focus on students' beliefs, values, goals, and cognitive processes. Table 7.2 presents an overview of the various cognitive theories. Of the cognitive theories reviewed, goal theory may provide the most useful framework for teachers as it focuses on the reasons that children engage in or avoid achievement activities. In a later section, we will discuss how teachers can create an instructional environment to promote an intrinsic learning orientation in their classrooms.

Individual Differences in Achievement Motivation

Why are some students confident of their ability to succeed, whereas others express serious doubts about their abilities? Why are some students more motivated to learn than others? In this section, we will examine three sources of individual differences: conceptions of ability, early learning experiences and parenting practices, and socioeconomic influences.

Ability Differences

Research suggests that students often develop unrealistic views of their abilities. We have already seen how girls are likely to underestimate their abilities in mathematics and science, whereas boys may underestimate their reading or verbal abilities. Such differences in ability perceptions can influence children's motivation to participate and to achieve in different academic domains, especially if the activity is perceived as inappropriate for one's gender.

Table 7.2	Cognitive Theories of Achievement Motivation
Theory	**Description**
Expectancy-value	Emphasizes people's expectations for success and achievement values. People are highly motivated when they expect and want to do well on an achievement activity.
Self-efficacy	Emphasizes people's judgments of how well (or poorly) they will perform a task given the skills they have and the circumstances they face. People are highly motivated to achieve when they believe they can perform a task or an activity successfully.
Attribution	Emphasizes people's interpretations of their success. People are highly motivated to achieve when they attribute successes to ability and failures to lack of effort or use of appropriate strategy.
Achievement goals	Emphasizes people's reasons for engaging in achievement activities. People are highly motivated to achieve when they want to develop or demonstrate competence, but these two goal orientations are associated with very different patterns of learning. People show greater cognitive engagement in, and persistence at, achievement activities when they are learning oriented. They want to learn for the sake of learning.
Self-determination	Emphasizes people's judgments of causality. People are intrinsically motivated when they attribute their behavior to internal rather than external causes.

Focus on Research

Illusory Incompetence

What causes some high-achieving students to experience motivational problems? Deborah Phillips and Marc Zimmerman (1990) hypothesized that some highly capable students develop unrealistically low estimates of their abilities. Phillips studied the self-perceptions and achievement aspirations of fifth- and ninth-grade students who scored above the seventy-fifth percentile on a standardized achievement test. Approximately 20 percent of fifth-graders and 16 percent of ninth-graders seriously underestimated their level of ability. The results also showed that approximately 28 percent of the children who underestimated their ability in fifth grade were in the low-perceived competence in the ninth grade. By the ninth grade, girls mostly made up the group that underestimated their abilities. The results further showed that when compared to more confident peers, children who seriously underestimated their actual ability and children whose self-perceptions of ability declined between the fifth and ninth grade were viewed by their mothers as less capable and by both parents as not performing up to their potential. This study demonstrated that high ability does not always guarantee feelings of competence or optimal motivation. Parents help shape the way children perceive their abilities.

Researchers have also examined the motivational orientations of students with different measured abilities. Their work suggests that both low and high achievers may develop motivational problems if they lack confidence in their abilities. For example, Marijo Renick and Susan Harter (1989) found that students with a diagnosed learning disability generally have more negative perceptions of their abilities, which in turn, lessens their intrinsic motivation to learn. Other evidence suggests that high-ability students can have serious motivational problems if they underestimate their abilities, have low-achievement expectations, or give up easily on tasks that are well within their level of ability. The Focus on Research box describes how high-ability students can develop an illusion of incompetence. It is important to remember that even though students get good grades, they may not have the self-confidence they need to maintain a learning focus in the classroom or to take on challenging tasks.

Carol Dweck and Elaine Elliot (1983) suggest that students not only hold different *perceptions* of their abilities but also use different *conceptions* of ability for judging their competence. Some students believe that their ability level is fixed and cannot be improved through practice or effort; they have an **entity theory of ability.** Other students have an **incremental theory of ability,** because they believe they can improve their ability by investing greater effort or by trying different strategies. Dweck and Elliot maintain that these different conceptions of ability are *unrelated* to objective measures of ability such as grades or achievement test scores. Table 7.3 describes links between students' conceptions of ability, goals, and mastery-oriented versus learned helpless behavioral patterns.

> *Some students think their ability is a fixed entity that cannot be improved through practice or effort. Others have an incremental view of ability, believing they can improve their ability by investing greater effort or by employing different strategies.*

Early Learning Experiences and Parenting Practices

To explain individual differences in children's achievement motivation, many theorists focus on early learning experiences that can help children develop a sense of competence and efficacy. This research focuses on the following sorts of questions.

Table 7.3	Links between Theories of Intelligence, Goals, Perceived Ability, and Learning Patterns				
Theory of Intelligence	**Goal Type**	**Dominant Concerns**		**Perceive Ability**	**Behavioral Response**
Entity (Ability is fixed)	Performance	Is my ability adequate?		High	Mastery
				Low	Helpless
Incremental (Ability is malleable)	Learning	How can I improve?		High	Mastery
				Low	Mastery

SOURCE: After Dweck & Leggett (1988).

- Do parents encourage children from an early age to explore and to try new things?
- Do parents provide appropriate levels of support when children attempt new activities?
- Do parents provide consistent standards by which children can judge their accomplishments?
- Do parents communicate high- or low-achievement expectations to their children?
- Do parents react harshly to disappointing performances?

Early research by Susan Harter (1978) maintained that successful early learning experiences give children the confidence to deal effectively and competently with their environment. As a result, these children become intrinsically motivated. They develop an internal set of mastery standards to judge their accomplishments and a strong sense of confidence in their abilities (i.e., self-efficacy). Conversely, students whose motivation is primarily extrinsic are less likely to have developed these mastery standards early. This can occur if young children experience a history of failure or disapproval in response to their early learning efforts. Alternatively, some children are rewarded from an early age for their accomplishments, so that they become dependent on external incentives for their source of motivation.

More recently, researchers have analyzed differences in parent-child relations. This research suggests that parenting styles that are either too controlling or too permissive can damage children's motivation and achievement patterns (Dornbusch, Ritter, Leiderman, Roberts, & Fraleigh, 1987; Ginsburg & Bronstein, 1993; Grolnick & Ryan, 1989). In contrast, parenting styles that support children's independence are generally associated with higher levels of intrinsic motivation and perceived competence. Examples of supportive parenting style might include (a) giving children input into decision making; (b) stating expectations in a suggestive rather than in a directive way; (c) acknowledging children's needs and feelings; and (d) providing choices and alternatives.

Parenting styles that support the development of children's independence are generally associated with higher levels of intrinsic motivation and perceived competence.

Gender Differences in Achievement Motivation

As we discussed, gender-role socialization begins quite early in children's development. By the preschool years, children sex-type activities as either masculine or feminine. And gender differences in children's perceptions of abilities are evident by the early elementary years (Eccles et al., 1993; Eccles, 1984; Eccles et al., 1998; Eccles-Parsons et al., 1983; Harter, 1982). Cultural stereotypes, along with gender-role socialization, can have a strong impact on students' motivation to choose and to excel in different achievement domains.

In general, gender differences in various measures of motivation are most pronounced in gender-stereotyped domains. For example, as discussed, boys have higher competence beliefs than girls for mathematics and sports, whereas girls have higher competence beliefs than boys for reading and English (Eccles, 1984; Eccles et al, 1993; Eccles-Parsons et al., 1983; Eccles, Wigfield, & Schiefele, 1998; Marsh, Craven, & Debus, 1991; Wigfield et al., 1991). Similar patterns emerge for children's and adolescents' achievement values. Boys value sports more than girls, whereas girls place a higher value than boys on English, social activities, and instrumental music (Eccles et al., 1993; Wigfield et al., 1991). Gender differences, favoring boys, are also found in students' valuing of science achievement (Kahle & Meece, 1984). By high school, gender differences in the valuing of mathematics appear (Eccles, 1984). There is also some evidence to suggest that girls report greater anxiety than boys about their mathematics performance (Meece et al., 1990), especially when they are asked to perform difficult timed mathematics tests (Spencer & Steele, 1995). Girls' negative affective reactions can lead them to lower the value of mathematics achievement or to avoid mathematics altogether. Gender differences in students' competency beliefs and achievement values are found even when students have equivalent skills in those areas. Additionally, the magnitude of the gender effect increases after puberty when young people begin to experience greater social pressure to conform to gender-role expectations.

According to the motivation theories we have discussed, gender differences in competency and value perceptions can affect achievement behaviors. For example, Eccles and her colleagues have shown that expectancy and value beliefs are important predictors of adolescents' enrollment and performance in mathematics (Eccles-Parsons et al., 1983; Eccles, 1984). Eccles (1984, 1987) maintains that gender differences in math-related competency and value perceptions can help explain women's underrepresentation in advanced high school mathematics and science classes. Unfortunately, this lack of advanced preparation often limits women's opportunities to pursue careers in the scientific, technological, and engineering.

Gender differences in motivation are most pronounced in gender-stereotyped domains such as mathematics, science, or sports.

Ethnic and Racial Differences in Achievement Motivation

Cultural stereotypes can also make it difficult for minority youths to develop positive perceptions of their abilities and to value their schooling experiences. There are, however, surprisingly few studies on racial and ethnic differences in students' motivation. For the most part, studies have focused on comparisons between African American and white students. In reviewing this research literature, Sandra Graham (1984) found very few ethnic or racial differences in students' need for achievement locus of control, achievement attributions, and ability perceptions. One of the interesting patterns that emerges from this research is that African American students tend to maintain positive perceptions of their abilities, even when they are not doing as well as other students (Stevenson, Chen, & Uttal, 1990). Also, they continue to have high expectations for succeeding at tasks they previously failed (Graham 1994). Further, research suggests that African American students' competence and expectancy beliefs are not predictive of their school achievement (Stevenson et al., 1990; Graham, 1994; Mickelson, 1990).

Few ethnic differences are found in students' need for achievement, locus of control, achievement attributions, and ability perceptions.

These findings are difficult to interpret. One possibility is that African American students are using an adaptive strategy to protect their self-esteem in the face of failure (Graham, 1984). Another possibility is that teachers tend to have lower expectations for minority students' achievement, and perceptions of differential treatment in the classroom may lead African American students to discount the feedback they receive from their teachers about their abilities. Although some studies reveal that teachers have more negative expectations for their black and Mexican students than for their white students (Irvine, 1990; Dusek & Joseph, 1986), studies have not found large differences in teachers' responses to students in the classroom (Irvine, 1990; Miller, 1995). That is, it is not clear that teachers treat minority students differently from white students as a result of their different achievement expectations.

Currently, researchers are focusing on the factors that would lead ethnic minority students to reject the importance of their school experiences for their future and for their self-worth. Ogbu (1992) has argued that that Native, African, and Mexican Americans share a history of oppression and discrimination in the United States. To cope with the oppression, these groups develop an identity in opposition to the white, majority culture, and reject attributes valued by that culture. According to this analysis, educational achievement is associated with white culture, which leads ethnic minorities to *devalue* the importance of academic success. This pattern is particularly prevalent in minority youth, who perceive little or no relation between school achievement and access to good jobs in their community (Fordham & Ogbu, 1996).

Claude Steele (1992) has also argued that academic achievement has significant social costs but for different reasons. He maintains that mainstream society portrays African Americans as intellectually inferior, and a fear of confirming this negative stereotype leads African American students to "disidentify" with school by reducing their achievement efforts or by devaluing the importance of school achievement for their own feelings of self-worth.

These various explanations emphasize the complexity of factors that can influence the achievement motivation of ethnic minority students. An added complication is that studies reveal that most ethnic minority parents and their children highly value education and have high educational aspirations (Eccles et al., 1998). Additionally, recent research suggests that Afrocentric, rather than Eurocentric, values have a positive influence on academic achievement in African American youths (Spencer et al., in press). Finally, it is important to keep in mind that there is considerable variation in achievement motivation within any ethnic group. We have already discussed gender differences within ethnic groups. In the next section, we discuss the effects of social class. Most studies of racial and ethnic differences in achievement motivation have not taken into account the influence of economic factors (Graham, 1984; Eccles et al., 1994).

Some minority students may reject academic success because peers view it as "acting white."

Socioeconomic Influences

Socioeconomic factors can also affect children's motivation to learn and to do well in school. The motivational problems of students from low-income families are perhaps the most complex and difficult to address for several reasons. First, compared with middle-class families, poor families have weaker resources to support their children's learning outside of school. Economically disadvantaged students often need extra help in mastering basic and advanced skills, but placement in special programs increases the risk that they will perceive themselves as slow learners. Second, the home and community socialization patterns of disadvantaged students are poorly matched to the middle-class orientations of schools. As a result, disadvantaged students frequently experience adjustment and discipline problems (Braddock & McPartland, 1993). Additionally, economically disadvantaged students have difficulty seeing the relevance and importance of schoolwork for their future goals, due to high rates of unemployment in their communities and lack of financial

Economically disadvantaged students have difficulty seeing the relevance of schoolwork for future goals as a result of high rates of unemployment in their communities and lack of financial resources.

resources to further their education. Poor students are likely to attend schools with fewer resources for recruiting highly qualified teachers and for providing enriching educational experiences. Compounding the effects of poor school conditions, poor children live in neighborhoods with few public services, such as libraries, museums, and parks. There is also a scarcity of high-achieving role models in these communities.

As we learned in Chapter 4, early intervention programs such as Head Start are successful in improving the educational attainment of economically disadvantaged children. Some theorists believe that these programs better prepare these students for entry into school. They are able to maintain positive attitudes toward learning because they do not experience early failure in school. Thus, motivation may be an important pathway through which early intervention programs positively affect children's academic achievement and educational attainment.

Developmental Trends in Achievement Motivation

As children progress in school, they feel less intrinsically motivated to learn, more negative about their abilities, and more anxious about their school performance. Such negative changes in motivation are particularly evident as students move from elementary to middle school.

Most children begin elementary school with an intrinsic desire to learn and to master new skills that gradually fades as they progress in school. Harter (1981) reported a systematic shift from a predominantly intrinsic orientation in third grade to a more extrinsic orientation by the ninth grade. These shifts are more dramatic for some subjects than for others, but most children show significant declines in intrinsic motivation for reading, mathematics, science, and social studies by the seventh grade (Gottfried, 1985). Developmental changes in students' intrinsic motivation are generally accompanied by declining confidence and performance and by increasing anxiety (Harter & Connell, 1984). In other words, as children progress in school, they feel less intrinsically motivated to learn, more negative about their abilities, and more anxious about their school performance. Negative changes in motivation are particularly evident as students move from elementary to junior high school.

What explains the decline in students' intrinsic motivation during the school years? One explanation focuses on how students evaluate themselves at various ages. For example, kindergarten students start school with very optimistic perceptions of their abilities, with most claiming to be the smartest student in their class (Stipek, 1993). They also think that they can get smarter by just working harder. That is, young children often have an incremental view of their ability. As school learning becomes more difficult and increased effort does not always lead to success, children begin to develop a more realistic view of their abilities.

Developmental changes in children's conceptions of ability and their evaluation standards can lead to negative changes in intrinsic motivation.

The standards children use to judge their ability also change as they progress in school. Whereas young children judge their ability in terms of effort, older children tend to rely on social standards or normative information. That is, they judge their ability in terms of how others have done, but effort has a different meaning. Compared with younger children, older children have a more differentiated conception of ability (Nicholls, 1984). By late elementary school, children understand that ability and effort are separate entities and that high effort can compensate for low ability. Thus, high effort can imply low ability if other children perform as well or better with less effort. Exhorting students to work harder is less effective at this age, because it often implies that the teacher or parent thinks the student needs to compensate for lack of ability.

These developmental changes in ability perceptions help explain declines in motivation as children grow older. Because older children measure their ability in terms of normative standards, they find it increasingly difficult to demonstrate high ability. Changes in these evaluation standards can lead students to lower their expectations for success and to feel less competent. At the same time, adolescents' increased self-awareness is likely to

Focus on Teaching

Motivation researchers have identified a number of ways teachers can help promote an intrinsic orientation toward learning in the classroom (Ames, 1992; Brophy, 1987; Corno & Rohrkemper, 1985; Covington, 1992; Lepper & Hodell, 1989; Maehr & Midgley, 1991; Marshall, 1992; Meece, 1991; Nicholls, 1989). Some strategies for improving motivation in the classroom follow.

Provide Motivating Learning Activities

- Provide learning activities that are personally challenging, meaningful, and call for students' active participation in the learning process.

- Use a variety of learning activities. Even minor changes in format can have a significant impact.

- Stimulate students' curiosity by asking questions that are surprising or discrepant from students' current understanding.

Emphasize the Intrinsic Value of Learning

- Help students see the value of what they are learning for other subjects and real-life problems.

- Help students connect what they are learning to their lives outside school.

- Link learning material to current events or familiar experiences.

- Learning activities should have a worthwhile instructional objective.

Promote Positive Feelings of Competency and Efficacy

- Provide feedback that lets students know they are improving their skills (e.g., "You are really getting good at multiplying fractions.").

- Use learning activities that progressively build on one another, so students can see they are improving.

- Help students set realistic, short-term goals, so they can receive continual feedback about their progress.

- Support students' independent learning efforts.

- When students perform poorly, provide specific and informative feedback about how they can improve.

Recognize Personal Improvement

- Use improvement-oriented grading systems.

- Provide multiple opportunities for students to complete tasks.

- Use normative forms of evaluation cautiously. Avoid public forms of evaluation. If used, they should provide a way to recognize all students.

Increase Opportunities for Choice

- Let students design some learning tasks or choose how to complete a lesson.

- Let students help determine the criteria by which their assignments will be evaluated.

- Involve students in developing guidelines for classroom behavior.

Provide Opportunities for Peer Collaboration

- Organize cooperative learning, peer tutoring, and peer interactions opportunities.

- Use a combination of heterogeneous and homogeneous grouping arrangements.

- Establish a learning environment in which differences among students are accepted and valued.

Secondary classrooms tend to be more impersonal, formal, evaluative, and competitive than elementary classrooms. Changes in the school environment can lead to negative changes in motivation.

heighten their concerns about evaluations and their fears about "looking stupid." As a result, adolescents may show a greater ego involvement in learning activities and display the type of achievement behavior that is associated with an extrinsic motivational orientation.

A second explanation for motivational declines focuses on changes in the school environment, especially as students move from elementary to secondary school. For example, Jacquelynne Eccles, Carol Midgley, and Terry Adler (1984) identified a number of different ways elementary and secondary classrooms differ. Whereas students are generally with one teacher and the same peer group for most of the day in elementary school, secondary students may have a different teacher for every subject, and each class may have a different group of students. In addition, the secondary classroom is generally characterized by more whole-class instruction and public drill, less individualized instruction, and fewer opportunities for student choice and decision making. Also, secondary teachers tend to base students' grades on competitive or normative standards, but elementary school teachers are more likely to grade students on the basis of their individual progress. Students are often "tracked" in secondary schools, so the value of having high ability is very important to them. Also, the restricted range of ability in secondary classes increases competition between students, especially if teachers grade on a curve.

In summary, secondary classrooms tend to be more impersonal, formal, evaluative, and competitive than elementary classrooms. Additionally, students have fewer opportunities to manage and direct their own learning at a time when they are developing more sophisticated cognitive and problem-solving skills. Eccles and her colleagues argue that these grade-related changes in instructional practices lead to declines in students' ability perceptions and in their intrinsic motivation to learn.

Researchers are not yet sure whether declines in intrinsic motivation are a natural consequence of cognitive and social development or a reflection of changes in the school environment. From an educational standpoint, it is important to understand both points of view. As students mature, they are better able to integrate information about their abilities from various sources, and they become anxious about their ability to handle a competitive learning environment. Such conditions make it difficult for even the best students to maintain an intrinsic orientation toward learning. We end this discussion of motivation with a Focus on Teaching box on pages 427 and 428 containing some suggestions for how to create a positive motivational climate in the classroom.

Chapter Summary

Erikson's Theory of Psychosocial Development

www.mhhe.com/meece

- Erikson provided a framework for understanding children's personal development. His theory helps us understand the emergence of the self in early development, the need for self-sufficiency in the school years, and the search for identity in adolescence. According to Erikson, children need a safe and secure environment in order to develop a sense of trust. They also need opportunities to initiate activities and to learn about their different strengths and options for the future.

Foundations of Social and Emotional Development

- Children's social and emotional development begins with early attachment relations. Children need secure attachments with parents who are warm, responsive, and caring.

- Attachments with caregivers, including teachers, can affect many behaviors important for school success, including curiosity, attention, problem-solving behavior, and persistence.

- With development, children become better interpreters of people's emotions and better able to use this information in regulating their behavior. They also become better able to express and understand complex emotions such as embarrassment, guilt, and jealousy. Gender and cultural expectations can influence what emotions are expressed and how they are expressed.

- Self-control involves the deliberate use of cognitive or behavioral strategies to achieve a desired goal. It is important for establishing positive social relations, for adjusting to school, for learning, and for lowering the risk of adolescent health and safety problems.

- Between the ages of 5 and 12, children show an increased ability to use cognitive and behavioral strategies for controlling impulses, tolerating frustration, and delaying gratification.

- Schools can play an important role in the development of emotional competence in the classroom. Teachers need to (1) create a positive affective environment for students, (2) model how to exhibit and express emotions, (3) discuss emotions with students, and (4) provide explicit instruction regarding how to handle emotions and stress.

Development of Self-Conceptions

- Self-concept refers to a set beliefs, attitudes, ideas, and knowledge that people have about themselves. Young children describe themselves in terms of physical traits, whereas older children and adolescents use psychological traits (i.e., intelligent, trustworthy, caring, etc.) and abstract concepts (e.g., devout Catholic). In addition, as children mature, their self-concepts become more differentiated and integrated. They see themselves as having multiple abilities, and they begin to see links between their past, present, and future selves. As children become more introspective with age, they can become more self-conscious and self-critical. During the early school years, children's self-esteem increases as they achieve success in peer relations. Although there is considerable stability in children's self-esteem by the late elementary years, the school environment plays a very important role in helping children and adolescents maintain positive self-esteem. Teachers who show concern about students, involve students in decision making, and encourage self-sufficiency can have a positive influence on self-esteem. Schools and classrooms that are highly structured, controlling, and competitive can have a negative influence on self-esteem.

- Students' perceptions and evaluations of their abilities influence their performance in school. Doing well in school can bolster self-esteem, which, in turn, can affect how well students do in school later on. Once a child's sense of ability is firmly established, it can have a stronger influence on academic performance than grades, standardized test scores, and other measures of ability.

Ethnic and Gender-Role Identity

- Children begin to develop an awareness of ethnic differences early. By age 3, children can correctly identify skin color and their own ethnic group. Because of racial prejudices and stereotypes, it may be difficult for ethnic minority children to develop positive feelings of competency and worth. Early research suggested that a larger percentage of African-American and Native American children than white children misidentify with their ethnic group. This misidentification was presumed to indicate low self-esteem and self-hatred. Current research, however, suggests that this early work may have been based on faulty assumptions. Most studies today report little difference in white and African American children's self-perceptions if they are succeeding in school and are held in high regard by parents and peers. The racial composition of the school can also have an important influence on the self-concepts and self-esteem of ethnic minority youths.

- The work of forming an ethnic identity generally takes place in adolescence. Ethnic minority youths have four possible ways to resolve identity issues. They can assimilate to the dominant culture or become a marginal member of the dominant culture. Third, they can choose to associate only with their own ethnic group. Fourth, adolescents can become bicultural by maintaining ties to both cultures through a process of code switching. Unfortunately, some youths resolve their identity crisis by forming a negative identity. They totally reject the values of the dominant culture as well as their own.

- Gender-role identity is a key component of the self. During the school years, children acquire an understanding of what it means to be a male and female in our society. The gender-role concepts of young children tend to be very rigid and exaggerated. Therefore, the gender-role behaviors and attitudes of young children tend to be very sexist. Students' self-concepts of abilities reflect traditional sex stereotypes: Boys are better at physical, mathematical, and technical activities, and girls are better at verbal, social, and domestic activities. With cognitive maturity, children's gender-role concepts become more flexible and less absolute. Adolescents who have a blend of masculine and feminine traits (i.e., they are androgynous) tend to have high self-esteem, positive self-concepts, and good coping skills.

- Gender-role behaviors and attitudes are learned from the environment through the process of socialization. Parents are extremely influential socializers of gender norms. Considerable research suggests that they model sex-typed behaviors, they encourage boys and girls to engage in sex-typed activities, and they treat boys and girls differently. Along with the family and the mass media, schools have an important role in gender-role socialization. In books and television programs, male and female characters continue to perform in sex-stereotypic occupations and domestic roles. The school setting is an important place for confirming and consolidating gender-role conceptions. Unfortunately, the images of masculinity and femininity children are exposed to at school continue to be sex-stereotypic.

Development of Achievement Motivation

- In achievement situations, motivation refers to forces that initiate, sustain, and terminate behavior. Motivation has been defined as an enduring trait, a situational state, and a set of cognitions, values, and beliefs. Most contemporary theories of motivation fall within the cognitive model. These theories emphasize the importance of efficacy beliefs, achievement values, causal attributions, and achievement goals. Of these cognitive theories, goal theory may provide the most useful framework for teachers. When children are focused on learning goals, they define their competence in terms of improvement, focus on their efforts, perceive errors as a part of the learning process, attribute difficulties to lack of effort, and persist at finding the correct solution. With a learning focus, students use cognitive strategies that can enhance conceptual understanding and the long-term retention of information. In contrast, a performance orientation tends to be associated with lower levels of cognitive engagement in learning activities and with negative affect and task avoidance when learning tasks are difficult.

- The home environment is a source of individual differences in motivation. During early development, children need an opportunity to explore and to have an effect on their environment. Parenting styles that support children's independence are positively associated with higher levels of perceived competence and intrinsic motivation. Also, children who view their abilities as something that can be enhanced through effort and practice have higher levels of perceived competence and intrinsic motivation. When children perceive their abilities as fixed and unchangeable, it can have a negative effect on motivation. Motivation problems are prevalent among low-income children due to lack of resources at home to support learning, mismatches between the home and school environment, and the lack of educational and employment opportunities.

- As children progress in school, they report lower self-perceptions of ability, less control over learning, less intrinsic motivation to learn, and more anxiety about

431

grades and evaluation. It is believed that these changes result from both individual and environmental changes. As children mature cognitively, they are better able to evaluate and integrate different sources of information about their abilities. They are also better able to compare their abilities with those of others. But most theorists believe that declines in motivation result from changes in the school environment. As students progress in school, the learning environment becomes more structured, controlling, impersonal, and evaluative. These conditions make it difficult for students to maintain positive perceptions of their abilities and to sustain an intrinsic interest in learning.

Key Terms

achievement motivation (p. 415)

androgyny (p. 411)

attachment (p. 381)

emotional competence (p. 390)

emotions (p. 386)

empathy (p. 387)

entity theory of ability (p. 422)

ethnic identity (p. 405)

extrinsic motivation (p. 417)

gender constancy (p. 409)

gender-role socialization (p. 413)

gender schema (p. 410)

ideal self (p. 398)

identity (p. 380)

identity status (p. 402)

incremental theory of ability (p. 422)

intrinsic motivation (p. 417)

learned helplessness (p. 419)

psychological self (p. 394)

self-concept (p. 392)

self-conscious emotions (p. 387)

self-control (p. 388)

self-efficacy (p. 418)

self-esteem (p. 392)

social referencing (p. 387)

strange situation (p. 382)

temperament (p. 384)

Activities

1. Begin to collect books and stories you can use in your classroom to help your students understand their own and others' emotions. You might consider using books written about a particular emotional issue such as shyness, friends moving away, divorce, and so forth. Be sure to choose books that are appropriate for the age group you plan to teach. Share your resource file with your classmates.

2. Interview a group of elementary and middle school students to find out about their self-concepts. Be sure to include a wide age range, say, from 7- to 14-year-olds. Ask students to describe themselves ("Tell me about yourself") and follow up with more specific questions about what they are good at and what they like about themselves. Ask them if they could change anything about themselves, what would it be. Take detailed notes on the students' responses, then analyze them according to the following questions:

   a. Did the students describe themselves according to observable characteristics (gender, physical appearance, favorite activities) or psychological traits (friendly, happy, smart)?

   b. Did the characteristics of children's self-descriptions vary by age?

c. Did girls focus on different characteristics (e.g., physical appearance) than boys? Did girls describe themselves in less positive terms than boys?

d. What conclusions might you draw about the students' feelings of self-esteem from the interview?

3. Interview different ages (7 to 17 years) to learn about their motivation to read. Before you interview students, you may try to draft some questions using what you have learned about the factors that can influence student motivation. Example questions might be:

- How often do you read?
- Do you like to read? Why or why not?
- What kind of books do you like to read?
- Do you receive much encouragement to read from your teachers, parents, or peers?
- What do you think teachers should do to help motivate students to read who don't like to read?

Analyze students' responses for the factors that influence students' motivation to read. Do some students appear to be intrinsically motivated to read, while others need external incentives and encouragement? How did students' perceptions of their ability to read influence their interest in reading? Discuss how you might use the students' responses to enhance students' intrinsic motivation to read in your classroom.

4. Interview teachers at different grade levels to gather information on motivation strategies. Ask teachers to describe the strategies they use to motivate students. How do they use rewards and incentives in their classroom? Compare teachers' strategies to the ones presented on pages 427 and 428. Develop an action plan for creating a positive motivation climate in your classroom, and share it with your classmates.

Chapter 8

Peer Relations and Moral Development

Amy is a student in Mrs. Harrison's seventh-grade math class. Toward the end of the class period, the students are given some time to work on their math homework, but Amy is having difficulty focusing on her work. She is seated across from Dawn, who does not appear to like this arrangement. Amy tries to engage Dawn in a conversation but is ignored. She then tugs on Dawn's sweater, and Dawn tells her, "Stop it!" Amy shows Dawn her new ballpoint pen, but Dawn continues to ignore her. A few seconds later, Amy stabs Dawn with the pen. Dawn yells, "Ow!" Mrs. Harrison looks over at Amy and tells her to get back to work. Amy ignores the teacher and waits a few seconds, then asks Mrs. Harrison if she can use the bathroom pass. Mrs. Harrison says, "No," and Amy returns to her seat. As she passes Dawn, she again stabs her with the pen. Dawn yells, "You'd better stop!" Amy returns to her seat, then looks around the room for several minutes. Mrs. Harrison tells the class to get ready to change classes. As the students are lining up, Amy stabs Dawn with the pen very hard. Dawn becomes visibly angry this time, and yells, "I told you to stop it!" Dawn then hits Amy with her fists. The teacher tells Dawn to go sit in her seat. Amy laughs and walks out of the room.

Chapter opener photo: Corbis/CB039037.

How would you explain Amy's behavior? What would you want to know about this student? How might the teacher's behavior have contributed to Amy's problem? How would you respond if Amy were your student? Although the teacher in this vignette seems unbelievably "tuned out," the observation is based on events in a real classroom. Amy has apparently learned that she can get attention from others by picking on them. Generally, children like Amy have not learned socially appropriate ways of initiating and maintaining interactions with others. Unfortunately, Mrs. Harrison did not use an effective strategy for stopping Amy's behavior. Without effective and consistent guidance, students such as Amy can become increasingly noncompliant, aggressive, and difficult, which further reduces the likelihood they will develop positive relations with others.

Children are social beings, and they must learn the patterns of social life—how to initiate social interactions, how to interpret another person's behavior, how to care for others, how to assert themselves, and so on. Although children begin learning social skills before they enter school, the classroom provides a good training ground for practicing and improving these skills. Children with good social skills generally have little difficulty making friends at school, whereas children with poor social skills often run the risk of being ignored or rejected by peers. Furthermore, children with good peer relations tend to be more successful in school. It is important, therefore, to understand the development of peer relations and social skills in order to help children form positive social relationships and to function in a group.

In this chapter, we explore the development of children's abilities to relate and to care for others. We will discuss how children reason about their social world and form an understanding of its racial and ethnic diversity. We will also consider how children's social relationships with peers change over the course of development. We will also discuss why some children, such as Amy, are not able to cooperate, share, or care for others. By the end of this chapter, you will be familiar with ways that teachers can create a classroom environment that positively influences children's social and moral development.

> *Children with good social skills generally have little difficulty making friends at school, whereas children with poor social skills often run the risk of being ignored or rejected by peers.*

Understanding Others

> *The development of children's social understanding begins in infancy and continues well into the school; it also plays an influential role in shaping their social relations at school.*

To form social relationships, children need to develop an ability to think about the thoughts, feelings, and behaviors of others. Researchers use the term **social cognition** to refer to children's ability to think about their social world. In the previous chapter, we learned that children's social understanding begins in their early interactions with caregivers. Here the child learns that self is distinct from others and that others may have different wishes and desires. The development of children's social understanding continues well into the school years, and it plays an influential role in shaping their social relations at school. Efforts to help children with poor peer relations are often directed at helping children interpret the thoughts, feelings, and behaviors of others.

We will look at three important aspects of children's social cognition: (1) social perspective-taking skills, (2) person perceptions, and (3) race and ethnicity conceptions.

Understanding the Perspective of Others

The ability to understand the perspective of others is central to learning to relate to others. We will learn later that aggressive children often have difficulty with social problem solving, which involves taking the perspective of others and understanding the consequences of their actions on others. Interest in social perspective-taking skills can be traced back to Piaget's claim that young children are cognitively egocentric and incapable of understanding or taking the perspective of others.

Social awareness emerges early in infancy. These infants are relating to each other through touch.

Understanding the perspective of others begins in early infancy. The first step in this process is to understand that the self is distinct from others; that is, people have an independent existence. Researchers believe that this process begins to occur when infants show distress or gaze toward the door when their caregivers leave the room, but this differentiation is not fully complete until the second year. During the period known as the terrible twos toddlers use words such as *me* and *mine* to assert their differentiation from others. They also show signs of frustration and temper when their attempts to influence their caregivers' actions are not successful. However, toddlers can also comfort younger children in distress by hugging or kissing them, and they may even try to comfort an adult in pain (Flavell & Miller, 1998).

By age 3, children grasp simple causal relations between desires, outcomes, and emotions. They believe, for instance, that people will be happy when they get what they want (Wellman, 1990). They also understand that different people may have different desires. John Flavell and his colleagues found that 3-year-olds had little difficulty understanding that an adult might like coffee, even though they themselves do not (Flavell, Mumme, Green, & Flavell, 1992). Studies further show that young children will restate a request in clearer language if they think the listener's behavior indicated a lack of understanding (Shwe & Markman, 1997).

Although preschool children are making significant advances in social understanding and perspective taking, there is still much to be learned. Important shifts in children's social cognition occur between the ages of 5 and 7, as new cognitive skills mature. As discussed in Chapter 7, preschool children tend to describe themselves in terms of observable, concrete traits (e.g., I have brown eyes and like ice cream), whereas older children tend to use psychological traits (e.g., I am cheerful and smart). There are also important changes in children's perspective-taking abilities.

Robert Selman and his colleagues identified several distinct stages in children's role-taking abilities. To study children's **perspective-taking skills**, children of different ages were asked to respond to the following social dilemma:

Important shifts in children's social cognition occur between the ages of 5 and 7, as new cognitive skills mature.

Focus on Development

Stages of Social Perspective Taking

Levels of Social Perspective Taking	Approximate Age Range	Characteristics
Level 0: Undifferentiated and egocentric perspective taking	3 to 6 years	Children have an undifferentiated view of interpersonal situations. They are unable to recognize that other people may interpret the situation differently from them.
Level 1: Differentiated perspective taking	5 to 9 years	Children recognize that others may have different perspectives on a situation, but their interpersonal understanding is unilateral and one way. For example, they understand that giving a gift can make someone else happy, but they do not recognize that making another person happy can have a reciprocal effect.
Level 2: Reciprocal perspective taking	7 to 12 years	Children are able to put themselves in the shoes of another, and they realize others can do the same. For example, a child understands that another child may not like him because he gets the other person in trouble. Children can anticipate and consider thoughts and feelings of others.

Holly is an 8-year-old girl who likes to climb trees. She is the best tree climber in the neighborhood. One day while climbing down from a tall tree she falls off the bottom branch but does not hurt herself. Her father sees her fall. He is upset and asks her to promise not to climb trees anymore. Holly promises. Later that day, Holly and her friends meet Sean. Sean's kitten is caught up in a tree and cannot get down. Something has to be done right away or the kitten may fall. Holly is the only one who climbs trees well enough to reach the kitten and get it down, but she remembers her promise to her father. (Selman & Byrne, 1974, p. 805)

The researchers then asked the children their thoughts about different characters in the story. For example, they were asked:

Does Holly know how Sean feels about the kitten?

What will Holly's father think when he finds out?

If Holly and her father discussed the situation, what might they decide? (Selman & Byrne, 1974, p. 805)

Most elementary school children are able to consider another person's thoughts and feelings.

As shown in the Focus on Development box, Selman and his colleagues found there was a developmental progression in children's role-taking skills from preschool to early

Levels of Social Perspective Taking	Approximate Age Range	Characteristics
Level 3: Mutual perspective taking	10 to 15 years	Children are able to see their own, another person's, and their mutual perspectives from the viewpoint of a third person. That is, the adolescent can step out of the immediate interaction and consider how a teacher, parent, or peer might view each individual perspective as well as their mutual perspective.
Level 4: In-depth and societal-symbolic perspective taking	12 years on	Adolescents and adults are able to understand that a person's perspective may represent a larger societal point of view. For example, adolescents are able to understand that their parents may have different perspectives because their parents' generation had different beliefs, values, and expectations.

Adapted from Seligman (1980).

adolescence. About 80 percent of preschool children were unable to recognize that people in the story would have different perspectives. When asked what the father would think, the preschool child is likely to respond, "Happy because he likes kittens." In contrast, a 10-year-old is likely to respond: "He'll be mad at first, but then when he sees the kitten he'll understand why Holly climbed the tree and will not punish her."

This research indicates that important changes in children's social perspective-taking abilities take place in the elementary school years. Most 3- and 4-year-olds have difficulty understanding that another person may have values, moral beliefs, or ideas about social rules that are different from their own. Children between the ages of 6 and 12 can put themselves in the "other's shoes" and see themselves through the eyes of others. Most elementary school children are able to consider another person's thoughts and feelings. However, it is not until adolescence or adulthood that people are able to think about social relationships as part of a larger social system or to grasp the complexity of human behavior. For example, understanding ethnic differences involves recognizing that individuals may react a certain way because of their culture.

From an educational perspective, it is important to help children develop their role-taking skills. Children often have difficulties forming and maintaining friendships because they are unable to understand the other person's point of view and the reasons for the other person's behavior (Le Mare & Rubin, 1987). Perspective-taking skills are associated with prosocial behaviors such as helping or sharing (Eisenberg & Fabes, 1998). When children are able to understand the thoughts and feelings of others, they are more willing to share and help. As we will learn, perspective-taking skills also play an important role in moral development.

Describing Other People

In Chapter 7, we learned how children form conceptions of themselves. With development, these self-conceptions became more differentiated, complex, and abstract. We find the same pattern in children's perceptions and descriptions of other people.

Young children attend to people's observable features, such as their physical characteristics or favorite activities (Livesly & Bromley, 1973). For example a first grader might describe her new friend in this way: "She has brown hair, and lives by me. She has one brother, and he goes to another school. We like to play together."

Just as young children describe themselves in global, all-or-nothing terms, we can see the same trend in their descriptions of others. A person is either good or bad, and a good person also has many other positive traits (e.g., she is happy, friendly, and smart).

In middle childhood, children begin to move beyond surface characteristics to include more psychological traits in their descriptions. We observed this same trend in children's self-conceptions. For example, a 10-year-old may describe his classmate in this way: "He really looks weird and does silly things. I think he is really dumb and is always doing something disgusting in class."

This description includes some physical traits, but it also includes some personal traits that are readily observable, such as the child's lack of ability. However, this description is vague and superficial. Researchers believe that children's person perceptions at this age are based more on how they feel about the person than about the person's actual characteristics (Ruble & Dweck, 1995). Children's perceptions of other people become more balanced later in development. The child begins to focus on those inner traits and qualities that can be observed in many situations. In other words, the child is looking for traitlike characteristics that help them to understand and predict a person's behavior (Flavell & Miller, 1998). The discovery of personality traits that influence behavior across settings is an important development in person perception. The use of trait terms to describe people more than doubles by the age of 8 (Ruble & Dweck, 1995).

A more differentiated and complex view of other people does not emerge until adolescence when young people begin to see inconsistencies in their own behaviors and traits. They also begin to describe other people in terms of more subtle abstract terms and inner dispositions. For example, a 15-year-old may describe her friend this way: "I think he only acts that way when he is around certain people . . . he really cares about people."

In summary, there are important parallels between children's self-perceptions and person perceptions. We have learned that children's descriptions shift from a focus on perceptually salient characteristics (physical appearance) to inner psychological traits and needs. For educational purposes, it is important to recognize that children's thinking about other people is very rigid and evaluative. Young children are mostly concerned with who is good or bad (Ruble & Dweck, 1995). If another child is perceived as good, many other positive traits are attributed to that person. We observed this pattern when we discussed physical attractiveness. Someone who is physically attractive is also thought to be smart, friendly, successful, and so on. We will learn next how the rigidity of children's person perceptions influences their understanding of race and ethnicity.

A more differentiated and complex view of other people does not emerge until adolescence when young people begin to see inconsistencies in their own behaviors and traits.

Understanding Race and Ethnicity

A key component of person perception is understanding ethnic and racial diversity. As we have discussed, a more ethnically diverse group of children is entering schools today. For many children, their first opportunity to interact with someone from a different ethnic or racial group will occur in a school setting. **Prejudices** form when children develop a negative view of others based on their race or ethnicity. Thus, many teachers are faced with the difficult challenge of helping children to understand racial and ethnic diversity.

Social cognitive theory has been used to understand the development of children's race and ethnic conceptions (Bigler, Jones, & Lobliner, 1987; Black-Gutman & Hickson, 1996; Quintana, Castaneda-English, & Ybarra, 1999; Quintana, 1998). The Focus on Teaching box presents a developmental model that teachers can use to promote ethnic awareness and understanding in their classroom.

Ethnicity is a complex concept that many mature adults have difficulty defining and understanding. How do children develop this understanding? As we have already learned, children begin to form conceptions of gender at an early age. Young children also tend to describe people in terms of observable characteristics. Similarly, 3- and 4-year-olds are able to use skin color, hair, and other observable physical characteristics to categorize people into different racial groups. They can apply the labels of black and white to different pictures, dolls, and people by age 4. However, their ability to distinguish and label other ethnic groups, such as Asian Americans, Mexican Americans, and Native Americans may take longer because the distinctive features of these groups are less visible (Aboud, 1988). Children's conceptions of social groups are not stable and permanent at this point. A child might say, "I used to be white, but I went into the sun, and now I am brown" (Quintana, 1998, p. 33).

Although young children are just beginning to distinguish between racial and ethnic groups, they have already formed some racial biases and preferences. As you recall, young children process information in terms of single dimensions (e.g., length, size). They are unable to consider more than one dimension at the same time. When applied to social understanding, we find that young children tend to attribute positive attributes (e.g., friendly, kind, happy) to their own social group and negative traits to the other group (Bigler et al., 1997; Black-Gutman & Hickson, 1996; Quintana, 1998). More significantly, preschool children report more positive attitudes toward whites than other ethnic groups. This pro-white attitude is found for Caucasian children, as well as African Americans, Latinos, and Native Americans. What is interesting about this finding is that it appears to be unrelated to parental or peer attitudes (Quintana, 1998). Additionally, no racial bias is found in young children's preferences for playmates or social interactions. Researchers believe that young children's racial biases and preferences reflect the negative views and prejudices of the larger society. Evidence also suggests that children's pro-white attitudes may reflect their natural preference for light and bright objects at this age. Children's stories reinforce these preferences: Heroes are dressed in white, and villains all wear black. At present, the source of young children's racial attitudes are not clear.

By elementary school, children begin to form a more balanced view of ethnicity and race. Like gender, they understand the permanence of different ethnic or racial categorizations. With the development of concrete operations, children can group people into large social categories based on nonobservable features of ethnicity such as preferences for food, language, and activities (e.g., "He's Mexican because he speaks Spanish."). School-age children, who are also developing a concept of time and history, can also link ethnicity to heritage. Consequently, elementary school children have a *literal* definition of ethnicity. It

> *Researchers believe that young children's racial biases and preferences reflect the negative views and prejudices of the larger society.*

Focus on Teaching

Level of Ethnic Perspective Taking	Approximate Age Range	Description	Educational Implications
Level 0: Integration of affective and perceptual understanding of ethnicity	Early Childhood 3 to 6 years	Preschool children use physical characteristics (skin color and appearance) to classify and describe people racially. They also have pro-white racial bias and antiminority racial attitudes and prejudices that reflect wider societal views. Ethnic prejudice does not influence self-perceptions or behaviors toward other racial or ethnic groups at this age.	Young children may show strong preference for what color is used to depict skin color, and this color may not correspond to their own skin color. For example, African American children may prefer white skin. Children at this age benefit from activities that enable them to explore variations in skin color and appearances within and between racial groups. Young children may not respond positively to direct attempts to reduce racial prejudice, but it is important to present positive images of different ethnic or racial groups as concepts of social categories develop.
Level 1: Literal understanding of ethnicity and race	Middle Childhood 6 to 10 years	Children understand the permanence of racial or ethnic categorizations. Children use ancestry (e.g., My father is Chinese) and literal features of ethnicity (foods, activities, and language). A more balanced view of ethnicity emerges as children are able to think about multiple dimensions. Children have difficulty understanding prejudice and the social consequences of racial or ethnic status at this age.	Children benefit from learning about the history of different social groups, and the different customs, languages, and traditions that differentiate them. At this age, children can understand similarities and differences across and within different ethnic groups. For example, children can explore similarities and differences in families, communities, or schools. It is important for children to see positive images of their ethnic group to build ethnic pride.

Level of Ethnic Perspective Taking	Approximate Age Range	Description	Educational Implications
Level 2: Social and nonliteral perspective on ethnicity	Early Adolescence 10 to 14 years	Young adolescents are acquiring a social perspective of ethnicity. They show greater awareness of the social consequences of ethnicity such as differences in houses, neighborhoods, or possessions. Young adolescents believe that ethnic similarity is important for the formation of friendships and social groups. Minority adolescents also show an awareness of ethnic bias and prejudice toward their own group, even if it is not verbally or behaviorally manifested.	Young adolescents are able to discuss the social implications of ethnicity. Interventions that teach differences in languages, customs, and traditions are not as effective for this age group, because young adolescents are beyond literal definitions of ethnicity. Ethnic attitudes and prejudice are a source of conflict at this age and need to be addressed directly. Adolescents benefit from open discussions of ethnic prejudice. It is also important to emphasize interethnic similarities and to provide activities that promote intergroup cooperation.
Level 3: Ethnic group consciousness and ethnic identity	Adolescence 14 years and on	Older adolescents are developing a group perspective of ethnicity. This can lead to increases in stereotyping and ethnocentricism in adolescence. Adolescents are also actively exploring their own ethnic identity. Expressions of ethnicity are related to self-perceptions rather than objective status (e.g., My parents are Mexican, but I see myself differently).	At this age, it is important to recognize ethnic differences and to provide opportunities for young people to express their ethnic identity in productive ways. Racial stereotypes and prejudices need to be discussed openly and honestly, especially when they are the source of social conflict. It is important to provide activities that would promote positive interethnic relations and cooperation.

SOURCE: After Quintana (1998).

Elementary school children have a literal definition of ethnicity based on heritage, language spoken, and traditions.

is based on heritage, language spoken, and traditions (Quintana, 1998). Older children are also becoming more aware of individual differences within racial groups. It is these differences that enable the child to better predict what the person may say or do in a situation.

During the elementary school years, children become less biased in their racial attitudes. Minority children show an increase in positive attitudes toward their own group, and white children also show an increase in their positive attitudes toward minorities. At this stage of development, children benefit from learning about the history and traditions of different ethnic groups. They can also explore similarities and differences in families, communities, languages, and so on. However, it is difficult for elementary school children to understand the social features and implications of ethnicity, which involves a higher level of abstraction (Quintana, 1998).

During early adolescence, young people make an important transition to considering the social implications of ethnicity. Young adolescents (ages 10 to 14) show greater awareness of the social consequences of ethnicity, such as differences in houses, neighborhoods, and income. They have moved away from a literal definition to a social perspective of ethnicity. Young adolescents can now describe examples of prejudices and biases they have observed or experienced. Most significantly, young adolescents have developed an ability to understand how others may view their ethnicity. In Stephen Quintana's (1998) interviews with Mexican Americans, sixth graders were painfully aware that "Mexican kids are not the kind of kids other kids play with" (p. 38). As we have discussed previously, ethnic and racial stereotypes can make it difficult for minority youths to form a positive ethnic identity.

As young adolescents begin to understand the social implications of ethnicity, they begin to consider how others may view their ethnicity.

In adolescence, ethnic similarity becomes increasingly important in the formation of peer groups and friendships. When older adolescents are asked to describe their ethnic groups, there are more references to "us" and "we" than with younger children. It is believed that these references reflect a *group consciousness* of ethnicity that may serve as the foundation for forming an ethnic identity. Unfortunately, it tends to be associated with an increase in ethnocentrism and ethnic stereotyping in adolescence, until young people form a more "multicultural perspective of ethnicity" that involves a more sophisticated understanding of how ethnicity is only one of many dimensions of the self and others (Quintana et al., 1999).

Children's reasoning about ethnicity and race has important implications for educators (see the Focus on Teaching box, pp. 442–443). Efforts to increase racial and ethnic understanding need to be sensitive to the developmental patterns we discussed. Many children may enter school with negative attitudes and prejudices toward different social groups, but young children may not respond positively to direct attempts to reduce prejudice. Children benefit more from learning about the histories, customs, and traditions of different social groups. It is also important to point out the ways social groups are similar, even though they may look, speak, or act differently. Adolescents are able to consider the social implications of race and ethnicity, such as differences in housing, income, and job opportunities. Compared with younger students, they are better able to understand the effects of racism, prejudice, and discrimination. However, efforts to deemphasize ethnic differences may not be appropriate for youths who are developing an ethnic consciousness. Older adolescents need educators who can help them develop a healthy ethnic identity.

More than half of hate crimes in the United States are committed by young people under the age of 21.

Schools also share an important responsibility for promoting tolerance and for reducing prejudice. More than half of hate crimes in the United States are committed by young people under the age of 21 (Heller & Hawkins, 1994). The teaching of tolerance requires that all students develop a sensitivity to the negative, discriminatory tone of racial and ethnic slurs, jokes, and stereotypes. Many schools are fostering tolerance and understanding through antibias curriculum and innovative learning projects. For example, more than 30,000 teachers nationwide have been trained to use *Facing History and Ourselves* curriculum materials with their middle and high school students (Heller & Hawkins, 1994). By critically examining moral questions raised by incidences of genocide (the Holocaust,

Cambodia, and Armenia), these materials are designed to help young people reflect on their own identity, group membership, and obligations to others. The *Freedom Writers Diary*, discussed in Chapter 7, is another excellent example of students using a historical event to learn about racism and prejudice in their own lives.

Children's Peer Relations

During the school years, children begin spending more time with their peers until, by adolescence, they spend about two-thirds of their day with classmates or friends. Adolescents consider the time they spend with their peers as the most enjoyable part of their day (Csikzentmihalyi & Larson, 1984). But parents often worry about the negative influence of peers. Problems such as drug and alcohol abuse, juvenile delinquency, and sexual promiscuity are often attributed to the negative influence of peers. However, contrary to popular belief, most studies suggest that good peer relations are *necessary* for normal psychological development. Children who are at greatest risk for developing academic problems and antisocial behaviors are those with poor peer relations. These children often have problematic family relations as well.

Children who are at greatest risk for developing academic problems and antisocial behaviors are those with poor peer relations.

The Role of Peers in Children's Development

The term **peer** refers to a child of equal age or maturity. Peer relations tend to be more egalitarian and balanced than relations with parents and other adults. This equality provides a context for the development of many important interpersonal skills (Hartup, 1996). With peers, children can learn to make decisions and to resolve conflict without adult intervention. The peer group also provides an opportunity to experiment with different roles and identities, and peers provide feedback that children may not get from adults. Numerous studies show that positive peer relations can enhance children's feelings of competence, efficacy, and self-worth (Parker & Asher, 1987; Parker, Rubin, Price, & DeRosier, 1995; Rubin, Bukowski, & Parker, 1998; Rubin, Coplan, Nelson, Cheah, & Lagace-Seguin, 1999).

Peers also have an important influence on school success. We have already discussed how peers are important collaborators in learning situations. Peers help one another learn through modeling academic skills, assisting in problem solving, serving as a resource, and providing encouragement and support. Additionally, research suggests that peers influence how much children value achievement, how much they study, how well they perform in school, and which classes they take (Berndt & Keefe, 1992; Epstein, 1983; Kinderman, McCollam, & Gibson, 1996; Steinberg, Dornbusch, & Brown, 1992; Wentzel & Caldwell, 1997). High-achieving students tend to associate with peers who value success in school, whereas low-achieving students are generally friends with classmates who express less interest in getting good grades (Berndt & Keefe, 1996). Peer acceptance also promotes a sense of group belonging in school, which can promote higher school achievement (Wentzel & Caldwell, 1997). Additionally, there is evidence to suggest that peers play an important role in school adjustment. Children make a positive transition to kindergarten when they enter school with existing friends or are able to make friends easily (Ladd, 1990; Ladd & Price, 1987).

Studies show that positive peer relations can enhance children's feelings of competence, efficacy, and self-worth.

What happens when children are deprived of peer relations? Children with poor peer relations are known to experience low self-esteem, depression, poor school achievement, dropping out of school, and delinquent behavior (Parker & Asher, 1987; Parker et al., 1995; Savin-Williams & Berndt, 1990). As adults, these same children may experience mental health problems, marital instability, and erratic work lives.

In summary, peers help shape children's development in many important ways. The most common effects are:

- Peer relations provide opportunities for play and for exploring new roles.
- Peer relations provide a valuable context for learning and practicing social skills, such as social problem solving, perspective taking, and resolving conflict.
- Peer relations provide emotional and social support to enhance feelings of competency, efficacy, and self-worth.
- Peers provide valuable information about behavioral norms and expectations.
- Peer relations provide opportunities to develop close and intimate relationships with others.
- Peer relations play an important role in fostering school engagement, motivation, and achievement.

Many young people experience peer pressure to try alcohol, to smoke cigarettes, and to engage in sexual activities.

However, not all peer relations are alike. Some peer influences are not always positive. Early involvement with deviant peer groups, for example, is related to school dropout (Cairns & Cairns, 1994; Cairns, Cairns, & Neckerman, 1989). Many young people also experience peer pressure to try alcohol, to smoke cigarettes, and to engage in sexual activities. When children engage in delinquent activities for the first time (e.g., shoplifting, vandalism, truancy), it is generally in the presence of peers (Cole & Dodge, 1998).

Parents play an influential role in this process as well. Parents choose the neighborhoods, schools, churches, and youth organizations from which children select their friends. Parents and community members also serve as important role models. Children are more likely to try alcohol or cigarettes with their peers if they observe role models drinking or smoking (Kandel & Wu, 1995). In addition, children with poor parental relations are more susceptible to peer influences (Fletcher, Darling, Steinberg, & Dornbush, 1995; Fuligini & Eccles, 1993). Thus, both peer and parental relations are linked to the development of problem behaviors in children and adolescents. We will explore these influences when we discuss the development of aggression in children.

Peer Popularity and Rejection

Why do some children have so many friends and others have so few? Why are some children rejected? The key determinant to **peer popularity** is social competence, the ability to initiate and maintain positive interactions with others (Asher & Parker, 1993; Coie, Dodge, & Kupersmidt, 1990; Rubin, Coplin, Nelson, Cheah, & Lagace-Seguin, 1999). In conflict situations, they tend to use negotiation and compromise to maintain positive relations with peers (Hart, DeWolf, Wozniak, & Burts, 1992). Popular children tend to be friendly, helpful, cooperative, good-natured, and sensitive. They also do well in school and obey the rules at home and at school. As a result, popular children have good relations with both children and adults.

Popular children tend to be friendly, helpful, cooperative, good-natured, and sensitive.

Some children are neither popular nor rejected by their peers. Approximately 6 percent to 11 percent of elementary school children have no friends or are not nominated as friends (Rubin et al., 1999). Researchers refer to these children as **neglected peers.** They seem to be invisible in the classroom and tend to be shy and socially withdrawn (Coie et al., 1990). They do not have serious social problems, but they are not as skilled at making friends or initiating interactions as popular children. Although they spend a lot of time alone, they do not describe themselves as lonely. It is generally assumed that shy and withdrawn children are at greater risk than other children for dropping out of school or developing psychological problems later in life; however, research has not yet confirmed this hypothesis.

Peer rejection can have lasting consequences. Rejected children need special assistance from teachers to develop positive peer relations.

One of the key determinants of **peer rejection** is aggression (Coie et al., 1990; Rubin et al., 1999). Rejected children lack the social skills needed for initiating positive interactions and for resolving conflict. Peers and teachers describe rejected children as inattentive, aversive, threatening, hostile, and disruptive. As a result, rejected children are strongly disliked by most of their classmates. Aggressive children make up approximately 40 percent to 50 percent of the rejected children. Another group of children tend to be rejected because they are highly socially withdrawn, timid, and submissive (Parkhurst & Asher, 1992; Rubin et al., 1999). Thus, there are two distinct groups of rejected children—those who are aggressive and those who are socially withdrawn and submissive.

As suggested earlier, peer rejection has many costs. It is associated with academic difficulties, truancy, and high school dropout. It is also a predictor of adolescent crime and delinquency. Longitudinal studies indicate that the effects of childhood rejection can last well into adulthood (Rubin & Caplan, 1992; Reid, 1993). Rejected children who are aggressive have the greatest need for assistance in improving their peer relations.

Enhancing Peer Relations in the Classroom

Given the importance of peers in children's development, teachers need to create a classroom environment that promotes positive social relationships. How can teachers enhance peer relations? Providing preschool and primary children with play opportunities is an important training ground for social skills. Through play, children learn to understand others, to follow and lead, to express emotions, to build relationships, and to resolve problems. For elementary and secondary students, cooperative learning and peer tutoring activities can contribute to a positive peer culture in the classroom. These activities promote sharing, cooperation, and helping behaviors. Research suggests that the systematic use of cooperative learning activities can reduce the number of students who are socially isolated and improve

Rejected children lack the social skills for initiating positive interactions and for resolving conflict.

The systematic use of cooperative learning activities can reduce the number of students who are socially isolated and improve relations between students of different ethnic and social backgrounds.

Using Cooperative Learning to Promote Positive Peer Relations

Cooperative learning methods enable teachers to respond to the diverse needs of their students while at the same time promoting positive relations in the classroom. Cooperative learning takes many different forms, but most approaches involve heterogeneous groups of four or five members working together to accomplish a shared goal. Although each member of the team is individually accountable, each student must learn to depend on others for assistance. Cooperative learning methods may be used in any subject matter, from preschool through graduate school.

A number of different cooperative learning approaches have been in development. The most widely used approaches are the Jigsaw Classroom, the Student Teams Achievement Division, and a Group Investigation.

The Jigsaw Classroom (Aronson & Patnoe, 1996)

In this approach, six-member teams work on a learning task that is broken down into different parts. Each member is responsible for one part. During the first phase of the activity, members of each team who are responsible for the same part of the lesson meet to discuss their part. After mastering the material, they return to their original team to teach their part.

Student Teams Achievement Division (Slavin, 1994)

Here students are assigned to groups of four or five members to work on problems together. The teams assist one another during the learning phases, but take individual assessments. Team scores are based on each individual member's improvement; therefore, each member can contribute to the overall goal of earning a high score. This approach has been used for projects in mathematics, reading, and social studies, and works well with students from different ability levels and in different grades.

Group Investigation (Sharan, 1990)

In a group investigation, students work in two- to six-member teams on an independent and group assignment. The teacher chooses a topic (e.g., weather), but students get to choose an individual problem related to the topic. Students work on their problems individually and then meet with their team to integrate their findings and to develop a group report. The teacher and student jointly evaluate the group and individual projects.

Cooperative learning is perhaps one of the most extensively studied teaching approaches. Researchers have examined its influence on academic achievement, higher-order thinking, transfer and retention of learning material, moral development, social competencies, and many other outcomes (Johnson, Johnson, &

relations between students of different ethnic and social backgrounds (Hansell & Slavin, 1983). Cooperative learning activities have also been found to increase student motivation and achievement (Slavin, 1983). The Focus on Teaching box describes ways to use cooperative learning methods in the classroom.

Stanne, 2000; Slavin, 1995). Because cooperative learning methods were initially used in the classroom to improve intergroup relations (cross-race, cross-gender, etc.), these effects have received attention as well.

Although cooperative learning methods need to be carefully used in the classroom, there is general consensus about their benefits. The research clearly indicates that cooperative learning improves students' motivation to learn, interest in learning, and academic performance. It also contributes to a supportive and cooperative classroom environment. And perhaps most important, cooperative learning can improve interpersonal relations of students from different ethnic and socioeconomic backgrounds, as well as improve the social acceptance of students with learning disabilities and other handicaps (Sharan, 1980; Slavin, 1995).

David and Roger Johnson (1975, 1999), who developed a program called Learning Together, view cooperative learning methods as a vehicle for team building and for socioemotional development in the classroom. In their view, cooperative learning methods are used most effectively in the classroom when the following key elements are observed:

- *Interdependence.* Group activities need to be structured in ways that ensure each group member's effort is required for success and each member has something unique and important to contribute. Students need to believe they sink or swim together. If there is no shared goal, there is no cooperation.
- *Individual and Group Accountability.* Two levels of accountability need to be observed in cooperative learning approaches. The group is accountable for achieving a shared goal, and each member is evaluated in terms of his or her contribution to the group.
- *Building Interpersonal and Small Group Skills.* Cooperative learning activities are highly complex, involving teamwork as well as individual effort. Effective cooperative learning involves helping students be good listeners, leaders, decision makers, and team members. Learning to manage conflict constructively is also important for the overall success of cooperative learning programs. It should not be assumed that students know how to work as part of a team. These skills need to be explicitly taught or modeled.
- *Group Processes.* Group members need to discuss how the group is working together to meet its goals. The objective of these discussions is to identify ways of improving group effectiveness and relations.

When cooperating learning methods are used, careful attention needs to be given to group composition. It is best to balance groups in terms of ethnicity, gender, and ability. Teachers need to monitor groups to encourage equal participation of all members.

For neglected and rejected children, collaborative learning opportunities alone may not be enough to improve their social status in the classroom. These children may need more direct intervention in order to learn how to relate positively to others. Social skill training programs can teach unpopular children how to initiate positive interactions with peers, to

Teachers can enhance children's peer relations by using a combination of cooperative learning and social training activities in their classroom.

make and keep friends, to think about the consequences of their behavior before acting, and to use nonaggressive solutions for resolving conflict. These training programs work best when teachers provide opportunities for children to practice the social skills they have learned and to receive positive responses from others when they use the skills (Berndt & Keefe, 1992). In sum, teachers can enhance children's peer relations by using a combination of cooperative learning and individual training activities in the classroom. The next sections provide some suggestions concerning how teachers can help enhance prosocial behavior and reduce aggression in their classrooms.

Development of Prosocial and Aggressive Behavior

As we have seen, popular and rejected children differ in the ways they relate to their peers. Popular children are able to share and to cooperate, whereas rejected children have difficulty initiating interactions in positive ways. Let's examine how these different ways of relating to peers develop.

Development of Prosocial Behaviors

Most parents and teachers want their children to help, cooperate, and care for others. They also want their children to appreciate that other people's needs may be more important than their own. Defined as voluntary actions intended to benefit another person, **prosocial behaviors** emerge early in development when there are supportive relationships between children and caregivers (Eisenberg & Fabes, 1998). For example, some infants react emotionally to the crying of other babies and, by the end of the second year, children will approach and try to comfort another child who is crying or upset. Two- and 3-year-olds can exhibit a wide range of prosocial behaviors including sharing, helping, and caregiving. These prosocial behaviors often occur spontaneously, with little prompting or encouragement from others (Eisenberg, 1992).

Prosocial behavior increases in elementary years as children learn to interpret the thoughts, feelings, and behaviors of others.

Prosocial behavior increases during the preschool years. As their cognitive abilities develop, children learn to interpret what others may be feeling, thinking, and saying and to learn how their own actions affect others and themselves. As a result, they are better at anticipating how people will respond to them. They also learn to coordinate their actions with others and to work cooperatively toward a common goal.

Some studies suggest that prosocial behaviors continue to increase during the school years, but others report either no change or a decrease in prosocial behavior, depending on the ages studied, the research methods used, and the behavior setting (Radke-Yarrow, Zahn-Waxler, & Chapman, 1983). However, most studies indicate that older children are better able to deal with more subtle and abstract forms of distress. For example, after viewing a television report of a family killed in a fire, one 7-year-old commented, "I hope those children weren't so young so they had a chance to have some life before having to die" (Radke-Yarrow et al., 1985; p. 488).

Why are some children more prosocial than others? There are a number of possible explanations. Nancy Eisenberg and her colleagues have studied how children reason about prosocial behavior (Eisenberg & Fabes, 1998). Because young children are not able to take the perspective of others, they do not realize the need for prosocial behavior. In elementary school, children's reasoning about prosocial behavior reflects a concern about other's people approval, as well as a desire to behave in a stereotypically "good" way. At this age, children may help others to gain approval or to do the "right thing." Beginning in late elementary school and thereafter, children begin to show a genuine concern, or empathy, for the other person's well-being. By adolescence, prosocial behaviors are guided by internalized values about helping others or by feelings of guilt or pride about one's actions.

The home environment also plays an important role in the development of prosocial behavior. Children who observe prosocial behaviors modeled in the home are more likely to exhibit these behaviors in other settings, such as school. When parents are helpful and responsive, their children imitate these behaviors (Bryant & Crockenburg, 1980). Additionally, many parents foster prosocial behaviors by providing opportunities for children and adolescents to perform routine household tasks and chores that benefit others (Grusex, Goodnow, & Cohen, 1996). It is believed that these activities sensitize young people to the needs and welfare of others.

Discipline practices also have an important influence on the development of children's prosocial behaviors. In general, parents who use reasoning and induction as a method of disciplining children tend to have children who behave prosocially (Hoffman, 1994). These parents tend to emphasize the rights and needs of others, as well as the impact of the child's behavior on others. In contrast, power tactics that involve physical punishment, physical restraint, or unexplained prohibition ("I told you not to hit!") may act as an immediate deterrent but do little to help children learn prosocial behaviors.

The research on parenting and prosocial behavior has important implications for teachers. It suggests that teachers can increase children's prosocial behaviors by modeling such behaviors, by encouraging children to share, cooperate, and help others, and by using positive discipline strategies that help students to consider the effects of their behavior on others. Students also benefit from activities in which they help others. Class projects such as tutoring younger children, reading to elderly people, building a play area, or collecting food or clothes for needy children are ways to foster a concern for the welfare of others. Service learning projects for other students has as its goal the development of social responsibility (Waterman, 1997).

Development of Aggressive Behavior

Few topics have attracted as much attention as the development of aggression in children. According to a recent national survey of high school students, almost half of male students and one-quarter of female students in grades 9 through 12 reported having been involved in a physical fight, and 17 percent reported carrying a weapon such as a gun, knife, or club in the last 30 days (U.S. Department of Human Services, 2000). Although rates of youth violence have declined in recent years, violence continues to be the second leading cause of death among teenagers in the United States, and homicide is the leading cause of death for ethnic minority teens. Moreover, the tragic school shootings in recent years show that youth aggression and violence can happen anyway. More than 70 percent of adults believe a school shooting can happen in their own community (Henrich, Brown, & Aber, 1999). As the lives of more and more families are touched by violence, policy makers and concerned citizens seek ways to stop it. Although fewer than one percent of all violent deaths of children occur at school, many schools are now involved in violence prevention programs.

For the purpose of our discussion, **aggression** is defined as behavior that is intentionally aimed at harming or injuring another person (Parke & Slaby, 1983). It is important to keep in mind that not all aggression is violent in nature. Verbal abuse, destruction of property, harassment, derogatory racial or antigay remarks, obscene gestures, and even vicious gossip are different forms of aggression.

One of the most common forms of aggression in school settings is bullying behavior. It is estimated that more than 5 million schoolchildren are bullies or victims of bullies (Espelage, Bosworth, & Simon, 2000). **Bullying behavior** takes many forms—embarrassing people, hitting, destroying property, ridiculing, and so on. As described in the Focus on Research box, bullying behavior has long-term consequences for both the bully and the

By adolescence, prosocial behaviors are guided by internalized values about helping others or by feelings of guilt or pride about one's actions.

Teachers can increase children's prosocial behaviors by modeling such behaviors, by encouraging children to share, cooperate, and help others, and by using positive discipline strategies that help students to consider the effects of their behavior on others.

Focus on Research

Nearly three-quarters of a million students report being aware of incidents of physical harassment, robbery, and bullying at their school (National Center for Education Statistics, 1995). In 1999, one in 20 students missed school in a 30-day period because the student did not feel safe in school (Center for Disease Control, 1995). One of these students' strongest fears is peer harassment in the form of bullying.

Bullying is a subset of aggression, and is defined as a set of behaviors that is "intentional and causes physical and psychological harm to the recipient" (Smith & Thompson, 1991, p. 1). Researchers believe that bullying occurs as a way for the bully to attain social position within a peer group or have dominance over others (Olweus, 1978; Espelage et al., 2000). Bullying behavior is most prevalent in adolescent peer groups. As adolescents make the transition to a new school environment, bullying might be one way to establish status in a new peer group (Pellegrini & Bartini, 1999). Bullies generally lack the social skills for positive integration with peers, and they often become associated with deviant peer groups who support antisocial activities such as damaging property, fighting, and so on (Espelage et al., 2000). Boys are more likely to engage in bullying behaviors than girls; however, girls tend to use social alienation and verbal bullying as methods of intimidation. These behaviors may be more difficult to identify than the physical bullying behaviors exhibited by boys (Espelage et al., 2000; Roberts, 2000).

Several factors contribute to the bullying behavior of youth. Because bullying is a form of aggression, it shares the same developmental course. The home environment of the bully tends to be punitive and harsh (Espelage, Bosworth, Karageorge, & Daytner, 1996; Espelage et al., 2000). The slightest infraction may spark a verbal, emotional, and physical reaction from caregivers. Physical punishment is commonly used, and parents provide little in the way of modeling positive behaviors. Bullies spend a good deal of their time without adult supervision, and they are seldom disciplined for antisocial behavior. Researchers believe that children from these circumstances learn to gain power and status by attacking the weaknesses of others.

Bullying behavior has consequences for both the bully and the victim. The damage done to the victim's self-esteem may be long term and lead the victim to victim. The majority of bullying incidents occur near or within school buildings, and only 25 percent of students report that their teachers had intervened in bullying situations.

Current theories of childhood aggression stress the importance of both biological and environmental influences (Coie & Dodge, 1998; Lahey, Waldman, McBurnett, 1999; Loeber & Stouthamer-Loeber, 1998). That is, some children may be genetically predisposed to exhibit aggressive behaviors, but there are also important family, peer, and cultural influences to consider. Once aggression becomes a significant component of a child's life, it can gain strength and become self-reinforcing because it provides children with a way to control and to manipulate others (Cairns & Cairns, 1994). If left untreated, children who show an aggressive profile in kindergarten or first grade will continue to be aggressive throughout the school years (Cairns, Cairns, Nickerman, Gest, & Gariepy, 1988; Coie & Dodge, withdraw from school (Hanish & Guerra, 2000). For example, Dan Olweus (1993) reports that children who were bullied in middle school had low self-esteem 10 years later, and they were more likely to report social isolation and depression than peers who were not bullied. In some cases, bullying can increase aggression among victims (Hanish & Guerra, 2000). There are also long-term consequences for the bully. As they become adults, they are more likely to become involved in criminal activity and to display aggression toward spouses and children (Huesmann, Eron, Lefkowitz, Eron, Walder, & Huesman, 1977; Olweus, 1993).

Bullying is the most prevalent form of violence and aggression in schools. It often occurs in areas of the school building that are not well supervised. Attacks on the playground or in the hallway are common. To compound the problem, many victims do not report bullying incidents out of fear of additional harassment. Thus, teachers and other school personnel may not be aware that peer victimization is occurring.

What can educators do? The following are some recommended strategies:

- Many schools have adopted antibullying policies that encourage treating others with respect and care. Students need to understand that physical aggression and bullying are not acceptable ways of gaining popularity or leadership.

- Bullies need to be confronted by adults in a calm, rational way. One way to begin the conversation is to ask the student to explain the behavior (e.g., What is going on with you and David today?)

- Bullies are often sad and unhappy. Empathic listening can help identify the cognitive and affective problems associated with the bullying behavior.

- Bullies need to learn alternative ways of interacting with peers. Social skill training and anger management programs have been effective in reducing bullying behavior.

1991; Olweus, 1981). Moreover, as early as first grade, childhood aggression is predictive of other problem behaviors that can occur in later development, such as poor academic achievement, peer rejection, substance abuse, truancy, and delinquent behavior (Reid, 1993).

Age-Related Changes in Aggression

There are clear differences in the form and frequency of aggression in children. Adults are often surprised when they learn that toddlers and preschoolers are often *more* aggressive than elementary school children. Visit any day care center, and you will see 3- and 4-year-olds quarreling or playing tug-of-war with toys and other prized possessions (Fabes &

Once aggression becomes a significant component of a child's life, it can gain strength and become self-reinforcing, because it provides the child with a way to control and to manipulate others.

Eisenberg, 1992). To get their way, some children may hit, kick, pull hair, or bite. Physical aggression of this sort is more common among younger children because they have limited verbal and social skills. In most instances, the aggression is intended to obtain a desired object, not to hurt or to injure another person. When a child's behavior is intended to obtain an object or to protect a play space, it is known as **instrumental aggression.** If, on the other hand, the child's goal is to hurt or harm another person, it is known as **hostile aggression.**

With age, instrumental aggression declines. This decrease is due to the development of children's abilities to delay gratification (see Chapter 7). Also, as we learned earlier, older children are better able to take the perspective of others and to consider the consequences of their actions. When aggression is exhibited in elementary school and thereafter, it takes the form of hostile aggression. It is person-oriented and intended to hurt or harm the other person. Hostile aggression is much more frequent among school-aged children and adolescents than preschoolers. From about 4 years on, boys are more likely than girls to engage in aggressive behaviors. However, it is believed that social aggression, which is intended to damage peer relations, may be more common among girls than boys (Coie & Dodge, 1998).

Along with the developmental shift from instrumental to hostile aggression, there are also important changes in *how* aggression is expressed at different ages. Younger children with limited verbal skills tend to resolve disputes through physical aggression, but older children are more likely to use *verbal forms of aggression.* Teasing, ridiculing, and shouting are the preferred modes of aggression among older children. This developmental change in aggressive behavior is due not only to improved language skills but also to changes in adult expectations and rules. By late elementary school, most children know they should use their words and not their hands to resolve conflicts.

In some cases, verbal aggression can take the form of sexual harassment. A survey of 1,632 students in grades 8 through 11 indicated that peer harassment in the form of sexual comments or jokes was a widespread phenomenon in American secondary schools (Barringer, 1993). More than 75 percent of all girls and 56 percent of all boys reported that

Hostile aggression is behavior that is aimed at harming or injuring another person, whereas instrumental aggression is behavior aimed at obtaining an object or protecting a play space. With age, instrumental aggression decreases and hostile aggression increases.

SOURCE: James L. Shaffer.

Rough-and-tumble play is common among young children, especially boys. The intent is not to do harm but to have fun. In contrast to fighting, the children are generally laughing and smiling.

they had been the target of unwanted sexual comments, gestures, or looks. The source of this harassment was most often from peers, and these activities tended to have the most negative effect on girls.

Causes of Childhood Aggression

Many parents and educators believe that electronic media, especially television, is a major contributor to childhood aggression. Young people watch an average of 28 hours of television per week, and 80 percent of television shows contain some form of violence (Pellman, 2000). As described in the Focus on Research box, aggressive children tend to watch more violent television programs, but the relation between television viewing and aggression is not straightforward.

The causes of aggression depend on when it emerges in development (Lahey et al., 1999; Loeber & Stouthamer-Loeber, 1998). Researchers have identified three developmental courses for aggressive behavior: (1) early onset; (2) limited duration; and (3) late onset. Most, but not all, aggressive acts during adolescence and adulthood are committed by youths who show a persistent pattern of aggression since childhood (Loeber & Hay, 1997). Longitudinal studies reveal that children who show an early onset of aggressive behaviors tend to have a difficult and oppositional temperament during infancy (Lahey et al., 1999). These children often come from families characterized by a number of stressful conditions (e.g., economic problems, substance abuse, marital discord, or mental health disorders), which makes it difficult for parents to set consistent limits for their children, especially if the children themselves are difficult (irritable, hyperactive, impulsive). Inconsistent or ineffective parental discipline can set in motion a *coercive family process* (Patterson, 1982), and it is one of the strongest predictors of aggressive behavior in early development. Without effective guidance, the child becomes increasingly aggressive, impulsive, and noncompliant. If parents give in to such behavior, it increases the likelihood that children will respond to future requests for compliance with hostility, negativity, and resistance.

As parent-child interactions become more strained, some parents may either withdraw from the relationship or use physical punishment to bring about compliance. In either case, such parent-child interactions militate against the child's development of emotional control, academic skills, and social competence. As we will discuss in Chapter 9, parents who regularly use physical force to control people also provide an aggressive model for their children to emulate. Additionally, aggressive children receive little reinforcement when they do exhibit nonviolent, cooperative play with their siblings.

Peers also play a role in the development of aggression. Children with an early onset of aggression tend to have fewer well-behaving peers who can serve as positive role models (Cairns & Cairns, 1994; Cairns et al., 1989; Coie & Dodge, 1998; Lahey et al., 1998). Aggressive children often form friendships with other aggressive or delinquent youths. These associations tend to reinforce and sustain existing problem behaviors. For youths who do not show an early pattern of aggression, the influence of deviant peers is much stronger. These associations can place nonaggressive or moderately disruptive youths on a developmental pathway toward problem behavior (criminality, police arrests, violence) in adulthood (Lahey et al., 1999; Loeber & Stouthamer-Lober, 1998). However, it is important to point out that the late onset of aggression is also associated with poor parental monitoring and high neighborhood crime rates. These environmental conditions increase the likelihood that young people will come into contact with delinquent peers (Lahey et al., 1999).

In summary, there appears to be no one single cause for aggression. It is an interplay of the child's own characteristics, family environment, peer relations, community, and culture. In the next section, we discuss how schools can help reduce aggression and violence among youth.

Teasing, ridiculing, and shouting are the preferred modes of aggression among older children.

Parents who regularly use physical force to control people also provide an aggressive model for their children to emulate.

Focus on Research

A study of 2,500 network and cable channels revealed a high frequency of violent acts that previous research has linked to harmful consequences (Carter, 1996). Approximately 30 percent of the programs sampled contained violence. And 25 percent of the violent incidents involved handguns. By adolescence, young people have observed more than 100,000 acts of TV violence, including 20,000 murders (American Psychological Association, 1993). In most instances, perpetrators of violence go unpunished; few programs containing violence emphasize nonviolent alternatives for solving problems. The authors of this study recommended that TV producers limit violence and show negative consequences for violent acts. The study also recommended that policy makers pass federal legislation to require television manufactures to install program-blocking devices, known as V-chips, so that parents can limit children's viewing of violence.

What are the effects of TV violence on children? Most studies report a clear link between TV violence and aggression (American Psychological Association, 1993). For example, Bandura's (1969) early study with the Bobo doll discussed in Chapter 1 showed that preschool children who viewed a film depicting aggressive models exhibited more aggression in a free play situation than children who did not watch the film. In another early study, Friedrich and Stein (1973) asked children to watch one of three types of television shows daily for four weeks: cartoons and other programs ("Batman") showing aggression, programs depicting prosocial themes ("Mr. Rogers' Neighborhood"), and shows with neither prosocial nor aggressive themes. Children who watched the aggressive shows displayed more aggressive behavior after the intervention than the children who viewed the other shows did. The effects of TV violence can have long-term effects. Children with higher exposure to television violence were more aggressive ten years later (Eron, Huesmann, Lefkowitz, & Walder, 1996; Zuckerman & Zuckerman, 1985).

As suggested here, a heavy dose of TV violence early in childhood can have harmful consequences for later development. Exposure to violence on television not only increases the likelihood of aggression but also increases children's acceptance of aggression. That is, children may become indifferent to violence. While this research suggests a clear link between TV violence and aggression, researchers are still debating cause-and-effect relations (Huston & Wright, 1998). Do aggressive children watch more aggressive TV shows? Or does violence on TV cause children, regardless of their developmental history, to become more violent? There is some evidence to suggest that aggressive children, who may have aggressive models inside and outside the home, tend to watch a greater number of television shows with aggressive themes. Also, children who show a predisposition toward aggression are more susceptible to the influence of TV violence than are children who are not aggressive.

Thus, the effects of TV violence on aggression are clearly not straightforward or simple, but there is nevertheless a strong link between the two. One expert estimates that television violence is responsible for 10 percent of violent behavior in this country (ISR Newsletter, 1994). As violence among youth continues to receive public attention, more and more pressure will be placed on television producers to eliminate or to seriously reduce violence. Stay tuned.

School Efforts to Reduce Aggression

Currently, violence prevention among youth is one of our country's top priorities. The Gun-Free Schools Act of 1994 required public schools receiving federal funding to implement mandatory expulsion rules for any student caught bringing a firearm onto school property. However, throwing troubled students out of school is not the best solution to the problem. It only increases the likelihood that they will fall further behind academically and eventually drop out of school. School expulsion also places youths at greater risk for delinquency, because they are less likely to have adult supervision (Children's Defense Fund, 1996).

Several school-based intervention programs have been successful in reducing aggression. Many schools have also implemented programs that help aggressive, socially immature children develop missing interpersonal skills. As discussed

Many teachers today have training in conflict resolution to help young people resolve interpersonal problems constructively.

School expulsion also places youths at greater risk for delinquency, because they are less likely to have adult supervision.

SOURCE: Mary Kate Deny/Photo Edit.

earlier, aggressive children are less likely than nonaggressive children to notice and interpret social cues correctly, to generate socially desirable responses to social problems, and to evaluate the consequences of their actions (Reid, 1993). They also have difficulty carrying out nonaggressive solutions to problems. An intervention program based on this research would emphasize training to enable aggressive children and adolescents (1) to stop and think about social problems before reacting; (2) to interpret problems accurately; (3) to consider several possible solutions; and (4) to evaluate the consequences of their actions. These programs are most successful when they begin early in school and involve both parents and teachers in addressing the problem behavior (Coie & Dodge, 1998).

Along with programs focused on individual groups of students, many schools have also implemented schoolwide programs for improving the social skills and interpersonal relations of all students. **Conflict resolution programs** are being used in elementary, middle, and high schools to help students solve interpersonal problems peacefully (Porro, 1996; Walker, 1995). These programs help students to (1) define the problem; (2) identify possible solutions; (3) evaluate consequences for self and others; and (4) choose solutions that benefit both sides (called *win-win* solutions). Two widely-used programs of this type are (1) Teaching Students to Be Peacemakers (Johnson & Johnson, 1995), and (2) Resolving Conflict Creatively (RCCP, 1997). Both programs begin in the early grades and continue

Steps in conflict resolution are: defining the problem, brainstorming solutions, and choosing those solutions that benefit both sides.

Preventing Aggression by Promoting Social Competence

Second Step is a school-based violence prevention program geared toward children from preschool through grade 9. The program is designed to reduce aggression by promoting social competence. The curriculum is focused on three key social-emotional competencies: empathy, social problem solving, and anger management. Program lessons are taught by trained teachers twice a week in the regular classroom. Stories, puppets, videos, role play, and class discussions are used to promote key concepts. Students take an active role in solving class problems, deciding rules, and resolving conflict. "Remember the Day" activities are used at the end of the day to review and discuss certain targeted behaviors (e.g., How did you feel when you were left out?). There is also a school and family component to the program.

Initial lessons focus on empathy. Students discuss and identify different feelings, and practice communicating different feelings. This aspect of the curriculum is very similar to the PATHS program discussed in Chapter 7. Stories are used to help students understand other people's feelings. Role playing is also used to help students with perspective-taking skills (e.g., What do you say when a friend is angry?).

In the social problem-solving component of the program, students learn how to solve problems using five strategies. Students are taught to (1) identify the problem; (2) brainstorm solutions; (3) evaluate solutions by asking Is it safe? Is it fair? How might people feel? Will it work? (4) select a solution; and (5) evaluate if the solution worked. As before, stories and role-playing activities are used to help develop these competencies.

The third component of the Second Step program is anger management. In these lessons, students are taught to recognize anger cues in their bodies—situations that "trigger" angry responses (e.g., teasing and name-calling)—and then practice strategies to bring their anger under control. These strategies may include self-talk, which involves using language to calm emotions.

Evaluations have examined the effects of the program on second- and third-grade students in 49 classes. Behavioral observations revealed that physical aggression decreased from fall to spring among students who were enrolled in the Second Step program. Reductions were greatest in the least structured settings—the playground and lunchroom—where aggression most frequently occurs. In addition, prosocial behavior (taking turns, sharing) increased among students from the fall to the spring term. These results provide encouraging evidence that a school-based program focused on promoting social competencies can help to reduce aggression.

through high school. Formal evaluations show that schoolwide conflict resolution programs are successful in reducing the frequency of aggressive behaviors and in changing cognitive processes (e.g., hostile attributions, retaliation fantasies) associated with aggression (Aber, Jones, Brown, Chaundry, & Samples, 1998; Johnson & Johnson, 2000b; RRCR, 1997). Another successful school-based program for reducing aggression is described in the Focus on Teaching box.

Conflict resolution and social skill programs help foster a positive school climate. Studies have identified a number of other key characteristics of schools with low levels of violent behavior (see *Early Warning, Timely Response: A Guide to Safe Schools,* Dwyer, Osher, & Wager, 1998). In these schools, there is a clear focus on academics and all students receive support in achieving high standards. There are also clear expectations for appropriate behavior, and teachers are well trained in behavior management. There is a schoolwide discipline plan that actively teaches prosocial behaviors and holds students accountable for misbehavior. Additionally, there is ample opportunity for adults to spend quality, personal time with students and to foster a sense of connection and belonging. Finally, schools with lower levels of aggression and violence maintain close ties to the families and the communities they serve.

Unfortunately, many schools still use corporal punishment—spanking—to control children's behavior, which not only exposes children to aggressive behavior, but also sanctions violence as a way of dealing with people. Similar to coercive discipline at home, corporal punishment can unintentionally reinforce antisocial behavior. Schools are one of the few public institutions in which corporal punishment is permitted; this practice is illegal in the military and in federal prisons. Despite its negative influence on children, the Supreme Court has twice upheld the rights of school officials to use corporal punishment. Harsh methods of punishment can create a negative school climate. Aggression is greatly reduced when there is a positive, caring school climate (Dwyer et al., 1998; Walker, 1995).

Schools are one of the few public institutions in which corporal punishment is permitted; this practice is illegal in the military and in federal prisons.

Developmental Changes in Peer Relations

The development of children's peer relationships follows a predictable developmental sequence. As with other areas of development, children's peer relations show "patterns of increasing diversity, complexity, and integration" (Rubin et al., 1998, p. 633). There are developmental changes in (1) how children relate to their peers; (2) the quality of their friendships; and (3) the formation of peer groups. The Focus on Development box summarizes development changes in peer relations from the preschool years through adolescence.

Infancy and Early Childhood

During infancy, children's peer interactions are limited to watching, smiling, pointing, vocalizing, and responding to another peer's behavior. When infants gain mobility and communication skills, their social exchanges become more complex.

Toddlers are much more likely to initiate play, imitate, and direct positive affection toward a playmate. Toddlers also show preferences for interacting with peers who have certain characteristics. Toddlers engage in a form of "turn-taking" with preferred playmates. They respond to their peer's overtures, then observe and respond to their responses. These exchanges are evidence of a reciprocal relationship, which lays the foundation for the development of friendships (Rubin et al., 1998; Ross, 1982).

During early childhood, peer interactions become more frequent and more complex. As you know, the preschool period is an important time for the development of sociodramatic play. This form of play enables children to take on complementary roles and to come to some shared agreement as to their imaginary roles. Sociodramatic play is an important arena in which children learn to negotiate, share, take turns, and compromise. Additionally, preschool children begin to express preferences for playmates who are similar in age, sex, or behavioral tendencies. They also act differently when they are in the company of friends. They more frequently engage in both positive and negative interactions when they are with

Focus on Development

Development of Peer Relations

Developmental Levels	Approximate Age Ranges	Characteristics of Peer Relations
Early childhood	3 to 5 years	Shows preferences for certain peers; engages in turn-taking with preferred peers; friendships involve doing things together
Middle childhood	6 to 10 years	Peer groups are small and selective; peer groups are same sex; peer groups have distinct social structure; friendships are based on shared values and reciprocity; concerns about social acceptance increase
Early adolescence	10 to 14 years	Cliques of six to nine peers form; peer groups organize by sex and race; concerns about peer popularity increase; peer conformity is greatest
Late adolescence	14 to 20 years	Large organized crowds form based on reputation and stereotypes; conformity to peer pressures decline; mixed-sex cliques form as interest in dating increases; friendships are characterized by intimacy, closeness, and self-disclosure

Sociodramatic play is an important arena in which children learn to negotiate, share, take turns, and compromise.

friends than with nonfriends. Interestingly, friends are more likely than nonfriends to re-solve conflict through negotiation and to stay in close proximity following conflict resolution (Rubin et al., 1998).

During preschool, children's friendships are defined very concretely. A friend is some-one who "likes to play dolls with me," or "plays with me a lot" (Selman, 1980). Friend-ships are a matter of doing the same activities together.

Elementary Years

During the elementary years, children have many more opportunities to interact with peers across a wide range of settings (e.g., school, church, home, neighborhood). Each of these contexts are associated with different types of peer interactions. Peers must compete in some settings (i.e., sports), but cooperate in others (i.e., school).

During late childhood, there are marked changes in children's understanding of friend-ship. Whereas younger children's friendships were based on shared activities, older chil-dren emphasize the importance of shared rules and values. A *friendship* is a mutually agreed upon relationship in which each person responds to the other's needs and desires (Selman, 1980). In their words, a friend is someone who can "stick up for you." Older chil-dren view violations of trust—such as not telling the truth, breaking promises, or gossip-ing—as serious matters that can end a friendship.

Because friendships are based on mutual trust in middle childhood, school-age children may become more selective in the friendships. Girls especially tend to have a smaller network of close friends (Parker & Asher, 1993). Children's concerns about social acceptance increases in middle childhood. These concerns may be related to children's abilities to compare their popularity with other children. Also, a good deal of children's gossip at this age focuses on children's social relations—who are friends, enemies, and so on. Discussions, especially among girls, can also focus on real or imagined romantic relationships with peers (Rubin et al., 1998).

In late childhood, children begin to form **cliques.** These groups tend to be friendship-based and range in size from three to nine children of the same sex and same race (Kinderman, McCollom, & Gibson, 1995). These peer groups generally have an established social structure, with one or two members serving as the leaders. By 11 years, nearly all children are a member of a peer group, and 50 percent of their interactions take place in that context.

Adolescence

Important changes in peer relations occur in adolescence. As previously mentioned, adolescence spend one-third of their waking time with peers—double the amount of time they spend with parents and other adults (Csikszentmihalyi & Larson, 1984). Compared with middle childhood, peer interactions are less likely to occur under the guidance and supervision of adults in adolescence.

Conceptions of friendship change in adolescence. Adolescents desire more closeness and intimacy with friends (Buhrmester, 1996). Friendships are characterized by intimate self-disclosure and provide an important source of support. During adolescence, teenagers begin to use their friends more than their parents as their trusted confidants (Fischer, Munsch, & Greene, 1996). Although adolescents tend to have fewer friends than young children, their friends tend to be more stable and enduring for psychological reasons (Cairns et al., 1995).

Young adolescents are most susceptible to peer pressures, perhaps because of their greater concerns about social acceptance at this age.

SOURCE: Skjold Photographs.

During early adolescence, peer groups are organized by gender and ethnicity.

Table 8.1	Description of Adolescent Crowds	

Type of Crowd	Percent of Adolescents	Description of Crowd
Populars	23%	Have many friends; are well known; look good; attend social events; are cool
Normals	45%	Are average; go to social events for fun; don't have problems
Jocks	10%	Like sports; participate in physical activities
Brains	9%	Get good grades; are smart; have good academic skills
Toughs	7%	Use drugs/alcohol
Loners	6%	Belong to tiny groups; feel alone; are not accepted by others; do not conform

SOURCE: After Youniss, McClellan, & Strouse (1994).

Conformity to peer norms and expectations tends to be greater in early adolescence than in childhood. Young adolescents are most susceptible to peer pressures perhaps because of their greater concerns about social acceptance at this age (Brown, Clasen, & Eicher, 1986). Teens generally experience the greatest pressures to conform to norms concerning dress, musical preferences, and social activities (Brown, Lohr, & McClenahan, 1986). However, many teens also report that their peers exert a positive influence on their school involvement and achievement (Berdnt & Keefe, 1995; Brown et al., 1995). As previously discussed, peer pressures can lead to some unfavorable outcomes for teens who may experiment with drugs, alcohol, or sex.

The structure of peer groups also changes during adolescence. There is a general "degrouping" of cliques in adolescence, and a more encompassing *crowd* structure emerges. Adolescent **crowds** are "reputation-based collectives of similarly stereotyped individuals who may or may not spend much time together" (Brown, 1990, p. 177). Crowds have a larger membership than cliques, and they are not particularly conducive to close interpersonal relations. In fact, an adolescent does not need to be friends with any member of the crowd to belong. The adolescent just needs to act or dress like other members of the crowd.

If you think back to your own high school experience, you can probably recall some of these crowds and their labels: the jocks, loners, brains, or nerds. As Table 8.1 shows, adolescents' descriptions of crowds in their schools tend to be highly stereotypic. It is also clear that a majority of adolescents think of themselves as normal or popular.

Being a member of a particular crowd has important consequences for the adolescent's identity. First, crowds have different social status within the schools, and students gain esteem and status by belonging to one of the prestigious crowds. In most U.S. schools, it is some variation of the "jocks" and the "populars." Members of high-status groups spend more time with peers and friends than adolescents in low-status groups. Crowd labels also serve as a "prototype identity" for adolescents by reinforcing certain aspects of their self-conceptions (Brown et al., 1994, p. 133).

Adolescent peer groups change again when young people become interested in dating. One of the first changes that occurs is when separate male and female cliques come together for a shared activity such as a school dance or party. Shortly thereafter, couples begin to

Focus on Research

David Kinney (1993) mapped the evolution of a peer group structure and the inter-relations of adolescent crowds in a midwestern high school. On the basis of interviews and observations, he found that crowds evolved through three phases. As shown in Figure 8.1, the middle school social system comprised essentially two crowds: a small group of high-status "trendies" and a large group of low-status "dweebs." There was a clear boundary between the two groups. In early high school, the social systems of crowds became much more elaborate due to the broader range of extracurricular activities. The dweebs joined new crowds: "normals, "headbangers," "grits," and "punkers." The headbangers and trendies competed for top status, whereas the grits and punkers were at the bottom of the status hierarchy. There was more permeability in the boundaries among the higher-status groups than between the higher- and lower-status groups. By late high school, peer status was no longer an important factor in differentiating crowds. Headbangers and trendies were essentially equal, and the boundary between the grits and headbangers no longer existed. In fact, a new group formed—the "grit-headbangers." During the high late school years, a number of students changed crowd affiliations. However, some crowd boundaries remained. For example, the boundary between the grits and both the trendies and punkers remained impermeable.

Kinney concluded that two factors explained changes in adolescent crowds. First, crowds need to be similar to one another in status. Second, they must also be open to forming relationships with members of different crowds.

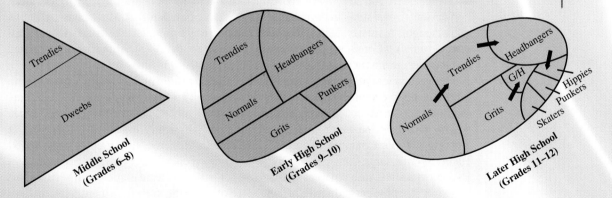

FIGURE 8.1 *Developmental Changes in Crowd Structure*
SOURCE: After Kinney (1993).

form within cliques, and the crowds begin to dissolve and disappear by late adolescence. The Focus on Research box describes changes in the social system of crowds in one school.

Summary of Peer Relations

Children's peers and friends play an important role in their development. As children develop, peer relations change from dyads focused on play to loosely organized crowds based on reputation and stereotypes. The peer culture of a school can either negatively or positively influence the learning environment. The influence of peers may be particularly critical during adolescence when peers fulfill needs that cannot be met by parents or other adults. Many young people report that the best part of school is spending time with their friends. Some researchers have thus argued that peers may be more important than teachers in fostering school engagement and achievement (Steinberg et al., 1992).

Gay and Lesbian Youth

Homosexual youth often experience considerable verbal and physical abuse from their peers, as well as social and emotional isolation from important social networks, including family and peers.

Changes in adolescents' peer relations raises some interesting questions and concerns for gay and lesbian youths. How do these young people negotiate the complexity of friendships, cliques, and crowds in adolescence? For young people who are homosexual, adolescence can be a difficult and traumatic period. They often experience considerable verbal and physical abuse from their peers, as well as social and emotional isolation from important social networks, including family and peers. Because gay and lesbian youths do not fit the heterosexual social norms of high school peer groups, they tend to experience the most negative and cruelest treatment of any social group (Gibson, 1989).

Depending on the study, it is estimated that 1 in 20 adolescents in the United States are gay, lesbian, or bisexual (Ginsburg, 1998). A large number of adolescents experiment with homosexual sex play, but for homosexual youths it is more than experimentation. A **homosexual orientation** is defined as a "consistent pattern of sexual arousal towards persons of the same gender encompassing fantasy, conscious attractions, emotional and romantic feelings, and sexual behaviors (Remafedi, 1975, p. 332). According to reports of adult lesbians and gays, same-sex attractions may occur before the age of 15. Teens who acknowledge this attraction can often recall a period of intense anxiety when they realized that they belonged to a social group that society often portrays in derogatory terms. **Homophobia** is an irrational fear and hatred of homosexuals, and it is pervasive in American high schools. For example, one study reported that 97 percent of students in Massachusetts public schools report regularly hearing homophobic remarks from their classmates (Massachusetts Governor's Commission on Gay and Lesbian Youth, 1993). Another study reported that the average high school student hears antigay epithets 25 times per day (Carter, 1997).

For gay and lesbian youth, schools can be a dangerous, as well as hostile, environment. Many choose to remain silent about their homosexuality. Those who choose to "come out" as teenagers risk verbal and physical abuse. Numerous reports indicate that gay and lesbian youths have been harassed, verbally abused, and physically assaulted (McFarland & Dupuis, 2001; Pinkington & D'Augelli, 1995; Savin-Williams, 1994). In his book *Breaking the Surface,* Greg Louganis, an Olympic champion diver who is gay, describes his adolescent experience with physical violence: "I got beat up often enough that it seems like a lot to me. The boys picked the fights and some of the girls cheered them on. I internalized all of it . . . I figured I must be wrong. They must be right to call me names and beat me up" (Louganis, 1995; p. 36).

Such negative experiences may account for the high rates of substance abuse among gay, lesbian, and bisexual youths. Studies reveal that approximately 60 percent of gay and lesbian adolescents abuse drugs or alcohol (Rotherman-Borus, Rosario, Van Rossem, Reid, & Gillis, 1995; Savin-Williams, 1994). Feelings of isolation and despair can also place homosexual adolescents at greater risk than other youths for suicidal ideation, suicide attempts, and completed suicide (Ramafedi, 1994). As we learned in Chapter 2, homosexual adolescents have the highest suicide rate of all young people.

Schools now have a legal responsibility to protect lesbian, gay, and bisexual youth from sexual harassment. A recent U.S. Supreme Court decision declared that school officials who ignore actions that create a sexually hostile environment for students are in violation of federal civil rights laws, and this protection extends to sexual minorities. To provide a safe educational environment for all students, many schools have developed anti-harassment policies and instituted staff development programs focused on the needs of gay and lesbian youths.

Moral Development

Schools are an important training ground for children's developing conceptions of moral behavior and ethical values. At school, students are faced with moral issues almost daily. Should they return a watch found on the playground? Should they report someone cheating on an exam? Should they hit when they are angry? Should the whole class be punished when one student is bad? Should they skip school? When should a student be expelled from school? Many school subjects also present children with moral questions to discuss and debate: Should animals be used in scientific research? Should the United States have used nuclear arms in World War II? When are dissent and protest appropriate? Works such as *Huckleberry Finn, Cry the Beloved Country, The Crucible,* and *The Diary of Anne Frank* present students with moral issues to consider. In short, schools have many opportunities to teach democratic principles and ethical values such as equality, justice, honesty, civility, tolerance, and respect for life (Damon, 1988; DeVries & Zan, 1994; Lickona, 1991).

In response to public concerns about juvenile violence, schools today are placing a greater emphasis on moral education and character development. In this last section, we will examine the development of children's moral reasoning. We will draw on Lawrence Kohlberg's (1969) theory of moral development to understand changes in children's conceptions of rules and fairness, and also discuss some other approaches to moral development. We will then discuss how teachers can create a classroom in which respect, responsibility, caring, and fairness are a part of the daily curriculum.

Kohlberg's Theory of Moral Development

Kohlberg's (1969) theory of moral development is based, in part, on the ideas presented in Piaget's *The Moral Judgment of the Child,* which was first published in 1932. One aspect of this study focused on how children develop respect for rules and a sense of social solidarity in the games they play among themselves. Piaget found that children progressed from *unilateral* to *mutual* respect for rules. Young children believe that rules are immutable, and terrible consequences will happen if rules are violated. As children gain experience in social interactions, particularly with peers, their understanding of rules change. Rules are increasingly viewed as pragmatic social agreements that allow everyone to participate equally in joint activities. Respect for rules is based on a concept of cooperation: To play fair, everyone must follow the same rules. Older children believe that rules for games can be changed, but only if everyone agrees.

Kohlberg extended Piaget's theory of moral judgment. He was mainly interested in how children and adults reason about moral issues in which different perspectives and values come into play. One of the most commonly used moral dilemmas can be described as follows. Heinz's wife is dying and needs a particular drug to save her. The drug is very expensive, and the druggist who invented it will not sell it at a price Heinz can afford. Heinz becomes desperate and considers stealing the drug for his wife. Should Heinz steal the drug? Why or why not?

In listening to individual responses to Heinz's dilemma, Kohlberg was not so interested in what action should be taken as in the thought processes involved. Kohlberg believed that moral judgment was a cognitive process in which a person must identify the issues, values, and perspectives in conflict, then order them in some logical hierarchy. In the Heinz dilemma, for example, the perspectives that are in conflict are those of the shopkeeper and Heinz. The values in conflict are property rights, loyalty and duty to a spouse, and right to life. Which value takes precedence over the other?

Three Levels of Moral Judgment

Using dilemmas such as the one of Heinz, Kohlberg identified six stages of moral development that he organized into three levels. His stage theory of moral development included the following cognitive development principles from Piaget's theory: each stage involves qualitatively different modes of thinking; each stage involves a restructuring of the thought processes and structures found at earlier stages; and the stages form an invariant sequence. In Kohlberg's theory, moral development progressed from *self-centered* to *rule-oriented* to *principled reasoning*. Unlike Piaget, however, Kohlberg did not believe his stages were universal. In fact, his studies show that not all adults reach the third level of moral reasoning. Progression through Kohlberg stages is dependent on role taking skills, abstract thinking, and socialization experiences. The six stages of Kohlberg's model of moral development are shown in Table 8.2.

Young children believe that rules are immutable, and terrible consequences will happen if the rules are violated.

According to Kohlberg's theory, people at the level of **preconventional moral reasoning** approach moral issues from a hedonistic perspective. They are not concerned with what society defines as the right way to behave, only with the concrete consequences of their actions. In the Heinz case, people at the preconventional level would say it is wrong for Heinz to steal because he may get caught and go to jail. Alternatively, they may say Heinz should steal the drug because he would feel sad if his wife died. At this stage, children say you should obey rules and laws because you might get punished or rewarded. This type of reasoning is very common among elementary school children, and declines between the ages of 10 and 13 (Hersh, Paolitto, & Reimer, 1979).

At the level of **conventional moral reasoning,** children accept and obey society's rules for right and wrong behavior even when there is no punishment or reward. They look to others, especially authority figures, for guidance, and obey rules to please others and to gain their approval. Kohlberg referred to this reasoning as a "good boy/good girl" orientation. If you recall, children's prosocial behavior at this age was motivated by gaining social approval as well. Later on, when children enter the "law and order" stage, they look to society as a whole for guidelines as to what is right and wrong. At this stage, children want to be good members of society. Whereas people at the preconventional level would say it is wrong to steal because it is against the law, conventional individuals might say Heinz should steal the drug because it is what a good husband should do. This stage of moral development is very common among older elementary school children, most secondary students, and many adults (Hersh et al., 1979).

In Kohlberg's theory of moral development, people progress from self-centered thinking, to rigid adherence to existing rules, to personally constructed moral principles.

The third level of moral judgment is called **postconventional moral reasoning.** At this level, individuals have developed their own set of ethical principles to define what is morally right and wrong. This level is rarely achieved before college, and some people never achieve it (Colby, Kohlberg, Gibbs, & Lieberman, 1983; Turiel, 1998). Postconventional individuals view rules and laws as social contracts achieved through a democratic process. Society's rules should be obeyed not because they are the "law" but because they protect basic human rights such as equality, justice, freedom, and life. Laws should be disobeyed when they are not determined through a democratic process or when they violate ethical principles. During the Vietnam War, for example, the voting age was lowered to 18 years, because 19- and 20-year-old men were being drafted in to the military before they had an opportunity to vote. Many men refused to fight in this war, because they believed it violated basic human rights, such as self-determination and the value of human life. Other

		Child Responses to
Stage	**Characteristics**	**Heinz Dilemma**

Level One: Preconventional	*Stage 1: Obedience-punishment orientation.* The child obeys rules to avoid punishment. *Stage 2: Instrumental and relativist orientation.* Each person's needs to take care of his or her own needs.	*Pro:* Maybe he won't get caught. *Con:* He will go to jail. *Pro:* The wife needs the drug and the husband will be lonely if she dies. *Con:* The storekeeper needs the money for his store.
Level Two: Conventional	*Stage 3: "Good girl"—"Nice boy" orientation.* Good people do nice things. Good behavior is what pleases other people. Intentions are important in judging goodness and badness. *Stage 4: Law and order orientation.* Good behavior is obeying laws and rules. It is important to do one's duty and respect authority.	*Pro:* He will show his wife he is a good husband. *Con:* Other people will think he is is bad. *Pro:* A husband has a duty to take care of his wife when she is sick. *Con:* It is against the law to steal.
Level Three: Postconventional	*Stage 5: Social-contract orientation.* Laws and rules exist to benefit everyone and to preserve human rights. Rules and laws are established by mutual agreement. *Stage 6: Universal ethical principle orientation.* General universal principles (justice, fairness, equality) determine what is right and wrong. Unjust laws may be broken when they conflict with moral principles.	*Pro:* The law was not intended when someone was dying. *Con:* If he steals the drug, other people who need the drug cannot buy it. *Pro:* Saving a person's life is more important than property. *Con:* He will be guilty because he was not living up to his own moral standards.

Table 8.2   Kohlberg's Stages of Moral Reasoning

powerful examples of postconventional reasoning can be found in the civil rights movement of the 1960s. In his writings and speeches, Martin Luther King, Jr., argued that people had a *moral responsibility* to challenge laws that were unjust, but they must be willing to accept the penalty. In his view, any law that degraded people was unjust. Thus, the reasoning behind King's call to change segregation laws through civil disobedience illustrated the highest level of Kohlberg's stages of moral development.

Links between Moral Reasoning and Behavior.

Kohlberg's theory assumes that moral judgments and moral actions are highly linked. People at higher stages of moral development should behave morally. Is there research evidence to support this assumption? A very early study by Hartshorne and May (1928) suggested that children were less likely to cheat if their moral judgments were consistent with those of adults (Rest, 1983). However, most experimental studies examining relations between cheating behavior and moral reasoning show a more mixed set of results (Rest, 1983). For the most part, studies report less cheating among children and adults at higher stages of moral development, but some studies report no relation between reasoning and behavior.

Other researchers have examined moral judgments in real-life situations. As part of a large-scale investigation of student activism in the 1960s, a group of University of California, Berkeley, psychologists examined relations between students' stages of moral reasoning and their participation in the Free Speech Movement of 1964/1965 (Haan, Smith, & Block, 1968). The results of this study showed that college students at the conventional level were less likely to protest against the administration's decision to limit civil rights activities on campus. In contrast, a greater number of students at the postconventional level participated in the demonstration and were arrested for their actions. It may be that school administrators would prefer students to blindly obey rules, but then who would question laws or rules that are unjust or morally wrong?

Ethic of Care versus Justice

In her 1982 book *In a Different Voice,* Carol Gilligan challenged some of Kohlberg's ideas because they were based on men. When Kohlberg applied his scheme, women were characterized as conventional rather than postconventional thinkers, because they tended to emphasize the feelings of others. In the Heinz case, women would typically want to resolve the conflict in a way that was mutually satisfying for both parties. They had difficulty rank ordering individual rights according to some logical hierarchy. Gilligan (1982) argued that Kohlberg's view of justice was individualistic, rational, and detached. Women are socialized to take responsibility for the well-being of others. Therefore, they are likely to make moral decisions based on an **ethic of care,** which emphasizes connections between people, as well as on an **ethic of justice.** At the highest stage of Gilligan's model of moral development, individuals must balance their own needs with their responsibility to others. Gilligan's research reminds us that caring and compassion are also important aspects of moral behavior that should be encouraged and developed.

Kohlberg's stages of moral development equated morality with justice, but several theorists have expanded his definition of morality to include the notion of human caring, which is central to feminine thinking.

The ethic of care serves as the foundation for Nel Noddings's ideas about caring in schools (Noddings, 1992). In Noddings's view, schools must be places where children receive care and learn to care for others. She writes, "The primary aim of every teacher must be to promote growth of students as competent, caring, loving, and lovable people" (p. 154). One of the loudest complaints of students in our schools is, "They don't care." Noddings maintains that schools must become caring communities in which children feel understood, respected, and recognized. In addition, schools must encourage a sense of caring for the self, for others, for the environment, and for the world of ideas. Such themes as war, poverty, crime, intolerance, humanity, and environmental concerns should be addressed in any subject area. Moreover, learning in the subject areas should help students confront great existential questions: What is the meaning of life? What is important? How shall I live? Caring is a crucial component of any educational program for children.

Creating a Moral Community in the Classroom

Kohlberg believed that children acquire basic moral values by participating in social institutions such as the family and school. Higher stages of moral development are generally observed in children and adolescents who come from warm and supportive homes in which

Opportunities to participate in democratic processes are key to facilitating students' moral development. Such experiences also promote a sense of school belonging.

parents set standards for acceptable behavior and provide reasons for *why* certain behaviors are inappropriate. These parents use an *authoritative* parenting style (see Chapter 9) and recognize that children have individual needs that should be considered in establishing and enforcing rules. More importantly, controversial topics and moral issues are openly discussed in these families.

In a similar way, teachers can help promote children's moral development. First, children need models of moral and prosocial behavior at school. Teachers need to establish a warm, caring, and supportive environment in which *all* children are treated with care, respect, and compassion. They need to model acceptance and respect for the feelings of others. Teachers should avoid favoritism, sarcasm, or any other behavior that embarrasses or humiliates a child (Lickona, 1991). Most important, teachers need to stop physical or verbal abuse. As we have discussed, far too many young people comment that their teachers did not respond to bullying behavior, name-calling, or derogatory ethnic or sexual remarks. All children deserve a safe and supportive school environment. In his book The *Moral Intelligence of Children*, Robert Coles writes:

> Character is ultimately who we are expressed in action, in how we live, in what we do, and so the children around us know: they absorb and take stock of what they observe, namely us—we adults living and doing things in a certain spirit, getting on with one another in our various ways. Our children add up, imitate, file away what they've observed and so very often later fall in line with the particular moral counsel we willingly or quite unselfconsciously have offered them. (p. 7)

Discipline practices at school can also promote or impede children's moral development. Like authoritative parents, teachers need to use an **inductive method of discipline**. This disciplinary method serves an educational function because it gives students reasons for why certain behaviors are unacceptable. For example, a teacher who disciplines through

Focus on Teaching

Teaching Self-Discipline in the Classroom

Numerous discipline approaches are used in schools today. Some are based on behaviorist principles of rewards and punishments, while others emphasize the management styles of teachers (organization, monitoring, withitness). The important goal of any discipline program is the development of self-discipline. Research on parenting practices (see Chapter 9) emphasizes the importance of inductive discipline approaches that enable children to understand the consequences of their actions on others, to take responsibility for their actions, and to develop decision-making skills. The following discipline approaches can be used to help children learn self-discipline in the classroom.

The Dreikurs Model: Discipline Through Democratic Teaching

In the Dreikurs model, teachers and students agree on rules and share in responsibility for establishing a classroom climate that is conducive to learning. Dreikurs refers to his approach as *democratic discipline.* Teachers spend time talking with students about how their actions affect others and about their choices of behaviors. A key element of this program is the use of *logical consequences* for "inappropriate" behavior choices. In Dreikurs's view, all behavior produces a corresponding result. Helping someone with his or her work has a pleasant or good consequence, whereas talking while others are trying to work has a negative consequence for others. When students misbehave, there should be a logical consequence for their action that is jointly agreed on by the students and teacher. Disturbing others means being removed from the group, hurting someone at recess means no recess, and throwing paper on the floor means picking it up. The

induction would point out how cheating hurts the cheater as well as other students in the class. Discipline practices that focus on the consequences of misbehavior for self and others help children to develop self-control and self-discipline. It also promotes the development of empathy, compassion, and cooperation (Maccoby & Martin, 1983). When children are simply punished for disobedience, it does not promote the understanding that leads to higher levels of moral development. The Focus on Teaching box features two classroom discipline approaches that incorporate these ideas.

Another way teachers can promote moral development in the classroom is through presenting moral issues and dilemmas. Kohlberg believed that schools should incorporate moral issues into the curriculum. As stated earlier, many school subjects present moral issues that can be discussed. For example, the Boston Tea Party can be used to discuss protest and dissent as well as to teach values such as justice, fairness, and democracy. Many guidebooks are available to help teachers teach values through the curriculum (see Lickona, 1991). In discussing controversial topics or moral issues, teachers need to help students consider different points of view, to share their thoughts and feelings, and to listen to one another. In this way, class discussions can help promote perspective-taking and communication skills.

Finally, students need opportunities to participate in democratic processes. On this point, Piaget (1932/1965) wrote:

Teachers need to establish a warm, caring, and supportive environment in which all children are treated with care, respect, and compassion.

470

consequences are discussed, explained, and jointly agreed upon. When consequences are logical, students begin to see that their choices have certain consequences. They will realize that poor choices have negative consequences for self and others. In Dreikurs's view, the use of logical consequences helps students learn inner discipline. For more information about this approach, see *Maintaining Sanity in the Classroom* (Dreikurs, 1982).

Cooperative Discipline

Dreikurs's discipline approach served as the foundation for Cooperative Discipline developed by Linda Albert (1989/1996). This approach also calls for a democratic style of teaching in which students are given choices and input into decision making. However, Albert's approach emphasizes the importance of analyzing the goals of students' misbehavior. In her view, students choose to misbehave to get extra attention, to gain power, to seek revenge, or to avoid failure. The teacher's role is to help students make better behavior choices. Albert provides specific, concrete strategies to use when students misbehave. Albert also believes students need to be given continual encouragement through what she calls Cooperative Discipline's "Three C's" approach. Teachers need to (1) help students feel *capable;* (2) *connect* positively with teachers and classmates; and (3) *contribute* significantly to the class, school, and community. Thus, the Cooperative Discipline approach emphasizes the importance of redirecting behavior while creating a positive classroom community for students. For more information about this approach, see *Cooperative Discipline* (Albert, 1996).

> How are we to bring children into the spirit of citizenship and humanity which is postulated by democratic societies? By the actual practice of democracy at school. It is unbelievable that at a time when democratic ideas enter into every phase of life, they should have been so little utilized as instruments of education. (p. 366)

Echoing Piaget's views, Kohlberg also believed that democratic governance should be at the heart of any moral education program. Traditionally, teachers and school administrators make decisions and rules, and then impose them on students. In Kohlberg's view, this power should be shared between teachers and students. He advocated the use of community meetings within the school to give students greater participation in the governing process. Many teachers use class meetings for this purpose. A class meeting involves the whole class, lasts for 15 to 30 minutes, and is most effective when done regularly. Some teachers end or start the school day with a class meeting.

   Class meetings can occur at any grade level. Some kindergarten teachers begin their school year by asking their students, Why do we need rules? What should the rules for this classroom be? What should happen if someone disobeys a rule? The class meeting can be used to discuss classroom rules, problems, or conflict situations, but it does not have to be limited to those topics. The class meeting can also be used to plan activities and to discuss ways of improving the classroom or school environment.

Class meetings help to promote a sense of community as well as an understanding and respect for the democratic process.

471

Class meetings are important forums for discussing ethical issues and events inside and outside school. For example, the teacher can pose the following sorts of questions: Should animals be dissected in science classes? Should public schools provide free education to children of immigrants when money for education is scarce? Should Congress reduce spending on Social Security in order to balance the budget? In sum, class meetings help to promote a sense of community as well as an understanding and respect for the democratic process. Students learn about democracy through experiencing it firsthand.

Chapter Summary

www.mhhe.com/meece

Understanding Others

- Researchers use the term *social cognition* to describe children's understanding of other people's thoughts, feelings, and behaviors.

- Perspective taking involves the ability to take another person's point of view. Perspective-taking abilities develop gradually during the elementary school years. Children are not able to view situations or themselves from another's perspective until the late or middle childhood years. Perspective-taking abilities are important for social relations and moral development, in which other points of view must be considered.

- There are parallels between children's self-conceptions and person perceptions. With development, children's perceptions of other people become more differentiated and focused on psychological traits that can be observed in many different situations.

- Children can categorize people into racial and ethnic categories at a young age. Due to society's racial biases, young children develop a pro-white orientation that decreases in elementary school when children develop a more balanced view of ethnicity. Adolescents can think about ethnicity from a social perspective and consider its social implications (e.g., differences in housing, income, opportunities).

Peer Relations

- Peer relations are necessary for normal psychological development. Positive peer relations can influence children's feelings of efficacy, competence, and self-worth. Peers can also influence students' school achievement. When deprived of positive peer relations, children may experience low self-esteem, poor school achievement, and depression.

- The ability to initiate and maintain positive interactions with others is the main predictor of peer popularity. Popular children tend to be friendly, cooperative, sensitive, and good-natured. Rejected children tend to be aggressive, hostile, and disruptive. Some children are neither popular nor rejected by their peers. Neglected peers tend to be shy and withdrawn.

- Teachers can enhance children's peer relations in a number of ways. Cooperative learning activities are particularly effective in promoting positive peer relations, if the activities are carefully structured and monitored. Children need opportunities to play, to cooperate, to share, and to negotiate problems. Some children may need special training in how to interact positively with others and to resolve conflict.

- Prosocial behaviors involve acts of caring, helping, sharing, and cooperating with others. These behaviors develop early but continue to increase in frequency as children mature cognitively and learn how their actions affect others. The capacity to know and feel another person's emotional state is an important determinant of prosocial behavior that is shaped by early childhood experiences. Parents and teachers can foster the development of prosocial behavior in children by modeling such behavior and by helping children reflect on how their behavior affects others.

- Aggression is defined as behavior that is intentionally aimed at harming or injuring another person. Young children use physical force to obtain an object or to get their way because they have limited social and verbal skills. However, this type of instrumental aggression is not intended to harm another person. Hostile aggression is more frequent among elementary and high school-age children, and it generally takes the form of teasing, ridiculing, and shouting as children grow older.

- Bullying behavior is one of the most common forms of aggression in school settings. This form of aggression has a negative impact on the school environment, as well as long-term negative consequences for both the victim and bully.

- Most, but not all, aggressive acts in adolescence are committed by young people with a long history of aggression. The causes of aggression depend on its age of onset. The early onset of aggression evolve from a complex interplay of the child's temperament and family environment, whereas peers play a more important role in its late onset. Once aggression emerges as a way to control people's behavior, it is often difficult to change, because it becomes self-reinforcing.

- Schools are becoming more and more involved in efforts to reduce aggression and violence among youths. Conflict resolution and peer mediation programs, which help children acquire the skills they need to resolve conflict, are becoming more widespread. Many schools are also implementing programs to help aggressive, immature children to develop missing social skills. These programs are most successful when combined with interventions to improve academic skills and to enhance parent-child relations.

Developmental Changes in Peer Relations

- Development of children's peer relations follows a predictable pattern. Young children show preferences for playmates, and interactions are based on shared activities. Small selective peer groups of the same sex develop in elementary school. Friendships are mutual and reciprocal.

- The peer group structure changes in adolescence when cliques and crowds emerge. Cliques of peers who share similar interests and activities provide a more intimate setting for developing enduring and intimate friendships. Crowds are larger groups of peers, who share a certain social reputation. Crowds dissolve when interest in dating begins.

- Approximately 1 in 20 adolescents in the United States is gay, lesbian, or bisexual. Homophobia is pervasive in American high schools, and it places gay and lesbian youth at considerable risk for physical and verbal abuse from peers. Schools have a legal responsibility to provide a safe and supportive atmosphere for all youth.

Moral Development

- Kohlberg's theory of moral development focuses on children's conceptions of rules, fairness, and justice. Preschool children believe rules should be obeyed because they lead to rewards or punishment, whereas elementary children view rules as important for maintaining social order. Elementary-age children want to please others and to obtain social approval. By late adolescence and adulthood, people begin to understand that rules are intended to help protect basic human rights such as equality, justice, and freedom.

- Gilligan argued that women are likely to make moral decisions based on an ethic of care, which emphasizes connections among people, as well as an ethic of justice. Women are socialized to care for others, and they tend to resolve moral conflicts in ways that preserve social relations and connections. Noddings argues that schools are an important place for the development of caring and compassion.

- Schools must be caring communities in which children feel understood, respected, and recognized. Schools must also help children learn how to care for themselves, others, the environment, and the world of ideas.

Key Terms

aggression (p. 451)

bullying behavior (p. 451)

cliques (p. 461)

conflict resolution programs (p. 457)

conventional moral reasoning (p. 466)

crowds (p. 462)

ethic of care (p. 468)

ethic of justice (p. 468)

homophobia (p. 464)

homosexual orientation (p. 464)

hostile aggression (p. 454)

inductive method of discipline (p. 469)

instrumental aggression (p. 454)

neglected peers (p. 446)

peer (p. 445)

peer popularity (p. 446)

peer rejection (p. 446)

perspective-taking skills (p. 437)

postconventional moral reasoning (p. 466)

preconventional moral reasoning (p. 466)

prejudices (p. 441)

prosocial behaviors (p. 450)

Activities

1. Develop an observational procedure for collecting information on children's prosocial and aggressive behavior. Observe three or four elementary school children in different settings (classroom, playground, cafeteria, etc.). Try to observe children of different ages or gender. Record instances of helping, sharing, taking turns, as well as instances of fighting, teasing, name-calling, and shouting. Be sure to record the events that preceded and followed the action. Analyze your observations for the frequency of prosocial and aggressive behaviors. Were there age or gender differences in the frequency of different behaviors? How did the setting of the observation influence children's behavior? What events tended to precede or follow acts of kindness or aggression? Discuss whether your findings fit with those described in the text.

2. Interview children of different ages about their conceptions of friendship (e.g., What is a friend?). Follow up with questions about what types of activities they like to do with their friends. How do children's conceptions of friendship change over development? Do boys and girls engage in different activities with their friends? Discuss how your findings fit with those described in the text.

3. Peer relations have an important influence on the classroom and school environment. Interview several teachers of different grade levels to ascertain their views of peer relations in their schools. Are peer groups segregated by gender, ethnicity, or social class? Is it easy or difficult for children to join different peer groups in the school? Ask teachers to describe the strategies they use to develop positive peer relations in their classroom. Share your results with classmates.

4. Interview a small group of teenagers (six to eight) of different age and gender groupings to learn about their feelings of guilt. Use the following instructions to interview each student.

> We all do things we are sorry about, or that aren't nice. Sometimes we get into trouble for these things. Sometimes no one finds out. What things have you felt bad about doing? It might have been something that your parents got mad at you about, or a teacher, or maybe no one knew, but you still felt bad. . . . Write down what happened and why you felt guilty. Think of three (different) times you felt like this. (Williams & Bybee, 1994, p. 619)

After interviewing your students, analyze their responses for the nature of the incident mentioned (interpersonal problems, fights with friends or families, lying, negative thoughts about a person, fighting, neglecting responsibilities, etc.). Next, analyze the responses for age and gender differences. Were older students more concerned about violating the rights of others than about violating rules? Were they more likely to mention situations that involved the violation of ethical standards or ideals? Were girls more likely to mention situations that involved caring for others, trust, and compassion? Were boys more likely to mention issues of fairness and justice? Discuss how your results fit with research on moral development.

Chapter 9

The Family: Partners in Education

Mr. Chavez is a ninth-grade English teacher at Drew Magnet School. He is preparing for back-to-school night, and hopes that more of his students' parents will attend this year than previous years. Many of his students come from single-parent families, and a large number come from homes where the first language is not English. These families are generally the hardest to reach. Mr. Chavez's school is beginning a new Family-School Partnership supported by state funds. The school plans to establish a family resource center to provide adult education classes, social services, and other family support programs. Also the school is establishing a new governance structure to give parents a strong voice in school policies and operations. During the summer, Mr. Chavez attended a continuing education program to learn new ways of working with parents of adolescents. His teacher education program provided little preservice training in this area. In fact, his college professors stressed the importance of home visits and parent involvement for the early grades only. At the summer program, Mr. Chavez learned that these programs have important benefits for adolescents and their families as well. He also learned about changing family demographics and different techniques for fostering communication with parents.

It is almost time for parents and students to arrive, and Mr. Chavez takes one more look around his classroom. His classroom has attractive displays of literature and writing from different cultures. He has also prepared a video that shows some of the projects he hopes to do

Chapter Opener Photo: James L. Shaffer.

477

with his classes. He will also demonstrate how parents can access the school's homework hotline from their homes. Mr. Chavez recruited someone from the community to help with translation. As he places the school's new parent handbook on a table near the door, parents begin to arrive.

Parents are children's first teachers, and students are most successful in school when educators and teachers work together as partners.

Parents are children's first teachers, and students are most successful in school when educators and teachers work together as partners. Too often, parents do not feel welcome at their child's school, or they feel their needs and interests are not taken into account. At the same time, teachers complain that parents are not helping to support their students' learning at home.

In this chapter, we will learn how educators can build partnerships with parents. The chapter begins by looking at the family as a system. We will then examine variations in family structures, and ethnic differences in family values and parenting practices. We will also consider several critical issues for educators. How can teachers help children cope with family transitions, such as divorce? What are the signs of child maltreatment, and what causes it? This chapter will also provide important information on the benefits and barriers of parental involvement in education, and on the strategies schools and teachers can use to build partnerships with families.

Conceptions of the Family

Function of the Family: Socialization

The family is the child's primary source of support and nurture in early development. For many of us, our earliest memories are ones that involve a family event—a birthday party or a holiday celebration. There are also occasions when a certain sound or smell can trigger a memory of a special time shared with a grandparent. Of course, there are also memories of family conflicts and disappointments. For better or worse, families have a lasting influence on children's development.

For centuries, families have been viewed as the social unit with primary responsibility for preparing the child to be a productive and competent member of society. This process has been termed **socialization** and concerns the rearing of children such that they may "function adequately within the requirements of the social group or groups among whom they live" (Maccoby, 1992, p. 1006). Maccoby (1992) identifies "adequate functioning" as the acquisition of those cognitive and behavioral tools which will enable individuals to (1) avoid deviant behavior; (2) contribute to the economic support of self and family; (3) form and sustain close relationships with others; and (4) be able to rear children themselves one day.

Families are the social unit with primary responsibility for preparing the child to be a productive and competent member of society.

Although socialization has long been a matter of interest for child development researchers, ideas about the direction and complexity of this process have changed. Early theories of family socialization were broad, attempting to explain all of parenting and child development in a few basic principles. Parents were viewed as "all powerful" because they constructed and shaped the child's environment. For example, Sigmund Freud proposed that parents' handling of developmental tasks, such as weaning and toilet training, established lifelong patterns of thought and behavior. As we have learned, attachment theorists still view the early years of life as pivotal in establishing basic emotional and behavioral patterns. For behaviorists, such as John Watson and B. F. Skinner, successful child rearing was simply a matter of managing children's learning experiences in various circumstances so as to strengthen proper behavior and extinguish undesired behavior. However, psychoanalytic and behavioral views of the family provide a limited view of family dynamics. In fact, psychoanalytic theorists were among the first to recognize that to help an emotionally troubled child, it is necessary to change the family system (Minuchin, 1985).

The Family as a System

Most child development theorists today view family interactions as part of a highly complex system (Bronfenbrenner & Morris, 1998; Bugental & Goodnow, 1998; Cox & Paley, 1997; Sameroff, 1994). From a systems perspective, parents shape their children, but the children influence them as well. A baby's temperament, for instance, elicits different responses from caregivers, which, in turn, sets in motion another pattern of responses. In a systems view of the family, parent-child interactions are mutual and reciprocal.

Family systems are also adaptive through processes of self-stabilization and self-organization. Families and the interactions of their members tend toward equilibrium, or homeostasis, exhibiting some resistance to change instigated by external forces. Sameroff (1994) has identified a number of family codes that help guide and organize behavior within the family system. Family beliefs, myths, stories, and rituals create a sense of history and tradition within a family and ease the day-to-day interactions of family members. However, the tendency of family systems to resist change can lead to problems when negative interaction patterns become ingrained and rigid (Katz & Gottman, 1997).

> *Most child development theorists today view family interactions as part of a highly complex system.*

SOURCE: Bill Aron/ PhotoEdit.

There are many ways parents can support their child's learning in school. This family is visiting a science museum together.

When change does occur in one element of the system, it affects the structure and functioning of the whole because of the interdependence that characterizes complex systems. The behavior of one family member affects the behavior of other family members. For example, the behaviors of a parent struggling with alcoholism will influence her relationships with her children and likely their relationships with each other. Likewise, one child's exceptional performance in sports or academics will have repercussions for his parents and siblings.

From a systems perspective, the family is part of larger social systems, such as neighborhoods, communities, and cultures. These other systems can affect the interactions within a family. For example, a dangerous neighborhood can lead parents to be highly restrictive in their parenting approach to protect their children from harm (Kelly, Power, & Wimbush, 1992). Also, as we will learn, various cultures and subcultures have different expectations for children's development, which can influence how parents and children relate within the family unit.

From a systems perspective, the family is part of larger social systems— neighborhoods, communities, and cultures.

The ecological theory of Urie Bronfenbrenner represents a systems approach for understanding family dynamics (Bronfenbrenner, 1979, 1986; Bronfenbrenner & Morris, 1998). If you recall from Chapter 1, Bronfenbrenner views children as embedded in multiple social systems that interact in complex ways to influence development (see Figure 9.1). In Bronfenbrenner's model, the **microsystem** was the child's immediate environment (the family, peer group, school), and the **mesosystem** was the interactions among components of the microsystem. For example, parents may meet with teachers or other school personnel to develop a management plan for a child who is having behavioral or academic problems in school.

The **exosystem** was composed of elements that may influence the child's development but only indirectly. Their impact is typically felt through their effect on elements of the

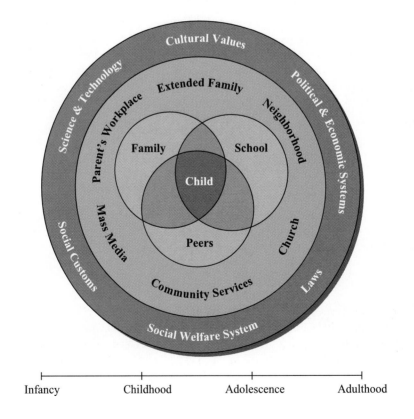

FIGURE 9.1

Bronfenbrenner's Ecological Model

SOURCE: After Bronfenbrenner (1979).

microsystem, such as the family. For example, a parent's work may affect the child through its control over the amount of time the parent has for interaction with the child or through the level of economic support it provides for meeting the child's needs.

The **macrosystem** represented the larger culture and possibly subcultures in which the individual lives, including ideologies, traditions, and values. Elements of the macrosystem include regional identity, nationality, ethnicity, and religious affiliation. Children growing up in rural, southern United States may have notably different experiences than those in the cities of the northeastern or western United States. More broadly, children living in Brazil will likely undergo a somewhat different socialization process than those living in Australia.

Family systems and their interrelationships also change over time. Bronfenbrenner refers to this level of influence as the **chronosystem.** The chronosystem represents the timing and patterning of events in an individual's life and the position of that individual's life in the larger flow of historical time. Both the child and the child's environment experience changes. For example, understanding and fostering the developing language and writing abilities of a child today will likely demand consideration of the increasing availability of electronic media for developing skills in those areas. Also, as the child progresses from preschool to adolescence, family influences give way to peers and school as important elements of the child's social environment.

In summary, conceptions of the family have changed from a simple focus on parents' effects to a complex system of interactions and processes operating at multiple levels. A child responds not only to a specific parental behavior but also to the setting, the relationship between the parent and child, and various other factors. As we will see in the next section, recent theories strive to address the broader milieu of social, economic, and cultural systems in which families and children are embedded.

Conceptions of the family have changed from a simple focus on parents' effects to a complex system of interactions and processes operating at multiple levels.

Variations in Family Structures

One aspect of the family system which has received much attention is the particular configuration of people who live together in a given family unit—usually called **family structure.** Numerous family structures exist in addition to the "traditional" family structure of a father, a mother, and several children. More and more children are living in single-parent households for at least part of their growing years. And many children experience a variety of family structures over the span of childhood and adolescence. Figure 9.2 provides data on the trends in family structures in the United States.

The following sections describe some of the variations in family structure and findings regarding their impact on children's developmental outcomes. Yet, even when researchers compare the development of children in specific family structures, there are many other factors that need to be examined to explain the child's development.

Many children experience a variety of family structures over the span of childhood and adolescence.

Single-Parent Families

In 1998, about 28 percent of all children under 18 lived with one parent (U.S. Bureau of the Census, 1998). The majority of these children, approximately 84 percent, lived with their mother, and 40 percent of these children lived with mothers who had never been married. Single-father homes were more likely to include a divorced father (44 percent) than a never-married father (33 percent). No other adults were present in the household for approximately 56 percent of children living with single parents.

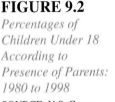

FIGURE 9.2

Percentages of Children Under 18 According to Presence of Parents: 1980 to 1998

SOURCE: U.S. Census Bureau, Statistical Abstract of the United States (1999).

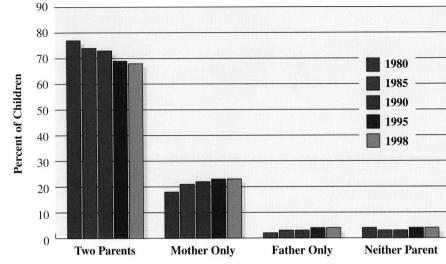

About 28 percent of all children under 18 lived with one parent.

Single parents face a number of difficulties, including sole care of children, limited economic resources, and role overload.

There are multiple pathways into single parenthood. Divorce produces the largest proportion of single parents. Other parents are widowed or assume single parenting because a spouse is out of the household due to work or incapacitation. For example, one parent may be serving in the military or is imprisoned. Also, a large number of women become single parents by having children out of wedlock. In 1998, more than 32 percent of births were to unmarried women (U.S. Department of Health and Human Services, 2000). The majority of single mothers are very young, but an increasing number of older, financially capable women are choosing to become parents outside of marriage by such means as artificial insemination and adoption. These different entries into and experiences of the single-parent family affect the relationships within it and the likely outcomes for children's development. The Focus on Research box describes difficulties associated with adolescent pregnancies.

Single parents face a variety of difficulties. Of paramount concern are the experiences of role overload and economic strain (Gongla & Thompson, 1987). Single parents face feelings of overwhelming responsibility as the sole caregiver and provider for their children. They must perform all of the child care tasks that can be shared in two-parent households. Even a less-involved parent in a two-parent family can provide some additional emotional and practical support to which single parents lack access. Not surprisingly, many single parents report feeling drained emotionally by their role as sole caregiver. High rates of poverty, low educational levels, and high mobility among single parents contribute additional stress.

Single Mothers

Most single parents (85 percent) are mothers. Single mothers face inordinate economic strain as a result of historical trends such as their lower levels of educational attainment, less-developed job skills, and lower wages than jobs performed by men (McLanahan & Sandefur, 1994). Also, single teenage mothers and single divorced mothers are especially likely to experience insufficient or decreased financial resources. Figure 9.4 shows the levels of family income associated with different family structures.

Single mothers who work outside the home must divide their time between work and children, often neglecting their own personal needs. Such role overload coupled with economic strain can result in poorer parenting (McLoyd, 1998).

Focus on Research

Teenagers as Mothers

Over the last several years teenage pregnancy rates have been declining (Curtin & Martin, 2000). The 1999 pregnancy rate for women aged 15 to 19 was approximately 50 per 1,000 births, a 3 percent drop from 1998 and the lowest rate recorded in the 60 years data have been systematically gathered. The most recent relative high point was recorded in 1991 when 62 per 1,000 births were to teenage mothers.

Despite this trend of decreasing percentages of teenage pregnancies, the concerns faced by teenage mothers and their children warrant attention. Social and economic disadvantage, poor academic performance and educational prospects, family or community history of out-of-wedlock births, and early sexual activity are among the factors thought to contribute to the likelihood of a teenage girl's becoming a mother (Brooks-Gunn & Chase-Lansdale, 1995; Rauch-Elnekave, 1994). Some of these factors are especially salient among different racial or ethnic groups. For example, African Americans report earlier sexual activity than Hispanic and European Americans, and African and Hispanic Americans are much more likely to come from socially and economically disadvantaged backgrounds. Such trends are likely to explain the differences in teen pregnancy rates shown in Figure 9.3

Becoming a teenage parent often serves to continue the pattern of negative life circumstances for the young woman and her child. Teen mothers are more likely to drop out of school (Furstenberg, Brooks-Gunn, & Chase-Lansdale, 1989). As a result, they are often poorly prepared for finding employment and may find themselves in need of public assistance to care for their and their babies' needs (Sullivan, 1993). Consequences for children of teenage mothers may be more severe. Higher levels of aggression and impulsive behavior and more delinquency often appear in these children (Chase-Lansdale, Brooks-Gunn, & Paikoff, 1991). Developmental and cognitive delays are also more common among children of younger

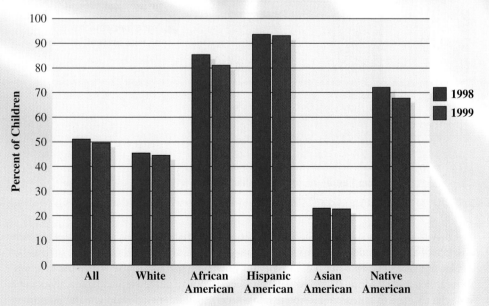

FIGURE 9.3

Teenage Births by Ethnicity of Mother in 1998 and 1999, per 1000 Births.

SOURCE: Curtin & Martin, (2000).

mothers and may contribute to eventual academic problems including grade failure (Hetherington, 1998). And when these children become adolescents themselves, they show early sexual activity and increased risk of teen parenthood.

Prevention efforts have focused on providing accurate information to children and adolescents regarding sexuality and its risks. Schools have implemented a variety of programs employing a range of approaches, from promoting abstinence as a responsible choice to training in the appropriate and consistent use of contraceptives. Because of very strong moral and political opinions in this area, evaluations of various programs are often equivocal.

Once a teenager has become a parent, what can be done to avoid or ameliorate the negative consequences previously described? Support from the family of the teen mother can go a long way to help especially in providing child care and training in effective parenting (Apfel & Seitz, 1991). Such support can also come from public sources such as the schools. A number of programs have begun to provide child care for children of students and parenting classes for those students; these programs have had promising results. Encouraging teenage mothers to continue their education yields other obvious benefits, such as enabling her to improve her eventual employability and to forestall or even escape from disadvantaged economic circumstances.

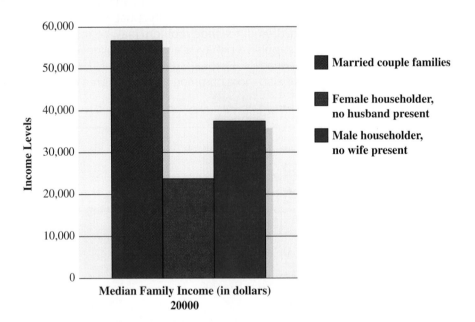

FIGURE 9.4
Median Family Income by Family Structure in 1999
SOURCE: U.S. Census Bureau, (1999).

Early research on single mothers and their children focused solely on the effects of the absence of a father. Studies identified a number of potentially harmful outcomes, such as behavior problems and less-masculine traits for boys who lacked a close father-son relationship (Biller, 1981). More recent investigations have looked at the various factors associated with the absence of a male figure in the household and children's developmental outcomes.

Absence or loss of a father is associated with economic deprivation, decreased parental resources, and decreased community resources. Each of these factors has been linked to less favorable outcomes for children. Thus, the effects of a single-mother family are strongly linked to the economic and community resources available to the family.

Single Fathers

Although the number of single fathers with custody of their children has increased in recent decades, this family form still constitutes only about 15 percent of all single-parent families (U.S. Bureau of the Census, 1999). These single fathers also suffer role overload as they try to manage singlehandedly the roles of caregiver and provider.

Men do not face the historical economic constraints faced by women in terms of lower status and lower-paying jobs. Consequently, single fathers tend not to suffer financially as single mothers do. They may, however, face less-optimal career options be-

SOURCE: Steve Skjold/ Photo Edit.

The number of single-mother families is growing. The effects of the family structure are linked to the economic and community resources available to the family.

cause of their parenting responsibilities. Working overtime or accepting a promotion that requires a greater time commitment at work may not be possible.

The pathway into single parenthood may affect the success and satisfaction that single fathers experience. Fathers who feel emotionally attached to their children or who question the parenting ability of their ex-partners often fight for custody. When consequently granted custody, such fathers describe the father-child relationship in very positive terms (Risman, 1986).

The age and sex of the child also play a role in the parenting of single fathers. Single fathers are more likely to parent older children. Mothers, on the other hand, more often raise infants and toddlers, who require more attention to their physical needs. Also, single fathers more often care for boys rather than girls. Fathers who raise daughters often question their parenting abilities and express concerns about providing appropriate guidance for their daughters, especially in dealing with topics such as sexuality in adolescence (Greif, 1985).

Single fathers do not face the historical economic constraints faced by women in terms of lower status and lower-paying jobs.

Single Parents and Children's Development

Because of the stigma attached to single-parent families, much of the research has focused on expected negative outcomes for children. Moreover, most studies have focused on the effects of female-headed households. Research on the influence of fathers on children's development

Focus on Research

Increasing interest in the role of fathers in children's lives has become evident among both researchers and shapers of public policy. Consequently, more attention has been given to fathers in the research literature and in the collection and analysis of data by government agencies (Lamb, 1997; Tamis-LeMonda & Cabrera, 1999).

A few statistics on fathers as caregivers may help to put this interest in perspective. In 1993, one in five fathers (2.9 million) provided care for at least one child under age 15 while the mother of the child worked. About two-thirds of those fathers (1.9 million) were considered the child's primary caregiver (U.S. Bureau of the Census, 1997). Also, the proportion of fathers providing primary care for their preschool children increased from 16 percent in 1988 to 18 percent in 1993. The traditional role of fathers within families has been that of economic provider, but changes in society (e.g., increased maternal employment) are leading fathers to also adopt the role of caregiver. In some cases, this is done out of economic necessity given the high cost of child care, but in other instances couples decide to have a child with the expectation of both parents sharing care.

Whereas earlier research on father involvement tended to focus on the simple presence or absence of the father, more recent investigations have attempted to delineate characteristics of different types of involvement. One model (Lamb, Pleck, Charnov, & Levine, 1987) suggests that father involvement can be characterized in terms of engagement (i.e., contact and interaction), accessibility (i.e., presence and availability), and responsibility (i.e., provision of resources and meeting the child's needs). These aspects of involvement may be further differentiated and can perhaps exert distinctive influences on outcomes for children.

What are some of the documented effects of father involvement on children? When fathers are primary caregivers for their children, they show more affection for them, they seem more attuned to their play behavior, and the children show a preference for their fathers in stressful situations (Geiger, 1996). In terms of children's cognitive development, positive links have been noted between father involvement and children's IQ and school success in middle childhood and adolescence. Benefits accrue also for the child's social competence.

It is important to recall that the family is a system of interacting members situated within a number of other social and cultural systems. The effects previously described reflect multiple intersecting processes through which father involvement impacts the child. Likewise, multiple factors interact to determine the extent of a given father's involvement with his child. Such factors include the father's mental health, his and the mother's expectations concerning his involvement in caregiving, and the level of support in the community and society for paternal involvement in the lives of children.

is a relative new area of inquiry. A discussion of recent research on paternal influences on children's development is presented in the Focus on Research box on the facing page.

Children from single-parent families do show a greater risk of negative consequences in the areas of educational attainment and sexual activity (McLanahan & Sandefur, 1994). Children from two-parent families have higher grade point averages, test scores, and attendance records than children from single-parent families. Given these patterns, it should not seem so surprising that being from a single-parent family doubles a child's risk of dropping out of school. Children from single-parent families are also less likely to attend or eventually graduate from college. With regard to sexual activity, girls from single-parent families report earlier onset of sexual activity and show a higher rate of teenage pregnancy.

As we will see with other family effects, those just reported for children of single-parent families are not as simple as they appear. For example, race and ethnicity moderate the relationship between having a single parent and teenage pregnancy risk. Whereas coming from a single-parent family versus a two-parent family doubles the risk for European Americans and Hispanic Americans, it only increases the risk by 25 percent for African Americans (Wu & Martinson, 1993). Similarly, the risk of school dropout is different for single-parent children of different racial or ethnic backgrounds and the levels of educational attainment. Youths of highly educated white parents are three times more likely to drop out of school if they come from a single-parent home than if they come from a two-parent home.

Several other factors can influence children of single-parent families. For example, children of widowed mothers tend to resemble children of two-parent families in terms of the outcomes mentioned earlier. Also, the presence of other adults in the home, such as a grandmother, can help offset the negative consequences faced by many single-parent children (Kellam, Ensminger, & Turner, 1997).

Some of the differences found between children of single parents when compared to children raised by two parents can have either positive or negative influences. Many children of single parents assume more responsibility around the house and may be given a larger role in family decision making. When children are burdened with inappropriate adult demands in terms of household and family responsibilities, however, they may develop feelings of incompetence or resentment. Similarly, it can be emotionally demanding and detrimental if a single parent turns to a child as a confidant. On the other hand, if the increased practical and emotional responsibilities are not excessive, children may develop a stronger sense of self-sufficiency and maturity (Hetherington, 1999).

Gay and Lesbian Families

Estimates of the number of gay and lesbian parents raising children vary widely. The stigma attached to homosexuality by some segments of society leads some parents not to disclose their homosexual identity for fear of harassment of themselves or their children. Some fear legal intervention to remove their custody or visitation rights. The large number of openly homosexual parents raising children today is a recent historical phenomenon.

Disclosure or concealment of one's sexual orientation can be a key issue for many homosexual parents as there are stresses associated with both options. Playing "straight" for friends and family out of fear of rejection, persecution, or discrimination can be emotionally taxing. One study found that lesbian mothers in stable relationships who were open about their sexual orientation were psychologically healthier than those who hid their lesbian identity (Rand, Graham, & Rawlings, 1982). Disclosure to their children seems to be more difficult for gay fathers than for lesbian mothers (Bozett, 1989). A number of other factors also affect parental decisions regarding disclosure. For example, living and working in a

Children from two-parent families have higher grade point averages, test scores, and attendance records than children from single-parent families.

Many children of single parents assume more responsibility around the house and may be given a larger role in family decision making.

The stigma attached to homosexuality by some segments of society leads some parents not to disclose their homosexual identity for fear of harassment of themselves or their children.

supportive environment in which a diversity of lifestyles is accepted and appreciated may make disclosure easier. Financial resources and ethnic background may also play a role in whether such an environment is available (Casper, Schultz, & Wickens, 1992).

There is great diversity among families with gay and lesbian parents. Most children of homosexual parents come from an earlier heterosexual union before the parent assumed a homosexual identity. However, a growing number of single and partnered gays and lesbians are choosing parenthood after assuming a homosexual identity. Options such as the use of donors or surrogates and adoption are allowing many lesbian women and gay men to become parents (Patterson, 1992). Homosexual parents also come from a variety of socioeconomic and ethnic backgrounds. Unfortunately, much of the research on gay and lesbian parents has been with a fairly homogeneous population of white, middle- to upper-middle-class, well-educated parents in urban areas. Consequently, the findings reviewed in this section should be viewed as limited in their generalizability until additional information is gathered on more diverse subgroups of homosexual parents.

As with the other "nontraditional" family structures discussed previously, much of the research on homosexual families has been either explicitly or implicitly comparative. Researchers have examined the similarities and differences between homosexual and heterosexual parents and between their respective children.

In general, gay parents and heterosexual parents are more similar than different. No differences are found between gay and heterosexual fathers on measures of their motives for parenthood, their sex-role orientation, or their involvement and intimacy with their children (Bigner & Jacobsen, 1989; Robinson & Skeen, 1982). However, lesbian mothers favor less-traditional sex-role socialization, and lesbian couples share parenting more equally than do heterosexual couples (Green, Mandel, Hotvedt, Gray, & Smith, 1986; Patterson, 1995).

Research comparing children of homosexual and heterosexual parents has focused primarily on issues of gender, sexual identity, and social adjustment. The results have revealed very few differences in outcomes for the two groups of children. No evidence for differences in gender identity or gender role behavior has been found (Green, 1978; Green et al., 1986; Patterson, 1992). Similarly, the majority of children of both homosexual and heterosexual parents grow up to assume a heterosexual orientation (Bailey, Bobrow, Wolfe, & Mikach, 1995; Tasker & Golombok, 1997). Children of gay and lesbian parents exhibit good relations with peers and adults, and they resemble children of heterosexual parents on measures of social competence, self-concept, locus of control, and moral judgment.

Children of gay and lesbian parents exhibit good relations with peers and adults, and they resemble children of heterosexual parents on measures of social competence, self-concept, locus of control, and moral judgment.

Implications for Educators

The structures of families are clearly changing. Although a majority of children today live in two-parent families, not all children will fit this pattern. We have discussed the increase in the number of single parents and gay and lesbian parents. Children may also live with aunts, grandparents, or foster parents.

It is important for teachers to be sensitive to variations in children's family circumstances. When you talk about families, it might be best to use the word *parents* rather than mothers and fathers. It is also important to avoid making generalizations about single-parent families. Although these families have special challenges, the impact of this family structure on children is primarily linked to limitations in economic resources, rather than the absence of a second parent. To increase parent involvement in school activities, special arrangements may be necessary to accommodate the busy schedules of single parents. Finally, it is important to bear in mind that the effect of various family structures on children is dependent on community resources. Schools can play an important role in strengthening family relationships.

Ethnic Diversity of Families

Along with changes in family structures, the ethnic composition of families is rapidly changing as well. For those working with children and their parents, it is important to understand the cultural values and child-rearing practices of different ethnic groups in the United States. We examine cultural variations in this section. As is the case with any summary, the descriptions here involve generalizations; it is important to remember that great diversity exists within ethnic groups as a result of such factors as country of origin, recency of immigration, and socioeconomic status (Marín & Marín, 1991; Tanaka, Ebreo, Linn, & Morera, 1998).

For those working with children and their parents, it is important to understand the cultural values and child-rearing practices of different ethnic groups in the United States.

African American Families

African Americans currently represent one of the largest ethnic minority groups within the United States. While significant numbers are recent immigrants from Africa or the Caribbean, the large majority are descendants of African slaves. Consequently, the experiences of African American families and children have been shaped by lingering vestiges of segregation and discrimination and a search for a positive ethnic identity (Comer & Poussaint, 1992).

Changing social and economic forces have been linked to marked changes in family life among African Americans during the past few decades. Black families in the United States have become more diverse in composition and structure than white families (Farley & Allen, 1987) as a result of such interrelated trends as decreasing employment among black males (Bowman, 1995) and declining rates of marriage (Gadsden, 1999). A majority of African American children live in mother-only households (Taylor, 1998). Also, a sizable proportion of African Americans live in urban settings in vulnerable neighborhoods where there is limited access to good schools and to secure, well-paying jobs (Gadsden, Smith, & Jordan, 1996). As can be seen in Figure 9.5, the median individual and household incomes for African Americans are significantly below the national average.

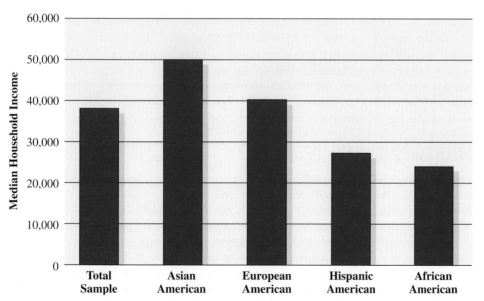

FIGURE 9.5

Median Household Income of Selected Ethnic Groups in 2000

SOURCE: U.S. Census Bureau (1999).

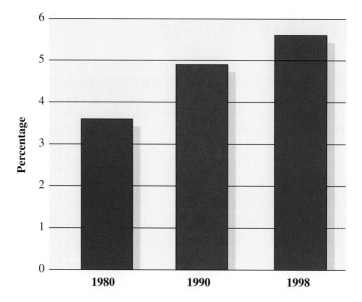

FIGURE 9.6

Percentage of Children Under 18 Living in Home of Grandparents from 1980 to 1998

SOURCE: U.S. Census Bureau (1999).

Child-rearing practices of African Americans emphasize the important of traits such as assertiveness, independence, and self-confidence.

African American families recognize and voice concern about their poor socioeconomic situations and the public perception of them (Gadsden, 1999). Moreover, these families possess certain attributes that may serve to ameliorate the negative effects of such challenges. African Americans express high expectations for themselves, their children, and their communities (Gadsden, 1999). Child-rearing practices emphasize important traits such as assertiveness, independence, and self-confidence (Lewis, 1975). Additionally, the African American community holds very egalitarian views of the division of labor between men and women (Scanzoni, 1985; Scott-Jones & Nelson-LeGall, 1986). African Americans also place great value on interpersonal relationships (Willis, 1992) and are more likely than whites to live in extended households made up of grandparents, uncles, aunts, cousins, godparents, and others (Farley & Allen, 1987). These extended families constitute an informal support network (Cherlin & Furstenberg, 1986; Comer & Poussaint, 1992) for the African American family and provide a range of services including monetary assistance, child care and child rearing, and emotional support (Stack & Burton, 1993). In some instances children may even be sent to live with members of the extended family, such as grandparents or aunts (Miller, 1993; McDaniel, 1994).

As can be seen in Figure 9.6, the number of children living with their grandparents is increasing. The trend of grandparents providing primary care for their grandchildren is discussed further in the Focus on Research box.

Hispanic American Families

The Hispanic population of the United States is rapidly increasing. Nearly two-thirds of this group are of Mexican origin. Puerto Rico and Cuba provide the next two largest groups followed by a variety of Central and South American countries (U.S. Census Bureau, 2000c). Many Hispanic Americans have immigrated here within the last two generations (Leyendecker & Lamb, 1999) to search for better socioeconomic circumstances and work opportunities or to escape from war or political tensions in their countries of origin. Although Hispanic families tend to be larger and divorce rates tend to be low (Zuniga, 1992), Hispanic families in the United States are more likely than non-Hispanic white families to be headed by a female with no spouse present, and Hispanics are less likely to be married

Focus on Research

Grandparents as Caregivers

More and more grandchildren are living in the homes of their grandparents. It is estimated that approximately 4 million children today are being raised by a grandparent (U.S. Census Bureau, 1999). Rates vary according to race and ethnicity, however, with black children more likely to live with a grandparent (12 percent) than white (4 percent) or Hispanic (6 percent) children. Given reports that African American grandparents are more likely than those of other ethnicities to function as surrogate parents (Szinovacz, 1998) and that African American grandmothers in low- and moderate-income families often play a key role in child care (Pearson, Hunter, Ensminger, & Kellam, 1990), the higher rate of grandparent-grandchild coresidence for black families is not so surprising. Of those children living with their grandparents in 1998, parents were completely out of the picture for over a quarter of them.

Grandparents may become caregivers of their grandchildren for a variety of reasons. Parents may no longer be able to provide primary care for their children as a result of death or incarceration, or they may simply abandon them. In some cases, parental mental illness, substance abuse, or child maltreatment may also lead grandparents to step in as caretakers of their grandchildren. Although legal guardianship is awarded to grandparents in many cases, sometimes these arrangements are informal, which may lead to a number of obstacles when grandparents seek assistance for the children.

Grandparents who have assumed responsibility for rearing their grandchildren often receive little support or help from other family members. They may experience mixed feelings of anger and guilt with regard to their children's inability to parent and often feel overwhelmed by the responsibility themselves (Burton & Dilworth-Anderson, 1991; Kluger & Aprea, 1999). Many seek out help from social agencies, and hundreds of support groups have sprung up around the United States, providing everything from emotional support to political voice.

There are a number of things that educators can do to help "grandfamilies" (Rothenberg, 1996). For example, educators might help caregiving grandparents by reviewing school policies that may need to be modified to accommodate them, providing information about school programs (e.g., after-school) which could lighten the caretaking load, offering referrals to health and social services as needed, and encouraging involvement in the school's activities. The grandchildren themselves could benefit from educators' acknowledgment that adjustment difficulties are possible and provide opportunities to build their resilience. Teachers and other school personnel should recognize that the children may feel "different" from peers because of their family status and should not compound the discomfort by calling attention to it.

than non-Hispanic whites (U.S. Census Bureau, 2000c). As for African Americans, the median individual and household incomes for Hispanics are below the national averages (see Figure 9.5).

The interdependent, collectivistic quality of Hispanic culture is often noted and contrasted with the more independent, individualistic character of United States society

(Leyendecker & Lamb, 1999) in general. Marín and Marín (1991) describe two basic cultural values, among others, which support and promote the more collectivist nature of Hispanic life: familialism and simpatía. **Familialism** refers to a strong identification with and attachment to both the nuclear and extended family and the feelings of loyalty, respect, duty, and reciprocity which accompany such familial attachment. **Simpatía** embodies the felt need for behaviors such as conformity and empathy, which promote harmonious, pleasant social relations. These cultural values consequently translate into socialization goals of fostering the development of qualities such as cooperation and proper demeanor in children in order to promote social integration into the family and larger community (Leyendecker & Lamb, 1999). Interdependence in extended families may play a role as a protective force through its implications for the development of a supportive network which shares in child rearing and the development of multiple significant relationships between children and adults (Buriel & De Ment, 1997; Suarez-Orozco & Suarez-Orozco, 1994).

Hispanic culture emphasizes interdependent and collectivist values, and child-rearing practices promote feelings of loyalty, respect, and duty to the family.

Hispanics may also tend to have more traditional views with regard to the roles of men and women (Leadbeater & Bishop, 1994). Male dominance and female submissiveness have been identified as common patterns in Hispanic social interactions. Whereas women are viewed as having primary responsibility for caregiving and life within the household (Zuniga, 1992), men make many of the decisions regarding the outside world. However, the level of traditionalism in gender roles is also related to levels of education and work involvement of women. Evidence suggests a range of roles is possible, including shared decision making (Mirande, 1988).

Asian American Families

Asian Americans account for approximately 4 percent of the total population of the United States. The largest proportions of Asian Americans are Chinese and Filipino with additional substantial numbers of Japanese, Asian Indians, Koreans, and Vietnamese (U.S. Census Bureau, 1993a). More recent immigrant groups escaping political and social unrest in Southeast Asia make up smaller numbers of the Asian American total. Early Asian immigrants to the United States often served as farm workers or laborers, while in recent decades greater numbers have come in search of educational and professional job opportunities (Chan, 1992). Divorce rates are low among Asian Americans, and rates of single-parent households are comparable for Asian Americans and white Americans (U.S. Census Bureau, 2000a).

Education is highly valued in many Asian cultures, and both children and parents ascribe great weight to effort in the pursuit of academic success.

Although the median household income for Asian Americans is well above the national figure (see Figure 9.5), poverty rates are also higher for this group than for whites in the United States (U.S. Census Bureau, 2000a). Asian and Pacific Islander families tend to be larger than white families in the United States. Recency of immigration also plays a substantial role in the social and economic status of Asian Americans (Tanaka, Ebreo, Linn, & Morera, 1998).

Traditional Asian culture places great emphasis on connectedness and collectivistic values (Markus & Kitayama, 1991). Consequently, there is a strong focus on family and harmony within Asian American groups. The individual is traditionally socialized to subordinate the self to the group and develop personal virtues such as patience, perseverance, restraint, and humility. Parents might be expected to sacrifice their own desires in the interest of providing the best possible opportunities for their children, while at the same time the children learn to show similar deference to the family's concerns (Chan, 1992). Education is also highly valued in many Asian cultures, and both children and parents ascribe great weight to effort in the pursuit of academic success (Stevenson & Lee, 1990). By doing well in school, children are seen as bringing honor to their family and improving their

SOURCE: Michael
Newman/Photo Edit.

Education is highly valued in Asian American families. These families often have a special time for
schoolwork in the home, and parents are highly involved in these activities.

own chances of job success. Such independent achievement in the service of promoting the
family's social status is encouraged (Lin & Fu, 1990). The interdependence of family members emerges also in the presence of multiple caregivers in the traditional Asian home
where grandparents and older siblings also play a role in the socialization of young children. For example, older siblings are expected to model socially acceptable behaviors and
may be scolded for not setting a good example (Chan, 1992).

Native American Families

Native Americans constitute less than 1 percent of the total population of the United States,
and they are scattered among more than 300 tribes which vary greatly in size. The largest
tribes include the Cherokee, Navajo, Chippewa, Sioux, and Choctaw, and nearly one-half of
the Native American population live in the western United States (U.S. Census Bureau,
1993b). Despite common portrayals, only about one-fifth of Native Americans live on reservations; the majority live in cities. Although the majority of Native American families have
both husband and wife present, the proportion of female-headed households is higher than
the national average. Native American families also tend to be multigenerational and slightly
larger than the national average (Joe & Malach, 1992). A smaller proportion of the Native
American population than of the total population is in the workforce, and Native Americans
show higher rates of employment in service, farming, craft, and laborer occupations than the
total population (U.S. Census Bureau, 1993b). Consequently, the income levels of this group
are lower than national figures, and the poverty rate is high (Harjo, 1993; Joe & Mallach,
1992). This dire economic situation is even worse for those living on reservations, where almost half the population live in poverty (U.S. Census Bureau, 1993b).

When the values and customs of Native Americans are discussed, attention must be
given to the centrality of tribal identity (Yellowbird & Snipp, 1998) as practices can vary

greatly from tribe to tribe according to historical traditions and level of contact with the larger society of the United States (Price, 1976). Nevertheless, Native Americans do share some common beliefs with regard to harmonious coexistence with nature and others (Attneave, 1982). Coupled with this focus on harmony is a tendency toward wholistic thinking, which emphasizes the interrelatedness of all things (Tharp, 1994). For a wholistic thinker, the whole must be understood as a complete functioning entity, not in terms of its individual components and their individual characteristics.

The entire Native American community plays a role in socializing children. It might not be uncommon for any member of the group to offer correction or praise to a child (Suina & Smolkin, 1994). Children are incorporated into the daily activities of the group and learn by observing and imitating adults. Much value is placed on the sharing of traditions and rituals, especially through teaching stories and oral histories. Respect for the past also appears in the reverence for elders in Native American communities; these elders play central roles in the spiritual, social, and cultural aspects of the community (Yellowbird & Snipp, 1998). Moreover, some Native Americans have described a "good Indian child" as one who shows respect to elders (Joe, 1994).

Family Influences on Development

Having addressed some of the diversity among families with regard to composition and ethnicity, we turn now to a discussion of the various ways families influence children's development. Families structure the environment in which children mature both directly and indirectly. In this section, we will discuss the characteristics of parents that foster and maintain children's adaptive development.

Parenting Characteristics and Styles

Parents ideally strive to produce socially mature and competent children who are capable of satisfactory participation in society. How do parents accomplish this goal? Are certain behaviors more often associated with parents' effective performance of their socialization task? This section will discuss some of the various dimensions of parenting behavior which researchers have examined in their attempts to identify and understand what constitutes optimal (and less than optimal) parenting. Among the characteristics receiving attention here are warmth, responsiveness, and control, as well as constellations of parenting qualities referred to as parenting styles.

Warmth

As with many other concepts we have discussed, parental warmth is a difficult construct to define. Yet most researchers and laypersons include in their definition of the term a level of

SOURCE: David Young-Wolff/Photo Edit.

Parents who are warm, responsive, and authoritative have a possible influence on their children's school achievement.

care and acceptance expressed toward a child by a parent and contrast it with hostility. A warm parent shows affection and empathy toward a child and an interest in the child's feelings and actions. Such nurturant behaviors are positively associated with children's development of prosocial behavior and moral standards, and the presence of higher self-esteem and higher intellectual abilities (Maccoby, 1980; Schaefer, 1989; Zahn-Waxler, Radke-Yarrow, & King, 1979). Also, the finding that children are more likely to imitate and identify with an affectionate model (Bandura, 1969) suggests a possible mechanism by which children might come to comply with and adopt parental values (MacDonald, 1992). Conversely, a lack of warmth or hostility in parent-child interactions is associated with delinquency, aggression, and a range of other problem behaviors (Hetherington & Martin, 1986; Olweus, 1980).

A warm parent shows affection and empathy toward a child and an interest in the child's feelings and actions.

Responsiveness

Responsiveness can be thought of as a parent's prompt, contingent, and appropriate reaction to a child's behavior (Bornstein & Tamis-LeMonda, 1997). When an infant cries, a parent who checks to see what is bothering the child or what the child needs is considered responsive. Likewise, the parent who notices when his 5-year-old shows great interest in a butterfly resting on a flower and engages her in a discussion about it is exhibiting responsiveness. Parents who notice their children's signals, interpret them appropriately, and respond in a sensitive manner have children who show more optimal social and cognitive outcomes such as more secure attachment, greater social competence, more emotional expressivity, higher cognitive functioning, and more rapid language development (Bornstein, 1989; Nicely, Tamis-LeMonda, & Grolnick, 1999). Responsive parenting has also been found to predict children's resilient adjustment in the face of adversity (Wyman et al., 1999). An absence of responsiveness has been linked to an increase in the risk of disruptive behavior problems (Wakschlag & Hans, 1999).

Parents who notice their children's signals, interpret them appropriately, and respond in a sensitive manner promote the development of social and cognitive competencies.

SOURCE: Michael Newman/Photo Edit.

Parents who provide explanations for rules and discuss why certain behaviors are desirable or undesirable can help children learn self-discipline.

Control and Discipline

Until children develop the ability to regulate their own behavior, the job of control falls most often on parents. Attempts to foster desired behaviors and

Focus on Research

Studies reveal that nearly all children in the United States experience some form of corporal punishment, although it may differ in frequency and severity (American Academy of Pediatrics, 1998; Strauss, 1994; Strauss & Stewart, 1999). **Corporal punishment** is defined as the use of physical punishment with the intention of causing a child to experience physical pain, but not injury, as a means of reducing an undesirable behavior (Strauss, 1994, p. 4). Forms of corporal punishment range from slapping the hand of a child about to touch a dangerous or fragile object to hitting a child with an object, such as a hairbrush, paddle, or belt.

The most common form of legal corporal punishment in the United States is spanking, which involves hitting a child with an open hand on the buttocks or extremities. In a 1995 national survey of parents, 94 percent spanked a child that year (Strauss & Stewart, 1999). About a third of the sample reported they had spanked a child under the age of one year. However, the frequency of spanking was highest among children aged 2 to 12 years, whereas only 14 percent of parents reported spanking their children after the age of 13 years. Boys generally experience more corporal punishment than girls, and frequency rates also differ by parental age, ethnicity, and social class (Strauss, 1994).

Is corporal punishment an effective form of discipline? Spanking a child for an undesirable behavior can temporarily stop or reduce a behavior, but its effectiveness decreases with subsequent use. To maintain the effectiveness of spanking over time, the intensity with which it is delivered must systematically increase. This pattern can quickly escalate into abuse (American Academic of Pediatrics, 1998). There are a number of other negative consequences that need to be considered, including the following:

- Spanking a child under the age of 18 months can cause physical injury, when the child is unlikely to understand the connection between behavior and punishment (American Association of Pediatrics, 1998).

- Spanking provides children with aggressive models. Children who are spanked show higher rates of aggression and delinquency in later development (American Association of Pediatrics, 1998; Strauss, 1994).

- The frequent use of spanking creates a negative family climate of rejection. The child associates the presence of a parent with hitting, which negatively affects the quality of the parent-child relationship.

eliminate unwanted behaviors begin early on as parents try to quiet a crying baby or to prevent the toddler's newfound walking ability from leading to a tumble down the stairs.

Parents differ in how they exert control over children. Researchers have examined the different child behavior outcomes of parents who use power-assertive versus inductive discipline techniques (Hoffman & Saltzstein, 1967). With **power-assertive discipline,** parents attempt to influence their children's behavior by use of commands and imperatives for which no reason other than "I said so" is given. Such parents seem to coerce their children

- The use of spanking as the primary means of discipline undermines the effectiveness of other discipline approaches, such as reinforcing desirable behaviors, imposing logical consequences, or removing privileges.

In general, child development researchers agree that corporal punishment is not an effective form of discipline. It teaches the child neither self-control nor self-discipline, and it can damage the parent-child relationship or cause injury to the child.

Of course, as we have discussed, parents need to stop undesirable behaviors when they occur. Some actions, such as touching a hot stove or biting another child, require immediate responses to stop the behavior. What are some alternatives to corporal punishment? First, it is important to protect children from potentially dangerous or risky situations (e.g., installing safety latches on cupboards). For young children, it is best to stop a behavior with a firm no, then remove the object from the child's hand or the child from the dangerous situation. Reasoning, verbal cues, and reprimands are ineffective for stopping undesirable behaviors in infants and toddlers (American Association of Pediatrics, 1998).

For older children, time-out, logical consequences, or removal or privileges are effective strategies for reducing and eliminating undesirable behaviors. As we discussed in Chapter 8, the application of logical consequences teaches children their behavior produces a corresponding result. The logical consequence for breaking a neighbor's window is to help pay for a new one. An example of time-out is removing the child from a play or social situation for a short period of time. For older children, this strategy generally involves denying participation in activities (grounding the child for the weekend) or losing privileges (no television or computer games for a specific period of time). These three discipline strategies (logical consequences, time-out, loss of privileges) are most effective when combined with the following: (1) an immediate consequence when the behavior first occurs; (2) a consistent response when the problem behavior continues to occur; and (3) a clear but calm explanation of why the behavior is inappropriate and what consequence the child can expect when the behavior occurs. It is also important to remember that the best discipline approach is one that provides children with positive role models, parental warmth and affection, opportunities to choose and evaluate different available options, and positive reinforcement to increase desirable behaviors.

into compliance with the typically rigid rules they enforce, often by means of yelling and hitting. As discussed further in the Focus on Research box, such restrictive and hostile discipline techniques have been shown to be ineffective and, in fact, to lead to elevated levels of disruptive behavior problems and aggression in children (Chamberlain & Patterson, 1995; Stormshak et al., 2000). On the other hand, parents who use **inductive discipline** offer explanations for their rules and even solicit reasons from their children for why certain behaviors might be more desirable or appropriate in certain circumstances. Consequently,

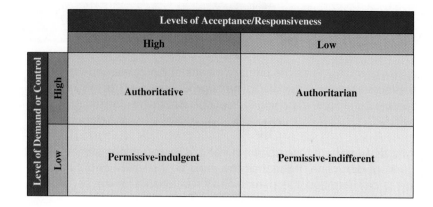

FIGURE 9.7

Dimensions of Parenting Styles

SOURCE: Based on Maccoby & Martin (1983).

these children are found to engage in more prosocial behavior and to expect enhanced relations with peers (Hart, DeWolf, & Burts, 1992).

Other issues in the discipline of children revolve around principles of reinforcement. Reinforcement of desirable behavior has been argued to be a more effective strategy to promote learning than punishment. Parents might attempt to forestall the appearance of unwanted behavior by providing attention and other reinforcements for positive behaviors (Wierson & Forehand, 1994). A child might be praised for making up his bed, for example. When less desirable behavior does appear, parents may simply ignore (i.e., withhold reinforcement from) minor inappropriate behaviors such as whining or fussiness with the effect that a child learns such actions gain nothing. Removing a child for a short time from the situation in which his unwanted behavior is being reinforced (e.g., "time-out") has also been shown to reduce negative behaviors. All such responses, whether reinforcement for a positive behavior or discipline for a negative behavior, should be delivered in a consistent and timely fashion. Allowing a child to "get by" with unacceptable behavior sometimes or giving repeated warnings without following through on the consequences sends a confusing message and results in continued misbehavior.

Restrictive and hostile discipline techniques are ineffective and may lead to elevated levels of disruptive behavior problems and aggression in children.

Parenting Styles

None of these parenting characteristics occurs separate from the others. Parents typically show a combination of levels of warmth, responsiveness, and control. Diana Baumrind (1967, 1971) identified some of the more common constellations of parenting behaviors, referred to as **parenting styles,** and traced some of their apparent effects on children's developmental outcomes. In Baumrind's original work, three parenting styles were identified: authoritarian, permissive, and authoritative. By examining parenting along the two dimensions of control and responsiveness, as shown in Figure 9.7, Eleanor Maccoby and John Martin (1983) provided a reformulation of Baumrind's work and further distinguished permissive-indulgent and permissive-indifferent parenting. The distinguishing characteristics of each parenting style are as follows:

- **Authoritarian parents** are high on the control dimension but low on responsiveness. Characterized by low warmth and little positive involvement with their children, these parents set rigid rules and discipline harshly with the expectation that the rules will be obeyed because of parental authority.
- **Authoritative parents** show warm, responsive involvement with their children and set appropriate and clear standards for behavior. They

communicate openly with their children, providing rationales for rules and showing respect for their children's rights and opinions. In these ways, authoritative parents encourage children's autonomy and independence appropriate for their age with the result that children develop social competence.

- **Permissive-indulgent parents** are highly warm and responsive to their children but place few demands or expectations on them. Rules which may exist are not clearly communicated or enforced so that children are left to make their own decisions and regulate their own behavior.
- **Permissive-indifferent parents** also leave it to their children to make their own decisions and control their own behavior by placing few demands on them, but in this case such a situation results more from neglect. Appearing emotionally detached, permissive-indifferent parents show little or no involvement in the lives of their children.

Authoritative parenting is also related to school success from early childhood through adolescence.

As shown in Table 9.1, each parenting style has important consequences for children's development. A number of positive child competencies are associated with authoritative parenting styles, such as self-reliance and social responsibility. As we discussed in Chapter 4, an authoritative parenting style also promotes intellectual development. Authoritative parenting is related to school success from early childhood through adolescence (Baumrind, 1978; Dornbusch, Ritter, Roberts, & Fraliegh, 1987; Steinberg et al., 1995). In contrast,

Table 9.1	Parenting Styles and Children's Development
Parenting Style	**Outcomes**
Authoritative	Self-reliance Social responsibility Higher levels of achievement
Authoritarian	Social incompetence Anxiety about social comparison Failure to show initiative Poor communication skills Lower school performance Lower self-esteem
Permissive-indulgent	Expect to get their own way Show little respect for others Never learn to control their own behavior Lower school performance
Permissive-indifferent	Social incompetence Lack self-control Lower school performance

SOURCE: Maccoby & Martin (1993).

children with authoritarian parents typically have lower grades in school and lower self-esteem. Children of indifferent-uninvolved parents tend to have the most negative profile of all. As adolescents, these children are at greatest risk for developing problem behaviors. The patterns for academic achievement shown in Table 9.1 are generally found across different ethnic groups, but European American and Hispanic American adolescents may benefit the most from authoritative parenting (Steinberg et al., 1995). Also, as we discussed, an authoritarian parenting style may particularly benefit young people in neighborhoods with crime and violence (Kelley et al., 1992).

Developmental Changes in Family Relations

Different issues and tasks take center stage in family interactions as children mature, and the manner in which they are handled is thought, in some cases, to lay the groundwork for future development.

Over the course of development the relationships between parents and their children undergo considerable change. Different issues and tasks take center stage in family interactions as children mature, and the manner in which they are handled is thought, in some cases, to lay the groundwork for future development. Parents must adjust their parenting practices to the growing competencies of the child. As you might imagine, an authoritative parenting style may facilitate this process because there is more give-and-take in the parent-child relationship. Let's look at how parent-child relations change in childhood and adolescence.

Movement Toward Coregulation

As we learned in Chapter 7, the behavior of children in infancy and early childhood is mainly controlled and regulated by parents. As children mature, there is a gradual shift toward **coregulation,** whereby control is shared by parents and children (Maccoby, 1984).

In middle childhood, children begin to spend less time with their families and more time in contexts outside the home, such as in school and peer activities. Parents may spend only half as much time with children in a variety of activities, such as caregiving, reading, and playing, when they are between the ages of 5 and 12 as they did when they were younger (Hill & Stafford, 1980).

During a period of coregulation in middle childhood, parents continue to provide broad, general guidelines for acceptable behavior while children regulate their own everyday behavior.

Children have also reached a point in their development where they can begin to manage their daily activities and assume responsibility for their behavior. Parents begin to expect more from them in terms of proper behavior. With children's increasing cognitive abilities, parents are able to reason with them about their behavior and its consequences. As a result, less physical discipline is used by parents of school-age children than by parents of preschoolers (Collins, Harris, & Susman, 1996).

As children demonstrate they can manage daily routines and responsibilities, there is a gradual shift in control from parents to child. Parents continue to provide broad, general guidelines for acceptable behavior while children regulate their own everyday behavior. This coregulation period provides parents with an opportunity to continue monitoring and supporting children at a distance while strengthening children's self-monitoring and decision-making skills with regard to appropriate behavioral standards. Eleanor Maccoby (1984) provides the following description of parents' and children's roles in coregulation:

> First, [parents] must monitor, guide, and support their children at a distance—that is, when their children are out of their presence; second, they must effectively use the times when direct contact does occur; and third, they must strengthen in their children the abilities that will allow them to monitor their own behavior, to adopt acceptable standards of [good] conduct, to avoid undue risks, and to know when they need parental support and guidance. Children must be willing to inform parents of their whereabouts, activities, and problems so that parents can mediate and guide when necessary. (pp. 191–192)

The process of coregulation in middle childhood prepares children for adolescence and adulthood, when they will assume responsibility for their own care and decisions.

Movement Toward Autonomy

During adolescence, parents must make further adjustments in parenting practices as young people strive for a sense of independence or **autonomy.** If you recall, adolescence marks the beginning of a young person's search for identity. Young people are establishing themselves as separate individuals, with their own identity, values, and goals for the future.

Adolescents find themselves in a position of desiring more independence but still needing the support of their parents. And parents of adolescents are often at a point in their own lives where other concerns (e.g., work, health, care of their own parents) clamor for their attention. Consequently, the idea of yielding more responsibility to the adolescents is attractive, but parents may remain unsure of the level of autonomy to grant. This mutual ambivalence on the part of both parents and adolescents with regard to balancing dependence and independence sets the stage for adolescent-parent conflict.

Interestingly, the arguments between adolescents and their parents typically center on what could be considered fairly mundane issues of household responsibilities, finances, privileges, and issues of personal taste in areas such as music and clothing. Adolescents and their parents have very similar beliefs on the "bigger" issues of religion, politics, and problems of society (Holmbeck, 1996; Youniss, 1989). However, the day-to-day issues of contention may seem very significant to adolescents who see them as instances in which they would like to begin exercising control over their own lives.

The frequency of adolescent-parent conflict appears highest in early adolescence (Laursen, Coy, & Collins, 1998). The task for parents and adolescents is to maintain a sense of closeness while roles are being renegotiated. It requires considerable mutual respect, flexibility, and openness in the parent-child relationship. Most adolescents and their parents handle this transition without excessive discord. As many as 20 percent of adolescents may experience difficulty establishing their autonomy, but a complete rupture of the parent-child relationship is rare unless there is prolonged, intense conflict (Brook, Brook, Gordon, Whitehouse, & Cohen, 1990).

In summary, an important component of the family system is that it must constantly change and adjust to the development of its members. With development, parents must adjust to the growing competencies and independence of their children. At the same time, parents may be experiencing changes in their health, job, or marital status that can make adjustments difficult to manage. The family is one of the few social systems that requires so many changes and adjustments from its members.

While roles are being renegotiated, the developmental task for parents and adolescents is to maintain a sense of closeness, which requires considerable mutual respect, flexibility, and openness.

Sibling Relationships

Most American children (80 percent) will have at least one sibling. Siblings play a unique and important role in children's development. They serve as role models, playmates, teachers, and sources of emotional support. In some families, siblings also care for younger children. Like the parent-child relationship, sibling relations also change with development.

For an older sibling, the arrival of a new baby can be both exciting and distressing. A parent's involvement with the older child will generally decline at this time. Many young children may become withdrawn, clingy, or demanding when a new baby is introduced into the family, but this distress can be avoided or reduced if parents are responsive to the older child's needs for attention and affection (Howe & Ross, 1990).

By the infant's second birthday, a sibling relationship begins to take shape. The younger child will imitate and attempt to play with the older sibling. By age 4, the young sibling will talk more to the older sibling than to his or her mother (Brown & Dunn, 1992). If they are close in age, siblings relate to each other as equals, much like peers.

Sibling conflict tends to increase during middle childhood. Some researchers believe that this conflict is due to the children's increased ability to make comparisons (Brody, Stoneman, & McCoy, 1994). One sibling may feel the other sibling is receiving more parental attention, approval, or affection, which can cause resentment. This effect may be especially strong if the father shows favoritism toward one child more than the other (Brody, Stoneman, & McCoy, 1994).

Though conflict may increase during the school years, siblings are also a source of companionship and support. Older siblings appear to be better teachers than friends when it comes to learning tasks (Azmitia & Hesser, 1993). However, as younger siblings mature and become more independent, they are less likely to accept direction from older brothers and sisters. As adolescents become more involved with friends, they may spend less time with siblings (Furman & Buhrmester, 1992).

The quality of sibling relationships is affected by parenting practices. Children whose parents are warm and supportive tend to develop positive sibling relationships. A similar pattern is found when there are warm, harmonious relationships between parents. In contrast, coercive, hostile, or negative relationships within the family can spill over to the sibling relationship.

> *Many young children may become withdrawn, clingy, or demanding when a new baby is introduced into the family, but this distress can be avoided or reduced if parents are responsive to the older child's needs for attention and affection.*

Birth Order Effects

Does the child's position in the family make a difference? **Birth order** has to do with the child's position in the family—first born, middle child, and so on. Numerous books and articles have been written about birth order effects in the family. The Focus on Research box describes a series of studies on birth order and intellectual development.

In general, most studies show birth order effects. Parents typically have higher expectations for first-born children than for later-born children, and they use stricter discipline. As a result, first-born children tend to be high achievers. They are also more conforming and obedient than their younger siblings. By the time other children arrive, parents are more realistic in their expectations and more confident in their parenting practices (Baskett, 1985). Later-born children tend to be more popular with peers (Eaton, Chipperfield, & Sinbeil, 1989).

> *Children whose parents are warm and supportive tend to develop positive sibling relationships.*

Single-Child Families

As we have seen, sibling relationships play an important role in children's development. Children without siblings—only children—are often portrayed as selfish and spoiled. Contrary to this image, children growing up in one-child families tend to be just as socially competent and well adjusted as other children. In fact, they tend to have higher levels of self-esteem and motivation than other children. They also do better in school (Falbo, 1992). Nevertheless, being an only child does have its disadvantages. In one study, only children expressed concerns about not getting to experience the closeness of a sibling relationship and about caring for elderly parents on their own (Hawkins & Knox, 1978).

> *Contrary to popular belief, children growing up in one-child families tend to be just as socially competent and well adjusted as children in larger families.*

Maltreatment of Children

Much of the chapter has focused so far on the ways in which families can provide support for children's positive, adaptive development with occasional identification of family circumstances that are not so beneficial. Now, however, we will address the circumstances

Focus on Research

Birth Order, Family Size, and Intelligence

The issue of birth order effects on behavior is a long-standing one. Over the years various researchers have associated birth order with a variety of personality outcomes and also with general intellectual functioning. At least three different models have been offered to explain the observed negative relation between birth order and intelligence in cross-sectional data.

According to the resource dilution model (Blake, 1981), the more children there are in a family, the thinner the family's resources are stretched. This includes the time and affection available from parents as well as material resources that might be supportive of children's intellectual development. Consequently, later-born children enter a setting in which there is less of everything to go around and face the prospect of less-optimal development.

The confluence model (Zajonc & Markus, 1975) suggests that after age 11 a negative relationship is seen between birth order and IQ at varying family sizes and between family sizes and IQ at varying birth orders because earlier children enjoy a "tutoring" advantage. That is, the older siblings become teachers of the younger siblings, and playing that role fosters their improved cognitive development. At younger ages a number of other factors are thought to influence intellect so there may appear to be no relationship between birth order, family size, and intelligence or the relationship may be positive.

Finally, the admixture hypothesis argues that birth order and family size are caused by factors outside the family, such as the distribution of intelligence among parents in the population (Page & Grandon, 1979). According to this view, the apparent connection between birth order and intelligence operates in the reverse direction of that posed by the resource dilution and confluence models. Moreover, the admixture hypothesis locates the relationship at the level of between-family influences as opposed to within the family as in the other models.

Using the National Longitudinal Study of Youth (NLSY) data set, a group of investigators recently examined the pattern of IQ scores within and across families (Rodgers, Cleveland, van den Oord, & Rowe, 2000). The NLSY data showed that later-born siblings had lower IQ scores in comparison to their earlier-born siblings, regardless of family size. However, a negative relationship did appear between family size and IQ: children in larger families in the NLSY data had IQ scores lower than those of children in smaller families. These findings were interpreted as demonstrating that the apparent within-family effect of birth order on intelligence is better explained by between-family factors, such as parental education and income levels.

surrounding the actual maltreatment of children, often by members of their families or family acquaintances. With knowledge of the risk factors, signs, and effects of child maltreatment, educators can better identify and more sensitively meet the needs of child victims.

Definitions of abuse and neglect are based on basic assumptions about children and the responsibilities of their caregivers. Several decades ago, it was not uncommon for young people to receive a "good strapping" to ensure their obedience. But today hitting a child with an object would be viewed as abusive. Most experts use the following definition to describe child abuse: "An abused or neglected child is a child whose physical or mental health or welfare is harmed or threatened with harm by the acts or omissions of his/her parent or other person responsible for his/her welfare" (Tower, 1992).

Child maltreatment can take different forms. **Physical abuse** includes physical injury caused by the child's caretaker, including beating, kicking, punching, burning, and so forth. By definition, the injury was not an accident. **Neglect** is a more common form of abuse, and it involves inattention to the basic needs of a child, such as food, clothing, medical care, supervision, and housing. Neglect is chronic, and generally affects all the children in the household. **Emotional maltreatment** involves rejecting a child and showing a consistent lack of concern for the child's emotional well-being. Finally, **sexual abuse** includes any contacts between the child or adult in which the child is being used for sexual stimulation. Sexual abuse may take place within the family, referred to as incest, or may involve caretakers outside the family, such as a relative, friend, or baby-sitter.

Child maltreatment can take a number of different forms including physical abuse, neglect, emotional maltreatment, and sexual abuse.

How prevalent is child abuse and neglect? In 1998, there were an estimated 903,000 victims of child maltreatment. After peaking around 15 per 1,000 children in the early 1990s, the rate of victimization has decreased to approximately 13 per 1,000 children in 1998 (U.S. Department of Health and Human Services, 2000). Over half of the confirmed victims suffered neglect, and almost a quarter suffered physical abuse. Almost 12 percent were victims of sexual abuse. Psychological abuse and medical neglect each accounted for 6 percent or fewer. Sadly, about a quarter of victims were subjected to multiple types of maltreatment.

Younger children are at greater risk for child abuse than older children.

A number of factors have been identified which place children at increased risk for suffering maltreatment. Younger children are at greater risk than older children: children under age 3 had a rate of 14 instances of maltreatment per 1,000 children in 1998, and almost 80 percent of the fatalities resulting from abuse and neglect that year were under age 5. Children who have recurrent illnesses, who are handicapped, or who are stepchildren also have elevated risk for becoming victims of maltreatment (Daly & Wilson, 1996; Sherrod, O'Connoer, Vietze, & Altemeier, 1984).

What factors lead to child maltreatment? Research has shown that often a number of factors in combination lead to physical abuse and neglect. Among those specifically identified in the literature are family stresses such as poverty and conflict, poor education, and social isolation (Coulton, Korbin, Su, & Chow, 1995; Goodman, Emery, & Haugaard, 1998; Trickett, Aber, Carlson, & Cicchetti, 1991; Zigler & Hall, 1989). Abusive parents typically have unrealistic expectations for their children and poor behavioral management skills. They tend to interpret their children's actions as willful disobedience, and they use physical force to control the child. Child abuse is one social problem that is found across education and income levels. Although much attention has been given to the idea of intergenerational transmission of maltreatment, only about 30 percent of individuals who suffered maltreatment become abusers themselves (Cicchetti & Toth, 1998).

Child abuse is associated with poverty, poor education, and social isolation.

The most severe consequences of child maltreatment are, of course, physical damage or death of the child, and more than 1,000 children died of abuse and neglect in 1998 (U.S. Department of Health and Human Services, 2000). There are also serious emotional, cognitive, and social consequences for child victims (Cicchetti & Toth, 1998). Many children who are mistreated show affective scars, including sadness, fear, anger, and depression. In addition, these children may experience difficult social relations with peers as a result of their more aggressive and less cooperative behavior or their failure to initiate social contact. Such effects can spill over into a child's school functioning, leading to poorer achievement and standardized test scores and repetition of grades. Child victims of sexual abuse may exhibit anxious, depressed, and withdrawn affect or occasional aggressive tendencies.

Helping Abused Children

Educators can contribute to both the identification and support of victims of child maltreatment and to prevention efforts. Both federal and state laws require reports of suspected child maltreatment by various professionals, including teachers. Consequently, teachers need to familiarize themselves with the warning signs of abuse and neglect. Some general indicators of child abuse and neglect are as follows:

- *Physical indicators:* Skin or bone injuries. These injuries may be concealed by clothing, as most adults recognize that abuse needs to be concealed. When there are numerous bruises at various stages of healing, abuse may be present. Injuries to the abdomen can cause swelling, tenderness, and vomiting. Head injuries result in dizziness, blackouts, retinal detachment, and, in severe cases, death.
- *Behavioral indicators:* Children who are being abused may change their behavior, becoming more aggressive, destructive, withdrawn, or uncommunicative. They may want to stay at school to avoid returning home. Children who are being abused will sometimes try to abuse other children. Fears, nightmares, and excessive concerns about cleanliness may also be symptoms of child abuse.
- *Academic performance:* Child abuse and neglect is generally associated with a sudden decline in academic performance or interest in learning. Maltreated children have a higher likelihood of failing or repeating a grade. Children who are hungry or who need glasses to read cannot learn, and these signs of neglect will be reflected in their school achievement.

Of course, a sudden change in behavior, affect, or academic performance does not prove that child abuse or neglect exists. However, it is important to monitor warning signs and to report this information to a school administrator, nurse, or counselor.

Because of the covert nature of child maltreatment, identification of victims can be difficult. It is no secret, however, that many children die from abuse or neglect because *no one would help or get involved.* As educators, it is important to understand your ethical and legal responsibility in reporting child abuse and neglect. For a concerned citizen, it is important to advocate for community-based services for families including parenting classes, medical care, adequate housing, job training, and quality day care programs. Additionally, educators can help stop the use of corporal punishment in our schools. If teachers and principals can use physical force to punish a child, then parents are likely to believe it is acceptable for them to do so as well to their children.

Precocious interest in sexual topics and seductive types of behavior have also been noted in these children (Kendall-Tackett, Williams, & Finkelhor, 1993).

Adults who work with children have a legal and ethical responsibility to report suspected child abuse. The Focus on Teaching box suggests ways educators can identify and support victims of child abuse.

Family Transitions: Divorce and Remarriage

Children tend to benefit from regularity, consistency, and continuity in family life. Regardless of their age, any change in family life can be both disruptive and upsetting to children and adolescents. In this section, we will consider the impact of two family transitions on children's development: the effects of divorce and remarriage. In both cases, the effects of family change are transmitted through changes in the parent-child relationship. Factors outside the family, such as social support and economic resources, can modify the impact of family transitions. Also, the child's own characteristics (age and gender) can play a role in this process. It is important to recognize that some children may experience multiple family transitions over the course of childhood and adolescence (e.g., a divorce may be followed by a remarriage). The effects of multiple transitions may be more enduring than those associated with a single transition (Amoto & Booth, 1991).

Divorce

Approximately half of all first marriages in the United States today end in divorce, and over 1 million children are involved in divorces each year.

Approximately half of all first marriages in the United States today end in divorce, and more than 1 million children are involved in divorces each year (Kirn, 2000). Regardless of their age, divorce is difficult for both children and adults. In the years immediately after a divorce, children become more defiant, more negative, more aggressive, depressed, or angry. If they are of school age, their school performance typically drops for at least a short time (Furstenberg & Cherlin, 1991; Hetherington, 1989; Hetherington & Clingempeel, 1992). Some children show long-term behavior problems, depression, poor school performance, acting out, low self-esteem, and later difficulties with intimate heterosexual relationships, but there is disagreement about these lasting negative effects (Hetherington, 1999; Kirn, 2000; Wallerstein, Lewis, & Blakeslee, 2000).

Numerous factors have been identified as being potentially influential in the ability of children to adaptively negotiate the life transitions associated with divorce. These include (1) the child's age and gender; (2) the level of conflict between parents; (3) the custodial arrangement; (4) the income level of the custodial parent; and (5) the quality of parenting provided. Let's look at a few of these effects.

Not surprisingly, the child's age is an important factor. Children who are young at the time of their parents' divorce may experience substantial anxiety and exhibit strong emotional reactions, but their cognitive immaturity may benefit them over time. When interviewed 10 years after the divorce of their parents, adolescents in one study hardly recalled their own earlier fears or the conflict between their parents (Wallerstein, Corbin, & Lewis, 1988).

Children are at higher risk for adjustment problems when parents remain embittered and hostile for a long time after the divorce.

Along with age, a child's gender can also influence the effects of divorce. During the school years, the negative effects of divorce appear to be stronger for boys than for girls (Hetherington, 1989, 1991). In adolescence, however, there are signs that girls are more disrupted by a divorce than are boys. For example, early-maturing girls from divorced families, compared with their male counterparts, experience more conflict with their mothers and more difficulties in heterosexual relationships (Hetherington, 1989, 1991).

Another factor that influences children's adjustment to divorce is conflict between parents (Amato, 1993). The emotionally charged nature of separations and divorces may overwhelm the child. Children fare better in divorced families with low conflict between the separated parents (Bishop & Ingersoll, 1989; Hetherington, 1999). Children are at higher risk for adjustment problems when the parents remain embittered and hostile for a long time after the divorce (Hetherington, 1999).

There is a long-standing trend in the United States for the custody of minor children to be awarded to mothers. In the last couple of decades, more fathers have asked for and been given custody, and a growing number of divorcing parents arrange for joint custody and/or shared living arrangements in which children spend part of each week or month with each parent. Whereas some studies have found support for a custody arrangement in which children are placed with the same-sex parent (Furstenberg, 1988; Santrock & Warshak, 1986), others have found no relative benefits of same-sex parental custody over opposite-sex parental custody (Downey & Powell, 1993).

Of course the most important consideration is that children will want, and benefit from, continuing contact with their noncustodial parent. Children experience successful relationships and visitation with noncustodial parents when visitation patterns are established early, are routine, and are governed by genuine efforts to "parent," as opposed to entertain the child (Thompson & Laible, 1999).

The psychological and economic well-being of the custodial parent often ranks as powerful predictors of children's postdivorce adjustment. Income plays a crucial role in the adjustment of parents and children who have experienced divorce. Fathers typically do not experience the dramatic decrease in income that mothers do following divorce (Santrock & Warshak, 1986). Approximately 60 percent of custodial mothers are awarded some level of child support. Of those, about 42 percent receive the full payment and 27 percent receive partial payment (U.S. Bureau of the Census, 2000), but the amounts received are typically insufficient for raising children (Teachman & Paasch, 1994).

> *Economic resources and social support are often crucial for the adjustment of parents and children who have experienced divorce.*

The quality of parenting typically declines in the year following divorce as parents become preoccupied with their own needs and transition issues, dealing with the depression and confusion often associated with divorce. These preoccupations inhibit the parents' ability to respond sensitively to their children. As a result, their parenting style changes, becoming almost neglectful as they fail to adequately monitor their children's behavior or set explicit rules or limits (Hetherington, 1989). This pattern may persist for several years, even after remarriage, but often, beginning in the second year after the divorce, parents grow more effective in their child-rearing practices (Hetherington & Clingempeel, 1992; Hetherington, Cox, & Cox, 1982; Hetherington, Stanley-Hagan, & Anderson, 1989).

Remarriage and Stepfamilies

Most children live in a single-parent household for approximately five years following a divorce. More than two-thirds of divorced parents will eventually remarry (Glick, 1989). A small minority of stepfamilies involve partners who both bring children from a previous marriage to form what is called a **blended family.** This family configuration includes a biological parent, a stepparent, and children. Figure 9.8 shows a child's portrait of her blended family. As you can see, Heather views herself as belonging to two blended families.

> *More than two-thirds of divorced parents will eventually remarry, and remarriage often provides additional resources for promoting healthy development of children.*

Remarriage often provides additional resources for promoting healthy development. There are likely to be economic benefits, especially for women who remarry, as well as added emotional and child-rearing support (Zill, 1994; Zill, Morrison, & Coiro, 1993). The new spouse who becomes involved with his or her stepchildren can share the tasks of care and supervision and may provide an additional positive adult role model in the home.

However, the addition of a new stepparent to the family can cause disruption and stress, requiring further adjustment for both adults and children who may still be attempting to deal with issues raised by divorce. Some mothers, for example, exhibit heightened conflict, disengagement, low monitoring and control, and poor communication with their children during the early months of a remarriage transition (Hetherington & Clingempeel, 1992; Hetherington & Stanley-Hagan, 1999).

FIGURE 9.8

Heather (Age 9) and Her Blended Families

When compared with children in first marriages, children in stepfamilies appear to experience more adjustment problems.

Another issue facing individuals in stepfamilies is unrealistic expectations. A great deal of uncertainty often exists in stepfamilies concerning who is part of the family and what the rights and responsibilities of various members are. Attempts to force a stepfamily to fit the model of a traditional biological family can cause problems to worsen and lead to new ones (Bray & Burger, 1993). Successful adjustment seems to result when families recognize that building a family takes time and that stepparents cannot replace biological parents but must develop an alternative, perhaps nontraditional, parenting role.

Research on children in stepfamilies has followed behind research on divorced families. Children of all ages show behavior problems following remarriage of their parents. When compared to children in first marriages, children in stepfamilies appear to be less well adjusted; they exhibit more behavioral and emotional problems, poorer academic achievement, lower social competence, and less social responsibility (Hetherington & Clingempeel, 1992; Hetherington & Jodl, 1994).

As with the discussion of the effects of divorce, the child's age and sex must be taken into account in discussions of what outcomes are probable. Whereas younger children are likely to eventually form an attachment to and accept a stepparent, adolescents experience more of the difficulties previously listed. In one study, children who were 9 years or older when their mother remarried displayed more problems than those whose mothers remarried when they were younger (Hetherington, 1993).

Both boys and girls show signs of emotional stress and behavioral disruption following the remarriage of their custodial parent. Over time, however, the presence of a stepfather seems to improve well-being in boys. In contrast, girls remain less warm and responsive toward stepfathers (Amato & Keith, 1991; Hetherington & Clingempeel, 1992).

Whereas a close relationship between parents in nondivorced families is related to positive child outcomes, the closer the parents' own relationship in remarried families, the more problems the children display (Hetherington, 1989). In cases in which the mother and children lived alone for some years and developed a very close relationship, the new closeness of the mother and stepfather may lead to resentment and resistance on the part of the children, setting them up for other problematic behaviors (Hetherington & Jodl, 1994).

Children's relationships with their biological parents are more positive than with their stepparents, regardless of whether a stepmother or stepfather family is involved. Even so, stepmothers are usually more involved and more active in child rearing than are stepfathers, who may remain distant and disengaged, showing little involvement or rapport with their stepchildren (Fine, Voydanoff, & Donnelly, 1993). With increasing complexity in the stepfamily structure comes increasing difficulties in the child's adjustment. The highest level of behavioral problems is typically seen in blended families in which both parents bring children from a previous marriage.

Some researchers have moved beyond simple comparisons based on family structure to examine the influence of parenting behaviors in blended families. For example, stepparents, especially stepfathers, show more punitive and critical parenting and less nurturant and responsive parenting. Such parenting patterns have been related to the lower school grades and higher rates of delinquency shown by children in these families when compared to children in two-natural-parent families (Dornbusch et al., 1987; Hetherington & Clingempeel, 1992).

Helping Children Cope with Family Change

As we have noted in previous sections, children thrive best under conditions in which their needs are met with regularity and consistency. However, changes in family structure and status do occur over the course of development for many children, and research on how children cope with such changes can provide useful information to educators.

Depending on whether children move as a result of a divorce or the remarriage of parents, the school may be one of the few places of continuity for them. As such, the school and school personnel can serve as supports for both the child and parents during these transitions. Providing a stable, predictable school environment may help parents and children cope while changes are occurring elsewhere. The Focus on Teaching box (p. 510) discusses how educators can help children cope with family transitions.

The school may be one of the few places of continuity for children who are experiencing family transitions.

Maternal Employment and Child Care

Since the 1960s, there has been a steady increase in the number of women entering the workforce. Throughout the following 30 years, the number of women in the labor force with children under the age of 18 more than doubled. Due to increases in the number of women working outside the home, more and more children under the age of 6 spend part of their day being cared for by someone other than their parents. Approximately 13 million children receive some form of early child care, whereas millions more school-age children attend after-school and summer programs while their parents work. In this section we consider the effects of maternal employment and child care on children's development.

Maternal Employment and Children's Development

Over the past two decades, having a working mother has become more the norm rather than the exception. Between 1980 and 1998, the percentage of children living in families in which both parents worked full time increased from 17 percent to 31 percent (U.S. Department of Health and Human Services, 2000). In addition, the number of children living with single mothers who are employed increased by one-third from 1993 to 1998. It has been argued that the employment of a mother outside the home is something of an economic necessity for single-mother and minority households due to the more dire economic circumstances faced by these groups (McLoyd, 1993). Despite these trends, compared with fathers, mothers engage in more work restructuring to allow for family commitments, are more likely to follow less consistent patterns of work with more workforce entries and

Focus on Teaching

Helping Young People Cope with Family Change

The school often plays a key role in determining how children cope with family transitions. Children spend much of their time in school, where the continuity of care can offer a stable and safe environment. Research evidence suggests that children who experience a caring and supportive school environment experience fewer adjustment problems than children who experience authoritarian, permissive, or neglectful environments (Hetherington, 1993).

Despite the high rates of divorce in the United States, there is still some stigma associated with divorce. It is not uncommon to hear adults refer to a divorced family as a "broken home." Additionally, many children's stories do not portray stepfamilies, especially stepmothers, in a favorable light. These misconceptions and stereotypes can add to children's adjustment problems. Therefore, it is important for educators not to view divorce and remarriage as having negative consequences for all children. As we have learned, many factors determine how children cope with a family transition.

As young people experience a divorce or remarriage, change in behavior is expected. Younger children may draw attention to themselves by acting out or becoming withdrawn. Older children may show more serious signs of distress, in some cases reaching the level of depression. For all children in these circumstances, lack of concentration, preoccupation, and disruption of normal schedules are likely to occur at some point.

During a family transition, students will need extra support, attention, and care at school. The following practices are effective for helping children of divorce, but are useful for other family changes as well (Freeman & Couchman, 1985; Frieman, 1993, 1997):

exits, and are more likely to work fewer hours (Karambayya & Reilly, 1992). There are also inequities in terms of household responsibilities in dual-earner families: while some fathers do increase their overall level of involvement in child care and household chores, mothers retain responsibility for the larger portion even when they work as much as their husbands (Pleck, 1997). And one recent study found that in "high-power" dual-career families, it is more often the wives who utilize scaling-back strategies to buffer the family from work intrusions (Becker & Moen, 1999). Such strategies include placing limits on work commitments, deciding to have a one-career family, and trading off responsibilities.

Early studies of the effects of maternal employment on children began just as women were moving into the workforce in greater numbers and were often predicated on the expectation that there would be some detriment to children who did not have a full-time caregiver at home. But in a number of those early studies researchers discovered that the independence fostered in children who had working mothers could be beneficial and lead to higher achievement motivation, higher competence, and higher educational and occupational goals (Hoffman, 1989; Hock, 1978; Woods, 1972). Also, children of working mothers tend to have less sex-stereotyped views of gender roles. In general, much of the continuing research in this area has found similarities between children of full-time homemaker mothers and mothers employed outside the home on a range of cognitive and behavioral measures (Gottfried, Bathurst, & Gottfried, 1994; Lerner & Abrams, 1994; Richards & Duckett, 1994).

- Provide opportunities for students to discuss and express their feelings.

- Maintain consistent expectations and routines.

- Encourage supportive communication.

- Use curriculum materials that present positive images of different family configurations.

- Inform parents about their children's progress or difficulties.

- Encourage parents to be honest, direct, and supportive with their children.

It is also important to consult school policies regarding contact with custodial and noncustodial parents. Most schools will have policies concerning the release of children from school, parental access to records and school functions, communication responsibilities, and so forth.

Finally, it is important to inform school counselors and other support personnel when children are experiencing considerable difficulty adjusting to family changes. There are a number of individual and group counseling approaches that can help students understand their feelings, feel good about themselves and their parents, and develop new coping skills.

Evidence for some potential difficulties has been found. Children for whom maternal employment was associated with decreased monitoring of their activities are more likely to show poor school performance and to experience behavior problems (Crouter, MacDermid, McHale, & Perry-Jenkins, 1990). This illustrates a point we have made before that understanding what influences children's development requires attention to more than whether children fall into a particular status—for example, whether their mother works outside the home or not. Instead, the context in which the family faces a particular experience and the effect of that experience on more proximal processes within the family must be explored. In this case, the mother's work status influences her ability to maintain supervision of her children, and if no other supports are present in the family or community—a grandparent or trusted neighbor, for example—to assist her in monitoring them, then adverse consequences may result.

Another example of this need to consider process and context involves the mother's attitudes about and satisfaction with her work. When a mother feels forced into employment for economic reasons and does not derive any satisfaction from the job she is doing, that will likely affect her overall mood and thereby her interactions with her children (Lerner & Galambos, 1988; Greenberger & Goldberg, 1989). Feelings of guilt, depression, or resentment could then interfere with her parenting and thereby hinder her children's adaptive development.

The independence fostered in children who had working mothers could be beneficial and lead to higher achievement motivation, higher competence, and higher educational and occupational goals.

511

Early Child Care and Children's Development

A variety of arrangements are used to care for children under the age of 6 when their parents are working. Approximately 25 percent of America's infants and preschoolers are cared for by a relative, whereas one-third attend a day care center. Figure 9.9 shows the various child care arrangements. The patterns are similar across different ethnic groups (Singer, Fuller, Keiley, & Wolf, 1998).

Approximately 25 percent of America's infants and preschoolers are cared for by a relative, whereas one-third attend a day care center.

The study of day care on children's development has a long history. However, until recently, information was rather equivocal. In 1991, the National Institute of Child Health and Human Development (NICHD) funded a comprehensive study of early child care. The study includes 1,364 mothers and newborns in 12 U.S. cities, and it examines a wide range of developmental outcomes, including attachment relations, problem behavior, emotional regulation, cognitive skills, and so on. The results thus far reveal few straightforward effects related to child care. Children in child care are just as likely to form secure attachments as children with maternal care (NICHD Early Child Care Network, 1997). Additionally, child care was not related to problem behavior such as aggression or poor self-control, regardless of the age of entry into child care (NICHD Early Child Care Network, 1998). Moreover, recent evidence reveals no significant effects of child care on children's cognitive and language development (NICHD Early Child Care Network, 2000). In fact, there was a slight advantage for children in child care centers, perhaps due to the increased exposure to developmentally stimulating materials and opportunities to interact with same-aged peers.

Recent research shows few effects of day care on children's cognitive, language, emotional, and social development, when children receive high-quality care.

One of the most important findings of this research is that the quality of child care programs matters. Results are less favorable in lower-quality programs. What defines high-quality child care? There are a number of factors, as follows:

- Low ratio of children to caregivers
- Well-trained and experienced staff
- Ample opportunities for educational, language, and social stimulation
- Low staff turnover
- Effective communication between parents and caregivers (Bredekamp & Copple, 1997)

The definition of low adult-to-child ratios varies by age. The National Association for the Education of Young Children (NAEYC) recommends an adult-to-child ratio of 1 to 3 for

FIGURE 9.9

Who's Minding the Children?

SOURCE: U.S. Department of Commerce (1997).

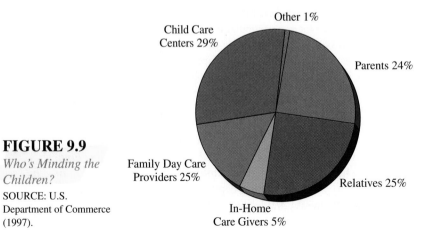

Other 1%
Child Care Centers 29%
Parents 24%
Family Day Care Providers 25%
Relatives 25%
In-Home Care Givers 5%

infants; 1 to 5 for children aged 1 to 2 years; 1 to 6 for children aged 2 to 3 years; and a ratio of no more than 1 to 10 for older children. Additionally, small group sizes are also important. Large groups of children with many adults is not as optimal as small groups with the same adult-to-child ratios. As with parent-child relationships, a key component of high-quality child care is warm, attentive, and responsive relationships. Unfortunately, high-quality child care is beyond the reach of many families due to its high cost and limited availability (Children's Defense Fund, 2000).

After-School Care and Children's Development

For many families, the problem of day care is resolved to some degree when children enter school. With older children, the concern is focused on the hours after school. Most schools dismiss students around 3 P.M., whereas most working parents are not able to leave work much before 5 P.M. This gap between parents' work schedules and children's school schedules can add up to 20 to 25 hours per week.

What happens to children when they leave school? Figure 9.10 shows the type of care students receive before and after school. Referred to as "latchkey children," approximately 12 percent of all children, ages 5 to 12, go home to an empty house. Children left unsupervised after school often spend their time watching television. Of even greater concern is the issue of safety. When left unsupervised, young people are more likely to engage in delinquent activities or to experiment with tobacco, alcohol, or drugs (Galambos & Maggs, 1991; Schwartz, 1999). Nearly half of all juvenile crime is committed between the hours of 2 P.M. and 8 P.M. Moreover, the U.S. Department of Justice reports that children are at greater risk for being victims of violent crime in the hours after school. Although these statistics are alarming, they do not apply to all children. Studies show that older children and adolescents can manage well on their own if they are mature, if the neighborhood is safe, and if there are guidelines for emergencies, and so on (Lamb, 1998). Children and adolescents who generally spend their unsupervised time away from the home tend to be at greater risk for problem behaviors.

As with parent-child relationships, a key component of high-quality child care is warm, attentive, and responsive relationships.

Approximately 12 percent of all children, ages 5 to 12, go home to an empty house.

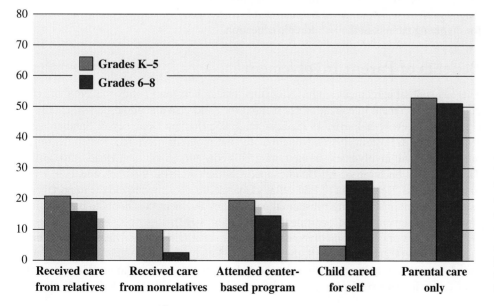

FIGURE 9.10

Before- and After-School Arrangements for Children in Grades K–8

SOURCE: National Center for Educational Statistics (2000).

After-school programs can provide children with safe, supervised care. The options for after-school care may include 4-H Clubs, Boys and Girls Clubs, the YMCA, Big Brothers/Big Sisters, and church programs, to name a few. Public facilities such as libraries and community centers may provide after-school care in some communities. There is also a growing number of school-based programs. It is estimated that 20,000 public schools now offer after-school or extended-day programs. Many of these programs provide not only recreational or curricular activities, but also tutoring and enrichment programs, such as homework assistance, science clubs, or computer classes.

After-school programs have resulted in improved school attendance, improved school achievement, and reduced high-risk behavior.

At issue is how much "schooling" should take place after school. Some experts argue that school-based programs that focus on academics neglect other areas of youth development. As we have discussed, young people need opportunities to participate in physical activities, to develop positive relations with adults, to engage in creative activities, and so on. If youths perceive after-school care as extended classroom time, they may lose interest in these programs.

Though evaluations of after-school programs are limited, the findings for some programs are encouraging (Fashola, 1998; Dryfoos, 1999; Posner & Vandell, 1999). For example, some school-based programs have resulted in improved school attendance, improved school achievement, and reduced high-risk behavior (Dryfoos, 1999). The effects are particularly positive for low-income children (Posner & Vandell, 1994).

Family Involvement in Children's Education

Teachers today are well aware that they need to form partnerships with parents and families if they want to best meet the needs of their students.

Talk to any schoolteacher or administrator, and they will comment on how difficult it is to get all parents involved in their children's education. Clearly, some parents are more involved than others, and some schools have better parental involvement than others. As we know, parents are children's first teachers. Parents have a significant impact on their children's development from birth, and this influence continues well beyond the adolescent years. Teachers today are well aware that they need to form partnerships with parents and families if they want to best meet the needs of their students. In this section, we explore (1) the benefits of parental involvement, (2) the family, school, and community characteristics that contribute to high levels of parental involvement; and (3) the most promising methods for involving parents in their children's education.

Benefits of Parent Involvement

There is general agreement among educators, researchers, and policy makers that active parental involvement in education is essential for children's and adolescents' school success (Carer, Lewis, & Farris, 1998; Epstein, 1995; Hoovey-Dempsey & Sandler, 1995, 1996; Sander & Epstein, 1998). Numerous federal programs have recognized the importance of parental involvement in their children's education, including Head Start, Follow Through, the Education of All Handicapped Children Act (PL-94-142), and Title 1 programs. The U.S. Department of Education's Goals 2000 also emphasized the importance of establishing and maintaining substantial parental involvement in schools to promote high student achievement (U.S. Department of Education, 1992).

The benefits of parental involvement in education are fairly clear. There are benefits for parents, teachers, and, most of all, the students. When parents become involved at school, they learn ways to help and to support their children's learning at home. They also gain confidence in their own parenting abilities and in their abilities to help their children succeed in school. By becoming involved in their children's schooling, parents also reinforce the importance and value of education (Hoover-Dempsey & Sandler, 1995).

Through increased contact with parents, teachers can increase their understanding of their students' cultural backgrounds, needs, and strengths. They can also acquire a better understanding of the stresses their students encounter in their daily lives that affect their performance in school. Addition-

SOURCE: Daemmrich/ Stock Boston.

Parental involvement in school activities has important benefits for their children's learning and school adjustment.

ally, increased contact with parents can help teachers understand the goals they have for their children. One of the most consistent findings in research on parent-school relations is that "teachers have very different views of parents than parents have of themselves" (Epstein, 1996, p. 216). This knowledge base is likely to lead (1) to an increased sense of efficacy for teachers in helping parents support their children's learning, and (2) to the use of effective instructional strategies in the classroom (Haynes & Ben-Avie, 1996; Epstein, 1988).

Not surprisingly, parental involvement at school has important benefits for children's and adolescents' learning. Early research suggested that parental involvement had positive effects on homework completion, student achievement, school attendance and adjustment, academic motivation, attitudes toward school, and educational aspirations, even after the effects of student ability and family economic resources are taken into account (Becher, 1984; Christenson, Rounds, & Gorney, 1992; Graue, Weinstein, & Walberg, 1983). Also, students who drop out of school report that their parents rarely attended school events or helped them with their homework (Rumberger, Ghatak, Poulos, Ritter, & Dornbusch, 1990).

The effects of parent involvement on students' educational outcomes are not always straightforward. Joyce Epstein (1996), a leading expert on home-school partnerships, points out that the effects may depend on the type and quality of parental involvement. If parent-teacher contact mainly focuses on academic or behavioral problems, it can lead parents to form negative expectations for their children as well as to participate less in school activities and events. Similarly, poorly designed parental involvement practices can lead to negatives outcomes for students and for schools (Epstein, 1996; Scotts-Jones, 1987).

When parents become involved at school, they learn ways to support their children's learning at home and gain confidence in their own parenting abilities.

Why Do Parents Become Involved?

Although most schools sponsor various programs and events for their children's parents, these events are not very well attended by parents. The results of a 1996 national survey of various programs for parents at public elementary schools (kindergarten to eighth grade) are shown in Figure 9.11. The programs included open houses or back-to-school nights; sports events or field days; arts events (plays, dance, or musical performances), science fairs, or other academic events; and parent-teacher conferences. The results of this survey indicated that a majority of public elementary schools (84 percent to 97 percent) hold various programs for parents, but less than half of the schools surveyed reported that these events were well attended by "most or all parents" (U.S. Department of Education, 1996).

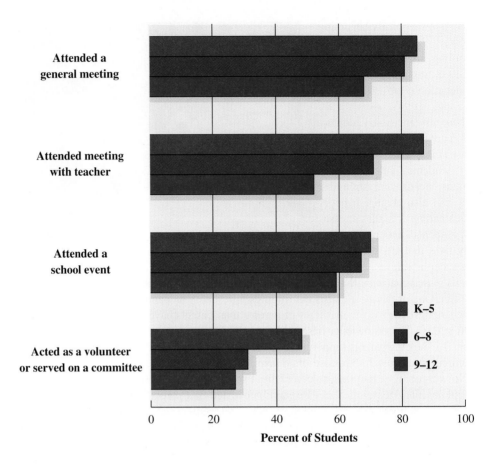

FIGURE 9.11

Percent of Students Whose Parents Attend a School Activity

SOURCE: National Center for Educational Statistics (2000).

In general, as Figure 9.11 shows, parents were most likely to attend conferences with their child's teachers than any other type of school event.

Parental involvement in their children's school is influenced by a number of factors, including their belief systems, economic resources, social networks, and history with schools. It is also influenced by various teacher, school, and community characteristics, but questions concerning parental involvement are typically phrased in terms of "Why are parents not more involved in their children's education?" (Eccles & Harold, 1996). We will look at parental characteristics first, then consider school influences on parental involvement.

Parental involvement in their children's school is influenced by a number of factors, including their belief systems, economic resources, social networks, and history with schools.

Parental and Familial Characteristics

Studies have shown that parental involvement is related to the parents' educational level, economic status, and family size (Dauber & Epstein, 1989). In general, parents with limited income and education are less likely to report high levels of involvement in school activities. As Figure 9.12 suggests, parent involvement also varies by family structure (e.g., one- versus two-parent families). Parental involvement in school activities also varies by the age of the children. Approximately 70 percent of children in grades 3 to 5 have children who attend three or more school activities (PTA meetings, parent-teacher conferences, school events, etc.) during the academic year. This figure declines to 53 percent for students in grades 6 to 8 and to 39 percent for students in grades 9 to 12. See Figure 9.11 for national figures for parental involvement rates by grade levels.

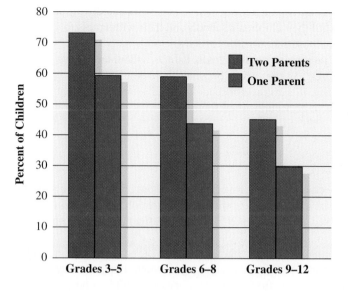

FIGURE 9.12

Percent of Children Whose Parents Attend Three or More School Activities Each Year: 1999

SOURCE: U.S. Department of Health and Human Services (2000).

Often ethnic minority families are less involved in their children's education. Many factors contribute to their low levels of parental involvement, including their own negative experiences as students (Ritter, Mont-Reynard, & Dornbusch, 1993). Because of cultural differences, many of these parents may not understand teacher expectations for getting involved in their children's education. Language barriers can compound these problems as well.

However, these family status variables alone do not fully explain parental decisions about involvement in their children's education (Hoover-Dempsey & Sandler, 1997). Many parents are able to nurture their children's school achievement even when faced with discouraging or difficult home situations. It is important, therefore, to go beyond family characteristics. Interestingly, research suggests that parental beliefs and attitudes play an important role in determining involvement in their children's schooling (Eccles & Harold, 1996; Hoover-Dempsey & Sandler, 1997). Examples include the following:

- **Efficacy beliefs.** It is important for parents to have confidence in their abilities to help their children with schoolwork. Parents become less sure of their abilities to help children with schoolwork as the children move up in grades or take more specialized classes.
- **Parents' perceptions of their children's abilities.** Parents' confidence in their children's ability to succeed in school, as well as their perceptions of the educational/occupational opportunities available to their children, can influence parental involvement in schooling.
- **Parents' perceptions of their role in their children's education.** It is important for parents to believe that they can play an active role in their children's education, and that their involvement can make a difference in their children's school achievement.
- **Parents' attitudes toward school.** It is important for parents to believe that the school wants them to be involved in their children's education, and that school personnel want to help, not blame, parents when their children have difficulties at school. It is important to recognize that many parents from minority and poor populations did not have positive experiences in school

themselves. Parents' early experiences with schools undoubtedly influence their attitudes toward their children's schools and their willingness to participate again in those schools.

- **Compatibility of parent and school goals.** Parents undoubtedly have goals for their own children. As our society becomes more ethnically and linguistically diverse, it is critical for schools to understand that parents want their children to have an accurate representation of their culture of origin and its history.

School and Teacher Characteristics

Along with parent and family characteristics, aspects of the school environment also influence the level of parents' involvement in their children's education. In fact, many of the parent characteristics discussed previously are likely to be affected by their children's school environment.

As discussed, there is a strong relationship between the age of the child and the level of parental involvement. There is generally more parent involvement in elementary schools because the school is located close to the children's home, and children have only one teacher. The organization of middle and high schools, on the other hand, are more complex, and teachers are responsible for larger groups of students. Keeping parents informed of each student's interests and progress can become an overwhelming task. Many secondary teachers report insufficient time to implement effective parent involvement strategies, as explained in this interview:

> Every teacher is basically responsible for notifying absent students' parents everyday, but it doesn't happen because we are supposed to do this in addition to making sure the halls are cleared, in addition to the lesson plans, in addition to other responsibilities. For example, I am a second year teacher…, a new dad…, and I coach varsity sports. I find it exceedingly difficult to make the time to call…[I] want to, but between lesson plans, and making out final exams, it's hard. (Sanders & Epstein, 1998, p. 29)

There are many reasons for creating school and family partnerships, but the most important reason is to help young people succeed in school and in later life.

Teachers' attitudes toward parent involvement seem to vary by grade level as well. Compared to teachers of younger students, high school teachers are less likely to encourage parent involvement. In fact, some evidence suggests that they actively discourage parent involvement unless there is a problem (Dornbusch & Ritter; Eccles & Harold, 1996; Epstein & Dauber, 1991; Hoover-Dempsey, Basslet, & Bussie, 1987). Yet research suggests that parent involvement is just as important for older students as for younger students. Parent involvement activities can positively influence students' academic achievement (Clark, 1983; Ginsburg & Hanson, 1986), homework completion (Keith, Reimer, Fehrman, Pottebaum, & Ausberg, 1986), and high school graduation rates (Delgado-Gaitan, 1988; Conklin & Dailey, 1981).

Encouraging Parental Involvement in Education

How can educators foster high levels of parental involvement? Traditionally, we think of parent involvement in school as attending PTA meetings, school events, and parent-teacher conferences. However, strategies for involving parents in their children's education can take many different forms. Parents can support their children's learning at home and volunteer in their child's classroom. Technology can be used to link parents and children to a network for help with homework. Remember Mr. Chavez? He was implementing some parent involvement strategies in his classroom (videos of class projects, homework hot line), but his school as a whole was also establishing a family resource center to provide adult education classes. Some schools also have a home-school coordinator to develop outreach programs for families and children.

Joyce Epstein has developed a framework for developing effective partnerships (Epstein, 1992). This framework and sample practices are presented in the Focus on Teaching box. Epstein believes that there are many reasons for creating school and family partnerships, but the most important reason is to help young people succeed in school and in later life. In implementing parent involvement practices, it is important to remember the following (Moles, 1996):

- Parents are the first and foremost teachers of their children.
- Families have vast opportunities to influence children by instruction and by example.
- All parents want their children to do well in school and have good futures.
- Parents want to work with schools to aid their children's education (pp. 249–250).

Fostering Resiliency in Children and Adolescents

Schools play an important role in fostering resiliency in young people. As discussed in earlier chapters, resiliency is commonly defined as a person's ability to develop competence in the face of adversity and hardship (Masten & Coatsworth, 1998). We have learned that families can promote children's positive development when they provide close affectionate relationships, models of appropriate behavior, and support and supervision. However, we have also learned that family circumstances can sometimes threaten children's well-being and healthy development. For these children, schools can help promote resilient actions. A favorite teacher or a coach can become an important role model for children experiencing difficulty at home or needing extra attention. The resiliency-building capacity of schools is a relatively new area of research (Henderson & Milstein, 1996). In this last section, we will examine how schools can foster resiliency in youth, regardless of family circumstances.

Schools play an important role in fostering resiliency in young people.

Resilient youth have a number of defining characteristics (Henderson & Milstein, 1996; Werner & Smith, 1992; Marsten & Coatworth, 1998). The ones most commonly mentioned across research studies include:

- **Social competence.** Resilient children have easygoing dispositions, and they easily adapt to different situations. They are socially skilled and able to attract the attention, support, and affection they need from peers, parents, and other adults.
- **Cognitive competence.** Resilient children have good problem-solving and intellectual abilities. They take initiative, set realistic goals, and monitor their progress. They are also resourceful in seeking help from others and in avoiding risky or harmful circumstances.
- **High self-esteem.** Resilient children are confident in their abilities to succeed. They have a sense of purpose and foresee a positive future for themselves.

It is also important to emphasize that resiliency is not just a list of individual child traits and characteristics—it is process (Henderson & Milstein, 1996). Resiliency is learned in families, schools, and communities.

Focus on Teaching

Five Types of Parent Involvement

On the basis of years of research across the country, Joyce Epstein has developed a framework for helping schools design effective school and family partnership programs. Some strategies (such as communicating, volunteering) can be implemented by individual teachers, whereas others involve the school as a whole.

Type 1: Parenting
Help all families establish home environments that support learning.

- Make home visits at transition points to elementary, middle, and secondary school.

- Hold educational programs for parents on parenting and child-rearing skills.

- Establish family support programs to help parents with health, nutrition, and other services.

Type 2: Communicating
Design effective forms of communication to reach parents.

- Hold parent-teacher conferences with each parent at least once a year.

- Use language translators for language minority families

- Send weekly or monthly folders home for review.

- Make regular phone calls, write newsletters, and use other communications.

Type 3: Volunteering
Recruit and organize help and support.

How can schools foster resiliency? Any effort that increases young people's social skills, cognitive abilities, and self-esteem helps to foster resiliency. Research has identified a number of school characteristics that can foster resiliency and positive development (Bernard, 1991; Comer, 1984; Henderson & Milstein, 1996; Rutter, Maughan, Mortimore, Ouston, & Smith, 1979):

- **Encourage strong commitment and connections to school.** Numerous studies show that a positive connection to the school environment or to teachers functions as a protective factor in young people's lives. Youths who report

520

- Establish school and classroom volunteer programs to assist students, teachers, administrators, and parents.

- Maintain a parent room or family center for volunteer work, meetings, and resources for families.

- Take annual surveys of parents to identify talents and needs.

Type 4: Learning at Home
Provide ideas to parents about how they can help children with learning at home.

- Run programs to provide parents with information on the skills required in all subjects at each grade.

- Provide information on homework policies and how parents can monitor their children's homework at home.

- Create family literacy and math programs.

Type 5: Decision Making
Include parents in school decisions and recruit parent leaders.

- Establish active PTA/PTO or other parent organizations in the school, including advisory councils, and committees for curriculum, safety, and so on.

- Develop advocacy groups to work for school reform and improvements.

- Develop networks to link families to parent representatives.

SOURCE: Epstein (1997).

strong attachment to their schools are less likely to engage in problem behaviors and to drop out of school. When schools are safe, supportive, and caring communities, young people are more likely to form a connection to school.
- **Set and communicate high expectations.** Research on both successful schools and youth resiliency emphasizes the importance of setting high expectations for all students. Schools with high expectations for behavior and achievement have lower rates of delinquency, drug use, teen pregnancy, and other problem behaviors. Through relationships that convey high expectations, students learn to believe in themselves.

- **Provide meaningful learning opportunities.** Schools that foster young people's resiliency provide opportunities to engage in meaningful learning activities that are related to their interests, culture, and developmental levels. Young people need opportunities for problem solving, goal setting, critical inquiry, self-reflection, and helping others. Grouping practices need to be inclusive and to promote cooperation and shared responsibility for learning.
- **Opportunities for participation.** Young people need opportunities for meaningful involvement and participation within the school. They need opportunities for leadership, for helping others, and for determining policies that affect them. Participation in athletics, extracurricular activities, and school governance can foster a sense of belonging and connection for young people.

In summary, children grow up in many overlapping worlds: families, peers, schools, and communities. Each context has its own set of risk and protective factors. Schools have the power and resources to promote the development of competency and resiliency in youth.

Chapter Summary

www.mhhe.com/meece

Conceptions of the Family

- Families are the social unit with the primary responsibility for preparing (or socializing) the child to be a productive and competent member of society.
- Early theories (psychoanalytic and learning theories) of family socialization focused on the effects of parents on children's development. Parents were viewed as "all powerful" because they created and shaped the child's environment. This view of the family is limited.
- A family is a highly complex system of interactions and processes operating at multiple levels. Parents influence children as much as children influence them. Change in any member of the family system can influence other members of the system. The family is also embedded in larger social systems—neighborhoods, communities, and culture—that can affect interactions within the family. Bronfenbrenner's ecological theory of children's development is an example of a systems approach.

Variations in Family Structures

- The structure of families is changing. Whereas most children grow up in two-parent families, there is an increasing number of children being raised in single-parent families. The majority of these families are headed by single mothers who face a number of challenges and difficulties. Single fathers tend to face fewer economic hardships.
- Children from single-parent families tend to be less successful in school than children from two-parent families. Girls from single-parent families may show an

early onset of sexual activity. The presence of economic resources and other adults in the household can offset the negative consequences of a single-parent family.

- There are few differences between homosexual and heterosexual parents. Children of gay and lesbian parents exhibit good relations with peers and adults, and they resemble children of heterosexual parents on measures of social competence, self-concept, locus of control, and moral judgment.

Ethnic Diversity of Families

- African Americans currently represent the largest minority group in the United States. Child-rearing practices in African American families tend to emphasize assertiveness, independence, and self-confidence. There are more egalitarian gender roles, and African Americans derive support and resources from the extended family.

- The number of Hispanic American families is steadily growing. These families tend to be larger, but divorce rates are low. Child-rearing practices in Hispanic American families emphasize interdependence, family obligation, conformity, and cooperation.

- Asian American families also emphasize the importance of social harmony and interdependence. The child is taught patience, perseverance, restraint, and humility. Asian American children are expected to do well in school to bring honor to the family.

- The traditions of Native American families differ by tribal identity. Yet most families value harmony and connectedness. The entire Native American community plays a role in raising children. Children are expected show great respect for the past and for their elders.

Family Influence on Development

- The family environment can be characterized in terms of differences in warmth, responsiveness, and control. These dimensions form constellations of parenting behaviors, called parenting styles. There are four types of parenting styles: authoritarian (high control, low warmth/responsiveness); authoritative (high control; high warmth/responsiveness); permissive-indulgent (low control, high warmth/responsiveness), and permissive-indifferent (low control, low warmth/responsiveness).

- Authoritative parenting is associated with the most positive outcomes for children. Children of authoritative parents are self-reliant and socially responsible, and perform well in school. Children with authoritarian parents have lower self-esteem and lower achievement than children of authoritative parents. Children of permissive-indifferent parents have the most negative profile of all.

- Relationships between children and parents change over the course of development. In early development, children are mainly controlled and regulated by parents. There is a gradual shift toward coregulation during middle childhood, whereby control is shared by parents and children. In adolescence, young people strive for independence. This period is generally characterized by conflict until parent and child roles are renegotiated.

- Sibling relationships play a unique and important role in children's development. Siblings serve as role models, playmates, teachers, and sources of emotional support. Like parent-child relations, sibling relationships change with development.

Children whose parents are warm and responsive tend to develop positive sibling relationships.

- Child maltreatment can take many different forms, including physical abuse, neglect, emotional maltreatment, and sexual abuse. Younger children are at greater risk for maltreatment than are older children. A number of social and economic factors contribute to child abuse, including poor parental education, family poverty and conflict, and social isolation. Child abuse has serious cognitive, emotional, and social consequences for the child, and, in some cases, it can lead to death. Federal and state laws require all professionals who work with children to report suspected cases of child abuse. It is important too for educators too learn about reporting procedures.

Family Transitions: Divorce and Remarriage

- Approximately half of first marriages end in divorce. The effects of divorce on a child are not straightforward and are related to the child's age and sex, the level of conflict between parents, the income level of the custodial parent, and the quality of the parenting provided. In general, most children are not adversely affected by divorce, despite the significant problems they face during the transition.

- Many children live in a blended family consisting of a biological parent, a stepparent, and children. The remarriage of a parent has both positive and negative consequences for the child. On the one hand, it brings added resources and support to the family, but, on the other hand, it requires further adjustment for children who may still be reconciling issues raised by their parents' divorce. As with divorce, the effects of remarriage are shaped by the child's characteristics and the quality of parenting provided.

- The school can provide continuity of care and stability for children experiencing a change in the family. During a family transition, young people will need extra support, attention, and care at school. It is important to maintain consistent rules and routines, and to provide opportunities for children to discuss their feelings.

Maternal Employment and Child Care

- More mothers with children under the age of 18 are working outside the home than ever before. Most studies show no effects related to maternal employment on children's development. Negative effects are likely to occur when maternal employment is associated with decreased monitoring of children's activities.

- A large number of children under the age of 6 receive some form of early child care, with approximately one-third attending a day care center. Early findings on the effects of day care were equivocal. Recently, new evidence shows few negative effects of day care on children's development when children attend high-quality day care programs. Quality is defined in terms of a low ratio of children to caregivers; a well-trained staff; opportunities for educational, language, and social stimulation; and low staff turnover.

- Many school-age children today also attend some form of after-school program. These programs are offered by churches, community organizations, and public facilities. Many programs are also offered by schools, but some experts are concerned that school care is neglecting important areas of youth development. A limited body of research suggests that school-based programs can result in improved school attendance and achievement, particularly for low-income children.

Family Involvement in Children's Education

- There is general agreement that active parental involvement in education is important for children's school success. When parents become involved in school activities, they devise ways of supporting their children's learning at home. Through increased contact with parents, teachers can increase their understanding of their students' cultural backgrounds, needs, and strengths.

- Parent involvement varies by family structure and grade level. Two-parent families are more involved in their children's schooling than single parents. Also, rates of parent involvement are higher for younger than for older students. Parental beliefs and attitudes play an important role in determining whether or not parents will become involved in their child's schooling.

- The organization of schools and teacher attitudes can discourage parental involvement. Many teachers report they have insufficient time to implement effective practices for working with parents, and high school teachers are less likely to perceive the value of parent involvement for their students.

- A number of effective parent involvement strategies have been identified. These include enhancing parenting skills, communicating regularly and effectively with parents, recruiting classroom volunteers, encouraging parents to help their children with learning at home, and including parents in school governance.

- Schools play an important role in fostering resiliency in youth. Any effort that enhances children's cognitive abilities, social competence, and self-esteem is resiliency building. Schools can foster resiliency by encouraging a strong connection to school, communicating high expectations, providing meaningful learning opportunities, and encouraging participation.

Key Terms

authoritarian parenting (p. 498)

authoritative parenting (p. 498)

autonomy (p. 501)

birth order (p. 502)

chronosystem (p. 481)

coregulation (p. 500)

corporal punishment (p. 496)

emotional maltreatment (p. 504)

exosystem (p. 480)

familialism (p. 492)

inductive discipline (p. 497)

macrosystem (p. 481)

mesosystem (p. 480)

microsystem (p. 480)

neglect (p. 504)

parenting styles (p. 498)

permissive-indifferent (p. 499)

permissive-indulgent (p. 499)

physical abuse (p. 504)

power-assertive discipline (p. 496)

sexual abuse (p. 504)

simpatía (p. 492)

socialization (p. 478)

Activities

1. Interview children of different ages to learn about their families. Find out what kind of activities they do with their parents and siblings. Also, ask about the activities they do with their friends. You might ask your interviewees to draw a picture of their families, and to describe what they would like to change about their families. Compare and

contrast responses across the different age groups. What themes emerge regarding how children spend time with families? How do the activities differ from ones they do with friends? Are there any interesting changes with age? Discuss what you learned with your classmates.

2. Begin to develop a resource file for helping children to cope with family change. Look for books and other reading materials on divorce and remarriages that children can read on their own. Review these materials for misconceptions about families. Collect additional professional materials on ways to support and help children who are experiencing a change in the family.

3. Interview school and community agency officials to learn more about policies and procedures concerning child maltreatment. What are your legal responsibilities as a teacher? What are the steps for reporting child maltreatment? Invite speakers to your class to discuss indicators and consequences of child abuse.

4. Interview teachers of different grade levels to gather information on the parent involvement. Ask teachers to describe the strategies they use to communicate with parents, to involve them in classroom activities, and to support children's learning at home. Find out which strategies seem to be most effective. Compare the list with the ones described in Epstein's parent involvement framework (see Focus on Teaching, pp. 520–521). Share your summary with classmates.

Adams, M. J. (1990). *Beginning to read: Thinking and learning about print*. Cambridge, Mass.: MIT Press.

Adelman, C. (1991). *Women at thirtysomething. Paradoxes of attainment*. Washington, D.C.: U.S. Department of Education.

Ainsworth, M. D., Blehar, M., Waters, E., & Wall, S. (1978). *Patterns of attachment*. Hillsdale, N.J.: Erlbaum.

Aitchison, J. (1985). Predestinate grooves: Is there a preordained language "program"? In V. P. Clark, P. A. Eschholz, & A. F. Rosa (eds.), *Language: Introductory readings* (pp. 90–111). New York: St. Martin's Press.

Albert, L. (1996). *Cooperative discipline*. Circle Pines, Minn.: American Guidance Service.

Alexander, K., & Entwisle, D. (1988). Achievement in the first two years of school: Patterns and processes. *Monographs for Research in Child Development, 53* (no. 2).

Alexander, K. L., Entwisle, D. R., & Horsey, C. S. (1997). From first grade forward: Early foundations of high school dropout. *Sociology of Education, 70,* 87–107.

Alexander, K. L., & Entwisle, D. R. (1988). Achievement in the first 2 years of school: Patterns and processes. *Monographs of the Society for Research in Child Development, 53* (2, Serial No. 218).

Alexander, K. L., Entwisle, D. R., & Drauber, S. L. (1995). *On the success of failure. A reassessment of the effects of retention in the primary grades*. New York: Cambridge University Press.

Alexander, K. L., Natriello, G., & Pallas, A. (1985). For whom the school bell tolls: The impact of dropping out on cognitive performance. *American Sociological Review, 50,* 409–420.

Alexander, P. A. (1996). The past, present, and future of knowledge research: A reexamination of the role of knowledge in learning and instruction. *Educational Psychologist, 31,* 89–92.

Allen, V. (1986). Developing contexts to support second language acquisition. *Language Arts, 64,* 61–67.

Allington, R. L. (1977). If they don't read much, how they ever gonna get good? *Journal of Reading 21,* 3761.

Amato, P. R. (1993). Children's adjustment to divorce: Theories, hypotheses, and empirical support. *Journal of Marriage and the Family, 55,* 23–38.

Amato, P. R., & Booth, A. (1991). Consequences of parental divorce and marital unhappiness for adult well-being. *Social Forces, 69,* 895–914.

Amato, P. R., & Keith, N. (1991). Parental divorce and adult well-being: A meta-analysis. *Journal of Marriage and the Family, 53,* 43–58.

American Academy of Pediatrics (1998). Guidance for effective discipline (RE9740). *Pediatrics, 101* (4), 723–728.

American Association of University Women Educational Foundation (1995). *How schools shortchange girls: The AAUW Report*. Washington, D.C.: Author.

American Association of University Women Educational Foundation (1998). *Gender gaps: Where schools still fail our children*. Washington, D.C.: Author.

American Psychiatric Association (1994). *Diagnostic and statistical manual of mental disorders* (Fourth Edition). Washington, D.C.: Author.

Amey, C., & Campbell, F. (1991). Poverty, early childhood education, and academic competence: The Abcederian experiment. In A. Huston (ed.), *Children reared in poverty* (pp. 190–221). New York: Cambridge University Press.

Anderson, D., & Levin, S. (1976). Young children's attention to "Sesame Street." *Child Development, 47,* 806–811.

Anderson, R. C., Hiebert, E. H., Scott, J. A., & Wilkinson, I. A. G. (1985). *Becoming a nation of readers: The report of the commission on reading*. Washington, D.C.: National Institute of Education.

Andersson, T., & Magnusson, D. (1990). Biological maturation in adolescence and the development of drinking habits and alcohol abuse among young males: A prospective longitudinal study. *Journal of Youth and Adolescence, 19,* 33–42.

Anglin, J. M. (1993). Vocabulary development: Amorphological analysis. *Monographs of the Society for Research in Child Development, 58* (Serial No. 238).

Apfel, N. H., & Seitz, V. (1991). Four models of adolescent mother-grandmother relationships in black inner-city families. *Family Relations, 40,* 421–429.

Applebee, A. N. (1978). *The child's concept of story*. Chicago: University of Chicago Press.

Applebee, A. N. (1981). *Writing in the secondary school*. Urbana, Ill.: National Council for Teachers of English.

Applebee, A., Langer, J., & Mullis, I. (1986). *Writing trends across the decade, 1974–84*. Princeton, N.J.: Educational Testing Service.

Applebee, A., Langer, J., & Mullis, I. (1988). *Who reads best: Factors related to reading achievement in grades 3, 7, and 11*. Princeton, N.J.: Educational Testing Service.

Applebee, A., Langer, J., Mullis, I., & Jenkins, L. (1990). *The writing report card, 1984–88. Findings from the nation's report card*. The National Assessment of Educational Progress. Princeton, N.J.: Educational Testing Service.

References

Archambault, R. (1964). *John Dewey on education: Selected writings*. New York: Modern Library.

Aries, P. (1962). *Centuries of childhood*. New York: Random House.

Arnett, J. (1992). Reckless behavior in adolescence: A developmental perspective. *Developmental Review, 12,* 339–373.

Arnett, J. J. (1999). Adolescent storm and stress reconsidered. *American Psychologist, 54,* 317–326.

Aronson, E., & Patnoe, S. (1996). *The jigsaw classroom* (2nd ed.). Boston: Addison-Wesley.

Aro, H., & Taipale, V. (1987). The impact of timing of puberty on psychosomatic symptoms among fourteen- to sixteen-year-old Finnish girls. *Child Development, 58,* 261–268.

Ashworth, K., Hill, M., & Walker, R. (1994). Patterns of childhood poverty: The dynamics of spell. *Journal of Policy Analysis and Management, 18,* 658–680.

Aslin, R. N., Jurczyk, P. W., & Pisoni, D. B. (1998). Speech and auditory processing during infancy: Constraints on and precursors to language. In W. Damon (gen. ed.), D. Kuhn, & R. Stiegler (vol. eds.), *Handbook of child psychology, Vol. 2: Cognition, perception, and language* (pp. 147–198). New York: John Wiley.

Attneave, C. (1982). American Indians and Alaska Native families: Emigrants in their own homeland. In M. McGoldrick, J. Pearce, & J. Giordano (eds.), *Ethnicity and family therapy* (pp. 55–83). New York: The Guilford Press.

Atwell, N. (1987). *In the middle: Writing, reading, and learning with adolescents*. Portsmouth, N.H.: Boynton/Cook.

Au, K. H. (1993). *Literacy instruction in multicultural settings*. Fort Worth: Harcourt Brace Jovanovich.

Au, K., & Kawakami, A. (1985). Research currents: Talk story and learning to read. *Language Arts, 62,* 406–411.

Au, K., & Mason, J. (1981). Social organizational factors in learning to read: The balance of rights hypothesis. *Reading Research Quarterly, 17,* 115–152.

Au, K., & Mason, J. (1983). Cultural congruence in classroom participation: Achieving a balance of rights. *Discourse Processes, 6,* 145–167.

August, D., & Hakuta, K. (1997). *Improving schooling for language-minority children. A research agenda*. Washington, D.C.: National Academy of Press.

Azmitia, M., & Hesser, J. (1993). Why siblings are important agents of cognitive development: A comparison of siblings and peers. *Child Development, 64,* 430–444.

Baharudin, R., & Luster, T. (1998). Factors related to the quality of the home environment and children's achievement. *Journal of Family Issues, 19* (4), 375–403.

Bailey, D., & Nelson, D. (1995). The nature and consequences of Fragile X syndrome. *Mental Retardation and Developmental Disabilities Research Reviews, 1,* 238–244.

Bailey, J. M., Bobrow, D., Wolfe, M., & Mikach, S. (1995). Sexual orientation of adult sons of gay fathers. *Developmental Psychology, 31,* 124–129.

Baillargeon, R. (1994). Physical reasoning in young children: Seeking explanations for impossible events. *British Journal of Developmental Psychology, 12,* 9–33.

Baillargeon, R., Spelke, E. S., & Wasserman, S. (1985). Object permanence in 5-month-olds. *Cognition, 20,* 191–208.

Baker, L., & Brown, A. L. (1984). Metacognitive skills and reading. In P. D. Pearson (ed.), *Handbook of reading research* (pp. 353–394). New York: Longman.

Baldwin, A. (1967). *Theories of child development*. New York: John Wiley.

Bandura, A. (1969). Social learning theory of identifactory processes. In D. A. Goslin (ed.), *Handbook of socialization theory and research* (pp. 213–262). Chicago: Rand-McNally.

Bandura, A. (1986). *Social foundations of thought and action: A social cognitive perspective*. Englewood Cliffs, N.J.: Prentice Hall.

Bandura, A. (1989). Social cognitive theory. In R. Vasta (ed.), *Annuals of child development* (vol. 6, pp. 1–60). Greenwich, Conn.: JAI Press.

Bandura, A., Ross, D., & Ross, S. (1963). Imitation of film-mediated aggressive models. *Journal of Abnormal and Social Psychology, 66,* 3–11.

Banks, J. (1994). *An introduction to multicultural education*. Boston: Allyn & Bacon.

Banks, J. (1994). *Multiethnic education: Theory and practice* (3rd ed.). Boston: Allyn and Bacon.

Baringa, M. (1996). Learning defect identified in the brain. *Science, 273,* 867–868.

Barkley, R. A. (1998). *Attention–deficit hyperactivity disorder: A handbook for diagnosis and treatment* (2nd ed.). New York: Guilford Press.

Barnes, D. (1989). "Fragile X" syndrome and its puzzling genetics. *Science, 243,* 171–172.

Barnett, W. S., & Boocock, S. S. (1998). *Early care and education for children in poverty promises, programs, and long-term results* (SUNY series, youth social services, schooling, and public policy: SUNY series, early childhood education. Albany: State University of New York Press.

Baroody, A. (1987). *Children's mathematical thinking*. New York: Teachers College Press.

Baroody, A., & Bartels, B. (2000). Using concept maps to link mathematical ideas. *Mathematics Teaching in the Middle Schools, 5*(9), 604–609.

Barr, H. M., Streissguth, A. P., Darby, B. L., & Sampson, P. D. (1990). Prenatal exposure to alcohol, caffeine, tobacco, and aspirin: Effects on fine and gross motor performance in 4-year-old children. *Developmental Psychology, 26*, 339–348.

Bartlett, E. J. (1982). Learning to revise: Some component processes. In M. Nystrand (ed.), *What writers know: The language, process, and structure of written discourse*. New York: Academic Press.

Baskett, L. M. (1985). Sibling status effects: Adult expectations. *Developmental Psychology, 21*, 441–445.

Bates, E. (1976). *Language and context: The acquisition of pragmatics*. New York: Academic Press.

Battle, E. S., & Lacey, B. (1972). A context for hyperactivity in children, over time. *Child Development, 43*, 757–773.

Baumrind, D. (1967). Current patterns of parental authority. *Genetic Psychology Monographs, 75*, 43–88.

Baumrind, D. (1967). Child care practices anteceding three patterns of preschool behavior. *Genetic Psychology Monographs, 75*, 43–88.

Bayley, N. (1969). *The Bayley scales of infant development*. New York: Psychological Corporation.

Beals, D. E. & DeTemple, J. M. (1993). Home contributions to early language and literary development. In D. Lea and C. Kenzer (eds.), *Examinary central issues in literary research theory and practice: Full second yearbook of the National Reading Conference* (pp. 207–216). Chicago: National Reading Conference, Inc.

Beals, D. E., DeTemple, J. M., & Dickinson, D. K. (1994). Talking and listening that support early literacy development of children from low-income families. In D. K. Dickinson (ed.), *Bridges to literacy: Children, families, and schools*. Cambridge, Mass.: Blackwell.

Beauchamp, C. K., & Moran, M. (1985). Acceptance of sweet and sour tastes in 2-year-old children. *Appetite, 5*, 291–305.

Becher, R. M. (1984). *Parent involvement: A review of research and principles of successful practice*. Urbana-Champaign, IL: ERIC Clearinghouse on Elementary and Early Childhood Education (ED 247-032).

Becker, H. J. (2000). Who's wired and who's not: Children's access to and use of computer technology. *The future of children: Children and computer technology*, Vol. 10, 44–75.

Becker, P. E., & Moen, P. (1999). Scaling back: Dual-earner couples' work-family strategies. *Journal of Marriage and the Family, 61*, 995–1007.

Becker, D. M., Yanek, L. R., Koffman, D. M., & Bronner, Y. C. (1999). Body image preferences among urban African Americans and whites from low income communities. *Ethnicity and Disease, 9* (3), 377–86.

Bednar, R. L., Wells, M. G., & Peterson, S. R. (1995). *Self-esteem* (2nd ed.). Washington, D.C.: American Psychological Association.

Begley, S. (1999). Shaped by life in the womb. *Newsweek, 134* (13), 50–57.

Begley, S. (2000). Getting inside a teen brain. *Newsweek, 135* (9), 58–59.

Behrman, R., & Kliegman, R. (1990). *Nelson essentials of pediatrics*. Philadelphia: W. B. Saunders.

Bellugi, U. (1970). Learning the language. *Psychology Today, 4*, 33.

Belsky, J. (1981). Early human experience: A family perspective. *Developmental Psychology, 17*, 2–23.

Bempechat, J., & Drago-Severson, E. (1999). Cross-national differences in academic achievement: Beyond ectic conceptions of children's understandings. *Review of Educational Research, 69*, 287–314.

Benbow, C. (1986). Physiological correlates of extreme intellectual precocity. *Neuropsychologia, 24*, 719–725.

Benbow, C. (1992). Academic achievement in mathematics and science of students between 13 and 23: Are there differences among students in the top one percent of mathematical ability? *Journal of Educational Psychology, 84*, 51–61.

Bender, B., Linden, M., & Robinson, A. (1987). Environment and developmental link in children with sex chromosome abnormalities. *Journal of the Academy of Child and Adolescent Psychiatry, 26*, 499–503.

Berk, L. (1986). Relationship of elementary school children's private speech to behavioral accompaniment to task, attention, and task performance. *Developmental Psychology, 22*, 671–680.

Berk, L., & Garvin, R. (1984). Development of private speech among low-income Appalachian children. *Developmental Psychology, 20*, 271–286.

Berliner, D., & Biddle, B. (1995). *The manufactured crisis. Myths, fraud, and the attack on America's public schools*. New York: Addison Wesley.

Bernard, B. (1991). *Fostering resiliency in kids: protective factors in the family, school, and community*. Portland, Ore.: Western Regional Center for Drug-Free Schools and Communities, Northwest Educational Laboratory.

Berndt, T. (1999). Friends' influence on students' adjustment to school. *Educational Psychologist, 34*, 15–28.

Bertalanffy, L. von (1968). *General systems theory*. New York: Braziller.

Bigler, R., Jones, L., & Lobliner, D. (1997). Social categorization and the formation of intergroup attitudes in children. *Child Development, 68*, 530–543.

References

Bigner, J. J., & Jacobsen, R. B. (1989). Parenting behaviors of homosexual and heterosexual fathers. In F. W. Bozett (ed.), *Homosexuality and the family* (pp. 173–186). New York: Harrington Park Press.

Biller, H. B. (1981). Father absence, divorce, and personality development. In M. E. Lamb (ed.), *The role of the father in child development* (pp. 489–552). New York: John Wiley.

Birch, S., & Ladd, G. (1996). Interpersonal relationships in the school environment and children's early school adjustment. In J. Juvonen & K. Wentzel (eds.), *Social motivation: Understanding children's school adjustment* (pp. 199–225). New York: Cambridge University Press.

Bishop, S. M., & Ingersoll, G. M. (1989). Effects of marital conflict and family structure on the self-concepts of pre- and early adolescents. *Journal of Youth and Adolescence, 18,* 25–38

Bissex, G. (1980). *GYNS AT WRK: A child learns to write and read.* Cambridge, Mass.: Harvard University Press.

Bjorklund, D. F. (1995). *Children's thinking: Developmental function and individual differences.* New York: Brooks/Cole.

Bjorklund, D. F., Muir-Broadus, J. E., & Schneider, W. (1990). The role of knowledge in the development of strategies. In D. F. Bjorklund (ed.), *Children's strategies: Contemporary views of cognitive development* (pp. 93–128). Hillsdale, N.J.: Erlbaum.

Black, B., & Greenough, W. (1986). Induction of pattern in neural structure by experience. In M. Lamb, A. Brown, & B. Rogoff (eds.), *Advances in developmental psychology* (vol. 4, 1–41). Hillsdale, N.J.: Erlbaum.

Black-Gutman, D., & Hickson, F. (1996). The relationship between racial attitudes and social-cognitive development in children: An Australian study. *Developmental Psychology, 32,* 448–456.

Blake, J. (1981). Family size and the quality of children. *Demography, 18,* 421–442.

Bloom, B. (1964). *Stability and change in human characteristics.* New York: John Wiley.

Bloom, B. (1985). *Developing talent in young people.* New York: Ballantine.

Bloom, L. (1970). *Language development: Form and function in emerging grammars.* Cambridge, Mass.: MIT Press.

Blum, R. W. Beuhring, T., Shew, M., Bearinger, L. H., Sieving R. E., & Resnick, M.D. The effects of race/ethnicity, income and family structure on adolescent risk behaviors. *American Journal of Public Health, 90* (12), 1879–1884.

Blumsack, J., Lewandowski, L., & Waterman, B. (1997). Neurodevelopmental precursors to learning disabilities: A preliminary report from a parent survey. *Journal of Learning Disabilities, 30,* 228–237

Blyth, D., Simmons, R., & Zakin, D. (1985). Satisfaction with body image for early adolescent females: The impact of pubertal timing within different school environments. *Journal of Youth and Adolescence, 14,* 207–225.

Board on Children and Families (1995). Immigrant children and their families: Issues for research and policy. *The Future of Children, 5,* 72–89.

Boateng, F. (1990). Combating deculturalization of the African-American child in the public school system. In K. Lomotey (ed.), *Going to school. The African–American experience.* Albany, N.Y.: State University of New York Press.

Bong, M. & Clark, R. (1999). Comparison between self-concept and self-efficacy in academic motivation research. *Educational Psychologist, 34,* 139–153.

Booth, A., & Dunn, J. (1996). *Family-school links: How do they affect educational outcomes.* Mahwah, N.J.: Erlbaum.

Bornstein, M. (1989). Maternal responsiveness: Characteristics and consequences. *New Directions for Child Development, 43.*

Bornstein, M., & Tamis-LeMonda, C. S. (1997). Maternal responsiveness and infant mental abilities: Specific predictive relations. *Infant Behavior and Development, 20,* 283–296.

Bouchard, T., Jr., & McGue, M. (1981). Familial studies of intelligence: A review. *Science, 212,* 1055–1059.

Bowerman, M. (1973). *Early syntactic development: A cross-linguistic study with special reference to Finnish.* Cambridge, England: Cambridge University Press.

Bowlby, J. (1969). *Attachment and loss: Vol. 1. Attachment.* New York: Basic Books.

Bowman, P. (1995). Coping with provider role strain: Adaptive cultural resources among Black husband-fathers. *Journal of Black Psychology, 16* (2), 1–21.

Bosworth, K., Espelage, D. L., & Simon, T. R. (1999). Factors associated with bullying behavior in middle school students. *Journal of Early Adolescence, 19* (3), 341–362.

Boyd, B. (1997). Teacher response to superhero play: To ban or not to ban? *Childhood Education,* Fall volume, 23–28.

Bozett, F. W. (1989). Gay fathers: A review of the literature. *Journal of Homosexuality, 18,* 137–162.

Bracey, G. (1995). *Final exam: A study of the perpetual scrutiny of American education: Historical perspectives on assessment, standards, outcomes, and criticism of U.S. public schools.* Bloomington, Ind.: TECHNOS Press.

Bradley, R., & Caldwell, B. (1984). 174 children: A study of the relationship between the home environment and early cognitive development in the first five years. In A. W. Gottfried & A. E. Gottfried (eds.), *The home environment and early cognitive development*. New York: Academic Press.

Bradley, R. H., & Caldwell, B. M. (1984). The relation of infants' home environments to achievement test performance in first grade: A follow-up study. *Child Development, 55*, 803–809.

Bradley, R. H., Caldwell, B. M., & Rock, S. L. (1988). Home environment and school performance: A ten-year follow-up and examination of three models of environmental action. *Child Development, 59*, 852–867.

Bradley, R., Caldwell, B., Rock, S., Barnard, K., Gray, C., Siegel, L., Ramey, C., Gottfried, A., & Johnson, D. (1989). Home environment and cognitive development in the first 3 years of life: A collaborative study involving six sites and three ethnic groups in North America. *Developmental Psychology, 25*, 217–235.

Braine, M. D. S. (1976). Children's first word combinations. *Monographs of the Society for Research in Child Development, 41* (Serial No. 164).

Braumind, D. (1967). Child care practices anteceding three patterns of preschool behavior. *Genetic Psychology Monographs, 75*, 43–88.

Braverman, P. K. (2000). Sexually transmitted diseases in adolescents. *Medical Clinics of North America, 84* (4), 869–889, vi–vii.

Bray, J. H., & Burger, S. H. (1993). Developmental issues in stepfamilies research project: Family relationships and parent-child interactions. *Journal of Family Psychology, 7*, 76–80.

Bredekamp, S., & Copple, C. (1997). *Developmentally appropriate practice in early childhood programs*. Washington, D.C.: National Association for the Education of Young Children.

Britton, J. (1970). *Language and learning*. New York: Penguin Books.

Britton, J., Burgess, T., Martin, N., McLeod, A., & Rosen, J. (1975). *The development of writing abilities* (pp. 11–18). London: Macmillan Education.

Brody, G. H., & Flor, D. L. (1998). Maternal resources, parenting practices, and child competence in rural, single-parent African American families. *Child Development, 69*, 803–816.

Brody, G. H., Stoneman, A., & McCoy, J. K. (1994). Forecasting sibling relationships in early adolescence from child temperaments and family processes in middle childhood. *Child Development, 65*, 771–784.

Brody, N. (1992). *Intelligence*. New York: Academic Press.

Bronfenbrenner, U. (1979). *The ecology of human development: Experiments by nature and design*. Cambridge, Mass.: Harvard University Press.

Bronfenbrenner, U. (1986). Ecology of the family as a context for human development: Research perspectives. *Developmental Psychology, 22*, 723–742.

Bronfenbrenner, U., & Morris, P. A. (1998). The ecology of developmental processes. In W. Damon (gen. ed.), & R. M. Lerner (vol. ed.), *Handbook of child psychology: Vol. 1. Theoretical models of human development* (pp. 993–1028). New York: John Wiley.

Brook, J. S., Brook, D. W., Gordon, A. S., Whiteman, M., & Cohen, P. (1990). The psychological etiology of adolescent drug use: A family interactional approach. *Genetic, Social and General Psychology Monographs, 116*, 110–267.

Brooks-Gunn, J., Britto, P. R., & Brady, C. (1999). Struggling to make ends meet: Poverty and child development. In M. E. Lamb (ed.), *Parenting and child development in "nontraditional" families* (pp. 279–304). Mahwah, N.J.: Erlbaum.

Brooks-Gunn, J., & Chase-Lansdale, P. L. (1995). Adolescent parenthood. In M. H. Bornstein (ed.), *Handbook of parenting: Vol. 3. Status and social conditions of parenting* (pp. 113–149). Mahwah, N.J.: Erlbaum.

Brooks-Gunn, J., & Warren, M. (1989). Biological and social contributions to negative affect in young adolescent girls. *Child Development, 60*, 40–55.

Brophy, J., & Good, T. (1974). *Teacher-student relationships: Causes and consequences*. New York: Holt, Rinehart, & Winston.

Brown, A. (1997). Transforming schools into communities of thinking and learning about serious matters. *American Psychologist, 52*, 399–413.

Brown, A. L., Bransford, J. D., Ferrara, R. A., & Campione, J. C. (1983). Learning, remembering, and understanding. In W. Dammon (series ed.), & J. H. Flavell & E. M. Markman (vol. eds.), *Handbook of child psychology: Vol 3. cognitive development* (pp. 77–166). New York: John Wiley.

Brown, A. L., & Campione, J. C. (1990). Communities of learning and thinking, or a context by any other name. In D. Kuhn (ed.), *Developmental perspectives on teaching and learning thinking skills* (pp. 108–126). Basel, Switzerland: Karger.

Brown, A. L., & Smiley S. S. (1978). The development of strategies to study text. *Child Development, 49,* 1076–1088.

Brown, J. R. & Dunn, J. (1996). Talk with your mother or your sibling? Developmental changes in early family conversation about feelings. *Child Development, 67,* 789–802.

Brown, R. (1973). *A first language: The early stages.* Cambridge, Mass.: Harvard University Press.

Brown, R., Cazden, C. B., & Bellugi, U. (1969). The child's grammar from I to III. In J. P. Hill (ed.), *Minnesota symposium on child psychology (Vol. 2)* (pp. 28–73). Minneapolis: University of Minnesota Press.

Bruer, J. T. In search of brain-based education. *Phi Delta Kappan, 80,* 649–657.

Bryant, B. K., & Crockenberg, S. B. (1980). Correlates and dimensions of prosocial behavior: A study of female siblings with their mothers. *Child Development, 51,* 529–554.

Bryant, D., Clifford, R., & Peisner, E. (1991). Best practices for beginners: Developmental appropriateness in kindergarten. *American Educational Research Journal, 28,* 783–803.

Buchanan, C., Eccles, J. S., & Becker, J. (1992). Are adolescents victims of raging hormones? Evidence of activational effects of hormones on moods and behavior at adolescence. *Psychological Bulletin, 111,* 62–107.

Buchanan, C. M., Eccles, J. S., & Becker, J. B. (1992). Are adolescents the victims of raging hormones: Evidence of activational effects of hormones on moods and behavior in adolescence. *Psychological Bulletin, 111* (1), 62–107.

Buchanan, C. M., Maccoby, E. E., & Dornbusch, S. M. (1992). Adolescents and their families after divorce: Three residential arrangements compared. *Journal of Research in Adolescence, 2* (3), 261–291.

Bugental, D. B., & Goodnow, J. J. (1998). Socialization processes. In W. Damon (gen. ed.), & N. Eisenberg (vol. ed.), *Handbook of child psychology: Vol. 3. Social, emotional, and personality development* (pp. 389–462). New York: John Wiley.

Buoye, A. (1998). Differentiating the effects of industrial and team sports participation on students' grade. Unpublished Master's Thesis, Notre Dame University. South Bend, Ind.

Bureau of the U.S. Census (1984). *Conditions of Hispanics in America Today.* Washington, D.C.: U.S. Government Printing Office.

Bureau of the U.S. Census (1987). *The Hispanic Population in the United States: March 1986 and 1987.* Washington, D.C.: U.S. Government Printing Office.

Buriel, R., & De Ment, T. (1997). Immigration and sociocultural change in Mexican, Chinese, and Vietnamese American families. In A. Booth, A. C. Crouter, & N. Landale (eds.), *Immigration and the family* (pp. 165–200). Mahwah, N.J.: Erlbaum.

Burling, R. (1959). "Proto-Bodo." *Language, 35,* 433–453.

Burton, L., M., & Dilworth-Anderson, P. (1991). The intergenerational roles of aged black Americans. *Family Review, 6,* 311–330.

Bus, A. G., van Ijzendourn, M. H. & Pelleguini, A. (1995). Joint book ready makes for success in learning to read: A meta-analysis on intergenerational transmission of Literacy. *Review of Educational Research, 65,* 1–21.

Byrne, B. M. (1986). Self-concept academic achievement relations: An investigation of dimensionality, stability, and causality. *Canadian Journal of Behavioral Science, 18,* 173–186.

Caine, R. N., & Caine, G. (1994). *Making connections: Teaching and the human brain.* New York: Addison Wesley.

Cairns, R., & Cairns, B. (1994). *Lifelines and risks. Pathways of youth in our time.* New York: Oxford University Press.

Cairns, R. B., Cairns, B. D., Neckerman, H. J., Gest, S. D. & Gariepy, J. L. (1988). Social networks and aggressive behavior: Peer support or peer rejection? *Developmental Psychology, 24,* 815–823.

Cairns, R. B., Cairns, B. D., & Neckerman, H. J. (1989). Early school dropout: Configurations and determinants. *Child Development, 60,* 1437–1452.

Caldwell, B., & Bradley, R. (1978). *Home observation for measurement of the environment.* Little Rock: University of Arkansas at Little Rock.

Caldwell, B. M. (1973). Infant day care—The outcast gains respectability. In P. Robey (ed.), *Child care—who cares? Foreign and domestic infant and early childhood development policies.* New York: Basic Books.

Caldwell, B. M., & Bradley, R. H. (1984). *Home observation for measurement of the environment.* Little Rock: University of Arkansas.

Calfee, R. (1994). Critical literacy: Reading and writing for a new millennium. In N. Ellsworth, C. Hedley, & A. Baratta (eds.), *Literacy: A redefinition* (pp. 19–38). Hillsdale, N.J.: Erlbaum.

Calsyn, R. & Kenny, D. (1977). Self-concept of ability and perceived evaluations by others. Cause or effect of academic achievement. *Journal of Educational Psychology, 69,* 136–145.

Camp, B. W., Blom, G., Hebert, F., & van Doornick, W. (1977). "Think Aloud": A program for developing self-control in young aggressive boys. *Journal of Abnormal Psychology, 5,* 157–169.

Campbell, F. A., & Ramey, C. T. (1993, March). *Mid-adolescent outcomes for high risk students: An examination of the continuing effects of early intervention.* Paper presented at the biennial meeting of the Society for Research in Child Development, New Orleans.

Campbell, F., & Ramey, C. (1994). Effects of an early intervention on intellectual and academic achievement: A follow-up study of children from low income families. *Child Development, 65* (2), 684–698.

Campbell, S. B. (1990). *Behavior problems in preschool children.* New York: Guildford Press.

Campbell, J. R., Hombo, C. M., & Mazzeo, J. *NAEP 1999 trends in academic progress: Three decades of student performance.* Washington, D.C.: U.S. Department of Education, Office of Educational Research and Improvement.

Caplan, N., Choy, M., & Whitmore, J. (1992, February). Indochinese refugee families and academic achievement. *Scientific American,* 36–42.

Caplan, P. J., & Caplan, J. B. (1999). *Thinking critically about research on sex and gender* (2nd ed.). New York: Addison Wesley Longman.

Capon, N., & Kuhn, D. (1979). Logical reasoning in the supermarket: Adult females' use of a proportional reasoning strategy. *Developmental Psychology, 15,* 450–452.

Carlson, E. A., Jacobvitz, D., & Sroufe, L. A. (1995). A developmental investigation of inattentiveness and hyperactivity. *Child Development, 66,* 37–54.

Carlsson-Paige, N., & Levin, D. E. (1995). Can teachers resolve the war-play dilemma? *Young Children, 50,* 62–63.

Carnegie Council on Adolescent Development (1989). *Turning Points: Preparing American youth for the 21st century.* Washington, D.C.: Carnegie Council on Adolescent Development.

Carnegie Task Force on Learning in the Primary Grades (1996). *Years of promise: A comprehensive learning strategy for American children.* New York: Carnegie Corporation of New York.

Carraher, T., Carraher, D., & Schleinman, A. (1985). Mathematics in the streets and in the schools. *British Journal of Developmental Psychology, 3,* 21–29.

Carrasquillo, A. (1993). Whole native language instruction for limited-English-proficient students. In A. Carrasquillo & C. Hedley (eds.), *Whole language and the bilingual learner* (pp. 3–19). Norwood, N.J.: Ablex.

Carskadon, M. (1999). When worlds collide. Adolescent need for sleep versus societal demands. *Phi Delta Kappan, 80* (5), 348–353.

Carter, K. (1997, March 7). Gay slurs abound. *Des Moines Register,* 3.

Casanova, U. (1995). Bilingual education: Politics or pedagogy? In O. Garcia & C. Baker (eds.). *Policy and practice in bilingual education* (pp. 15–24). Bristol, Pa.: Multilingual Matters.

Case, R. (1985). *Intellectual development: A systematic reinterpretation.* New York: Academic Press.

Casper, V., Schultz, S., & Wickens, E. (1992). Breaking the silences: Lesbian and gay parents and the schools. *Teachers College Record, 94,* 109–137.

Caspi, A. (1998). Personality development across the life course. In W. Dammon (series ed.) & N. Eisenberg (vol. ed.), *Handbook of child psychology, Vol. 3. Social, emotional, and personality development* (pp. 311–388). New York: John Wiley.

Caspi, A., Lynam, D., Moffitt, T., & Silva, A. (1993). Unraveling girls' delinquency: Biological, dispositional, and contextual contributions to adolescent misbehavior. *Developmental Psychology, 29,* 19–30.

Caspi, A., & Moffitt, T. (1991). Individual differences and personal transitions. The sample case of girls at puberty. *Journal of Personality and Social Psychology, 61,* 157–168.

Caspi, A., & Silva, P. A. (1995). Temperamental qualities at age 3 predict personality traits in young adulthood: Longitudinal evidence from a birth cohort. *Child Development, 66,* 129–161.

Cassidy, J., & Berlin, L. J. (1994). The insecure/ambivalent pattern of attachment: Theory and research. *Child Development, 65,* 971–991.

Cattell, R. B. (1971). *Abilities: Their structure, growth, and action.* Boston: Houghton Mifflin.

Cazden, C. (1972). *Child language and education.* New York: Holt, Rinehart & Winston.

Ceci, S. (1990). *On intelligence...more or less: A bioecological treatise on intellectual development.* Englewood Cliffs, N.J.: Prentice Hall.

Ceci, S. (1991). How much does schooling influence general intelligence and its cognitive components? A reassessment of the evidence. *Developmental Psychology, 27,* 703–722.

Ceci, S., & Williams, W. (1993). Schooling, intelligence, and income. *American Psychologist, 52,* 1051–1058.

Centers for Disease Control and Prevention (1994, August 29). Zidovudine for the prevention of HIV transmission from mothers to infants. *Morbidity and Mortality Weekly Report, 43,* 577–581.

Cernoch, J. M., & Porter, R. H. (1985). Recognition of maternal axillary odors by infants. *Child Development, 56,* 1593–1598.

Chall, J. S., Jacobs, V. & Baldwin, L. (1990). *The reading crisis: Why poor children fall behind.* Cambridge, Mass.: Harvard University Press.

Chamberlain, P., & Patterson, G. R. (1995). Discipline and child compliance in parenting. In M. H. Bornstein (ed.), *Handbook of parenting: Vol. 4. Applied and practical parenting* (pp. 205–226). Mahwah, N.J.: Erlbaum.

Chan, S. (1992). Families with Asian roots. In E. W. Lynch & M. J. Hanson (eds.), *Developing cross-cultural competence* (pp. 121–150). Baltimore: Paul H. Brookes Publishing Company.

Chao, R. K. (1994). Beyond parental control and authoritarian parenting style: Understanding Chinese parenting through the cultural notion of training. *Child Development, 65,* 1111–1119.

Chase, W. G., & Simon, H. A. (1973). Perception in chess. *Cognitive Psychology, 4,* 55–81.

Chase-Lansdale, L., Brooks-Gunn, J., & Paikoff, R. L. (1991). Research and programs for adolescent mothers: Missing links and future promises. *Family Relations, 40,* 396–403.

Chavkin, N. F. (ed.), *Families and schools in a pluralistic society.* Albany: State University of New York Press.

Checkly, K. (1997). The just seven . . . and the eighth. A conversation with Howard Gardner. *Educational Leadership,* September 1997, pp. 8–13.

Chen, C., Lee, S., & Stevenson, H. (1996). Long-term prediction of academic achievement of American, Chinese, and Japanese Adolescents. *Journal of Educational Psychology, 88,* 750–759.

Chen, C., Stevenson, H., Haywood, C., & Burgess, S. (1995). Culture and academic achievement: Ethnic and cross-national differences. In P. Pintrich & M. Maehr (eds.), *Advances in motivation and achievement. Culture, motivation and achievement,* Vol. 9, pp. 119–152. Greenwich, Conn.: JAI Press, Inc.

Chen, X., Hastings, P. D., Rubin, K. H., Chen, H., Cen, G., & Stewart, S. L. (1998). Child-rearing attitudes and behavioral inhibition in Chinese and Canadian toddlers: A cross-cultural study. *Developmental Psychology, 34,* 677–686.

Cherlin, A. J., & Furstenberg, F. F. (1986). *The new American grandparent: A place in the family, a life apart.* New York: Basic Books.

Chess, S., & Thomas, A. (1984). *Origins and evolution of behavior disorders.* New York: Brunner/Mazel.

Chi, M. T. H. (1978). Knowledge structure and memory development. In R. Siegler (ed.), *Children's thinking: What develops?* Hillsdale, N.J.: Erlbaum.

Chi, M. T. H., Feltovich, P. J., & Glaser, R. (1981). Categorization and representation of physic problems by experts and novices. *Cognitive Science, 5,* 121–152.

Chi, M. T. H., & Koeske, R. D. (1983). Network representation of a child's dinosaur knowledge. *Developmental Psychology, 19,* 29–39.

Children's Defense Fund (1996). *Yearbook 1996. The state of American's children.* Washington, D.C.: Author.

Children's Defense Fund (1999). *Yearbook 1999. The state of American's children.* Washington, D.C.: Author.

Children's Defense Fund (2000). *Yearbook 2000. The state of American's children.* Washington, D.C.: Author.

Chomsky, C. (1970). *Reading, writing, and phonology.* Harvard Educational Review, 40, 297–309.

Chomsky, N. (1957). *Syntactic structures.* The Hague, The Netherlands: Mouton.

Chomsky, N. (1965). *Aspects of the theory of syntax.* Cambridge, Mass.: MIT Press.

Chomsky, N. (1986). *Knowledge of language: Its nature, origin and use.* New York: Praeger.

Christenson, S., Rounds, R., and Gorney, D. (1992). Family factors and student achievement: An avenue to increase students' success. *School Psychology Quarterly, 7,* 178–206.

Cicchetti, D., & Toth, S. L. (1998). The development of depression in children and adolescents. *American Psychologist, 53,* 221–241.

Clarizio, H. F. (1997). Conduct Disorder: Developmental considerations. *Psychology in the Schools, 34,* 253–265.

Clark, H., & Clark, E. (1977). *Psychology and language.* New York: Harcourt Brace Jovanovich.

Clark, L. A., Kochanska, G., & Ready, R. (2000). Mothers' personality and its interaction with child temperament as predictors of parenting behavior. *Journal of Personality and Social Psychology, 79,* 274–285

Clark, M. L. (1991). Social identity, peer relations, and academic competence of African American adolescents. *Education and Urban Society, 24* (1), 41–52.

Clark, V. P., Eschholz, P. A., & Rosa, A. F. (eds). (1985). *Language: Introductory readings.* New York: St. Martin's Press.

Clarke, S. C. (1995). Advance report of final marriage statistics, 1989 and 1990. *Monthly Vital Statistics Report, 43* (12), suppl. (DHHS Publication No. [PHS] 95-1120). Hyattsville, Md: National Center for Health Statistics.

Clay, M. M. (1980). *Reading: The patterning of complex behavior* (2nd ed.). Portsmouth, N.H.: Heinemann.

Clay, M. M. (1985). *The early detection of reading difficulties* (3rd ed.). Portsmouth, N.H.: Heinemann.

Clay, M. M. (1991). *Becoming literate: The construction of inner control.* Portsmouth, N.H.: Heinemann.

Cohen, B. (1980). *Issues related to transferring reading skills from Spanish to English.* Bilingual Education Paper Series. New York: Research & Development.

Cohen, F. (1984). *Clinical genetics in nursing practice.* Philadelphia: Lippincott.

Cohen, N. J., & Minde, K. (1981). The "hyperactive syndrome" in kindergarten children: Comparison of children with pervasive and situational symptoms. *Journal of Child Psychology and Psychiatry, 24,* 443–455.

Cohn, D. A. (1990). Child-mother attachment of six-year-olds and social competence at school. *Child Development, 61,* 152–162.

Coie, J. D., & Dodge, K. (1998). Aggression and antisocial behavior. In W. Dammon (series ed.), & N. Eisenburg (vol. ed.), *Handbook of child development, Vol. 3. Social, emotional and personality development* (pp. 779–862). New York: John Wiley.

Coie, J. D., & Dodge, K. A. (1983). Continuities and changes in children's sociometric status. A five-year longitudinal study. *Merrill-Palmer Quarterly, 29,* 261–282.

Coie, J. D., Dodge, K., & Kuperschmidt, J. B. (1990). Peer group behavior and social status. In S. K. Asher and J. D. Coie (eds.), *Peer rejection in childhood* (pp. 17–59). New York: Cambridge University Press.

Coles, R. (1997). *The moral intelligence of children.* New York: Random House.

Collins, W. A., Maccoby, E. E., Steinberg, L., Hetherington, E. M., & Bornstein, M. H. (2000). Contemporary research on parenting: The case for nature and nurture. *American Psychologist, 55,* 218–232.

Collins, W. A., Harris, M. L., & Susman, A. (1996). Parenting during middle childhood. In M. H. Borstein (ed.), *Handbook of parenting: Vol 1. Children and parenting* (pp. 65–90). Mahwah, N.J.: Erlbaum.

Comer, J. (1989). Educating poor minority children. *Scientific American, 259* (9), 42–48.

Comer, J. (1985). The Yale-New Haven Primary Prevention Project: A follow-up. *Journal of the American Academy of Child Psychiatry, 24,* 154–160.

Comer, J. O., & Haynes, H. D. (1999). The dynamics of school change: Response to the article, "Comer's School Development Program in Prince George's County, Maryland: A theory-based evaluation," by Thomas D. Cook et al. *American Educational Journal, 36* (3), 599–607.

Comer, J. P., Haynes, H. D., Joyner, E. T., & Ben Avie, M. (1996). *Rallying the whole village: The Comer process for reforming education.* New York: Teachers College Press.

Comer, J. P., & Poussaint, A. F. (1992). *Raising black children.* New York: Penguin Books.

Compas, B. E., Connor-Smith, J. K., Saltzman, H., Thomsen, A. H., & Wadsworth, M. (2001). Coping with stress during childhood and adolescence: Problems, progress, and potential in theory and research. *Psychological Bulletin, 127,* 87–127.

Compas, B., Ey, S., & Grant, K. (1993). Taxonomy, assessment, and diagnosis of depression during adolescence. *Psychological Bulletin, 114,* 323–344.

Conger, R., Conger, K., Elder, G., Lorenz, F., Simons, R., & Whitbeck, L. (1992). A family process model of economic hardship and adjustment of early adolescent boys. *Child Development, 63,* 526–541.

Conklin, M. E., & Dailey, A. R., (1981). Does consistency of parental encouragement matter for secondary students? *Sociology of Education, 54,* 254–262.

Conner, J. M., Schackman, M., & Serbin, L. A. (1978). Sex-related differences in response to practice on a visual-spatial test and generalization to a related test. *Child Development, 49,* 24–29.

Cook, B. G. (2001). A comparison of teachers' attitudes toward their included students with middle and severe disabilities. *The Journal of Special Education, 34,* 203–213.

Cook, B. G., Semmel, M. I., & Gerber, M. M. (1999). Attitudes of principals and special education teachers toward inclusion: Critical differences of opinion. *Remedial and Special Education, 20,* 199–207, 256.

Cook, B. G., Tankersley, M., Cook, L., & Landrum, T. J. (2000). Teachers' attitudes toward their included students with disabilities. *Exceptional Children, 67,* 115–135.

Coon, H., Fulker, D., DeFries, J. C., & Plomin, R. (1990). Home environment and cognitive ability of 7-year-old children in the Colorado Adoption Project: Genetic and environmental etiologies. *Developmental Psychology, 26,* 459–468.

Cooper H., Nye, B., Charlton, K., Lindsay, J. & Greathouse, S. (1996). The effects of summer vacation on achievement test scores: A narrative and meta-analysis review. *Review Educational Research, 66,* 227–269.

Coulton, C. J., Korbin, J. E., Su, M., & Chow, J. (1995). Community level factors and child maltreatment rates. *Child Development, 66,* 1262–1276.

Cox, M. J., & Paley, B. (1997). Families as systems. *Annual Review of Psychology, 48,* 243–267.

Craik, F. I. M., & Lockhart, R. S. (1972). Levels of processing: A framework for memory research. *Journal of Verbal Learning and Verbal Behavior, 12,* 599–607.

Crain-Thoreson, C., & Dale, P. S. (1992). Do early talkers become early readers? Linguistic precocity, preschool language, and emergent literacy. *Developmental Psychology, 28,* 421–429.

Cramer, C., & Davidhizar, R. (1999). FAS/FAE: impact on children. *Journal of Child Health Care, 3* (3), 31–54.

Cratty, B. J. (1986). *Perceptual and motor development in infants and children* (3rd ed.). Englewood Cliffs, N.J.: Prentice Hall.

Crnic, K., & Greenberg, M. (1987). Maternal stress, social support, and coping: Influences on early mother-child relationships. In C. Boukydis (ed.), *Research on support for parents and infants in the postnatal period* (pp. 25–40). Norwood, N.J.: Ablex.

Crosbie-Burnett, M., & Helmbrecht, L. (1993). A descriptive study of gay male stepfamilies. *Family Relations, 43,* 394–399.

Crouter, A. C., MacDermid, S. M., McHale, S. M., & Perry-Jenkins, M. (1990). Parental monitoring and perceptions of children's school performance and conduct in dual- and single-earner families. *Developmental Psychology, 23,* 649–657.

Crowehurst, M., & Piche, G. L. (1979). Audience and mode of discourse effects on syntactic complexity in writing at two grade levels. *Research in the Teaching of English, 13,* 101–109.

Csikszentmihalyi, M., & Larson, R. (1984). *Being adolescent: Conflict and growth in the teenage years.* New York: Basic Books.

Csikszentmihalyi, M., & Rathunde, K., & Walen, S. (1993). *Talented teenagers: The roots of success and failure.* New York: Cambridge University Press.

Cullinan, B. E. (ed.). (1987). *Children's literature in the reading program.* Newark, Del.: International Reading Association.

Cullinan, B. E. (ed.). (1992). *Invitation to read: More children's literature in the reading program.* Newark, Del.: International Reading Association.

Cummings, M. E., & O'Reilly, A. W. (1997). Fathers in family context: Effects of marital quality on child adjustment. In M. E. Lamb (ed.), *The role of the father in child development* (pp. 49–65). New York: John Wiley.

Cunningham, A. E., & Stanovich, K. E. (1991). Tracking the unique effects of print exposure in children: Associations with vocabulary, general knowledge, and spelling. *Journal of Educational Psychology, 83,* 264–274.

Cunningham, P. M. (1995). *Phonics they use: Words for reading and writing.* New York: HarperCollins.

Curtin, S., & Martin, J. (2000). *Births: Preliminary data for 1999. National Vital Statistics Reports, 48* (14). Washington, D.C.: U.S. Department of Health and Human Service, Centers for Disease Control and Prevention.

Curtiss, S. (1977). *Genie: A psycholinguistic study of a modern-day "wild child."* New York: Academic Press.

Dahl, R. E. (1999). The consequences of insufficient sleep for adolescents, *Phi Delta Kappan, 80* (5), 354–359.

Daly, M., & Wilson, M. (1996). Violence against stepchildren. *Current Directions in Psychological Science, 5,* 77–81.

Damico, J., & Oller, J. W., Jr. (1980). Pragmatic versus morphological/syntactic criteria for language referrals.

Language, Speech, and Hearing Services in Schools, 11, 85–94.

Damon, W. (1999). Moral development of children. *Scientific American, 281,* 72–79.

Daniels, H. A. (1985). Nine ideas about language. In V. Clark, P. Eschholz, & A. Rosa (eds.), *Language: Introductory readings* (pp. 18–36). New York: St. Martin's Press.

Dauber, S. L., & Epstein, J. L. (1993). Parents' attitudes and practices of involvement in inner-city elementary and middle schools. In N. F. Chavkin (ed.), *Families and schools in pluralistic society* (pp. 53–71). Albany: State University of New York Press.

DeCasper, A. (1980). *Newborn preference for maternal voice: An indication of early attachment.* Paper presented at the meeting of the Southeastern Conference on Human Development, Alexandria, Va.

Decker, S. N., & DeFries, J. C. (1980). Cognitive abilities in families with reading disabled children. *Journal of Learning Disabilities, 13,* 517–522.

DeFries, J. C., Fulker, D. W., & LaBuda, M. C. (1987). Evidence for a genetic etiology in reading disability of twins. *Nature,* 537–539.

DeGarmo, D. S., Forgatch, M. S., & Martinez, C. R., Jr. (1999). Parenting of divorced mothers as a link between social status and boys' academic outcomes: Unpacking the effects of socioeconomic status. *Child Development, 70,* 1231–1245.

DeLoache, J. S. & DeMendoza, O.A.P. (1987). Joint picture book interactions of mothers and one-year-old children. *British Journal of Developmental Psychology, 5,* 11–123.

Delgado-Gaitan, C. (1988). The value of conformity: Learning to stay in school. *Anthropology and Educational Quarterly, 19* (4), 354–381.

Delgado-Gaitan, C., & Trueba, H. (1991). *Crossing cultural borders.* New York: Falmer Press.

Delpit, L. D. (1988). The silenced dialogue: Power and pedagogy and educating other people's children. *Harvard Educational Review, 58,* 280–298.

Delpit, L. D. (1990). Language diversity and learning. In S. Hynds & D. L. Rubin (eds.), *Perspectives on talk and learning.* Urbana, Ill.: National Council for Teachers of English.

Denham, S. (1998). *Emotional development in young children.* New York: Guildford Press.

DeVries, R. (1990). *Constructivist early education: Overview and comparisons with other programs.* Washington, D.C.: National Association for the Education of Young Children.

Dewey, A. (1983). *Pecos Bill.* New York: Mulberry Books.

Diagnosis and Treatment of Attention Deficit Hyperactivity Disorder. NIH Consensus Statement Online 1998. Nov. 16–18, 16 (2).

Diaz, R M. (1983). Thought and two languages: The impact of bilingualism on cognitive development. *Review of Research in Education*, 10, 23–54.

Dorman, G. J. (1984). *How to multiply your baby's intelligence*. Garden City, N.Y.: Doubleday.

Dornbusch, S., & Ritter, P. (1996). Parents of high school students: A neglected resource. *Educational Horizons*, 66 (2), 75–77.

Dornbusch, S., Ritter, P., Liderman, P., Roberts, D., & Fraleigh, M. (1987). The relation of parenting styles to adolescent school performance. *Child Development*, 58, 1244–1257.

Dornbusch, S., Ritter, P., & Steinberg, L. (1991). Community influences on the relation of family statuses to adolescent school performance: Difference between African-American and non-Hispanic whites. *American Journal of Education*, 99, 543–567.

Downey, D. B., & Powell, B. (1993). Do children in single-parent households fare better living with same-sex parents? *Journal of Marriage and the Family*, 55, 55–71

Dreikurs, R. (1982). *Maintaining sanity in the classroom*. New York: Harper & Row.

Driver, R., Gruesne, E., & Tiberghein, A. (1985). *Children's ideas in science*. Philadelphia: Open University Press.

Dryfoos, J. (1990). *Adolescents at risk: Prevalence and prevention*. New York: Oxford University Press.

Dryfoos, J. (1994). *Full–service schools: A revolution in health and social services for children, youth, and families*. San Francisco: Jossey Bass.

Dryfoos, J. (1999). The role of school in children's out-of-school time. *The Future of Children. When School Is Out*, 9 (2), 117–132.

Dubas, J., Graber, J., & Petersen, A. (1991). A longitudinal investigation of adolescents' changing perceptions of pubertal timing. *Developmental Psychology*, 27, 580–586.

DuBors, D. L., Tevendale, H. D. Burk-Braxton, C., Suenson, L., & Hardesty, J., (2000). Self-system influences during early adolescence: Investigation of an integrature model. *Journal of Early Adolescent*, 12–43.

Duckworth, E. (1964). Piaget rediscovered. In R. Ripple & V. Rockcastle (eds.), *Piaget rediscovered* (pp. 1–5). Ithaca, N.Y.: Cornell University Press.

Duncan, G. J., & Brooks-Gunn, J. (eds.) (1997). *Consequences of growing up poor*. New York: Sage.

Duncan, G. J., & Rogers, W. (1988). Longitudinal aspects of childhood poverty. *Journal of Marriage and the Family*, 50, 1007–1021.

Duncan, P., Ritter, P., Dornbusch, S., Gross, R., & Carlsmith, J. (1985). The effects of pubertal timing on body image, school behavior, and deviance. *Journal of Youth and Adolescence*, 14, 227–236.

Durst, R. (1987). Cognitive and linguistic demands of analytic writing. *Research in the Teaching of English*, 21, 347–376.

Dwyer, K., Osher, D., & Wager, C. (1998). *Early warning, tiimely response: A guide to safe schools*. Washington, D.C.: U.S. Department of Education. Available online: http://www.ed.gov/goffices/OSERS/OSEP/earlywrn.html.

Dyson, A. H. (1993). *Social worlds of children learning to write in an urban primary school*. New York: Teachers College Press.

Eaton, J., Anderson, C., & Smith, E. (1984). Students' misconceptions interfere with science learning: Case studies of fifth-grade students. *Elementary School Journal*, 64, 365–379.

Eaton, W. O., Chipperfield, J. G., & Singeil, C. E. (1989). Birth order and activity level in children. *Developmental Psychology*, 25, 668–672.

Eccles, J., Midgley, C. M., Wigfield, A., Buchanan, C. M., Reuman, D., Flanagan, C., & Mac Iver, D. (1993). Development during adolescence. The impact of stage-environment fit on young adolescents; experiences in schools and in families. *American Psychologist*, 48 (2), 90–101.

Eccles, J. S. & Barber, B. L. (1999). Student council, volunteering, basketball, or marching band: What kind of extra-curriculum involvement matters? *Journal of Adolescent Research*, 14, 10–43.

Eccles, J., Jacobs, J., & Harold, R. (1991). Gender role stereotypes, expectancy effects, and parents' role in the socialization of gender differences in self-perceptions and skill acquisition. *Journal of Social Issues*, 46, 182–201.

Eccles, J. S., & Harold, R. D. (1993). Parent-school involvement during the early adolescent years. *Teachers College Record*, 94 (3), 568–587.

Eccles, J. S., & Harold, R. D. (1996). Family involvement in children's and adolescents' schooling. In A. Booth & J. Dunn (eds.), *Family school links* (pp. 3–34). Mahwah, N.J.: Erlbaum.

Eccles, J., Lord, S., & Midgley, C. (1991). What are we doing to early adolescents: The impact of educational contexts on early adolescents. *American Journal of Education*, 99, 521–542.

Eccles, J., Midgley, C., & Adler, T. (1984). Grade-related changes in school environment: Effects on achievement motivation. In J. G. Nichols (ed.), *Advances in Motivation and Achievement* (Vol. 3). New York: Academic Press.

References

Eccles, J. S., & Harold, R. D. (1991). Gender differences in sport involvement: Applying the Eccles' expectancy-value model. *Journal of Applied Sport Psychology, 3,* 7–35.

Echols, L. D., West, R. F., Stanovich, K. E., & Zehr, K. S. (1996). Using children's literacy activities to predict growth in verbal cognitive skills: A longitudinal investigation. *Journal of Educational Psychology, 88,* 296–304.

Edelsky, C., Altwerger, B., & Flores, B. (1991). *Whole language: What's the difference?* Portsmouth, N.H.: Heinemann.

Edin, K., & Lein, L. (1997). *Making ends meet: How single mothers survive welfare and low-wage work.* New York: Sage.

Eisenburg, N. & Fabes, R. A. (1998). Prosocial development. In. W. Dammon (series ed.) & N. Eisenburg (vol. ed.), *Handbook of child psychology, Vol. 4. Social-ization, personality, and social development.* (pp. 701–778). New York: John Wiley.

Eisenburg, N., Martin, C. L., & Fabes, R. A. (1996). Gender development and gender effects. In D. C. Berliner & R. C. Calfee (eds.), *The handbook of educational psychology,* (pp. 358–396). New York: McMillan.

Eisner, E. W. (1991). Rethinking literacy. *Educational Horizons, 69,* 120–128.

Elkind, D. (1967). Egocentrism in adolescence. *Child Development, 38,* 361–375.

Elkind, D. (1981). *The hurried child: Growing up too fast too soon.* Reading, Mass.: Addison Wesley.

Elkind, D. (1983). *The hurried child.* Reading, Mass.: Addison Wesley.

Elliot, A. J. (1981). *Child language.* Cambridge, England: Cambridge University Press.

Emery, R. E. (1999). *Marriage, divorce, and children's adjustment* (3rd ed.). Newbury Park, Calif.: Sage

Ensminger, M., & Alexander, K. (1993). Paths to high school graduation or dropout: A longitudinal study of first-grade cohorts. *Sociology of Education, 65,* 95–113.

Entwisle, D., & Alexander, K. (1993). Entry into school: The beginning school transition and educational stratification in the United States. *Annual Review of Sociology, 19,* 401–423.

Entwisle, D., & Hayduk, L. (1982). *Early schooling: Cognitive and affective outcomes.* Baltimore: Johns Hopkins Press.

Entwisle, D., & Stevenson, H. W. (1987). Schools and development. *Child Development, 58,* 1149–1150.

Epstein, J. L. (1995). School/family/community partnerships: Caring for the children we share. *Phi Delta Kappan, 76* (9), 701–712.

Epstein, J. L. (1996). Perspectives and previews on research and policy for school, family, and community partnerships. In A. Booth & J. Dunn (eds.), *Family school links: How do they affect educational outcomes?* (pp. 209–246). Mahwah, N.J.: Erlbaum.

Epstein, J. (1987). Parent involvement: What research says to adjustments. *Education and Urban Society, 19* (2), 119–136.

Epstein, J. L. (1988). How do we improve programs for parent involvement? *Educational Horizons, 66,* 58–59.

Epstein, J. L., & Connors, L. J. (1992). Six types of involvement in the middle grades and high schools. *The Practitioner, 18* (4), 1–8.

Erickson, F., & Mohatt, G. (1982). Cultural organization of participant structures in two classrooms of Indian students. In G. D. Spindler (ed.), *Doing the ethnography of schooling: Educational anthropology in action* (pp. 132–174). New York: Holt, Reinhart & Winston.

Ericsson, K. A., Krampe, R., & Tesch-Romer, C. (1993). The role of deliberate practice in the acquisition of expert performance. *Psychological Review, 100,* 363–406.

Erikson, E. H. (1958). *Young man Luther: A study of psychoanalysis and history.* New York: Norton.

Erikson, E. H. (1963). *Childhood and society.* New York: Norton.

Erikson, E. H. (1969). *Gandhi's truth: On the origins of militant nonviolence.* New York: Norton.

Eron, L. D., Huesman, L. R., Lefkowitz, M. M., Walder, L. O. (1996). Does television violence cause aggression? In D. F. Greenberg (ed.), *Criminal Careers* (Vol. 2, pp. 311–321). Aldershot, England: Darmouth Publishing.

Ervin-Tripp, S. (1964). Imitation and structural change children's language. In E. H. Lenneberg (ed.), *New directions in the study of language* (pp. 163–189). Cambridge, Mass.: MIT Press.

Espelage, D., Bosworth, K., & Simon, T. (2000). Examining the social context of bullying behaviors in early adolescence. *Journal of Counseling and Development, 78,* 326–333.

Ezzell, C. (2000). Beyond the human genome. *Scientific American, 283* (1), 64–69.

Fagot, B., & Kavanaugh, K. (1991). Observations of parent reactions to sex-stereotyped behavior: Age and sex effects. *Child Development, 62,* 617–628.

Falbo, T. (1992). Social norms and the one-child family: Clinical and policy implications. In F. Boer & J. Dunn (eds.), *Children's sibling relationships* (pp. 71–82). Hillsdale, N.J.: Erlbaum.

Farley, R., & Allen, W. (1987). *The color line and the quality of life in America.* New York: Oxford University Press.

Fashola, O. (1998). *Review of extended-day and after-school programs and their effectiveness*. (Report No. 24). Baltimore: Johns Hopkins University, Center for Research on the Education of Students Placed at Risk.

Federal Interagency Forum on Child and Family Statistics (2000). *America's children: Key national indicators of well-being, 2000*. Washington, D.C.: U.S. Government Printing Office.

Feinman, S., & Lewis, M. (1983). Social referencing at ten months: A second order effect on infants' responses to strangers. *Child Development, 54*, 878–887.

Feldlaufer, H., Midgley, C., & Eccles, J. S. (1988). Student, teacher, and observer perceptions of the classroom before and after the transition to junior high school. *Journal of Early Adolescence, 8*, 133–156

Fenzel, L. M. (2000). Prospective study of changes global self-worth and strain during the transition to middle school. *Journal of Early Adolescence, 20*, 93–116.

Ferreiro, R., & Teberosky, A. (1982). *Literacy before schooling*. Portsmouth, N.H.: Heinemann.

Field, T. M., Schanberg, S. M., Scafidi, F., Bauer, C. R., Vega-Lahr, N., Garcia, R., Nystrom, J., & Kuhn, C. M. (1986). Effects of tactile/kinesthetic stimulation on preterm neonates. *Pediatrics, 77*, 654–658.

Field T. M. (1990). *Infancy*. Cambridge, Mass.: Harvard University Press.

Fine, M. A., Voydanoff, P., & Donnelly, B. W. (1993). The relations between parental control and warmth and child well-being in stepfamilies. *Journal of Family Psychology, 7*, 222–232.

Fischer, J. L., Munsch, J., & Greene, S. M. (1996). Adolescence in intimacy. In G. R. Adams & R. Montemayor (eds.), *Psychosocial development during adolescence* (Vol. 8, pp. 95–129). Thousand Oaks, Calif.: Sage.

Fischer, M. (1990). Parenting stress and the child with attention deficit hyperactivity disorder. *Journal of Clinical Child Psychology, 19*, 337–346.

Fisher, K. (1980). A theory of cognitive development: The control and construction of hierarchies of skills. *Psychological Review, 87*, 477–531.

Fix, M., & Passel, J. S. (1994). *Immigration and immigrants: Setting the record straight*. Washington, D.C.: Urban Institute.

Flaks, D. K., Ficher, I., Masterpasqua, F., & Joseph, G. (1995). Lesbians choosing motherhood: A comparative study of lesbian and heterosexual parents and their children. *Developmental Psychology, 31*, 105–114.

Flavell, J., Beach, D., & Chinsky, J. (1966). Spontaneous verbal rehearsal in memory task as a function of age. *Child Development, 37*, 283–299.

Flavell, J. H. (1985). *Cognitive development* (2nd ed.). Englewood Cliffs, N.J.: Prentice Hall.

Flavell, J. H., Green, F. L., & Flavell, E. (1986). Development of knowledge about the appearance-reality distinction. *Monographs of the Society of Child Development, 51* (1, Serial No. 22).

Flavell, J. H., & Miller, P. (1998). Social Cognition. In W. Damon (gen. ed.), & D. Kuhn & R. Siegler (vol. eds.), *Handbook of child psychology, Vol. 2: Cognition, Perception, and Language* (pp. 851–898). New York: John Wiley.

Flavell, J. H., & Miller, P. H. (1998). Social cognition. In D. Kuhn & R. Siegler (eds.). *Handbook of child psychology, Vol. 2: Cognition, perception, and language* (4th ed., pp. 851–898). New York: John Wiley.

Flavell, J. H., Mumme, D. L., Green, F. L., & Flavell, E. R. (1992). Young children's understanding of different types of beliefs. *Child Development, 63*, 960–977.

Fletcher, A., Dailiry, N. E., Steinburg, L., & Dornbusch, S. M. (1995). The company they keep: Relation of adolescents' adjustment and behavior to their friends' perception of authoritative parenting in the social network. *Developmental Psychology, 31*, 300–310.

Florio-Ruane, S. (1985). *Creating your own case study*. Unpublished manuscript. Michigan State University.

Fordham, S. (1996). *Blacked out dilemmas of race, identity, and success at Capitol hill*. Chicago: University of Chicago Press.

Forness, S. R., Kavale, K. A., & Walker, H. M. (1999). Identifying children at risk for antisocial behavior: The case for comorbidity. In Gallimore, R., Bernheimer, L. P., MacMillan, D. L., Speece, D. L., & Vaughn, S. (eds.), *Developmental perspectives on children with high-incidence disabilities*. Mahwah, N.J.: Erlbaum.

Forum on Child and Family Statistics (1999). *America's children: Key national indicators of well-being, 1999*. Washington, D.C.: U.S. Government Printing Office.

Fox, G. L., & Kelly, R. F. (1995). Determinants of child custody arrangements at divorce. *Journal of Marriage and the Family, 57*, 693–708.

Freedom Writers (1999). *The freedom writers diary*. New York: Doubleday.

Frey, K., Hirschstein, M. K., & Guzzo, B. A. (2000). Second step: Preventing aggression by promoting social competence. *Journal of Emotional and Behavioral Disorders, 8*, 102–113.

Friedlander, B. (1970). Receptive language development in infancy. *Merrill-Palmer Quarterly, 16*, 7–51.

Frieman, B. B. (1993). Separation and divorce: Children want their teachers to know—meeting the emotional needs of preschool and primary school children. *Young Children, 48* (6), 58–63.

Frieman, B. B. (1997). Two parents—two homes. *Educational Leadership, 54* (7), 23–25.

Fuligni, A. J. (1997). The academic achievement of adolescents from immigrant families: The roles of family background, attitudes, and behavior. *Child Development, 68,* 351–363.

Fuligini, A. J., & Eccles, J. S. (1993). Perceived parent-child relationships and early adolescents' orientations toward peers. *Developmental Psychology, 29,* 622–632.

Furham, S. (1988). Racelessness as a factor in black students' school success: Pragmatic Strategy on Pyretic Victory? *Harvard Educational Review, 58,* 54–84.

Furman, W., & Buhrmester, D. (1992). Age and sex differences in perception of networks of personal relationships. *Child Development, 63,* 103–115.

Furstenberg, F. F., Jr. (1988). Child care after divorce and remarriage. In E. M. Hetherington & J. D. Arasteh (eds.), *Impact of divorce, single-parenting, and stepparenting on children* (pp. 245–261). Hillsdale, N.J.: Erlbaum.

Furstenberg, F. F., Jr., Brooks-Gunn, J., & Chase-Lansdale, L. (1989). Teenaged pregnancy and child bearing. *American Psychologist, 44,* 313–320.

Furstenberg, F. F., Jr., & Cherlin, A. J. (1991). *Divided families: What happens to children when parents part.* Cambridge, Mass.: Harvard University Press.

Furstenberg, F. F., Jr., & Nord, C. W. (1985). Parenting apart: Patterns of childrearing after marital disruption. *Journal of Marriage and the Family, 47,* 893–904.

Gadsden, V. L. (1999). Black families in intergenerational and cultural perspective. In M. E. Lamb (ed.), *Parenting and child development in "nontraditional" families* (pp. 221–246). Mahwah, N.J.: Erlbaum.

Gadsden, V. L., Smith, R. R., & Jordan, W. J. (1996). The promise of desegregation: Tendering expectation and reality in achieving quality schooling. *Urban Education, 31* (4), 381–402.

Galambos, N. L., & Maggs, J. L. (1991). Out-of-school care of young adolescents and self-reported behavior. *Developmental Psychology, 27,* 644–655.

Galda, L., Cullinan, B. E., & Strickland, D. S. (1993). *Language, literacy, and the child.* Fort Worth: Harcourt Brace.

Garber, H. (1988). *The Milwaukee project: Preventing mental retardation in children at-risk.* Washington, D.C.: American Association on Mental Retardation.

Garcia, E. E. (1994). "Hispanic" Children: Effective Schooling Practices and Related Policy Issues. In N. Ellsworth, C. Hedley, & A. Baratta (eds.), *Literacy: A redefinition* (pp. 77–87). Hillsdale, N.J.: Erlbaum.

Gardner, H. (1983). *Frames of mind: The theory of multiple intelligences.* New York: Basic Books.

Gardner, H. (1993). The relationship between early giftedness and later achievement. In G. R. Bock & K. Ackrill (eds.), *The origins and development of high ability* (pp. 175–182). New York: John Wiley.

Gardner, H. (1999). *Intelligence reframed multiple intelligences for the 21st century.* New York: Basic Books.

Gardner, H., & Hatch, T. (1989). Multiple intelligences go to school. *Educational Researcher, 18,* 4–10.

Garland, A., & Zigler, E. (1993). Adolescent suicide prevention. *American Psychologist, 48,* 169–182.

Ge, X., Conger, R. D., & Elder, G. H. (1996). Coming of age too early: Pubertal influences on girls' vulnerability to psychological distress. *Child Development, 67,* 3386–4000. *Findings from three longitudinal studies.* Unpublished manuscript. University of North Carolina-Chapel Hill.

Geiger, B. (1996). *Fathers as primary caregivers.* Westport, Conn.: Greenwood.

Gelman, R. (1969). Conservation acquisition: A problem of learning to attend to relevant attributes. *Journal of Experimental Child Psychology, 7,* 167–187.

Gelman, R. (1972). Logical capacity of very young children: Number invariance rules. *Child Development, 43,* 75–90.

Gelman, R., & Baillargeon, R. (1983). A review of Piagetian concepts. In J. Flavell & E. Markman (eds.), *Handbook of child psychology: Cognitive development,* Vol. 3 (pp. 167–230).

Gelman, R., & Gallistel, C. R. (1978). *Children's understanding of number.* Cambridge, Mass. Harvard University Press.

Gelman, R., & Meck, E. (1983). Preschoolers' counting: Principles after skills. *Cognition, 13,* 343–359.

Gelman, R., & Shatz, M. (1976). Appropriate speech adjustments: The operation of conversational constraints on talk to two-year-olds. In M. Lewis & L. Rosenblum (eds.), *Conversation, interaction, and the development of language.* New York: John Wiley.

Gentry, R. (1982). An analysis of the developmental spellings in *Gnys at Wrk. The Reading Teacher, 36,* 192–200.

Gesell, A., & Ilg, F. (1946). *The child from five to ten.* New York: Harper Brothers.

Gesell, A., Ilg., F., & Ames, L. (1956). *Youth: The years from ten to sixteen.* New York: Harper Brothers.

Gibson, E. J., & Walk, R. D. (1960). The "visual cliff." *Scientific American, 202,* 64–71.

Gibson, E., & Radar, N. (1979). Attention: The perceiver as performer. In G. Hale & M. Lewis (eds.), *Attention and cognitive development* (pp. 1–22). New York: Plenum.

Gilligan, C. (1982). In a different voice. Cambridge, Mass.: Harvard University Press.

Ginsburg, G. S., & Bronstein, P. (1993). Family factors related to children's intrinsic/extrinsic motivational orientation and academic performance. Child Development, 64, 1461–1474.

Ginsburg, H., & Opper, S. (1988). Piaget's theory of intellectual development (3rd ed.). Englewood Cliffs, N.J.: Prentice Hall.

Gleason, J., Berko, J., & Weintraub, S. (1976). The acquisition of routines in child language. Language in Society, 5, 129–136.

Gnepp, J., & Chilamkurti, C. (1988). Children's use of personality attributions to predict people's emotional and behavioral reactions. Child Development, 59, 743–754.

Goldberg, M. F. (1997, March). Maintaining a focus on the child. Phi Delta Kappan, pp. 557–559.

Golden, D. (1994, July). Building a better brain. Life Magazine, pp. 62–70.

Goleman, D. (1995). Emotional Intelligence. Why it can matter more than IQ. New York: Bantam.

Golombok, S., & Tasker, F. L. (1996). Do parents influence the sexual orientation of their children? Findings from a longitudinal study of lesbian families. Developmental Psychology, 32, 3–11.

Gongla, P. A., & Thompson, E. H., Jr. (1987). Single-parent families. In M. B. Sussman & S. K. Steinmetz (eds.), Handbook of marriage and the family (pp. 397–418). New York: Plenum.

Good, T., & Brophy, J. (1972). Behavioral expression of teacher attitudes. Journal of Educational Psychology, 63, 617–624.

Goodlad, J. (1984). A place called school. New York: McGraw-Hill.

Goodman, G. S., Emery, R. E., & Haugaard, J. J. (1998). Developmental psychology and law: Divorce, child maltreatment, foster care, and adoption. In W. Damon (gen. ed.) & I. E. Sigel & K. A. Renninger (vol. eds.), Handbook of child psychology: Vol. 4. Child psychology in practice. New York: John Wiley.

Goodman, K. (1976). Reading: A psycholinguistic guessing game. In H. Singer & R. Ruddell (eds.), Theoretical modes and processes of reading (2nd ed.) (pp. 497–508). Newark, Del.: International Reading Association.

Goodman, K. (1986). What's whole in whole language? Portsmouth, N.H.: Heinemann.

Goodman, K. (1992). I didn't found whole language. The Reading Teacher, 46, 188–199.

Goodman, K., & Goodman, Y. (1979). Learning to read is natural. In L. B. Resnick & P. S. Weaver (eds.), Theory and practice of early reading (Vol. 1). Hillsdale, N.J.: Erlbaum.

Goodman, Y. (1978). Kid-watching: An alternative to testing. National Elementary Principal, 10, 41–45.

Goodnow, J. (1985). Change and variation in ideas about childhood and parenting. In I. E. Sigel (ed.), Parent belief systems (pp. 235–270). Hillsdale, N.J.: Erlbaum.

Gopnik, A., Meltzoff, A., Kuhl, P. (1999). The scientist in the crib: Minds, brains and how children learn. New York: William Morrow.

Gortmaker, S., Dietz, W., & Cheung, L. (1990). Inactivity, diet, and the fattening of America. Journal of the American Dietetic Association, 90, 1247–1252.

Gottfried, A. E., Bathurst, K., & Gottfried, A. W. (1994). Role of maternal and dual-earner employment status in children's development: A longitudinal study from infancy through early adolescence. In A. E. Gottfried & A. Gottfried (eds.), Redefining families: Implications for children's development (pp. 55–97). New York: Plenum Press.

Gould, S. J. (1981). The mismeasure of man. New York: Norton.

Graber, J. A., Lewinsoh, P. M., Seeley, J. R., & Brooks-Gunn, J. (1997). Is psychopathology associated with the timing of pubertal development? Journal of the American Academy of Child and Adolescent Psychiatry, 36, 1768–1776.

Graham, S. (1994). Motivation for African Americans. Review of Educational Research, 64, 55–117.

Grant, C. A., & Gomez, M. L. (1996). Making schooling multicultural: Campus and classroom. Englewood Cliffs, N.J.: Prentice Hall.

Graue, M. E., Weinstein, T., & Walberg, H. J. (1983). School-based home instruction and learning: A quantitative analysis. Journal of Educational Research, 76 (6), 351–360.

Graves, D. H. (1979). What children show us about revision. Language Arts, 56, 312–319.

Graves, D. H. (1983). Writing: Teachers and children at work. Portsmouth, N.H.: Heinemann.

Green, R. (1978). Sexual identity of 37 children raised by homosexual or transsexual parents. American Journal of Psychiatry, 135, 692–697.

Green, R., Mandel, J. B., Hotvedt, M. E., Gray, J., & Smith, L. (1986). Lesbian mothers and their children: A comparison with solo parent heterosexual mothers and their children. Archives of Sexual Behavior, 15, 167–184.

Greenberg, J. (1995). Making friends with the Power Rangers. Young Children, 50, 60–61.

Greenberg, M., Kusche, C. A., Cook, E. T., & Quamma, J. (1995). Promoting emotional competence in school-aged children: The Effects of the PATHS curriculum. *Development and Psychopathology, 7*, 117–136.

Greenberger, E., & Goldberg, W. A. (1989). Work, parenting and the socialization of children. *Developmental Psychology, 25*, 22–35.

Greenfield, P., & Cocking, R., (eds.) (1994). *Cross–cultural roots of minority child development*. Hillsdale, N.J.: Erlbaum.

Greenough, W. T., Black, J. E., & Wallace, C. S. (1987). Experience and brain development. *Child Development, 58*, 539–559.

Greif, G. L. (1985). *Single fathers*. Lexington, Mass.: Heath.

Grinsberg, R. W. (1998). "Silenced voices inside our schools." *Initiatives, 58*, 1–15.

Gronlund, G. (1992). Coping with Ninja Turtle play in my kindergarten classroom. *Young Children, 48*, 21–25.

Gross, D., & Harris, P. L. (1988). False beliefs about emotion: children's understanding of misleading emotional displays. *International Journal of Behavioral Development, 11*, 475–488.

Grumbach, M., Roth, J., Kaplan, S., & Kelch, R. (1974). Hypothalamic-pituitary regulation of puberty in man: Evidence and concepts derived from clinical research. In M. Grumbach , G. Gave, & F. Mayer (eds.), *Control of onset of puberty*. New York: John Wiley.

Grusec, J. E., Goodnow, J. J., & Cohen, L. (1996). Household work and the development of concern for others. *Developmental Psychology, 32*, 999–1007.

Guildford, J. P. (1967). *The nature of human intelligence*. New York: McGraw-Hill.

Hack, M., Klein, N., & Taylor, G. (1995). Long-term developmental outcomes of low birth weight infants. *The Future of Children, 5*, 176–196.

Hagen, J., & Hale, G. (1973). The development of attention in children. In A. Pick (ed.), *Minnesota symposium on child psychology*, Vol. 7 (pp. 117–140). Minneapolis: University of Minnesota Press.

Hagerman, R. J. & Silverman, A. C. (1991). *Fragile X syndrome: Diagnosis, treatment, and research*. Baltimore: Johns Hopkins University Press.

Hakuta, K. (1986). *The mirror of language*. New York: Basic Books.

Hakuta, K., & Garcia, E. E. (1989). Bilingualism and education. *American Psychologist, 44*, 374–379.

Hakuta, K., & Gould, L. J. (1987). Synthesis of research on bilingual education. *Educational Leadership, 44*, 38–45.

Hale-Benson, J. (1990). Visions for children: Educating Black children in the context of their culture. In K. Lomotemy (ed.), *Going to school: The African-American experience*. Albany.: State University of New York Press.

Hall, G. S. (1904). *Adolescence: Its psychology and its relations to physiology, anthropology, sociology, sex, crime, religion, and education*. New York: Appleton-Century-Crofts.

Hallahan, D. P., & Kauffman, J. M. (2000). *Exceptional learners. Introduction to special education* (8th ed.). Boston: Allyn & Bacon.

Hamilton, R., & Ghatala, E. (1994). *Learning and instruction*. New York: McGraw-Hill.

Haney, P. & Durlak, J. (1998). Changing self-esteem in children and adolescents: A meta-analytic review. *Journal of Clinical Child Psychology, 27*, 423–433.

Hanish, L., Guerra, N. (2000). Children who get victimized at school: What is known? What can be done? *Professional School Counseling, 4* (2), 113–119.

Hanrich, C. C., Brown, J. L., Aber, J. L. (1999). Evaluating the effectiveness of school-based violence prevention: Developmental approaches. *Social Policy, Report*, Vol. XIII, Society for Research in Child Development.

Harjo, S. S. (1993). The American Indian experience. In H. P. McAdoo (ed.), *Family ethnicity: Strength in diversity* (pp. 199–207). Newbury Park, Calif.: Sage.

Harman, D. (1987). *Illiteracy: A national dilemma*. New York: Cambridge University Press.

Harrell, J., McMurray, R., Bangdiwala, S., Frauman, A., Gansky, A., & Bradley, C. (1996). The effects of a school-based intervention to reduce cardiovascular disease risk factors in elementary school children: The cardiovascular health in children (CHIC) study. *The Journal of Pediatrics, 128*, 797–805.

Harris, A. J., & Sipay, E. R. (1990). *How to increase reading ability* (9th ed.). New York: Longman.

Harris, J. R. (1998). *The nurture assumption: Why children turn out the way they do*. New York: The Free Press.

Harris, K., & Graham, S. (1985). Improving learning disabled students' composition skills: Self-control strategy training. *Learning Disability Quarterly, 8*, 27–36.

Harrison, J. (1985). Functions of language attitudes in school settings. *Language in Society, 22*, 1–21.

Harste, J. (1989). *New policy guidelines for reading: Connecting research and practice*. Urbana, Ill.: National Council for Teachers of English.

Harste, J., Short, K., & Burke, C. (1988). *Creating classrooms for authors: The reading writing connection*. Portsmouth, N.H.: Heineman.

Harste, J., Woodward, V., & Burke, C. (1984). *Language stories and literacy lessons*. Portsmouth, N.H.: Heinemann.

Hart, B., & Risley, T. R. (1992). American parenting of language-learning children: Persisting differences in family-child interactions observed in natural home environments. *Developmental Psychology, 28*, 1096–1105.

Hart, C. H., DeWolf, D., Wozniak, P., & Burts, D.C. (1992). Maternal and paternal disciplinary styles: Relations with preschoolers' playground behavioral orientations and peer status. *Child Development, 63*, 879–892.

Hart, C. H., DeWolf, D. M., & Burts, D. C. (1992). Linkages among preschoolers' playground behavior, outcome expectations, and parental disciplinary strategies. *Early Education and Development, 3*, 265–283.

Hart, E. L., Lahey, B. B., Loeber, R., Applegate, B., & Frick, P. J. (1995). Developmental changes in attention-deficit hyperactivity disorder in boys: A four-year longitudinal study. *Journal of Abnormal Child Psychology, 23*, 729–750.

Harter, S. (1986). Processes underlying the construct, maintenance, and enhancement of the self-concept in children. In J. Seils & A. Greenwald (eds.), *Psychology perspectives on the self*, Vol. 3 (pp. 137–181). Hillsdale, N.J.: Erbaum.

Harter, S. (1990). Causes correlates and the functional role of global self-work: A lifespan perspective. In R. Steinberg & J. Kolligian, Jr. (eds.) *Competence considered* (pp. 67–97). New Haven, Conn.: Yale University Press.

Harter, S. (1993). Causes and consequences of low self-esteem in children and adolescents. In R. F. Baumeister (ed.) *Self-esteem: The puzzle flow self-regard.* (pp. 87–116). New York: Plenum Press.

Harter, S. (1999). *The construction of the self.* New York: Guildford Press.

Harter S. (1998). The development of self-representations. In W. Damon (series ed.) & N. Eisenberg (vol. ed.) *Handbook of child psychology. Vol. 3: Social, emotional and personality development* (pp. 553–618). New York: John Wiley.

Harter, S. & Pike R. (1984). The pictorial scale of perceived competence, motivation orientation, and anxiety in segregated and mainstreamed educable mentally retarded children. *Journal of Education Psychology, 77*, 217–230.

Harter, S., & Whitesall, N. (1989). Developmental changes in children's understanding of single, multiple, and blended emotional concepts. In C. Saarni, & P. Harris (eds.), *Children's understanding of emotions* (pp. 81–116). Cambridge, England: Cambridge University Press.

Harter, S., Whitesall, N., & Lowalski, P. (1992). Individual differences in the effects of educational transitions on young adolescents' perception of competence and motivational orientation. *American Educational Research Journal, 29*, 77–807.

Hartup, W. W. (1996). The company they keep: Friendships and their developmental significance. *Child Development, 67*, 1–13.

Hartup, W. W., and Stevens, N. (1999). Friendships and adaptation across the lifespan. *Current Directions in Psychological Science, 8* (3), 76–79.

Harwood, R. L., Miller, J. G., & Irizarry, N. L. (1995). *Culture and attachment: Perceptions of the child in context.* New York: Guilford.

Hasslebring, T. S., & Glaser, C. H. W. (2000). Use of technology to help students with special needs. *Future of Children. Children and Computer Technology,* Vol. 10 (pp. 102–122). [available online www.futureofchildren.org].

Haston, A. C. and Wright, J. C. (1998). Mass media and children's development. In I. Sejel & K. A. Renninjer (vol. eds.), W. Damon (editor-in-chief), *Handbook of Child Psychology* (5th ed., pp. 999–1058) New York: John Wiley.

Hayman, N. & Comer, J. (1990). Helping black children succeed: The significance of some social factors. In K. Lomotey (ed.), *Going to school: The African-American experience.* Albany: State University of New York Press.

Haynes, N., & Ben-Avie, M. (1996). Parents as full partners in education. In A. Booth and J. Dunn (eds.), *Family school links: How do they affect educational outcomes?* (pp. 45–56). Mahwah, N.J.: Albaum.

Heath, S. B. (1983). *Ways with words: Language, life, and work in communities and classrooms.* Cambridge, England: Cambridge University Press.

Hedges, L., & Nowell, A. (1995). Sex differences in mental test scores, variability, and numbers of high scoring individuals. *Science, 269*, 41–45.

Heller, C., & Hawkins, J. A. (1994). Teacher tolerance: Notes from the front line. *Teachers College Record, 95*, 337–369.

Henderson, E. (1990). *Teaching spelling.* Boston: Houghton Mifflin.

Henderson, N., & Milstein, M. M. (1996). *Resiliency in schools: Making it happen for students and educators.* Thousand Oaks, Calif.: Corwin Press.

Herman-Giddens, M., Slora, E., Wasserman, R., Bourdony, C., Bhapkar, M., Koch, G., & Hasemeier, C. (1997). Secondary sexual characteristics and menses in young girls seen in office practice: A study from the Pediatric Research in Office Settings Network. *Pediatrics, 88*, 505–512.

Herrnstein, R., & Murray, C. (1994). *The bell curve: Intelligence and class structure in America.* New York: Free Press.

Hess, R. D., & Azuma, H. (1991). Cultural support for schooling: Contrasts between Japan and the United States. *Educational Researcher, 20,* 2–8, 12

Hiebert, E. H. (ed.). (1991). *Literacy for a diverse society: Perspectives, practices, and policies.* New York: Teachers College Press.

Hetherington, E. M. (1989). Coping with family transitions: Winners, losers, and survivors. *Child Development, 60,* 1–14.

Hetherington, E. M. (1991). The role of individual differences and family relationships in children's coping with divorce and remarriage. In P. A. Cowan & E. M. Hetherington (eds.), *Family transitions* (pp. 165–194). Hillsdale, N.J.: Erlbaum.

Hetherington, E. M. (1993). An overview of the Virginia longitudinal study of divorce and remarriage with a focus on early adolescence. *Journal of Family Psychology, 7,* 1–18.

Hetherington, E. M. (1998). Social capital and the development of youth from nondivorced, divorced, and remarried families. In A. Collins (ed.), *Relationships as developmental contexts: The 29th Minnesota symposium on child psychology.* Hillsdale, N.J.: Erlbaum.

Hetherington, E. M. (1999). Should we stay together for the sake of the children? In E. M. Hetherington (ed.), *Coping with divorce, single parenting, and remarriage: A risk and resiliency perspective.* Mahwah, N.J.: Erlbaum.

Hetherington, E. M., & Clingempeel, W. G. (1992). Coping with marital transition. *Monographs of the Society for Research in Child Development, 57* (2–3, Serial No. 227).

Hetherington, E. M., & Jodl, K. M. (1994). Stepfamilies as settings for child development. In A. Booth & J. Dunn (eds.), *Stepfamilies: Who benefits? Who does not?* (pp. 55–79). Hillsdale, N.J.: Erlbaum.

Hetherington, E. M., & Martin, B. (1986). Family interaction. In H. C. Quay & J. C. Werry (eds.), *Psychopathological disorders of childhood* (3rd ed., pp. 332–390). New York: John Wiley.

Hetherington, E. M., & Stanley-Hagan, M. M. (1995). Parenting in divorced and remarried families. In M. H. Bornstein (ed.), *Children and parenting* (Vol. 4). Hillsdale, N.J.: Erlbaum.

Hetherington, E. M., & Stanley-Hagan, M. M. (1999). Stepfamilies. In M. E. Lamb (ed.), *Nontraditional families.* Hillsdale, N.J.: Erlbaum.

Hetherington, E. M., Stanley-Hagan, M. M., & Anderson, E. R. (1989). Marital transitions: A child's perspective. *American Psychologist, 44,* 303–312.

Hill, C. R., & Stafford, F. P. (1980). Parental care of children: Time diary estimate of quantity, predictability, and variety. *Journal of Human Resources, 15,* 219–239.

Hirsch, B. J., & Rapkin, B. D. (1987). The transition to junior high school: A longitudinal study of self-esteem, psychological symptomatology, School life, and social support. *Child Development, 58,* 1235–1243.

Hiscock, M., & Kinbourne, M. (1987). Specialization of the cerebral hemisphere: Implications for learning. *Journal of Learning Disabilities, 20,* 130–142.

Hoch, J. (1985). Remodeling old models of intelligence. In B. B. Wolman (ed.), *Handbook of intelligence* (pp. 267–300). New York: John Wiley.

Hock, E. (1978). Working and nonworking mothers with infants: Perceptions of their careers, their infants' needs, and satisfaction with mothering. *Developmental Psychology, 4,* 37–43.

Hockett, C. (1968). *The state of the art.* (J. Linguarum, series minor, 73). The Hague, The Netherlands: Mouton.

Hoff-Ginsberg, E. (1991). Mother-child conversation in different social classes and communicative settings. *Child Development, 62,* 782–796.

Hoffman, L. W. (1989). Effects of maternal employment on the two-parent family. *American Psychologist, 44,* 283–292.

Hoffman, M. L. (1994). Discipline and internalization. *Developmental Psychology, 30,* 26–28.

Hoffman, M. L., & Saltzstein, H. D. (1967). Parent discipline and the child's moral development. *Journal of Personality and Social Psychology, 5,* 45–57

Hohmann, M., & Weikart, D. (1995). *Educating young children: Active learning practices for preschool and child care programs.* Ypsilanti, Mich.: High/Scope Educational Foundation.

Holloway, S. D., Kashiwagi, K., Hess, R. D., & Azuma, H. (1986). Causal attributions by Japanese and American mothers and children about performance in mathematics. International *Journal of Psychology, 21,* 269–286.

Holmbeck, G. N. (1996). A model of family relational transformations during the transition to adolescence: Parent-adolescent conflict and adaptation. In J. A. Graber & J. Brooks-Gunn (eds.), *Transitions through adolescence: Interpersonal domains and context* (pp. 167–199). Mahwah, N.J.: Erlbaum.

Hoover-Dempsey, K., & Sandler, H. (1995). Parental involvement in children's education: Why does it make a difference? *Teachers College Record, 97,* 310–331.

Hoover-Dempsey, K. & Sandler, H. (1997). Why do parents become involved in their children's education? *Review of Educational Research, 67,* 3–42.

Howe, N., & Ross, H. S. (1990). Socialization perspective taking and the sibling relationship. *Developmental Psychology, 26,* 160–165.

Howes, C., & Matheson, C. C. (1992). Contextual constraints on the concordance of mother-child and teacher-child relationships. In R. C. Pianta (ed.), *New directions in child development, Vol. 57. Relationships between children and non-parental adults* (pp. 25–90). San Francisco: Jossey-Bass.

Howes, C., & Wu, F. (1990). Peer interactions and friendships in an ethnically diverse school setting. *Child Development, 61, 537–541.*

Hubel, D. H., & Wiesel, T. N. (1970). The period of susceptibility to the physiological effects of unilateral eye closure in kittens. *Journal of Physiology, 206, 419–436.*

Huesmann, L. R., Eron, L. D., Lefkowitz, M. M., & Walder, L. O. (1984). Stability of aggression over time and generations. *Developmental Psychology, 20, 1120–1134.*

Huffman, L. C., Mehlinger, S. L., & Kerivan, A. S. (2000). Risk factors for academic and behavioral problems at the beginning of school. In *Off to a good start: Research on the risk factors for early school problems and selected federal policies affecting children's social and emotional development and their readiness for school.* Chapel Hill: University of North Carolina, Frank Porter Graham Child Development Center.

Huggins, S. L. (1989). A comparative study of self-esteem of adolescent children of divorced lesbian mothers and divorced heterosexual mothers. In F. W. Bozett (ed.), *Homosexuality and the family* (pp. 123–135). New York: Harrington Park Press.

Hunt, K. (1977). Early blooming and late blooming syntactic structures. In C. Cooper & L. Odell (eds.), *Evaluating writing: Describing, measuring, judging* (pp. 91–106). Urbana, Ill.: National Council for Teachers of English.

Hunter, C. S. J., & Harman, D. (1979). *Adult illiteracy in the United States.* New York: McGraw-Hill.

Huston, A. C., & Wright, J. C. (1998). Mass media and children's development. In W. Dammon (series ed.) & I. Sigel & A. Renniger (vol. eds.), *Handbook of child psychology, Vol. 4, Child Psychology in Practice* (pp. 999–1058). New York: John Wiley.

Hyde, A., & Bizar, M. (1989). *Thinking in context: Teaching cognitive processes across the elementary school curriculum.* New York: Longman.

Hyde, J. S., Fennema, E., & Lamon, S. J. (1990). Gender differences in mathematics performance: A meta-analysis. *Psychological Bulletin, 107, 139–155.*

Hyde, J. S., & Linn, M. (1988). Gender differences in verbal ability. A meta-analysis. *Psychological Bulletin, 104, 53–69.*

Hyde, J. S., & McKinley, N. M. (1997). Gender differences in cognition: Results from meta-analyses. In P.

J. Caplan, M. Crawford, J. S. Hyde, & J. T. E. Richardson (eds.). (pp. 30–51). *Gender Differences in Human Cognition.* New York: Oxford University Press.

Hymel, S., Comfat, C., Schoreit-Reichl, K., & McDougall, P. (1996). Academic failure and school dropout: The influence of peers. In J. Juvonen & K. R. Wentzel (eds.), *Social maturation: Understanding children school adjustment.* New York: Cambridge Press.

Hymes, D. (1974). *Foundations in sociolinguistics.* Philadelphia: University of Pennsylvania Press.

Imedadze, N. V. (1978). On the psychological nature of child speech formation under condition of exposure to two languages. In E. M. Hatch (ed.), *Second language acquisition: A book of readings.* Rowley, Mass.: Newbury House.

Ingrassia, M. (1995, April 24). The body of the beholder. *Newsweek,* pp. 66–67.

International Association for the Evaluation of Educational Achievement (1997). *Science achievement in the middle school years.* U.S. Department of Education, National Center for Educational Statistics.

Irvine, J. (1990). *Black students and school failure. Policies, practices, and prescriptions.* New York: Praeger.

Itard, J. (1962). *The wild boy of everyone.* New York: Appleton-Century-Crofts.

Jackson, A. W., & Davis, G. A. (2000). *Turning points 2000: Educating adolescents in the 21st Century.* New York: Teachers College Press.

Jacobvitz, D., & Sroufe, L.A. (1987). The early caregiver-child relationship and attention deficit disorder with hyperactivity in Kindergarten: A prospective study. *Child Development, 58 (6), 1488–1495.*

Jencks, C, & Phillips, M. (1998). The black-white test score gap: An introduction. In C. Jencks & M. Phillips (eds.), *The Black-White Test Score Gap* (pp. 1–51). Washington, D.C.: Brookings Institution Press.

Jensen, A. R. (1973). *Educability and group differences.* New York: Harper & Row.

Jerald, C. D., & Orlofsky, G. F. (1999). Raising the bar on school technology. *Education Week, 19, 58–108.*

Jerison, H. J. (1973). *Evolution of the brain and intelligence.* New York: Academic Press.

Jeynes, W., & Littell, S. (2000). A meta-analysis of studies examining the effect of whole language instruction on the literacy of low-SES students. *The Elementary School Journal, 101 (1), 21–33.*

Joe, J. R. (1994). Revaluing Native-American concepts of development and education. In P. M. Greenfield & R. R. Cocking (eds.), *Cross-cultural roots of minority child development* (pp. 107–114). Hillsdale, N.J.: Erlbaum.

Joe, J. R., & Malach, R. S. (1992). Families with Native American roots. In E. W. Lynch & M. J. Hanson

References

(eds.), *Developing cross-cultural competence* (pp. 89–119). Baltimore: Paul H. Brookes Publishing Company.

Johnson, D. W., & Johnson, R. T. (1999). Learning together and alone: Cooperative, competitive, and individualistic learning (5th ed.). Boston: Allyn Bacon.

Johnson, D. W. & Johnson, R. T. (2000). *Teaching students to be peacemakers: Results of twelve years of research.* Unpublished manuscript, University of Minnesota.

Johnson, D. W., Johnson, R. T., & Stanne, M. B. (2000). *Cooperative learning methods: A meta-analysis.* Unpublished manuscript, University of Minnesota.

Johnston, L., Bachman, J., & O'Malley, P. (1999). *Monitoring the future.* Ann Arbor, Mich.: Institute for Social Research.

Jones, G., & Carter, G. (1994). Verbal and nonverbal behavior of ability-grouped dyads. *Journal of Research on Science Teaching, 31,* 603–619.

Jones, L. (1984). White-black achievement differences. *American Psychologist, 39,* 1207–1213.

Jordon, W. (199). Black high school students' participation in school-sponsored sports activities: Effects on school engagement and achievement. *Journal of Negro Education,* 68 (1), 54–70.

Josselson, R. (1988). The embedded self: I and Thou revisited. In D. K. Lapsley & F. C. Power (eds.), *Self, ego, and identity: Integrative approaches* (pp. 91–106). New York: Springer-Verlag.

Josselson, R. (1988). *Finding herself: Pathways to identity development in women.* San Francisco: Jossey-Bass.

Juell, C., Griffith, P., & Gough, P. (1986). The acquisition of literacy: A longitudinal study of children in first and second grade. *Journal of Educational Psychology, 78,* 243–255.

Kagan, J. (1998). Biology and the child. In W. Dammon (series ed.) & N. Eisenberg (vol. ed.), *Handbook of child psychology, Vol. 3. Social, emotional, and personality development* (pp. 177–236). New York: John Wiley.

Kamii, C. (2000). *Young children reinvent arithmetic. Implications of Piaget's theory.* New York: Teachers College Press.

Kandel, D., & Logan, J. (1984). Patterns of drug use from adolescence to young adulthood, I: Periods of risk for initiation, continued use, and discontinuation. *American Journal of Public Health, 74,* 660–666.

Kaplan, D., Damphouse, K., & Kaplan. H. (1996). Moderating effects of gender of the relationship between not graduating from high school and psychological dysfunction in young adulthood. *Journal of Educational Psychology,* 88, 760–774.

Kaplan, D., Damphouse, K., & Kaplan, H. (1996). Mental health implications of not graduating from high school. *Journal of Experimental Education, 62,* 105–123.

Karambayya, R., & Reilly, A. H. (1992). Dual earner couples: Attitudes and actions in restructuring work for family. *Journal of Organizational Behavior, 13,* 585–601.

Karmiloff-Smith, A. (1979). *A functional approach to child language: A study of determiners and reference.* Cambridge, England: Cambridge University Press.

Katz, L. F., & Gottman, J. M. (1997). Buffering children from marital conflict and dissolution. *Journal of Clinical Child Psychology, 26,* 157–171.

Kaufman, A., & Kaufman, N. (1983). *Kaufman assessment battery for children: administration and scoring manual.* Circle Pines, Minn.: American Guidance Service.

Keating, D. (1990). Adolescent thinking. In S. Feldman & G. Elliot (eds.), *At the threshold: The developing adolescent* (pp. 54–90). Cambridge, Mass.: Harvard University Press.

Keeney, T., Cannizzo, S., & Flavell, J. (1967). Spontaneous and induced verbal rehearsal in a recall task. *Child Development, 38,* 953–966.

Keith, T. Z., Reimers, T. M., Fehrman, P. G., Pottebaum, S. M., & Aubey, L. W. (1986). Parental involvement, homework, and TV time: Direct and indirect effects on high school achievement. *Journal of Educational Psychology, 78* (5), 424–434.

Kellam, S. G., Ensminger, M. E., & Turner, R. J. (1997). Family structure and the mental health of children. *Archives of General Psychiatry, 34,* 1012–1022.

Kelley, M. L., Power, T. G., & Wimbush, D. D. (1992). Determinants of disciplinary practices in low-income black mothers. *Developmental Psychology, 63,* 573–582.

Kellog, R. (1970). *Analyzing children's art.* Mountain View, Calif.: Mayfield.

Kendall-Tackett, K. A., Williams, L. M., & Finkelhor, D. (1993). Impact of sexual abuse on children: A review and synthesis of recent empirical studies. *Psychological Bulletin, 113,* 164–180.

Keniston, A., & Flavell, J. (1979). A developmental study of intelligent behavior. *Child Development, 50,* 1144–1152.

Kessen, W. (1979). The American child and other cultural inventions. *American Psychologist, 34,* 815–820.

Kett, J. (1977). *Rites of passage: Adolescence in America, 1790 to present.* New York: Basic Books.

Kim, K., & Smith, P. K. (1998). Childhood stress, behavioral symptoms and mother-daughter pubertal development. *Journal of Adolescence, 21* (3), 231–240.

Kimball, M. (1989). A new perspective on women's math achievement. *Psychological Bulletin, 105,* 198–214.

Kimura, D. (1989, November). Monthly fluctuations in sex hormones affect women's cognitive skills. *Psychology Today*, 63–66.

Kinderman, T., McCollam, T., & Gibson, E. (1996). Peer networks and students' classroom enjoyment during childhood and adolescence. In J. Juvonen and K. R. Wentzel (eds.), *Social maturation understanding children school adjustment*. New York: Cambridge University Press.

Kinney, D. (1993). From "nerds" to "normals": Adolescent identity recovery within a changing social system. *Sociology of Education*, 66, 21–40.

Kirn, W. (2000, September 25). Should you stay together for the kids? *Time*, 156, 75–82.

Klahr, D., & MacWhitney, B. (1998). Information processing. In W. Damon (editor-in-chief) and D. Kuhn & R. S. Siegler (vol. eds.), *Handbook of child psychology* (5th ed., Vol. 2; pp. 631–678.) New York: John Wiley.

Klesges, R. (1993). Effects of television on metabolic rate: Potential implications for childhood obesity. *Pediatrics*, 19 (2).

Klig, K.C., Hyde, J. S., Showers, C. J., & Buswell, B. N. (1999). Gender differences in self-esteem: A meta analysis. *Psychological Bulletin*, 125, 470–500.

Klima, E., & Bellugi, U. (1966). Syntactic regulation in the speech of children. In J. Lyons & R. Wales (eds.), *Psycholinguistics papers* (pp. 183–208). Edinburgh, Scotland: Edinburgh University Press.

Kluger, M. P., & Aprea, D. M. (1999). Grandparents raising grandchildren: A description of the families and a special pilot program. *Journal of Gerontological Social Work*, 32, 5–17.

Kolata, G. (1986). Obese children: A growing problem. *Science*, 232, 20–21.

Kopp, C. B., & McCall, R. B. (1982). Predicting later mental performance for normal, at-risk, and handicapped infants. In P. B. Baltes & O. G. Brim (eds.), *Life-span development and behavior* (Vol. 4). New York: Academic Press.

Kozol, J. (1985). *Illiterate America*. New York: Anchor/Doubleday.

Kozol, J. (1991). *Savage inequalities: Children in America's schools*. New York: Crown.

Krashen, S. D., & Terrell, T. D. (1983). *The natural approach: Language acquisition in the classroom*. New York: Pergamon Press.

Kress, Gunther. (1982). *Learning to write*. London: Routledge & Kegan Paul.

Kreutzer, M. A., Leonard, C., & Flavell, J. H. (1975). An interview study of children's knowledge about memory. *Monographs of the Society for Research in Child Development*, 40 (1, serial no. 159).

Kubow, P. K., Wahlsstrom, K. L., & Bemis, A. (1999). Starting time and school life, Reflections from educators and students, *Phi Delta Kappan*, 80 (5), 366–371.

Labov, W. (1972). The logic of nonstandard English. *Language in the inner city: Studies in the black English vernacular*. Philadelphia: University of Pennsylvania Press.

Ladd, G., & Price, J. (1987). Predicting children's social and school adjustment following from preschool to kindergarten. *Child Development*, 58, 1158–1189.

Lahey, B. B., Waldman, I. D., & McBurnett, K. (1999). Annotation: The development of antisocial behavior: An integrative causal model. *Journal of Child Psychology and Psychiatry*, 40, 699–682.

Lamb, M. E. (ed.), (1997). *The role of the father in child development* (3rd ed.). New York: John Wiley.

Lamb, M. E., (1998). Nonparental child care: Contex, quality, correlates, and consequences. In W. Damon (ed.) and I. Siegel & A. Renniger (vol. ed.), *Handbook of child psychology*, Vol. 4, (pp. 73–134). New York: John Wiley.

Lamb, M. E., Pleck, J. H., Charnov, E. L., & Levine, J. A. (1987). A biosocial perspective on paternal behavior and involvement. In J. B. Lancaster, J. Altman, A. Rossi, & L. R. Sherrod (eds.), *Parenting across the lifespan: Biosocial perspectives* (pp. 11–42). New York: Academic Press.

Landry, S. H., Smith, K. E., Swank, P. R., & Miller-Loncar, C. L. (2000). Early maternal and child influences on children's later independent cognitive and social functioning. *Child Development*, 71, 358–375.

Langer, J. (1991). Literacy and schooling: A socio-cognitive perspective. In E. H. Hiebert (ed.), *Literacy for a diverse society* (pp. 9–27). New York: Teachers College Press.

Langlois, J., & Stephen, C. (1981). Beauty and the beast: The role of physical attractiveness in peer relationships and social behavior. In S. Brehm, S. Kassin, & S. Gibbons (eds.), *Developmental social psychology: Theory and research* (pp. 152–168). New York: Oxford University Press.

Laosa, L. M. (1990). Psychosocial stress, coping, and development of Hispanic immigrant children. In F. C. Serafica, A. I. Schwebel, R. K. Russell, P. D. Isaac, & L. B. Myers (eds.), *Mental health of ethnic minorities* (pp. 38–65). New York: Praeger.

Laquer, T. W. (1983). Toward a culture ecology of literacy in England, 1600–1850. In D. P. Resnick (ed.), *Literacy in historical perspective* (pp. 43–57). Washington, D.C.: Library of Congress.

Larson, R., & Richards, M. H. (1994). *Divergent realities: The emotional lives of mothers, fathers, and adolescents*. New York: Basic Books.

References

Laursen, B., Coy, K. C., & Collins, W. A. (1998). Reconsidering changes in parent-child conflict across adolescence: A meta-analysis. *Child Development*, 69, 817–832.

Laurson, B., Coy, K. C., & Collins, W. A. (1998). Reconsidering changes in parent-child conflict across adolescence. *Child Development*, 69, 817–832.

Lauson, R. (1995). Secrets in the bedroom: Adolescents private use of media. *Journal of Youth and Adolescence*, 24, 535–550.

Lavine, L. (1977). Differentiation of letterlike forms in pre-reading children. *Developmental Psychology*, 13, 89–94.

Lazar, I., Darlington, R., Murray, H., Royce, J., & Snipper, A. (1982). Lasting effects of early education: A report from the Consortium for Longitudinal Studies. *Monographs of the Society for Research in Child Development*, 47 (Serial no. 195).

Le Mare, L. J., & Rubin, K. H. (1987). Perspective taking and peer interaction: Structural and developmental analyses. *Child Development*, 58, 306–315.

Leadbeater, B. J., & Bishop, S. J. (1994). Predictors of behavior problems in preschool children of inner-city Afro-American and Puerto Rican adolescent mothers. *Child Development*, 65, 638–648

Leaper, C. (ed.). *Childhood gender segregation: Cause and consequences*. San Francisco: Jossey-Bass.

Lee, S. (1996). *Unraveling the "model minority" stereotype. Listening to Asian American youth*. New York: Teachers College Press.

Lee, V., & Bryk, A. (1986). Curriculum tracking as mediating the social distribution of high school achievement. *Journal of Education Psychology*, 78, 81–395.

Lee, V., Loeb, S., & Lubeck, S. (1998). Contextual Effects of prekindergarten classes for disadvantaged children on cognitive development: The case of chapter 1. *Child Development*, 69, 479–494.

Lee, V., & Marks, L. (1990). Sustained effects of the single-sex secondary school experience on attitudes, behaviors, and values in college. *Journal of Educational Psychology*, 82, 578–590.

Lemonick, M. (2000). Teens before their time. *Time*, 156, (18), 67–74.

Lenneberg, E. H. (1967). *Biological foundations of language*. New York: John Wiley.

Lenneberg, E. H. (1969). On explaining language. *Science*, 164, 635–643.

Leopold, W. F. (1954). A child's learning of two languages. Georgetown University Round Table on Languages and Linguistics, 7, 19–30. Reprinted in E. M. Hatch (ed.), *Second Language Acquisition: A book of readings*. Rowley, Mass.: Newbury House, 1978.

Lerner, J. V., & Abrams, L. A. (1994). Developmental correlates of maternal employment influences on children. In C. B. Fisher & R. M. Lerner (eds.), *Applied developmental psychology*. New York: McGraw-Hill.

Lerner, J. V., & Galambos, N. L. (1988). The influences of maternal employment across life: The New York Longitudinal Study. In A. E. Gottfried & A. W. Gottfried (eds.), *Maternal employment and children's development: Longitudinal research* (pp. 59–83). New York: Plenum.

Leu, D., & Kinzer, C. (1995). *Effective reading instruction* (3rd ed.). Englewood Cliffs, N.J.: Merrill.

Levin, D. E. (1994). *Teaching young children in violent times: Building a peaceable classroom*. Cambridge, Mass.: Education for Social Responsibility.

Lewis, D. (1975). The black family: Socialization and sex roles. *Phylon*, 36, 221–237.

Lewis, M. (1992). *Shame: The exposed self*. New York: Free Press.

Leyendecker, B., & Lamb, M. E. (1999). Latino families. In M. E. Lamb (ed.), *Parenting and child development in "nontraditional" families* (pp. 247–262). Mahwah, N.J.: Erlbaum.

Lieberman, A. F., Weston, D. R., & Paul, J. H. (1991). Preventive intervention and outcome with anxiously attached dyads. *Child Development*, 62, 199–209.

Lin, C-Y. C., & Fu, V. R. (1990). A comparison of child-rearing practices among Chinese, immigrant Chinese, and Caucasian-American parents. *Child Development*, 61, 429–433.

Linn, M. C., & Hyde, J. S. (1989). Gender, mathematics, and science. *Educational Researcher*, 18, 17–19, 22–27.

Linn, M., & Petersen, A. (1985). Emergence and characterization of sex differences in spatial ability: A meta-analysis. *Child Development*, 56, 1479–1498.

Linney, J., & Seidman, E. (1989). The future of schooling. *American Psychologist*, 44, 343–348.

Lipsitz, J., Mizell, M. H., Jackson, A. W., & Austin, L. M. (1997) Speaking with one voice: A manifesto for middle-grades reform. *Phi Delta Kappan*, 78, 533–540.

Livesly, W. J., & Bromley, D. B. (1993). *Person perception in childhood and adolescence*. New York: John Wiley.

Livson, N., & Peskin, H. (1980). Perspectives on adolescence from longitudinal research. In J. Abelson (ed.), *Handbook of adolescent psychology* (pp. 47–98). New York: John Wiley.

Lloyd, D. (1976). Prediction of school failure from third-grade data. *Educational Psychological Measurement*, 38, 1193–1200.

Loban, W. (1976). *Language Development: Kindergarten through grade 12*. Urbana, Ill.: National Council for Teachers of English.

Lobel, A. (1990). *Allison's zinnia*. Fairfield, N.J.: Greenwillow Books.

Locke, J. (1902). *Some thoughts on education*. Cambridge, Mass.: Cambridge University Press.

Loeber, R., & Stouthamer-Loeber, M. (1998). Development of juvenile aggression and violence: Some common misconceptions and controversies. *American Psychologist, 53*, 242–259.

Lomax, E., Kagan, J., & Rosenkrantz, B. (1978). *Science and patterns of child care*. San Francisco: W. H. Freeman.

Long, M., & Porter, P. (1985). Group work, interlanguage talk, and second language acquisition. *TESOL Quarterly, 19*, 207–228.

Lu, M. C., Lin, Y. G., Prietto, N. M., & Garite, T. J. (2000). Elimination of public funding of prenatal care for undocumented immigrants in California: A cost/benefit analysis. *American Journal of Obstetrics and Gynecology, 182* (1 Pt 1), 233–239.

Lummis, M., & Stevenson, H. W. (1990). Gender differences in beliefs and achievement: A cross-cultural study. *Developmental Psychology, 26*, 254–263.

Lundy, A., & Rosenberg, J. A. (1987). Androgyny, masculinity & self-esteem. *Social Behavior & Personality, 15*, 91–95.

Luster, T., & McAdoo, H. (1995). Factors related to self-esteem among African American youths: A secondary analysis of the High/Scope Perry Preschool Data. *Journal of research on Adolescence, 5*, 451–468.

Lyntton, H., & Romney, D. (1991). Parents' sex-related differential socialization of boys and girls: A meta-analysis. *Psychological Bulletin, 109*, 267–296.

Lyons, J. J. (1995). The past and future directions of federal bilingual education policy. In O. Garcia & C. Baker (eds.), *Policy and practice in bilingual education* (pp. 1–14). Bristol, Pa.: Multilingual Matters.

Lyons, T. A. (1983). Lesbian mothers' custody fears. *Women and Therapy, 2*, 231–240.

Maccoby, E. (1998). *The two sexes: Growing up apart, coming together*. Cambridge, Mass.: Belknap Press.

Maccoby, E. E. (1980). *Social development: Psychological growth and the parent–child relationship*. New York: Harcourt Brace Jovanovich.

Maccoby, E. E. (1984). Middle childhood in the context of the family. In W. A. Collins (ed.), *Development during middle childhood: The years from six to twelve*. Washington, D.C.: National Academy Press.

Maccoby, E. E. (1992). The role of parents in the socialization of children: An historical overview. *Developmental Psychology, 28*, 1006–1017.

Maccoby, E. E., & Martin, J. (1983). Socialization in the context of the family: Parent-child interactions. In E. M. Hetherington (ed.) & P. H. Mussen (series ed.), *Handbook of child psychology. Vol. 4, Socialization, personality, and social development* (pp. 1–101). New York: John Wiley.

Maccoby, E. E., & Mnookin, R. H. (1992). *Dividing the child: Social and legal dilemmas of custody*. Cambridge, Mass.: Harvard University Press.

Maccoby, M. E., & Jacklin, C. N. (1974). *The psychology of sex differences*. Palo Alto, Calif.: Stanford University Press.

MacDonald, K. (1992). Warmth as a developmental construct: An evolutionary analysis. *Child Development, 63*, 753–773.

Macionis, J. (1991). *Sociology* (3rd ed.). Englewood Cliffs, N.J.: Prentice Hall.

Madden, N., Salvin, R., Karweit, N. Dolan, L., & Wasik, B. (1993). Success for all: Longitudinal effects of a restructuring program for inner-city elementary schools. *American Educational Research Journal, 30*, 123–148.

Magnusson, D., Stattin, H., & Allen, V. (1985). Biological maturation and social development: A longitudinal study of some adjustment processes from mid-adolescence to adulthood. *Journal of Youth and Adolescence, 14*, 267–283.

Mahoney, J. L. (2000). School extracurricular activity participation as a moderator in the development of antisocial patterns. *Child Development, 71* (2), 502–516.

Main, M., & Solomon, J. (1990). Procedures for identifying infants as disorganized/disoriented during the Ainsworth strange situation. In M. Greenberg, D. Cicchetti, & E. M. Cummings (eds.), *Attachment in the preschool years: Theory, research and intervention* (pp. 121–160). Chicago: University of Chicago Press.

Malina, R. M., & Bouchard, C. (1991). *Growth, maturation, and physical activity*. Champaign, Ill.: Human Kinetics.

Manly, R., Rickson, H., & Standeven, B. (2000). Children and adolescents with eating disorders: Strategies for teachers and school counselors. *Intervention in School and Clinic, 35*, 228–231.

Manly R., Rickson, H., & Standeven, B. (2000). Children and adolescents with eating disorders: Strategies for teachers and school counselors. *Intervention in School and Clinic, 35*, 228–231.

Manning, B. H. (1988). Application of cognitive behavior modification: First and third graders' self-management of classroom behavior. *American Educational Research Journal, 25*, 193–212.

References

Mariani, M., & Barkley, R. S. (1997). Neuropsychological and academic functioning in preschool children with attention deficit hyperactivity disorder. *Developmental Neuropsychology, 13,* 111–129.

Marín, G., & Marín, B. V. (1991). *Research with Hispanic populations.* Newbury Park, Calif.: Sage.

Marjoribanks, K. (1987). Ability and attitude correlates of academic achievement: Family group differences. *Journal of Educational Psychology, 79,* 171–178.

Markus, H. R., & Kitayama, S. (1991). Culture and the self: Implications for cognition, emotion, and motivation. *Psychological Review, 98,* 224–253.

Marsh, H. (1993). The effects of participation in sport during the last two years of high school. *Sociology of Sport Journal, 10,* 18–43.

Marsh, H., Byrne, B., & Yeung, A. S. (1999). Casual order of academic self concept and achievement: Reanalysis of a pioneer study and revised recommendations. *Educational Psychologist, 34,* 155–167.

Marsh, H. W. (1988). Casual effects of academic self-concept on academic achievement: A reanalysis of Newman (1984). *Journal of Experimental Education, 56,* 100–103.

Marsh, H. W. (1989). Effects of attending single-sex and coeducational high schools on achievement, attitudes, behavior, and sex differences. *Journal of Educational Psychology, 81,* 70–85.

Marsh, H., & Yeung, A. S. (1997). Casual effects of academic self-concept on academic achievement: Structural equation models of longitudinal data. *Journal of Educational Psychology, 89,* 41–54.

Mash, E. J., & Johnston, C. (1982). A comparison of mother-child interactions of younger and older hyperactive and normal children. *Child Development, 53,* 1371–1381

Mash, E. J., & Johnston, C. (1983). Sibling interactions of hyperactive and normal children and their relationship to reports of maternal stress and self-esteem. *Journal of Clinical Child Psychology, 12,* 91–99.

Mason, J., & Allen, J. B. (1986). A review of emergent literacy with implications for research and practice in reading. In E. Rothkopf (ed.), *Review of research in education* (pp. 3–47). Washington, D.C.: American Education Research Association.

Massachusetts Governor's Commission on Gay and Lesbian Youth (1993). Making schools safe for gay and lesbian youth: Breaking the silence in schools and in families. Boston: Author.

Masten, A. S., Coatsworth, J. D. (1998). The development of competence in favorable and unfavorable environments: Lessons from research on successful children. *American Psychologist, 53,* 205–220.

Matas, L., Arend, R. A., & Scroufe, L. A. (1978). Continuity of adaptation in the second year: The relationship between quality of attachment and later competence. *Child Development, 49,* 547–556.

Mauer, D., & Mauer, C. (1988). *The world of the newborn.* New York: Basic Books.

Maxwell, R. J. (1996). *Writing across the curriculum in middle and high schools.* Needham Heights, Mass.: Allyn & Bacon.

McCall, R. B., Applebaum, M. I., & Hogarty, P. S. (1973). Developmental changes in mental performance. *Monographs of the Society for the Research in Child Development, 38* (Serial no. 150).

McCaul, E. J., Donadlson, G. A., Colsdarci, T., & Davis, W. (1992). Consequences of dropping out of school: Findings from the high schools and beyond. *Journal of Educational Psychology, 85,* 198–207.

McCollum, P. (1991). Cross-cultural perspectives on classroom discourse and literacy. In E. Hiebert (ed.), *Literacy for a diverse society* (pp. 108–121). New York: Teachers College Press.

McDaniel, M. A., Waddill, P. J., & Einstein, G. O. (1988). A contextual account of generation effect: A three factor theory. *Journal of Memory and Language, 25,* 521–536.

McDaniel, A. (1994). Historical racial differences in living arrangements of children. *Journal of Family History, 19,* 57–77.

McFarland, W., & Dupuis, M. (2001). "The legal duty to protect gay and lesbian students from violence in school." *Professional School Counseling, 4* (3), 171–179.

McLanahan, S., & Sandefur, G. (1994). *Growing up with a single parent: What hurts, what helps?* Cambridge, Mass.: Harvard University Press.

McLoyd, B. (1990). The impact of economic hardship on black families and children. Psychological distress, parenting, and socioeconomic development. *Child Development, 61,* 311–346.

McLoyd, V. (1993). Employment among African-American mothers in dual-earner families: Antecedents and consequences for family life and child development. In J. Frankel (ed.), *The employed mother and the family context* (pp. 180–226). New York: Springer.

McLoyd, V., Jayaratne, T., Ceballo, R., & Borquez, J. (1994). Unemployment and work interruption among African-American single mothers: Effects on parenting and socio-emotional functioning. *Child Development, 65,* 562–589.

McNeill, D. (1966). Developmental psycholinguistics. In F. Smith & G. A. Miller (eds.), *The genesis of language: A psycholinguistic approach* (pp. 15–84). Cambridge, Mass.: MIT Press.

Meece, J. L. (1987). The influence of school experiences on the development of gender schemata. In L. Liben & M. Signorella (eds.). *Children's gender schemata (New Directions for Child Development*, no. 38, pp. 57–74). San Francisco: Jossey-Bass.

Meece, J. L. (1991). The classroom context and children's motivational goals. In M. Maehr & P. Pintrich (eds.), *Advances in achievement motivation research* (Vol. 7, pp. 261–285). New York: Academic Press.

Meece, J. L., Wigfield, A., & Eccles, J. (1990). Predictors of math anxiety and its consequences for young adolescents' course enrollment intentions and performance in mathematics. *Journal of Educational Psychology, 82*, 1–11.

Meeus, W. Iedema, J. Helsen, M. & .Vollebergh, W. (1999). Patterns of adolescent identity development: Review of literature and longitudinal analysis: *Development Review, 19,* 591–621.

Meichenbaum, D. (1977). *Cognitive-behavior modification: An integrative approach.* New York: Plenum Press.

Meichenbaum, D., & Asarno, J. (1978). Cognitive behavioral modification and metacognitive development: Implications for the classroom. In P. Kendall & S. Hollon (eds.), *Cognitive-behavioral interventions: Theory, research, and procedures* (pp. 11–33). New York: Academic Press.

Meichenbaum, D., & Goodman, J. (1971). Training impulsive children to talk to themselves: A means of developing self-control. *Journal of Abnormal Psychology, 77,* 115–126.

Melnick, M., & Sabo, D. (1992). Educational effects of interscholastic athletic participation on African-American and Hispanic youth. *Adolescence, 27* (106) 295–308.

Menyuk, P. (1976). Relations between acquisition of phonology and reading. In J. T. Guthrie (ed.), *Aspects of reading acquisition.* Baltimore: Johns Hopkins University Press.

Meyer, D. K. (1993). What is scaffolded instruction? Definitions, distinguishing features, and misnomers. In D. J. Leu & C. K. Kinzer (eds.), *Examining central issues in literacy research, theory, and practice:* Forty-second Yearbook of the National Reading Conference, pp. 41–54. Chicago: National Reading Conference.

Mickelson, R. A. (1990). The attitude-achievement paradox among black adolescents. *Sociology of Education, 63,* 44–61.

Midgley, C., Feldlaufer, H., & Eccles, J. S. (1989). Changes in teacher efficiency and student self-and task-related beliefs during the transition to junior high school. *Journal of Educational Psychology, 81,* 247–258.

Miller, A. (1993). Social science, social policy, and the heritage of African American families. In M. B. Katz (ed.), *The "Underclass" debate: Views from history* (pp. 254–289). Princeton, N.J.: Princeton University Press.

Miller, P. (1993). *Theories of developmental psychology* (3rd ed.). New York: Freeman.

Miller, P., & Weiss, M. (1981). Children's attention allocation, understanding of attention, and performance on the incidental learning task. *Child Development, 52,* 1183–1190.

Miller, S. A. (1988). Parents' beliefs about children's cognitive development. *Child Development, 59,* 259–285.

Miller, S. A. (1995). Parents' attributions for their children's behavior. *Child Development, 66,* 1557–1584.

Mills, G. E. (2001). *Action research: A guide for the teacher researcher.* Columbus, Ohio: Merrill.

Milunsky, A. (1989). *Choices, not chance.* Boston: Little, Brown.

Minuchin, P. (1985). Families and individual development: Provocations from the field of family therapy. *Child Development, 56,* 289–302.

Minuchin, P., & Shapio, E. (1983). The school context for social development. In P. Mussen (series ed.) & E. M. Hetherington (vol. ed.), *Handbook of Child Development* (pp. 197–276). New York: John Wiley.

Mirande, A. (1988). Chicano fathers: Traditional perceptions and current realities. In P. Bronstein & C. P. Cowan (eds.), *Fatherhood today: Men's changing role in the family* (pp. 93–106). New York: John Wiley.

Mischel, H. N., & Mischel, W. (1983). The development of children's knowledge of self-control strategies. *Child Development, 54,* 603–619.

Mischel, W., Ebbensen, E. B., & Zeiss, A. R. (1972). Cognitive and attentional mechanisms in delay of gratification. *Journal of Personality and Social Psychology, 21,* 204–218.

Mischel, W., & Moore, B. (1980). The role of ideation in voluntary delay of symbolically presented rewards. *Cognitive Therapy and Research, 4,* 211–221.

Mitchell, A. (1929) *Children and movies.* Chicago: University of Chicago Press.

Miura, I., Okamoto, Y., Kim, C., Steere, M., & Fayol, M. (1993). First graders' cognitive representation of number and understanding of place value: Cross-national comparisons—France, Japan, Sweden, and the United States. *Journal of Educational Psychology, 85,* 24–30.

Modell, J., & Goodman, M. (1990). Historical perspectives. In S. Feldman & G. Elliot (eds.), *At the threshold: The developing adolescent* (pp. 93–122). Cambridge, Mass.: Harvard University Press.

Moely, B., Hart, S., Leal, L., Santulli, K., Koa, N., Johnson, T., & Hamilton, L. (1992). The teacher's role in facilitating memory and study strategy in the elementary school classroom. *Child Development, 63,* 653–672.

Moffett, J. (1968). *A student-centered language arts curriculum, grades K–13: A handbook for teachers.* New York: Houghton Mifflin.

Moffitt, T. (1990). Juvenile delinquency and attention-deficit disorder: Developmental trajectories from age 3 to 15. *Child Development, 61,* 893–910.

Moffitt, T., Lynam, D., & Silva, P. (1994). Neuro-psychological tests predicting persistent male delinquency. *Criminology, 32,* 277–300.

Moles, O. C. (1996). New national directions in research and policy. In A. Booth, & J. Dunn (1996). *Family-school links. How do they affect educational outcomes?* (pp. 247–254). Mahwah, N.J.: Erlbaum.

Moll, L. (1990). *Vygotsky and education: Instructional implications and applications of sociohistorical psychology.* New York: Cambridge University Press.

Morrison, F., Smith, S., & Dow-Ehrensberger, M. (1995). Education and cognitive development: A natural experiment. *Developmental Psychology, 34,* 789–799.

Moshman, D., & Franks, B. (1986). Development of the concept of inferred validity. *Child Development, 57,* 153–165.

Moskowitz, B. (1985). The acquisition of language. In V. P. Clark, P. A. Eschholz, & A. Rosa (eds.), *Language: Introductory readings* (pp. 45–73). New York: St. Martin's Press.

Munio, G. & Adams, G. (1977). Ego identity formation in college students and working youth. *Development Psychology, 13,* 523–524.

Murray, D. (1985). *A writer teaches writing* (2nd ed.). Boston: Houghton Mifflin.

Mussen, P., & Jones, M. (1957). Self-conceptions, motivations, and interpersonal attitudes of late- and early-maturing boys. *Child Development, 28,* 243–256.

Mutas, L., Arend, R., & Sroufe, L.A. (1978). Continuity of adaptation in the second year: The relationship between quality of attachment and later competence. *Child Development, 49,* 542–556.

National Assessment of Educational Progress. (1981). *Reading, thinking, and writing: Results from the 1979–80 national assessment of reading and literature.* Denver: National Assessment of Educational Progress.

National Center for Educational Statistics (1995). *Third International Mathematics and Science Study, Videotape classroom study, 1995–1995.* Washington, D.C.: U.S. Department of Education, Office of Research and Educational Improvement.

National Center for Education Statistics (1993). *The condition of education.* Washington, D.C.: U.S. Department of Education, Office of Education Research and Improvement.

National Center for Education Statistics (1995). *The condition of education.* Washington, D.C.: U.S. Department of Education, Office of Education Research and Improvement.

National Center for Educational Statistics (1997). *Digest of educational statistics, 1997.* Washington, D.C., Government Printing Office.

National Center for Educational Statistics (1999). *Digest of educational statistics, 1999.* Washington, D.C.: U.S. Government Printing Office.

National Center of Educational Statistics (1998). *The condition of education.* Washington, D.C.: U.S. Department of Education, Office of Educational Research and Improvement

National Center for Educational Statistics (2000a). *Digest of educational statistics, 1999.* Washington, D.C.: Department of Education, Office of Research and Educational Improvement.

National Center for Education Statistics (2000b), *America's Kindergarteners. Findings from the Early Childhood Longitudinal Study, Kindergarten Class of 1998–99.* Washington, D.C.: U.S. Department of Education, Office of Educational Research and Improvement.

National Center for Educational Statistics (2000c). *National Assessment of Educational Progress (NAEP), 1999 long-term trend assessment.* Washington, D.C.: U.S. Department of Education, Office of Education and Improvement.

National Center of Educational Statistics (2000d). *The condition of education.* Washington, D.C.: U.S. Department of Education, Office of Educational Research and Improvement.

National Institutes of Health (1998). *Autism.* Washington, D.C.: Department of Health and Human Services.

National Institutes of Health (2000). *AIDS in infants and children.* Washington, D.C.: Department of Health and Human Services.

National Institute of Mental Health (1995). *Learning disabilities.* Washington, D.C.: Department of Health and Human Services.

National Institute of Mental Health (2000). *Attention deficit hyperactivity disorder: Questions and answers.* Washington, D.C.

National Research Council (1996). *National Science Standards.* Washington, D.C.: National Academy Press.

National Research Council (1997). *The new Americans. Economic, demographic and fiscal effects of immigration.* Washington, D.C.: National Academy Press.

National Research Council (1999). *Starting out right: A guide to promoting children's reading success.* Washington, D.C.: Author.

National Research Council (2000). *From neurons to neighborhoods.* Washington, D.C.: National Academy Press.

Natriello, G., McDill, E. L., & Pallas, A. M. (1990). *Schooling disadvantaged children: Racing against catastrophe.* New York: Teachers College Press.

Natriello, G., Pallas, A. M., & McDill, E. (1986). Taking stock: Renewing our research agenda on the causes and consequences of dropping out. *Teachers College Record, 87,* 430–440.

Needle, R. H., Su, S. S., & Doherty, W. J. (1990). Divorce, remarriage, and adolescent substance use: A prospective longitudinal study. *Journal of Marriage and the Family, 52,* 57–169.

Neilans, T., & Israel, A. (1981). Towards maintenance and generalization of behavior change: Teaching children self-regulation and self-instructional skills. *Cognitive Therapy and Research, 5,* 189–195.

Neisser, U., Boodoo, G., Bouchard, T. J., Jr., Ceci, S. J., Halpern, D. F., Loehlin, J. C., Perloff, R., Sternberg, R. J., & Urbina, S. (1996). Intelligence: Knowns and unknowns. *American Psychologist, 51,* 77–101.

Nelson, K., & Hudson, J. (1988). Scripts and memory: Functional relationships in development. In F. Weinert & M. Perlmutter (eds.), *Memory development: Universal changes and individual changes* (pp. 147–168). Hillsdale, N.J.: Erlbaum.

Nelson, N. W. (1998). *Childhood language disorders in context: Infancy through adolescence.* Boston: Allyn and Bacon.

Newman, D., Griffin, P., & Cole, M. (1989). *The construction zone: Working for cognitive change in school.* New York: Cambridge University Press.

Nicely, P., Tamis-LeMonda, C. S., & Grolnick, W. S. (1999). Maternal responsiveness to infant affect: Stability and prediction. *Infant Behavior and Development, 22,* 103–117.

NICHD Early Child Care Network (1997). The effects of infant child care on infant-mother attachment security: Results of the NICHD study of early child care. *Child Development, 68* (5), 860–879.

NICHD Early Child Care Network (1998). Early child care and self-control, compliance, and problem behavior at twenty-four and thirty-six months. *Child Development, 69* (4), 1145–1172.

NICHD Early Child Care Network (2000). The relation of child care to cognitive and language development. *Child Development, 71,* 960–980.

Noddings, N. (1992). *The challenge to care in schools.* New York: Teachers College Press.

North Carolina Department of Public Instruction (1998). *Public school enrollment data.* Raleigh, N.C.: Author.

Oakes, J. (1985). *Keeping track: How schools structure inequality.* New Haven, Conn.: Yale University Press.

Oakes, J. (1990). Opportunities, achievement, and choice: Women and minorities. In C. Cazden (ed.), *Review of research in education* Vol. 16 (pp. 153–222). Washington, D.C.: American Educational Research Association.

Oakes, J. (1991). Limiting Opportunity: Students race and curricular differences in secondary vocational education. *American Journal of Education, 91,* 801–820.

Oakes, J. (1995). Two cities' tracking and within-school segregation. *Teachers College Record, 96* (4), 681–691.

Oakes, J., & Stuart, A. (1998). Detracking for high student achievement. *Educational Leadership, 55* (6), 38–42.

Ochs, E., Schieffelin, B., & Platt, M. (1979). Propositions across utterances and speakers. In E. Ochs & B. Schieffelin (eds.), *Developmental pragmatics* (pp. 251–268). New York: Academic Press.

Oden, S., Schweinhart, S., & Weikart, D. (2000). *Into adulthood. A study of the effects of Head Start.* Ypsilanti, Mich.: High/Scope Educational Research Foundation.

Offord, D. R., & Bennett, K. J. (1994). Conduct disorder: Long-term outcomes and intervention effectiveness.

Ogbu, J. (1978). *Minority achievement and caste.* San Diego, Calif.: Academic Press.

Ogbu, J. (1987). Variability in minority school performance: A problem in search of an explanation. *Anthropology & Education Quarterly, 18,* 508–523.

Ogbu, J. (1988). Literacy and schooling in subordinate cultures: The case of black Americans. In E. Kintgen, B. Kroll, & M. Rose (eds.), *Perspectives on literacy,* (pp. 227–242). Carbondale, Ill.: Southern Illinois University Press.

Ogbu, J. & Fordham, S. (1986). Black students' school success: Coping with the "burden of acting white." *Urban Review, 18,* 176–206.

Okagaki, L., & Frensch, P. A. (1998). Parenting and children's school achievement: A multiethnic perspective. *American Educational Research Journal, 35,* 123–144.

References

Okagaki, L. & Steinberg, R. (1993). Parental beliefs and children's school performance. *Child Development, 64,* 36–56.

Olweus, D. (1980). Familial and temperamental determinants of aggressive behavior in adolescent boys: A causal analysis. *Developmental Psychology, 16,* 644–666

Olweus, D. (1981). Continuity in aggressive and inhibited withdrawn behavior patters. *Psychiatry and Social Services, 1,* 141–159.

Olweus, D. (1993). Victimization by peers: Antecedents and long-term outcomes. In K. H. Rubin & J. B. Asendorpf (eds.), *Social withdrawal, inhibition, and shyness in childhood* (pp. 315–341). Hillsdale, N.J.: Erlbaum.

O'Malley, J. M. (1982). *Children's English and services study: Educational and needs assessment for language minority children with limited English proficiency.* Rosslyn, Va.: Inter-American Research Associates.

Orlofsky, J. L. (1997). Sex role orientation, identity, formative, and self-esteem in college men and women. *Sex Roles, 3,* 561–374.

Orton, S. T. (1937). *Reading, writing, and speech problems in children.* New York: Norton.

Page, E. B., & Grandon, G. (1979). Family configuration and mental ability: Two theories contrasted with U.S. data. *American Educational Research Journal, 16,* 257–272.

Paikoff, R., & Brooks-Gunn, J. (1991). Do parent-child relationships change during puberty? *Psychological Bulletin, 110,* 47–66.

Paivis, A. (1971). *Imagery and verbal processes.* New York: Holt, Rinehart, and Winston.

Paley, V. G. (1988). *Bad guys don't have birthdays.* Chicago: University of Chicago Press.

Palinscar, A. S., & Brown, A. L. (1984). Reciprocal teaching of comprehension-fostering and comprehension monitoring activities. *Cognition and Instruction, 1,* 117–175.

Palinscar, A. S., & David, Y. M. (1991). Promoting literacy through classroom dialogue. In E. Hiebert (ed.), *Literacy for a diverse society* (pp. 122–140). New York: Teachers College Press.

Paris, S., & Jacobs, J. (1984). The benefits of informed instruction for children's reading awareness and comprehension. *Child Development, 55,* 2083–2093.

Paris, S. G., Lipson, M. Y., & Wixon, K. (1983). Becoming a strategic reader. *Contemporary Educational Psychology, 8,* 293–316.

Paris, S. G., & Winograd, P. W. (1990). How metacognition can promote academic learning and instruction. In B. J. Jones & L. Idol (eds.), *Dimensions of thinking and cognitive instruction* (pp. 15–51). Hillsdale, N.J.: Erlbaum.

Parke, R., & Slaby, R. G. (1983). The development of aggression. In E. M. Hetherington (ed.), *Handbook of child development, Vol. 4. Socialization, personality and social development* (4th ed., pp. 547–641). New York: John Wiley.

Parker, J. G., & Asher, S. R. (1987). Peer relations and later adjustment: Are low-accepted children at risk? *Psychological Bulletin, 102,* 357–389.

Parker, J. G., Rubin, K. H., Price, J., & DeRosien, M. E. (1995). Peer relationships, child development, and adjustment: A developmental psychopathology perspective. In D. Cicehetti and D. Cohen (eds.), *Developmental psychopathology, Vol. 2. Risk, disorder, and adaptation.* (pp 96–161). New York: John Wiley.

Patterson, C. J. (1995). Families of the lesbian baby boom: Parents' division of labor and children's adjustment. *Developmental Psychology, 31,* 115–123.

Patterson, C. J., & Chan, R. W. (1999). Families headed by lesbian and gay parents. In M. E. Lamb (ed.), *Nontraditional families.* Hillsdale, N.J.: Erlbaum.

Patterson, G. R., Capaldi, D., & Bank, L. (1991). An early starter model for predicting delinquency. In D. J. Pepler & K. H. Rubin (eds.), *The development and treatment of childhood aggression* (pp. 139–168). Hillsdale, N.J.: Lawrence Erlbaum.

Patterson, G. R., DeBaryshe, B. D., & Ramsey, E. (1989). A developmental perspective on antisocial behavior. *American Psychologist, 44,* 329–335.

Pearson, J. L., Hunter, A. G., Ensminger, M. E., & Kellam, S. G. (1990). Black grandmothers in multi-generational households: Diversity in family structure and parenting involvement in the Woodlawn community. *Child Development, 61,* 434–442.

Pellegrini, A. D., & Galda, L. (1993). Ten years after: A reexamination of symbolic play and literacy research. *Reading Research Quarterly, 28,* 162–175.

Pellegrini, A. D., Brody, G. H., & Seigel, I. E. (1985). Parents' book reading habits with their children. *Journal of Educational Psychology, 77,* 332–340.

Pellegrini, A., & Bartini, M. (1999). *A longitudinal study of bullying, victimization, and peer affiliation during the transition from primary school to middle school.* Paper presented at the 107th American Psychological Association Conference, Boston, MA.

Pellegrini, A. D., Huberty, P., & Jones, I. (1995). The effects of recess timing on children's playground and classroom behaviors. *American Educational Research Journal, 32,* 845–864.

Pellegrini, A. D., & Smith, P. K. (1998). Physical activity play: the nature and function of a neglected aspect of playing. *Child Development, 69* (3), 577–598.

Pellett, T. L., & Harrison, J. M. (1992). Children's perceptions of the gender appropriateness of physical activities: A further analysis. *Play and Culture, 5*, 305–313.

Pellman, H. (2000). What parents need to know about children and the media. *Pediatrics, 18*, 4–6.

Perfetti, C., Beck, I., & Hughes, C. (1985). Reading acquisition and beyond: Decoding includes cognition. *American Journal of Education, 93*, 40–60.

Petersen, A., Compas, B., Brooks-Gunn, J., Stemmler, M., Ey, S., & Grant, K. (1993). Depression in adolescence. *American Psychologist, 48*, 155–168.

Petersen, A., & Taylor, B. (1980). The biological approach to adolescence: Biological change and psychological adaptation. In J. Adelson (ed.), *Handbook of adolescent psychology* (pp. 117–155). New York: John Wiley.

Peterson, C., & McCabe, A. (1991). Linking children's connectives use and narrative macrostructure. In A. McCabe & C. Peterson (eds.), *Developing narrative structure*. Hillsdale, N.J.: Erlbaum.

Phelan, P., Davidson, A. L., & Yu, H. C. (1998). *Adolescents' worlds: Negotiating family, peers, and schools.* New York: Teachers College Press.

Philips, S. U. (1983). *The invisible culture: Communication in the classroom and community on the Warm Springs Indian Reservation.* New York: Longman.

Phinney, J. S. (1990). Ethnic identity in adolescents and adults: A review of research. *Psychological Bulletin, 108*, 499–514.

Phinney, J., & Devich-Navalino, M. (1997). Variation in bicultural identification among African American and Mexican American Adolescents. *Journal of Research on Adolescence, 7*, 3–32.

Phinney, J., Ong A. & Madden, T. (2000). Cultural values and intergenerational value discrepancies in immigrant and non-immigrant families. *Child Development, 71*, 528–539.

Phinney, J. S., & Rosenthal, D. A., (1992). Ethnic identity in adolescence: Process, context, and outcome. In G. R. Adams, T. P. Gullotta, & R. Montemayer (eds.), *Adolescent identity formation* (pp. 145–172). Newbury, Calif.: Sage.

Piaget, J. (1926). *The language and thought of the child.* London: Routledge & Kegan Paul.

Piaget, J. (1951). *The child's conception of the world.* New York: The Humanities Press.

Piaget, J. (1952). *The origins of intelligence in children.* New York: International Universities Press.

Piaget, J. (1954). *The origins of intelligence.* New York: Basic Books.

Piaget, J. (1962). *Play, dreams, and imitation in children.* New York: Norton.

Piaget, J. (1964). Development and learning. In R. Ripple & V. Rockcastle (eds.), *Piaget rediscovered* (pp. 7–20). Ithaca, N.Y.: Cornell University Press.

Piaget, J. (1967). *Six psychological studies.* New York: Random House.

Piaget, J. (1969). *Science of education and the psychology of the child.* New York: Viking.

Piaget, J. (1976). *Judgment and reasoning in the child.* Totowa, N.J.: Littlefield, Adams.

Piaget, J., & Inhelder, B. (1956). *The child's conception of space.* London: Routledge & Kegan Paul.

Pianta, R. C. (1994). Patterns of relationships between children and kindergarten teachers. *Journal of School Psychology, 32*, 15–32.

Pianta, R., C. (1999). *Enhancing relationships: Between children and teachers.* Washington, D.C.: American Psychological Association.

Pianta, R. C., & Harbers, K. (1996). Observing mother and child behavior in a problem-solving situation at school entry: Relations with academic achievement. *Journal of School Psychology, 34*, 307–322.

Pianta, R. C., Rimm-Kaufman, S. E. & Cox, M. J. (1999). Introduction: An ecological approach to the kindergarten transition. In R. C. Pianta, & M. J. Cox, *The transition to kindergarten* (pp. 3–12). Baltimore: Paul H. Brookes Publishing Company.

Pianta, R. C., & Steinberg, M. (1992). Relationships between children and kindergarten teachers from the teachers' perspective. In R. C. Pianta (ed.), *Beyond the parent: The role of other adults in children's lives* (pp. 61–80). San Francisco: Jossey-Bass.

Pianta, R. C., Steinberg, M., & Rollins, K. (1995). The first two years of school: Teacher-student relationships and deflections in children's classroom adjustment. *Development and Psychopathology, 7*, 297–312.

Pilkington, N. W., & D'Augelli, A. R. (1995). Victimization of lesbian, gay, and bisexual youth in community setting. *Journal of Community Psychology, 23*, 34–56.

Pinker, S. (1994). *The language instinct: How the mind creates language.* New York: William Morrow.

Pinnell, G., DeFord, D., & Lyons, C. (1988). *Reading recovery: Early intervention for at-risk first graders.* Arlington, Va.: Educational Research Service.

Pintrich, P., & Schunk, D. (1996). *Motivation in education: Theory, practice, and applications.* Englewood Cliffs, N.J.: Merrill.

Pipher, M. (1994). *Reviving Ophelia: Saving the selves of adolescent girls.* New York: Ballantine Books.

Pleck, J. H. (1997). Paternal involvement: Levels, sources, and consequences. In M. Lamb (ed.), *The role of the father in child development* (pp. 66–103). New York: John Wiley.

Plomin, R. (1989). Environment and genes: Determinants of behavior. *American Psychologist, 44*, 105–111.

Plomin, R. (1990). *Nature and nurture*. Pacific Grove, Calif.: Brooks/Cole.

Plomin, R. (1990). The role of inheritance in behavior. *Science, 248*, 183–188.

Plomin, R., & DeFries, J. (1980). Genetics and intelligence: Recent data. *Intelligence, 4*, 15–24.

Plomin, R., DeFries, J., & Loehlin, J. (1977). Genotype-environmental interaction and correlation in the analysis of human behavior. *Psychological Bulletin, 24*, 738–745.

Porter, R. H., Cernoch, J. M., & McLaughlin, F. J. (1983). Maternal recognition of neonates through olfactory cues. *Physiology and Behavior, 30*, 151–154.

Portes, A. (1997). Immigration theory for a new century: Some problems and opportunities. *International Migration Review, 31*, 799–825.

Portes, P. R. (1999). Social and psychological factors in the academic achievement of children of immigrants: A cultural history puzzle. *American Educational Research Journal, 36*, 489–507.

Posner, J. K., & Vandell, D. (1994). Low income children's after-school care: Are there beneficial effects of after-school programs. *Child Development, 65*, 440–456.

Pressley, M. (1998). *Reading instruction that works: The case for balanced teaching*. New York: Guildford Press.

Pressley, M., & Ghatala, E. S. (1990). Self-regulated learning: Monitoring learning from text. *Educational Psychologist, 25*, 19–34.

Pressley, M., Wharton-McDonald, R., Allington, R., Block, C. C., & Morrow, L. (1998). *The nature of effective first grade literacy instruction*. (CELA Research Rep. No. 11007). Albany State University of New York at Albany, The National Center on English Learning and Achievement. [http://cela.albany.edu/1stgradelit/index.html]

Price, J. A. (1976). North American Indian families. In C. H. Mindel & R. W. Haberstein (eds.), *Ethnic families in America: Patterns and variations* (pp. 248–270). New York: Elsevier

Public Agenda (1997). *Getting by: What American teenagers really thing about their schools*. New York: Public agenda.

Puma, M. J., Jones, C. C., Rock, D., & Fernandez. R. (1993). *Prospects: The Congressionally Mandated Study of Educational Growth and Opportunity. Interim Report*. Bethesda, Md.: Abt Associates.

Purcell Gates, V. (1995). *Other people's words: The cycle of low literacy*. Cambridge, Mass.: Harvard University Press.

Quintana, S. (1998). Children's developmental understanding of ethnicity and race. *Applied and Preventive Psychology, 7*, 27–45.

Quintana, S. (1999). Role of perspective-taking abilities and ethnic socialization in development of adolescent ethnic identity. *Journal of Research on Adolescence, 9* (2) 161–184.

Ramey, C. T., & Campbell, F. A. (1984). Preventive education for high-risk children: Cognitive consequences of Carolina Abecedarian Project. *American Journal of Mental Deficiency, 88*, 515–523.

Ramey, C. T., & Campbell, F. A. (1991). Poverty, early childhood education, and academic competence: The Abecedarian experiment (pp. 190–221). In A. C. Huston (ed.), *Children in poverty: Child development and public policy*. New York: Cambridge University Press.

Rand, C., Graham, D. L. R., & Rawlings, E. I. (1982). Psychological health and factors the court seeks to control in lesbian mother custody trials. *Journal of Homosexuality, 8*, 27–39.

Rank, M. R., & Hirschl, T. A. (1999). The economic risk of childhood in America: Estimating the probability of poverty across the formative years. *Journal of Marriage and the Family, 61*, 1058–1067.

Rauch-Elnekave, H. (1994). Teenage motherhood: Its relationship to undetected learning problems. *Adolescence, 29*, 91–104.

Raudenbush, S., Rowan, B., & Cheong, Y. (1993). Higher order instructional goals in secondary schools: Class, teacher, and school influences. *American Educational Research Journal, 30*, 523–553.

Read, C. (1975). *Children's categorization of speech sounds in English* (National Council for Teachers of English Research Report No. 17). Urbana, Ill.: National Council of Teachers of English.

Reid, J. (1993). Prevention of conduct disorders before and after school entry: Relating interventions to developmental findings. *Development and Psychology, 5*, 243–262.

Remafedi, G. J. (1987). Adolescent homosexuality: Psychosocial and medical implications. *Pediatrics, 79*, 331–337.

Remafedi, G. (1999). Sexual orientation and youth suicide. *Journal of the American Medical Association, 282* (13), 1291–1292.

Resnick, M. D., Bearman, P. S., Blum, R. W., Bauman, K. E., Harris, K. M., Jones, J., Tablro, J. Beuhring, T., Sieving, R. E., Shew, M., Ireland, M., Bearinger, L. H., Udry, J. R. Protecting adolescents from harm. Findings from the National Longitudinal Study of Adolescent Health. *Journal of the American Medical Association, 278* (10), 823–832.

Reyes, M. de la Luz. (1995). A process approach to literacy using dialogue journals and literature logs with second language learners. In O. Garcia & C. Baker (eds.), *Policy and practice in bilingual education* (pp. 200–215). Bristol, Pa.: Multilingual Matters.

Reynolds, A. J., & Wahlberg, H. J. (1991). A structural model of science achievement. *Journal of Educational Psychology, 83*, 97–107.

Rheingold, H., & Joseph, J. (1977). *Speech to newborns by nursery personnel*. Paper presented at the meeting of the Society for Research in Child Development, New Orleans.

Richards, M. H., & Duckett, E. (1994). The relationship of maternal employment to early adolescent daily experiences with and without parents. *Child Development, 65*, 225–236.

Rileigh, K. (1973). Children's selective listening to stories: Familiarity effects involving vocabulary, syntax, and intonation. *Psychological Reports, 33*, 255–266.

Risman, B. J. (1986). Can men "mother"? Life as a single father. *Family Relations, 35*, 95–102

Ritchie, D., Price, V., & Roberts, D. F. (1987). Television, reading, and reading achievement: A reappraisal. *Communication Research, 14*, 292, 315.

Ritter, P. L., Mont-Reynaud, R., & Dornbusch, S. M. (1993). Minority parents and their youth: Concern, encouragement, and support for school achievement. In N. F. Chavkin (ed.), *Families and schools in a pluralistic society* (pp. 107–120). Albany: State University of New York.

Roberton, M. A. (1984). Changing motor patterns during childhood. In J. Thomas (ed.), *Motor development during childhood and adolescence* (pp. 48–90). Minneapolis, Minn.: Burgess.

Roberts, W. B. (2000). The bully as victim: Understanding bully behaviors to increase effectiveness of interventions in bully-victim dyad. *Professional School Counseling, 4* (2), 148–155.

Rodgers, J. L., Cleveland, H. H., van den Oord, E., & Rowe, D. C. (2000). Resolving the debate over birth order, family size, and intelligence. *American Psychologist, 55*, 299–612.

Roeser, R., Midgley, C., & Urban, T. (1996). Perceptions of the school psychological environment an dearly adolescents' psychological and behavioral functioning in school: The mediating role of goals and belong. *Journal of Educational Psychology, 88*, 408–422.

Rogler, L. (1994). International migrations: A framework for directing research. *American Psychologist, 49*, 710–718.

Rogoff, B. (1981). Schooling and the development of cognitive skills. In H. C. Triandis & A. Heron (eds.), *Handbook of cross-cultural psychology*, Vol. 4 (pp. 233–294). Boston: Allyn & Bacon.

Rogoff, B. (1990). *Apprenticeship in thinking: Cognitive development in social context*. New York: Oxford University Press.

Rogoff, B., Ellis, S., & Gardner, W. (1984). Adjustment of adult-child instruction according to child's age and task. *Developmental Psychology, 20*, 193–199.

Rogoff, B., & Morelli, G. (1989). Perspectives on children's development from cultural psychology. *American Psychologist, 44*, 343–348.

Romo, H. D., & Falbo, T. (1996). *Latino high school graduation: Defying the odds*. Austin: University of Texas Press.

Roschelle, J. M., Pea, R. D., Hoadley, C. M., Gordin, D. N., & Means, B. M. (2000). Changing how and what children learn in school with computer-based technologies. *The Future of Children. Children and Computer Technology, Vol. 10*, 76–101.

Rosenberg, R. N., & Pettigrew, J. W. (1983). Genetic neurological diseases. In R. N. Rosenberg (ed.), *The clinical neurosciences* (pp. 33–165). New York: Churchill Livingston.

Rosenblatt, L. M. (1988). *Writing and reading: The transactional theory* (Tech. Rep. No. 416). Urbana, Ill.: Center for the Study of Reading.

Rosenshine, B., & Meister, C. (1992). The use of scaffolds for teaching higher-order cognitive strategies. *Educational Leadership, 26*, 275–280.

Ross, S., Smith, L., Casey, J. & Slavin, R. (1995). Increasing the academic success of disadvantaged children: An Examination of alternative early intervention programs. *American Educational Research Journal, 32*, 73–800.

Rothbart, M. K., & Bates, J. E. (1998). Temperament. In W. Dammon (series ed.) & N. Eisenberg (vol. ed.), *Handbook of child psychology, Vol. 3, Social, emotional, and personality development* (pp. 105–176). New York: John Wiley.

Rothbaum, F., Weisz, J., Pott, M., Miyake, K., & Morelli, G. (2000). Attachment and culture: Security in the United States and Japan. *American Psychologist, 35*, 1093–1104.

Rothenberg, D. (1996). *Grandparents as parents: A primer for schools* (Report No. EDO-PS-96-8). Urbana, IL: ERIC Clearinghouse on Elementary and Early Childhood Education. (ERIC Document Reproduction Service No. ED 401 044).

Rotheram-Borus, M. S., Rosaris, M., Van Russem, R., Reid, H., Gellis, R. (1995). Prevalence, course, and predictors of multiple problem behaviors among gay and bisexual male adolescents. *Developmental Psychology, 31*, 75–85.

Rousseau, J. (1911). *Emile*. New York: Dutton.

References

Rubin, K., Bukowski, W., & Parker, J. (1998). Peer interactions, relationships, and groups. In W. Dammon (series ed.) & N. Eisenburg (vol. ed.), *Handbook of child psychology, Vol. 4: Socialization, personality, and social development*. (4th ed., pp. 619–700). New York: John Wiley.

Rubin, K., Coplan, R. J., Nelson, L. J., Cheah, C. L., & Legace-Segurn, D. G. (1999). Peer relationships in childhood. In M. H. Bornstein & M. E. Lamb (eds.), *Developmental Psychology* (4th ed., pp. 451–503). Hillsdale, N.J.: Erlbaum.

Rubin, K. H., Nelson, L. J., Hastings, P., & Asendorpf, J. (1999). The transaction between parents' perceptions of their children's shyness and their parenting styles. *International Journal of Behavioral Development, 23*, 937–958.

Ruble, D., & Dweck, C. S. (1995). *Self-conceptions, person conceptions, and their development*. In N. Eisenberg (ed.), *Social Development* (pp. 109–139). Thousand Oaks, Calif.: Sage Publications.

Rueda, R. (1986). Metacognition and passing: Strategic interactions in the lives of students with learning disabilities. *Anthropology and Education Quarterly, 17*, 145–165.

Ruff, H. A., Capozzoli, M., & Weissberg, R. (1998). Age, individuality, and context as factors in sustained visual attention during the preschool years. *Developmental Psychology, 34* (3), 454–464.

Rury, J. L. (1991). *Education and women's work: Female schooling and the division of labor in urban America, 1870–1930*. Albany: State University of New York Press.

Rutter, M. (1983). School effects on pupil progress. Research findings and policy implications. *Child Development, 54*, 1–29.

Rutter M., Maughan, B., Mortimore, P., Ouston, J., & Smith, A. (1979). *Fifteen thousand hours: Secondary schools and their effects on children*. Cambridge, Mass.: Harvard University Press.

Saarni, C., Mumme, D. L., & Campos, J. J. (1998). Emotional development: Action, communication, and understanding. In W. Dammon (series ed.) & N. Eisenberg (vol. ed.), *Handbook of child psychology, Vol. 3: Social, emotional, and personality development* (5th ed., pp. 237–309). New York: John Wiley.

Safe Kids (1999). *National Safe Kids Campaign: 1999 Public Policy Priorities*. Washington, D.C.: Safe Kids.

Sagi, A., Donnell, F., van Ijzendoorn, M. H., Mayseless, O., & Aviezer, O. (1994). Sleeping out of home in a kibbutz communal arrangement: It makes a difference for infant-mother attachment. *Child Development, 65*, 992–1004.

Sameroff, A. J. (1994). Developmental systems and family functioning. In R. D. Parke & S. G. Kellam (eds.), *Exploring family relationships with other social contexts* (pp. 199–214). Hillsdale, N.J.: Erlbaum.

Sameroff, A. J., Seifer, R., Barocas, R., Zax, M., & Greenspan, S. (1987). Intelligence quotient scores of 4-year-old children: Social-environmental risk factors. *Pediatrics, 79*, 343–350.

Sanders, M., & Epstein, J. (1998, August). *School-family-community partnerships in middle and high schools from theory to practice* (CRESPAR Report No. 22). Baltimore: Johns Hopkins University, Center for Research on the Education of Students Placed at Risk.

Santrock, J. W., & Warshak, R. A. (1986). Development, relationships, and legal/clinical considerations in father-custody families. In M. E. Lamb (ed.), *The father's role: Applied perspectives*. New York: John Wiley.

Savin-Williams, R. (1994). The disclosure to families of same-sex attractions by lesbian, gay, and bisexual youths. *Journal of Research on Adolescence, 3*, 49–68.

Scanzoni, J. (1985). Black parental values and expectations of children's occupational and educational success: Theoretical implications. In H. P. McAdoo & J. McAdoo (eds.), *Black children: Social, educational, and parental environments* (pp. 113–122). Beverly Hills, Calif.: Sage.

Scarr, S. (1992). Developmental theories for the 1990s: Development and individual differences. *Child Development, 63*, 1–19.

Scarr, S., & McCartney, K. (1983). How people make their own environments: A theory of genotype environmental effects. *Child Development, 54*, 424–435.

Schaefer, E. S. (1989). Dimensions of mother-infant interaction: Measurement, stability, and predictive validity. *Infant Behavior and Development, 12*, 379–393.

Schickendanz, J. (1986). *More than the ABCs: The early stages of reading and writing*. Washington, D.C.: National Association for the Education of Young Children.

Schneider, B., & Stevenson, D. (1999). *The ambitious generation: America's teenagers, motivated, but directionless*. New Haven, Conn.: Yale University Press.

Schon, I. (1985). *Books in Spanish for children and young adults: An annotated guide*. Metuchen, N.J.: Scarecrow Press.

Schon, I. (1986). *Basic collection of children's books in Spanish*. Chicago: American Library Association.

Schunk, D. H. (2000). Learning theories. An educational perspective (3rd ed.). Upper Saddle River, N.J.: Merrill.

Schunk, D. S., & Cox, P. D. (1986). Strategy training and attributional feedback with learning disabled students. *Journal of Educational Psychology, 78*, 201–209.

Schwartz, W. (1996). *A guide to choosing an after-school program: For parents/about parents.* New York, NY: ERIC Clearinghouse on Urban Education.

Schweinhart, L. J., & Weikert, D. (1997). *Lasting differences: The High/Scope Perry Preschool Curriculum Comparison study through age 23.* (Monographs of the High/Scope Educational Research Foundation, 12). Ypsilanti, Mich.: High/Scope Press.

Scott-Jones, D. (1984). Family influences on cognitive development and school achievement. *Review of Research in Education, 11,* 259–304.

Scott-Jones, D. (1987). Mother-as-teacher in the families of high- and low-achieving low-income black first graders. *Journal of Negro Education, 56,* 21–34.

Scott-Jones, D. (1995). Parent-child interactions and school achievement. In B. A. Ryan, G. R. Adams, T. P. Gullotta, R. P. Weisberg, & R. L. Hampton (eds.), *The family-school connection: Theory, research and practice* Vol. 2, pp. 75–107. Thousand Oaks, Calif.: Sage.

Scott-Jones, D., & Nelson-LeGall, S. (1986). Defining black families: Past and present. In E. Seidman & J. Rappaport (eds.), *Redefining social problems* (pp. 83–100). New York: Plenum.

Segalowitz, S. J., & Lawson, S. (1995). Subtle symptoms associated with self-reported mild head injury. *Journal of Learning Disabilities, 28,* 309–319.

Seginer, R. (1983). Parents' educational expectations and children's academic achievements: A literature review. *Merrill-Palmer Quarterly, 29,* 1–23.

Seitz, S., & Stewart, C. (1975). Imitations and expansions: Some developmental aspects of mother-child communication. *Developmental Psychology, 11,* 763–768.

Selman, R. (1980). *The growth of interpersonal understanding.* New York: Academic Press.

Selman, R. L. & Byrne, D. F. (1974). A structural-developmental analysis of levels of roletaking in middle childhood. *Child Development, 45,* 803–806.

Sènèchal, M., & Cornell, E. H. (1993). Vocabulary acquisition through shared reading experiences. *Reading Research Quarterly, 28,* 360–375.

Sènèchal, M., LeFevre, J., Hudson, E., & Lawson, E. P. (1996). Knowledge of storybooks as a predictor of young children's vocabulary. *Journal of Educational Psychology, 88,* 520–536.

Shapiro, J. (1995). Home literacy environment and young children's literacy knowledge and behavior. In W. Linek & E. Sturtevant (eds.). *Generations of literacy: Seventeenth yearbook of the College Reading Association* (pp. 288–300). Harrisonburg, Va.: College Reading Association.

Sharan, S. Cooperative learning and helping behavior in the multi-ethnic classroom. In H. C. Foot, M. J. Morgan, & R. H. Shute (eds.), *Children helping children.* New York: John Wiley.

Sharan, S., & Sharan, S. (1992). *Expanding cooperative learning through group investigation.* New York: Teachers College Press.

Sharp, D., Cole, M., & Lave, C. (1979). Education and cognitive development: The evidence from experimental research. *Monographs of the Society for Research in Child Development, 44* (1–2, Serial No. 178).

Shaw, D. S., & Vondra, J. I. (1993). Chronic family adversity and infant attachment security. *Journal of Child Psychology and Psychiatry and Allied Disciplines, 34,* 1205–1215.

Sheilds, M. K., & Behrman, R. E. (2000). Children and computer technology: Analysis and recommendations. *The Future of Children: Children and Computer Technology,* Vol 10, 4–30.

Sherman, A. (1997). *Poverty matters: The cost of child poverty in America.* Washington, D.C.: Children's Defense Fund.

Sherrod, K. B., O'Connor, S., Vietze, P. M., & Altemeier, W. A., III (1984). Child health and maltreatment. *Child Development, 55,* 1174–1183.

Shields, C. M., & Oberg, S. L. (1999). What can we learn from the data? Toward better understanding of the effects of multitrack year-round schooling. *Urban Education, 24,* 125–155.

Shino, P., & Behrman, R. (1995). Low-birth-weight: Analysis and recommendations. *The Future of Children, 5,* 4–18.

Shoda, Y., Mischel, W., Peake, P. (1990). Predicting adolescent cognitive and self-regulatory competencies from preschool delay of gratification: Identifying diagnostic conditions. *Developmental Psychology, 26,* 978–986.

Shumow, L., Vandell, L., & Kang, K. (1996). School choice, family characteristics, and home-school relations: Contributions to school achievement? *Journal of Educational Psychology, 99,* 451–460.

Shuy, R. (1967). *Discovering American dialects.* Urbana III.: National Council for Teachers of English.

Shuy, R. (1980). Vernacular black English: Setting the issues in time. In M. F. Whiteman (ed.), *Reactions to Ann Arbor: Vernacular black English and education.* Arlington, Va.: Center for Applied Linguistics.

Shwe, H. I., & Markman, E. M. (1997). Young children's appreciation of mental impact of their communication signals. *Developmental Psychology, 33,* 630–636.

Siegler, R. S. (1998). *Children's thinking* (3rd ed.). Englewood Cliffs, N.J.: Prentice Hall.

Siegler, R. S., Robinson, M., Liebert, D. E., & Liebert, R. M. (1973). Inhelder and Piaget's pendulum problem: Teaching preadolescents to act as scientists, *Developmental Psychology*, 9, 97–101.

Silberman, M. L. (1971). Teachers' attitudes toward elementary school students. *Journal of Educational Psychology*, 60, 402–407.

Silbereisen, R., Petersen, A., Albrecht, H., & Kracke, B. (1989). Maturational timing and the development of problem behavior: Longitudinal studies in adolescence. *Journal of Early Adolescence*, 9, 247–268.

Simmons, R., & Blyth, D. (1987). *Moving into adolescence*. New York: Aldine de Gruyter.

Simmons, R., & Blyth, D. (1987). *Moving into adolescence. The impact of pubertal change and school context*. Hawthorne, N.Y.: Aldine de Gruyter.

Simmons, R., Black, A., & Zhou, Y. (1991). African-American versus White children and the transition into junior high school. *American Journal of Education*, 99, 481–520.

Simmons, R. et al. (1987). The impact of cumulative change in early adolescence. *Child Development*, 5, 1220–1234.

Simons, R. L., Lin, K.-H., Gordon, L. C., Conger, R. D., & Lorenz, F. O. (1999). Explaining the higher incidence of adjustment problems among children of divorce compared with those in two-parent families. *Journal of Marriage and the Family*, 61, 1020–1033.

Singer, J. D., Fuller, B., Keiley, M. K., & Wolf, A. (1998). Early child-care selection: Variation by geographic location, maternal characteristics, and family structure. *Developmental Psychology*, 34, 1129–1144.

Singer, J. L., & Singer, D. G. (1976). Imaginative play and pretending in early childhood. In A. Davids (ed.), *Child personality and psychopathology* (pp. 69–112). New York: John Wiley.

Sinha, C. G., & Walkerdine, V. (1978). Conservation: A problem in language, culture and thought. In N. Waterson & C. Snow (eds.), *The development of communication*. London: John Wiley.

Skinner, B. F. (1957). *Verbal behavior*. New York: Appleton-Century-Crofts.

Slavin, R. E. (1995). *Cooperative learning: Theory, research, and practice* (2nd ed.). Boston: Allyn Bacon.

Slavin, R. E. (1994). *Using team learning* (4th ed.). Baltimore, Md.: Johns Hopkins University, Center for Research on Elementary Schools.

Slavin, R. E., & Madden, N. A. (1999). School practices that improve race relations. *American Educational Research Journal*, 16 (2), 169–180.

Slavin, R. E., Karweit, R. E., & Madden, N. L. (1989). *Effective programs for children at risk*. Boston: Allyn & Bacon.

Sleeter, C. E., & Grant, C. A. (1987). An analysis of multicultural education in the United States. *Harvard Review*, 57, 421–444.

Sleeter, C. E., & Grant, C. A. (1988). *Making choices for multicultural education: Five approaches to race, class, and gender*. Columbus, Ohio: Merrill.

Slobin, D. I., & Welsh, C. A. (1973). Elicited imitation as a research tool in developmental psycholinguists. In C. A. Ferguson & D. I. Slobin (eds.), *Studies of child language development* (pp. 485–497). New York: Holt, Rinehart & Winston.

Smith, M. L., & Shepard, L. A. (1988). Kindergarten readiness and retention: A qualitative study of teachers' beliefs and practice. *American Educational Research Journal*, 25, 307–333.

Smith, N. B. (1975). Cultural dialects: Current problems and solutions. *The Reading Teacher*, 29, 137–141.

Smith, P. K., & Thompson, D. (1991). Dealing with bully/victim problems in the U.K. In P. K. Smith and D. Thompson (eds.), *Practical approaches to bullying* (pp. 1–2). London: Fulton.

Smitherman, G. (1985). "It bees dat way somtime": Sounds and structures of present-day black English. In V. Clark, P. Eschholz, & A. Rosa (eds.), *Language* (4th ed., pp. 552–568). New York: St. Martin's.

Smoll, F., & Schutz, R. (1990). Quantifying gender differences in physical performance: A developmental perspective. *Developmental Psychology*, 26, 360–369.

Snow, C. (1977). The development of conversation between mothers and babies. *Journal of Child Language*, 4, 1–22.

Snow, C. (1986). Conversations with children. In P. Fletcher & M. Garman (eds.), *Language acquisition: Studies in first language development* (pp. 69–89). Cambridge, England: Cambridge University Press.

Snow, C., & Ferguson, C. A. (1977). *Talking to children: Language input and acquisition*. Cambridge Mass.: Cambridge University Press.

Snow, C., Burns, M. S. and Griffin, P. (1998). *Preventing reading difficulties in young children*. Washington, D.C.: National Academy Press.

Society for Research in Child Development (1990, Winter). *Report of the Committee for Ethical Conduct in Child Development Research*, pp. 5–7.

Sousa, D. (1995). *How the brain learns. A classroom teacher's guide*. Reston, Va.: National Association of Secondary Prinicipals.

Sowers, S. (1982). Six questions teachers ask about invented spelling. In T. Newkirk & N. Atwell (eds.),

Understanding writing (pp. 47–54). Boston, Mass.: Northeast Regional Exchange.

Spangenberg-Urbschat, K., & Pritchard, R. (1994). Kids come in all languages: Reading instruction for ESL students. Newark, Del.: International Reading Association.

Spear, K. (1988). *Sharing writing: Peer response groups in English classes.* Portsmouth, N.H.: Boynton/Cook.

Spearman, C. (1927). *The abilities of man.* New York: Macmillan.

Spencer, M., & Dornbusch, S. M. (1990). Challenges in studying minority youth. In S. Feldman & G. Elliot (eds.), *At the threshold: The developing adolescent* (pp. 255–276). Cambridge, Mass.: Harvard University Press.

Spiegel, D. L. (1992). Blending whole language and systematic direct instruction. *The Reading Teacher, 46,* 38–47.

Spring, J. (1994). *The American school. 1642–1993* (3rd ed.). New York: McGraw-Hill.

Sroufe, L. A. (1982). Attachment and the roots of competence. In H. E. Fitzgerald and T. H. Carr (eds.), *Human Development: Annual Editions.* Guilford, Calif.: Duskin.

Sroufe, L. A. (1996). *Emotional development: The organization if emotional life in early years.* New York: Cambridge Press.

Sroufe, L. A., Fox, N. E., & Pancake, V. R. (1983). Attachment and dependency in developmental perspective. *Child Development, 54,* 1615–1627.

Stack, C. B., & Burton, L. (1993). Kinscripts. *Journal of Comparative Family Studies, 24,* 157–170.

Stahl, S. A. (1992). Saying the "p" word: Nine guidelines for exemplary phonics instruction. *The Reading Teacher, 45,* 618–625.

Stanovich, K. E. (1986). Matthew effects in reading: Some consequences of individual differences in the acquisition of literacy, *Reading Research Quarterly, 16,* 360–407.

Steinberg L. (1996). *Beyond the classroom: Why schools reform has failed and what parents need to do.* New York: Simon & Shuster.

Steinberg, L., Dornbusch, S. M., & Brown, B. B. (1992). Ethnic differences in adolescent achievement. *American Psychologist, 47,* 723–729.

Steinberg, L., Lamborn, S. D., Dornbusch, S. M., & Darling, N. (1992). Impact of parenting practices on adolescent achievement: Authoritative parenting, school involvement, and encouragement to succeed. *Child Development, 63,* 1266–1281.

Sternberg, R. (1984). How can we teach intelligence? *Educational Leadership, 38–48.*

Sternberg, R. (1985). *Beyond IQ: A triarchic theory of human intelligence.* New York: Cambridge University Press.

Stevenson, H., & Lee, S. (1990). Contexts of achievement. *Monographs for Research in Child Development, 55* (1–2 serial no. 221).

Stevenson, H. W., Chen, C., & Uttal, D. (1990). Beliefs and achievement: A study of Black, white, and Hispanic children. *Child Development, 61,* 508–523.

Stevenson, H. W., & Lee, S. (1990). Contexts of achievement: A study of American, Chinese, and Japanese children. *Monographs of the Society for Research in Child Development, 55* (1–2, Serial No. 221).

Stevenson, H. W., & Sigler, J. W. (1992). *The learning gap: Why our schools are failing and what we can learn from Japanese and Chinese education.* New York: Simon & Schuster.

Stigler, J., & Hiebert, J. (1999). *The teaching gap: Best ideas from the world's teachers for improving education in the classroom.* New York: Free Press.

Stigler, J., Gallimore. R., & Hiebert, J. (2000). Using video surveys to compare classrooms and teaching across cultures: Examples and lessons for the TIMSS video studies. *Educational Psychologist, 35,* 87–100.

Stigler, J., Gonzales, P., Kawanka, T., Knoll, S., & Serrano, A. (1999). *The TIMSS videotape classroom study: Methods and findings from an exploratory research project on eighth–grade mathematics instruction in Germany, Japan, and the United States.* Washington, D.C.: U.S. Department of Education, National Center for Educational Statistics.

Stiglitz, E. (1990). Caught between two worlds: The impact of a child on the lesbian couple's relationship. *Women and Therapy, 10,* 99–116.

Stiles, J., Bates, E. A., Thai, D., Trauner, D., & Reilly, J. (1999). Linguistic, cognitive, affective development in children with prenatal and perinatal focal brain injury: A ten-year overview from the San Diego Longitudinal Project. In C. Rovee-Collier (eds.), *Advances in infant research* (Vol. 13), Norwood, N.J.: Ablex.

Stipek D. & MacIver, D. (1989). Developmental change in children's assessment of intellectual competence. *Child Development, 60,* 521–538.

Stone, J. L., & Church, J. (1957). *Childhood and adolescence: A psychology of the growing person.* New York: Random House.

Stormshak, E. A., Bierman, K. L., McMahon, R. J., Lengua, L. J., & The Conduct Problems Prevention Research Group. (2000). Parenting practices and child disruptive behavior problems in early elementary school. *Journal of Clinical and Child Psychology, 29,* 17–29.

References

Stranger, J. D. F. & Gridenia, N. (1999). Media in the home 1999: The fourth annual survey of parents and children. Philadelphia: Annenbery Public Policy Center, University of Pennsylvania.

Strauss, C., Smith, K., Frame, C., & Forehand, R. (1985). Personal and interpersonal characteristics associated with childhood obesity. *Journal of Pediatric Psychology, 10*, 337–343.

Strauss, M. A. (1994). *Beating the devil out of them. Corporal punishment in American families.* New York: Lexington Books.

Strauss, M. A., & Stewart, J. H. (1999). Corporal punishment by American parents: National data on prevalence, chronicity, severity, and duration, in relation to child and family characteristics. *Clinical Child and Family Psychology Review, 2* (2), 55–70.

Strickland, D. S., & Morrow, L. M. (1989). Developing skills: An emergent literacy perspective. *The Reading Teacher, 43,* 82–83.

Stronge, J. H., & Reed-Victor, E. (2000). *Educating homeless children.* Larchmont, N.Y.: Eye on Education.

Suarez-Orozco, C., & Suarez-Orozco, M. M. (1994). The cultural psychology of Hispanic immigrants. In T. Weaver (ed.), *Handbook of Hispanic cultures in the United States, Vol. 2: Anthropology* (pp. 129–146). Houston: Arte Publico Press.

Subrahmanyam, K., Kraut, R. E., Greenfield, P. M., & Gross, E. F. (2000). The impact of home computer use on children's activities and development. *The Future of Children. Children and Computer Technology, Vol. 10,* 123–144.

Sue, S., & Okazaki, S. (1990). Asian-American educational achievements: A phenomenon in search of an explanation. *American Psychologist, 45,* 913–920.

Suina, J. H., & Smolkin, L. B. (1994). From natal culture to school culture to dominant society culture: Supporting transitions for Pueblo Indian students. In P. M. Greenfield & R. R. Cocking (eds.), *Cross-cultural roots of minority child development* (pp. 115–130). Hillsdale, N.J.: Erlbaum.

Sullivan, M. L. (1993). Culture and class as determinants of out-of-wedlock childbearing and poverty during late adolescence. *Journal of Research on Adolescence, 3,* 295–316.

Summerville, M., & Kaslow, N. (1993, March). *Racial differences in psychological symptoms, cognitive style, and family functioning in suicidal adolescents.* Paper presented at the biennial meeting for the Society for Research in Child Development, New Orleans.

Szinovacz, M. (1998). Grandparents today: A demographic profile. *The Gerontologist, 38,* 37–52.

Tallal, P. (1980). Auditory temporal perception, phonics, and reading disabilities in children. *Brain Language, 9,* 182–198.

Tanner, J. (1978). *Fetus into man: Physical growth from conception to maturity.* Cambridge, Mass.: Harvard University Press.

Tanaka, J. S., Ebreo, A., Linn, N., & Morera, O. F. (1998). Research methods: The construct validity of self-identity and its psychological implications. In L. C. Lee & N. W. S. Zane (eds.), *Handbook of Asian American psychology* (pp. 21–79). Thousand Oaks, Calif.: Sage.

Tasker, F. L., & Golombok, S. (1997). *Growing up in a lesbian family: Effects on child development.* New York: Guilford.

Taylor, B. M., Fryre, B. L. and Marayama, G. H. (1990). Time spent reading and reading growth. *American Education Research Journal, 27,* 351–372.

Taylor, R. L. (1998). Black American families. In R. L. Taylor (ed.), *Minority families in the United States* (pp. 19–45). Upper Saddle River, N.J.: Prentice Hall.

Tchudi, S., & Yates, J. (1983). *Teaching writing in the content areas: Senior high school.* Washington, D.C.: National Education Association.

Teachman, J. D., & Paasch, K. M. (1994). Financial impact of divorce on children and their families. *The Future of Children, 4,* 63–83.

Teale, W. H. (1978). Positive environments for learning to read: What studies of early readers tell us. *Language Arts, 55,* 922–932.

Teale, W., & Sulzby, E. (eds.) (1986). *Emergent literacy.* Norwood, N.J.: Ablex.

Templeton, S., & Spivey, E. (1980). The concept of word in young children as a function of level of cognitive development. *Research in the Teaching of English, 14,* 265–278.

Terman, L. (1925). *Genetic studies of genius, Vol. 1: Mental and physical traits of a thousand gifted children.* Stanford, Calif.: Stanford University Press.

Terman, L., & Oden, M. H. (1959). *Genetic studies of genius, Vol. 4: The gifted group at midlife.* Stanford, Calif.: Stanford University Press.

Tharp, R. G. (1989). Psychocultural variables and constants: Effects on teaching and learning in schools. *American Psychologist, 44,* 349–359.

Tharp, R. G. (1994). Intergroup differences among Native Americans in socialization and child cognition: An ethnogenetic analysis. In P. M. Greenfield & R. R. Cocking (eds.), *Cross-cultural roots of minority child development* (pp. 87–105). Hillsdale, N.J.: Erlbaum.

Tharp, R., & Gallimore, R. (1988). *Rousing minds to life: Teaching learning and schooling in social context.* New York: Cambridge University Press.

Tharp, R., & Gallimore, R. (1989). *Rousing minds to life: Teaching, learning, and schooling in social context.* Cambridge, England: Cambridge University Press.

Thomas, J. R. (1984). Children's motor skill development. In J. R. Thomas (ed.), *Motor development during childhood and adolescence* (pp. 91–104). Minneapolis: Burgess.

Thompson, R. A. (1998). Early brain development and social policy. *Policy and Practice in Public Human Services*, 56, 66–77.

Thompson, R. A. (2000). The legacy of early attachments. *Child Development, 71* (1), 145–152.

Thompson, R. A., & Laible, D. J. (1999). Noncustodial parents. In M. E. Lamb (ed.), *Parenting and child development in "nontraditional" families* (pp. 103–123). Mahwah, N.J.: Erlbaum.

Thorndike, R., Hagen, E., & Sattler, J. (1986). *The Stanford-Binet Intelligence Scale: Guide for administering and scoring* (4th ed.). Chicago: Riverside Publishing.

Tower, C. C. (1992). *The role of educators in the prevention and treatment of child abuse and neglect.* Washington, D.C.: U.S. Department of Health and Human Services.

Triandis, H. (1990). Cross-cultural studies of individualism and collectivism. In J. Berman (ed.), *Nebraska symposium on motivation, Vol. 37: Cross-cultural perspectives* (pp. 41–133). Lincoln: University of Nebraska Press.

Triandis, H. (1995). Individualism and collectivism. Boulder, Colo.: Westview.

Trickett, P. K., Aber, J. L., Carlson, V., & Cicchetti, D. (1991). Relationship of socioeconomic status to the etiology and developmental sequence of physical child abuse. *Developmental Psychology, 27,* 148–158.

Troy, M., and Sroufe, L. A. (1987). Victimization among preschoolers: Role of attachment relationship history. *Journal of the American Academy of Child and Adolescent Psychiatry, 26* (2), 166–172.

Tuandas, H. (1995). *Individualism and Collectivism.* Boulder, Colo.: Westview.

Tudge, J. (1993). Processes and consequences of peer collaboration: A Vygotskian analysis. *Child Development,* 63, 1364–1379.

Tudge, J., & Rogoff, B. (1989). Peer influences on cognitive development: Piagetian and Vygotskian perspectives. In M. H. Bornstein & J. S. Bruner (eds.), *Interaction in human development* (pp. 17–40). Hillsdale, N.J.: Erlbaum.

Turiel, E. (1998). The development of morality. In W. Dammon (series ed.) & N. Eisenberg (vol. ed.), *Handbook of child psychology, Vol 3: Social, emotional, and personality development* (pp. 863–932). New York: Wiley.

Urban Institute (2000). One in five U.S. children are children of immigrants [On-line]. Available http://www.urban.org/news/press/CP_000911.html

U.S. Bureau of the Census (1993a). *We the Americans: Asians* (Series WE-3). Washington, D.C.: U.S. Government Printing Office.

U.S. Bureau of the Census (1993b). *We the First Americans* (Series WE-5). Washington, D.C.: U.S. Government Printing Office.

U.S. Bureau of the Census (1997). *My daddy takes care of me! Fathers as care providers* (Current Population Reports, Series P70-59). Washington, D.C.: U.S. Government Printing Office.

U.S. Bureau of the Census (1998). *Marital status and living arrangements: March 1998 (update)* (Current Population Reports, Series P20-514). Washington, D.C.: U.S. Government Printing Office.

U.S. Bureau of the Census (1999). *Statistical abstract of the United States* (119th ed.). Washington, D.C.: U.S. Government Printing Office.

U.S. Bureau of the Census (2000a). *The Asian and Pacific Islander population in the United States: March 1999* (Current Population Reports, Series P20-529). Washington, D.C.: U.S. Government Printing Office.

U.S. Bureau of the Census (2000b). *Child support for custodial mothers and fathers: 1997* (Current Population Reports, Series P60-212). Washington, D.C.: U.S. Government Printing Office.

U.S. Bureau of the Census (2000c). *The Hispanic population in the United States: March 1999* (Current Population Reports, Series P20-527). Washington, D.C.: U.S. Government Printing Office.

U.S. Bureau of the Census (2000d). *Poverty in the United States: 1999* (Current Population Reports, Series P60-210). Washington, D.C.: U.S. Government Printing Office.

U.S. Centers for Disease Control and Prevention (1996). Guidelines for school health programs to promote lifelong healthy eating. *Morbidity and Mortality Weekly Report, 45, 3.*

U.S. Department of Education. (1991). *The condition of bilingual education in the nation: A report to the Congress and the president.* Washington, D.C.: U.S. Department of Education.

U.S. Department of Education (1999). Twenty-first Annual Report to Congress on the Implementation of the Individuals with Disabilities Education Act. Washington, D.C.: Author.

U.S. Department of Health and Human Services (2000). *Trends in the well-being of America's children and youth 2000.* Washington, D.C.: Author.

U.S. Department of Health and Human Services (2000). *Child maltreatment 1998: Reports from the states to the National Child Abuse and Neglect Data System.* Washington, D.C.: U.S. Government Printing Office.

U.S. Department of Labor and U.S. Department of Education. (1988). *The bottom line: Basic skills in the workplace.* Washington, D.C.: Office of Public Information, Employment and Training Administration, U.S. Department of Labor.

Vacca, J. A., Vacca, R., & Grove, M. K. (1991). *Learning to Read* (2nd ed.). New York: HarperCollins.

Vacca, J. A., Vacca, R. T., & Grove, M. K. (1995). *Reading and Learning to Read* (2nd ed.). New York: HarperCollins.

Vacca, R. T., & Rasinski, T. V. (1992). *Case studies in whole language.* Fort Worth: Harcourt Brace Jovanovich.

Valencia, S. (1990). Assessment: A portfolio approach to classroom reading assessment: The whys, whats, and hows. *The Reading Teacher, 44,* 338–340.

Van den Boom, D. C. (1995). Do first-year intervention effects endure? Follow-up during toddlerhood of a sample of Dutch irritable infants. *Child Development, 66,* 1798–1816.

Vander Zanden, J. (1993). *Human development* (5th ed.). New York: McGraw-Hill.

Vaughn, B., & Langlois, J. (1983). Physical attractiveness as a correlate of peer status and social competence in preschool children. *Developmental Psychology, 19,* 561–567.

Vaughn, S., & Elbaum, B. (1999). The self-concepts and friendships of students with learning disabilities: A developmental perspective. In R. Gallimore, L. P. Bernheime, D. L. MacMillian, D. L. Speece, & S. Vaughn. (eds). *Developmental perspectives on children with high-incidence disabilities* (pp. 81–110). Mahwah, N.J.: Erlbaum.

Volterra, V., & Taeschner, T. (1978). The acquisition and development of language by bilingual children. *Journal of Child Language 5,* 311–326.

Vurpillot, E. (1968). The development of scanning strategies and their relation to visual differentiation. *Journal of Experimental Child Psychology, 6,* 632–650.

Vygotsky, L. S. (1962). *Thought and language.* Cambridge, Mass.: MIT Press.

Vygotsky, L. S. (1978). *Mind in society: The development of higher psychological processes.* Cambridge, Mass.: Harvard University Press.

Vygotsky, L. S. (1987). Thinking and speech. In *The collected works of L. S. Vygotsky, Vol. 1: Problems of general psychology.* (N. Minick, trans.). New York: Plenum Press.

Wakschlag, L. S., & Hans, S. L. (1999). Relation of maternal responsiveness during infancy to the development of behavior problems in high-risk youths. *Developmental Psychology, 35,* 569–579.

Wallerstein, J. S., Corbin, S. B., & Lewis, J. M. (1988). Children of divorce: A 10-year study. In E. M. Hetherington & J. D. Arasteh (eds.), *Impact of divorce, single parenting, and stepparenting on children.* Hillsdale, N.J.: Erlbaum.

Wallerstein, J. S., Lewis, J. M., & Blakeslee, S. (2000). *The unexpected legacy of divorce: A 25-year landmark study.* New York: Hyperion.

Walker, D. (1995). School violence prevention. *Eric Digest, Number 94.* Eugene, OR: ERIC Clearinghouse on Educational Management.

Walker-Andrews, A. S. (1997). Infants' perception of expressive behavior: Differentiation of multimodal information. *Psychological Bulletin, 121,* 437–456.

Ward, L. M. (1995). Talk about sex: Common themes about sexuality in prime-time television programs children and adolescents view most. *Journal of Youth and Adolescence, 24,* 595–616.

Warren, C., Harris, W., & Kann, L. (1995). *Adolescent health: State of the nation—pregnancy, sexually transmitted diseases and related risk behaviors among U.S. adolescents* (Monograph Series No. 2). Atlanta: Centers for Disease Control and Prevention, Division of Adolescent and School Health, Surveillance and Evaluation Research Branch.

Wartella, E. A., & Jennings, N. (2000). Children and computers: New technology—old concerns. *Future of children. Children and Computer Technology, Vol. 10,* 31–42.

Washington, V. (1988). The black mother in the United States: History, theory, research, and issues. In B. Birns & D. F. Hay (eds.), *The different faces of motherhood* (pp. 185–213). New York: Plenum.

Waterman, A. (1982). Identity development from adolescence to adulthood: An extension of theory and review of research. *Developmental Psychology, 18,* 341–358.

Waterman, A. (1999a). Identity, the identity statuses, and identify status development: A contemporary statement. *Developmental Review, 19,* 591–621.

Waterman, A. (1999b). Issues of identity formation revisited: United States and the Netherlands. *Developmental Review, 19,* 462–479.

Waterman, A. S. (1997). An overview of service learning and the role of research and evaluation in service-learning programs. In A. S. Waterman (ed.), *Service Learning* (pp. 4–24), Mahwah, N.J.: Erlbaum.

Waterman, A. S. (1999). Issues of identity formation revisited: United States and The Netherlands. *Developmental Review, 19,* 462–479.

Weaver, P., & Schonhoff, F. (1984). *Subskill and holistic approaches to reading instruction* (3rd ed.). New York: Longman.

Wechsler, D. (1958). *The measurement and appraisal of adult intelligence* (4th ed.). Baltimore: Williams & Wilkins.

Wechsler, D. (1991). *Wechsler Intelligence Scale for Children* (3rd ed.). San Antonio: Psychological Corporation.

Wehlage, G., Rutter, R., Smith, G., Lesko, N., & Fernadez, R. (1989). *Reducing the risk: Schools as communities of support*. New York: Falmer Press.

Weiler, J. (1998). The athletic experiences of ethnically diverse girls. *ERIC/CUE Digest*. New York, NY: ERIC Clearhouse in Urban Education.

Weiner, B. (1979). A theory of motivation for some classroom experiences. *Journal of Educational Psychology*, *71*, 3–25.

Weir, R. H. (1962). *Language in the crib*. The Hague The Netherlands: Mouton.

Wierson, M., & Forehand, R. (1994). Parent behavioral training for child noncompliance: Rationale, concepts, and effectiveness. *Current Directions in Psychological Science*, *3*, 146–150.

Weiss, M. J., & Hagen, R. (1988). A key to literacy: Kindergarteners' awareness of the functions of print. *The Reading Teacher*, *41*, 574–578.

Wellman, H. (1988). The early development of memory strategies. In F. Weinert & M. Perlmutter (eds.), *Memory development: Universal changes and individual differences* (pp. 3–29). Hillsdale, N.J.: Erlbaum.

Wellman, H. (1990). *The child's theory of mind*. New York: Cambridge Press.

Wellman, H., & Estes, D. (1986). Early understanding of mental entities: A reexamination of childhood realism. *Child Development*, *57*, 910–923.

Wellman, H., & Gelman, R. (1998). Knowledge acquisition in foundational domains. In W. Dammon (series ed.) & D. Kuhn, & R. Siegler (vol. eds.), *Handbook of child psychology*, *Vol. 2: Cognition, perception, and language* (pp. 523–573). New York: John Wiley.

Wellman, H. M. (1990). *The child's theory of mind*. Cambridge, Mass.; MIT Press.

Wells, G. (1985). *Language development in the preschool years*. New York: Cambridge University Press.

Wells, G. (1986). *The meaning makers: Children learning language and using language to learn*. Portsmouth, N.H.: Heinemann.

Wenglinsky, H. (1998). *Does it compute? The relationship between educational technology and student achievement*. Princeton, N.J.: Educational Testing Service.

Wentzel, K. (1996). Social goals and social relationships as motivators of school adjustment. In J. Juvonen & K. R. Wentzel (eds.), *Social motivation: Understanding children's school adjustment*. (pp. 226–248). New York: Cambridge University Press.

Wentzel, K., & Caldwell, K. (1997). Friendship, peer acceptance, and group membership: Relations to academic achievement in middle school. *Child Development*, *68*, 1198–1209.

Werner, E. E. (1999). Risk and protective factors in the lives of children with high-incidence disabilities. In R. Gallimore, L. P. Bernheimer, D. L. MacMillan, D. Speece, & S. Vaughn (eds.), *Developmental perspectives on children with high-incidence disabilities*.(pp. 15–32). Mahwah, N.J.: Erlbaum.

Werner, E. E., & Smith, R. S. (1992). *Vulnerable but invincible: A study of resilient children*. New York: McGraw-Hill.

Wertsch, J. (1985). *Vygotsky and the social formation of mind*. Cambridge, Mass.: Harvard University Press.

Wertsch, J., & Tulviste, P. (1992). L. S. Vygotsky and contemporary developmental psychology. *Developmental Psychology*, *28*, 548–557.

Wesley College Center for Research on women (1992). *American Association of University women Report: How schools shortchange girls*. Washington, D.C.: AAUW.

Whitehurst, G. J., Lonigan, C. J. (1998). Child development and emergent literacy. *Child Development*, *68*, 848–872.

Wigfield, A. (2000). Facilitating children's reading motivation. In L. Baker, M. J. Dreher, & J. Guthrie (eds.), *Engaging young readers*. New York: Guildford Press.

Wigfield, A., & Guthrie, J. (1997). Relations of children's motivation for reading to the amount and breadth of their reading. *Journal of Educational Psychology*, *89*, 420–432.

Willis, W. (1992). Families with African American roots. In E. W. Lynch & M. J. Hanson (eds.), *Developing cross-cultural competence* (pp. 121–150). Baltimore: Paul H. Brookes Publishing Company.

Winner, E. (2000). The origins and ends of giftedness. *American Psychologist*, *55*, 159–169.

Wolf, N. (1991). *The beauty myth: How images of beauty are used against women*. New York: William Morrow.

Wolfe, D. P. (1989). Portfolio assessment: Sampling student work. *Educational Leadership* (April) 35–39.

Wood, D., Bruner, J. S., & Ross, G. (1976). The role of tutoring in problem solving. *Journal of Child Psychology and Psychiatry*, *17*, 89–100.

Woods, N. B. (1972). The unsupervised child of the working mother. *Developmental Psychology*, *6*, 14–25.

Wood, T., Cobb, P., & Yackel, E. (1992). Change in learning mathematics: Change in teaching mathematics.

In H. Marshall (ed.), *Redefining student learning: Roots of educational change*. Norwood, N.J.: Ablex.

Wrobel, G. D. (1999). The impact of school starting time on family life. *Phi Delta Kappan, 80* (5), 360–365.

Wu, L., & Martinson, B. (1993). Family structure and the risk of premarital birth. *American Sociological Review, 58*, 210–232.

Wyman, P. A., Cowen, E. L., Work, W. C., Hoyt-Meyers, L., Magnus, K. B., & Fagen, D. B. (1999). Caregiving and developmental factors differentiating young at-risk urban children showing resilient versus stress-affected outcomes: A replication and extension. *Child Development, 70*, 645–659.

Yaden, D., Rouge, D., & MacGellivency, L. (1999). *Emergent literacy: A polyphony of perspectives.* (Report Number 1-005). University of Michigan, Center for the Improvement of Early Reading Achievement.

Yellowbird, M., & Snipp, C. M. (1998). American Indian families. In R. L. Taylor (ed.), *Minority families in the United States* (pp. 226–248). Upper Saddle River, N.J.: Prentice Hall.

Youniss, J. (1989). Parent-adolescent relationships. In W. Damon (ed.), *Child development today and tomorrow* (pp. 379–392). San Francisco: Jossey-Bass.

Youniss, J., McCellen, J. A., & Strouse, D. (1994). "We're popular, but you are snobs": Adolescents describe their crowds. In R. Montemayor, G. R. Adams, & T. P. Gallota (eds.), *Personal relationships during adolescence* (pp. 102–122). Thousand Oaks: Sage

Yussen, S. R., & Bird, J. E. (1979). The development of metacognitive awareness in memory, communication, and attention. *Journal of Experimental Child Psychology, 28*, 502–508.

Zahn-Waxler, C., Radke-Yarrow, M., & King, R. A. (1979). Child-rearing and children's prosocial initiations toward victims of distress. *Child Development, 50*, 319–330.

Zajonc, R. B., & Markus, G. (1975). Birth order and intellectual development. *Psychological Review, 82*, 74–88.

Zigler, E., & Hall, N. W. (1989). Physical child abuse in America: Past, present, and future. In D. Cicchetti & V. Carlson (eds.), *Child maltreatment: Theory and research on the causes and consequences of child abuse and neglect.* New York: Cambridge University Press.

Zill, N. (1994). Understanding why children in stepfamilies have more learning and behavior problems than children in nuclear families. In A. Booth & J. Dunn (eds.), *Stepfamilies: Who benefits? Who does not?* (pp. 97–106). Hillsdale, N.J.: Erlbaum.

Zill, N., Morrison, D. R., & Coiro, M. J. (1993). Long-term effects of parental divorce and parent child relationships, adjustment, and achievement in young adulthood. *Journal of Family Psychology, 7*, 91–103.

Zill, N., Nord, C. W., & Loomis, L. S. (1995). *Adolescent time use, risky behavior and outcomes: An analysis on national data.* Rockville, Md.: Westat.

Zimmerman, B. J. (1990). Self-regulated learning and academic achievement: An overview. *Educational Psychologist, 25*, 3–18.

Zimmerman, B. J., & Martinez-Pons, M. (1990). Student differences in self-regulated learning: Relating grade, sex, and giftedness to self-efficacy and strategy use. *Journal of Educational Psychology, 82*, 51–59.

Zoccolillo, M. (1993). Gender and the development of conduct disorder. *Development and Psychopathology, 5*, 65–78.

Zuniga, M. E. (1992). Families with Latino roots. In E. W. Lynch & M. J. Hanson (eds.), *Developing cross-cultural competence* (pp. 151–179). Baltimore: Paul H. Brookes Publishing Company.

Glossary

A

ability grouping The practice in elementary school of grouping children according to their presumed academic ability; thought by some, when not used in conjunction with other grouping possibilities, to stigmatize and limit children's potential, particularly minority students, at an early age; see *tracking*.

accommodation A term used by Piaget to describe how children change existing schemes by altering old ways of thinking or acting to fit new information in their environment; contrast with *assimilation*.

achievement motivation An internal mechanism that energizes, directs, and terminates achievement behavior; explained by theorists variously as an enduring psychological need, an environmentally activated state, or a set of cognitions and beliefs.

action research Research conducted by teachers, administrators, and other change agents in the school to improve the educational environment for their students. The goal of action research is to understand a specific problem or to improve teaching practices within a specific classroom or school settings.

adaptation One of two basic principles referred to by Piaget as invariant functions; the ability of all organisms to adapt their mental representations or behavior to fit environmental demands; contrast with *organization*.

adolescent egocentrism A cognitive limitation emerging in adolescence, characterized by difficulty distinguishing thoughts about one's own thinking from their thinking about the thoughts of others. This limitation may manifest itself in heightened self-absorption and self-consciousness.

age norms The estimated age, often established by *cross-sectional studies*, at which certain psychological or behavioral characteristics emerge.

aggression Behavior that is intentionally aimed at harming or injuring another person; see *instrumental aggression*, *hostile aggression*.

alphabetic system The structure of some languages, including English, whereby single shapes in the written language make up letters, which in turn, are linked to specific sounds; contrast with *ideographic system*.

amniotic sac A structure present at implantation of the zygote that begins to function and mature during the embryonic period. See *placenta*.

androgens Sex hormones generally associated with male characteristics, yet produced and present in both sexes.

androgyny A blend of masculine and feminine traits that develop gradually as young people mature and become more flexible in their attitudes toward *gender-typed behaviors* through encounters with new activities and interests.

animism According to Piaget, children's inclination during the *preoperational stage* to attribute intentional states and human characteristics to inanimate objects.

anorexia nervosa An eating disorder, mainly affecting adolescent girls between the ages of 14 and 18, characterized by a 25 percent to 50 percent loss in body weight through excessive dieting and exercise; usually treated with a combination of hospitalization and family counseling.

assimilated A personal attitude and stance of a minority member characterized by adopting the norms, attitudes, and behaviors of the dominant culture and rejecting one's ethnic or racial culture.

assimilation A term used by Piaget to describe how children mold new information to fit their existing schemes in order to better adapt to their environment; contrast with *accommodation*.

attachment The close, affective relationship formed between a child and one or more caregivers.

attention deficit hyperactive disorders (ADHD) Behavior, diagnosed by a qualified professional, characterized by inattention, impulsivity, and unusual or excessive activity.

attribution theory A cognitive theory of motivation that examines how individuals interpret their successes and failures in achievement situations.

authentic assessment A currently preferred performance assessment method with the underlying principle that students are more apt to understand a concept that has real-life application.

authoritarian parenting A parenting style characterized by rigid rules and often unrealistic expectations for children; contrast with *authoritative* and *permissive*. It is high on the demand/control dimension but low on acceptance/responsiveness. It is also characterized by low warmth and little positive involvement. Rigid rules are set with the expectation they will be followed due to parental authority.

authoritative A parenting style characterized by high levels of warmth, acceptance, and responsiveness as well as reasonable expectations for children and firmly enforced rules; contrast with *authoritarian* and *permissive*.

authoritative parenting A style of parenting characterized by warm, responsive involvement, and the setting of appropriate and clear standards for behavior. The child's autonomy is encouraged by providing rationales for rules and showing respect of her rights and opinions.

autism A lifelong developmental disability that is neurologically based and affects the functioning of the brain; disabilities vary from mild to severe and include deficits in verbal and nonverbal communication, problems with reciprocal social interaction, and a restrictive set of activities and interests.

automaticity A factor in the development of children's attentional processes whereby familiarity with an object or task allows them to use it or perform without thinking.

autonomy The ability to be independent and self-motivated; to control and assume responsibility for one's own actions.

B

basic sense of trust In Erikson's theory, the first stage of psychosocial development, in which infants must form a sense that their caregivers and their environment are safe, secure, and predictable; establishes a foundation for confidence in one's self. See Table 6.1.

behavioral geneticist Scientists who study the degree to which psychological traits, such as sociability, aggression, and mental abilities, are inherited.

biculturalism The maintaining of ties of both the dominant and ethnic culture and developing an identity that allows the child to alternate between dominant and ethnic identities depending on the situation.

bidilectal An ability to speak several varieties of English, including *SAE* and a home *dialect.*

bilingual The ability to speak two languages.

bilingual-bicultural program A learning program focused on producing balanced learners who are competent in both English and their home language; contrast with *transitional bilingual program.*

bilingual education A perspective or approach to teaching children that uses at least two languages during instruction, usually a child's native language and the second language the child is acquiring.

binge drinking Drinking five or more alcoholic drinks in a row.

birth order The child's position in the family, whether born first, second, last, and so forth.

blended family A family configuration that includes a biological parent, stepparent, and child. It is formed when two partners bring together children from a previous marriage.

blind Those who have either 20/200 vision or a 20 percent or less field of vision; see *low vision.*

bulimia nervosa An eating disorder characterized by binge eating followed by vomiting or use of laxatives to purge the body; more common among older teens and young adults. This disorder generally is associated with a distorted body image and an inability to control one's impulses; treatable through family and individual therapy.

bullying behavior The most common form of aggression often taking the form of embarrassing people, hitting, destroying property, and ridiculing.

C

case study A research design for in-depth investigation of a person or small group of individuals; not a reliable source for generalized statements beyond those investigated in the study.

causal relationship When the results of a study indicate there is a systematic cause-and-effect result between two factors.

centration A developmental limitation present during the *preoperational stage* that makes young children focus their attention on only one aspect, usually the most salient, of a stimulus.

cephalocaudal One of two patterns characterizing growth in infancy; growth begins at the head and proceeds downward. As a result, the infant's brain, neck, and trunk develop before the legs.

chromosomes The structures that carry the genes; composed of long threadlike molecules of deoxyribonucleic acid (DNA).

chronosystem Term used by Bronfenbrenner to refer to involving the timing and patterning of events in an individual's life and the position of that individual's life in the larger flow of historical time.

circular reactions Piaget's term for patterns of behavior during the *sensorimotor stage* that are repeated over and over again as goal-directed actions.

class inclusion A concept acquired during the *concrete operational stage* that involves children's understanding of hierarchies; knowledge that objects in a subcategory (tulips) must be smaller than the superordinate category (flowers).

classical conditioning A behavioral principle of learning by which a new response is learned through the pairing of two stimuli. The response that naturally occurs in the presence of one stimulus (food) which begins to occur following the presentation of a second stimulus (bell) when the two stimuli are repeatedly paired.

classification A mental operation achieved during the *concrete operational stage* that allows children to impose order on their environment by grouping things and ideas according to common elements.

clinical interview method An interview technique attributed to Piaget of probing children's reasoning processes; a way of combining *performance assessments* and *interviews.*

clique A small peer group, generally same sex and same race, that has a clear social structure with one or two members serving as leaders.

code-switching A personal attitude and stance, usually by a minority member, characterized by successful shuttling between the dominant and one's ethnic or racial culture.

coercive family process A family dynamic characterized by inconsistent, ineffective, or punitive parental discipline during early development that leads to aggressive behavior in children.

cognitive behavior modification Meichenbaum's developmental program that helps children control and regulate their behavior; children are taught self-regulatory strategies to use as a verbal tool to inhibit impulses, control impulses and frustration, and promote reflection.

collaborative consultation A teaching partnership that often accompanies cooperative or *team teaching* and is characterized by a consultative relationship in which both special and general educators discuss academic and social behavior problems in the general classroom to meet the needs of all children.

collective monologue A characteristic conversational pattern of preschoolers who are unable to take the perspective of others and thus make little effort to modify their speech for their listener so that remarks to each other seem unrelated.

communication disorders Individuals characterized by specific impairments in speech and/or language.

communicative competence Learning to use language in an appropriate manner; knowing what words and structures to use on what occasion. This is the major area of linguistic growth during childhood, through adolescence, and continuing into adulthood.

compensation One of three basic mental operations including *negation* and *identity* needed to perform Piagetian *conservation* tasks; a form of *reversibility* which involves an understanding that one operation can compensate for the effects of another operation. In Piaget's *conservation* of liquid task, the height of one glass can compensate for the breadth of another glass.

componential intelligence One of three components of intellectual behavior in Sternberg's *triarchic model of intelligence* involving such skills as the ability to allocate mental resources, to encode and store information, to plan and monitor, to identify problems, and to acquire new knowledge; contrast with *experimental intelligence* and *contextual intelligence*.

comprehension An active process in which readers strive to construct a meaningful interpretation of written or oral information.

concrete operational stage The period of life from 7 to 11 years old when, Piaget believed, children's thinking becomes less rigid, and they begin to use mental operations, such as *classification*, *conservation*, and *seriation* to think about events and objects in their environment.

conditional knowledge Children's understanding about why learning strategies are effective in specific situations; contrast with *declarative knowledge* and *procedural knowledge*.

conflict resolution program School-based intervention programs designed to help students acquire the skills they need to resolve conflict; components include defining the problem, brainstorming about possible solutions, and choosing solutions that benefit both sides (called win-win solutions).

conservation A mental operation in the *concrete operational stage* that involves the understanding that an entity remains the same despite superficial changes in its form or physical appearance.

constructivist approach An approach to learning which purports that children must construct their own understandings of the world in which they live. Teachers guide this process through focusing attention, posing questions, and stretching children's thinking; information must be mentally acted on, manipulated, and transformed by learners in order to have meaning.

context knowledge A *decoding* strategy; using the surrounding text and one's background knowledge to identify an unknown word; contrast with *phonic knowledge* and *sight word knowledge*.

contextual intelligence One of three components of intellectual behavior in Sternberg's *triarchic model of intelligence involving* the ability to adapt to a changing environment or to shape the environment to capitalize on one's abilities or skills; contrast with *componential intelligence* and *experiential intelligence*; also see *practical intelligence*.

conventional level According to Kohlberg, the second level of moral judgment, characterized by individuals who accept society's rules for right and wrong and obey authority figures; contrast with *preconventional level* and *postconventional level*.

corporal punishment Use of physical punishment with the intention of causing a child to experience physical pain, but not injury; used as a means for reducing or eliminating undesirable behavior in children.

corregulation Control of behavior shared by parents and children; develops in middle childhood.

correlational coefficient The statistic that measures the strength of relations between two measures (e.g., self-esteem and school achievement); expressed in a positive or negative ratio from 1.0 to +1.0.

correlational study A widely used design for developmental research studying what different factors influence one another or go together; such studies are not able to test cause-and-effect hypotheses.

critical literacy   The ability to use written language to solve problems and to communicate.

critical period   (1) Periods of development during which certain basic structures are formed or a child is most vulnerable or responsive to environmental influences. (2) Lenneberg's hypothesis that language development has a biological basis and there is a time in infancy when particular neurological faculties develop. It states that if certain internal or external conditions related to language development are missing, then a child will never be able to acquire language.

cross-sectional study   A study that gathers information simultaneously on one or more aspects of development among children of different age groups.

cross-sequential study   A study that follows a group of different-aged children for 2 or 3 years; can reliably identify antecedents and stability of behavior patterns during the course of the study.

crowds   The largest adolescent group that is made up of individuals with similar reputations and stereotyped identities that is not conducive to close interpersonal relations.

crystallized intelligence   In intelligence theories, one of two kinds of intelligence that develops from learning experiences; measured by word fluency, general information, and vocabulary and verbal comprehension; contrast with *fluid intelligence*.

cumulative deficit effect   A phenomenon found in some studies showing that under poor environmental conditions, differences in IQ scores among races increase with age.

curriculum casualty   A school situation in which a child's needs clash with the learning and behavioral expectations of the educational system.

D

deaf   Those who cannot hear or understand speech; see *hard of hearing*.

deaf-blindness   A condition characterized by the unique debilitating effects of hearing and vision impairments.

declarative knowledge   Children's understanding about what learning strategies are available to help them; contrast with *procedural knowledge* and *conditional knowledge*.

decoding   The process that readers use to determine the oral equivalent of written words.

deferred imitation   A Piagetian concept in *representational thinking* in which children are able to repeat a simple sequence of actions or sounds after the sequence is observed; an early form of *representational thinking*.

deoxyribonucleic acid (DNA)   Long threadlike molecules that twist around to form a double helix and make up chromosomes; believed to contain about 100,000 genes, the basic units of heredity; see *dominant gene* and *recessive gene*.

depression   An affective disorder characterized by disturbances in cognitive and behavioral functioning that last longer than 2 or 3 weeks; symptoms include an inability to concentrate, feelings of hopelessness, weight changes, an inability to have fun, and thoughts of death.

development   The systematic and successive changes that follow a logical or orderly pattern over a long period of time and enhance a child's adaptation to the environment.

dialect   A variation of a single language spoken by members of a speech community; contrast with *accent*; see *social dialect*.

direct instruction   A teaching strategy in which the teacher explains, demonstrates, and then provides supervised practice for a learning task.

discontinuous process   The emergence of drives, needs, and cognitive processes in a series of discrete stages of maturation that influence the way a child relates to the environment; psychoanalytic and cognitive development (Piagetian) theories argue that development is a series of discrete stages.

dizygotic twins   Two siblings who come from separate eggs that are released at the same time from an ovary and are fertilized; also known as fraternal twins.

dominant gene   A gene inherited from one parent, such as brown hair, that will mask the expression of a *recessive gene* from the other parent.

Down syndrome   A genetic disorder of varying degree that is due to the presence of an extra twenty-first chromosome or a piece of one, causes a range of physical and mental handicaps, and occurs in 1 out of 800 live births. Mothers over the age of 35 have an increased risk of conceiving a child with this disorder, because of their longer exposure to environmental substances. The presence of this abnormality can be detected through the genetic screening process amniocentesis in the fourth month of pregnancy.

E

ectoderm   The outermost layer of the embryonic structure that will develop into the nervous system and skin.

effectance motivation   According to White, an inherent need that propels individuals to engage in activities from which they can derive a sense of personal mastery or competence.

egocentric speech   One of three stages of children's use of language identified by Vygotsky during which children begin to use speech to regulate their behavior and thinking through spoken aloud self-verbalizations; contrast with *social speech* and *inner speech*.

egocentrism   The tendency to think about, see, and understand the world from one's own perspective; an inability to see objects or situations from another's perspective.

ego-oriented goals   See *performance-oriented goals*.

elaboration   A memory encoding strategy in which one forms a personally meaningful mental image of items to be remembered.

embryonic period   The second stage of prenatal development marked by the implantation of the *zygote* and lasting from weeks 2 to 8, during which all the basic structures of the child (the central nervous system, the skeleton, and the internal organs) are established and begin to function.

emergent literacy   The concept that literacy learning is ongoing from birth.

emotional competence   The understanding, expression, and regulation of emotions. Also called emotional intelligence.

emotional maltreatment   Rejection and consistent lack of concern for another's emotional well-being.

emotional or behavior disorders   Characterized by significantly different psychosocial development from one's peers, including hyperactivity, aggression, withdrawal, immaturity, and learning difficulties.

empathy   The ability to know and feel another person's emotional state.

encode   To process information and place into memory through the use of cognitive strategies such as *elaboration*, *organization*, and *rehearsal*.

endoderm   The innermost layer of the embryonic structure that will develop into the digestive tract and vital organs.

English as a second language (ESL)   A special language learning program for nonnative speakers that focuses narrowly on learning the target language.

entity theory of ability   A theory of intelligence, proposed by Dweck, whereby students believe their ability level is fixed and cannot be improved through practice or effort; contrast with *incremental theory of ability*.

episodic memory   Long-term memory storage of personal or autobiographical events or information, as well as information about the place, time, and order of events.

equilibration   Piaget's concept that refers to our innate tendency of self-regulation to keep our mental representations in balance by adjusting them to maintain organization and stability in our environment through the processes of *accommodation* and *assimilation*.

estrogens   Sex hormones generally associated with female characteristics, yet produced and present in both sexes; crucial to the maturation of the reproductive system, breast development, and the onset of ovulation and menstruation in females.

ethic of care   Gilligan's argument that women are socialized to take responsibility for the well-being of others and therefore emphasize connections between people as well as of justice.

ethnic identity   Refers to one's sense of self concerning racial or ethnic group membership.

ethnicity   Refers to a group of people, such as Japanese, Cuban, or Italian, who share a common nationality, cultural heritage, and language; contrast with *race*.

event sampling   A technique used to record observations of a certain selected behavior, such as aggression.

exceptionality   An umbrella term to describe all who receive special education—children with disabilities as well as children who are gifted.

exosystem   In Bronfenbrenner's theory, the system that influences the child's development only indirectly.

expectancy-value theory   A cognitive model of motivation which stresses that individuals are more apt to engage in and persist at learning activities when they expect and want to succeed.

experiential intelligence   One of three components of intellectual behavior in Sternberg's *triarchic model of intelligence* involving the ability to cope with new situations in an effective, efficient, and insightful manner; contrast with *componential intelligence* and *contextual intelligence*.

experimental study   After careful selection and matching on a number of variables, participants are randomly assigned to either an experimental or a control group to measure any difference between the groups for a particular outcome, known as the dependent variable; any significant variance between the two groups' outcome measure would support the hypothesis that the treatment caused the outcome.

expert versus novice studies   A research paradigm that shows that more knowledgeable individuals are better able than novices to group or organize information in meaningful patterns suggests that advances in children's thinking processes are explained by both quantitative changes in their thinking processes and qualitative changes in how knowledge is organized.

external locus of control   A pattern of attributing events to factors outside one's control; a characteristic of children with learning disabilities; see *locus of causality*.

externalizing problems   The kinds of difficulties a majority of children with emotional and behavioral disorders experience, including argumentative, aggressive, antisocial, and destructive actions; contrast with *internalizing problems*.

extrinsic motivation   A need to learn or act that rises from external contingencies, such as winning an award, parental demands, or to achieve a high grade; contrast with *intrinsic motivation*.

F

familialism   The strong identification with and attachment to both the nuclear and extended family, and the feelings of loyalty, respect, duty, and reciprocity which accompany such familial attachment.

Glossary

family structure   The configuration of people who live together in a given family unit.

feeling of inferiority   In Erikson's fourth stage of psychosocial development, children 7 to 11 years old can develop negative attitudes about their abilities and competencies if a parallel internal *sense of industry* is not encouraged (see Table 6.1).

fetal period   The third and longest stage of prenatal development, from 8 weeks until birth, during which time the fetus increases in size; eyelids, fingernails, taste buds, and hair form; and the respiratory system matures to enable breathing after birth.

fine motor skills   Involve small body movements and small muscle coordination and control.

fluid intelligence   In intelligence theories, one of two kinds of intelligence that reflects innate cognitive abilities; measured by the speed of information processing, memory processes, ability to detect relationships, and other abstract thinking skills; contrast with *crystallized intelligence*.

formal logic   The development during the *formal operational stage* of the cognitive tools for solving many types of logical problems; examples are *propositional* and *hypothetico-deductive thinking*.

formal operational stage   During the period of life between 11 and 12 years of age and onward during which, Piaget believed, children begin to apply formal rules of logic and to gain the ability to think abstractly and reflectively; thinking shifts from the real to the possible; see *formal logic*.

fragile-X syndrome   A genetic disorder more common in male than female offspring due to the presence of an X chromosome that appears to be pinched or very thin in one area and is likely to break during cell division. May cause mild retardation in females; will cause varying degrees of retardation in males and is associated with both physical (cleft palate, eye disorders) and mental (hyperactivity) deficits. This disorder can be detected through genetic screening.

functionally literate   Able to read and write well enough to negotiate daily life.

G

gender constancy   The understanding by around age 4 or 5 that one's sex is permanent and cannot be altered by changes in clothing, hairstyle, or activities.

gender-role conceptions   The images we have of ourselves as males and females.

gender-role identity   Children's perceptions of themselves as a female or male.

gender-role socialization   The process by which children learn the attitudes and behavior that society defines as appropriate for their gender; see *gender-typed behavior*. Same as sex-role socialization.

gender schema   Children's understanding of gender and gender-role expectations.

gender-typed behavior   Preferences demonstrated by the age of 3 for choosing toys and activities; can be influenced by stereotypical social values.

general intellectual factor   In intelligence theories, the idea that a general ability factor (g) underlies all intellectual functioning. Someone with a high general intelligence is expected to do well on all intellectual tests.

generalizability   An important determination, in judging the quality of a study, of whether or not the findings apply or do not apply to groups other than the one studied.

genes   A unit of the chromosome by which hereditary characteristics are transmitted.

genotype   A person's genetic characteristics as determined by the genes a person inherits from both parents for any particular trait; contrast with *phenotype*.

germinal period   The first stage of prenatal development, encompassing the first 2 weeks of fetal development. The fertilized egg rapidly divides, travels down the fallopian tube to the uterus, and prepares for implantation.

giftedness   Individuals identified with a minimal IQ score of about 130 and above-average academic achievement, usually 2 years above grade level.

goal theory of motivation   A cognitive theory of motivation that emphasizes students' personal reasons for choosing, performing, and persisting at various achievement levels.

grammar   Language rules that extend from the simplest level of combining sounds to the complex level of extended conversations including phonology, semantics, syntax, pragmatics, and the lexicon; see Figure 5.1.

gross motor skills   Involve the movement of the head, body, legs, arms, and large muscles; see Table 2.7.

guided participation   Rogoff's term used to describe transferring responsibility for a task from the skilled partner to the child in a mutual involvement between the child and the partner in a collective activity. Steps include choosing and structuring activities to fit the child's skills and interests; supporting and monitoring the child's participation; and adjusting the level of support provided as the child begins to perform the activity independently.

H

habituation procedure   A technique researchers use to study infant memory by assessing changes in the intensity of infants' responses to various forms of stimulation over a period of time.

hand dominance   A preference for using either the right or left hand that develops around the age of 5 for more than 90 percent of all children.

hard of hearing   Those who have sufficient hearing to enable them to understand speech; may require amplification of speech through a hearing aid; see *deaf*.

heritability   The proportion of observed variance for a behavior that can be ascribed to genetic differences among individuals in a particular population; a population statistic that applies only to the sample from which it is derived.

hierarchial classification   A mental operation learned during the *concrete operational stage* that allows children to organize concepts and objects according to how they relate to one another in a building-block fashion. For example, all matter is composed of molecules and molecules are made up of atoms, which, in turn, are made up of protons, electrons, and neutrons.

holophrases   Refers to single words intended to convey more complex meaning typically utilized by children aged 18 to 24 months.

homophobia   An irrational fear and hatred of homosexuals.

homosexual orientation   Consistent sexual attraction toward persons of the same gender that includes fantasies, conscious attraction, romantic feelings, or sexual behaviors.

horizontal decalage   Piaget's term for children's inconsistency in thinking within a developmental stage; explains why, for instance, children do not learn *conservation* tasks about numbers and volume at the same time.

hostile aggression   In 3- and 4-year-old children, behavior that is intended to hurt or harm another person; see *aggression*. Contrast with *instrumental aggression*.

hypothalamus   A structure at the base of the brain that controls the pituitary gland.

hypothesis   A statement of prediction derived from a theory that has not yet been tested.

hypothetico-deductive thinking   A form of *formal logic* achieved during the *formal operational stage* Piaget identified as the ability to generate and test hypotheses in a logical and systematic matter.

I

ideal self   The image of the self created during middle childhood that is developed by comparing one's real self to a set of desired characteristics including the expectations, values, and ideals of peers and adults.

identity   (1) In Piaget's theory, one of three basic mental operations including *negation* and *compensation* needed to perform *conservation* tasks; involves an understanding of cognitive constancy, that people, objects, and quantities remain unchanged despite changes in appearance. (2) In Erikson's theory, the fifth stage of psychosocial development when adolescents commit themselves to a set of beliefs, values, and adult roles in forming a basic sense of self. If adolescents are unable to explore alternative roles and options, they will experience a parallel internal state of *role confusion*; see Table 6.1.

identity achievement   Marcia's term for an adolescent's determination of definite goals or choices after having explored different options.

identity foreclosure   The state adolescents are in when they have not explored different possibilities but have committed to specific choices.

identity moratorium   Marcia's term for an adolescent's exploration of different occupational plans, ideological stances, and personal relationship when she is not ready to make a choice or commitment.

identity versus identity confusion   In Erikson's theory, the central issue that defines adolescence whereby the adolescent must feel his identity informed by his past, future, and current identities, and how he sees himself and how others see him.

ideographic system   The structure of some languages, including Chinese, whereby each character in the written language represents the meaning of an individual word; contrast with *alphabetic system*.

imaginary audience   The belief that one is constantly being watched and evaluated, which is an expression of adolescent egocentrism, defined by Elkind as resulting from the inability of adolescents to distinguish between their thoughts about themselves and their thoughts about others.

incremental theory of ability   A theory of intelligence, proposed by Dweck, whereby students believe their ability level can improve through a greater investment of effort or by trying different strategies; contrast with *entity theory of ability*.

inductive discipline   A discipline technique in which parents offer explanation for their rules and ask children to reflect on their behavior; helps children develop self-control and self-discipline.

infant attachment   The process by which infants form strong affectional ties with their caregivers; generally takes place within the first 6 months of age and is important for the development of a basic sense of trust that can have long-term effects on an infants' later emotional and cognitive development.

infant mortality   A term referring to the number of infants that die within the first year of life, often caused by a short gestation period or low birth weight.

inner speech   One of three stages of children's use of language identified by Vygotsky during which children internalize their self-verbalizations and are able to manipulate language in their heads to think about problem solutions and action sequences. A self-regulatory process by which children guide their own thinking and behavior; also called private speech; contrast with *social speech* and *egocentric speech*.

insecure-avoidant attachment   In Ainsworth theory, a behavior pattern in which infants appear indifferent to the departure of their mothers and avoid the parent when they return. Distinguished from secure attachment.

insecure-disorganized attachment   Another form of insecure attachment in which infant shows disorientation and contradictory behavior in Ainsworth's Strange Situation. Distinguished from secure attachment.

insecure-resistant attachment   In Ainsworth theory, a behavior pattern in which infants show high levels of distress upon separation, but ambivalence when parent returns.

instrumental aggression   In young children, behavior that is intended to obtain an object, to protect a play space, or to get one's way; behavior that is not intended to hurt or harm another person; see *aggression*. Contrast with *hostile aggression*.

instrumental conditioning   See *operant conditioning*.

intelligence quotient (IQ)   Represents a score obtained by comparing a child's *mental age* score with other children's of the same chronological age; currently determined through a deviation IQ score procedure.

interactional perspective   A theory that supports the interplay of innate and environmental influences on a child's development.

intercoder reliability   See *interobserver reliability*.

interindividual variation   Differences in developmental needs from one child to the next; see *intraindividual variation*.

internalization   Vygotsky's term for the process of constructing a mental representation of external physical actions or cognitive operations that first occur through social interaction.

internalizing problems   The kinds of problems some children with emotional and behavioral disorders experience, including depression, withdrawal, anxiety, and obsession; contrast with *externalizing problems*.

interobserver reliability   A reliability estimate used in interview and observation studies whereby more than one person observes or codes the same events and a percentage of agreement is computed to guard against subjective interpretations and judgments; also called *intercoder reliability*.

interview   A *self-report* measure in which subjects are asked a standard set of questions.

intraindividual variation   The unique pattern of strengths and needs related to each child's physical, cognitive, social, and emotional growth; see *interindividual variation*.

intrinsic motivation   A desire to learn or act that arises from internal sources of curiosity, interest, enjoyment, and innate strivings for mastery and growth; contrast with *extrinsic motivation*.

intuitive theory   Piaget's explanation for young children's attempts to explain natural phenomena by using their personal experiences; characterized by *animism*.

invented spelling   Unconventional ways children spell words in their early attempts at writing.

L

language   A symbolic system in which a series of sounds make words to represent an idea, an object, or a person and eventually becomes the medium through which we think.

language acquisition device (LAD)   Chomsky's idea that children are born with a mechanism in their brains that enables them to recognize the universal rules that underlie all languages and the structure and grammar of their native language.

lateralization   Specialization of the two hemispheres of the brain.

lateralized   A theory about cognitive functioning suggesting that each of the two cerebral hemispheres of the brain, the left side and the right side, performs a special set of functions and becomes the dominant center of brain functioning.

learned helplessness   A feeling of helplessness that develops when one encounters difficult or failure, especially in situations when one does not have control. This reinforces low self-confidence.

learning-oriented goals   Outcome desired because of the child's intrinsic interest in learning something new.

limited English proficiency (LEP)   A minimal knowledge of *Standard American English (SAE)*; often characteristic of nonnative speakers.

literacy   Constructed meaning; meaning created through the interaction of reader or writer and written text.

literate environment   A place in which children encounter print with authentic purposes and adults value and participate in reading and writing.

literate thinking   The ability to think and reason like a literate person within a particular society; see *literacy*.

locus of causality   In *attribution theory*, the motivational source, either internal or external, to which people attribute their actions or achievements.

logical rule of class inclusion   A mental operation achieved during the *concrete operational stage* that allows children to understand the relationship of something's whole to its parts; see *class inclusion*.

logical rule of progressive change   The understanding which develops during the *concrete operational stage* that various stimuli can be ordered in terms of increasing and decreasing size.

logical rule of transitivity   The understanding which develops during the *concrete operational stage* that objects in the middle of a series are both shorter and longer than others; a necessary concept in solving *seriation* problems.

Logico-mathematical knowledge   In Piaget's theory, the type of knowledge as the mental construction of relationships involved in the concrete operations of seriation, classification, and conservation, as well as various formal operations that emerge in adolescence.

longitudinal study   A study that collects different types of data (e.g., early experiences, education, personality characteristics) on a regular basis and tracks the development of a group of children over a number of years.

long-term memory   A component of the information processing system into which information passes from *short-term memory* if it has been transformed or worked on in some personally meaningful way; has a large capacity, and can store information indefinitely.

low birth weight   Many premature and some full-term babies who weigh less than 5.5 pounds or 2,500 grams at birth.

low vision   Those who cannot read newsprint-size letters, even with corrective lenses; see *blind*.

M

macrosystem   In Bronfenbrenner's model, the larger culture and possibly subculture in which the individual lives— including ideologies, traditions, and values. Elements of the macrosystem include regional identity, nationality, ethnicity, and religious affiliation.

marginality   Living within a dominant culture but remaining estranged or alienated from it.

mastery oriented   When the desired outcome is the ability to perform, rather than attainment of new knowledge.

matrix classification   In Piaget's theory, a concept achieved during the *concrete operational stage* that involves ordering items by two or more attributes, such as by both size and color.

memory script   A mental representation of often-repeated events in a child's daily life; a basic method for organizing and interpreting familiar experiences.

memory strategy   A cognitive operation, such as repeating a list of items over and over again, that will help one to remember abstract, unfamiliar, or meaningless information.

menarche   The beginning of a girl's menstrual cycle; generally the last physical change to occur in puberty.

mental age (MA)   The score represented by the number of test items a child gets correct that was formerly used in calculating an IQ score; see *intelligence quotient*.

mental retardation   Characterized by a lower than normal level of intelligence and developmental delays in specific adaptive behavior.

mesoderm   The middle layer of the embronic structure that will become the skeleton and muscles.

mesosystem   In Bronfenbrenner's model, interactions among components of the microsystem.

metacognition   Knowledge about one's own thinking; involves an understanding of how memory works, what tasks require more cognitive effort, and what strategies facilitate learning; plays an important role in children's cognitive development during the middle childhood years and in the development of self-regulated learning.

metalinguistic awareness   The ability to think and talk about the relationship between print and sound in a language; for instance, a child's ability to identify the first sound as making the difference between the words *rat* and *bat*.

microsystem   In Brofenbrenner's model, the child's immediate environment (the family, peer group, school).

mitosis   The process through which chromosomes produce duplicate copies of themselves and divide into new cells; each new cell has 23 pairs of chromosomes.

mixed speech   A single language system lasting until about 2 years of age in which a *simultaneous bilingual* combines features of both languages he or she is exposed to.

monozygotic twins   Two siblings who come from the same fertilized egg and contain the same genetic instructions; also known as identical twins.

motherese   A type of child-directed speech also known as parentese in which parents or caregivers modify language they direct toward their children from birth; thought to assist children's language development by simplifying structure to make language acquisition simpler.

multidimensional conception of intelligence   The concept that intelligence represents several different mental abilities or intellectual competencies; contrast with *unitary conception of intelligence*.

multilingual   The ability to speak more than two languages.

multimodal approach   A teaching method effective with children having an *attention deficit disorder* that combines educational support, psychological counseling, behavioral management at school and home, and medical management using a psychostimulant.

myelin   The fatty substance that coats neurons and dendrites to enable *myelination*.

myelination   The second of two changes during brain development after birth; the process during which neurons and dendrites become coated with a fatty substance (*myelin*) to enable neural impulses to travel faster.

N

natural experiment Studies that use natural settings (home, school, playground) in which to study children to avoid skewing experimental evidence due to overly controlled laboratory-like settings that do not resemble the real world.

naturalistic observation An observation situation that uses real life environments in which to collect data; see *natural experiment*.

need to achieve In motivation theory, a person's desire to excel in achievement situations.

negation In Piaget's theory, one of three basic mental operations including *compensation* and *identity* needed to perform *conservation* tasks; a form of *reversibility* which involves an understanding that operations can be undone (negated) or can have an inverse relationship (subtraction is the inverse of addition).

negative identity A possible outcome for ethnic or racial minority young people who fail to establish a strong sense of self and reject their community's values as well as those of the dominant culture.

neglect A form of child abuse involving inattention to basic needs such as food, clothing, and medical care.

neglected peers Children who are seldom chosen as work or play partners by their peers.

neo-Piagetian theory Cognitive developmental models that add greater specificity to developmental changes while maintaining the basic assumptions of Piaget's theory.

neurons Long thin cells within the central nervous system, different from other cells because they are not closely packed, that are formed during the first 5 months of gestation.

neurotransmitters Chemicals released by *neurons* that cross over *synapses* in the central nervous system to communicate with other neurons.

niche-picking The tendency of older children to choose an environment that compliments their heredity as part of the active gene-environment effect described by Sandra Scarr and her associates.

O

obesity A greater than 20 percent increase over average body weight for an individual's age, sex, and body build; contributing factors can be heredity, unhealthy diet, lack of exercise, abnormal metabolism, and family trauma.

object permanence Piaget's term for an infant's understanding during the *sensorimotor stage* that objects continue to exist even when they can no longer be seen or acted on.

operant conditioning A behavioral principle of learning through which behavior is increased or extinguished by rewards and punishments; same as *instrumental conditioning*.

organization (1) In Piaget's theory, one of two basic principles referred to as invariant functions that guide children's intellectual development; the innate predisposition to integrate simple physical patterns or mental schemes into more complex systems; contrast with *adaptation*. (2) In information processing theory, a memory encoding strategy in which one tries to group items to be remembered into meaningful categories.

P

parenting style Common patterns of parenting styles including authoritarian, permissive, and authoritative.

partial participation A teaching approach in which a student from a separate special classroom spends time in the general classroom engaged with activities modified to fit his or her abilities; see *reverse mainstreaming*.

peer A person equal in age, rank, or maturity to another person.

peer popularity One whose presence or opinion is sought after by others of the same age; the key determinants are the abilities to initiate and to maintain positive interactions with others.

peer rejection Ignoring or avoiding those who are strongly disliked by their peers; those rejected are often inattentive, aversive, threatening, hostile, and disruptive.

performance assessment A method of collecting information that measures children's ability to perform specific cognitive or physical tasks correctly.

performance-oriented goals One type of achievement goal identified by motivation theorists, whereby students are motivated to achieve by a desire to demonstrate high ability or to avoid negative evaluations of ability; same as ego-oriented goals. Contrast with *task-oriented goals*.

permissive-indifferent parenting A style of parenting in which children are left to make their own decisions and regulate their own behavior that often results from or leads to neglect.

permissive-indulgent A style of parenting in which parents are very warm and responsive, and put few demands or expectation on their children. Rules are not clearly communicated or enforced, leaving children to make their own decisions and regulate their own behavior.

permissive parenting A parenting style characterized by a lack of rules and expectations for children and by inconsistent discipline; contrast with *authoritative* and *authoritarian*.

personal fable A second aspect of adolescent egocentrism that follows from the belief in an imaginary audience, resulting in an increased concern about appearance and behavior as an expression of one's uniqueness and sense of self-importance.

perspective taking skills   One of the important aspects of the development of social cognition that involves being able to imagine what others may be thinking and feeling.

phenotype   A person's observable physical and behavioral characteristics; when individuals receive a recessive gene from one parent and a dominant gene from another, their *genotype* will be different from their phenotype.

phonemic awareness   The ability to connect the distinctive sounds, or phonemes, in words to letters.

phonic knowledge   A *decoding* strategy; the rules for combining sounds to make words and the stress and intonation patterns of a language (Figure 5.1); contrast with *context knowledge* and *sight word knowledge*.

physical abuse   Purposeful bodily injury caused by another.

physical disabilities   Congenital or acquired disabling conditions that result from damage to the central nervous system, either to the brain or the spinal cord.

physical knowledge   One of three types of knowledge as described by Piaget; knowing the attributes of objects such as their number, color, size, and shape; knowledge is acquired by acting on objects, experimenting, and observing reactions.

pincer grasp   Develops at the end of the first year of life as an infant learns to use the thumb and index finger to pick up small objects.

pituitary gland   A small endocrine gland near the base of the brain responsible for the release of hormones affecting growth.

placenta   A structure present at implantation of the zygote that begins to function and mature during the embryonic period. This structure, the *umbilical cord*, and the *amniotic sac* make up the life support system for the developing embryo.

plasticity   The ability of the brain, especially in the early years of development, to change.

polygenetic traits   Human characteristics, such as intelligence, skin color, and height, that result from the combination or interaction of two or more genes.

postconventional level   According to Kohlberg, the third level of moral judgment, characterized by individuals who develop their own set of principles to define what is morally right and wrong; contrast with *preconventional level* and *conventional level*.

power assertive discipline   A discipline style in which parents attempt to control their children's behavior by use of commands and imperatives based solely on their authority.

practical intelligence   Sternberg's theory that an intelligent person can use skills effectively in a particular context; involves applying *contextual intelligence* to everyday problems; see Figure 4.8.

pragmatics of language   The strategies for using language appropriately in different contexts, such as turn-taking, interrupting, beginning a new topic appropriately; see Figure 5.1.

preconventional level   According to Kohlberg, the first level of moral judgment, characterized by individuals who approach moral issues from a hedonistic or pleasure-oriented perspective; contrast with *conventional level* and *postconventional level*.

prejudice   Unfounded negative feelings toward a person because of his or her membership in a group.

prenatal development   The time from conception to birth; follows a universal sequence that is mainly directed by genetic influences but also can be affected by environmental factors.

preoperational stage   The period of life from 2 to 7 years old when, Piaget believed, children demonstrate an increased ability to use symbols (gestures, words, numbers) to represent real objects in their environment.

primary sex characteristics   Changes in the gonads (testes and ovaries) and the development of eggs and sperm stimulated by a change in the levels of sex hormones in male and female adolescents during puberty.

private speech   See *inner speech*.

procedural knowledge   Children's understanding about how learning strategies should be applied; contrast with *declarative knowledge* and *conditional knowledge*.

propositional logic   A form of *formal logic* achieved during the *formal operational stage* that Piaget identified as the ability to draw a logical inference between two statements or premises in an "if-then" relationship.

prosocial behavior   Actions stemming from an appreciation that others' needs are as important or more important than one's own; supportive actions, such as sharing, helping, and care giving.

proximal-distal   One of two patterns characterizing growth in infancy; development begins in the center and proceeds outward. As a result, the organs develop before the arms or hands.

psychological need   An internal tension or conflict that leads to or influences a person's goal-directed behavior.

psychological self   A developmental gain during which adolescents begin to understand that they have an inner self—thoughts and feelings hidden from others unless they share them.

puberty   Refers to the period in which a young person becomes capable of sexual reproduction; the average age of onset for girls is 10 to 12 years old and for boys, 12 to 14 years old.

Q

qualitative changes The emergence of discrete competencies and behaviors during different stages of development. Those theorists who view development as discontinuous.

questionnaire A *self-report* measure that contains carefully written questions for subjects to answer; a very common method of data collection.

R

race Refers to a group of people, such as African Americans or Asian Americans, who share biologically transmitted traits that are defined as socially significant, such as skin color or hair texture; contrast with *ethnicity*.

rating scale A form of questionnaire or interview in which research subjects are asked to rate themselves or others on a set of dimensions, such as aggression, temperament, and intelligence.

reaction range A concept used by researchers to understand an individual's unique, genetically determined response to environmental influences. Genes may determine the upper and lower boundaries for development, but the reaction range defines the degree to which the environment can affect development.

reading readiness approach An outdated conception of literacy development that emphasized a set of skills children needed to master before beginning formal reading instruction; contrast with *emergent literacy*.

realism According to Piaget, children's inclination during the *preoperational stage* to confuse physical and psychological events in their attempts to develop theories of the internal world of the mind.

recall memory A form of information retrieval that involves the free recall of information without any cues or prompts to aid the process; requires more cognitive effort than *recognition memory*; children display better recall memory as they get older.

recessive gene A gene inherited from one parent, such as blond hair, not always expressed, because its genetic directions are masked by a *dominant gene* of the other parent. A child needs to inherit a recessive gene from each parent for the gene to be expressed.

reciprocal determinism Defined by Bandura's social learning theory as a bidirectional relationship between a child and his or her social environment; children have as much an influence on their environment as it has on them.

reciprocal teaching Palincsar and Brown's learning model designed to help poor readers acquire comprehension skills.

Teachers and students take turns being the discussion leader, and through collaborative learning dialogues, students learn how to regulate their own understanding of what they are reading.

recognition memory A basic form of information retrieval that involves recognizing a familiar stimulus when it is seen, heard, or experienced again; requires less cognitive effort than *recall memory* tasks; infants are able to display recognition memory by attending more to an unfamiliar than a familiar stimulus.

reflective abstraction A concept that allows children to use information they already have acquired to form new knowledge that begins to emerge during the *concrete operational stage* but more characteristic of adolescent thinking.

rehearsal The first memory encoding strategy to be learned, involving the repetition of information over and over again to assist with recall.

reinforcement A repeated response to an action in which individuals modify their behavior on the basis of the expected response.

reliability The consistency or precision of a measurement when repeated under similar circumstances; can be tested by administering the same test several times within a short interval of time (e.g., a few weeks) to check the consistency of results over time.

representational thinking A Piagetian concept that develops during the *preoperational stage* in which children gain the ability to use words to stand for real objects.

research design The plan or structure of an investigation, which is determined in part by the investigator's research question.

resiliency The capacity of young people to cope with difficult and challenging circumstances in their lives to develop competence.

retrieval strategy Any of the cognitive operations a learner might use to recover information from memory.

reverse mainstreaming A teaching approach in which students from the general classroom spend some time in the separate special classroom, interacting with children with disabilities in learning activities; see *partial participation*.

reversibility A concept achieved during the *concrete operational stage* that allows children to mentally reverse operations; involves an understanding that actions can be undone and is important for understanding *conservation* problems.

role confusion In Erikson's fifth stage of psychosocial development, adolescents can experience uncertainties about themselves and their future if they are unable to explore different roles and options; contrast with *identity*.

S

scaffolding The process by which adults provide support to a child who is learning to master a task or problem by performing or directing those elements of the task that are beyond the child's ability.

scheme Also referred to as schema (pl. schemata) in some research areas; in Piaget's theory, the physical actions, mental operations, concepts, or theories people use to organize and acquire information about their world.

script See *memory script*.

secondary sex characteristics Changes in genitals, breasts, and the growth of facial, pubic, and body hair stimulated by a change in the level of sex hormones in male and female adolescents during puberty.

secular trend A shift in normative patterns of development exemplified in today's average adult height and the onset of puberty.

securely attached In Ainsworth's theory, infants who are distressed by parental separation and easily comforted by the parent upon return. Distinguished from insecure attachment.

selective attention A development that allows children to focus their attention on task-relevant information and ignore irrelevant information so they use their cognitive resources more efficiently.

self-concept The beliefs, attitudes, knowledge, and ideas people develop or construct about their personality, physical skills, and mental abilities; see *self-esteem*.

self-conscious emotions Feeling such as pride, shame, and guilt requiring a connection between one's actions and feelings that involve an evolving sense of self; generally emerges between the ages of 2 and 4.

self-control Being able to control negative emotions, persist at difficult and challenging activities, and inhibit impulses.

self-determination In motivation theory, the ability to act independently and to choose one's own course of action.

self-efficacy In motivation theory, an individual's judgment of personal ability to perform a task given the skills he or she possesses and the circumstances he or she faces; according to Bandura, shaped by prior experience, peer models, and corrective feedback.

self-esteem Personal evaluation of one's own traits, abilities, and characteristics; a judgment of one's own worth, value, or competence; see *self-concept*.

self-evaluation A cognitive strategy that encourages children to record their performance and compare it to their target goals.

self-instruction A cognitive strategy that encourages children to use internal speech to guide them through a task in a step-by-step manner; see *inner speech*.

self-monitoring A cognitive strategy that encourages children to keep track of their own comprehension, understanding, and learning progress.

self-regulated learning Children's increasing regulation and control of their own learning processes due to their development of their metacognitive knowledge.

self-report A method of collecting information in which individuals being studied report on themselves through *questionnaires*, *rating scales*, or *interviews*.

semantic memory Long-term memory storage of information, skills, and concepts of a general nature. Much of what is learned in school is included in semantic memory.

semantics The meaning of words; only certain strings of sounds are meaningful as words and words are related in complex networks and have special properties; see Figure 5.1.

semiotic functioning See *representational thinking*.

sense of guilt In Erikson's third stage of psychosocial development, children 3 to 6 years old can develop guilt feelings if their caregivers demand too much self-control or initiative; contrast with *sense of initiative*.

sense of industry In Erikson's theory, the fourth stage of psychosocial development in which children 7 to 11 years old must begin to identify their strengths and to take pleasure in their accomplishments; if they are unsupported in their mastery efforts, a parallel internal *feeling of inferiority* or inadequacy may develop. See Table 6.1.

sense of initiative In Erikson's theory, the third stage of psychosocial development in which children 3 to 6 years old develop a sense of purpose and direction and learn to balance their actions with the demands of others. If children are unable to live up to parental expectations, a parallel *sense of guilt* will develop; see Table 6.1.

sensorimotor stage The period of life from birth to 2 years old when children acquire what Piaget believed are the building blocks of symbolic thinking and human intelligence—schemes for two basic competencies, goal-directed behavior, and *object permanence*.

sensory register According to information processing theories, the place where information is stored in the cognitive process for a few milliseconds until it is recognized or lost; each sense has its own sensory register.

separation The rejection of the dominant culture by the minority who then only associates with members of his or her own minority group.

seriation In Piaget's theory, the understanding that develops during the *concrete operational stage* that involves the ability to order objects in a logical progression, such as from shortest to tallest; important for understanding the concepts of number, time, and measurement.

Glossary

sex chromosome The twenty-third chromosome; humans have two types, X and Y; females have two X chromosome, and males have an X and a Y chromosome.

sex-linked characteristic Some recessive traits carried on the female *sex chromosome*, such as baldness, color blindness, and hemophilia; generally expressed in male rather than female offspring.

sex-role socialization The process by which children acquire the knowledge, skills, and traits appropriate for their gender.

sexual abuse Contacts between the child and adult in which the child is being used for sexual stimulation.

short-term memory A component of the information processing system into which information passes and is held for a brief period of time once it has been interpreted or encoded in terms of prior knowledge; also known as working memory; contrast with *long-term memory*.

sight word knowledge A *decoding* strategy; the developing recognition and understanding through exposure of the meaning of words; contrast with *context knowledge* and *phonic knowledge*.

simpatía The felt need for behaviors, such as conformity and empathy, which promote harmonious, pleasant social relations.

simultaneous bilingual Learning several languages at the same time.

social cognition A Piagetian concept defined as knowledge about people, including their thoughts, feelings, and actions.

social comparison A developmental change that occurs during the school years as children begin to compare themselves with others in terms of actions or abilities.

social desirability A tendency of individuals to overestimate desirable behavior and underestimate undesirable behavior on *self-report* measures.

social dialect Speech patterns of a particular ethnic, social, or regional group.

social knowledge In Piaget's theory, this type of knowledge is derived in part through interactions with others. Examples of this knowledge include mathematical words and signs, languages, musical notations, as well as social and moral conventions.

social referencing The process of incorporating facial cues into response sequences in infants.

social speech One of three stages of children's use of language identified by Vygotsky that is used primarily for communicative purposes in which thought and language have separate functions; contrast with *egocentric speech* and *inner speech*.

socialization The social processes in which a child is prepared to be a productive and competent member of society.

specific learning disabilities A wide range and varying degrees of characteristics children exhibit that classify them as exceptional and require special accommodations for learning situations.

stability of IQ In intelligence theories, the degree to which an IQ score remains constant over time; central to the *heritability* of intelligence issue. For instance, if IQ is not stable over time, researchers could point to the influence of environmental factors in the outcome of people's intellectual potential.

standard American English (SAE) The language of instruction in schools.

standard deviation A statistical estimate used with IQ scores that represents the average amount individual scores within a sample vary from the mean.

standardized tests of intelligence The most common method of assessing individual differences in cognitive development; referred to as the psychometric approach.

statistically significant When the relation between two measures is stronger than would have been predicted by chance.

Strange Situation Ainsworth procedure for assessing behaviors of caregivers and children; used to establish quality of attachment.

strategic learner Any learner who uses cognitive strategies (attention, encoding, memory, and retrieval) to enhance his or her learning.

structured immersion A method for serving English-learning students in which children receive up to a year of intensive training in English before they are placed in an English-speaking classroom.

structured observation An observation situation that uses a carefully controlled setting and standardizes the conditions under which data are collected.

submersion A "sink or swim" approach to teaching students with limited proficiency in English in which learners are placed into a monolingual, English classroom without any instructional support.

substance abuse Frequent or excessive use of a drug, including cigarettes, alcohol, and marijuana.

successive bilingualism A person who learns the dominant language (English) but retains his or her native language as well (Spanish); the stages of language development will be different from *bilingual* or *multilingual* learners; see *mixed speech*.

synapses The tiny gaps between *neurons* in the central nervous system where fibers from different neurons come close together but do not touch and *neurotransmitters* cross over.

syntax The structure of language; the way words are combined to form phrases and sentences.

T

task-oriented goals   One type of achievement goal identified by motivation theorists, similar to *intrinsic motivation*, whereby students are motivated to achieve by a desire to improve or develop their competencies; same as learning-oriented goals. Contrast with *performance-oriented goals*.

telegraphic speech   Early speech that is characterized by typically short, simple sentences composed primarily of content words: "Kendall swim pool."

temperament   An infant's characteristic style of responding to the environment and includes activity level, predictability, and emotionality; believed to be early component of personality development.

teratogen   Any environmental substance or disease (alcohol, caffeine, radiation, caustic chemicals, chicken pox, AIDS) that can have an adverse effect on a fetus during prenatal development.

testosterone   Hormone affecting the development of the penis, testes, and other organs of the reproductive system in males.

test-retest reliability   A measure used to determine the consistency of a test's results; see *reliability*.

theory   A set of general rules, assumptions, propositions, and principles used to explain facts; a developmental theory provides a framework for observing, interpreting, and explaining children's changes over time.

theory of multiple intelligences   Gardner's proposal that there are at least seven different intelligences: linguistic, logical-mathematical, musical, spacial, bodily-kinesthetic, interpersonal, and intrapersonal; see Table 4.1.

time sampling   A technique used to record on a coding sheet all observations listed that happen within a predetermined length of time, say, within a 5-minute time frame.

tracking   The ongoing practice in middle and high schools of grouping students according to their presumed academic ability; thought by some to limit learning and achievement opportunities due to the kinds and quality of instruction and to students' resulting low motivation and self-esteem; see *ability grouping*.

traumatic brain injury (TBI)   An acquired injury to the brain from either an open or closed head injury that has significant impact on learning, including problem solving, speech and motor abilities, psychosocial behavior, and information processing; learning difficulties may be permanent or temporary, depending on the location and extent of the injury.

triangulation   The use of multiple data collection methods to compare findings across sources and to find consistent patterns.

triarchic model of intelligence   Sternberg's concept that intelligence is divided into contextual, experiential, and componential subcomponents; see *componential intelligence*, *contextual intelligence*, and *experiential intelligence*; see also *multidimensional conception of intelligence*.

U, V

umbilical cord   A structure present at implantation of the zygote that begins to function and mature during the embryonic period. See *placenta*.

validity   The degree to which a research instrument or test accurately measures what it claims to measure.

W

whole language   A language philosophy characterized by a set of beliefs including the purpose of language is to create and share meaning; language is language, regardless of whether it is spoken or written; language is best learned by using it in a social context for authentic purposes.

working memory   See *short-term memory*.

writing across the curriculum   A program approach in which writing is incorporated into all subject areas, from music to mathematics.

Z

zone of proximal development   A concept in Vygotsky's theory regarding children's potential for intellectual growth rather than their actual level of development; the gap between what children can do on their own and what they can do with the assistance of others (see Figure 3.10).

zygote   The human cell that is formed by the union of the female egg and male sperm and contains one set of 23 chromosomes from the mother and another set of 23 chromosomes from the father.

Text Credits

Figure 1.1. Excerpt "Teacher's Beliefs and Practices . . . " From "Kindergarten Readiness and Retention" by Smith and Shepard in *American Educational Research Journal,* Fall 1988, Vol. 25, No. 3, pp. 330–331.

Figure 1.11. From "A Portrait of America's Children." From the Children's Defense Fund. Copyright © 2000 Children's Defense Fund. Reprinted with permission.

Focus on Teaching. Adapted from "The Use of Technology to Enhance Mathematics Achievement" by Clem Annice in Geoffrey E. Mills (ed.) *Action Research: A Guide for the Teacher Researcher,* 2000, pp. 70–71. Reprinted by permission of Prentice-Hall, Inc., Upper Saddle River, NJ.

Figure 1.20. "Guidelines for Conducting Research with Children." From Society for Research in Child Development Committee on Ethical Conduct in Child Development. Reprinted with permission.

Figure 2.9. "Early Brain Development" by J. L. Conel. From *The Postnatal Development of the Human Cortex,* Vol. I-VIII. Cambridge, Mass.: Harvard University Press. Copyright © 1939, 1975 by the President and Fellows of Harvard College. Reprinted by permission of the publisher.

"Barney: Keep making gold . . ." From *Bad Guys Don't Have Birthdays* by Paley, 1988, p. 19. Reprinted by permission of The University of Chicago Press.

Focus on Development. From *Analyzing Children's Art* by Rhoda Kellogg. Copyright © 1970, 1968 by Rhoda Kellogg. Reprinted by permission of Mayfield Publishing Company.

Focus on Research. Adapted from "First Graders' Cognitive Representation of Number and Understanding of Place Value: Cross-national comparisons—France, Japan, Korea, Sweden, and the United States" by Miura, Okamoto, Kim, Steer, and Fayol in *Journal of Educational Psychology,* 1993, Vol. 85, pp. 24–29. Copyright © 1993 by the American Psychological Association. Reprinted with permission.

Focus on Teaching. Adapted from "Genetics" in *National Science Education Standards,* pp. 64–66. Copyright © 1996 by the National Academy of Sciences, Washington, D.C. Reprinted with permission.

Focus on Research. From "Reciprocal Teaching of Comprehension Fostering and Comprehension-Monitoring Activities" by Annemarie Sullivan Palincsar and Ann L. Brown in *Cognition and Instruction,* 1984, 1(2), p. 161. Copyright © 1984 Lawrence Eribaum Associates, Inc. Reprinted with permission.

Figure 4.3. From "The Development of Scanning Strategies and their Relation to Visual Differentiation" by Elaine Vccrpillot in *Journal of Experimental Child Psychology,* Vol. 6: 632–650. Copyright © 1968 by Academic Press. Reproduced by permission of the publisher.

Figure 4.7. From "Network Representation of a Child's Dinosaur Knowledge" by Michelene T.H. Chi and Randi Diamon Koeske in *Developmental Psychology,* 1983, Vol. 19, No. 1. Published by the American Psychological Association. Reprinted by permission of Michelene T.H. Chi.

Name Index

Name Index

Name Index

Name Index

Subject Index

Subject Index